"ASPECT" GEOGRAPHIES

A GEOGRAPHY OF TOURISM

"ASPECT" GEOGRAPHIES

A GEOGRAPHY
OF TOURISM

H. ROBINSON, B.A., M.Ed., Ph.D.

*Head of Department of Geography and Geology and
Dean of the Faculty of Arts,
The Polytechnic, Huddersfield*

MACDONALD AND EVANS

MACDONALD & EVANS LTD
8 John Street, London WC1N 2HY

First published March 1976

©

MACDONALD AND EVANS LIMITED
1976

ISBN: 0 7121 0721 5

Other "Aspect" Geographies
A GEOGRAPHY OF MANUFACTURING
A GEOGRAPHY OF SETTLEMENTS
BIOGEOGRAPHY

Filmset in Photon Times 11 on 12 pt by
Richard Clay (The Chaucer Press), Ltd, Bungay, Suffolk
and printed in Great Britain by
Fletcher & Son Ltd, Norwich

Introduction to the Series

THE study of modern geography grew out of the medieval cosmography, a random collection of knowledge which included astronomy, astrology, geometry, political history, earthlore, etc. As a result of the scientific discoveries and developments of the seventeenth and eighteenth centuries many of the component parts of the old cosmography hived off and grew into distinctive disciplines in their own right as, for example, physiography, geology, geodesy and anthropology. The residual matter which was left behind formed the geography of the eighteenth and nineteenth centuries, a study which, apart from its mathematical side, was encyclopaedic in character and which was purely factual and descriptive.

Darwinian ideas stimulated a more scientific approach to learning, and geography, along with other subjects, was influenced by the new modes of thought. These had an increasing impact on geography, which during the present century has increasingly sought for causes and effects and has become more analytical. In its modern development geography has had to turn to many of its former offshoots—by now robust disciplines in themselves—and borrow from them: geography does not attempt to usurp their functions, but it does use their material to illuminate itself. Largely for this reason geography is a wide-ranging discipline with mathematical, physical, human and historical aspects: this width is at once a source of strength and weakness, but it does make geography a fascinating study and it helps to justify Sir Halford Mackinder's contention that geography is at once an art, a science and a philosophy.

Naturally the modern geographer, with increasing knowledge at his disposal and a more mature outlook, has had to specialise, and these days the academic geographer tends to be, for example, a geomorphologist or climatologist or economic geographer or urban geographer. This is an inevitable development since no one person could possibly master the vast wealth of material or ideas encompassed in modern geography.

This modern specialisation has tended to emphasise the importance of systematic geography at the expense of regional geography, although it should be recognised that each approach to geography is incomplete without the other. The general trend, both in the universities and in the school examinations, is towards systematic studies.

This series has been designed to meet some of the needs of students pursuing systematic studies. The main aim has been to provide introductory texts which can be used by sixth-formers and first-year university students. The intention has been to produce readable books which will provide sound introductions to various aspects of geography, books which will introduce the students to new ideas and concepts as well as more detailed factual information. While one must employ precise scientific terms, the writers have eschewed jargon for jargon's sake; moreover, they have aimed at lucid exposition. While, these days, there is no shortage of specialised books on most branches of geographical knowledge, there is, we believe, room for texts of a more introductory nature.

The aim of the series is to include studies of many aspects of geography embracing the geography of agriculture, the geography of manufacturing industry, biogeography, land use and reclamation, food and population, the geography of settlement and historical geography. Other new titles will be added from time to time as seems desirable.

H. ROBINSON
Geographical Editor

Preface

INTEREST in recreation seems suddenly to have exploded upon the geographical scene and many geographers are now turning their attention to it. Tourism is merely an aspect of recreation but, so far, few geographers have shown much interest. This book attempts to provide an introduction to the geography of tourism. The idea arose out of the writer's attempt to initiate a Degree in Tourism. On the Continent and elsewhere in the world universities have undergraduate courses in tourism and, in view of the growing importance to the U.K. of the tourist industry, it would seem that we ought to be following suit. Our tourist industry has in fact been neglected for far too long.

Writing a book on tourism is not a particularly easy task since information about the tourist industry varies widely from country to country. This dearth of factual information helps to explain the inequality in the treatment of the industry in some of the countries dealt with here. Some Chapters deal with aspects of tourism which the purist will claim bear little relation to geography, but I have included them because I feel they are necessary to a proper understanding of the phenomenon of tourism. On the other hand, I have omitted any reference, other than of an incidental kind, to the hotel and catering industry, one of the major components of the tourism activity, since it has little geographical relevance. I have attempted to justify tourism as an appropriate study for the geographer, but it is probably best thought of as an aspect of applied geography.

The book is organised into a number of parts: first, some consideration is given to the tourism phenomenon itself, its historical background, the factors affecting demand, and the elements of tourism; secondly, the problems of measurement, the dimensions of tourism, and the spatial patterns are looked at; thirdly, transport, the significance of tourism and its planning are discussed; next there is a section on the tourist and the environment, more especially in relation to the U.K.; and, finally, regional tourism is considered.

A short bibliography of source material is appended: these sources have been used in the writing of this book, although I have culled information from all manner of sources—magazines, newspapers, bank bulletins, etc. I have found Michael Peter's *International Tourism* and J. Alan Patmore's *Land and Leisure* especially useful and wish to acknowledge my indebtedness to these two pioneer studies. I gratefully acknowledge my thanks to all those authors, editors and publishers who have so graciously allowed me to use quotations, often at considerable length, maps and diagrams in this book, especially to the editors of the *Financial Times*, *International Tourism Quarterly*, *Geography*, *Geographical Magazine* and *Tourism Planning and Research Ltd*. I am indebted to my colleague, Mr Colin Bamford, for his assistance in Chapters VIII, IX and X; also to my two colleagues, Dr D. A. Kirby and Dr B. J. H. Brown, who read and commented upon many of the Chapters. I wish also to give my thanks to my friend Ivan Veselic of Kosice, Czechoslovakia, for procuring the figures relating to tourist movements in Eastern Europe and to Professor S. Medlik of the University of Surrey for his kindness and help. Lastly to my dear wife who for so many years now has had to endure the clattering of my typewriter and been denied my company during so many evenings.

H.R.

Contents

Chapter   *Page*

INTRODUCTION TO THE SERIES   v
PREFACE   vii
LIST OF ILLUSTRATIONS   xv
LIST OF TABLES   xvii
INTRODUCTION   xxi
    The tourist phenomenon   xxi
    Geography and tourism   xxii
    The geography of tourism as applied geography   xxiv

PART ONE: THE GROWTH AND PHENOMENON OF TOURISM

I. THE GROWTH OF TOURISM   3
    Early travel   3
    The origin of the annual holiday   4
    The development of spas   6
    The growth of seaside resorts   9
    The Grand Tour   11
    The Victorian Age   13
    The heyday of the resorts   15
    The post-war era   16

II. THE EVOLUTION OF DEMAND   18
    Leisure   18
    Affluence   21
    Mobility   23
    Present-day factors   25

III. TOURIST MOTIVATION   29
    The why of tourism   29
    Behavioural aspects   30

Chapter		Page
IV.	THE ELEMENTS OF TOURISM	40
	The basic components	40
	The geographical components	41
	The elements of tourism	42

PART TWO: THE MEASUREMENT AND DIMENSIONS OF TOURISM

V.	THE MEASUREMENT OF TOURISM	53
	The tourist: a definition	53
	Some problems	54
	Counting tourists	55
	Methods of measurement	56
	The importance of measurement	58
	Market analysis	59
	The problem of seasonality	60
VI.	INTERNATIONAL TOURIST FLOWS	64
	Recreational travel: the new migration	64
	The dimensions of world tourism	64
	International tourist movements	66
	The interpretation of international tourist flows	72
	Future trends	75

PART THREE: SOME ASPECTS OF THE TOURIST INDUSTRY

VII.	THE ORGANISATION OF TOURISM	81
	The role of organisation	81
	National tourism organisation	82
	The British Tourist Authority	85
	Travel agents and tour operators	89
	U.K. agents and operators	90
	Holiday camps and Club Méditerranée	92
VIII.	TRANSPORT AND TOURISM	94
	Circulation: its importance	94
	Speed, cost and load	95
	Determinants of spatial interaction	96
	Transport and tourism	97
	Summary	117

Chapter   *Page*

IX.   THE ECONOMIC AND SOCIAL SIGNIFICANCE
        OF TOURISM   120
        Domestic and foreign travel   120
        Balance of payments   121
        Domestic effects   125
        Employment   128
        Investment in tourism   130
        Other economic implications and problems   136
        The social significance of tourism   137

X.   PLANNING FOR TOURISM   142
        Tourism in the developing countries   142
        The imperative of planning   143
        The formulation of a tourist programme   144
        The assessment of national tourist attractions   146
        Essential basic services   147
        Investment planning   148
        The management of tourism   150
        Overall conclusions   151

PART FOUR: THE TOURIST AND
            THE ENVIRONMENT

XI.   THE TOURIST AND THE TOWN   155
        Tourist resorts   155
        The attributes of resort towns   157
        Facilities and amenities   158
        Morphology and shape   160
        Architecture and landscape features   163
        Parks and playgrounds   165
        Cultural, social and historical attractions   167
        Classification of resorts   168
        Problems of a resort: Blackpool   172
        Conservation of urban amentities   174

XII. THE TOURIST AND THE COUNTRYSIDE   178
        The resources of the countryside   178
        Man's use of the countryside   180
        Pressures and problems   181
        Second homes   182
        The framework of countryside control   184

          Areas of outstanding natural beauty   190
          Encroachment on the countryside   190
          Use of water areas   192
          The Broads   195
          Farmhouse holidays   196
          Land lost for recreation   197
          The Lea Valley Regional Park   198

XIII.   THE TOURIST AND THE COAST   201
          The use of the coast   201
          Pressures on the coast   202
          The state of the coast   204
          "The mess on the coast"   207
          Planning policies   210
          Heritage coasts   212
          The coast of North Wales and tourism   213

        PART FIVE: REGIONAL TOURIST
                 DEVELOPMENT

XIV.   TOURISM IN THE UNITED KINGDOM   221
          Domestic tourism   221
          Foreign tourism   235

XV.   INTRODUCTION TO TOURISM IN EUROPE
          The European travel market
          Current trends and problems

XVI.   TOURISM IN WESTERN AND CENTRAL
          EUROPE   255
          Eire   255
          The Scandinavian countries, Finland and Iceland 257
          The Benelux countries   260
          France   263
          Tourist regions   269
          West Germany   281
          Switzerland   286
          Austria   292

XVII.   TOURISM IN SOUTHERN EUROPE   297
          Spain   297
          Problems and future planning   305

Chapter		Page
	The Canary Islands	309
	Portugal	310
	Italy	316
	Yugoslavia	324
	Greece	330
	Malta	333
XVIII.	TOURISM IN EASTERN EUROPE AND THE SOVIET UNION	336
	Eastern Europe	336
	Russia	341
XIX.	TOURISM IN NORTH AMERICA	347
	North American leisure	347
	Domestic tourism	348
	The American overseas tourist	353
XX.	LATIN AMERICA	363
	Mexico	364
	The West Indies	369
	South America	378
	Uruguay	384
	Chile	385
	Peru	385
	Argentina	386
XXI.	AFRICA AND THE NEAR EAST	390
	The Atlas Region	393
	Egypt	403
	Turkey	405
	Lebanon	408
	Israel	411
	Jordan	414
	West Africa	416
	East Africa	418
	The Republic of South Africa	422
XXII.	TOURISM IN THE REST OF THE WORLD	429
	The Indian Ocean Islands	431
	India	436

Chapter   *Page*
      Sri Lanka   438
      Singapore   440
      Hong Kong   442
      Taiwan   444
      Korea   445
      Japan   446
      Australia   450
      New Zealand   453

APPENDIX   457
  I.   Bibliography   457
 II.   Areas of outstanding natural beauty   461

INDEX   463

List of Illustrations

Fig.		Page
1.	Model of the tourist industry	xxx
2.	Seasonality in tourism: some examples	62
3.	Growth of world tourist arrivals (1960–71)	65
4.	Growth of world tourist receipts (1960–71)	70
5.	Pattern of world tourism receipts	71
6.	British Tourist Board's organisational structure	87
7.	English Tourist Boards	88
8.	British motorways	106
9.	Circular flow of money in the economy	122
10.	Planning model	144
11.	Shapes of resorts	161
12.	National Parks and Areas of Outstanding Natural Beauty: England and Wales	188
13.	Inland waterways	194
14.	Coastal development and protection	203
15.	The use of beaches	206
16.	The coast of North Wales	214
17.	Tourism flows in U.K.: millions of nights and £m (1970)	222
18.	Percentages of British holiday-makers visiting the various regions (1950, 1960 and 1970)	225
19.	Destination of holiday-makers: Devon	226
20.	Tourist numbers: tourist regions of Great Britain	227
21.	Origins of holiday-makers: selected areas of Britain (1968)	230
22.	Seasonality of foreign visitor arrivals in Britain	234
23.	Europe: map of tourist arrivals and receipts (1970)	245
24.	Arrivals of West Europeans outside Europe	246
25.	Tourist movements to and within Northern Europe	247
26.	Tourist movements to and within Central Europe	247
27.	Tourist movements to and within Western Mediterranean	248
28.	Tourist movements to and within Eastern Mediterranean	249
29.	France: stays in various regions and abroad	267

Fig.		*Page*
30.	Tourism developments in Languedoc–Roussillon	276
31.	French winter sports resorts in the Alps	280
32.	Switzerland: tourist centres and communications	286
33.	Austria: tourist centres	292
34.	Spain: graph of visitors and foreign exchange earnings (1951–70)	298
35.	Regional distribution of tourism in Spain	303
36.	Spain: tourism features	307
37.	Foreign visitors to Italy	317
38.	Italy: tourism features	320
39.	The Dalmatian holiday coast	326
40.	Numbers of nights spent by visitors at leading Yugoslavian tourist centres (1965)	328
41.	National Parks and National Scenic Trails: United States	351
42.	Brazil: tourism features	380
43.	Tourist centres: Morocco, Algeria and Tunisia	392
44.	Tourist centres: the Near East	404
45.	National Parks and Game Reserves: East Africa	420
46.	South Africa: tourism features	424
47.	Graph of Japanese departures overseas	447

Tables

Table   *Page*

1.   Comparison of national annual paid and public holidays   21
2.   An index of projected changes in recreation-related factors
     at quinquennial intervals (1960–85)   22
3.   Age groups and holidays   25
4.   Proportion of people not taking holidays in relation to
     income   26
5.   Proportion of people going abroad in relation to social
     class   26
6.   Peters' inventory of tourist attractions   41
7.   Geographical components of tourism   42
8.   Volume of international tourism in the world   66
9.   International tourist movements   67
10. Earnings from international tourism   69
11. Receipts from international tourism by regions   69
12. Transport used to reach holiday destinations in Great
     Britain   98
13. Modes of transport in tourism   98
14. Types of transport used on longest part of journey to
     holiday destination (1960 and 1969)   102
15. Types of transport used on longest part of journey to
     holiday destination (1969) by region of destination   104
16. Inclusive tour charter traffic from U.K. airports   112
17. Passengers by non-scheduled services as a percentage of
     total air passenger traffic to Spain (1967)   112
18. A. Scheduled air fares (summer 1973). B. Inclusive tour
     comparisons (summer 1973)   113
19. A. 85 per cent load factor. B. 100 per cent load factor   114
20. Comparison of scheduled airlines and inclusive tour char-
     ter operating costs   115
21. Value of tourism compared with that of commodity exports
     (1967)   124
22. The value of £ in relation to other foreign currencies   125

Table		Page
23.	Estimates of the tourism multiplier	127
24.	Structure of British hotel industry by size and location (1970)	133
25.	Grants and loans under Hotel Development Incentives Scheme (at 31st August, 1972)	134
26.	English Tourist Board: grant applications by counties at 31st March, 1973	135
27.	Growing membership of societies	181
28.	Coastal eyesores by geographical county	208
29.	Numbers of the U.K. population taking a holiday at home or abroad, 1951–73	221
30.	Proportion of U.K. population taking holidays	223
31.	Estimated holiday expenditure (1951–71)	224
32.	Timing of holidays in Britain: A. Main holidays; B. Additional holidays	232
33.	Accommodation used on main holidays in Britain	233
34.	Main European destinations of British holiday-makers	237
35.	Overseas visitors to the U.K.	239
36.	European foreign holiday traffic	244
37.	Visitors to European countries (from all countries)	250
38.	Visitors to European countries (from other O.E.C.D. European countries)	250
39.	Visitors to European countries (from the U.S.A. and Canada)	251
40.	International tourist receipts and expenditures of European countries	252
41.	Receipts from international tourism as a proportion of exports of goods and services (1969)	253
42.	Tourism in the countries of northern Europe	258
43.	Frontier arrivals in France (1970)	269
44.	West German tourist destinations and expenditures (1970)	282
45.	Principal visitors to the West German Federal Republic (1970)	283
46.	Switzerland: foreign arrivals (1970)	291
47.	Austria: principal arrivals (1970)	294
48.	Spain: tourism by nationalities	299
49.	Visitors: Portugal with Madeira	310
50.	Portugal: frontier and hotel arrivals	311
51.	Portugal: foreign tourist movements by nationality (1971)	313
52.	Visitors to Italy	316

Table		Page
53.	Yugoslavia: chief foreign arrivals (1970)	325
54.	International tourist traffic to and from Czechoslovakia	339
55.	Visitors from communist countries to Czechoslovakia and Czech visitors to communist countries	340
56.	Arrivals in East European countries	341
57.	U.S. travellers to overseas areas	354
58.	Destination of U.S. travellers overseas	354
59.	U.S. travellers visiting selected European countries (1970)	354
60.	Total visitor arrivals to U.S.	355
61.	U.S.: origins of foreign overseas visitors	357
62.	Canada: tourist arrivals (1970)	361
63.	Canada: foreign tourist receipts by main visitor groups (1970)	361
64.	Patterns of Latin American tourism	363
65.	Selected tourist arrivals: Latin American countries	365
66.	Mexico: tourism account	365
67.	Brazil: foreign tourist arrivals (1971)	383
68.	Peru: foreign tourist arrivals (1970 and 1971)	386
69.	Africa and the Near East: tourist arrivals (1972)	391
70.	Numbers of tourists entering the Maghreb (1966–72)	394
71.	Morocco: tourist arrivals by country of origin	396
72.	Tunisia: tourist arrivals (1961–71)	398
73.	Turkey: country of origin of tourists	407
74.	Lebanon: tourist arrivals (1968–72)	409
75.	Israel: average duration of a tourist's stay (1967)	413
76.	Visitors to selected West African countries (1972)	417
77.	Foreign visitors in East African countries	422
78.	Tourist arrivals and receipts in Asia and Australia (1970)	430
79.	Tourist arrivals in the Indian Ocean Alliance	432
80.	Visitors to Hong Kong (1972)	443
81.	Visitors to Taiwan	445
82.	Major destinations of Japanese travellers (1972)	448
83.	Tourist statistics: Australia	451
84.	Australia: principal overseas visitors (1971–72)	452
85.	Australia: source of arrivals	453

Introduction

THE TOURIST PHENOMENON

TRAVEL, from the very earliest historical period, has had a fascination for man: the urge to discover the unknown, to explore new and strange places, to seek changes of environment and to undergo new experiences. Travel to achieve these ends is not new, but tourism, as we understand the term today, is of relatively modern origin. Tourism is distinguishable by its mass character from the travel undertaken in the past. The mass movement of people annually from their home location to some other temporary location for a few days or weeks is a growth very largely, if not entirely, of the period following the Second World War.

The annual migration of large numbers of people began rather more than a hundred years ago but the present-day exodus, especially in relation to international tourism, is essentially a post-war phenomenon.

Over the past fifteen years in particular—since the world began to settle down after the years of readjustment immediately following 1945—there has been an astonishingly rapid increase in both domestic and international tourism. The United Nations reported that in the ten-year period between 1955–65 the number of tourist arrivals (in some sixty–seventy countries) trebled, from around 51 million to over 157 million. Such an increase in such a short period of time is quite phenomenal, but this apparently is only the beginning for, according to estimates worked out by I.U.O.T.O., the *International Union of Official Travel Organisations*, alternatively known as the *World Tourism Organisation*, there will be something of the order of 1000 million tourists on the move throughout the world by 1980. This estimate has been arrived at on a modest annual growth rate of 5 per cent, although in actual fact international tourism has been expanding at the rate of about 12 per cent *per annum* over the past fifteen years.

This rapid increase in tourism is the outcome of many factors, such as increased leisure, higher standards of living and improved education, but above all the developments in the means of speedy transport and communication. During the past fifteen years there has been a remarkable increase in the number of long-distance journeys undertaken by tourists, and since the average holiday period is still of two–three weeks' duration such extended journeys would have been well-nigh impossible but for the accelerated developments in transport. Such improvements in transport have made it possible for millions of people to travel to far-away places, places which only a few generations ago were regarded as being almost entirely inaccessible. Today the holiday-maker can be transported a thousand miles or more in a matter of a few hours.

It is not generally realised, as Peters[1] has pointed out, that tourism is the largest single item in the world's foreign trade and is increasing in importance every year. According to I.U.O.T.O. estimates total world receipts from international tourism in 1967 amounted to £6000m exclusive of transportation costs which, if added, would probably increase this figure by about one-third. The receipts from domestic tourism were estimated by I.U.O.T.O. to be of the order of £20,000m. If these be added to the receipts from international tourism then the expenditures on tourism, £26,000m or thereabouts (1969), come close to equalling the entire national income of the United Kingdom. By any standards this is pretty big business and clearly of great economic significance. Tourism is important for two very obvious reasons: (*i*) in many countries, especially Western European countries and those of North America, the tourist trade is now a major activity employing large numbers of people; and (*ii*) the receipts from tourism form a very valuable invisible export, are especially important as a dollar earner, and frequently contribute substantially to the balance of payments. As a factor of significance in the economy of a country or in the balance of trade, tourism is a comparatively recent phenomenon, but it is one of rapidly growing importance.

GEOGRAPHY AND TOURISM

This essentially modern development is of a great interest to the economist and sociologist. What, it may be asked, is the justification for treating tourism as a geographical study? At least six arguments may be advanced in answer.

(*i*) However one defines the discipline of modern geography, it cannot be denied that it is particularly concerned with the nature of environments, the location of phenomena such as settlement, and spatial distributions and relationships. Tourism is very much concerned with spatial conditions—the location of tourist areas and the movements of people between place and place—and so geography has a fundamental role to play in examining the spatial interplay of tourist demand and satisfaction.

(*ii*) The phenomenon of tourism is closely related to the structure, form, use and conservation of the landscape. The impact of tourism upon the landscape is basically twofold: the changes which tourism brings to the physiognomy of the landscape in the form of hotels and other kinds of accommodation and installations for the tourist industry and the attempts to preserve and conserve the natural landscape through the setting up of national parks, nature reserves, etc. Tourism thus obviously affects land use but leads to two different, almost conflicting, landscape effects. Geography has an important part to play in the reconciling of tourist activity with other demands upon particular environments.

(*iii*) Boesch [2] has drawn attention to "the influence of tourism upon particular levels of the formal structure [of the landscape], as may be exemplified by characteristic changes in demographic composition." The development of tourism led, for instance, to large numbers of people being attracted to mountain areas, *e.g.* the Alps, which provided a new source of livelihood for the indigenes. This development came at a time when these regions were beginning to lose their populations because they were unable to compete with agricultural production in more favoured regions and farming provided a very precarious livelihood. Many other marginal areas have been likewise rescued from economic disaster and depopulation through the development of tourism. As Christaller [3] has said, tourism by its very nature favours peripheral regions and is "a branch of the economy which avoids central places and the agglomerations of industry." Such economic and demographic changes have long engaged the attention of geographers.

(*iv*) Tourism is a commercial activity and therefore an aspect of economic geography. In many countries, especially in Western Europe and North America, the tourist trade is now a major industry employing large numbers of people in the provision of accommodation, catering, transport, entertainment, other service industries and the souvenir trade. In many of the less developed countries governments have seen the development of tourism as one solution to their regional problems. The dispersion of development to underdeveloped areas is perhaps the greatest benefit brought by tourism. This is a key factor in the promotion of economic growth. Thus tourism is patently a topic for geographical study and Boesch [4] says "Recreational studies are multifarious and complex, constituting a fruitful field for research in economic geography."

(*v*) Another feature of geographical interest relates to the role of tourism in international trade and as an import/export item in the economy of a country. Tourism, as has already been pointed out, is now the largest single item in the world's foreign trade and amounts to something of the order of £8000m a year. Tourism may play a very important role in a country's balance of payments. For example, the invisible exports accruing from tourism may be, as in the cases of Spain and Eire, equal to the values of major export items. The amount of money spent abroad by American tourists is quite staggering and this clearly brings important economic benefits to the tourist destination countries such as Mexico, the Bahamas, Britain, etc.

(*vi*) Finally, tourism has important and far-reaching social and cultural effects and these are of great concern to the geographer. The social benefits of tourism centre around the money brought into underdeveloped areas by the industry. The provision of infrastructure —the construction of roads, and systems of electricity supply, water supply and sewage disposal, hospitals, churches, schools and shops —becomes necessary when an area is developed for tourism. An increase in tourism also brings in its train enhanced employment for there are normally considerable developments in service industries— such as food processing—and in luxury trades. Again, tourists bring with them their own cultural ideas, practices and demands and these may have a profound effect upon the indigenous cultures as, for instance, has occurred in Spain, where fishing villages have mushroomed into tourist resorts and social constraints have been greatly weakened.

In view of these arguments it may be conceded that the study of tourism comes within the purview of geography and should be seriously studied by the geographer. Perhaps the geography of tourism may most appropriately be thought of as applied geography.

THE GEOGRAPHY OF TOURISM AS APPLIED GEOGRAPHY

Applied geography may broadly be defined as the application of geographical methods of survey, investigation, analysis and representation in a practical direction, *e.g.* physical and regional planning, urban development. The sphere of applied geography differs from traditional or classical geography, Leszczycki says, in having four characteristic features: (*i*) the investigation or research carried out is directed towards a practical end; (*ii*) the work implies the critical evaluation of the phenomena studied; (*iii*) the practical purpose of the studies requires that the results be represented quantitatively; and (*iv*) the studies, since they must take into account the possibilities of further future development, should be able to give perspectives and scientifically based forecasts.[5] Leszczycki goes on to say that applied geographical studies either provide solutions to concrete problems, providing an evaluation and a new perspective or have an important practical value even though the research was, in the first place, not specifically commissioned to solve an existing problem on the ground.

If these criteria are used, a good case can be made for treating the geography of tourism as an aspect of applied geography, for the geographical study of tourism embraces all four features mentioned above. The problems connected with tourist travel and recreation, says Leszczycki, "have grown steadily in importance from the social point of view [and the studies that have been made] are very complex . . . not only research dealing with aspects of natural environment valuable for recreation and tourist travel, such as landscape or climate, dealt with by physical geography; but also anthropogenic aspects valuable for recreation or tourist travel, from the point of view of culture, as well as such phenomena as recreational trips, economic problems connected with the services for tourists and the social and cultural problems which result from tourist and recreational travel. This last group of problems belongs to cultural and economic geography. But as all these studies, economic as well as physical, aim at solving but one complex problem, they can be considered as a special branch of applied geography, namely recreational geography. . . ."[6]

It will now be clear that tourism touches geography at many points, that it is an appropriate study for the geographer and that it offers a fertile field for investigation by him. This book, therefore, seeks to provide an introduction to the study of tourism and to consider some of the geographical implications in that study.

The expansion of tourism has many ramifications which are of concern to the geographer: migrations of people, changes in transport, increased accessibility, changes in land use, urban development, cultural diffusion, etc. In view of this great and increasing expansion, it is rather surprising that so few geographers, until recently, have directed their attention to tourism. A pioneer in this field was, of course, Professor E. W. Gilbert and recently J. A. Patmore has made a notable contribution in his study of land use and leisure activities.[7]

The Tourist

To begin with, it might be useful to identify "the tourist." The officially accepted definition of a tourist is a person travelling for a period in excess of twenty-four hours in a country other than that in which he normally resides.[8] Such a definition is not entirely satisfactory since it excludes the holiday-maker who is touring within his homeland; to most people such a touring holiday-maker is also a tourist. Is it possible to draw a distinction between the terms "holiday-maker" and "tourist"? Strictly speaking, the tourist is a person who travels round from place to place or, in other words, makes a tour but many, perhaps most, tourists travel to a destination and stop there a while. On arriving at his destination, the holiday-maker makes his holiday. It would appear difficult to draw a distinction between the tourist and the holiday-maker unless the holiday-maker is one who makes a holiday in his own homeland while the tourist makes it outside his homeland. And where does the Englishman who goes to Scotland, the Isle of Man or Wales fit in? Is he a tourist or is he just making a holiday?

The officially accepted definition given above includes, in addition to those people who are quite patently tourists, businessmen who are travelling abroad on business and students who are staying abroad for periods of time; but it does not include those on day excursions or military personnel stationed in foreign countries. While the majority of businessmen no doubt mix business with pleasure, one is not entirely convinced that the businessman is truly identifiable as a tourist. Nor the student either, for the temporary migrant worker is not classed as a tourist.

While the given definition is reasonably well accepted, it must be admitted that definitions of tourist entry among the different countries vary; this means that there are shortcomings in the data which are supplied and which one might wish to use for the purposes of analysis.

What motivates the tourist? Why does he take a holiday, why does he engage in travel? This question of motivation will be explored more fully later, but it may be noted in passing that there is a variety of reasons, several of which may operate at the same time, although many take a holiday for a particular reason. Again, why does the tourist choose to go to a particular spot? What influences his choice? This question will also be considered subsequently. There are many other questions of interest: how long does he holiday? What means of transport does he use? What kind of accommodation does he prefer? How much money does he spend? What are his holiday habits: does he visit the same place time and again or does he prefer to ring the changes? All these questions are worthy of study.

Growth of Tourism

Holidays and recreation, in one form or another, are common to all civilisations but the annual holiday, in the sense that we understand it today, is essentially a product of the West. The surge of people to the coast and the country every summer is very much a modern phenomenon, and the idea of "going abroad" is (although it has roots in the past) a very recent development indeed. Until about a century ago, only the well-to-do and leisured could afford to take a holiday away from home. The majority of resorts were, therefore, small and in the main provided only genteel accommodation; they functioned very largely as centres of fashion and privilege as well as therapeutic centres.

"[Patterns in] holiday and recreation..." says L. J. Lickorish, "have ... been slow to evolve."[9] During the nineteenth century, however, the revolution in transport—the introduction of the railway—and the emergence of a middle-class with time and money to spare for recreation, led to the growth of the modern holiday industry and, as Lickorish says "... the pattern of holiday-making—the traditional week or fortnight by the sea—and the design of resorts—centred around the promenade, main street and railway station—reflect the habits ... of the nineteenth century."[10]

Nineteenth-century patterns of tourism lingered on well beyond 1900, only gradual changes resulting from improved transport and a new philosophy of holiday-making. By far the greatest developments have occurred since the end of the Second World War, arising from the substantial growth in leisure time, affluence and mobility. Today (at least in advanced countries), the majority of people can afford an annual holiday. In Britain, for example, in 1970, 34·5 million people took a holiday away from home; this represents nearly 60 per cent of the population. The corresponding figure for 1950 was 25 million or approximately 50 per cent of the population. The number of Britons who travelled abroad in 1950 and 1970 were respectively 1·25 and 5·75 million. Thus, not only is holiday-making increasing but the horizons of holiday travel are continually expanding as standards of living and personal incomes increase and the popularity of road, sea and air travel becomes greater.

Two other aspects of the growth of tourism should be mentioned. First is the rapid growth in the taking of "second holidays" of longer or shorter duration and, at least in the case of the more affluent members of society, in the establishment of what may be called "recreation homes," *e.g.* seaside flatlets, country cottages, caravans, cruising boats, etc. "It is in ... multiple holidays," says Lickorish, "that the biggest [domestic] growth in ... Britain is taking place."[11] This trend is also evident in other developed countries, *e.g.* the U.S.A., France and Denmark. Secondly, more and diverse types of holiday and recreation are becoming popular. For example, in addition to comparatively recent developments such as the holiday camp, caravan and coach tour, there are even newer fashions such as yachting, trail-riding, safari and archaeological holidays. This growth in demand for travel and in variety of tourist activity is making for great specialisation within the industry.

Nature of Tourism

Three important points made during the Estoril Seminar[12] indicate the changes which have taken, and are taking, place in tourism and which are fundamentally changing its nature. In the first place, the whole concept of pleasure travel has changed quite drastically during the past thirty years. Foreign travel in pre-war days was for the more affluent, leisured and well-educated members of society who enjoyed travel for its own sake and who were content to enjoy scenery, works of art and the flavour of foreign places. This concept, however, has been replaced by "tourism"—something which is altogether different. The present-day traveller has a different kind of background, and his ideas about travel are very different. He comes from a wider social background and his tastes and desires are much more varied; his leisure time is much more restricted and, accordingly, he wishes to pack into it as much as possible.

Secondly, there has been what is aptly termed the "democratisation" of leisure pursuits. Winter sports, for example, were not so very long ago an activity almost exclusively confined to the wealthier members of the population. The "commercialisation" of many hobbies or leisure-time activities such as riding, boating, shooting, hitherto rather exclusive pursuits, has made them available to the ordinary man who is interested. Large numbers of people are now also going abroad to participate in the more exciting and exotic activities of mountaineering, water-skiing, underwater swimming, pony-trekking and the like.

Thirdly, there has been the development of what is generally termed "social tourism." This kind of tourism, epitomised in the British holiday camp, not only by-passes the usual facilities provided by the traditional tourist resorts but is responsible for the opening up and development of new areas. "Organised for very large groups of people, constructing its own specially-designed low-price accommodation and very often providing its own entertainment and other services, 'social tourism' is able to bring vast numbers of tourists into remote and relatively undeveloped regions."[13]

Organisation of Tourism

G. Janata in a paper on tourism commented: "Tourism has arrived; aided and abetted by improved communications, education, higher incomes and freedom of movement, to influence . . . consumer behaviour and the growth, location and stratification of the industry, including the hotel and catering industry."[14] No one would question the validity of this statement but it may be useful for us to clarify the term "industry" as applied to tourism. Strictly speaking, tourism, like recreation, is not an industry: it is an activity; but, in economic terms, it creates a demand or provides a market for a number of quite separate and varied industries. In some areas tourism represents the major part of the market, in others a complementary, but frequently highly profitable, demand for accommodation, catering, transport, entertainment and other services designed largely, perhaps even primarily, for a residential or industrial community (*see* Fig. 1).

If we look at tourism in economic terms, *i.e.* demand (or production) and supply, we can, says Janata, divide tourism into two sectors, the dynamic sector and the static sector.[15] Within the dynamic sector fall the economic activities of (*i*) the formation of the commodity, (*ii*) the motivation of demand, (*iii*) the provision of transport. Translated into practical terms, the dynamic aspects embrace the activities of tour operators, travel agents, transport undertakers and ancillary agencies. The static sector looks after the "sojourn" part of tourism, the demand for accommodation, food, and refreshment in the main, the chief provider of which is the hotel and catering industry, although there are also other ancillary services involved.

Many economic activities are involved in, and support, tourism, which for convenience we will now refer to as the tourist industry.

Character of the Tourist Industry

First, tourism is "a multi-dimensional phenomenon"; many and varied activities each make their own separate and individual contribution to a comprehensive service to tourists. However, these activities, though separate, are interdependent. Such interdependence implies a need for co-operative effort and common policies, but "the diversity and . . . [small size] of many units make the formulation of any national

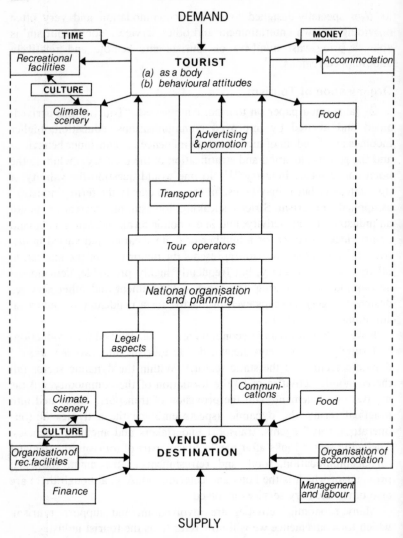

FIG. 1.—*A model of the tourist industry.*

plan by voluntary means impracticable and therefore uneconomic." [16] Nevertheless, some measure of co-operation and co-ordination has been achieved between tourist centres, hoteliers and tour operators.

Secondly, the industry is marked by a "widely differing economic performance"—tourism is dependent upon so many varied activities that a situation can arise "where weak links in the chain of services and facilities adversely affect the progress of otherwise healthy sectors of the industry."[17] A good example of this is the seaside resort of Whitby which has become far less viable as a resort because of inadequate transport links, especially since it lost its railway connections, which left it almost marooned.

Thirdly, the industry is primarily a service industry and a large proportion of those actively engaged in it find employment in tertiary occupations, *e.g.* catering, transport, travel agency work. The industry is also marked by a fairly distinct seasonal rhythm: there are few places in Britain, other than London and Stratford-on-Avon, which have an all-year-round trade. This means that casual work and seasonal unemployment are often distinguishing features of the industry, especially in the typical resort town. This unsatisfactory situation could be improved by the staggering of holidays, the promotion of second and out-of-season holidays at reduced prices, etc. Anything which will help to lengthen the tourist season will help the industry generally.

Finally, the industry is essentially a dynamic one. It is dominated by the changing ideas and attitudes of its customers and must be prepared to show a much greater degree of sensitivity and willingness to adjust to new conditions than it has in the past.

Economic Value of Tourism

Tourism has become the largest single item in the world's foreign trade, currently of the order of £8000m a year. The industry, which in 1960–65 showed a growth rate of between 12 and 15 per cent, continues to expand (though at a rather reduced rate: in 1973 at about 9 per cent on the world average), hence the economic value of tourism is substantial.

Tourism helps a country's economy in a variety of ways. In countries where the industry is fairly well developed, it provides employment on a large scale; in some areas or towns it is the preponderant employer of labour. International tourism can also assist the balance of payments, for example, in countries such as Spain, Mexico and Jordan where tourist receipts represent a substantial proportion of the exports—44, 39 and 28 per cent respectively in 1970—tourism is vital. Equally significant, although less immediately obvious, are the multiplier effects; the extent of these effects is difficult to measure, although, as Peters has said, "it is hard to visualise a multiplier of less than two."[18] The importance of "secondary" expenditure, which is inherent in tourism, cannot be over-estimated. Tourism also aids a national economy in that it can help to develop and revitalise regional economies more quickly than many other industries and, by its very nature, tends to favour peripheral regions which are the very ones needing an injection of economic capital.

Tourism can also be a useful instrument of social policies. The social benefits are largely a product of the money brought into under-developed areas by the industry. As already noted, the provision of infrastructure—communications, shops, hospitals, churches, schools, etc.—all become necessary when an area is developed for tourism. The provision of "service" industries is also very useful as the local indigenous population would not otherwise be able to support these facilities. The provision of recreational facilities, ostensibly for the benefit of the tourist, also benefit the health and welfare of the people living within the region. The biggest single social advantage that tourism brings is, however, that of employment.

The Tourist Countries

Tourism is highly developed in Western Europe and in North America, but elsewhere, although the potential is certainly present, development is slight. In view of the economic advantages to be gained from tourism, many of the developing countries have tended to seize upon tourism as offering a quick and easy way of promoting economic development and of solving their balance of payments difficulties. But even if countries such as Algeria, Iran and the Philippines possess the natural resources for tourist development, these in themselves are not enough, for they lack the infrastructure which is essential for successful tourist development. Many of them without doubt will be able to build up a thriving tourist industry, but it must be a rather slow process since there are many difficulties to be overcome. Certainly a tourist industry of any appreciable size cannot evolve overnight.

Countries such as France, Switzerland and Italy, which already possess a highly developed tourist industry have the principal problem of maintaining and expanding that industry. Countries such as Yugoslavia, Turkey, Tunisia and Morocco, where the industry is already of some considerable significance, need careful planning and appropriate investment if it is to be a very important factor in the national economy. Regions such as South America, Africa and South-eastern Asia have latent possibilities for tourist development, but tourism is likely to be of a rather limited nature. Countries such as Mongolia, Ethiopia and Haiti have possibilities for tourist development which are very strictly limited because their climates are unpleasantly extreme, or because they are rather remote and isolated, or because they lie away from areas of high income and high population density which supply the tourists, or because their low level of overall development is such that they lack even the basic facilities required by tourism.

This introduction should be looked upon as the foundation upon which all the subsequent discussion rests and should be related to the rest of the text during the reading of the book.

NOTES

1. M. Peters, *International Tourism*, Hutchinson, 1969, p. 4.

2. H. Boesch, *A Geography of World Economy*, D. Van Nostrand Co., 1964, p. 228.

3. W. Christaller, "Some Considerations of Tourist Location in Europe," Papers Regional Science Association XII, 1964, pp. 95–105.

4. *Op. cit.*. p. 229.

5. S. Leszczycki, "Applied Geography or Practical Application of Geographical Research," *Problems of Applied Geography II*, PWN–Polish Scientific Publishers, 1964, p. 15.

6. *Op. cit.*. p. 17.

7. *Land and Leisure*, David and Charles, 1970.

8. Committee Report to the Council of the League of Nations, 1937.

9. "Planning for Tourism," in *Recreation Research and Planning*, ed. T. L. Burton, George Allen & Unwin, 1970, p. 167.

10. *Idem.*

11. *Op. cit.*. p. 168.

12. *Tourism Development and Economic Growth*, O.E.C.D., 1966.

13. *Tourism Development and Economic Growth*, p. 12.

14. Presented at Ealing College of Technology, 18th May, 1971.

15. *Op. cit.*

16. *Annual Report*, English Tourist Board, 1971, p. 18.

17. *Annual Report*, English Tourist Board, 1971, p. 18.

18. *Op. cit.*, p. 241.

the way to a maze of high hedges and high, for mature design which simply the curious detective-author looked to level of investigation, when such that they make even the best bafflingly subjected by matter.

This introduction should be looked upon as one introduction upon which all the subsequent discussion rests, and should be situated to the rest of the text setting the shaping of the book.

NOTES

1. Myth Valuation, mimeo, The one discussion, Volume 4.

2. H. Innes, Topographisch deb and Grange, D. Verlichtigheid, 1964.

3. W. Christaller, Theory of analytisch graff Translation and structure.... Prentice Reprise of Science Association, VII., 1964 pp. 3-10.

4. The same page 179

5. E. V. Chapter in Applied Geography... Practical Applications and Vocabularies, Press Co. Fonction of geographic Geography 2, NWN pulled-Ocean, Push Co., Baltic, 1958.

6. Ibid all Land page, ibid., Charter 16.

7. mimeo Read.. in the Council.. Ch. I Lagrange Manтом, 1932.

8. W. Phillip and Land Group... Intervaller, Regional and Plantation of J. at Basus, Georges Allan & Unwin, 19604.

9. Ibid. 94

10. page. 85, 57

11. Ibid., 55

12. Schumacher by economics and Resources Volume 3, ALC. 37a, 1966.

13. Nusellschafter, quantitative Economic Board....

14. Research and change in Page Q Geography, 1961 May 1961.

15. Op.

16. Annual Report, Board, Cotton Board, 1941 p. 16.

17. Annual report, British Social Board, 1941 p. 18.

18. Op cit. India.

Part One

THE GROWTH AND PHENOMENON OF TOURISM

Chapter I

The Growth of Tourism

THE annual holiday is an important feature of modern social life in the West. The migration of millions of people to the coast and country every summer is essentially a modern phenomenon, while the idea of "going abroad" for a holiday is a very recent phenomenon indeed. The institution of the annual holiday, which is very largely of English origin, has had important social repercussions: it has led to a greater mobility of the population, created a new industry, now of substantial proportions, resulted in the growth of many towns of distinctive function, and broadened the horizons of millions. This practice of taking a holiday raises several interesting queries: how did the holiday arise? why does it take the form it does? and why do people go where they do? To begin this study of the geography of tourism, it will not be inappropriate to try to answer these questions.

EARLY TRAVEL

Travel is not the same as tourism, although travel is an essential ingredient. Man has travelled from the very earliest times: much of it in the beginning was largely unconscious and indeterminate although it would seem that with the development of civilisation conscious travel in order to explore and see the world began and there are frequent early references attesting this. Shulgi, ruler of ancient Babylonia, claimed to have protected roads and built rest houses for respectable wayfarers; Homer's *Odyssey* records the wanderlust of the ancient Greeks and Herodotus' *Travels* his own extensive journeying; Plutarch speaks of "globetrotters who spend the best part of their lives in inns and boats"; while in the Book of Daniel there is the statement that "Many shall run to and fro, and knowledge shall be increased."[1]

Travel received a great stimulus from the easy communications and security of the Roman Empire. The significance of the Roman roads cannot be over-emphasised for whither they went so did civilisation. Numerous itineraries and guide-books were published giving routes, the names of roads, distances between places and the times required in travelling to them. For the Romans, Greece was at first the great goal of travel but the adoption and spread of Christianity subsequently led to numerous pilgrims making their way to the Holy Land and we hear of many—including many women, such as St Sylvia of Aquitaine, Fabiola, Melania, Paula and Etheria—undertaking the pilgrimage.[2]

The safety and security created by the *Pax Romana* disappeared with the collapse of the Roman Empire. As the Barbarians swept across Europe most of the towns decayed, the great roads fell into disuse and crumbled away, and it became dangerous to travel since the countryside was infested with brigands. Not until the *Völkerwanderung* was over and a semblance of authority, law and order restored was it prudent again to go travelling, and after about A.D. 1000 people began once more to journey around. A measure of security was found in the large numbers of people who during medieval times began to travel, chiefly on pilgrimages, for no one travelled for pleasure in the modern sense. Pilgrimage, whether to Canterbury, Santiago de Compostela or the Holy Land, became a social feature of the age. There is in existence a fourteenth-century travellers' guide which provides pilgrims with detailed information about the countries and regions they would pass through and the types of hostelries they would encounter *en route.*

The Renaissance marked the next important stage in the history of travel. The great navigations of the late fifteenth and early sixteenth centuries "shattered the narrow horizons of medieval communities and stirred Renaissance man's restlessness and curiosity"[3] and the nobility and the wealthy began to travel abroad. This came to be a particular habit of the English gentry and "English milords had almost the monopoly of tourist travel in Europe, and their requirements became the standard of inns from Calais to Venice."[4] The Grand Tour, about which more will be said later, began in the sixteenth century and came to be looked upon as an essential part of the education of every young gentleman. The eighteenth century became the great age of travel, which was not to be equalled until the present century.

THE ORIGIN OF THE ANNUAL HOLIDAY

The term "holiday" derives, of course, from holy days, days associated with religious observances, though now it is generally used in a secular sense meaning a respite from the routine of workaday life and a time of leisure, amusement and recreation. Public holidays were a feature of ancient Rome, and among the most enjoyable was the

Saturnalia—the feast of Saturn—in December, when all classes indulged in feasting and frolic, and even the slaves were permitted privileges. In Christian Europe certain days commemorating religious festivals and saints' days became holy days on which there was cessation from work, with fasting and prayer. An Act (incidentally, still on the Statute Book) was passed in England in 1552, in the reign of Edward VI, "for the keeping [of] holidays and fasting days." Subsequently, though public and semi-official offices in England frequently closed on certain saints' days, there were no general public holidays until the time of the Industrial Revolution.

The modern concept of the annual holiday is very largely an outcome of the Industrial Revolution, which wrought drastic social as well as economic, changes. The English holidays of Christmas, Easter and Whitsuntide—the so-called bank holidays—are traditional holidays occurring at the great religious festivals; the other bank holiday, the August bank holiday, was only introduced in 1871. In addition, there gradually emerged the week's holiday. As a result of the revolution in industry and the change in the economic system, it gradually became customary, more particularly during the nineteenth century, for holidays to be negotiated directly between the employer and his work-people. In some parts of the country these negotiated holidays were taken in consecutive days at a particular time of the year and out of this grew the "wakes" weeks in Lancashire, the "tides" and "feasts" in the West Riding, and the "fair" holidays in Glasgow. "The 'wakes weeks' of the North of England," says Pimlott "are descended from the village wakes which in the Middle Ages were held on the eve of the . . . festival [of the patron saint]."[5]

The custom of a holiday in the summer season, coinciding with the local fairs and feasts as well as with the better weather, gradually grew throughout the nineteenth century. Such set weeks are still widely recognised in many industrial centres; for example, in Bradford the annual holiday is traditionally fixed at Bowling Tide, the second or third week in August. These set weeks had an obvious advantage from the industrial point of view in that a factory could close down completely for a period thereby obviating the disorganisation caused by small groups of people taking their holidays over an extended period.

"The dissociation of the notion of a holiday from religion has been a gradual process, which is not yet wholly at an end, but it was one of the prerequisites for the development of holidays in the modern sense. The other main prerequisite was economic and social: there had to be reasonably good facilities for travel and a considerable section of the population in the position to use those facilities. In other words the annual holiday would not have developed but for the secularisation of social life and the technical conquests which are features of our modern civilisation. As the sphere of religion has narrowed, as wealth has increased and has been more widely disseminated, and as communications have improved, so conditions have become more congenial for its growth."[6] Although these conditions favoured and facilitated the practice of taking holidays away from home, they do not explain it: some stimulus, some incentive, was needed. This stimulus came from a rather strange and unexpected quarter.

It has been customary to believe that in late medieval and early modern times the population was largely immobile, that people were born, lived and died in tightly circumscribed surroundings, seldom, if ever, moving far from their native heath. Modern research has, however, tended to show that people, as a whole, were considerably more mobile than had hitherto been thought. Nevertheless, it is probably still true to say that the vast majority lived within fairly narrow horizons. A small proportion, however, did move about and as Pimlott says "In the time of Elizabeth there were already many travellers on the roads of England, lawyers following the Judges on their circuits, students going to the Universities, adventurous young men making their way to seek their fortunes in London, members of Parliament, courtiers, officials, merchants, players, vagabonds."[7] Only a few were travelling like the modern tourist because they loved travel for its own sake or were searching for a new recreational experience. Before people generally came to do that, two innovations were required: first, a change of mental attitude, a new outlook towards pleasure and enjoyment, and the secularisation of social life and, second, the creation of centres of *divertissement* which provided accommodation and entertainment. Such innovations did eventually come about although, as Pimlott remarks "the first was unlikely to occur in advance of the latter, and the latter might seem to presuppose the former."[8] This dilemma was resolved "as an incidental result of a seemingly irrelevant advance in medicine—the trust which in the sixteenth and seventeenth centuries the medical profession began once again to place in the therapeutic qualities of the mineral waters."[9]

THE DEVELOPMENT OF SPAS

The medical profession was largely responsible for the growth of holidaying away from home. During the seventeenth century doctors increasingly began to recommend the medicinal properties and healing qualities of mineral waters. The idea of the healthful and curative properties of mineral waters was no new thing, however, for the ancient Greeks had their "Asclepian sanctuaries" where the ailing indulged in bathing, exercise and dieting and during the Roman Empire health resorts associated with springs and baths were widespread. In England, both Bath and Buxton were important centres. With the coming of Christianity the water cures and bathing centres of classical times lost favour: the early Christians looked upon bathing centres as haunts of wickedness and promiscuity.

The custom of medicinal bathing lapsed during the Middle Ages but with the Renaissance the cult revived. Centres of medicinal bathing and water cures became known as *spas*. The term is derived from the Walloon word, *espa*, meaning a fountain, and is taken from the town of Spa in Belgium. This watering place was founded as early as 1326 by Collin le Loup, an ironmaster of Liège, who apparently was cured of an ailment by the chalybeate springs. Spas on the continent were developed some two to three hundred years before they became popular in England. Nevertheless, it does seem that even in medieval England pilgrimages were sometimes undertaken to springs or holy wells which were credited with magical properties and that Bath was a centre to which the sick of all classes resorted. The Elizabethan *Poor Law Act* of 1601 gave special dispensation at Bath and free treatment was provided by the Church. Many of the spas which subsequently emerged in England had their origin in the pre-Reformation holy wells. Holy wells were a very common feature and the place name is to be found on most O.S. 1-inch sheets.

The efficacy of mineralised waters to cure gout, dropsy, stomach complaints, even barrenness in women, was firmly believed in by the medical practitioners of the seventeenth century, although at this time science had not revealed their true chemical properties or fully discovered how to use them medicinally. One well-known seventeenth-century doctor of Tunbridge Wells claimed that spa waters "with their saponary and detersive quality, clean the whole ... body of man from all feculency and impurities. No remedy is more effectual in hypochondriacal and hysterick fits ...."[10]

Thus the vogue of "taking the waters" began, and doctors despatched their invalid patients to Bath and Tunbridge Wells and a few other places where mineral springs were known to exist. A search for new mineral springs began in earnest, for the discovery of mineralised waters meant potential prosperity and places were quick to capitalise such good fortune. For example, Scarborough found springs, which were charged with minerals, gushing out of the cliffs and with this discovery it began to flourish; it still styles itself "Queen of Watering Places." By the end of the eighteenth century there were literally hundreds of spas, great and small, in existence: Bath, Tunbridge Wells, Cheltenham, Epsom, Harrogate and Buxton are only the most famous of numerous watering places which included, for example, Ashby de la Zouch, Boston (near Leeds), Dinsdale-on-Tees, Ilkley, Malvern, Llandrindod Wells and Shap.

Bath and Tunbridge Wells became the most popular and most fashionable of the English watering places, but Bath was pre-eminent. In origin a Roman settlement and centre of relaxation, its modern revival stemmed from royal patronage in Stuart times. During the eighteenth century, with Richard "Beau" Nash as its "master of ceremonies," Bath reached the pinnacle of its fame, though its supremacy as a watering place is still undisputed. Epsom and Tunbridge Wells became famous during the seventeenth century and, though they owed their origin to medicinal springs and wells, their fame and prosperity grew and rested in their social pleasures rather than in their clinical cures. Tunbridge Wells in particular became a great frivolling centre for Charles II's court. Tunbridge Wells is of special interest, as Pimlott remarks, for, unlike Bath, it had no past history and its development illustrates the interplay of three of the principal factors making for the development of a fashionable resort—the approval of the medical profession, local enterprise (in this case the accidental discovery and development of mineral springs by Dudley, Lord North), and Court patronage.[11]

Thus the spas developed and, though at first they were in the nature of sanatoria, visited for reasons of health by the sick and ailing of all classes, and could in no sense be called holiday resorts, they became increasingly centres of *divertissement* to which the rich and fashionable flocked whether their ailments were real, fancied or non-existent. The spas came to play an important role in English social life. "Although both their collective name and their original character came from the Continent," says Addison "the development of spa life in England was characteristically English. With our chronic perversity, having become far more solemn than our neighbours in health we became far more jovial in sickness. The Abbé Le Blanc noticed this. He said: 'They are much deceived who think that the waters of Bath are like those of Bourbon, where only infirm, paralytic or valetudinarian persons are to be found. This is the place in all England to enjoy good health, and to turn it to account.'"[12] After the Restoration the medical men quickly lost control of the spas which became no longer primarily health resorts; rather they turned into centres of amusement and diversion, with assembly rooms, musical entertainments, recreational games (including amorous pursuits) and gambling. By the end of the seventeenth century the three principal watering places, Bath, Tunbridge Wells and Epsom, were "more fam'd for Pleasure than Cures." The popularity of the spas continued throughout the eighteenth century and so fashionable did the habit of "taking the waters" become that Horace Walpole, writing in 1790, commented sardonically "One would think that the English were ducks; they are forever waddling to the waters."

However, notwithstanding the astonishing development and success of the spas (though some, it is true, had only a transitory existence) "the number whom the spas could accommodate and the number who could afford to stay at them were ... both small. The fashionable watering places counted for little except in the lives of the highest strata of society. The lesser ones were frequented by the provincial gentry and the citizens from the immediate vicinity. For the rest of the community except in the special case of London they served only their primary purpose as a cure." [13]

By the middle of the nineteenth century some of the earlier spas had begun to decline but the introduction of the German practice of hydrotherapy gave others a new lease of life and even led to the establishment of some new Victorian spas, *e.g.* Woodhall Spa. But the First World War marked the end of an era and the social changes of the post-war years led both to the rapid decline of the spas as curative centres and to fundamental changes in the function of spa towns.

THE GROWTH OF SEASIDE RESORTS

The second stage in the development of holiday resorts centred on the movement to the coast which, in turn, led to the growth of the seaside resort. Water, again, provides the fascination and motivating factor. The sea and sea bathing are among the more important ingredients of any English seaside resort. The practice of bathing in the sea for pleasure is a comparatively recent development: the motive in bathing was at first essentially curative. Sea bathing is usually said to have begun at Scarborough, already known for its spa, about 1730, though bathing is attested at Whitby even earlier. At Brighton (or Brighthelmstone as it was commonly called until the nineteenth century), the practice is first recorded in 1736.

This new habit of sea bathing gained popularity through the recommendations by the medical profession of its therapeutic value. As early as 1667 Dr Robert Whitie had urged sea bathing for gout. In 1702, Sir John Floyer, in his *History of Cold Bathing*, said: "since we live on an Island, and have the Sea about us, we cannot want an excellent Cold Bath, which will both preserve our Healths, and cure many Diseases, as our Fountains do." Seaside resorts for bathing, however, only date from the middle of the eighteenth century and the real impetus for the movement to the sea may be said to have been provided by Dr Richard Russell, a Brighton physician, who argued that sea water was as effective for medical use, internally and externally, as spa waters. Sea water, he said, was "a Kind of common Defence against the Corruption and Putrefaction of Bodies." Russell maintained that sea water was effective against many maladies and should be used in the treatment of, among other diseases, cirrhosis, dropsy, gout, gonorrhoea and scurvy. Russell not only urged the value of sea bathing but insisted that sea water itself—a full pint of it—should be drunk! And so gradually the habit of sea bathing became established and the seaward movement began.

As a result of this new vogue, Brighton soon came to rival Bath as a health resort. In the latter part of the eighteenth century the influx of visitors to Brighton, all anxious to drink the waters, bathe in the briny or enjoy the salubrious climate, grew to great proportions. Royal patronage set the seal on Brighton's prosperity. The Prince Regent, later George IV, became a regular visitor to Brighton and thereby gave it fame; the gentry and genteel followed suit and secured the prosperity of the place. The famous Pavilion was built at this time as a royal residence. The fad of sea bathing followed the fad of taking waters; and the growth of seaside resorts was set in motion. William Cowper in his poem *Retirement* (1782) gently ridicules the gathering momentum of the seaward movement:

> "Your prudent grandmammas, ye modern belles,
>   Content with Bristol, Bath and Tunbridge Wells,
>   When health required it would consent to roam,
>   Else more attached to pleasures found at home.
>   But now alike, gay widow, virgin, wife,
>   Ingenious to diversify dull life,
>   In coaches, chaises, caravans and hoys,
>   Fly to the coast for daily, nightly joys,
>   And all, impatient of dry land, agree
>   With one consent to rush into the sea."

Seaside resorts were modelled at first on the spas: they were furnished with promenades, assembly rooms and libraries and held balls, musical concerts and lectures, while masters of ceremonies organised the entertainment. Like the spas, many of them owed much to royal patronage. Just as Brighton was indebted to the Prince Regent, so Weymouth owed much to the visits of George III, Worthing and Southend to the patronage of Princesses Adelaide and Charlotte, and Cowes, later, to Queen Victoria.[14]

The growth of the English seaside resort was greatly stimulated by the French Revolutionary and Napoleonic Wars. Hostilities placed restrictions on foreign travel and those who formerly had made the Grand Tour, visiting Paris, Geneva, Florence and Rome, now contented themselves with trips to Brighton, Margate, Scarborough and Weymouth. Napoleon, incidentally, was also indirectly responsible for the seaside bands, long an essential feature of seaside resorts, since the south coast was sprinkled with military camps whose brass bands captivated the ladies with their stirring martial music.

English holidays at this time, however, could be and doubtless often were, dull and dreary. The gentility and snobbery of the "refined" resorts added up to dullness and ennui and Charles Lamb with some exasperation wrote: "We have been dull at Worthing one summer, duller at Brighton another, dullest at Eastbourne a third, and are at this moment doing dreary penance at—Hastings!" The only interesting diversions seem to have been flirting with the fair ladies and watching the bathers. People at first bathed in the nude and this led to inquisitive onlookers congregating to watch. To discourage such "peeping Toms," bathing machines, which could be trundled into deep water, appeared. But the impolite sightseers were, apparently, not to be outdone and took to using telescopes. The ladies countered this by adopting bathing dress, a costume soon so concealing that the disappointed sightseers were constrained to complain:

> "The ladies dressed in flannel cases
> Show nothing but their handsome faces."

During the latter part of the nineteenth century there was a gradual revolt against the genteel dullness and propriety of the seaside resort and at newer resorts such as Blackpool greater opportunities for revelry presented themselves. But before proceeding to trace these later developments, some reference must be made to the Grand Tour.

THE GRAND TOUR

The Continental holiday shows clear traces of its descent from the Grand Tour of the seventeenth and eighteenth centuries. The first allusion to the Grand Tour occurred in 1670 but, as Fairbairn pointed out, it was initially an Elizabethan concept. "From Tudor times three types of people made their way to Europe, stimulated by different circumstances, but all conspiring to develop and influence that phenomenon which by the seventeenth century became known as the Grand Tour. First the end of the Wars of the Roses and the gradual achievement of law and order under the strong Tudor monarch sent a mass of out-of-pocket gallants into Europe as travellers and mercenaries. Next the development of the printing press and the arrival of Renaissance learning from Italy encouraged more students to travel. Thirdly the evolution of a rich and stable monarchy helped to create a class of professional statesmen and diplomats."[15] People then, particularly diplomats, merchants and scholars, began to travel on the Continent in considerably greater numbers than they had ever done before. To help create a class of professional diplomats young men were placed in the entourage of ambassadors "for in so travelling they shall suck the experience of many." But there were some who feared the ill effects of foreign travel with all its temptations upon young and yielding gentlemen and Robert Cecil, Queen Elizabeth's great minister, was disgusted with his son who had become too enamoured of foreign ways roundly charging him with being "a spending sot, meet only to keep a tennis-court." However, the numbers of people going abroad at this time were small, for foreign travel was subject to strict Government control; furthermore, foreign travel was still a very hazardous business.

"[In the seventeenth century] ... increasing numbers of potential diplomats, men becoming rich through England's growing foreign trade and scholars in search of European learning, began to legitimise the gallants' jaunts which thus imperceptibly merged into the educative and political institution known as the Grand Tour."[16] Pimlott draws attention to two factors which stimulated continental tourism during late Stuart and early Hanoverian times: the intellectual atmosphere of the Restoration period and the peace following the Utrecht settlement (1713): both fostered and favoured the idea of the Grand Tour.[17] By the middle of the eighteenth century it had become fashionable for the upper classes to travel abroad and probably about 20,000 travellers a year crossed the Channel; according to Horace Walpole an estimated 40,000 people passed through Calais during the two years 1763–5, while Edward Gibbon was told that in 1785 there were more than 40,000 Englishmen touring or resident on the Continent. The Grand Tour seems to have reached the height of its popularity in the years immediately following the Seven Years War (1756–63) but by this time its aim seems to have largely degenerated into the pursuit of pleasure and many inveighed against its corrupting influence. Within a few years, however, the Grand Tour was to be brought to a sudden end: the Revolution in France and the Wars of Napoleon which plunged the whole of the Continent into turmoil resulted in a cessation in travel. As Fairbairn said: "The Napoleonic Wars broke the continuity, and thereafter the old order of things changed: the Tour had become overnight the memory of a dying generation. Then again a new type of traveller was emerging with specific reasons for travel: to study agriculture, botany or art."[18]

One of the interesting aspects of the Grand Tour was its conventional and regular form. As early as 1678 John Gailhard, in his *Compleat Gentleman*, had prescribed a three-year tour as customary. A generally accepted itinerary was also laid down which involved a long stay in France, especially in Paris, almost a year in Italy visiting Genoa, Milan, Florence, Rome and Venice, and then a return by way of Germany and the Low Countries via Switzerland. Of course, there were variations to this itinerary but this was the most popular route: it was generally believed that "there was little more to be seen in the rest of the civil world after Italy, France and the low Countries, but plain and prodigious barbarism."[19]

THE VICTORIAN AGE

When the Prince Regent and his bucks were enjoying themselves at Brighton very few other people in England took holidays. Outside wealthy circles, few ever travelled very far from their immediate neighbourhood. Movement about the country was severely limited, partly because of expense but partly because of the difficulties of road transport. The building of the new turnpike roads and, later, of the railways made it possible for people to venture further afield. The coming of the railways in particular exercised a profound effect upon the fortunes of the seaside resort since they brought a new mobility, allowing people to move relatively freely, quickly and cheaply from one place to another. The introduction of "excursion trains," as early as the 1840s made possible the day trip to the coast and Pimlott concluded that the advances in third-class railway travel "were a major cause of the accelerated growth of the popular seaside resort in the 'seventies and 'eighties."[20]

Any improvement in transport was likely to have immediate repercussions upon travel, and even before the advent of the railway the new steamboats, providing cheaper and more rapid transport, illustrated this. Margate, which became the first popular resort, owed its popularity to the steamer services. As early as 1765 sailing ships carrying wheat up to London were each taking some sixty to seventy passengers downstream to Margate on their return journey and by 1802 "hoys" were carrying 20,000 passengers in the season to that seaside resort. After the coming of the steamboats, increasing numbers travelled down river from London and in 1830 Margate had more than 100,000 visitors and as an account of the time stated "visitors, like mackerel, are valued only by the shoal and the amusements are consequently chiefly adapted for the Million." Nor was this the only case of water transport; as Cosgrove and Jackson say: "Steamers, long before the coming of the railway, had conveyed hundreds of thousands of Liverpudlians across the Mersey to New Brighton or even further to Rhyl and Llandudno, and had initiated the Manx holiday industry." [21] The railways, however, "had a much more pervasive influence. ... Entirely new resorts were created by their arrival—Cleethorps had its origin in 1849 when the main Grimsby line was completed and branch lines in 1871–3 and 1877 created Skegness and Mablethorpe respectively." [22]

During the early years (1830–70) most of the visitors to the seaside resorts were day excursionists, for the working classes had not as yet secured regular holidays nor sufficient incomes to enable them to undertake any prolonged stay: regular holidays were still reserved for the upper and middle classes, especially the latter. Blackpool, for example, was very much a "middle-class creation" and it remained their preserve until the 1860s.

In Brighton, the aristocracy were beginning to yield place to the middle classes and there were even complaints of rowdy elements from London invading the resort. Some resorts managed to preserve their "select" nature, however. Saltburn, for instance, was successful in preventing cheap day excursions being run to the town until quite late in its development; the result was the emergence of nearby Redcar as a playground for industrial Teesside.

At this time, all the important resorts, with the exception of Scarborough and Margate, were on the South Coast; these were Brighton, Hastings and Dover. In the north of England, Blackpool, Southport and Bridlington were still very small places only just beginning to emerge as resorts.

By 1900 this situation had been completely transformed and there were over sixty places officially listed as seaside resorts; three of the major ones (Scarborough, Blackpool and Southport) in the north of England.

THE HEYDAY OF THE RESORTS

From about 1870 the seaside resorts became increasingly and preponderantly proletarian playgrounds. The gradual introduction of regular holidays and better wages made it possible for large numbers to indulge in a holiday away from home and during the summer season working-class families moved *en masse* to the seaside, usually to the larger resorts which had more to offer in the way of amenities. The result of this expansion in holiday-making led to a rapid growth of the resorts and their population increased from a total of 390,000 in 1851 to 1,155,000 in 1901.

Until the First World War, the pre-eminent mode of transport was the railway for the motor car was still in its infancy. This had the effect of concentrating development at particular points along the coast. Moreover, easy accessibility was important and this tended to stimulate regional development: resorts grew to serve nearby industrial populations, for example the Durham and north Yorkshire coast (Hartlepool, Seton Carew, Redcar) served the Durham coalfield and Teesside, the Fylde coast (Blackpool, Fleetwood) served north Lancashire and parts of the West Riding, the North Wales coast (Rhyl, Colwyn Bay, Llandudno) served south Lancashire and the northwest Midlands, and the Gower Peninsula and Glamorgan coast (Penarth, Barry, Mumbles) served the South Wales coalfield.

While in the beginning the seaside resorts developed because of their natural resources, *i.e.* the sea and the beach, soon the more popular thriving resorts turned their attention to the provision of additional amenities and recreational facilities, or what may be termed "created resources." After 1870 there was substantial investment by both municipalities and individuals in the provision of these "created resources." As Pimlott has said: "The capital invested in the seaside resorts in this period of expansion was enormous. Large sums were sunk by private persons in hotels, boarding houses, shops, residences and places of entertainment, and private enterprise accounted for most of the capital investment. But municipal activity was by no means negligible. Existing piers were enlarged and new ones built at the public expense: parades, parks, ornamental gardens were laid out and improved; road and sea defence works were undertaken; baths, bandstands, aquaria and other amenities were provided. In its turn the capital invested gave employment in a hundred different ways—directly in the building industry, to the hotel and boarding-house keepers and the domestic staffs who waited upon the visitors, to the shopkeepers, restaurateurs, entertainers and all the others who attended immediately to their requirements, indirectly on the railways, in the luxury industries, and to all those who supplied the raw materials and the manufactures which were consumed."[23] Some indication of the immense sums of money spent in enhancing the amenities of resorts is provided by the case of Blackpool, where the local authority in the inter-war period spent nearly £3m providing new and improved promenades, parks, gardens and swimming pools.

THE POST-WAR ERA

The long period of spectacular growth of the seaside resorts came to an end in 1939 with the outbreak of the Second World War. For five years their functions very largely lapsed and when, at the end of hostilities they began to resuscitate their former activities they found that a new philosophy of holiday-making had begun to emerge and that many of the old traditions had gone.

The post-war era, with longer holidays, increasing affluence, the surge in motor-car ownership, the growth of cheap foreign package tours as well as the growth in "activity" holidays, has seen radical changes both in the spirit and location of holiday-making. These changes will be discussed later: suffice it to say that many of the resorts have suffered lean times in recent years and some, such as Blackpool, are having to give serious thought to their futures.

Perhaps the greatest and most significant development in modern tourism has been the quite spectacular growth of holidays abroad. In Britain alone something like 8 million people annually are holidaying abroad. There are many factors responsible for this but chiefly it is due to the extraordinary development of the inclusive ("package") tour which has transformed the holiday habits of millions. The motor car, too, has had a big impact on holiday-making and been responsible for the rapid growth in the touring, camping and caravanning type of holiday which largely, if not entirely, ignores the traditional resort town. These and other themes will be explored in later chapters.

NOTES

1. "The Art of Travel," M.D., the Medical Newsmagazine, July, 1967, reprinted in R. W. McIntosh, *Tourism: Principles, Practices, Philosophies*, Grid Inc., 1972.

2. *See* D. Brooke, *Pilgrims Were They All*, Faber & Faber, 1937.

3. McIntosh, *op. cit.*, p. 16.

4. McIntosh, *op. cit.*, p. 17.

5. J. A. R. Pimlott, *The Englishman's Holiday*, Faber & Faber, 1947, p. 22.

6. Pimlott, p. 22.

7. *Op. cit.*, pp. 22–3.

8. *Op. cit.*, p. 23.

9. W. Addison, *English Spas*, Batsford, 1951, p. 2.

10. Dr Madan, quoted in Addison, *op. cit.*, p. 2.

11. Pimlott, *op. cit.*, p. 27.

12. Addison, *op. cit.*, p. 3.

13. Pimlott, *op. cit.*, pp. 33–4.

14. *See* E. W. Gilbert, "The Growth of Inland and Seaside Health Resorts," *Scottish Geographical Magazine*, January, 1939.

15. A. N. Fairburn, "The Grand Tour," reproduced from *The Geographical Magazine*, London, Vol. XXIV, 1951, pp. 118–27.

16. Fairburn, *op. cit.*

17. Pimlott, *op. cit.*, p. 68.

18. Fairburn, *op. cit.*

19. Fairburn, *op. cit.*

20. *Op. cit.*, p. 164.

21. I. Cosgrove and R. Jackson, *The Geography of Recreation and Leisure*, Hutchinson, 1972, p. 37.

22. Cosgrove and Jackson, *op. cit.*, p. 37.

23. *Op. cit.*, p. 179.

Chapter II

The Evolution of Demand

IN the preceding chapter we gave a brief resumé of the historical development of holiday-making in Britain. A number of factors were alluded to which have been mainly responsible for the more recent growth of this important social phenomenon: increased leisure, holidays with pay, higher living standards, and greater mobility. Let us look a little more closely at these.

LEISURE

Holiday-making and tourism are, of course, only a part of the much wider field of leisure. Holiday-making and tourism cannot be indulged in unless one has the leisure or available time for its pursuit. Leisure does not *necessarily* result in holidaying, although it does tend to promote it. We have already indicated that increased leisure was a significant factor in the development of tourism, and increasing leisure is likely to stimulate tourist demand still further.

Relatively few people have thought very seriously about the implications of the growth of leisure in the twentieth century. One of the few who have is Michael Dower and in 1965 he drew attention to the great challenge which growing leisure presented: "Three great waves have broken across the face of Britain since 1800 ... the sudden growth of dark industrial towns ... the thrusting movement along far-flung railways ... the sprawl of car-based suburbs. Now we see ... the surge of a fourth wave which could be more powerful than all the others ... *leisure.*"[1] The Duke of Edinburgh has said: "we are on the threshold of the age of leisure ... we have to concentrate on providing facilities of the right sort and in the right place, and properly organised."

D. C. Mercer, discussing the demand for outdoor recreation has said that the demand situation in any area at a given time is made up of six interrelated elements:

(*i*) the *size* of the population;
(*ii*) the *amount* and *timing of leisure* enjoyed by the population;

(*iii*) the *mobility* of the population;
(*iv*) the *age* and *income* structure of the population;
 (*v*) the *recreational activities* engaged in by the population which, in turn, is dependent on
(*vi*) the *opportunities* available for recreation.

Although here we are more especially interested in the second of these components, "from the geographer's point of view, two variables are of interest above all others . . . the *distance* separating a population from its recreation areas; and . . . the *mobility* of that population in terms of car ownership and usage."[2]

Prior to the Industrial Revolution the aristocracy had a virtual monopoly of leisure. The agricultural labourer and the town artisan enjoyed breaks on Sundays and certain Saints' Days it is true but prolonged holidays were unknown. At first, the revolution in industry tended to aggravate rather than assuage the situation for the factory system with its inflexible working day and long hours militated against any rest from labour. With rare exceptions, the system was merciless. Gradually as time went on some workers did manage to arrange short holidays, usually coinciding in the North with the local patronal festivals, but for the majority respite from work was largely limited to Christmas, Easter and Whitsuntide. The first really significant change came in 1871 when Sir John Lubbock's *Bank Holiday Act* introduced the August Bank Holiday break to give four recognised annual public holidays.

During the middle and late nineteenth century, a series of statutes defined maximum working hours and conditions of labour for various categories of workers and guaranteed certain holidays to employees without loss of pay; for example, in 1842, the *Coal Mines Act* laid down the maximum hours of work per week for miners; in 1850, a weekly half-day break was made compulsory for women and children working in factories; and in 1878 the *Factories' and Workshops' Act* was passed. With the rise of Trade Unionism, the Unions sought systematically not only to secure improvements in basic wages and working conditions but also to obtain longer periods of annual holiday with pay.

Holidaying for the masses throughout the Victorian era was almost entirely confined to day excursions. The extended holiday was very much the privilege of the upper class and the more prosperous middle class. As Pimlott has said, around 1900 a holiday "was taken for granted as a luxury which could be enjoyed at a certain level of income but which there was no special hardship in going without."[3]

Nevertheless, the practice of going away for a week's holiday gradually gained ground, especially during the inter-war period as holidays with pay increasingly became usual. However, the normal working week remained fairly stable at about 45 hours until 1960 after which time a steady reduction in the standard weekly hours of work began to take place until it now stands at about 40.* The reduction in the length of the official working week is almost certain to continue: for example, in the summer of 1971 the Engineers' Trades Union lodged a claim for a 35-hour week; it is expected to drop to about 30 hours by the end of the century.[4] Already in the United States hundreds of firms now operate a three-day working week. The reduction in the working hours has meant that most workers now have a clear two-day weekend and this makes it possible for people, if they so wish, to go away for the weekend, either to a "second home" or resort or comparable place of relaxation. With the reduction in the length of the official working week has gone an extension of the basic holiday period from one to two or three weeks. Detailed information about the numbers of workers receiving paid annual holidays is far from adequate but sample surveys by *The Industrial Society* and the *Pilot National Recreation Survey*[5] provide some useful data. It has been estimated that in 1950 approximately 80 per cent of all industrial workers had one week's paid annual holiday; today it is virtually 100 per cent. Probably something of the order of 75 per cent of all workers now receive two weeks' paid holiday and 50 per cent three weeks.

It is interesting to compare the situation in Britain with that in the Continental countries, especially the countries of the European Community, and Table 1 summarises this situation.

These figures may come as something of a surprise to many and if the British worker believes that no one else in Europe works as hard as he does the Table goes a long way to show that indeed this is so. Among the countries of the European Community Italy alone has not got a legally enforced minimum holiday.

The considerable increase that is likely in holiday time in the future cannot fail to react on tourism. Already, partly as a result of increased leisure, there has been a rapid expansion in the taking of second holidays, as well as in day and weekend excursions and in the growth of second homes. The past decade has seen a big growth in these "multiple holidays."

---

* By standard working week is meant the weekly hours of work mutually agreed upon by employers and unions for each category of work, or that which is statutorily defined by legislation.

TABLE 1

Comparison of national annual paid and public holidays

Country	Minimum annual paid holidays (*in days*)	*Public holidays*	*Total*
France	24	9	33
Belgium	18	10	28
Netherlands	18–23	6–7	24–30
Luxembourg	18–24	10	28–34
W. Germany	15–24	10–13	25–37
Italy	12–20	17	29–37
United Kingdom	15 (generally)	6	21

AFFLUENCE

Increased leisure does not in itself beget tourism; there are in fact many socio-economic factors—income, age, occupation and education —which are important. Income obviously will have an important effect. Burton, discussing recreation generally, says: "the available data do suggest a strong correlation between income and recreation. Broadly, as income rises so does participation in most recreation pursuits."[6] This statement is equally applicable to holiday-making and tourism, which is but a special aspect of recreation.

We are living in what has been called an "age of affluence" and have already seen that tourism has been, and is, influenced by the economic considerations of holidays with pay and increases in real income. Income is therefore the second basic factor in the evolution of demand; as Lickorish has said: "Tourism, holiday-making and recreation are a function of wealth."[7]

When annual holidays first became a recognised feature of social life, they were given without remuneration. As wages were low, people had to be thrifty to enable them to live for a week without wages, let alone go away on holiday. Even as late as 1925 it was estimated that only about $1\frac{1}{2}$ million manual workers had paid holidays. Thereafter, however, there was a rapid improvement and by 1937 nearly 8 million workers received holidays with some kind of pay. The *Holiday with Pay Act* 1938, had the effect of encouraging voluntary agreements in respect of paid holidays. After the war the situation improved dramatically and by 1950 something like 80 per cent of all industrial workers were receiving one week's holiday with pay. At present the figure is practically 100 per cent. During recent years there has also been a substantial increase in the length of holidays with pay, many employees receiving two, and a considerable proportion three, weeks' paid holiday. Professional people and "white collar" workers fare better in this respect than manual workers, although there has been all-round progress. Even in 1965 when the *Pilot National Recreation Survey* was undertaken the returns showed that some 44 per cent of workers were receiving up to two weeks' paid annual holiday, an additional 19 per cent had two to three weeks', and a further 8 per cent enjoyed between three and four weeks'. Table 2 shows, along with other recreation-related factors, a projection of the average length of annual holidays with pay.

TABLE 2

An index of projected changes in recreation-related factors at quinquennial intervals (1960–85)

	Year					
Factor	1960	1965	1970	1975	1980	1985
1. Population	100	103	106	110	113	117
2. Home students in full-time higher education	100	165	195	240	315	395
3. Real income per head	100	115	130	155	180	200
4. Number of cars in use	100	165	220	280	330	380
5. Length of standard working week	100	95	90	85	80	75
6. Average length of annual holiday with pay	100	110	125	150	180	200

Source: T. L. Burton, *Economic Aspects of Selected Outdoor Recreation Enterprises in Rural Britain,* unpublished Ph.D. thesis, University of London, 1967.

The second economic consideration one must bear in mind is the increase in real income. For more than a decade now there has been an appreciable increase in real income; in general, wages have risen at a faster rate than the cost of living. Although there has been general inflation since the war, Britain is currently suffering a phase of acute inflation and it is difficult to predict how long this will continue. According to the official cost-of-living index, the value of money has halved during the past twenty years; on the other hand, wages have more than doubled—in many cases trebled and sometimes even quadrupled—over the same period so that on the average everyone is appreciably better off. In general, people have more money coming into their households than ever before—personal incomes increased by $10\frac{1}{2}$ per cent between 1969 and 1970.[8] After allowing for tax payments and higher national insurance contributions, however, real personal income rose by 9 per cent. Even this, however, is not as great as it seems for the rise in prices reduced the figure to $3\frac{1}{2}$ per cent. Nevertheless, there is an appreciable and continuing rise in real incomes. Real *per capita* income is the most difficult of all factors to forecast but Burton, taking the period 1960–80, says it "will probably rise by an amount somewhere between 50 and 100 per cent."[9]

Personal disposable incomes, *i.e.* incomes after tax has been deducted, are larger than ever before. A reflection of this is that in 1970 personal savings increased by $8\frac{1}{2}$ per cent over the 1969 figure and consumer spending also went up by $8\frac{1}{2}$ per cent. Over the decade 1960–70 the pattern of consumer spending changed quite markedly: the amount spent on food, the largest single item, decreased from about 25 to 20 per cent while the money spent on entertainment, recreation and travel increased. In 1970 the second biggest spending was on travel, entertainment and "other services" which amounted to $18\frac{1}{2}$ per cent of total consumer spending.[10] Total holiday expenditure was of the order of £1000m, while the amount spent on holidays abroad was £350m.

MOBILITY

The third important factor in the evolution of demand is increasing mobility. There is actual mobility, such as the motor car has provided, so that people are no longer anchored to a particular holiday centre as they tended to be when they mostly travelled by train, and there is speed of movement, which economises on time and therefore makes it possible for people with only two weeks or even one week of holiday to travel to distant places. Accessibility is a most important factor in holiday travel and the holiday destination.

Patmore has written: "As opportunities for recreation have increased, so has the mobility which enables those opportunities to be seized. The very nature of the transport available in any period has done much to determine the location, and even the form, of recreational pursuits. Paradoxically, much early escape from the oppressive confines of an urban environment was channelled by the railway to other towns, the nascent resorts. As late as 1927 Albert Demangeon could write that 'British civilisation wears an urban semblance even in its recreation.' Even before the advent of the railway, some coastal resorts had become popular because of their accessibility by water. Margate is a classic instance"[11] (*see* p. 14). Especially important from the viewpoint of mass recreation was the introduction of the excursion train with its cheap fares and, as Patmore has said, "the success of excursion trains clearly demonstrated the demand for cheap pleasure travel."[12]

The railway dominated communications for almost one hundred

years. The gradual spread of the network opened up many areas and made many places hitherto not very accessible easy to get to. But a railway system is not a flexible instrument of communications and the railways tended rather to concentrate and restrict movement to particular channels—in this context to a number of seaside resorts which were already beginning to emerge. Until the Second World War the railway continued to carry the majority of holiday travellers; in 1950 travel by train was still the most popular form of transport for holiday-makers spending two or three weeks on the Continent. At that time there were slightly less than $2\frac{1}{2}$ million private cars in the United Kingdom (compared with 13 million in 1970) and the numbers who took their cars abroad were relatively few. Air travel, too, had not come into its own with respect to holiday travel; indeed, to fly was widely regarded as something of an adventure and Thos. Cook's, the leading travel agent, went out of their way to reassure tourists who were a little apprehensive about travelling by air—in their travel brochure it stated: "Travel by air is indeed pleasant." At that time the latest thing in air travel was the turbo-prop Viscount which had a speed of around 300 m.p.h.

After 1950, when the difficulties and restrictions of the immediate post-war years had begun to straighten themselves out, there were rapid developments in transport—car ownership multiplied, the motor coach appeared in increasing numbers and the coach tour became popular, while air transport gained rapidly in popularity. Car ownership, above anything else, has had very important repercussions upon recreation generally. Not only has it affected the annual holiday in that it has made the touring holiday more popular and enabled people to travel farther afield (because car travel is cheaper than rail), but it has greatly stimulated the half-day, full-day or weekend excursion either into the country or to the coast. The level of car ownership seems likely to continue to increase, especially as incomes, and more particularly real incomes, rise and it has been estimated that by 1980 there will be something approaching 20 million cars in Britain, approximately half as many again as at the beginning of the 1970s. The extent to which the motor car will be used for holiday purposes in the future is, however, not easy to assess. Burton says: ". . . It depends upon a much wider range of factors, including traffic congestion, the extent to which recreation facilities that are provided in urban areas can act as alternatives to visits by car to the countryside and, not least, unknown technological innovations in forms of mass transport."[13] In the immediate future, however, it seems certain that much greater use of the motor car will be made in tourism, for two significant developments are facilitating greater usage of the car. The construction of motorways is making speedy travel over long distances by car easy, and making more remote places more accessible. The development of "Motorail"—the carrying of cars over extended distances by train—is making it possible for holiday-makers to use their cars in holiday areas, a facility which could not be enjoyed if, as formerly, tourists travelled by train because of the long, tedious and tiresome car journeys involved.

There are also the great advances made in air travel, more particularly, of course, for overseas holiday-making. Now jets reach 600 m.p.h. and the tourist can reach a far distant holiday area, such as Malta, Cyprus, Tunis or the Canary Islands, in a matter of a few hours. Air fares, too, in spite of increased fuel costs are still relatively cheap. The enormous expansion in air traffic for holiday purposes will be dealt with in greater detail later.

PRESENT-DAY FACTORS

In addition to the factors of leisure time, disposable income and increased mobility, consideration must be given to such things as age, education, social class and cost, which are all significant factors in influencing current demand.

Age, and sex also, affects demand. Table 3 gives a breakdown, according to age, of the people in Britain participating in holidays at home.

TABLE 3
Age groups and holidays

Age group	Percentage
16–24	58
25–34	60
35–54	63
55–64	62
over 65	46

Clearly the elderly, partly because of increasing infirmity but also partly because of reduced income, are less prone to take holidays away. It is interesting to note also that women show a greater proclivity to go away on holiday than men. Family circumstances also exert an important influence; families which are in the child-rearing stage (*i.e.* approximately the 25–34 age group) tend to holiday, and certainly to travel, less—partly, of course, because of the expense. By the time a family man has reached his mid-forties he is usually well on his way towards reaching his maximum salary, has become largely relieved of supporting his children and substantially reduced his financial commitments (*e.g.* mortgage and the like) and hence is in a better position to indulge in holidays. When one looks at the figures of those who go abroad for their holidays it is found that only 26 per cent of those under 24 years of age and only 8 per cent of those over 65 venture out of the country; on the other hand, 32 per cent between the ages of 25 and 44 and 35 per cent between the ages of 45 and 64 go abroad.[14]

Levels of income form another important factor influencing tourism as well as participation in recreation pursuits generally. The *Pilot National Recreation Survey* clearly indicated that "in almost every pursuit, participation increases with income." This is also borne out by the figures of people taking home holidays at different levels of income. Table 4 shows the proportions of people who do not take a holiday, in relation to income levels.

TABLE 4

Proportion of people not taking holidays in relation to income

Income	Proportion taking no holiday (%)
Over £3500	17
£2500–3500	23
£1900–2500	23
£1500–1900	35
£1000–1500	45
Less £1000	59

These figures demonstrate quite clearly that the more affluent members of society are the ones who holiday most.

Income cannot always be equated with social class but there is a broad correlation between the two. Table 5 shows the proportions of people who go abroad, according to their social class.

TABLE 5

Proportion of people going abroad in relation to social class

Social group	Percentage of population	Proportion going abroad (%)
AB (Professional and managerial)	14	31
C₁ (Skilled working class)	21	29
C₂ (Unskilled working class)	37	29
DE (Poor and elderly)	28	12

Another important socio-economic factor which influences the demand for travel is education. Broadly speaking, the better educated members of the population have a higher propensity to travel; moreover, those with a better education travel more often. According to the evidence we have, education does seem to have some positive bearing on tourism and therefore, in view of the increase in the proportion of young people receiving full-time higher education, one can predict an increasing interest in, and enthusiasm for, travel.

Costs will always be an important factor generating or retarding tourism and especially holidaying abroad. The price levels of tourism are especially significant and, broadly speaking, countries receiving tourists must be able to compete with the costs of holidays in the generating countries. One of the reasons why so many British people have been attracted to Spain is the low cost of Spanish holidays. On the other hand, the French have tended to price themselves out of the market because of the high cost of food, accommodation, etc.

Surprisingly enough, until very recently the continental holiday was one of the very few things still cheaper than it was twenty years ago. For example, in 1950 a fortnight's holiday in Cyprus travelling by air cost £138 while a similar holiday in 1972 cost just over £100; similarly, a fortnight's holiday in southern Italy at, say, Amalfi or Salerno which cost about £80 in 1950 could in 1972 be had for about £10 cheaper. Since 1973, however, costs have increased substantially. Over and above such general reductions there are, of course numerous tour operators offering "package holidays" at bargain prices, though these, too, have suffered increases in costs. Because of these relatively low prices at a time when disposable incomes are rising it is now possible for many thousands of people to travel abroad for their holidays.

NOTES

1. "The Challenge of Leisure," Civic Trust, 1965, p. 5.

2. "The Geography of Leisure—A Contemporary Growth-Point," *Geography*, Vol. 55, pp. 261–72.

3. *The Englishman's Holiday*, p. 211.

4. M. Dower, "Leisure—It's Impact on Man and the Land," *Geography*, Vol. 55, 1970, pp. 253–60.

5. British Travel Association/University of Keele, 1969.

6. Introduction, *Recreation and Research Planning*, Allen & Unwin, 1970, p. 19.

7. "Planning for Tourism," in *Recreation and Research Planning*, ed. T. L. Burton, p. 169.

8. *National Income and Expenditure 1971*, Publication of the Government Statistical Service, H.M.S.O.

9. *Op. cit.*

10. *National Income and Expenditure 1971.*
11. *Land and Leisure*, David & Charles, 1970, p. 25.
12. *Idem*, p. 27.
13. *Recreation and Research Planning*, p. 257.
14. British Travel Association, 1967.

Chapter III

Tourist Motivation

THE WHY OF TOURISM

WHY do people these days engage in tourism? A study of tourist psychology and motivation reveals that individuals normally travel for more than one reason, and for many, perhaps the majority, tourism is the outcome of a combination of motivations. On the other hand, it should be recognised that some are urged to take a holiday for one particular reason alone. Those who can afford the time and money frequently go to the winter sports for the specific purpose of skiing, skating and tobogganing. Many Britons are enticed to the Mediterranean lands by the attraction of nothing other than abundant sunshine, blue skies and warm seas. Numerous Americans visit Europe just to look at the "old homeland" and at such historic centres as London, York, Bruges, Amsterdam, Heidelberg, Rome and Venice.

McIntosh has said that basic travel motivators may be grouped into four categories:[1]

(*i*) *Physical motivators*, which are related to physical relaxation and rest, sporting activities, and specific medical treatment; all are connected with the individual's bodily health.

(*ii*) *Cultural motivators*, which are connected with the individual's desire to travel in order to learn about other countries and their peoples and their cultural heritage expressed in art, music, literature, folklore, etc.

(*iii*) *Interpersonal motivators*, which are related to a desire to visit relatives or friends, or to escape from one's family, workmates or neighbours, or to meet new people and forge new friendships, or simply to escape from the routine of everyday life.

(*iv*) *Status and prestige motivators*, which are identified with needs of personal esteem and personal development; these are related to travel for business or professional interests, for the purposes of education or the pursuit of hobbies.

If we break down and elaborate upon these categories, we can say that people engage in tourism for eight main reasons:

(*i*) For relaxation and refreshment of body and mind, which is becoming ever more necessary in modern life with its speed, stress and strain.

(*ii*) For health purposes: to secure fresh air and sunshine, and often winter warmth, and sometimes to take, and bathe in, medicated waters or undergo special treatments of a medical kind.

(*iii*) For active participation in a wide variety of sporting activities such as walking, mountaineering, skiing, sailing, fishing, shooting, surfing, pony-trekking, etc.

(*iv*) For sheer pleasure, fun and excitement; the individual's need for pure pleasure is very strong indeed and travel and holiday-making form a simple way of satisfying this demand.

(*v*) For interest in "foreign parts," especially in places having important historical or cultural associations or places holding special festivals in art, drama, music, etc.

(*vi*) For interpersonal reasons: to visit one's relatives, to meet new people and seek new friendships, or even to escape for a while from one's usual associates.

(*vii*) For spiritual purposes as, for example, the making of pilgrimages to sacred religious sites or holy places.

(*viii*) For professional or business reasons, *e.g.* attending conventions related to the professions, industry or commerce, or to some organisation to which the individual belongs.

BEHAVIOURAL ASPECTS

It may not be entirely inappropriate here to take a quick glance at some of the behavioural aspects of man, since these are not without some significance to the tourist industry. Man is a social animal and gregariousness is a feature of human society; he is dependent as an individual upon social membership. One of the instinctive emotional tendencies of the individual is to seek the company of his fellow men and to remain with them when they have been found. This may help to explain why families persist in going to crowded seaside resorts, why they will put up with crowded beaches, restaurants, places of amusement, etc. and why they will tolerate queueing in traffic jams to get to a holiday resort. It helps to explain also the success of holiday fellowship centres and "holiday camps" which carry socialisation to an extreme; also, such kinds of holiday as organised coach tours, caravan holidays and ocean cruises. Many tourists participate in such holidays as much because they enjoy being members of an organised group as because they enjoy meeting people.

It should not be forgotten, however, that while there are many who are never content unless they are part of a crowd, there are some who shun crowds and eschew contact with people as much as possible: they are the ones who want mountains and beaches to themselves and will go to endless trouble to discover quiet, unknown spots.

Social stratification also still tends to exert a strong influence upon tourism. Formerly, the upper classes—the titled, the wealthy and the leisured—went to the winter sports centres and holidayed in the off-season. Resorts such as Blackpool and Margate were not for them; it was Deauville or Nice or some other five-star resort. Such social snobbery still persists and for the sake of "keeping up with the Jones'" people will purchase a caravan, buy a boat, go on a cruise or indulge in a winter sports holiday. It's all good for the tourist business, even though it may entail an overdraft at the bank. As one climbs in the social and economic scale one often moves from boarding house to private hotel, from private hotel to two or three star hotel, and so on. Such social attitudes reflect the natural tendency of individuals to display and assert themselves among their fellow men and to find satisfaction in gaining their admiration.

Associated with these attitudes is the element of fantasy, escapism. A holiday is, very often, simply an escape from the routine existence of everyday working life. For instance, until the Second World War, the typical Lancashireman's or Yorkshireman's idea of a holiday was a spree—a brief break from his working life when he "lived like a lord," liberally and without stint. Throughout the year he paid his holiday money into the Works Holiday Club so that he could spend it all on one week's riotous and extravagant living. His idea of a good time was to consume beer, ice-cream, oysters and whelks in large quantities, recline at ease in a deck-chair and doze in mid-afternoon—denied him during fifty weeks of the year—dance in the ballroom, have a mild flirtation, paddle in the sea or build castles in the sand. Holidays become a wonderful opportunity for escapism: Annies become Helens, typists become private secretaries, fathers become directors, the daily help becomes a housekeeper, and the mink coat has been left at home in case it should be stolen!

Ethnocentrism (the belief of a group in the superiority of its own society) and exhibitionism are interesting aspects of social behaviour which are particularly relevant to tourism. Needless to say, such patterns of social behaviour create delicate and difficult problems to hoteliers and tour operators.

Curiosity is a human attribute of great significance to tourism. Many individuals are motivated by an urge to experience something new. The more intelligent the person—this does not always mean the better educated—the more likely is he to persist in searching for new experiences.

Another aspect of particular relevance to tourism is social communication: social organisation is only made possible and maintained by communication. But the most significant aspect of communication—ignoring for the moment developments in transportation—is the use of mass media, *i.e.* the press, radio, television, film, etc. for advertising purposes. People are very prone to be influenced by advertisements, and tourist agents and operators are not slow to press psychology into service. We have just mentioned the significance of curiosity as a motivating factor, but the most powerful incentive is not the unknown, but the partially known; hence the advertiser titillates the potential tourist with glossy, brightly coloured brochures or films and television pictures which are highly selective and flattering. Such allurements are specially designed to entice the tourist—and they do so with remarkable success. All manner of inducements are used, such as "English spoken here," "private beach," etc.

Man's physiological needs—fresh air, food, drink, rest, comfort, etc. necessary for the maintenance of general bodily wellbeing—are equally important as a motivating factor. Hence the stress which is so often laid by hoteliers and tour operators upon such items as cuisine, the wine cellar, beds, lounges, bathing pools, etc. There are indeed many tourists who are drawn to a particular place simply because of the guarantee of good food and a comfortable environment. Some countries, notably Switzerland, Austria and the Netherlands, appreciating the importance of this, have gained a high reputation for good food, comfort, cleanliness and service.

Tourism Motivators

Refreshment of body and mind

Industrialisation, urbanisation, motorisation, the "rat-race," etc. have created great pressures in modern life: speed, stress and strain have made it more necessary than ever before for people to relax periodically and undergo refreshment of body and mind. What form this relaxation and refreshment takes naturally varies with the individual.

To some, relaxation is secured by a change of environment or a different mode of life. Many find the change of air, the changed environment and the amusement and gaiety of the seaside resort quite sufficient to dispel their tensions. Others, more venturesome, seek the sunshine and excitement of foreign places and find that the holiday abroad possesses a magic virtue. To some, perhaps the minority, the annual holiday has a different meaning: it provides an opportunity to leave behind the din and clatter, drudgery and rush of day to day existence. For a brief spell one can seek and enjoy the quietude and tranquillity of a little-known seaside spot bereft of crowds and clamour but full of sand and sea, or stay in some pleasant country village which, perhaps, boasts an old inn with character, comfort and cuisine of a high order. Here in such a placid and peaceful environment the fatigue of body and mind is smoothed away and a new vigour and vitality instilled. But, whatever form the holiday takes, relaxation and refreshment are sought in some measure by the holiday-maker who is anxious to get away from it all for a little while.

Health

Doctors have long recommended the general benefits to be gained from fresh air and sunshine. In former times, when tuberculosis was a common ailment, patients were urged to seek a temporary home in regions which had unpolluted air, equable conditions and plenty of life-giving sunlight. In Switzerland, for instance, many sanatoria were established for these reasons and in many cases these sanatoria laid the foundations for future resort development. Davos in Switzerland, for example, now an important winter sports centre, started off as a health resort; located on the sheltered, sunny north-west (*adret*) side of the Landwasser valley at an elevation of over 1520 m (5000 ft), it lay above the mists, enjoyed abundant sunshine and pure air and, capitalising on these natural advantages, a German doctor called Spengler, founded the *Kurhaus* (1867) and started the village on its career as a health resort.[2] Madeira, now an increasingly popular holiday island, also found initial favour as a retreat for English consumptives. Many with asthmatic and bronchial troubles take advantage of the Cornish Riviera or comparable places with mild winters. Again, many travel to spas and clinics for curative baths and medical treatment. In some countries great store is still placed in spa treatments, probably nowhere more so than in the Soviet Union where there are numerous sanatoria along the Black Sea coast, *e.g.* at Sochi, or in the foothills of the Caucasus, *e.g.* at Kislovodsk.

Participation in sports

One of the interesting recent developments in tourism and holiday-making generally is the great increase in holidays involving physical activities. Burton has pointed out how the pattern of recreational activities has changed: there has been a decided swing from the more passive aspects of recreation to a more active or participatory involvement. This would seem to be linked in some ways to higher living standards (largely geared to increases in real and disposable incomes); the sedentary and monotonous character of so many jobs creates its own reaction: people tend to demand activity and excitement during their leisure hours which provide an antidote to the inertia and tedium of their working life. Thus there has been a great upsurge in sporting holidays. Whereas in the past many holiday-makers participated in a desultory way in sports, enjoying an occasional swim, round of golf, game of tennis, etc. large numbers these days make sport the *raison d'être* of the holiday: they go away primarily to indulge in a sporting activity to which all their energies are directed, whether it be hiking, mountaineering, skiing, sailing, fishing, surfing, underwater swimming, pony-trekking, etc. Perhaps the most notable of all these sporting holidays, at least in Britain, is the tremendous enthusiasm which has developed for sailing in recent years.

Pleasure

"Perhaps uppermost of all individual travel motivations is simply the motivation for satisfying a person's need for pure pleasure," says McIntosh. "Travel has the unique quality of being able to satisfy this desire...."[3] The individual's need for pure pleasure is very strong indeed: fun, excitement, sensual pleasures and romance. McDougall has said "... Happiness intensifies all pleasure, and every occasion of pleasure enriches our happiness."[4] The significance of the pleasure factor is, of course, not neglected by the travel agent and tour operator, who are astute psychologists when it comes to selling their wares: their brochures particularly emphasise the pleasurable aspects of holidays and travel. Moreover, it should be borne in mind that the anticipation of, and planning for, a holiday may be just as enjoyable as the actual holiday itself and forms part of the total pleasurable experience. "The romance of the trip is also a strong motivation, particularly in relation to honeymoon travel and also for those who are thrilled with the romantic aspects of seeing, experiencing and enjoying strange and attractive places."[5] Thus, while pleasure and romance are primary attributes of the holiday-travel experience, they are also very strong motivators.

Curiosity and culture

One principal reason for tourism is curiosity—about foreign lands, places and people. Mass media communications have made it possible for people to read about, hear and see "foreign parts," and appetites are whetted. The experiences of many during the Second World War brought an urge to travel more and, although it is difficult to prove, such wartime travel experiences may possibly have been one of the important factors which helped to trigger off the post-war travel boom. People whose parents ventured no further than Blackpool or Brighton, are now going further afield—to Scandinavia, Majorca, Tunisia. The increased interest shown by many in the art, architecture, music, literature, dance, folklore, sports and pastimes of other peoples' cultures or in archaeological and historical remains and monuments is but another aspect of curiosity, which has been partly stimulated by more education. International events, *e.g.* the Olympic Games, national celebrations, *e.g.* the fiftieth anniversary of the U.S.S.R., special festivals, *e.g.* the Oberammagau Passion Play, have great drawing power.

Interpersonal reasons

Much travel is undertaken for interpersonal reasons. There is considerable travel by people wishing to visit their relatives and friends. Large numbers of Americans visit "the old country" simply to see their families or because they *feel* Britain is their homeland. Many engage in travel because they like meeting new people and, indeed, many friendships have been made as a result of holiday acquaintances. There is also the other side: sometimes the individual feels that for the sake of his sanity he must get away from his relatives or neighbours or workmates for a little while or escape from the constraints and conventions of his normal everyday life. How often do people say they are going away on holiday simply "to get away from it all!"

Spiritual reasons

Many people are urged to travel for spiritual reasons. We have already seen that the wish to visit shrines and other holy places was one of the earliest motivators of travel. The making of pilgrimages to sacred religious sites or holy places is widespread in many parts of the world: in the Arab–Moslem world, for instance, the pilgrimage to Mecca or to other holy centres, such as Kairouan in Tunisia, remains a compelling act of faith. Among Europeans formal pilgrimages are now rare although religious centres, such as the Vatican, Jerusalem, Canterbury or St David's in Wales draw large numbers of tourists. Likewise, the small Pyrenean town of Lourdes, through its association with Bernadette Soubirous and the alleged miraculous properties of a local spring, has for over a hundred years drawn large numbers of pilgrims and the sick; it is estimated that over half a million people visit Lourdes every year. In the main, however, European tourists visit centres of religion and holy places out of interest rather than for personal reasons of faith, although this does not mean that they do not get any spiritual uplift at all from doing so.

Professional and business reasons

Large numbers of people travel for business or professional reasons. People increasingly have to travel around in connection with their occupational or professional interests. Conferences and conventions linked with politics, education, commerce, industry and the professions seem to proliferate year by year. Though some travel strictly for the business in hand, the majority link that business with pleasure and there are no doubt not a few who attend conferences and the like for the sake of their personal development and reputation and the enhancement of their own prestige. The tourist industry certainly benefits enormously from those who travel for business or quasi-business reasons.

Factors handicapping travel

To conclude this brief account of tourist motivation, it will be useful to look at the reasons why some people do not travel extensively or fail to travel at all. In a study made by Lansing and Blood, barriers to travel fell into five broad categories: (*i*) expense, (*ii*) lack of time, (*iii*) physical limitations, (*iv*) family circumstances, and (*v*) lack of interest;[6] to these we may add another factor, (*vi*) psychological deterrents.

There are financial constraints for every family, and holidays have to compete with other demands upon income. Cost would appear to be a major reason for not participating in holidays. Among the more poorly paid wage-earners there is not enough disposable income to support a holiday away from home. In pre-Second World War days, frequently the only way the working-man could afford an annual holiday was by making a weekly contribution to the holiday club run by the factory or other business concern. Today, although he may be much better paid, the pressures on his purse—often the instalments on his car, television or other household gadget, together with the weekly flutter on the pools and bingo—are frequently too great to leave anything for holidays.

Secondly, there are some who are inhibited by lack of time. Some people find it very difficult to leave their profession, business or job for even a brief period. A case in point is the small shop-keeper with perhaps a post office or paper round which must be serviced almost every day, year in year out. Of course there are some individuals in some walks of life who believe they are indispensable and will forego holidays.

Thirdly, physical limitations in the form of ill-health or incapacity may keep people at home. The elderly who are more prone to ailments and infirmity are, of course, especially affected and after the age of seventy relatively few indulge in extensive travel. In the elderly such common ailments as heart trouble, bronchitis and arthritis all militate strongly against mobility and the desire to go away; for most of them long journeys are tiring, changes in food are upsetting and a strange bed may cause sleeplessness.

Fourthly, family circumstances are often a limiting factor. Parents with young children find it inconvenient, harassing and expensive to go on holiday. The development of camping and caravanning has been a great boon to parents with family obligations and has greatly facilitated travel, nevertheless figures show that this factor is a significant barrier to travel. Indeed, family commitments of any kind, whether it be young children, tending the sick, or looking after the elderly, substantially affect the holiday travel situation.

A fifth factor is lack of interest in travel. This may be due to "unawareness of travel destinations which would bring adequate satis-factions for potential travellers"[7] but mainly, it would seem, it is due to a preference simply to stay at home. This latter condition may be due to a variety of factors: inertia, dislike of changing routine, dislike of travel, shyness of meeting people, etc. Lack of information on non-participants in Britain makes it impossible to say what proportion of the population prefers to stay at home and is not interested in travel but an enquiry carried out in the United States indicated that 26 per cent of the sample study indicated they would rather remain at home than go away.[8]

Finally, there are certain psychological factors which act as deter-rents to travel. It seems clear that some people have a reluctance to travel because of fears: of leaving the safety and security of their own homes; of meeting, and mixing with, other people; of being in foreign places and not knowing the language; of travel either by air or water; of being taken ill when they are abroad, etc. These fears are often largely responsible for the lack of interest just mentioned. McIntosh writes: "... An individual's home is safe, it is a place he knows thoroughly, and he is not required to maintain a façade there. He can be himself in his own home and no unusual demands are placed on him. ... On the other hand, the fact that ... home is so well known tends to produce boredom and the need to explore. An individual thus finds that he is possessed of two very strong drives: *safety* and *exploration*, and he must discover some means of reducing this conflict."[9]

Conclusion

In conclusion, we cannot perhaps do better than quote Dr Ernest Dichter who said: "What motivates the traveller of today is, in the final analysis, anchored within ourselves. It is an ambivalence, the desire to live in a cocoon, to be protected while at the same time to sail out and make the world our territory. The physical and financial potentialities which are just around the corner are powerful lures to break the psychological isolation within which we have been living for centuries. Daily newspapers are still full of daily violence resulting from fears of losing our identity, our language, and express our desire to stay within the pseudoprotection of national boundaries. In the world to come, which hopefully is not too far off, we will learn to become world citizens and to realise that this does not entail a loss of our identity but a first time discovery of the true, inner individuality and uniqueness that is independent of flags, currency and red or green border lines on a fictitious divided map of the globe which was created originally without such artificial frontiers. The travel motivator, whatever his professional label, has indeed one of the most exciting jobs of this century. To give people the courage to get out from behind the phony protection of their isolationism. What the travel motivator has to do is to match the physical promises with the even more important mental and psychological ones. We have to destroy the visible and invisible walls which have been erected by fearful people over the centuries."[10]

NOTES

1. R. W. McIntosh, *Tourism: Principles, Practices, Philosophies*, Grid. Inc., Columbus, Ohio, 1972, p. 52.
2. G. Taylor, *Urban Geography*, Methuen, 1949, p. 340.
3. *Op. cit.*, p. 60.
4. *Character and Conduct of Life*, Methuen, 5th edn. 1937, p. 106.
5. McIntosh, *op. cit.*, p. 60.
6. *The Changing Travel Market*, Braun-Brumfield, Inc., Ann Arbor, Michigan, 1964, p. 11.

7. McIntosh, *op. cit.*, p. 58.
8. McIntosh, *op. cit.*, p. 58.
9. *Op. cit.*, p. 59.
10. Extract from speech delivered at International Seminar held in Srinagar, Kashmir, October, 1967.

Chapter IV

The Elements of Tourism

THE BASIC COMPONENTS

THERE are three basic components of tourism: locale, transport and accommodation. The term "locale" is used to embrace the holiday destination and what it offers the tourist, *e.g.* sunshine, sightseeing, sporting facilities. To get to his destination, the holiday-maker has to travel and, therefore, some mode of transport is necessary. Finally, having reached his destination he must have some kind of accommodation providing food and sleep.

Tourism, as mentioned in the Introduction, can be divided into two sectors, the dynamic and the static. The dynamic sector embraces "the economic activities of (*i*) the formation of the commodity, (*ii*) the motivation of demand, and (*iii*) the provision of transport."[1] Unless the holiday-maker makes his own choice of destination and uses his own transport, this dynamic sector involves the activities of various agents, *e.g.* travel agencies, tour operators, carriers, etc. Even the individual making his own way often has to call upon the services of some of these agents, *e.g.* in securing a seat on a plane or a place on a car ferry. At the destination, the sojourn part of tourism—the static sector of the industry—is mainly provided for by the hotel and catering industry along with some other ancillary services which absorb the derived demand for accommodation, food and refreshment and provide some of the amenities desired by the tourist.

Attractions and amenities are the very basis of tourism: unless these are present the tourist will not be motivated to go to a particular place. But, of course, the needs and tastes of tourists vary widely: the attractions of one place to some people may be anathema to others. Again, it is important to emphasise that tourists' demands are very susceptible to change, for fashion is an important factor to be reckoned with. "Some countries," says Peters, "are extremely fortunate in that they have one asset so outstanding and unique that the tourist industry can largely depend on, and be promoted by, this feature. More often, the combination of a number of assets is necessary to create a strong enough appeal to secure a viable share of the market."[2] Peters has drawn up an inventory of the various attractions which are of significance in tourism and his five categories are given in Table 6.

TABLE 6

Peters' inventory of tourist attractions

1. *Cultural*
   Sites and areas of archaeological interest.
   Historical buildings and monuments.
   Places of historical significance.
   Museums.
   Modern culture.
   Political and educational institutions.
   Religion.
2. *Traditions*
   National festivals.
   Arts and handicrafts.
   Music.
   Folklore.
   Native life and customs.
3. *Scenic*
   Outstanding panoramas and areas of natural beauty.
   National Parks.
   Wildlife.
   Flora and fauna.
   Beach resorts.
   Mountain resorts.
4. *Entertainments*
   Participation and viewing sports.
   Amusement and recreation parks.
   Zoos and oceanariums.
   Cinemas and theatres.
   Night-life.
   Cuisine.
5. *Other attractions*
   Climate.
   Health resorts or spas.
   Unique attractions not available elsewhere.

   Source: *International Tourism*, Hutchinson, 1969, pp. 148–9.

THE GEOGRAPHICAL COMPONENTS

The attractions of tourism are, to a very large extent, geographical in their character, and Table 7 attempts to summarise them. Location and accessibility are important: whether a place has a coastal or inland position, and the ease with which a given place can be reached. Physical space may be thought of as a component for there are those who seek the wilderness and solitude. Scenery or landscape is a compound of landforms, water and the vegetative cover and has an aesthetic and a recreative value. Climatic conditions, especially in relation to the amount of sunshine, temperature and precipitation (snow as well as rain), are of special significance. Animal life may be an important attraction, firstly in relation to bird-watching or viewing game in their natural habitat and, secondly, for sporting purposes, *e.g.* fishing and hunting. Man's impact on the natural landscape in the form of his settlements, historical monuments and archaeological remains is also a major attraction. Finally, a variety of cultural features—ways of life, folklore, artistic expressions, etc.—provide valuable attractions to many.

TABLE 7

Geographical components of tourism

1. Accessibility and location.
2. Space.
3. Scenery:

    (*a*) Landforms, *e.g.* mountains, canyons, cliffs, volcanic phenomena, coral reefs.
    (*b*) Water, *e.g.* rivers, lakes, waterfalls, geysers, glaciers, the sea.
    (*c*) Vegetation, *e.g.* forests, grasslands, moors, heaths, deserts.

4. Climate: sunshine and cloud, temperature conditions, rain and snow.
5. Animal life:

    (*a*) Wildlife, *e.g.* birds, game reservations, zoos.
    (*b*) Hunting and fishing.

6. Settlement features:

    (*a*) Towns, cities, villages.
    (*b*) Historical remains and monuments.
    (*c*) Archaeological remains.

7. Culture: ways of life, traditions, folklore, arts and crafts, etc.

This emphasises the very important role which geography plays in the tourism activity. In tourism studies, much attention is usually directed to the economic aspects of the industry, to hotel and catering studies, and to transport, but all too often scant recognition is given to the role of geography in which, in fact, tourism is fundamentally founded: were there no geographical differences between place and place, tourism would not exist.

THE ELEMENTS OF TOURISM

There are six principal elements or ingredients which predispose towards tourism development. These elements, which are the fundamental attractions of tourism, are:

    (*i*) good weather,
    (*ii*) scenery,

(*iii*) amenities,
(*iv*) historical and cultural features,
 (*v*) accessibility,
(*vi*) accommodation.

There are, of course, other factors in the situation which are sometimes of consequence such as hospitality, currency exchange rates and political control formalities which may add to (or detract from) the above attractions, but usually they are of much less significance.

Good Weather

Fine weather with warmth and sunshine is one of the most important attractions of a tourist area. Good weather is a particularly important ingredient in holidaying—it can make or mar a holiday—and its significance, at least in Britain, is reflected in such advertising as "Come to *sunny* Sandsea." Most of the seaside resorts in England are on the warmer south, and sunnier east, coasts. The south Cornish coast has become the English Riviera because of the mildness of its winter, a mildness which permits sub-tropical vegetation to flourish. But generally speaking, the weather in the United Kingdom is notoriously fickle and there is a woeful lack of sunshine. Not surprisingly, therefore, large numbers of Britons are enticed to the Mediterranean lands by the attraction of nothing other than the promise of seven consecutive days of sunshine. Countries such as Spain, Italy and Greece in Europe and states such as California and Florida in the United States which are able to guarantee fine weather in summer, and in fact capitalise on this, have become important areas of tourism.

Areas with attractive winter climates—winter warmth or sunshine—are also likely to become centres of tourist attraction. In the United States, Florida has become an important winter holiday area since it is one of the few parts of the Republic to enjoy warm winters; as a result, tens of thousands of Americans flee to Florida to escape the winter cold. Large numbers of Americans, and Europeans too, spend a winter holiday in the Bahamas and the West Indies for the same reason: there is the growing popularity in Britain of Christmas cruises to the West Indies. The popularity of the winter sports centres of Alpine France, Switzerland and Austria rests in part upon the weather: it may be cold and the ground covered in snow but there is, usually, abundant sunshine and very clear, crisp air. It is more than doubtful whether the Alpine winter sports centres would be as well patronised as they are if the skies were overcast and sunless.

Nor should one forget the importance in tropical climates of cool upland areas which frequently have developed "hill station resorts," *e.g.* Simla in India.

Climate, then, is of particular significance to tourism and there are many areas which because of their fine exhilarating climates are potential tourist areas. Vilhjalmur Stefansson long campaigned to promote the possibilities of some parts of the Arctic lands as tourist areas, calling it "the friendly Arctic." The Russian scholar, Professor Otto J. Schmidt, wrote: "[People] . . . are unanimous in praising its beauty—its colours and shapes, the particular charm of the landscape—in summer as well as winter . . . it is the ideal country for tuberculosis nursing-homes and holiday hotels. . . ."[3]

While we must recognise the importance of climate and the singular importance of sunshine as a factor in tourism, there must be usually attractions other than plentiful sunshine otherwise the hot desert areas of the world, the Sahara, etc. would be major tourist areas.

Scenery

Scenic attractions are, perhaps, the second most important factor in tourism. Dramatic mountain scenery and coast scenery exert a strong fascination and the tourist visiting the Alps or the Pyrenees or the Norwegian or Dalmatian coasts for the first time cannot but be impressed by their physical majesty. When water is added, beauty is added to sheer physical splendour. What would the Trossachs, the English Lake District or the Alps be without their lakes?

Prior to the middle of the eighteenth century "nature in the raw" had little appeal and mountains in particular were disliked and avoided. The Romantic Movement was largely responsible for this changed attitude. The reaction against the classical tradition and formal beauty led to an appreciation of Nature, individuality of expression and intensity of emotion. Until the Romantic Movement made its impact, grand landscapes had no appeal and during the era of the Grand Tour travellers avoided the Alps or made their way across them as expeditiously as possible. As Fairburn wrote: "Until 1763 Switzerland was not extensively visited; climbing the glaciers had not been introduced and the Alps were viewed simply as a very unnecessary stage in the journey to Italy. William Windham's expedition to Chamonix in 1741 and his subsequent paper to the Royal Society set the fashion of visiting the Savoy glaciers, and by 1780 there were as many as thirty visitors daily to the Temple of Nature above Chamonix. The Alpine scenery was not appreciated, for the travellers were more absorbed in protecting themselves against the cold and surmounting the 'uncouth rocks.' "[4]

Other types of scenery attract the tourist. In Britain, many find the rolling downs of Southern England, the intimacy of the Yorkshire Dales, the splendour of the purple moorlands of parts of the Pennines and the North York Moors, and the lush greenness of the border country between England and Wales quite irresistible. Great natural wonders, such as the Giants' Causeway of Northern Ireland, the geysers of Iceland, the glaciers of the Alps, Niagara Falls, the Grand Canyon of Colorado, the caves of the Central Massif in France, etc. are a source of great interest to many tourists and have become the basis of a tourist industry. At Kariba, the spectacular man-made dam and the vast lake impounded by it have stimulated a considerable tourist industry and one can imagine that Lake Nasser in Egypt will, in the future, join with the Pyramids as a "must" for the tourist visiting Egypt.

Amenities

Facilities for bathing, boating, recreation, dancing and amusement, are an important feature of any seaside resort, indeed of every tourist centre. Amenities are either (*i*) natural, *e.g.* beaches, sea bathing, possibilities of fishing, opportunities for climbing, viewing, etc. and (*ii*) manmade, *e.g.* entertainments of every kind and facilities which cater for the special needs of the visiting tourist.

Fine sandy beaches, sheltered, drenched in sunshine and offering good bathing conditions form a tourist attraction not lightly to be dismissed. The magnificent beaches of the Northumbrian coast (marred, however, by cool easterly winds and occasional sea frets), the sandy coves of Cornwall, the wide beaches of north Devon and the spacious sands of Cardigan Bay in Wales are especially popular in Britain. The forty-odd miles of Belgian coast, with a series of coast resorts from end to end, owes almost everything to the fine beaches created by the dune belt backing the shore. Some of the most famous resorts in the world, *e.g.* Palm Beach in Florida, Copacabana Beach (Rio de Janeiro), Montego Bay (Jamaica), Bondi Beach (Australia), owe much to their beautiful sands. Other natural amenities, such as spacious sheltered water for sailing, as, for instance, Poole Harbour, the Broads or Lake Windermere, or the opportunities for good fishing and shooting are often important.

Increasingly the holiday-maker in general has demanded entertainment and recreational facilities in larger and larger measure and what has come to be known as "development" has preoccupied the resort managements. Piers, promenades and parks, bathing pools and putting greens, theatres, cinemas and fun palaces, chair lifts, funiculars and illuminations are but some of the amenities provided. People's tastes change and their wants become more sophisticated and if a resort wishes to attract and keep its clientele it must move with the times and provide those amenities currently in vogue and in demand. Blackpool provides the classic example of how a fine and extensive sandy beach—the original factor in its development as a seaside resort—has been superseded by man-made amenities, *e.g.* the Tower, "the Golden Mile," the Pleasure Beach, which have made it the leading seaside resort in the country.

Historical and Cultural Factors

Features of historical or cultural interest exert a powerful attraction for many tourists. Think of the enormous drawing power of Stratford-on-Avon because of its association with Shakespeare, or of Pisa because of its famous leaning tower, or of Bruges because of its old-world charm, or of Oberammagau because of its Passion Play, or of Petra with its magnificent rock-cut temples, or the incomparable pyramids of Egypt. Antiquities, famous ruins, castles and cathedrals, temples and stately homes, art galleries and musical festivals all claim their pilgrims. Relics of the past, whether glorious or inglorious, have a strange fascination for many. Williams and Zelinsky have written: "The special favour enjoyed by Greece in the travel plans of the British and Americans may reflect not only the significant climatic, scenic and other standard tourist attractions but also something of a special aura—the after-glow of the classical past—that seems to create a particularly attractive image of Greece. . . ."[5] The popularity of Hellenic cruises reflects the same feeling for the past. Many Americans and Canadians visit Europe because of its long historical heritage, and of course many view Europe as their original homeland and harbour a sentimental attachment to it.

For any foreign visitor to England, London is a "must": this is not merely because it is the largest city in the country and the capital but because of its historical associations and traditions, its pageantry and entertainment and its many cultural attractions. In much the same way the visitor to France includes Paris in his itinerary, to Italy, Rome.

Many countries, particularly those which are still developing tourist industries, are using the legacy of their historical past as their principal tourist attraction. For example, Cambodia has capitalised on the ruins of Angkor, Peru on the long-lost but newly found Inca city of Macchu

Picchu. So far, however, most of these countries lack the infrastructure to take much advantage of the situation.

Accessibility

Tourist attractions of whatever kind would be of little value if their locations were inaccessible by normal means of transport. Physical isolation and inadequate transport facilities are, clearly, handicaps to tourism. Although the North-western Highlands of Scotland possess much grander scenery than the Grampians, relatively few tourists in Scotland go beyond the Caledonian Canal. The lack of good roads, often the lack of any motorable highways, discourages many holiday-makers from touring Yugoslavia. In pre-war days when the tiny Pyrenean Republic of Andorra was approached by little more than a mule track the number of visitors each year ran into hundreds; today it can be easily reached by a good motor road with the result that in the tourist season thousands of visitors flock to it weekly!

Aircraft have revolutionised travel. Places which not so long ago were completely inaccessible to those having only two weeks' holiday are now within easy striking distance. Iceland, Majorca, the Algarve and Crete are but a few hours' flying distance from Britain. Bermuda, about a thousand miles off the coast of North America, is regularly visited, often just for a weekend, by prosperous Americans. Within the United States where, because of the great distances, air travel is frequently more important than overland travel and where there is a fine network of air routes, the tourist enjoys an ease of access found in few other areas.

The nearness and easy accessibility of Brighton to London or of Blackpool to the Lancashire conurbations results in 100,000 visitors inundating these seaside resorts on a peak day in summer. The popularity of the Belgian coast resorts for the English holiday-maker is largely due to the ease with which they can be reached by boat. The extension of a motorway to the English Lake District has had a big impact on the region's tourist trade for it has brought the population of the Midlands within easy reach of the area; whereas places such as Bowness, Ambleside and Keswick have been invaded by as many as 20,000 visitors on a Bank Holiday, one can foresee this figure being doubled. Not everyone, of course, relishes this prospect but it is a good measure of what increased accessibility may mean.

Accommodation

Accommodation is a term loosely used to cover food and lodging: it really falls into the category of amenities but is so basic as to warrant separate treatment. Types of holiday accommodation have shown striking changes since 1950. There has been a marked decline in the use of boarding houses and small private hotels and many of these have been turned into holiday flatlets. The larger hotels are managing more or less to keep their share of the holiday trade: in many of the more popular areas abroad they are booming but elsewhere, particularly in the more traditional holiday resorts and in some seaside resorts in the United Kingdom many are having a lean time and some, in fact, have closed down. These changes in accommodation demand reflect the recent and growing demand for more informal types of accommodation, *e.g.* rented accommodation (flats, cottages, etc.), caravanning and camping. While camping and caravanning may seem to dispense with the need for accommodation this is not altogether so for campers and caravanners usually need camping sites, partly because random camping is seldom permitted and partly because travellers require use of water, cooking facilities, toilets, etc. for which they must be prepared to pay a camping or parking fee.

Accommodation may be an important tourist attraction; indeed, large numbers of tourists go to a particular spot simply because there is a first-class hotel there which provides excellent food, rooms and facilities. Some countries, of course, notably Switzerland, Austria and Holland, have gained a reputation for good food, comfort and cleanliness. The same applies, of course, to individual establishments. Many hotels pride themselves on their good cuisine and service, and good facilities will attract custom. The French Government, for example, paved the way for the tourist development of Corsica by launching a big hotel building programme.

Miscellaneous Factors

A variety of other factors may influence the choice of tourist destination. Hospitality is important. A friendly and welcoming attitude on the part of the nationals of the country visited will make the visitor feel at home and help him enjoy his holiday. Many a tourist has been discouraged from making a return visit to a country as a result of an inhospitable attitude he has encountered. The French Government mounted a campaign in the late 1960s to explain the advantages to be gained from a flourishing tourist trade and the value of being courteous and helpful to the visiting tourist.

It is very necessary, too, to have information bureaux where the foreign visitor who is unfamiliar with the country or resort, and who possibly cannot speak the language of the country, can readily acquire information about places of interest to visit, sports facilities, night-life, shopping, etc. Trained and competent couriers and local guides, who can speak the local language, are also needed.

So far as possible, all constraints upon visiting tourists—the need for passports, visas and the like—should be reduced or abolished. The United Nations' Rome Conference on Tourism recommended (1963) the gradual elimination within reason of all barriers, restrictions and formalities to facilitate international travel. Some countries have already gone a long way towards increasing facilitation; for example, many Western European countries have abolished visas between themselves and, in 1967, Bulgaria and Yugoslavia did away with entry permits for nationals of all countries on a unilateral basis. Apart from certain health, customs and currency restrictions, it is desirable that formalities should be reduced to a minimum and as much freedom given to the visitor as possible.

NOTES

1. G. Janata, "Tourism in H.N.D. Hotel and Catering Administration Courses." Paper given at Ealing Technical College, 18th May, 1971.

2. M. Peters, *International Tourism*, Hutchinson, 1969, p. 147.

3. Quoted by H. P. Smolka in *Forty Thousand Against the Arctic*, 1937.

4. A. N. Fairburn, "The Grand Tour," *Geographical Magazine*, London, Vol. XXIV, 1951, p. 125.

5. "On Some Patterns in International Tourist Flows," *Economic Geography*, October, 1970, pp. 549–67.

Part Two

THE MEASUREMENT AND DIMENSIONS OF TOURISM

Chapter V

The Measurement of Tourism

THE TOURIST: A DEFINITION

Who is a tourist? In this chapter on the measurement of tourism, we shall attempt first to define the term, although it should be said at the outset that the present definitions available are not very satisfactory. Realising the importance of collecting tourist statistics and of securing international compatibility, a committee of statistical experts of the League of Nations recommended in 1937 the acceptance of the following definition: the term "tourist" shall, in principle, be interpreted to mean any person travelling for a period of twenty-four hours or more in a country other than that in which he usually resides. The committee regarded the following persons as tourists:

(*i*) those travelling for pleasure and domestic reasons, including health;

(*ii*) those travelling to international meetings;

(*iii*) those travelling for the purposes of business;

(*iv*) those arriving in the course of a sea cruise, even though they may stay less than twenty-four hours.

According to the committee's recommendations, the following persons should not be regarded as tourists:

(*i*) those persons entering a country, with or without a contract, to take up an occupation;

(*ii*) those persons arriving to take up residence in a foreign country;

(*iii*) students and young persons in boarding schools;

(*iv*) those persons domiciled in frontier zones and crossing the frontier to work in the adjacent foreign country;

(*v*) those travellers passing through a country without stopping even though the journey be in excess of twenty-four hours.

Although there have since been slight modifications to these recommendations, basically they still stand and they have been used in the compilation of travel statistics by both individual countries for national purposes and by I.U.O.T.O. for collating international movements.

At the United Nations Conference on International Travel and Tourism held in Rome in 1963, a revised definition was prepared by I.U.O.T.O. and adopted;[1] the definition was: the term "visitor" describes any person visiting a country other than that in which he has his usual place of residence, for any reason other than following an occupation remunerated within the country visited. This definition covered two categories:

(*i*) *tourists:* temporary visitors staying over twenty-four hours in the country visited, the purpose of whose journey fell under one of the following two categories:

1. leisure, recreation, holiday, sport, health, study, religion;
2. business, family, friends, mission, meeting.

(*ii*) *excursionists:* temporary visitors staying less than twenty-four hours in the country visited, including cruise passengers.

The Tourism Committee of O.E.C.D. adopted in 1970 the I.U.O.T.O. definition, recommending that a tourist should be defined as a foreign resident staying in a country for over twenty-four hours, but recommended also that cruise passengers should be counted as a separate group. The Committee also reaffirmed that the five categories not regarded as tourists by the League of Nations' statistical committee be accepted. Thus the O.E.C.D. definition excludes foreigners taking up or continuing work or study in a country and travellers passing through a country without stopping, but includes businessmen's visits, diplomatic traffic and persons travelling to meetings, conferences or conventions of any kind.

The O.E.C.D. definition may be adopted with appropriate amendment for tourism within a single country: a person becomes a tourist if he visits a place for at least twenty-four hours; if for a shorter period, *i.e.* under twenty-four hours, he is counted as an excursionist.

SOME PROBLEMS

The United Nations Statistical Commission met in 1965 to discuss the definitions of the terms "tourist" and "visitor," but nothing was resolved; as Peters wrote: "the U.N. Commission considered the difficulty of collecting statistical data on tourism but omitted to define the methods of collection or, indeed, to improve the present unsatisfactory definition of a tourist."[2]

The generally accepted definition includes many types of people who would not call themselves tourists in the sense commonly used in the United Kingdom, where the term is normally limited to those travelling on holiday, visiting friends or relatives or going abroad to restore their health. Business travel is not normally thought of as tourism, although pleasure may be mixed with business. Some would question attending meetings and conferences as falling within the scope of tourism, even though travel be involved; nevertheless, as one writer comments "there is a very real sense in which organisers of conferences and conventions and the like select their venue with some regard to its pleasure and entertainment opportunities, no matter how serious and technical the subject matter of the conference may be."[3]

But there are other problems. For example, as the U.N. Statistical Commission pointed out in its 1965 meeting, as a result of the absence of frontier formalities, as happens in the case of the Scandinavian countries, it is virtually impossible to collect data in terms of the 1963 Rome definition. Again, it is not impossible for a visitor to obtain a permit to reside or take up employment in a country once he has crossed the frontier. Furthermore, figures or counts refer to events, *i.e.* entrances into a country, not individuals; for instance, a person, perhaps a businessman, visits a foreign country three times a year and, under the present system of counting, this is recorded as three distinct tourist visits.

COUNTING TOURISTS

McEwen has said that nearly all international tourists have three actions in common: (*i*) they cross international frontiers, (*ii*) they exchange their own currency for foreign currency, and (*iii*) they spend time outside their own country, and this implies using some form of accommodation.[4] It is possible to use these actions as methods for measuring international tourism, *i.e.* by enumerating arrivals at frontiers, by recording currency transactions and by recording numbers of nights in accommodation by foreign visitors. Unfortunately none of these ways is completely foolproof; each has its limitations in respect of recording and enumerating foreign visitors. Counting foreign visitor arrivals is the most usual and most widely adopted method.

The tourist statistician is basically concerned with arrivals and departures, and more particularly the former. In arriving at his figures he is, as indicated above, concerned with events rather than individuals and as far as he is concerned half a dozen visits by the same person is counted as six separate events or six tourist arrivals. There are certain difficulties in the matter of counting, chief of which perhaps is the risk of double counting and, indeed, absolute figures of tourists visiting almost every country tend to be inflated because of double counting; for example, a French tourist on his way to holiday in Portugal may travel by car for two days through Spain and on his return journey to France will also travel two days through Spain, hence his journey, *i.e.* his arrival in Spain, is recorded twice.

Counting may be undertaken in a number of different ways, for example, frontier arrivals, hotel arrivals. There can be wide discrepancies between frontier arrivals and arrivals at hotels as the following figures for Portugal clearly indicate: in 1971, frontier arrivals totalled 1,962,600 while hotel arrivals numbered 1,287,400. The difference between these two figures can, of course, be explained: the former figure embraces day excursionists, cruise passengers and second home owners. Using hotels (which is, perhaps, one of the best ways of measuring "real" tourist growth) is probably a much less satisfactory way of counting visitors than by frontier counts since if a visitor stays in two hotels during the course of his visit this is counted as two separate arrivals, while, on the other hand, stays in private accommodation are not counted. In practice tourists are difficult to count; events are easier to deal with and the statistician usually counts events. A point that should be noted is that very few countries concern themselves with outward travel and so have little information of the numbers going to foreign countries; for this reason most of the material which is available for analysis relates to the statistics of arrivals. Yet another point of note is that often it is difficult to make direct comparisons between the statistical data collected by different countries since the data collected is acquired on a different basis; for example, in some cases arrivals are recorded by nationality rather than by country of residence: hence it might be possible for a British Common Market bureaucrat working in Brussels to weekend in Amsterdam and such an arrival may be indistinguishable from a Scotsman spending his fortnight's summer holiday in the Netherlands.

METHODS OF MEASUREMENT

Let us turn now to the principal methods of measuring tourism. There are administrative procedures which assist measurement, for example, frontier arrivals may be counted by passports, visas, disembarkation cards and the like, or use may be made of registration at hotels, or even the cashing of traveller's cheques. Statistics of these various matters arise as a by-product of administration. Such statistics are not necessarily entirely accurate. Certainly they are not exhaustive, since they provide no socio-economic information about people. A second method is to use sample surveys. To secure statistically valid samples, adequate social survey mechanisms are required. The question arises, of course, as to how one contacts and identifies visitors; the contact may be made at the time of arrival or subsequently when the traveller returns home; in either case, he is asked to complete a questionnaire. The sample survey basis is independent of the administrative process and has the advantage of making contact with the tourist from whom all kinds of information relevant to the industry may be elicited. Furthermore, statistically identical surveys can be conducted in various countries.

The International Passenger Survey (I.P.S.) was originally designed by the Board of Trade for Balance of Payments purposes and is one kind of investigation, using the sample survey basis, used in Britain. A fraction of arrivals or departures are interviewed either at port or airport. A continuous survey can be carried out throughout the year, and much useful information culled from the traveller. Another method of investigation is that carried out by the British National Travel Survey (B.N.T.S.) which has operated since 1951 and which uses sample survey techniques. Questionnaires are sent to people after they have returned home from holiday, usually in the autumn. Some 5,000–6,000 surveys are usually undertaken and these give a fairly comprehensive cross-section. Full details of the holidays taken can be obtained, along with the socio-economic characteristics of the tourist. In this way important data can be collected from the informants which can be of great significance for the industry. The I.P.S. and B.N.T.S. surveys, taken together, should provide a good working basis for the analysis of the industry; the B.N.T.S. is invaluable for the marketing process. The British Tourist Authority has also undertaken *ad hoc* surveys.

The chief sources of tourism statistics are national returns, such as those issued by the British Tourist Authority in Britain or the national tourist offices of other countries, and the international travel statistics published by supranational bodies such as I.U.O.T.O. and O.E.C.D., although the annual statistics published by both these organisations are merely compilations from national tourist returns usually obtained by the administrative process. The point should be emphasised that problems of comparability of statistics do exist, that more precise international standards of measurement are needed and that there is room for more sample surveys.

THE IMPORTANCE OF MEASUREMENT

The question naturally arises: what is the value of tourism measurement? It is not merely that it is useful to know the numbers of tourist arrivals, especially for a series of consequent years, which will indicate whether the tourist trade in any particular country is growing, stagnant or declining, but that it is valuable to know the mode of arrival, the length of stay, the kind of accommodation used, the amenities desired by the traveller and the amount that he spends. Any information regarding the markets, the mode of transport used and the socio-economic characteristics of the visitors are all essential for tourism planning.

A regular return of the average length of stay is important for "changes in the average length of stay, either ... longer ... or shorter ... can be very significant in determining trends."[5] An intervening opportunity or a trend may appear that seriously affects a resort's or a country's trade. It may also point to a change in tourist fashion. It may reflect, as it has done in Greece and Eire, political influences.

In many countries, more particularly in cool temperate latitudes, tourism is concentrated into a relatively brief season; this is highly uneconomic from the point of view of use of tourism plant. Accordingly, many countries, including Britain, are attempting with some success to lengthen their tourist season. Statistics, relating to different modes of transport, can be broken down, on a monthly basis, and this will greatly help in determining seasonal trends.

Certain socio-economic information is invaluable to the destination country. Take, for instance, the French, visiting Portugal, who go in large numbers in the height of the summer season but show a strong predilection for camping and have a length of stay in hotels which is the lowest of all Portugal's visitors except for Spanish tourists. Changes in accommodation demands since 1950 have caused the Swiss to reappraise and refashion this sector of their flagging tourist industry, compelling them to undertake a drastic streamlining of their hotels and to provide extensive non-hotel accommodation.

The spending capacity of tourists should also be noted. By and large, the Americans and the West Germans are the biggest spenders and clearly it would seem sensible policy for tourist countries to cultivate these two countries which are not only the largest generators of tourist traffic but the freest spenders. Another financial aspect of importance is whether a tourist country should opt to develop mass package tourism (as Spain has done) or to encourage the more selective high- and medium-bracket income tourists (as Portugal has done).

MARKET ANALYSIS

Peters says that the majority of analyses undertaken show the tourist market to be made up of three elements: recreational travellers, business travellers and travellers for purposes other than pure recreation or business.[6]

Recreational travellers, who probably make up two-thirds or even more of the total, travel for holiday or pleasure purposes. In recreational travel: (*i*) the choice of destination lies in the hands of the traveller, subject to certain contingencies or restrictions such as political constraints, currency restrictions, availability of time, etc.; and (*ii*) the costs involved in transportation and at the destination are borne by the individual or his parents or perhaps a friend. The amount of income, and especially discretionary income, the amount of time at the traveller's disposal and the length of paid holiday, and the social and educational background of the traveller will all influence the choice of destination and the demand for foreign holiday travel, but the current fashion in a holiday destination or national controls designed to restrict travel abroad or even the marketing activities of other countries within the traveller's homeland may also exert an influence. Cost may well be the main factor and the opportunity of a cut-price "inclusive tour" may decide the holiday traveller's destination. Peters writes "that the recreational component of the travel market is highly price-elastic ... a reduction in price will usually lead to a more than proportionate increase in travel at certain price ranges."[7]

Business travel differs from recreational travel in three principal ways: (*i*) the destination of the business traveller is determined for him and is normally not influenced by personal considerations; (*ii*) the costs incurred in the business trip are borne by the company or firm; and (*iii*) business travel, which is regarded as an essential part of the business process, is not greatly affected by travel costs. In contrast to the recreational component of the travel market, the business component is usually considered to be relatively price-inelastic: reductions in the cost of travel would be unlikely to affect materially increases in business travel. Any increase in the volume of business travel is related essentially to expanding trade relationships. The business component of the travel market is expanding although its numerical growth rate does not show the spectacular increases which have occurred in recreational travel, particularly as a result of the developments in inclusive tour holidays. Business travel is a valuable part of the tourism industry, however, since the business traveller tends to be a higher spender than the holiday-maker. The business end of the travel market is highly specialised and is becoming more so; Arthur Sandles has said "This whole complex industry is now geared to providing what the business-man wants quickly and smoothly. Indeed, so specialised is business travel today that it has developed its own service industry. . . ."[8]

An aspect of business travel which has already grown rapidly, and is likely to continue to grow, is the international conference market. If delegates' expenses are paid by company, firm or organisation, such travel is classed as business travel. "International Convention traffic is currently one of the main growth sectors of the total tourist market. Estimates for 1972 suggested that the total number of international conventions was 6300, generating a total expenditure of £375m. These figures are expected to rise to a total of 15,500 conventions in 1980, with a total expenditure of £1500m. These estimates are fairly conservative, but even so, it is probable, on present trends, that [by 1980] . . . the size of the world market will have more than doubled. The value of the market will have quadrupled."[9]

The third sector of the travel market comprises those who travel for other than purely holiday or business reasons, and into this category fall those who travel for the purpose of visiting relatives or friends, for personal health reasons, for educational purposes, for attending international conferences when the cost is borne by the individual. There is no satisfactory all-embracing definition for this third group of travellers and so it is usual to categorise them as travellers for "other purposes."

These three groups of travellers are not mutually exclusive, for the private individual visiting friends or relatives frequently combines this with a holiday while the business traveller often includes a holiday break in his journey. For such reasons, statistics based on purpose of visit may be misleading and caution must be taken in their interpretation.

THE PROBLEM OF SEASONALITY

Tourism is not the only industry or economic activity afflicted by seasonality but it suffers more than most from seasonal changes: indeed, one of the most complex problems of tourist demand relates to this factor. Seasonality means that tourism plant is frequently used for only a limited part of the year and this, clearly, is uneconomic (*see* Fig. 2). Tourist areas in North-western Europe have a short season—often as little as three months—except in those centres or areas where business and conference travel helps to keep tourism at a reasonable level all the year round. A corollary of this seasonal usage is seasonal employment, which is a serious problem except in centres or areas which are fortunate in having two seasons in the year, *e.g.* certain mountain resorts which enjoy a summer season and a winter sports season. Some of the developing countries, which have recently established tourist industries, suffer particularly from seasonality because they are unable to fall back on the business tourist. Seasonality also places stresses and strains upon the transport system which has to cope with a sudden and greatly enlarged volume of passenger train and motor car traffic. Thus seasonality presents a problem not only in relation to employment but also in relation to investment.

Seasonality is most marked where "the industry is dependent upon holiday- rather than business-related travel."[10] The problem has, however, been vigorously attacked and a considerable measure of success achieved. Hoteliers and tour operators have made attempts both to prolong the holiday season and to smooth out seasonality, especially by offering out-of-season holidays in the winter and spring periods and by structuring prices to encourage holiday travel outside the peak period. Government, at both national and local levels, and also industry, have helped; for example, in England the August Bank Holiday was moved from the beginning to the end of August, holidays have been staggered and in some instances three-day weekends have been introduced; again, festivals of art, music and drama organised by local authorities, together with special celebrations, sporting events, conventions and such attractions as "illuminations," which have been successfully adopted by some English resorts, have all helped to prolong the season. The public, incidentally, is helping, too, for it is becoming fashionable to take a second holiday—usually during the winter season—and this clearly offers some promise of reducing seasonality; the growth in second home ownership should have a similar effect.

McIntosh has commented "The development of promotional fares by the carriers and the expansion of the number, timings and variety of tours offered have all helped to stimulate demand in the off-season. ... This trend will [probably] continue, and may grow ... with the trend towards the four-day work week in the United States and [its]

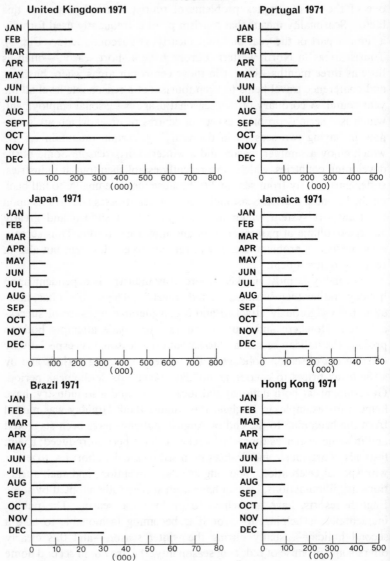

FIG. 2.—*Seasonality in tourism: some examples.* One of the chief problems of the tourist industry in many countries is its seasonal character. Clearly, tourism plant, often needing heavy investment, which is only used for a few months is uneconomic. In the U.K. the season at best is only six months long, apart from a few exceptions, and there is an undesirable peaking in July and August. Countries such as Hong Kong and Japan have a more equitably phased trade. Jamaica's busiest season is the winter period.

possible extension ... into Canada, Western Europe, Japan and other industrial countries. Increased efficiency and effectiveness of promotional programmes and better marketing also tend to offset the traditional seasonal patterns of demand. Festivals, special celebrations, special tours, lower rates, more year-round activities and the growing number of travellers in the market who can take vacations at other than the traditional peak periods of the year have combined to level out the demand patterns towards a more even demand throughout the year.

Any effort which can be made by a community to sustain and spread out the demand during usually slack or decreasing periods is well worth the effort. Business coming into the community at these times of the year is actually producing a profit in excess to what is produced by each dollar in the peak season. ... In most tourist service businesses, fixed costs are quite high in relation to operating costs and thus, increasing total yearly revenue, even modestly, produces proportionately higher profits."[11]

NOTES

1. Notwithstanding the attempts of I.U.O.T.O. to secure a universally accepted definition, there is no global acceptance of its definition and, accordingly, it remains difficult to get comparable tourist statistics on a world-wide basis.

2. Peters, *op. cit.*, p. 16.

3. *International Tourism Quarterly*. No. 1. March, 1973, p. 9.

4. *The European Tourist Markets*. Tourism Planning and Research Ltd., 1971. Section 1.2.2.

5. R. W. McIntosh, *Tourism: Principles, Practices, Philosophies*, Grid Inc., 1972, p. 210.

6. *International Tourism*, Hutchinson, p. 16.

7. *Idem*, p. 17.

8. "Key part of the market," Business Travel, Financial Times Survey, *Financial Times*, 23rd May, 1973.

9. Research Newsletter, No. 8, Spring, 1973, p. *ii. British Travel News*, No. 41, Spring, 1973.

10. *Economic Review of World Tourism*, I.U.O.T.O., 1970, p. 39.

11. *Op. cit.*, pp. 208–9.

Chapter VI

International Tourist Flows

RECREATIONAL TRAVEL: THE NEW MIGRATION

SEVERAL years ago, Dr R. I. Wolfe, in an important and perceptive paper bearing this title, drew attention to the fact that every age has had its own characteristic migrations and that these have been "symptoms of stress—as they continue to be in our own age." [1] He pointed out that in our own day there are three characteristic migrations: the almost world-wide drift of people into the cities, the journey to and from work which has led to large-scale commuting and recreational travel for pleasure. Though there is nothing new in recreational travel, its scale and its scope is unique to our age. First, however, we should look at the current dimensions of world travel, attempt to interpret the movements taking place and try to estimate future trends.

THE DIMENSIONS OF WORLD TOURISM

International tourism attracts much more attention than domestic tourism, probably because of the balance of payments problem. But to secure a full picture of the significance of tourism in the world, domestic tourism should be taken into account. Numerically, international tourism becomes almost insignificant when compared with domestic tourism. If one takes, for example, the United States, which is the largest generating country with respect to international tourism, the American Society of Travel Agents (A.S.T.A.), found in 1967 that some 124·6 million tourists (86 per cent of the total number of tourists) holidayed within the country as against some 20 million (14 per cent) who went abroad. Popovic says that "In 12 European countries where data were available (Austria, Belgium, France, F.R. Germany, Italy, Luxembourg, Netherlands, Norway, Portugal, Spain, Switzerland, Yugoslavia), of 834 million nights registered in tourist accommodation facilities in 1967 only 222 million or 27 per cent were of foreign tourists, while 612 million nights or 73 per cent were of domestic tourists, even though a considerable number of domestic tourists were not recorded at all."[2] In the United Kingdom in 1972 while 37·5 million people took holidays lasting four or more days only 8·5 million of them took foreign holidays. It becomes abundantly clear that domestic tourism is of very great importance. Precise figures of domestic tourism in the world at large are difficult to arrive at, but it seems likely that they are of the order of 1000 million annually.

If we turn our attention now to the volume of international tourism, it has been estimated that the total tourist arrivals in 1972 was around 180 million. International tourism is increasing each year but it has varied over the past decade (*see* Fig. 3); in the early 1960s the average annual increase was around 12 per cent but in the later 1960s it dropped to about 9 per cent. Since 1970 the rate of increase has picked up a little and it is anticipated that an average annual growth rate of

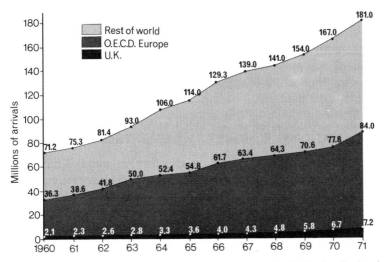

FIG. 3.—*Graph showing growth of world tourist arrivals (1960–71).* During the decade world tourist arrivals in the world more than doubled, reaching a total of around 180 million. Half of these were in the O.E.C.D. countries of Europe, which made Europe the outstanding tourist destination region in the world. Note how the U.K.'s growth as a tourist destination was considerably greater than the world average.

around 10 per cent will occur in the 1970s. Table 8 shows the volume of international tourism in the world during the ten years from 1961 to 1970.

Projections for the future are, of course, notoriously difficult to make, for all sorts of imponderables may be involved. Assuming an average annual rate of increase of around 10 per cent (although some

TABLE 8
Volume of international tourism in the world

Year	Tourist arrivals (m)	Increase from previous year (%)
1961	72	8
1962	80	10
1963	93	16
1964	106	14
1965	115	8
1966	131	14
1967	139	6
1968	141	2
1969	153	8
1970	168	9
1971	181	8

authorities think this growth rate will level out in the late 1970s), it would appear that by 1980 there will be more than 250 million arrivals: L. J. Lickorish has suggested the figure may be nearly 300 million.[3] Of course, even the recent growth rate of around 10 per cent cannot be sustained for very long; as Wolfe says "even a rate of 10 per cent yields an utterly ridiculous figure when extended over a century of growth: for every traveller at the beginning of the period there would be nearly 14,000 at the end."[4]

INTERNATIONAL TOURIST MOVEMENTS

International tourist arrivals are currently around 180 million annually. Table 9 gives international tourist movements for selected years. It will be seen that there is a remarkable geographical concentration. Europe is easily the principal destination region and in 1970 received almost 75 per cent of world total arrivals; North America ranked second with about 16 per cent. None of the other world regions could claim more than 4 per cent and Latin America, the Middle East, Africa, Asia and Australia combined had a mere 9·2 per cent. In 1973, the picture had not materially altered: 91 per cent of tourist movement took place in Europe and North America.

This clearly shows that over the period 1950–70 the shares of Europe and Australia rose while those of North America, Latin America and the Middle East declined.

The most important feature of current international tourist movements is the very high proportion (80 per cent) of travel generated by a dozen countries. These twelve "generators of tourism," as they are called, are: the United States, West Germany, the United Kingdom,

TABLE 9

International tourist movements

	Arrivals (m)				Regional share (%)			
	1950	1960	1967	1970	1950	1960	1967	1970
Europe	16·8	50·4	102·6	136·3	66·6	71·0	74·3	74·7
North America	6·2	15·2	23·3	30·0	24·6	21·4	16·9	16·1
Latin America	1·3	2·7	4·7	5·4	5·2	3·8	3·4	3·0
Middle East	0·2	1·4	2·5	3·4	0·8	2·0	1·8	1·7
Africa	0·5	0·4	1·9	2·6	2·0	0·6	1·4	1·4
Asia/Australia	0·2	0·9	3·0	5·3	0·8	1·2	2·2	3·1
TOTAL	25·2	71·0	138·0	183·0	100·0	100·0	100·0	100·0

Source: I.U.O.T.O. compiled from N.T.O. statistics.

France, Canada, Belgium, Netherlands, Italy, Switzerland, Sweden, Denmark and Austria. These countries, also, between them, claim some two-thirds of all tourist receipts. Although three countries, Spain, Mexico and Japan, are listed in the top twelve receiving countries, none of them falls into the category of the twelve biggest spenders.[5]

One can detect some significant trends, although none as yet are important; for example, there is a growing movement to some of the African countries, notably to those of the Atlas Lands and East Africa. Again, although still somewhat embryonic, there is a recent but perceptible growth in the movement of tourists to the Indian Ocean and South American areas. On the other hand, from Japan there is an ever-growing number of Japanese travelling abroad. There is a movement, still weak but growing gradually, of Latin Americans travelling abroad and principally for pleasure purposes since the numbers travelling for business reasons are very small.

Analysis of International Movements

The above presents a broad, if brief, picture of international tourist movements. Some closer scrutiny of these movements, however, is required. International tourist arrivals increased fivefold between 1950 and 1967, representing an annual rate of growth of the order of 10·5 per cent. But, as both Peters[6] and Popovic[7] have pointed out, this annual growth rate and the account of tourist movements and regional shares outlined above do not provide an altogether true picture of the extent of travel movements throughout the world. For instance, the totals given in Table 9 combine short-haul and long-haul traffic; in this context short-haul traffic is taken as that originating in one region and travelling only within that region whereas long-haul traffic is that which originates in one region but travels to another region. Approximately one-fifth of all tourist traffic falls into the long-haul category. The proportion of long-haul traffic is tending to increase and, although Europe gets nearly two-thirds of the total inter-regional traffic, there are encouraging signs that tourists are beginning to travel in increasing numbers to other long-distance destinations. In the case of the Middle East, Africa and Latin America there is a heavy dependence upon long-haul traffic and, indeed, over half of the tourists visiting these regions come from outside the destination region. On the other hand, in North America only a very small proportion, just over 5 per cent, of the arrivals may be categorised as long-haul traffic. In North America a high proportion of tourist arrivals represent short cross-frontier traffic, *i.e.* between the United States and Canada and between the United States and Mexico.

It is important to know whence tourists go from the various originating regions. We have already noted that statistics relating to outward travellers are seldom to be had since few countries keep records of departures, hence the numbers of travellers generated by the various regions must be deduced from arrival statistics. It is clear from such figures as are available that North America is the prime generating region in respect of long-haul traffic and accounts for some 60 per cent of the total, while Europe, ranking second, accounts for only about 20 per cent. The other regions are only responsible for around 5 per cent each. The predominance of North America is very largely due to the large numbers of United States and Canadian citizens who cross the North Atlantic to visit Europe. They are sufficiently affluent to indulge in long-distance travel while many are drawn to Britain and other countries of Europe because of ethnic and cultural ties. Many, moreover, visit Europe for business reasons since they have commercial interests there.

The short-haul traffic is of much greater importance than the long-haul traffic. "Real mass tourism," says Popovic, "is rather short- or medium-range tourism."[8] In 1967, Italy had 27·6 million foreign tourist arrivals, but some two-thirds (18 million) came from adjacent countries (France, Germany, Switzerland, Austria and Yugoslavia), a quarter (7 million) from the rest of Europe, and only 9 per cent (2·6 million) from the rest of the world. In the case of the United Kingdom, in 1969, the total number of foreign visitors was 5·8 million; of this number 2·5 million came from Western Europe, *i.e.* almost half, together with 0·7 million from Eire, 1·6 million from North America and 1·2 million from the Commonwealth countries. "Family ties" gave the United Kingdom a larger proportion of long-haul visitors than was characteristic of other European countries but, even so, the short- and medium-haul traffic was appreciably larger than the long-haul traffic.

Popovic has summed up the global picture in the following words "the impressive figures on the volume of world tourism, so frequently quoted, have to be taken with a grain of salt. Mass tourism and its tremendous economic significance is a phenomenon of developed countries. By importance, first comes domestic tourism, then tourism from neighbouring countries, then tourism from other countries within the region, and finally overseas (interregional) tourism, which represents only a very small fraction of international tourism."[9]

The Value of International Tourism

Tables 10 and 11 show, respectively, the foreign exchange earnings over the period 1961–71 and the receipts from world tourism, by regions, for three selected years.

World tourism receipts (*see* Fig. 4) have shown a continuous upward trend in the post-war era, although occasionally the rate of growth was

TABLE 10

Earnings from international tourism

Year	Foreign exchange earnings ($ billion)	Increase from previous year (%)
1961	6·8	10
1962	7·4	9
1963	8·2	10
1964	9·6	17
1965	11·0	14·5
1966	12·5	14
1967	13·4	7
1968	14·0	4
1969	15·3	9
1970	17·4	14
1971	19·9	14·5

Source: O.E.C.D., *Tourism in Member Countries* and I.U.O.T.O., *Economic Review of World Tourism.*

TABLE 11

Receipts from international tourism by regions

Region	Receipts (£m)			Regional share (%)		
	1950	1960	1967	1950	1960	1967
Europe	318	1399	3070	42·4	57·3	60·7
North America	238	496	930	31·7	20·3	18·4
Latin America	140	372	650	18·7	15·2	12·9
Middle East	9	32	80	1·2	1·3	1·6
Africa	32	63	90	4·3	2·6	1·8
Asia/Australia	13	82	230	1·7	3·3	4·6
TOTAL	750	2444	5050	100·0	100·0	100·0

Source: I.U.O.T.O. compiled from N.T.O. statistics.

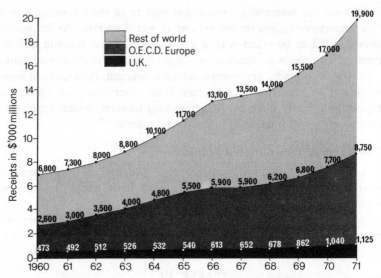

FIG. 4.—*Graph showing growth of world tourist receipts (1960–71)*. World tourist receipts almost trebled during the decade, reaching a total of almost $20,000m in 1971. Europe's share was about half; U.K. receipts more than doubled. Note the great upsurge in receipts since 1968, which very largely reflect inflation.

slow; this was most noticeable in 1967–68 when international difficulties, political and economic, coincided. But since 1969, until 1974 when there was a halt, the upward trend continued. As with the volume of international tourism, receipts from international tourism have shown an average annual growth of 9–10 per cent. I.U.O.T.O. predicted in 1974 an increase in world spending on international tourism of about 7 per cent *per annum*.

Although receipts from tourism showed a substantial increase between 1950 and 1960 and between 1960 and 1967 in every region, the regional shares dropped in the cases of North America, Latin America and Africa but increased in the cases of Europe, the Middle East and Asia/Australia. Clearly Europe is *the* great destination area (*see* Fig. 5) and receives the bulk of international tourist receipts. In 1967, the rate of growth in tourist receipts fell markedly and slackened off especially in Europe and in the Middle East; this drop would seem to reflect the economic recession in world economic conditions and the political upheaval in the Middle East. However, by 1969 some measure of political and economic stability had been achieved and a renewed upsurge in international tourism commenced.

The growth in international travel over the past twenty years has

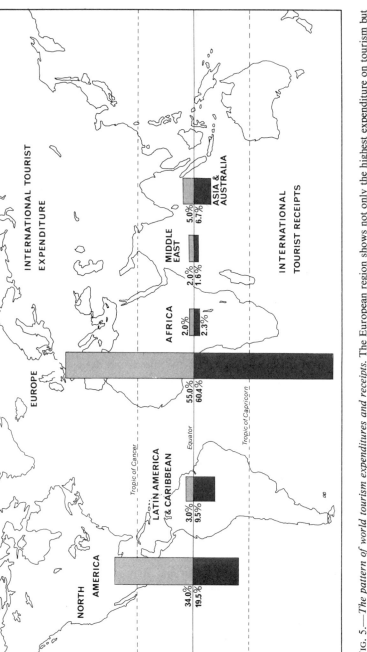

FIG. 5.—*The pattern of world tourism expenditures and receipts.* The European region shows not only the highest expenditure on tourism but enjoys the highest receipts. North America accounts for about one-third of the total international expenditure: tourist receipts, on the other hand, are relatively small. The proportion of world receipts enjoyed by Latin America, Africa and the Middle East declined over the past decade. With the rapid growth in the Japanese tourist market, one can expect to see expenditures in the Asian–Australian region grow markedly during the 1970s.

been remarkable. Total spending between 1950 and 1971 rose from $2 billion to $20 billion, an annual rise of 11 per cent. The tourist trade now accounts for 6 per cent of international trade. Eighty per cent of the spending takes place in Europe and North America and of this Europe has 60 per cent.

THE INTERPRETATION OF INTERNATIONAL TOURIST FLOWS

Williams and Zelinsky have made an enquiry into international tourist movements and attempted an interpretation of such movements.[10]

As a result of their enquiry, Williams and Zelinsky were able to postulate several findings; some of their interpretations are strongly based, others less so and of a more hypothetical nature.

First, international tourist flows do not occur in a random way but are patterned, exhibiting great stability from year to year, at least over a short-term period. It would seem that once a tourist flow has become established it has its own momentum; in other words, it tends to continue in its existing state of motion. Because of this impetus, it becomes possible to predict the tourist stream, at least in the fairly immediate future, with a considerable degree of assurance. This does not, of course, explain past or even present flows and although there is a lack of data to support speculation Williams and Zelinsky "strongly suspect that information fed back by previous tourists may go a long way towards explaining the short-term stability of tourist flow patterns."[11]

Discrepancies between actual and expected tourist flows are most easily and obviously explained in terms of spatial distance—greater distances involving greater travelling time and increased costs. For example, few Japanese or South African tourists visit Europe and one might readily interpret this in terms of the factors just mentioned. Travelling time and cost are clearly inhibiting factors in many cases; conversely, in numerous instances, distance seems not to count at all. For example, there is a surprisingly feeble tourist interchange between some contiguous countries, as between France and Germany, Austria and Switzerland and Austria and Italy. One might have surmised that geographical propinquity and easy accessibility would have stimulated tourist interaction but this clearly is not necessarily the case.

A second major hypothesis put forward by Williams and Zelinsky is that "the presence or absence of other types of international connectivity, past or present, will tend to stimulate or inhibit international tourist movements."[12] For instance, political associations, common cultural characteristics, commercial and business ties, migration links between countries, etc. often encourage tourist movements. The Americans visit Britain in large numbers partly because of their Anglo-Saxon affiliations, partly because of past and present political and commercial associations and partly because of shared culture traits. The considerable flow of Scandinavians, more especially Swedes, to West Germany and of Dutch to Britain are probably to be partially explained in terms of the close commercial ties which exist. Conversely, the lack of historical, cultural or commercial ties on the one hand or of politico-cultural antipathies and barriers on the other may explain the absence of tourist interaction between certain countries. For example, although Japanese tourists make a fair showing in the United Kingdom and West Germany (probably partly a result of the close commercial ties) until recently they were virtually absent in Portugal and Spain.[13] Again, in the immediate post-war years the antagonisms which developed between the Soviet Union and the West resulted in the "Iron Curtain" and a tight restriction of movement between the two; it is only in recent years that a tourist flow has begun to develop between Western Europe and the Soviet Union. South Africa's apartheid policy is repugnant to many who on principle would refrain from visiting that country, while, as Williams and Zelinsky say "Few American Negroes would think of spending a ... vacation in South Africa."[14]

A third point is the hypothesis of reciprocity, that is a tourist flow from country A to country B should generate a counterflow from B to A. It might be supposed that this would be likely to happen but, except in a few instances, this does not seem to occur. In the case of Austria and Italy where one might have expected, in view of geographical proximity and geographical contrasts, a fair degree of reciprocity, Williams and Zelinsky found that this was not so and that the flow from Austria to Italy exceeded the reverse movement in the order of 20 to 1. Williams and Zelinsky in fact found that the reciprocity hypothesis was much feebler than they had expected and came to the conclusion that flows in one direction are a poor and totally unreliable indicator of flows in the reverse direction. Such unequal flows may well reflect unequal standards of living.

Fourthly, there is the factor of appeal or attractiveness of one country for another: this usually resolves itself into contrasts—conditions of climate, scenery, cultural features, ways of life, etc. Britain provides an excellent example of this; weary of the damp, dull and fickle weather, there is in summer an exodus of Britons to the Mediterranean lands where for a week or a fortnight or even longer they can be assured of warmth and sunshine. Other factors are, of course, involved but there can be little doubt that sunshine is *the* great pulling force. "We might even suggest," say Williams and Zelinsky, "a certain 'heliotropic' [and also boreaphobic?] factor emerging from the evidence, namely a strong southward surge of sun-seeking, cold-shunning tourists. . . ." [15]

This quest for contrasting conditions of a physical or social nature is strikingly illustrated by the large numbers (running into millions each year) of tourists from northern and western Europe who seek their holidays in Spain, the Mediterranean region of France, Italy and Greece. The validity of the lure of desirable complementary factors is further established by the quite feeble movement of Austrians to Scandinavia or of Greeks to Spain. [16]

A fifth factor of considerable significance is economic: the cost of a holiday within the destination country. Costs fall into two broad categories: the cost of travel to one's destination and the cost of accommodation. Not only do costs vary from country to country but rates of foreign exchange may differ appreciably between one country and another. There can be little doubt that the high costs of food, accommodation, etc. in France, Belgium and Switzerland in post-war years have had the effect of diverting many British tourists to Portugal and Spain, and more recently to Yugoslavia, with their low-cost holidays. Another economic factor of great significance in more recent years has been the introduction of "package holidays"; the willingness of destination countries to join forces with tourist agencies in arranging package holidays has been responsible for big increases in the number of tourists visiting those countries. Charter flights, too, have had a tremendous impact upon tourist travel: cheapness of transport has made it possible for the tourist to travel to far-off lands which, otherwise, because of travelling time and cost, he would have been prevented from visiting. Low-budget holidays in Spain and the Balearic Islands have been largely responsible for the very rapid increase in the number of British tourists visiting Spanish holiday centres; recently, however, costs have begun to rise and it will be interesting to see what effects such increasing costs have. There is another aspect of the cost problem: as tourist areas become popular and more developed there is a tendency for costs to rise within those areas and this may have the effect of diverting tourists to other equally accessible and attractive areas within the same country with lower prices; this has occurred, for instance, in France where the lower costs in Brittany have siphoned off some of the tourists who formerly made for the Riviera.

Sixthly, there is the influence of what is termed intervening opportunities. The theory was formulated by the sociologist Stouffer: "The number of persons going a given distance is directly proportional to the number of opportunities at that distance and inversely proportional to the number of intervening opportunities." This "law" means that a tourist travelling from his home base to a distant destination will pause *en route* at attractive intermediate stopping places and may, in the extreme case, even forego reaching his proposed ultimate destination for nearer opportunities. An English tourist bound for Finland may, for example, break his journey and linger a while in Copenhagen, or a Frenchman destined for the Algarve in southern Portugal may be seduced by the glories of Andalusia and never reach the Portuguese frontier. The influence of intervening opportunities once affected the author who, bound for the North-western Highlands of Scotland, was captivated by the Northumbrian coast and hardly managed to get across the Border.

Seventhly, one can discern a distinct influence exerted by special world events such as Olympic Games, World Fairs and the like; these give rise to temporary surges of tourists. Often, though by no means inevitably, such international events stimulate a long-term expansion of tourism in the country where they are mounted. Williams and Zelinsky point out that the Olympic Games staged in Italy and Japan in 1964 and 1968 not only accelerated the flows of American visitors to those countries but seem to have generated a permanent expansion of the tourist business; on the other hand, they note the failure of the Brussels Fair of 1958 and the New York World Fair of 1964–65 to achieve any positive long-term effects.[17]

FUTURE TRENDS

International tourism accounts for only about one-fifth of total tourists. As already emphasised the domestic tourist market is immeasurably greater and probably totals around 1000 million at the present time. In the developed countries there has been a notable increase in the numbers of nationals taking a holiday, whether abroad or at home, during the past two decades and the assumption is that this trend will continue if social and economic conditions continue to improve. This has already been shown to be the case in some of the less well developed countries such as Spain, Yugoslavia and Greece where increasing prosperity at home has led to increasing numbers engaging in tourism.

As standards of living rise, as disposable incomes increase, as the length of holidays increase, as holidays with pay increase and as education improves there is likely to be an increase in tourism, whether it be of a domestic or international nature. As some of the developing countries grow, it may be anticipated that their nationals too will begin to participate in tourism. This has already begun to happen in Brazil and Mexico, although it should be recognised that this is still small-scale.

On the other hand, the tourism market is very sensitive to economic, social and political conditions: changes in costs, habits, fashions and conditions relating to international incidents and politics are apt to react strongly on tourism. Increasing costs, for example, may diminish demand. In Britain, for instance, the need for cut-throat competition among the tourist operators appears to be becoming drastically modified; many firms are in the red and many others have been taken over or gone out of business: they have been operating on too slender profit margins and this is no longer a viable way to operate. The current energy crisis has already resulted in appreciable price increases due to escalating transport costs, and may have longer-term effects of reduced air and motor transport. It is difficult at present to assess the precise effects which these difficulties will have upon the tourist industry in the future; the indications are that it will continue to grow but perhaps at a reduced rate.

It seems fairly certain that for a long time to come Europe and the Mediterranean will continue to be the principal tourist destination but there are clear indications that other areas will also attract tourists in the future, e.g. East and South Africa, the Indian Ocean islands, Southeast Asia. With improved air transport, many people are prepared to travel further and as the current tourist areas become increasingly congested it is very probable that more and more holiday-makers will seek out new, less frequented, destinations. As world population grows and urbanisation increasingly develops, it could well happen that those countries offering *space* will have a precious commodity avidly sought by international tourists.

With the exception of the United States and Canada, the chief tourist movements have in the past been generated by the more prosperous European countries. The 1970s, however, have seen Japan beginning to enter the tourist arena on a rapidly growing scale. In 1962 a mere 75,000 Japanese travelled abroad; by 1974 departures overseas had reached 1,250,000, a growth rate of around 30 per cent annually. Japan, therefore, represents a major and increasingly important tourist market and it seems certain that Japanese outward travel will represent a new tourist flow of great significance during the next decade or so.[18]

For some years now the leisure industry has been expanding rapidly and international tourism has been a major growth point. While it is difficult to foresee and project the future pattern of development, it seems reasonably certain that continued growth, even if at a rather slower rate, will take place. It will be interesting to see if UNESCO's estimate of 3000 million tourists (domestic and international) by A.D. 2000 is achieved![19]

NOTES

1. "Recreational Travel: the New Migration," *Canadian Geographer* X, 1, 1966, pp. 1–14.

2. V. Popovic, *Tourism in Eastern Africa*, Ifo-Institut für Wirtschaftsforschung München Afrika-Studienstelle, Weltforum Verlag, München, 1972, p. 10.

3. *British Travel News*, No. 43, Autumn, 1973, p. 30.

4. Wolfe, *op. cit.*, p. 3.

5. M. Peters, *International Tourism*, Hutchinson, 1969, p. 34.

6. *Op. cit.*, p. 36.

7. *Op. cit.*, p. 11.

8. *Idem.*

9. *Idem.*

10. E. Williams and W. Zelinsky, "On Some Patterns of International Tourist Flows," *Economic Geography*, October 1970, pp. 549–67.

11. *Op. cit.*

12. *Op. cit.*

13. However, it should be noted that rapidly increasing numbers (52,000 in 1972) have begun to visit Spain.

14. *Op. cit.*

15. *Op. cit.*

16. *Op. cit.*

17. *Op. cit.*

18. See E. Devas, *Japan—a major tourist market*, Tourism Planning and Research Ltd., 1973.

19. Reported in *Courier*, February, 1974, p. 36.

Part Three

SOME ASPECTS OF THE TOURIST INDUSTRY

Chapter VII

The Organisation of Tourism

THE ROLE OF ORGANISATION

ORGANISATION is the framework within which tourism works: it relates to the structure of the industry, and is concerned with the issues involved in, and the approaches to, tourism. Organisation is the function of purpose and is concerned with maximising the opportunities for tourism. The basic determinants of success in tourism are threefold:

> (*i*) attractions, *e.g.* climate, scenery, historical and cultural features;
> (*ii*) accessibility, *i.e.* distance of destination and transport facilities;
> (*iii*) amenities, *e.g.* accommodation, catering, entertainment.

An appropriate mix is necessary for success, and it is the task of the organisation to achieve this success. Organisation alone can make a success (or otherwise) of the tourist destination.

The organisation of tourism falls into two parts: first, there are the *sectors* of tourism, *i.e.* the various providers of tourist services—the transport services, the hotel and catering services, entertainments; secondly, there are the *levels* of tourist organisation—the activities concerned with tourism at national, regional and local levels. Thus there is at once a horizontal and a vertical organisation in the organisation of tourism.

Precisely how the tourist industry is organised in any country varies very widely, but there a number of considerations which help to influence the nature of the organisational set-up.

> (*i*) The political, economic and social system in a particular country will have an important bearing upon its tourist organisation; in some countries, such as Spain and the Soviet Union, the industry is centralised and largely dominated by the government, whereas in others, such as Britain and Austria, the industry is decentralised with a minimum of governmental interference.

(*ii*) The importance of tourism in the national economy is likely to influence the character of the organisation. Where tourism is well-developed and of substantial economic importance, the organisation is likely to be well developed also, and the government actively concerned, as happens in the case of France and in Italy.

(*iii*) The stage of tourism development reached by a country is also likely to have considerable influence; for instance, in countries where tourism is just beginning, as in many of the developing countries, quicker results can be achieved if the industry is centralised and under direct government control. In the developing countries direct governmental intervention would seem to be not only desirable but indispensable.

(*iv*) Certain historical considerations may influence the nature of the tourist organisation. For instance, in Switzerland traditional influences are very strong. Switzerland has a long history of tourism and there is, as one might expect, a highly developed tourist organisation, but it is one which reflects the federal character of the state and is strongly decentralised.

NATIONAL TOURISM ORGANISATION

All countries which are engaged in tourism have an official tourism organisation whose function is to co-ordinate the different activities of all the bodies interested in tourism development. This central organ with general responsibility for the overall development of the tourist industry is commonly called the National Tourist Organisation (N.T.O.), although sometimes it goes by other names, *e.g.* National Tourism Council, National Tourist Commission, State Tourist Corporation. With the growth and complexity of modern tourism, most countries have found it sensible to establish an N.T.O. under some title. There are cases, however, where an N.T.O. does not exist: where this occurs the responsibility is taken directly by a Ministry of Tourism or a Department of State.

"There is no set formula as to what constitutes the most satisfactory constitutional arrangement for the national tourism body. In some countries, tourism ranks as a full Ministry and in some its Minister enjoys Cabinet rank. Another arrangement frequently encountered is for Tourism to share a Minister with Information or, perhaps, Art and Sport. Other possibilities include attaching the tourism office to the Presidency of the Council; putting it in the charge of an Under-Secretary with an occasional voice in the Council of Ministers; or, alternatively, making it semi-autonomous and largely independent of the regular structure of government."[1] Some eighty-six countries possess an N.T.O. In the case of sixty-three the N.T.O. is a government department, frequently a Ministry, which makes and implements policy; twelve consist of Statutory Boards to which the government delegates the implementation of its policy, as in the instance of the British Tourist Authority; and eleven comprise Voluntary Organisations similar to the former British Travel Association which was a purely voluntary organisation and not a statutory organisation nor in a government department.

It will be apparent that national arrangements for the N.T.O. vary widely. As Peters says, "The degree and form of government interest, the responsibility for development and the extent of government financial aid depends on many factors. The extent of state responsibility for tourism varies widely from country to country and depends on the political structure of the country, the government's assessment of the potential value of tourism to the economy, the degree of private interest and the availability of public and private capital for tourism projects."[2]

Functions of the N.T.O.

The objects and functions of the N.T.O. are, primarily, to ensure that the maximum possible value from international tourism accrues to the country for its economic and social benefit. The functions of the N.T.O., however, will vary quite widely in relation both to (i) the degree of direct intervention that the government desires to exercise, and (ii) the level of development of the tourist industry in the country concerned.

Functional differences are reflected in the N.T.O.'s structure and in its constitutional status; in some instances it is part and parcel of the central machinery of government and the government operates directly and comprehensively in the tourism sector, in others, it is semi-autonomous and functions after the manner of a professional body and not as a deliberate tool of the government. "As a general rule, it may be said that this latter conception of the role of the national tourism office is more appropriate to countries where tourism is already fairly advanced and where the private sector is active in it. In countries which are only starting to develop their tourism potential or where it is desired to make a rapid push forward, the government will normally play a more active role itself in promoting tourism development and will use the tourism office as its administrative organ for the purpose."[3] As the Estoril Seminar concluded, its "functions ... may be solely advisory, or regulatory, or ... also be directly operational and promotional."[4]

The N.T.O. is therefore the organisation set up by, and entrusted by, the state to take on the responsibilities of tourism matters at the national level; it is the body generally responsible for the formulation and implementation of national tourist policy. It "can carry out its task most effectively and satisfactorily only when it has extensive competence, adequate resources and no hampering limitations on its activities."[5] Any National Tourist Organisation can only act efficiently if the following factors noted by Peters are present:

"(i) ... sufficient influence and authority to initiate, direct and carry through all the changes that will be necessary to expand the tourist industry in future years.

(ii) ... full support of the government and be able to influence the activities of a number of government departments on matters affecting tourism development and tourists.

(iii) ... full support and confidence of all the trades comprising the tourist industry.

(iv) ... be financed adequately by the government in order to carry out all the duties assigned to it, on a scale commensurate with the potential income from tourism.

(v) ... efficient personnel and technical officers, thoroughly experienced in the various trades in the tourist industry."[6]

At the Estoril Seminar in 1966, it was generally agreed that "the N.T.O. would normally undertake ... the following functions: (1) Research; (2) Information and promotion within the country; (3) Regularisation of standards of lodgings and restaurants; (4) Control of activities of private travel agencies; (5) Publicity overseas; (6) Technical and juridical problems; (7) International relations; (8) Development of selected tourist areas; (9) Overall tourism policy and promotion."[7]

The Organisation and Work of a National Tourist Office

The N.T.O. is therefore likely to be concerned with four main things: administration, production, marketing and financing.

The administration will be concerned with the personnel of the organisation, with the part to be played by tourism in the national plan, with liaison with other government departments, regional co-operation, legal problems and advisory services, etc.

The production part will be concerned with all those elements and activities which make up the tourism product. Production will include the inventory and assessment of the country's natural attractions and the development and protection of these assets, the listing, assessing and forecasting of the country's tourism plant, the requirements in infrastructure where tourist development is planned, the drawing up of plans for regional or area development, the establishment of close relations with the hotel and catering and transport sectors of tourism, the recruitment and training of personnel for the tourist industry, etc.

The marketing section will be concerned with research into the principal and potential tourist markets, their size, socio-economic characteristics, food and accommodation preferences, spending power and the like; with sales promotion, public relations, overseas offices, etc.; and collaboration with other countries in the same region.

Finally, the financial work will involve investment in, and financing of, tourism in the country. For example, it will provide financial assistance for approved tourist projects, it may approve loans or grants for hotels, the provision of amenities, etc., it will seek and encourage private investment in tourism projects and where these are not enough perhaps seek funds from international agencies such as the International Bank for Reconstruction and Development, as did Yugoslavia for the construction of its Adriatic Highway. The role of foreign participation in tourism development is especially important in many of the developing countries who have not the capital available for investment.

THE BRITISH TOURIST AUTHORITY

Prior to 1969, when the *Development of Tourism Bill* was presented to Parliament and passed to establish the British Tourist Authority, the organisation of tourism in Britain was mainly in the hands of the British Travel Association, a voluntary co-operative association whose aims were to promote travel to and within Britain and to improve travel facilities and tourist amenities. In the last year of its existence the British Travel Association had an income of £3·7m, 80 per cent of which came as a Government grant, and a staff of about 450, a third of whom were posted abroad. Wales, Scotland and Northern Ireland had their own "national" Travel Boards, and England was divided up into nine zones—North and North-east, North-west, Midlands, North Midlands, East, South-east, South, South-west and London. This regional organisation was supported by various local organisations, *e.g.* holiday resorts and district bodies. The Government had shown a lukewarm interest in tourism for some forty years and it had no positive policy.

Such responsibility as it assumed was delegated to the then Board of Trade.

The existing situation was fraught with problems and difficulties even though the British Travel Association did a good job within the limits of its powers and finances. The principal weaknesses and drawbacks were the lack of any clear-cut Government policy, the lack of any effective powers of the national tourist organisation, the weak regional organisation in most parts of the country, the un-co-ordinated and piecemeal development of facilities, and the diversity and inadequacy of the financial support.[8] By the late 1960s, the accelerating growth of tourism in Britain, the growing appreciation by the Government of the importance of tourism to the economy and the fact that the Government had already begun to intervene in the industry (e.g. registration and classification of hotels) and to grant it assistance (e.g. hotel improvement and building schemes) produced a climate favourable to change.

In restructuring tourism organisation in Britain, the Government had several options available: it could give development powers to the exisiting British Travel Association, but this was not considered to be a very appropriate solution for a voluntary membership organisation; it could give development powers to the then Board of Trade, but opinion generally was against this and Eire's experience reaffirmed the undesirability of this possible solution; it could create a new Government Department for the development and promotion of tourism (but as promotion is essentially a commercial activity, it seemed to many that the Civil Service ought not to be concerned with such matters, while many also thought that a Ministry might very well turn out to be a very second-rate department); there was the possibility of leaving the British Travel Association as the promotional organisation and creating a new development organisation, but it was generally thought that the separation of these functions was undesirable; or the Government could create a new statutory organisation combining promotion and development, an option which had the balance of advantages in its favour and which, ultimately, was chosen as the most appropriate course of action.[9]

The *Development of Tourism Act* 1969, provided for the establishment of a British Tourist Authority (B.T.A.) and Tourist Boards for Wales and Scotland with responsibilities for the promotion and development of tourism in Britain. The Act, at the same time, provided for financial assistance out of public funds for new hotel construction and for the extension, alteration and modernisation of existing hotels, and it enabled provision to be made for the registration of all establishments in which sleeping accommodation is provided by way of trade or business. Under the new statutory organisation, the Government was to be responsible for policy and finance, the National Tourist Organisation (the B.T.A.) for promotion and development, *i.e.* all overseas promotion and non-U.K. activities, the "Country" Boards (England, Wales and Scotland) for development and promotion within the U.K. (*see* Fig. 6).

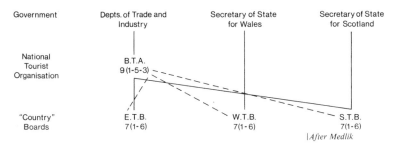

FIG. 6.—*The British Tourist Board's organisational structure.*

The B.T.A. Board comprises nine members: chairman, five members from the field of commerce and business and the three chairmen of the English, Welsh and Scottish Boards. The Country Boards each have seven Board members: a chairman and six members. Each of the Country Tourist Boards has an executive staff.

The establishment of the statutory organisation has brought clear benefits to the organisation of tourism in Britain. For the first time a top tourist organisation has been set up and given powers for development. The B.T.A. is the co-ordinating body, but the Country Boards are not subordinate. Priority is also given to regional organisation. As against these advantages, there are certain disadvantages, chiefly the failure of the Government to make a firm policy decision with respect to tourism in Britain and the limited progress made in financing the work of the B.T.A. For example, one Tourist Board chief has complained that the Government is starving the organisation of cash and the Yorkshire Tourist Board, for instance, had a budget of a mere £72,000 (in 1973), a totally inadequate income if the Board is to fulfil its function adequately.

The English Tourist Board has also set up eleven Regional Tourist Boards (*see* Fig. 7); these are:

    (*i*) The English Lakes Counties Tourist Board.
    (*ii*) Northumbria Tourist Board.
    (*iii*) Yorkshire Tourist Board.
    (*iv*) North-west Tourist Board.

FIG. 7.—*The English Tourist Boards.* There have been some changes in the former British Travel Association's regions since the *British Tourism Act.* Northumbria and Yorkshire have been carved out of the former North/North-East Region; the Lakes Counties have been separated out of the former North-West Region; the Midlands Region has been separated into the East and West Midlands; but the changes have been greatest in the south-eastern part of the country where a new Thames and Chilterns Board has been created, the East Region has been truncated, and Dorset has been incorporated into the West Country Region.

   (*v*) West Midlands Tourist Board.
  (*vi*) East Midlands Tourist Board.
 (*vii*) East Anglia Tourist Board.
(*viii*) The Thames and Chilterns Tourist Board.
  (*ix*) The London Tourist Board.
   (*x*) South-east England Tourist Board.
  (*xi*) West Country Tourist Board.

Sir Mark Henig, Chairman of the English Tourist Board, has described their task as being: "... to identify and promote the tourist attractions of their own regions within a broader English plan. They will provide the tourist with information, encourage the introduction of new tourist amenities and promote new types of holidays."[10] It should be noted that under the *Local Government Reorganisation Act* 1973 the Isle of Wight became a full County in its own right and became part of the English Tourist Board's administrative regional structure. Terms of association were agreed between the South-east England and the Isle of Wight Tourist Boards.

These regions were established on the basis of four criteria: they had to be geographical entities—natural tourist regions with community of interests and readily identifiable; they had to coincide with Local Authority Areas; it was desirable that they should tie up with the

Economic Planning Regions; and they had to be sufficiently large to enable them to function properly.

The Scottish Tourist Board suggested that seven tourist regions should be set up in Scotland.

(*i*) Highlands and Islands.
(*ii*) North-east.
(*iii*) East Central.
(*iv*) Clyde.
(*v*) Edinburgh and the Lothians.
(*vi*) Borders.
(*vii*) South-west.

Each region has its own Tourist Association and full-time staff, with an Executive Committee composed of representatives from the Local Authorities and from the tourist industry.

The Welsh Tourist Board divided Wales up into three regions: North, Central and South.

TRAVEL AGENTS AND TOUR OPERATORS

So far we have been concerned with the governmental or "official" organisation of tourism; let us now turn to the role of the private sector. In most countries which are at all concerned with the tourist industry, the private sector plays a very important role, not merely in selling the tourism product but often also in producing it, for many individuals, companies and corporations are involved in promoting, developing and financing tourism.

The travel agency has a history which goes back over a hundred years; it was pioneered in Britain by Thomas Cook. The function of the travel agent is, primarily, to give advice to potential tourists on the merits of alternative destinations, on the modes of transport available and the routes to be followed for a given destination, and to make the necessary arrangements for a chosen holiday, which may involve the booking of accommodation, transport or other relevant services. Because the agent has accumulated knowledge, expertise and contacts, he is a useful and sometimes invaluable, intermediary.

However, as Peters says, "although the main function of the agent is as a retailer [*i.e.* as a distributor of the tourism product], certain agents also act as 'manufacturers' of the product."[11] These "manufacturers" are commonly called tour operators. They plan, organise and sell tours. They make all the necessary arrangements—transport, accommodation, insurance, sight-seeing, often entertainment and other matters—and sell this "package" for an inclusive price. By mass-producing holidays in this fashion, the tour operators are able to procure substantial discounts from carriers, hoteliers, etc. and so offer their package deals at much reduced rates. Thus the holiday-maker not only gets his holiday for a much lower cost than if he made his own arrangements but is relieved of all the trouble of making his own arrangements. Against these very substantial advantages must be set the loss of freedom of choice and action. The tour operator may sell his tours directly to the public or through the channels of the retail agencies.

Since the Second World War tour operators have proliferated and all kinds of commercial undertakings have entered the field—in Britain, transport companies such as Wallace Arnold and Southdown, the Co-operative Wholesale Society and in West Germany mail-order firms. While most of the larger operators spread their activities widely, the smaller ones tend to specialise in particular fields, *e.g.* particular destinations or types of holiday.

U.K. AGENTS AND OPERATORS

Travel agents account for some four-fifths of all inclusive tour bookings and since the package holiday has increased in popularity the travel agency business has greatly expanded. Probably considerably more than half of the holidays taken abroad by British people now consist of inclusive packages. The total value of the package tour market in 1973 was probably in the region of £300m, as compared with £130m in 1968.[12] An Economic Intelligence Unit survey in 1968 for the Association of British Travel Agents showed that more than half of the total bookings were accounted for by 100 or fewer agents. In 2500 A.B.T.A. offices in Britain in 1966, some £280m was spent by the public; in 1974 this was more like £500m. But of the total amount spent in 1966 something between £150–160m, or about 55 per cent, was accounted for by some 60 agencies and 75 per cent of the total number of agencies were responsible for only just over one-fifth (£80m) of the total turnover. Agencies, of course, work on a commission basis and while, in 1968, the average turnover per employee was about £15,000, it was reckoned that this should be doubled for the business to be really profitable.

One of the biggest problems facing the agencies is the highly seasonal character of their business; there are slack periods in the year, when staff are under-employed. Since it was estimated that nearly two-thirds of agency running costs consist of wages, it will be clear that to maximise the use of labour is very necessary. The prospects for some of the smaller and less well known agencies would appear to be lean, especially since the major tour operators are selling more of their tours directly to the public, partly because of the dissatisfaction which most of the tour operators and carriers feel concerning the services carried out on their behalf by the travel agencies, although the E.I.U. report questioned the alleged reasons for their dissatisfaction and, in fact, their actual validity.

Only some 15 per cent of the tours are sold directly by the wholesalers, the vast majority of tours being sold through the retail travel agents.[13] In Britain there has been little attempt or success at marketing inclusive tours through the big mail-order firms, as there has been with conspicuous success in West Germany, although one or two of the smaller firms (such as Travel Club), sell by mail-order. Some tour operators have also considered selling their tours through outlets such as banks and supermarkets, but this idea has never been followed up.

Since 1965 there has been a clear trend towards specialisation and rationalisation. While the larger firms offer a wide range of holidays in many countries, some of the smaller ones cultivate special markets, only the upper end of the market, for example, offering a wider choice of resorts and higher quality hotels. The competition in the travel market has led to many of the smaller operators going out of business or, alternatively, being taken over by larger or more successful firms— Thomsons, for example, took over Lunn-Poly and Sunair. But even the giant operators can get into difficulties, as in the case of Clarksons, which lost money to the tune of several million pounds a year, and were bought by Court Line in 1974 (now also out of business). In the tour operating business profit margins are low and firms can easily get into difficulties.

While there has been a certain amount of horizontal integration in the travel trade, more notable has been the considerable vertical integration, particularly in Britain between airlines and tour operators. One of the early link-ups was between Universal Sky Tours Ltd. and Britannia Airways; subsequently Cosmos and Monarch Airlines linked up and Laker Airways purchased Arrowsmith Holidays and Lord Brothers. Tour operators have been somewhat chary of acquiring hotels, although Thomsons and Fortes Travel Division (Milbank and Hickie Borman) own some.

HOLIDAY CAMPS AND CLUB MÉDITERRANÉE

The Holiday Camp began in the 1930s particularly after 1937 when the enterprising Mr Butlin opened his Camp at Skegness (there had been some earlier ones, *e.g.* Heysham Holiday Camp and Cunningham's Camp at Douglas). The success of Butlin's venture led to many others being established. For harassed parents with young children and limited means, or for adolescents who enjoy an organised holiday with a surfeit of fun, amusement and entertainment and who hanker after a holiday romance, the Holiday Camp provides an almost ideal solution. Butlins, Pontins and others have developed a type of holiday which is very much a part of the British way of life, although the Camps do not suit or attract everyone.

A more recent Continental development which has had a spectacular success is the holiday village. The idea of the holiday village with its informality, easy friendships, sporting activities, night-life and good food, was conceived by a Frenchman, M. Gerard Blitz, who set up the first tented village in 1950 on the island of Majorca. Catering at first for the French, the Paris-based company, which owns and runs the Club Méditerranée, now not only serves the European market—where Club villages are found in France, Spain, Italy, Greece, Turkey, Yugoslavia, Israel, Egypt and North Africa—but has entered the Caribbean area, where it aims at the North American market, and has, or hopes to, set up villages in Hawaii, Brazil, Mauritius and Bali. In 1973 the Club had thirty-four centres around the world, and sells 300,000 holidays annually. During 1973–78 it is planned to increase sales by 60 per cent so that by 1978 Club Méditerranée will be catering for half a million holiday-makers.[14] One interesting feature is that the Club attracts little business from British holiday-makers; among the possible reasons for this are that cheap package holidays are strongly entrenched, that the British prefer to meet and mix with foreigners rather than go to an all English-speaking camp, and that Butlins, etc. already cater for this type of holiday in Britain.

NOTES

1. *Tourism Development and Economic Growth*, Estoril Seminar, O.E.C.D., 1967, p. 20.
2. Peters, *op. cit.*, p. 212.
3. *Tourism Development and Economic Growth*, p. 20.
4. *Idem*, p. 21.
5. R. W. McIntosh, *op. cit.*, p. 86.

6. *International Tourism*, pp. 207–8.

7. *Tourism Development and Economic Growth*, p. 21. Footnote.

8. S. Medlik, "Organisation of Tourism: Britain," Paper in Management Development Programme, University of Surrey, 1971.

9. Medlik, *op. cit.*

10. Quote from a speech at the Goldsmiths' Hall in the City of London to mark the first meeting of the Regional Tourist Board chairmen, Spring, 1972.

11. *International Tourism*, p. 228.

12. Special Report No. 1, "Package Holidays," *Retail Business* 141, November, 1969, p. 14.

13. *Idem*, p. 16.

14. G. Merrit, "British Beachhead Wanted," *The Financial Times*, 16th March, 1973.

Chapter VIII

Transport and Tourism

TOURIST travel is a manifestation of spatial interaction and implies a movement away from the place where people normally work and live. Transport, which makes travel possible, is therefore an integral part of tourism, involving moving very large numbers of people and demanding heavy investment and complicated organisation. It will be useful to look first, in general terms, at the factors affecting the demand for transport before discussing more specifically the role of transport in tourism.

CIRCULATION: ITS IMPORTANCE

The French term *circulation* is a useful term embracing all movement and communication, basic to the process of spatial interaction. The activity of tourism is intimately dependent upon communication and transportation since distance and time greatly influence it.

Travel by people, the spread of trade and the increased volume of traffic have been helped enormously by the development of new, more efficient and speedier means of transportation and by improved communications facilities. Contacts can be almost instantaneous and anything that happens can now be known the world over within the space of a few minutes. Clearly, these developments in transport and communications have, in effect, made the earth a much smaller place, and had a correspondingly powerful impact upon the travel and tourist industry. Space and time are intimately linked together and these days space, in the sense of distance, is often equated with time, a fact which is fundamental to the whole problem of the geography of communications and transport.

Human conceptions of territorial space, of spatial relationships and of physical distance have undergone a continuing evolution. Today, man's concept of territoriality (and especially in the tourist sense) is closely identified with the life and activities of specific places, while his concept of distance is measured rather in the time it takes him to reach his destination than in miles or kilometres. Regional variation essentially endows a place with particularity or uniqueness, and it is, of course, this regional differentiation which lies at the root of tourism—people wish to visit new, foreign places, strange to their experience.

The concept of spatial differentiation implies physical distance, for regionally different places are of necessity physically removed from one another. Every place on the earth's surface is spatially interrelated with every other place, but these relationships are not necessarily stable and unchanging; on the contrary, they tend to be dynamic and to change with time, outlook and with improved techniques of movement. For example, half a century ago a holiday in the Seychelles, or even in Morocco, was almost unthinkable to the vast majority of Britons.

Travellers or tourists are able to change their positions spatially only by the consumption of time: in other words, it takes time for individuals to be moved from one place to another. Spatial interchange, at the simplest level, implies three things: the local abundance of a commodity, an external demand for a commodity and the transference of a commodity from where it is obtained to the place of consumption. Translated into tourism terms, one can conceive of Mediterranean sunshine as the commodity and the sun-starved Britons as creating the external demand; but, in this instance, the sun cannot be brought to Britain so the Briton is transferred to the sun. Essential to the concept of tourist spatial interchange is this separation in space of the centre of demand (the market) from the point of consumption (the tourist destination); and this separation can be bridged only by the establishment of effective means of transport and communication—"space-adjusting techniques" as they have been called.[1]

Time is closely linked with distance, but time taken to make a journey is often associated with other things, *e.g.* speed and cost.

SPEED, COST AND LOAD

In transport, time is largely equated with speed of movement, but the saving of time (which cuts down costs) is associated with two other factors or conditions: the overcoming of certain obstacles or hindrances to movement and what is commonly called turn-round. There are often handicaps to directness and to speed of movement. Physical obstacles, *e.g.* mountains, rivers, shoal water or submerged reefs, may impede direct movement as also may economic and political conditions. Considerable time can be saved in transport by efficient terminal facilities, *e.g.* the avoidance of queueing, speedy loading and unloading, mechanised handling, etc. which facilitate a quicker turn-round.

If time is of no object, the traveller from Britain to the United States, for instance, may well prefer to go by sea and take advantage of a leisurely cruise; but if time is important he is likely to travel by air. Frequently to business men "time is money"; when this applies, quicker, though perhaps more costly, travel is, in the final reckoning, cheaper. Speed in transport can be achieved in a variety of ways: (*i*) by using new and more powerful methods of propulsion; (*ii*) by improving trackways to facilitate speedier movement; (*iii*) by guaranteeing full cargoes or passenger loads which enables transport to be organised to schedule; (*iv*) by improving terminal facilities, which allows a quicker turn round; and (*v*) by the adoption of new devices and inventions, such as radio communications, automatic signalling, radar, etc. which facilitate uncongested movement.

The quantity or load factor is of great importance in transport since, generally speaking, the greater the quantity, whether goods or passengers, carried the cheaper the cost. This is well illustrated by the increasing use of bulk carriers whether by sea, *e.g.* for oil, ores or by air, *e.g.* jumbo jets. The use of larger vehicles, however, often brings its own constraints, *e.g.* the need for a deeper draught of water, a firmer, superior and more costly trackway and in the case of aircraft a much longer runway.

The cost of carriage, whether of goods or people, is obviously a very important consideration in transport. Trade almost always follows the cheapest routes. Although the cheapest route is not necessarily the shortest route; neither is the quickest route always the shortest. Natural obstacles along the line of direct route may have to be avoided, although journeys round such hindrances may in fact take a shorter time than those through or over them. Sometimes a short route, though quicker than a longer one, is more expensive because of the need to use special equipment or vehicles whose running costs are heavy. In mountainous terrain, for example, rack railways, more powerful engines, bridging and tunnelling, etc. mean higher transport costs.

DETERMINANTS OF SPATIAL INTERACTION

Ullman has proposed a threefold system to explain interaction development and, since this has great relevance to recreational travel, some attention should be drawn to it. Ullman's bases for transportation and interaction are: complementarity, intervening opportunity and transferability.[2]

Areal differentiation does not of itself produce interchange; in order that two areas may interact there must be a demand in one and a supply in the other. Where such a relationship exists between two areas, they are said to be complementary. Let us apply this factor to tourism. Among British holiday-makers there is a great demand for sunshine; the Mediterranean lands of southern Europe have a plentiful supply of it; hence there is complementarity between the two. This complementarity generates interaction, a function of natural and cultural differentiation.

The second factor is that of *intervening opportunity*. Complementarity gives rise to interaction between two areas only when there is no intervening source of supply available. It will be dependent upon the absence of intervening sources of supply. As Ullman points out: "Florida attracts more amenity migrants from the Northeast of the U.S.A. than does more distant California."[3] In this case, Florida provides a nearer complementary source and creates an intervening opportunity, which results in the substitution of another area.

Interaction is thirdly influenced by the factor of *transferability*, that is "distance, measured in real terms of transfer and time costs."[4] In other words, if the distance or time required to make the journey between the market and the supply is too great and the cost is too high transferability will not take place, notwithstanding perfect complementarity and the absence of intervening opportunity. If transfer costs, in time and money, exceed the ability and willingness to pay, then interchange will be prevented. For example, a British tourist may have a desire to visit Jamaica but the journey there may be too long for the holiday time at his disposal or the cost of the journey may be too high for his pocket, hence interaction will not take place and an alternative destination, involving less travelling time and expense, will be substituted.

TRANSPORT AND TOURISM

Transport has been at once a cause and an effect of the growth of tourism: improved transport facilities have stimulated tourism; the expansion of tourism has stimulated transport.

Perhaps the single most important function of transport relates to accessibility. Accessibility is a term frequently used to mean the degree of access to a particular place in terms of distance, time or cost. Specifically the term also implies the number of opportunities available for a given travel cost, and reflects the quality of the transport network, *i.e.* the availability and quality of service provided. Accessibility has been a very important factor affecting the rise and growth of many individual resorts and tourist areas. Brighton, Southend, Blackpool and Southport have already been cited as examples in this context. Switzerland, again located almost at the geographical centre of peninsular Europe, is relatively easily accessible from most parts of the Continent and well situated to capture much of the European holiday traffic. Places which are inaccessible—in effect, places which are not well served with transport facilities—are unlikely to develop as important centres of tourism.

If we look at the transport used by the British to reach holiday destinations in Great Britain during the past twenty years we see quite marked changes and trends (*see* Table 12). Perhaps the most fundamental change has been the massive movement away from public transport and towards travel by car. In 1951 almost three-quarters of all holiday-makers travelled by bus, coach or train and just over a quarter by car; in 1970 the proportions were almost reversed, with only three in ten using public transport and almost seven in ten travelling by car.

TABLE 12

Transport used to reach holiday destinations in Great Britain

	1951 (%)	1955 (%)	1960 (%)	1965 (%)	1970 (%)
Car	27	34	47	60	68
Bus/Coach	27	33	21	21	15
Train	47	37	30	21	13
Other	na	na	10	9	4

Figures do not add up to 100%, since more than one mode of transport was used.

If we look at international travel over the same period we are struck most forcibly by the great expansion in air traffic: if people wish to travel long distances and have only limited holiday time at their disposal, air transport has a great advantage. The development of package tours, inclusive of transport costs (frequently by air at reduced rates) has also stimulated air transport.

Before the arrival of air transport, sea transport was the only means

TABLE 13

Modes of transport in tourism

Country	Road (%)	Rail (%)	Sea (%)	Air (%)
To: Spain (1969)	60·0	8·0	8·0	20·0
Algeria (1969)	46·5	—	8·4	45·1
Norway (1970)	90·0	1·0	2·0	7·0
Finland (1972)	33·9	—	54·6	11·5
Egypt (1970)	20·0	—	4·8	75·2

of travelling between, say, Britain and the United States. By modern standards of movement, water transport is slow and now that air transport charges are competitive, travel by sea is declining in importance. There are still many, however, to whom sea travel is in itself a pleasure and cruising holidays have grown in importance. A significant recent development is the air–sea link-up: holiday-makers are ferried by air to embarkation points for sea cruises; for example, many British tourists are flown to, say, Athens where they pick up Mediterranean cruise ships. In areas such as the Aegean and Caribbean, cruising is still the best and most comfortable way of touring around. There also remain some holiday areas where sea transport provides the only practicable transport; until a few years ago, the only way to get to Madeira was by boat; but with the opening of an airport on the island not only has an alternative mode of transport been provided but the number of tourists has escalated. The inception of air transport, and especially its growth in post-war years, made quick, easy, long-distance transport possible. Tourists with limited time at their disposal can now, if they so wish and can afford the fare, travel many hundreds, even thousands, of miles to a holiday destination. The Seychelles until 1971 had no tourist industry but with the building of an airport its isolation and inaccessibility were abolished overnight and immediately it began to attract visitors.

Railways

Reference has already been made to the important role played by the railways in the nineteenth-century development of holiday-making. Thousands took advantage of the new day excursions and one perspicacious gentleman, a certain Thomas Cook, sensing the possibilities, organised the first excursion special. On the 5th July, 1841, he arranged a special railway excursion between Leicester and Loughborough and 570 people went on the shilling trip.[5] Thomas Cook & Son Ltd. grew from this to be the first, and for long the largest, travel agency. The Great Exhibition of 1851 had a considerable impact on the growth of railway travel; it stimulated the development of cheap excursions and some 3 million people travelled to London by rail to visit the Exhibition. Patmore relates how "Fierce competition broke out for the Exhibition traffic from the West Riding between the Great Northern Railway on the one hand and the Midland and London & North Western Railways on the other. The return fare fell first to 15s, and ultimately to as little as 5s."[6] The railways provided, for the first time, cheap pleasure travel and, as the railway network spread, large areas of country and many coastal locations were opened up to the townsman.

Early railway travel must have been far from comfortable and not infrequently hazardous, but in the early 1870s first-class railway travel was introduced by an American, G. M. Pullman, who developed the Pullman coaches with their luxury furnishings and dining facilities. Long-distance travel could now be undertaken in comfort and with pleasure. Comparable travel in Europe was organised by the *Compagnie des Wagons-Lit.*

The great age of rail lasted for just about one hundred years and although motorised transport had appeared by the beginning of the twentieth century it was not until the 1930s that it began seriously to challenge railway transport. After the Second World War the real expansion in motor transport occurred and the railways began to suffer a rapid decline. Increasingly the railways became uneconomic and, although a railway modernisation scheme was introduced in 1955 with the intention of providing new rolling stock and extensive improvements, by 1970 it became necessary to cut back on services. The *Beeching Report* (1963) recommended the closure of many uneconomic lines and there has been a drastic curtailing of services since. The closing of many local lines brought difficulties to many rural areas and to many seaside resorts which were denied rail connections. Such action has not been limited to Britain; it is a feature characteristic of most countries of Western Europe and North America, and it seems inevitable that continued contraction will occur in most economically well-developed countries because of the ever-increasing competition from the motor car and aeroplane.

It is therefore paradoxical that the very things which have seemed to foretell the doom of railways, especially motor transport, are offering it in fact possibilities of a new lease of life. As a result of a growing population, urban expansion and growing congestion on the roads, Britain may soon need its railways more than ever before. Indeed, if railway transport could be made more speedy, more punctual, more efficient and more comfortable, many would probably return to travel by rail. For long-distance travel, railway transport is still hard to beat and, due to congestion on the roads, many tourists possessing a car are putting it on the trains, *e.g.* from Yorkshire one can have one's car carried to Scotland or Devon. Air travel is still relatively unreliable and, certainly in Britain, journeys by aeroplane often take more time than the distance merits; as a result, many countries are experimenting with new supertrains in an attempt to win back passengers from the airlines. Britain has an A.P.T., or advanced passenger train, at the test stage which will travel at up to 150 mph on existing track and at 186 mph on specially prepared track and experiments have been made with a 250 mph Hovertrain; France has a Turbotrain and is experimenting with an Aerotrain which, it is believed, will reach speeds of up to 200 mph; West Germany is working on the Transrapid, propelled by linear induction, which by 1980, it is claimed, will be in action and will travel at 300 mph; while Japan, which already has the best railway in the world, has its famous bullet train, running between Tokyo and Osaka, at 125 mph, and is experimenting with a 300 mph train using a magnetic field as track.[7]

Finally, it should be remembered that in Europe there is still a far-ranging network of railways and first-class travel is usually good. From London, for example, using the sea-links, one can journey to Vienna, Milan or Barcelona. If the Channel Tunnel were to be built the time-gap between train and plane to destinations on the Continent would be appreciably narrowed.

Roads and Motor Transport

The motor car has revolutionised holiday habits. "The car," says Patmore "brought incomparably greater freedom to recreational travel ... in the choice of destination ... in the timing of journeys ... to pause at a moment's whim."[8]

Although the first motor cars had come into operation by the end of the nineteenth century, up to the time of the First World War their numbers, in Britain, were small, less than 50,000, and were the toys of the wealthy. During the inter-war period, car ownership multiplied rapidly from 109,000 in 1919 to 2 million by 1939. After the Second World War the numbers jumped from 5 million in 1959 to over 14 million in 1973.

The car has become increasingly important in the pursuit of leisure and tourism. "The overall trend in tourism is towards greater use of the private car. In 1960, only 47 per cent of British holiday-makers travelled by car, but in 1969 this proportion had risen to 67 per cent [see Table 14]. The use of buses and coaches has declined from 21 per cent to 14 per cent, but the total using road transport is now four-fifths of all holiday-makers. The actual number of holiday-makers travelling by road has, of course, increased even more significantly as more people take a holiday away from home."[9]

The motor car is also important in international tourism. Large numbers of Britons travelling abroad do so by car as do large numbers of Continentals visiting Britain: "Of nearly two million holiday visitors from Europe in 1969, an estimated 19 per cent were motoring visitors.

TABLE 14

*Types of transport used on longest part of journey
to holiday destination (1960 and 1969)*

Method used	1960 (%)	1969 (%)
Train	30	16
Bus/coach	21	14
Car	47	67
Plane	2	1
Boat	5	2
Other	3	1
TOTAL MENTIONS	108 [1]	102 [1,2]

1. Totals do not add to 100 as some respondents mentioned more than one mode of transport.

2. Individual figures do not add up to total because of rounding.

Source: British Tourist Authority, National Travel Surveys.

The proportion of motoring visitors from more distant countries was naturally smaller, but nevertheless some 9 per cent of all foreign visitors arrived by car. In addition, it is estimated that over half a million visitors hire a car in this country for all or part of their stay."[10] As one would naturally expect, the use of road transport is appreciably greater in domestic than in international tourism; this is certainly to be expected in Britain since this country is an island, but the statement is equally true for other countries.

The provision of good motor roads and road services has a highly important role to play in the development of both domestic and international tourism. Referring to the latter, Sir Alexander Glen, Chairman of the British Tourist Authority, writing in 1970, said: "The numbers of those taking motoring holidays, especially from Europe, has trebled during the past two years and the potential market remains enormous. If we are to realise this potential we shall need to improve facilities at our ports. Roll on/roll off ferries already provide a highway to and from Europe and it is essential that formalities and procedures at both ends do not interrupt the flow. As new plans are being made to provide the U.K. motorist with more motorways and a better road system, let us not forget the importance of overseas visitors...."[11] Since foreign motoring tourists spend more than do non-motoring tourists, they contribute proportionately more to U.K. earnings from international tourism, and all motoring tourists bring benefits to the economy since they spread consumer spending more equitably throughout the tourist areas and more especially bring tourist money into outlying and marginal areas where previously little or nothing was earned.

In Britain there are marked regional variations in the use and pattern of road transport in relation to tourism. "To some extent these can be explained by the provision, or lack, of particular transport facilities for the main journey (the South-East, for example, is well served by public transport to all parts of the country and car-use is relatively low). It is noticeable, however, that those regions with the highest car-use (Cumberland and Westmorland, Northumberland and Durham, East Anglia, the South-West, Wales and Scotland) are those in which the attractions are dispersed rather than concentrated in a relatively small area. The desire for mobility in the holiday area is a major factor in determining the mode of transport used for the main journey from home."[12] Table 15 gives the type of transport used on the longest part of the journey to the holiday destination, in 1969, in terms of the region of destination.

The coming of the motor car, and especially its rapid growth in numbers, resulted in a big increase in traffic on an out-of-date road system, for not only were the width and road surface deficient but the pattern was still basically that which had been laid down by the Romans. And British roads were notoriously tortuous. Chesterton wrote "the rolling English drunkard made the rolling English road," but in truth the rolling road was largely the product of the land-owning system of the past when tracks went round field boundaries, thus giving us our innumerable dog-leg bends. Moreover, it had become customary for the roads to also carry water and sewage mains, gas pipes, electricity cables and telephone wires; thus there were severe problems facing road realignment. In fact, only the motorways are really free of these problems.

With the tremendous increase in road traffic, these problems of the existing road system soon became acute. Improved roads and dual carriageways were introduced in the 1930s and although these helped to speed up movement over long stretches sooner or later—at cross roads, where the road narrowed, at river bridging points or at the entry points to towns—the system became clogged and there was frightful congestion.

Another point to bear in mind is that increased road facilities inevitably generate more traffic, and as roads function as a terminal as well as a track accordingly, facilities for parking, either on or close to the road, must be made. Capital cities and many other towns, *e.g.* seaside resorts such as Blackpool, historic centres such as York, cultural centres such as Stratford-on-Avon, are great tourist attractions little equipped historically to provide facilities for the problems of a large influx of car-borne visitors.

TABLE 15

Types of transport used on longest part of journey to holiday destination (1969): by region of destination

Region of destination

Method used	Great Britain	Cumberland and Westmorland	Northumberland and Durham	North West and Isle of Man	Yorkshire	Midlands	East Anglia	South-East	South-West	Wales	Scotland
Train	16	9	14	16	17	16	12	25	13	10	17
Bus/coach	14	10	14	25	18	21	19	16	11	11	13
Car	67	76	71	55	65	61	70	60	76	78	67
Plane	1	0	0	1	0	0	0	0	0	0	1
Boat	2	0	0	9	0	0	0	3	0	0	2
Other	1	4	3	0	2	1	2	1	1	1	1
TOTAL MENTIONS [1,2]	102	100	102	105	102	100	101	104	101	101	102
Estimated persons aged 16+ (000)	18,550	320	250	1,520	1,080	900	1,170	4,290	4,460	2,300	2,270

1. Totals do not add to 100% as some respondents mentioned more than one mode of transport.
2. Individual figures may not add up to totals because of rounding.
Source: British Tourist Authority, National Travel Survey 1969.

In the 1930s the Germans pioneered the development of motorways with their *autobahnen*, although the motivation behind their construction was to a very considerable extent strategic and military. The rapid post-war expansion in motor transport in Britain and the inadequacy of the road system led to the development of motorways here as well. The *Motorways Plan*, published in 1946, aimed more particularly to aid the industrial development of the Midlands and the North-West. The M1 and the M6 were the first motorways to be opened. By the summer of 1971, 1326 km (829 miles) of motorway had been completed and an additional 419 km (262 miles) started. It is planned that Britain's motorway network will be approximately doubled to some 3219 km (2000 miles) by 1982. The aim is to link all air terminals, major seaports, industrial areas and every major city, and to create a motorway network which will enable anyone, once on it, to get anywhere within the system. Obviously the motorways have not been built primarily nor even secondarily for tourism, although there is no doubt that tourism will benefit from them (*see* Fig. 8). Already we have seen the impact which the northerly extension of the M6 has had on the Lake District (*see* p. 47). However, "the present motorway network is woefully inadequate in relation to tourist needs since it connects only the major centres of population, with the exceptions of Tyneside and Teesside, which have to rely on non-motorway sections of A1, Clydeside and the Portsmouth/Southampton area. Resort areas are served by motorways only if they happen to lie on or near to a route between two major population centres. In the majority of cases, tourist areas are not in such favoured positions and have to rely on all-purpose roads of varying standards to carry the ever-increasing amounts of tourist traffic. Tourism is unlikely to generate enough traffic to justify a motorway being built solely for tourist purposes. The traffic is very seasonal, the majority being in the six months from April to September, and there are marked peaks within the season at weekends, so although the traffic flow on a summer Sunday may seem sufficient to warrant new high-capacity roads, it must be remembered that such a high level of traffic occurs for only a few days a week for less than half the year. Average traffic levels over the year as a whole may not be sufficient to justify such a road, but the incidence of congestion is such that it imposes costs far in excess of those on similar roads with a more even distribution of traffic." [13]

In addition to the extended motorway plan, Mr Peter Walker (then Minister for the Environment) indicated in 1972 that he had proposals for an additional 2414 km (1500 miles) of what were termed "high quality strategic trunk routes," but there are fears that some areas such

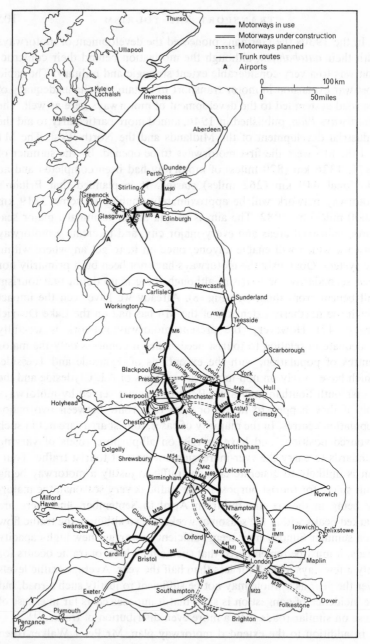

FIG. 8.—*British Motorways.* The map shows the motorway network in the summer of 1975. The growth of the network is having marked repercussions on the mobility of the tourist; for instance, the completion of the M6 to Carlisle has opened up the Lake District to the people of the Midlands.

as the South-West and East Anglia will remain poorly served for tourism. Indeed, current highway investment appraisal techniques do not work in favour of tourism. The same fears have been expressed in respect of Scotland. Although the Secretary of State for Scotland stated in the House of Commons that "the encouragement of tourism, which is an important part of our strategy for Scotland, is fully taken into account in planning the road programme" it is felt by many that insufficient consideration has been given to the needs of tourism and that the provision of roads for tourist needs in the present programme falls far short. The British Road Federation Report *Roads and Tourism* concludes: "It is essential given the present-day pattern of tourism that major emphasis be placed upon the provision of road access to and within the main tourist areas if the economic and social benefits from the growth of tourism are to be reaped. Poor access and heavy congestion will not only hinder this growth, but will also cause the environment to deteriorate if large numbers of vehicles have to use roads which were designed only for low traffic levels. Good, well-designed roads can help to stabilise the environment while at the same time enabling a large number of people to appreciate it."[14]

Improvements in road transport facilities stimulate tourism. The construction of the *Magistrale*, or Adriatic Highway, which runs all the way along the coast of Yugoslavia from Rijeka in the north to Titograd in the far south, has had a marked influence upon both the expansion of tourism and the growth of tourist centres in that country, especially in the south. As Hamilton has written: "The localisation of tourist centres in Yugoslavia prior to 1964 (the date of the opening of the Adriatic Highway) reflected the situation when accommodation and transport tended to localise visitors around main ports and railheads. Improved transport [and accommodation] facilities have led to the greater spatial dispersion of tourism."[15] The French, in developing their new holiday coast in Languedoc–Roussillon, saw the necessity of providing rapid and easy access to the six new resorts and a new autoroute is planned. The new motorway is to be set back a few miles from the coast and to by-pass the main inland towns; though running parallel to the coast, it is to be kept away from it. Access roads will serve each resort, but in every case these will terminate in car parks situated some distance from the sea and "from these points onwards all traffic must be on foot or by water so that there is no motor traffic near the beaches or running closely parallel to them."[16] Finally, reference may be made to the Autostrada del Sol which is being extended into southern Italy; this should help to open up the extremities of the country to the tourist and lead to the greater development of tourist resorts—still relatively few—in the south.

In conclusion, we may usefully quote what Peters has to say concerning the principles that must govern road development if tourism is to benefit. "The opening up of a country to tourists, and the development of new resort centres, in most cases is dependent on an adequate road system to spread tourists around the country. The principles to be incorporated ... should be:

(a) Safe, wide, scenic roads to resorts and other main attractions with good direct links between them.

(b) Secondary roads linking the principal road networks to provide a wide range of tours covering every important point of tourism interest.

(c) ... a system ... designed to encourage tourists to move around through all the regions of the country spreading the benefits from tourism as widely as possible.

(d) Elimination of 'dead-end' roads to avoid back-tracking by tourists who prefer to travel continuously on new routes."[17]

Water Transport

Transport by water makes a significant contribution to the development of travel on land and by air. The offshore islands of Britain, the Isle of Wight, the Isle of Man, Hebrides, etc. were entirely dependent upon sea links before the coming of the aeroplane, as in fact to a considerable extent they are still. The British Isles, because of their insular position, were dependent on various short sea crossings to the Continent, and travel between the Old World and the New likewise was totally dependent upon the ship. In the context of tourism today, we can think of water transport as fulfilling two main roles: ferrying and cruising.

Scheduled liner transport, formerly much used for inter-continental travel, has almost, if not quite, vanished. The first regular shipping services by steamers were inaugurated by Sir Samuel Cunard in 1840. He pioneered trans-Atlantic navigation and set the high standards of comfort and service which for long were associated with the Atlantic crossing. But, like the trans-continental railways, the long-distance liner services have fallen on hard times as a result of the growing competition from the airlines and now we see the great ocean-going liners acting as cruise ships for part of the year, although the bigger vessels are not always suitable for this role because of their great draught. P. & O.'s

45,000-ton *Canberra* is, for example, to be modified to enable it to engage more effectively in holiday cruising.

The expansion in international tourism has led to an increasing use of ferry-boats by tourists, especially motorised tourists, on short sea crossings. Large numbers of Britons holidaying in Ireland or on the Continent and considerable numbers of Continentals coming to Britain, use water transport. Although increasing use is being made of car ferries these are really mobile bridges and this mode of transport is likely to be drastically reduced if the Channel Tunnel eventually comes into operation.

The hovercraft was pioneered by Sir Christopher Cockerell in the 1950s, and the first Channel crossing by an air-cushion vehicle was made in 1959. The potential of hovercraft in the 1960s seemed great but the hope that they might radically alter transport patterns has faded. As ferries they have been operated in a number of places in the British Isles but few have proved to be really successful or to have survived as regular services. R. S. Tolley has drawn attention to the hovercraft's high operating costs and the physical limitations of its use and concludes, "The hovercraft ferry may continue for some time on specific routes which offer particular advantages for hovercraft operation, but the impact on the overall passenger ferry market seems likely to be minimal. Indeed, since 1970, more than a dozen new conventional cross-Channel ferries have been ordered, compared with only one new hovercraft." [18]

It is difficult to forecast the future of tourist sea transport. Long-distance sea travel will almost certainly continue to contract, although there will always be a limited demand for sea cruising, since this leisurely and attractive mode of travel has a great appeal. One of the most important recent developments in sea traffic has in fact been that of holiday sea cruises, especially in the Mediterranean and Caribbean, but it should be emphasised that compared with land-based activity this is comparatively small. "Sea travel," says McIntosh, "has evolved into a predominantly 'floating resort' or 'floatel' concept. This appealing idea has increased demand for sea travel, and cruises have grown in popularity in recent years. This elegant way of life will ... have a growing market as affluence and leisure time increase." [19] We have already noted the growing tendency for British holiday-makers to fly out to the cruise area and pick up the cruise ship; in the same way, many Americans fly to Miami and pick up a vessel there to make a circuit of the Caribbean. Secondly, there is an increasing tendency for cruise vessels to do less actual cruising and to make an increasing number of calls to enable passengers to see more places and undertake more shore excursions. In this way tourists can combine the advantages of life at sea with a sight-seeing touring holiday.

Air Transport

Improved methods of transportation have already been cited as one of the main reasons for the tremendous growth in tourism, and when one is looking at international as distinct from domestic tourism, then complementary developments in air transport are most outstanding. Although people were travelling by air before the Second World War, air transport for the masses is essentially a post-war phenomenon. This has been achieved through improved aircraft technology and the development of all-inclusive or package holidays. The overseas holiday now clearly reflects the rising standards of living within our society.

The great advantage of air travel is its speed, and destinations in Europe and beyond are now within easy reach of the tourist who has only a limited amount of time to spend away from home. This charac-teristic of speed, however, is only achieved at a cost because of the high capital outlay yet when one considers the ever increasing size of aircraft (a Lockheed Tristar for example holds over 300 passengers) coupled with intensive fleet utilisation, the cost of air travel has declined in real terms over the last twenty-five years.

New aircraft have tended to be larger, faster and cheaper to operate in terms of cost per seat-mile, and lower fares have succeeded in bringing increased revenue. Broadly speaking, one can differentiate between two groups of air traveller. On the one hand, there are those who travel to a specific destination for a given purpose—the business traveller or a family visiting friends. In such cases, demand can, to some extent be stimulated by improvements in the quality of service or by fare reductions, but as Williams[20] points out, such demand cannot really be created. For the tourist, however, "if a holiday can be devised at a particular resort which best satisfies his tastes at the price he is prepared to pay, traffic to that resort which would otherwise not exist is truly *created*." Furthermore, for tourists, the destination is influencable in so far as it is less important than is travel for other purposes. At a given price, however, there may be a choice between a holiday abroad or a holiday in the U.K., but as Williams says "a £30 holiday on the Costa Brava cannot compete with a £70 holiday on the Costa Brava, but it may compete with a £30 holiday at Clacton-on-Sea."[21]

For tourism purposes, the traveller has a choice between scheduled and non-scheduled services, but on the whole, it was the non-scheduled airlines that were initially (and obviously still are) more importantly employed to operate inclusive tour charters. From 1952 onwards, independent airlines were encouraged to expand in the inclusive tour market and, moreover, the State airlines were not allowed to keep any aircraft specifically for charter purposes. To control inclusive tour operations, a tour promotion agency and an airline had to make an application for a licence to operate a specified number of services to given destinations. These applications were then reviewed by the Air Transport Advisory Council and under the 1952 terms of reference, private airlines could apply for "associate agreement" rights to operate such services as long as these would not seriously conflict with established networks. The main defence of the scheduled operators was standard Provision 1, which resulted from Resolution 045 of I.A.T.A. (International Air Transport Association). This stipulated that the total price of an inclusive tour should not be less than the minimum scheduled fare applicable to the same destination. The result of all this was the rapid growth of inclusive tour charters operated by the independent airlines, and by 1959 around 180,000 passengers were carried on such flights.

The scheduled airlines (and B.E.A. in particular) were not happy about inclusive tour growth during the 1950s, since they saw this as a potential threat to their scheduled services to holiday resorts. Consequently, in 1960, the European scheduled operators went on the offensive by offering more competitive terms in the form of the inclusive tour basing or I.T.X. fare. Such fares are available to any travel agent who is willing to book blocks of inclusive tour seats on scheduled services. A discount of 16·6 per cent is offered, but the holiday as a whole must be sold at an all-inclusive price. These new rates proved to be very attractive and their success was not simply a matter of underpricing independent operators; while such fares were slightly more expensive than charters, they really provided a better quality of service to the customer in the form of greater comfort, more convenient departures and a more reliable service. Another factor responsible for the temporary set-back to the independents' inclusive tour growth was the 1960 *Civil Aviation* (*Licensing*) *Act*. As a result of this Act the Air Transport Licensing Board (A.T.L.B.) took on the role of financial investigator before granting a licence. The aim of this Act was to ensure the commercial stability of applicant airlines, and this was generally desirable to improve the public standing of the industry. The immediate effect, however, as shown in Table 16, was to force tour operators to

TABLE 16
e tour charter traffic (outward passengers carried) from U.K. airports (summer seasons 1961–68)

	1961	1962	1963	1964	1965	1966	1967	1968
U.K. Airlines								
Passengers (000)	225	222	261	397	555	898	1004	1279
Increase or decrease (%)	—	−1	+18	+52	+40	+62	+12	+27
Foreign airlines								
Passengers (000)	70	130	180	195	188	192	251	254
Increase or decrease (%)	—	+87	+38	+8	−3	+2	+31	+1
TOTAL								
Passengers (000)	295	352	441	592	743	1090	1255	1533
Increase or decrease (%)	—	+20	+25	+34	+26	+47	+15	+24

Source: Approximate figures provided by the A.T.L.B. based upon Board of Trade Airport Statistics.

turn to foreign airlines because of delays during the period of investigation. Nevertheless, in spite of these difficulties in the first years of the 1960s, later years saw the tremendous growth in inclusive tour traffic and prompted Edwards to say "We regard the record of inclusive travel traffic development as one of the most important credit items in the performance of British civil aviation in recent years ... we wish to stress here the great contribution made by the private sector in the development of inclusive tours."[22]

Statistics published by I.C.A.O. (International Civil Aviation Organisation) show that the share of non-scheduled operations in world air traffic doubled from 1960 to 1967: in 1960, the passenger-miles on non-scheduled services were only 8 per cent of world traffic but by 1967, this share had risen to 15 per cent. In Europe, the most striking example of all was the growth of non-scheduled air traffic to Spain. This is shown in Table 17.

Edwards then goes on to say "it is our belief that the trends described

TABLE 17
Passengers by non-scheduled services as a percentage of total air passenger traffic to Spain (1967)

Origin of traffic	*Non-scheduled (%) of total air passengers*
United Kingdom	69·2
Germany	79·7
Scandinavia and Finland	97·4
Netherlands	83·3

Source: European Civil Aviation Conference, quoted in Edwards (*op. cit.*) para. 226.

above will continue and that the demand for scheduled services, as we have previously known them, will become a smaller proportion of total air transport demand."[23]

The attraction of the inclusive tour is undoubtedly its price, and as we shall explain later, the cost of the all-in holiday is often less than the return air flight. Table 18 compares the price of scheduled air travel (18 (A)) and a comparable inclusive tour fares for equivalent destinations (18 (B)).

Spain is the largest attractor of tourists from the U.K., and the low season price of Thomsons all-inclusive holiday is less than the scheduled air fare, while the higher price for a peak season departure from London is slightly above this fare. The same is true for the Greek holiday, which involves an air flight of around 1700 miles. While these three examples are for travel on charter flights, the other two examples use pre-booked seats on scheduled air services, which are less of a saving to the customer, but will still work out cheaper than if the tourist were to make his own arrangements. Perhaps the best saving can be made on the tour to Indonesia, since modern hotel accommodation, sightseeing trips and stays in Singapore and Bangkok are all provided for over £100 less than the ordinary return fare. As we shall discuss later, the cost savings to the tour operator increase on such long-haul flights, enabling him to offer such an attractive package.

It will be useful next to consider the economics of inclusive tour

TABLE 18 (A)
Scheduled air fares (summer 1973)

1. London–Alicante	£48.65 ⎫	Cheapest night tourist return excursion
2. Manchester–Alicante	£62.95 ⎬	fares, minimum stay 6 days valid 1
3. London–Athens	£84.00	month
4. London–Tangier	£58.10 ⎭	
5. London–Djakarta	£573.50	Ordinary return fare

TABLE 18 (B)
Inclusive tour comparisons (summer 1973)

1. 14 nights *Benidorm* Hotel Ris Park (*via* Gatwick and Alicante)	£43	low
Thomson Holidays, Thomson's Britannia Airways	£55	high
2. As above but *via* Manchester and Alicante	£49	low
	£61	high
3. 14 nights *Mati* Hotel Attica Beach (*via* Luton and Athens) Thomson	£72	low
Holidays, Thomson's Britannia Airways	£83	high
4. 14 nights *Tangier* Hotel Chellal (*via* Heathrow, Malaga and Tangier)	£79	low
Exchange Travel Holidays Ltd., pre-booked seat on B.E.A.	£104	high
scheduled flight		
5. 21 nights *Indonesia* (includes Singapore and Bangkok) (*via* Heathrow		
and Amsterdam) Friendship Travel Centres Ltd., pre-booked seat on	£468	
Garuda/K.L.M./B.E.A. flights		

operation in more detail since this will give more insight into the reasons for the above situation and an appreciation of latest developments within the industry. The main components of an inclusive tour or package holiday are the cost of travel from a given origin and the cost of accommodation and food at the holiday destination. Certain other costs may also be involved, but the whole holiday is sold at an all-inclusive price, with little or no indication of the contributions of the constituent elements. The operation of inclusive tours involves the principle of "system design" of holidays started by T. E. Langton in 1930 (for coach holidays), and "matches" of accommodation with aircraft seats.[24] A

TABLE 19 (A)
85 per cent load factor

Cost item	Amount (£)	Percentage of total	Cost per head £	s	d
Charter of aircraft	1650	37·2	14	14	6
Aircraft catering	30	0·7		5	0
Hotel (14 nights)	1725	38·8	15	8	0
Ancillary transport	225	5·1	2	0	0
Gross profit margin	808	18·2	7	5	0
TOTAL	£4438	100·0	39	12	6
Gross profit margin	808	18·2	7	5	0
Advertising and promotion	280	6·5	2	11	0
Agent's commission	256	5·6	2	5	0
Running expenses	200	4·5	1	16	0
NET PROFIT	72	1·6		13	0

TABLE 19 (B)
100 per cent load factor

Cost item	Amount	Percentage of total	Cost per head £	s	d
Charter aircraft	£1650	31·5	12	10	0
Aircraft catering	32	0·6		5	0
Hotel (14 nights)	2033	38·9	15	8	0
Ancillary transport	225	4·3	1	14	0
Gross profit margin	1290	24·7	9	15	6
TOTAL	£5230	100·0	39	12	6
Gross profit margin	£1290	24·7	9	15	6
Advertising and promotion	290	5·5	2	4	0
Agent's commission	300	5·7	2	5	6
Running expenses	200	3·8	1	10	0
NET PROFIT	500	9·7	3	16	0

high-load factor is crucial for the profitability of the venture. The following example from Peters[25] illustrates this clearly.

The above example is based on the costs of mounting an inclusive tour from London to a popular Mediterranean resort such as Palma in 1969. The holiday tour is given a selling price of £39·62½ per head utilising a 132-seat Britannia. With 100 per cent load factor, the cost per passenger-mile falls from 0·92p to 0·75p. The net profit for the operator, however, rises from just £72 to £500. This is therefore a sevenfold increase, and while the example might seem a little outdated, it does bring home the importance of a high load factor for profitable tour operations.

In comparing scheduled and charter services, Edwards then gives a simple example. Assuming the same aircraft costs per hour, Table 20 summarises the argument.

TABLE 20

Comparison of scheduled airlines and inclusive tour charter operating costs

	Scheduled airline	Inclusive tour charter
Load factor (%)	60	85
Operating costs – short haul	8d (3·33p) per mile	5d (2·1p) per mile
	6½d (2·7p) per mile	4d (1·66p) per mile

Under Provision 1, an inclusive tour sold at the same price as the return scheduled fare would yield about £20 for a stage length of 800 miles and about £80 for a route of 4000 miles, which could be made available for hotel and meal costs at the destination. While the first figure is inadequate to cover a two-week summer season hotel cost, for the longer trip, the operator could provide accommodation for less than £80. Such a problem could also arise on routes shorter than this and as Edwards points out, it was for this reason in October 1968 that the A.T.L.B. made exceptions to the application of Provision 1 on tours operated to places like Rhodes (1700 miles). Even on quite short routes to popular resorts, winter hotel rates can be negotiated on a cheap basis, but Provision 1 prevented an operator from marketing these tours at a low promotional price.

In order to alleviate some of these problems, certain modifications to Provision 1 came into effect in October 1968. Firstly, for an experimental period, short winter holidays to most places in Europe and North Africa could be sold at 50 per cent of the normal tourist class return trip fare and in the case of longer holidays the minimum price could be 60 per cent of this fare level. Secondly, for inclusive tour holidays outside Europe, the minimum price could be set at either the lowest public return fare or at a minimum charge agreed by I.A.T.A. for a tour using scheduled services to the same destination. In spite of this, Edwards took the view that the A.T.L.B. was too restrictionist and that tour operators should be able to compete on a price basis. Consequently, they recommended that at least for an experimental period all minimum prices for inclusive tours should be abolished, and this was finally implemented. The relaxing of Provision 1 proved to be a great stimulus to the industry and resulted in tremendous growth of winter and second holidays as well as inclusive tours to places such as the Seychelles, Indonesia and the West Indies. In addition, prospects for enhanced growth of inclusive tour traffic across the North Atlantic greatly increased.

In spite of these developments, however, inclusive tour operation is a difficult business. While traffic continued to grow in the first years of the 1970s, profit margins slumped alarmingly, especially for the charter airlines. In the situation we have described, there is pressure on the airlines to cut margins, and this results in little being left in reserve to meet unexpected contingencies. Channel Airways, for example, had a particularly bad year in 1971 and the delays which were caused produced a good deal of adverse publicity. This unfortunately bears on all sections of the industry. In addition, the independent airlines have faced more intense pressure from scheduled carriers such as B.A.C. (*e.g.* Sovereign Holidays). In April 1973, Clarksons was sold, for just £1, having made successive losses in 1971 and 1972.

"System design" results in great benefits for the customer in the form of lower-priced holidays. By chartering a whole aircraft, a tour operator can effectively reduce the cost of travel and in addition, the operator will block-off a corresponding number of beds at the resort destination. By booking regular (say, fortnightly) flights and accommodation, the tour operator is also solving the occupancy problems of the foreign hotelier. In addition, both airline and hotelier are relieved of the burden of marketing costs as well as load factor problems.

During the 1960s, however, this early form of system design took on a more complex form. This followed the financial failures of three British independent airlines in 1961, with the consequent stranding of holiday-makers abroad. As Williams says, the obvious solution was to form an airline vertically integrated with a tour operator. Britannia Airways (then called Euravia) was formed, and was almost totally owned by Universal Sky Tours Ltd., at the time Britain's largest tour operator. Its founders were more concerned with reliability than profitability, but the latter also occurred following the tremendous growth in business. This was the forerunner of a new trend—other examples being Monarch Airlines and Cosmos, and Laker Airways purchased Arrowsmith Holidays and Lord Brothers, both reputable travel agencies.

A further extension of system design arose out of the tour operator's organisational control of the airline. This was the introduction of ten- and twelve-day holidays in order to overcome peaking problems and achieve better aircraft utilisation. As a marketing venture, these tend to be offered at rather lower prices than fourteen-day holidays, since weekend travel is not involved. The close relationship between airlines and tour promoters was not without problems—the collapse of British Eagle in 1968, for example, resulted in serious losses for Lunn-Poly.

These low prices charged for package holidays were obviously responsible for the tremendous growth of demand after the early 1960s, although this has slowed down since 1967 owing to adverse economic conditions. When it became clear that inclusive tour traffic had not really been responsible for any major diversion from scheduled traffic as illustrated by the continued growth of B.E.A.'s passenger volumes, Provision 1 was relaxed and this was a further stimulus to growth. The existence of Provision 1 had not been such a major problem for tour operators while they were developing markets in Spain and Italy in particular, but bearing in mind the increasingly refined aspects of system design, it became more of a serious problem. As Edwards points out, their complaints over Provision 1 related to three types of operation: (*i*) the introduction of tours to more distant destinations, (*ii*) the attempt to develop new tour traffic at low prices during the winter period, (*iii*) the introduction of short-duration tours (*i.e.* less than one week).[26]

SUMMARY

We are perhaps now in a position to summarise the role which transport plays in tourism, both at the domestic and international level. It is abundantly clear that air transport plays a dominant role in the inter-regional movement of tourists, which normally entails travel over long distances and frequently over water barriers as between, for example, North America and Europe. Air transport is also of growing importance in intra-regional travel, again where substantial distances are involved or geographical obstacles impede easy movement, *e.g.* between Britain and Greece or Sweden and Majorca. The rate of growth of international air traffic has persisted at around 15 per cent a year, and this increased use of air transport by tourists is the result of a number of factors: people have become more air-travel-minded, travel is immeasurably quicker and fares have generally decreased. The most decisive development, however, has been the development of inclusive tours in which travellers are carried on charter flights at rates substantially below those of normal scheduled services.

In Europe, where a short cross-frontier journey takes holiday-makers abroad, travel by rail is still very important, although rail transport is gradually being undermined by the continuing expansion in car ownership and road travel. Road transport—more especially by private car since bus and coach travel has contracted in recent years—is of paramount importance in domestic and intra-regional movements, especially where there are large tourist flows between neighbouring countries within the same continent, *e.g.* continental Europe. Whether the ever-increasing volume of cars on the roads and the attendant discomforts and frustrations of motoring will divert traffic back to the railways is unknown, but there are some who believe (especially as new and speedier trains are developed) that this will happen. However, the situation with respect to car travel is likely to get worse before it gets better, notwithstanding the extension of motorway networks.

Scheduled sea traffic, especially on the longer runs, has declined and seems likely to decline still further. On the other hand, there has been a boom in sea cruising and the use of ferry-boats by motorised tourists. It may be mentioned that the unfavourable exchange rates *vis-à-vis* the £ since 1973 have given a big fillip to British shipping lines since costs on British cruise ships have obviously not been adversely affected.

NOTES

1. J. E. Spencer and W. L. Thomas, *Cultural Geography*, Wiley, 1969, p. 424.

2. E. L. Ullman, "The Role of Transportation and the Bases for Interaction," in *Man's Role in Changing the Face of the Earth*, ed. W. L. Thomas, University of Chicago Press, 1956, pp. 862–80.

3. *Op. cit.*

4. Ullman, *op. cit.*

5. J. A. R. Pimlott, *The Englishman's Holiday*, Faber, 1947, p. 91.

6. *Land and Leisure*, David & Charles, 1970, p. 26.

7. J. Laffin, *Daily Telegraph Magazine*, No. 354, 6th August, 1971.

8. *Op. cit.*, p. 28.

9. *Roads and Tourism*, British Road Federation Report published in association with the British Tourist Authority, p. 5.

10. *Idem*, p. 8.

11. Foreword, *Roads and Tourism*.

12. *Roads and Tourism*, p. 6.

13. *Idem*, pp. 10–12.

14. *Idem*, pp. 14–15.

15. F. E. I. Hamilton, *Yugoslavia: Patterns of Economic Activity*, G. B. Bell & Sons, 1968, p. 304.

16. H. Thurston, "France Finds A New Holiday Coast," *Geographical Magazine*, London, February, 1969, p. 344.

17. M. Peters, *International Tourism*, Hutchinson, 1969, p. 203.

18. R. S. Tolley, "New Technology and Transport Geography: the Case of the Hovercraft," *Geography*, Vol. 58, July, 1973, pp. 227–36.

19. R. W. McIntosh, *Tourism: Principles, Practices, Philosophies*, p. 116.

20. J. E. D. Williams, "Holiday Traffic by Air," Brancker Memorial Lecture, 1968.

21. *Idem*.

22. *British Air Transport in the Seventies*, Report of Committee of Enquiry, H.M.S.O., Cmnd 4018, 1969, p. 22.

23. *Ibid*.

24. Williams, *op. cit*.

25. *Op. cit*., pp. 120–1.

26. *British Air Transport in the Seventies*, pp. 171–4.

Chapter IX

The Economic and Social Significance of Tourism

IN this chapter an attempt will be made to discuss the economic and social importance of tourism. Let us look first at the economic importance of the tourist industry.

The difference between the direct and indirect effects of expenditure on tourism should be emphasised. The direct effects relate to the actual expenditure involved in tourism, *e.g.* on transport, accommodation, food and drink, shopping, services, etc. The income received by the people providing such goods and services from tourists forms the direct impact on the economy. The indirect or secondary results of this expenditure on tourism arise from the fact that the trades directly involved in tourism, in order to meet the demands of tourists, must purchase from other trades and industries those goods and services, *e.g.* foodstuffs, furnishings, sporting equipment and facilities, which are needed to produce the things demanded by tourists. Thus, as Richards has pointed out, there are two sets of links between tourist spending and the economy: first, the broad consumption items, mentioned above, which have a direct effect and, second, the links between the trades directly involved in tourism and those trades and industries which supply the tourist trades with goods and services. It will now be clear that "the full impact of tourism on the economy is not just through expenditure on the front-line tourist trades. It embraces all those other industries which have been called upon at various stages of the process to supply goods and services. The outputs produced by these other industries outside the direct tourism sector are in a very real sense due to the needs of the tourists who spent the money in the first place and set the whole thing going."[1]

DOMESTIC AND FOREIGN TRAVEL

There are three separate elements in the tourist expenditure of any country: (*i*) the domestic expenditure, *i.e.* the money spent by nationals on holiday-making within their own country; (*ii*) expenditure by foreign tourists within the country in which they are taking a holiday; and (*iii*) the expenditure incurred by nationals who holiday abroad. The receipts from tourism in the first two cases are of a credit kind and are reflected in the National Income accounts. Tourist expenditure by nationals abroad is, however, of a debit nature, since the tourist is taking money out of the country; in other words, such expenditure must be set against the income from tourism in the home country. Elements (*iii*) should be set against (*ii*) in the Balance of Payments account.

The amount of money spent on tourism by nationals in their own country, *i.e.* on domestic tourism, will be governed by two things in particular. As we have already noted, the amount spent by a family on holiday-making is related to the amount of income, for the greater the income the more, in an absolute sense, is likely to be spent on consumer expenditure. Against this, however, must be set what is termed the marginal propensity to save (defined as the proportion of an income change which is saved) or the desire to devote part of increased income to saving; hence, if families save some of their income they must spend less on goods and services—for instance, on holidays. The act of saving withdraws money from the circular flow of income in the economy. Expenditure by foreign tourists within a country is an external source of additional income and forms an invisible export; thus foreign tourist expenditure adds to the circular flow of income and so is to be welcomed. Conversely, home tourist expenditure abroad constitutes a withdrawal or "leakage" from the flow since the expenditure creates income for foreign countries (*see* Fig. 9). If the expenditure on tourism abroad equals the expenditure of foreign tourists the two cancel each other out and the circular flow of income in the economy will be unchanged.

Expenditure by foreign tourists and expenditure by nationals on tourism abroad are important because they affect the Balance of Payments. Income from foreign tourism adds to the national income and, as an invisible export, may offset a loss on the visible trading account and be of critical importance in the overall financial reckoning. External expenditure on tourism may be a drain on the economy and sometimes governments—as happened in the United Kingdom in 1969–72—have had to fix a limit on the amount of money allowed for foreign tourism, *e.g.* in Britain it was set at £50 per head.

BALANCE OF PAYMENTS

The Balance of Payments shows the relationship between a country's total payments to all other countries and its total receipts from them; in

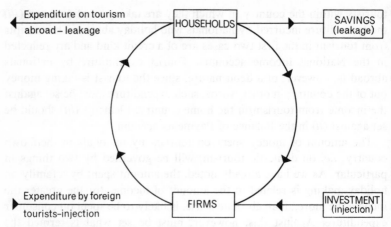

FIG. 9.—*Circular flow of money in the economy.* Households' savings, import expenditures, purchase and sales taxes are examples of withdrawals of money from the circular flow; gross investment, export incomes, and government expenditure are, on the other hand, additions to the circular flow of money. Whereas expenditure on tourism abroad represents a leakage in the national economy, expenditures by foreign tourists form an invisible export and so represent an injection into the economy.

other words, it may be defined as a statement of income and expenditure on international account. Payments and receipts on international account are of three kinds: (*i*) the visible balance of trade (relating to the import and export of goods); (*ii*) invisible items (relating to services such as shipping, insurance); (*iii*) capital transfers. The receipts from foreign tourism form an "invisible export" similar to the other "invisibles" which come from transportation and shipping, banking and insurance, income on investments, etc. Because most countries from time to time have serious problems with the balance of their international payments, much attention comes to be focused on tourism because of its potentially important contribution to, and effect upon, the Balance of Payments.

First, it should be emphasised that tourist receipts and expenditures are two wholly separate and different items and there is no inherent merit in achieving a balance between the two, although most countries do tend to show considerable concern with their own travel account and strive to secure a credit balance; as previously mentioned, it has not been unknown for a country to place restrictions on the foreign tourism expenditures of its nationals in order to improve the balance on the travel account. Tourism is a very useful means of earning much-needed foreign currency; indeed, it is almost without rival as a source, as such countries as Spain, Eire, Mexico and Panama have found. In such cases, foreign exchange receipts from international tourism are major earners of foreign currency and exceed the receipts from any other single industry. Clearly, therefore, receipts from international tourism may assume great significance in Balance of Payments calculations.

Secondly, one must be careful not to assume that the receipts from international tourism are always net, for sometimes expenditures are involved which must be set against them. As Peters has said: "certain imports associated with tourist expenditures must be deducted ... the importation of materials and equipment for constructing hotels and other amenities, and necessary supplies to run them; foreign currency costs of imports for consumption by international tourists; remittances of interest and profits on overseas investment in tourism enterprises, mainly hotel construction; foreign currency costs of conducting a tourism development programme, including marketing expenditure overseas."[2] From all this it will be apparent that it is not always easy to isolate and to evaluate precisely the net receipts from international tourism. In many of the islands in the West Indies, for example, the tourist industry has grown vigorously during the past few decades but unfortunately the islands have not benefited as much as they might have done because of the many leakages which have had to be set against income; much of the investment was foreign and interest charges had to be paid, much of the equipment, such as hotel furnishings, linen and crockery, had to be imported and paid for, while many foodstuffs (which might easily have been grown locally) were imported from the United States.

For many countries, particularly small countries, which are mainly dependent upon primary production, usually one or two basic cash crops, tourism often offers a more reliable form of income. Cosgrove and Jackson have shown (Table 21) that, in 1967, some twenty-six countries earned more than 10 per cent of the value of their commodity exports from their tourist industries.[3] Table 21 also reveals that seven countries obtained more than half of the value of their commodity exports from tourism.

In the case of some European countries, notably Spain, Portugal, Austria, Yugoslavia, Greece and Eire, the invisible earnings from tourism are of major significance as a source of income and have a very strong positive effect on the Balance of Payments. On the other hand, countries such as the United States and West Germany, the most important tourist-generating countries, have an expenditure on tourism abroad which is far in excess of the expenditure by foreign tourists, hence their invisible earnings from tourism are of relatively little significance in their Balance of Payments. In Britain, after a long period of

TABLE 21

Value of tourism compared with that of
commodity exports (1967) (commodity exports
value = 100)

Over 100:	Bahamas	250
50–100:	Bermuda	87
	Mexico	84
	Spain	82
	Jordan	59
	Lebanon	57
	Malta	52
25–50:	Barbados	41
	Portugal	39
	French Polynesia	36
	Jamaica	35
	Austria	33
	Fiji	26
	Greece	26
	South Vietnam	25
	Eire	25
	Kenya	25
10–25:	Tunisia	23
	United Arab Republic	20
	Switzerland	20
	Morocco	19
	Italy	16
	Cyprus	15
	Yugoslavia	12
	Canada	11
	Israel	10

Source: Cosgrove and Jackson, *The Geography of Recreation and Leisure*, statistics derived from *U.N. Yearbook 1968.*

running a deficit on the travel account, there was a rapid growth in the number of foreign visitors arriving in the late 1960s, which produced a credit balance; however, this balance has been gradually eroded as a result of the upsurge in the numbers now holidaying abroad each year. Britain's invisible earnings from tourism are none the less substantial: in 1974 the total earnings from foreign tourism were £830m, or £1,070m when fare payments are included. Since the total invisible exports amounted to £10,000m, tourism accounted for 10 per cent of total invisible earnings. Of the total value of exports, both visible and invisible, tourism accounted for 4·1 per cent.

Another economic issue which arises relates to the problem of currency exchange rates. The rates of currency exchange can have very important repercussions upon tourism because they can make holidays cheaper or more expensive. Devaluation of the currency implies that the currency becomes of less value within the country in which it takes place but, on the other hand, it means that foreigners get greater value for their money. For example, the floating of the British £ in 1972 meant that it is now worth less than formerly in most countries and the cost of European holidays to the British are now 15 to 20 per cent more, depending on the country visited, than in the summer of 1972. It should be recalled that the £ was also previously devalued in 1971* and in 1967, hence Continental holidays cost the British tourist appreciably more than they did in the past. In 1950 the £ bought 18 Swiss francs; in 1973 it bought 8; hence a holiday in Switzerland in 1973 cost the British tourist more than twice as much as it did in 1950. On the other hand, the Swiss traveller can enjoy a holiday in Britain for less than half its cost in 1950. There are, of course, other factors which have to be taken into consideration, such as inflation, and the cost of a holiday in Switzerland to the British traveller costs more not only because of the devaluation and the floating of the £ but also because of the rate of inflation in Switzerland was, until recently, worse than in Britain. In 1973, from the point of view of the British traveller, holidays in France, Germany and Switzerland were the most expensive, while holidays in Spain, Yugoslavia and North Africa were the most economical. Table 22 shows the value of the £ in relation to other selected currencies.

TABLE 22

The value of £ in relation to other foreign currencies

What £100 would buy	Before 1967 devaluation	Before 1971 devaluation	1972 pre-float of £	End of Jan. 1973	19th Feb. 1973	17th Sept. 1975
Swiss franc	1,212	1,039	1,002	857	810	561
German mark	1,110	878	827	751	712	540
Spanish peseta	16,750	16,827	17,100	15,107	14,200	12,025
Italian lira	174,700	150,800	152,300	138,400	147,000	148,500
French franc	1,382	1,334	1,323	1,199	1,140	923
Japanese yen	101,300	86,400	78,800	71,400	64,000	635,000

Source: National Westminster Bank.

DOMESTIC EFFECTS

Tourism is important economically in that, among other things, it provides a source of income, it provides employment, it brings infrastructural improvements, and it may help regional development. Each of these economic aspects may be dealt with discretely, but they are all intimately related and here are considered together. Let us first look at income.

Tourism as a source of income is not easy to measure, at least with

* This devaluation resulted from the floating of the £ and was not an official devaluation like that in 1967.

any degree of accuracy. This is because of the *multiplier effect*. The multiplier is an income concept; briefly it may be defined as the effect on total expenditure (and hence on total employment) of a certain amount of real capital investment, or an increase in expenditure by the consumer. The nature of the tourism multiplier and its effects may be described as follows. The money spent by the tourist in, say, paying his hotel bill will be used by the hotel management to defray the costs which it has incurred in meeting the demands of the visitor, *e.g.* such goods and services as food, drink, furnishings, electricity, laundering, entertainers. The recipients, in turn, use the money they have received to meet their financial commitments. And so on. In other words, tourist expenditure supports not only the tourist industry directly but helps indirectly to support numerous other industries which supply goods and services to the tourist industry. In this way money spent by tourists may be said to be used several times and to spread into various sectors of the economy. Every time the money changes hands it provides "new" income and the continuing series of conversions of the money spent by the tourist forms what the economist terms "the multiplier effect." The more times the conversion occurs, the greater is its beneficial effect on the economy. However, this transfer of money cannot go on indefinitely because of "leakages" which occur. Such leakages may consist of, for instance, imported foreign goods, interest on foreign investments, or savings which withdraw money from circulation, and any leakages of these kinds will reduce the stream of expenditure which in consequence will limit and reduce the multiplier effect.

Income generated by foreign tourist expenditure in countries possessing more advanced economies, which generally are more self-sufficient and less in need of foreign imports, will tend to have higher multipliers than countries which are less self-contained and need to support their tourist industries by substantial imports. However, as Peters comments "Even for those economies where there is a high import and leakage content, it is hard to visualise a multiplier of less than two."[4] If the developing countries are to gain the maximum economic benefits from their tourism industries, it would seem essential for them to control very strictly those imported items for tourists' consumption and to keep foreign investment expenditure for the purposes of tourism to a reasonable level, otherwise the benefits accruing from tourism will be cancelled by the leakages. The most significant leakages would appear to arise from expenditure on imports (*e.g.* food and drink, linen and crockery) but, fortunately, all these are items over which host countries are able, if they are so disposed, to exert some control; for instance, home-grown products could be substituted for imported foodstuffs and a significant saving effected. Such savings would help to increase the tourism multiplier which, in turn, would help the host country to derive the maximum economic benefits from its tourist industry.

The calculation of the tourism multiplier, however, is by no means easy and such estimates as have been made in the case of a number of economies (*see* Table 23) show very wide variations; Peters expresses the opinion that in these particular studies some of the multipliers were too high (as in the cases of the Far East, Pakistan and Eire) while others were probably much too conservative (as in the cases of Hawaii, Lebanon and Greece).[5] Any methods of quantification used to elicit the multiplying effect should use reliable and refined data and a generally accepted theoretical basis.

TABLE 23
Estimates of the tourism multiplier

Country	Estimated tourism multiplier	Source
Pacific and the Far East	3·2–4·3	*Future of Tourism in the Pacific and Far East*, Checchi and Co., 1961.
New Hampshire	1·6–1·7	*Economic Impact of Rrcreation, Vacation and Travel on New Hampshire*, 1962.
Hawaii	0·9–1·3	*Future Growth of Hawaiian Tourism*, Paul G. Craig, Ph.D., 1963.
Greece	1·2–1·4	*An Econometric Model of the Greek Economy*, Daniel B. Suits, 1964.
Pakistan	3·3	*Master Plan for the Development of Tourism in Pakistan*, 1965.
Ireland	2·7	*Study of the Economics of Tourism in Ireland*, 1966.
Lebanon	1·2–1·4	*Nouvelle étude prospective sur l'apport du tourisme au developpement economique du Liban*, Dr Pierre Gorra, 1967.

Source: M. Peters, *International Tourism*, 1969, p. 240.

In comparison with the above, Richards estimated in 1972 that the U.K.'s tourism multiplier was 2·95.

So far, in discussing the domestic effects of tourism, we have been mainly concerned with the direct effects: how visitor expenditure and government investment generate income which, in turn, affects employment by creating additional jobs. This matter of employment will be dealt with more fully in a moment but first let us look at two other domestic effects which the development of tourism brings in its train.

Indirect expenditure accruing from tourism is reflected in the income engendered in the non-tourist sectors of industry, *e.g.* in industries providing equipment, furniture, accessories used by hotel and catering establishments or in agriculture which provides meat, dairy produce, vegetables and fruit also required by the tourist industry or in the transport and communications industries, both of which impinge upon tourism in a variety of ways. Another aspect involves the improvements in infrastructure—roads, airports, electricity and gas supplies, sanitation and water supplies, etc.—which are undertaken in order to attract tourists or make it possible to attract tourists. These improvements may confer benefits upon the resident population by providing them with amenities which, hitherto, they had not enjoyed. Furthermore, the provision of an infrastructure may provide the basis or serve as an encouragement for greater economic diversification: a variety of secondary industries may be promoted which may, or may not, serve the needs of tourism. Thus, indirectly, tourist expenditure may be responsible for stimulating other economic activities.

Another important domestic effect relates to the regional aspects of tourist expenditure. Such expenditure is of special significance in marginal areas, such as parts of Scotland, Wales, South-western England and Western Eire, which are relatively isolated, economically underdeveloped, and have unemployment problems. Similarly the French Government in its Languedoc–Roussillon plan have created a series of new resorts partly to bring prosperity to an area which traditionally has been underdeveloped. The Italian Government is likewise attempting to develop tourism in southern and insular Italy—the Mezzogiornio—in order to help to redress the economic imbalance which has long existed between the north and the south. Tourism as a source of income and employment is of special importance where alternative resources are short or lacking altogether.

EMPLOYMENT

A second major direct economic effect of tourism relates to employment. The tourist industry is a labour-intensive service industry and so is a valuable source of employment: it employs large numbers of people and provides a wide range of jobs which extend from the unskilled to the highly specialised. In addition to those involved in management there are large numbers of specialist personnel required such as accountants, housekeepers, cooks, waiters and entertainers who, in turn, need even larger numbers of semi-skilled and unskilled workers such as front-of-house personnel, chambermaids, porters, kitchen staff, gardeners, etc. Moreover, it should be emphasised that tourism is also responsible for creating employment outside the industry in its more narrowly defined sense and in this respect, says McIntosh "it scores noticeably over other forms of new industry."[6] Those who supply goods and services to those directly involved in tourism equally are beneficiaries from tourism; such *induced employment* includes, for example, those involved in the construction industry, in furnishing and equipment industries and in farming and food supply.

Richards has analysed the importance of tourism to the British economy and drawn attention to its particular relevance in terms of employment. He has written: "There is one aspect which has been frequently emphasised in discussions of the economic benefits of investment in tourism . . . the creation or support of jobs—an argument which is used consistently in relation to tourism strategy in regions of Britain where unemployment is both high and persistent. Much of the debate has pivoted on cost-benefit arguments where costs of investment are set against the benefits (differently defined in different cases) of tourism. However, these discussions often miss an important variable in the situation, namely the amount of employment extra to the direct jobs —which is supported in other industries and activities connected with the tourist trades. . . . For every 100 jobs held in direct tourist trades approximately 60 jobs in other industries are indirectly dependent on tourism business. In economic jargon this is an employment multiplier of 1·6. . . . £1m of tourist expenditure attracted to Britain or generated within the country (domestic tourism also supports jobs) probably supports 860 jobs in the tourist trades, but in total terms supports about 1255 jobs throughout the economy. This type of comparison is of vital importance in assessing the benefits of an expansion of tourism in an existing area or of a new programme for tourism development. There are two reasons for this. First, it gives the proper basis for a true evaluation of tourism's job-creation potential. Secondly, it gives extra ammunition to fire at government officials when putting a case for public finance for tourism development, since such people often base their evaluations on the overall rather than the direct well-being to be expected from a given tourist programme."[7]

"Tourism as a source of employment," says Medlik "is particularly important for areas with limited alternative sources of employment, as is often the case in non-industrial areas deficient in natural resources other than scenic attractions and climate. Rough estimates suggest that even in Britain more than 5 per cent of the total working population earn their living mainly through tourism. There are many areas of Britain where more than 10 per cent of the working population is wholly or mainly engaged in catering for the visitor. The proportion is significantly higher in some regions and localities and over 20 per cent in some resorts." [8] However, in many tourist areas this employment is of a seasonal nature only. This is especially true of "marginal" areas where there are also few possibilities of alternative out-of-season employment. Strenuous efforts are for this reason being made to lengthen the season by such attractions as illuminations, festivals and reduced prices for out-of-season holiday-making.

In many of the developing countries, where chronic unemployment often exists, the promotion of tourism can be a great encouragement to economic development and, especially, employment. In such countries, a factor favouring tourism is its low requirement of costly "imported" manpower such as is frequently required for the operation of advanced industries. A study carried out in East Anglia in 1968 suggested that one new job was created for every $2400 of tourist expenditure. . . . [9] Blake and Lawless, discussing Algeria's tourist industry, commented: ". . . one job will be directly created for every six new hotel beds, and many more indirectly. This is a particularly important fact for some of the less-favoured parts of the country, notably the south, where employment opportunities are severely limited. Thus tourism can be an essential feature of regional economic development at least in respect of creating work." [10]

INVESTMENT IN TOURISM

Capital, according to the economist, is a factor of production and capital yields income, but capital is a scarce commodity. Tourism, like most other industries, demands considerable investment. The investor normally prefers to put his money into a venture where the return is quick and assured; hence the potential investor in tourism will require to know the probable return from any investment he might make and will compare it with the returns from investments in other sectors of business. The question thus arises: is tourism an attractive investment proposition?

One factor which undoubtedly influences the attractiveness of investment in tourism is concerned with the nature of such investment. From an economic point of view, it is characterised by the fact that a high proportion of the capital outlay is spent on fixed assets. In accommodation units, it is in land purchase, buildings and interior facilities such as furniture, carpets and kitchen equipment. Medlik estimated that 90 per cent of capital invested in hotel developments came into this fixed assets category.[11] Variable assets thus only account for a small proportion of the capital outlay, and stocks of food and drink (the main variable assets) also have a high rate of turnover. One implication of this situation is that the fixed costs of operation form a high proportion of total costs, and such fixed costs have to be paid whether or not the hotel is open to visitors. This is one of the reasons why many hotels remain open in off-peak periods, presumably in the hope that these costs can be covered. An associated point worthy of mention is that during the peak part of the season it is necessary for them to have a high bed occupancy rate.

How do the rates of return from investment in tourism compare with those from other industries? Medlik, referring to Reports from the Centre for Inter-Hotel Comparison (University of Surrey) says that after allowing for overhead costs such as depreciation and interest on capital employed, profit amounts on average to around 10 per cent of sales revenue.[12] This would appear to be quite an acceptable rate of return *vis-à-vis* other business ventures. He does, however, point out that there are differences in profitability depending on the sales mix of an establishment. Accommodation services (15 per cent) yield the highest rate of profit, whereas food (10 per cent) and liquor (7 per cent) are not as profitable in relative terms.

Therefore, on this basis, the overall profitability of an establishment depends very much on the weights within total revenue given to each of these classes of activity.

Further information on this important problem is provided by Peters and McIntosh who extend the scale of enquiry into public as well as private investment in tourism.

Peters writes: "Tourism should be regarded as a product which can only be successfully sold on a high-volume basis if the total product is competitively priced. Generally, tourism enterprises are not regarded as attractive investments from the point of view of return on capital and security. In many developing countries there is an obvious preference for investment in ventures with high profit potential or in readily realisable assets likely to produce quick profits. High profits or quick capital gains are unlikely in most types of tourism investments—many of which require large-scale investment in fixed assets, not easily realisable, and producing only comparatively small profits if efficiently operated."[13] Clearly, however, if tourism projects are to be initiated or expanded large-scale investment of either a private or public nature is required. Largely because the tourist industry usually requires heavy investment and large profits and quick returns are seldom forthcoming, public investment, at least initially, becomes necessary in most tourist developments of any magnitude (as in the Languedoc–Roussillon Scheme in France already referred to (p. 107). The provision of infra-structure is especially costly and this is something which normally has to be provided by the state.

McIntosh, discussing the difficulties in using capital/output ratios when it comes to measuring the value of tourism investment, especially in making international comparisons, says that, according to the avail-able evidence, it would appear investments in tourism yield a return which compares fairly favourably with that offered by other indus-tries.[14] Moreover, in comparison with some industries, *e.g.* the produc-tion of primary commodities which may suffer sudden and violent fluctuations, tourism offers a greater measure of stability; he believes that this may lead to an eventual change in attitude on the part of investors who may be prepared to accept lower returns on a long-term basis for reasonably stable prospects. He makes the further significant point that profitability is not always the only criterion of investment participation: "A simple comparison of rates of return from investments of different kinds may not, however, provide an adequate basis for policy decisions in national economic planning. Many developing coun-tries or areas are particularly concerned about foreign exchange earn-ings. Investments in tourism may have advantages in this field even when the rate of return appears to be lower than in other fields of investment. Similarly if an objective of economic policy is to ensure a rapid increase in the level of employment, the country concerned must take into account the employment-generating effects of an investment in tourism compared with other investment possibilities."[15]

The extent of direct government investment in tourism bears a close relationship to the degree to which it is developed; for example, in developing countries where it is desired to promote the industry much of the initial investment must be undertaken by the state. To attract private investment, such states must be prepared to provide the essential infrastructure for the industry and to create a favourable investment climate to encourage the private investor. Since most private investors seek a quick return for their capital outlay, special financial incentives, *e.g.* subsidies, credits, preferential rates of interest, must be offered to make investment in tourism attractive and to mobilise capital. Foreign investment is usually welcomed by most developing countries, largely because of their own acute shortage of capital resources, but foreign investment also invariably brings other advantages with it such as more realistic estimates of market potential, skills in hotel management, expertise in sales promotion and marketing.

A second important aspect of investment in tourism, and a particular feature of investment in hotels and catering, is the problem of obtaining finance. This problem is linked with the nature of the investment, as discussed above, and also with the structure of the industry. Table 24 shows this structure.

TABLE 24
Structure of British hotel industry by size and location (1970)

Location	All hotels—number of bedrooms							Licensed average	Unlicensed average
	Up to 10	11–25	26–50	51–100	Over 100	Total	Average		
London	430	525	134	105	115	1,309	40	117	16
Urban areas with pop. 100,000 and over	1,333	591	217	101	58	2,300	18	32	10
Urban areas with pop. under 100,000	5,069	1,474	367	135	30	7,075	11	14	8
Rural areas	3,741	812	144	33	3	4,733	9	11	6
Coastal	14,032	4,478	1,060	349	69	19,988	12	22	8
TOTAL	24,605	7,880	1,922	723	275	35,405	13	22	9

Source: Hotel and Catering E.D.C., Hotel Investment Study.

One of the attractions of the tourist industry is that it presents a business opportunity for persons with limited capital funds. Consequently, as shown in Table 24, the British industry is dominated by small establishments. In addition, of the 35,405 hotels, almost two-thirds are unlicensed. According to Medlik, the largest operator, Trust House Forte, owns 184 hotels—this is just over $\frac{1}{2}$ per cent of the total number of hotels although it represents $4\frac{1}{2}$ per cent of total bedroom capacity.[16] As the industry is very much dominated by single-proprietor ownership this can present problems when investment funds are required to finance an expansion of the scale of operation. There are many different sources of investment funds, but two main groups can be distinguished—(*i*) internal and (*ii*) external. Personal savings and retained profits or undistributed profits (in the case of joint-stock companies) are the main internal sources, and the first two are particularly important for the single-owner or partnership business. External sources are numerous, *e.g.* the commercial banks and building societies, but the biggest obstacle for the small business is one of being able to offer sufficient collateral to back the loan request. Trade credit, from furniture and equipment manufacturers, may be a useful source, although this is not likely to be of use for long-term investment. Private and public companies can, however, obtain finance for investment by the issue of shares—the former being a sale to a restricted number of people, whereas public companies such as Trust House Forte and Grand Metropolitan Hotels can offer shares to the general public *via* the Stock Exchange.

In addition to the sources already mentioned, various other bodies are becoming increasingly important sources—the Industrial and Commercial Finance Corporation (now part of Finance for Industry Ltd.) is willing to make loans of £5000 upwards to the hotel industry, and bearing in mind the problem of smaller operators, the Council for Small Industries in Rural Areas and its Scottish counterpart may provide loans for small hotels and other tourist establishments in rural areas and country towns in the Development Areas. The Highlands and Islands Development Board and the Ministry of Commerce in Northern Ireland also provide special incentives to encourage tourism in their area.

There are therefore many sources of finance for new investment in the industry, but perhaps the biggest stimulus to the industry came in 1969 with the hotel development incentives provided in the *Development of Tourism Act*. For hotel projects started before 1st April, 1971, and completed before March, 1973, grants of up to 25 per cent of eligible expenditure on the cost of providing new accommodation and installing certain items of fixed equipment, and in some cases loans, could be given by the English, Scottish and Wales Tourist Boards.

By February, 1972, the Chief Executive of the English Tourist Board writing in *Local Government Finance* estimated that "the E.T.B.'s estimated expenditure of public funds under Part II of the Act is £50m over the years 1970/75, rather under 10 per cent on loans which are at the Board's discretion and the balance of over 90 per cent in grants, where the Board is without discretion. This sum reflects capital investment of £300m, providing a present best estimate of 62,000 additional hotel bedrooms, perhaps some 110,000 additional beds and such other improvements as new lifts and bathrooms."

TABLE 25

Grants and loans under Hotel Development Incentives Scheme (at 31st August, 1972)

	Valid applications	Amount of grants (£m)	Total investment (£m)	No. of bedrooms
English Tourist Board	1,626	48·1	300·3	62,091
(of which) London	232	21·2	153·9	24,217
Scottish Tourist Board	442	5·3	27·2	5,366
Wales Tourist Board	426	3·5	13·9	4,713
TOTAL	2,494	56·9	341·4	72,170

Source: University of Surrey.

At the 31st March, 1973, the applications by county to the English Tourist Board were as outlined in Table 26.

From Table 26 it is obvious that around 40 per cent of all grants

TABLE 26

English Tourist Board—grant applications by counties at 31st March, 1973

County	Valid applications	New bedrooms	Amount applied for £
Bedfordshire	17	618	533,486
Berkshire	24	556	417,279
Buckinghamshire	13	445	344,381
Cambridgeshire	11	488	438,929
Cheshire	67	1,844	1,321,006
Cornwall	141	1,155	605,245
Cumberland	55	658	478,149
Derbyshire	13	101	50,862
Devon	238	2,171	1,349,545
Dorset	46	417	279,597
Durham	32	913	864,001
Essex	36	720	565,776
Gloucestershire	51	1,182	1,018,241
Hampshire	147	2,004	1,478,904
Herefordshire	14	101	55,294
Hertfordshire	40	1,177	977,431
Huntingdonshire	7	71	63,606
Isle of Wight	60	828	535,054
Kent	62	580	350,531
Lancashire	150	5,197	3,155,296
Leicestershire	23	978	605,776
Lincolnshire	26	299	253,245
London—G.L.C.	331	24,177	25,950,106
Norfolk	35	1,093	684,847
Northamptonshire	12	333	286,370
Northumberland	37	664	720,239
Nottinghamshire	17	259	175,723
Oxfordshire	20	282	210,694
Rutland	*	29	18,066
Shropshire	11	52	48,633
Somerset	65	1,036	679,092
Staffordshire	25	773	636,525
Suffolk	24	442	293,057
Surrey	42	1,285	1,097,548
Sussex	93	1,267	899,069
Warwickshire	78	3,120	2,670,141
Westmorland	39	369	271,598
Wiltshire	18	277	237,881
Worcestershire	16	168	153,271
Yorkshire	173	2,793	2,279,365

* Fewer than five applications.

applied for came from the London area, and this has been one criticism of the scheme. Yet London still remains the magnet for overseas visitors and the above situation certainly reflects the imbalance already in the market. A second criticism is that public money has been needlessly paid out, especially to large operators, and in certain cities (Liverpool is a good example) new developments are taking place in a market already working at low bed-occupancy rates. An earlier problem raised was that of the small business not being able to secure investment funds, and a final criticism of the scheme has been made on these grounds. In refuting this criticism, the English Tourist Board say that 82 per cent of claims (by February, 1972) were for grants below £20,000; indeed, 35 per cent were for grants of below £5000 and 10 per cent for below £500. With evidence such as this, the last criticism seems ill-founded and the Incentives Scheme would appear to be effective for all, and not just the large, operators, and does help to overcome some of the investment problems.

OTHER ECONOMIC IMPLICATIONS AND PROBLEMS

Tourism development gives rise to a variety of economic conflicts and problems and not least of these relates to land use. Tourist development makes demands on space: land must be made available for tourist activities. Fortunately tourism, as Christaller said, tends to avoid central places and makes much use of peripheral regions;[17] but frequently tourism needs clash with the demands of agriculture—the tourist destination may coincide with an area which is primarily devoted to arable or pastoral farming. Thus, inevitably, a conflict arises between the demands of tourism on the one hand and agriculture on the other. A good example of this conflict is to be seen in Provence, in southern France, where, as inland villages have been transformed into tourist centres, market gardening and the cultivation of flowers for the perfume industry have been pushed further inland.[18] This problem is further aggravated by the issue of public access, the provision of such access usually involving yet further demands upon agricultural land and often bringing in its train damage to farm property and hazards to farm stock. Any expansion of tourism in an area implies that increasing acreages must be made available for it and opened up to tourists, but this is as much a planning as an economic problem. Again, while the opening up of an area to tourism may provide new amenities for the tourist, it may also involve loss of amenity for the local residents and there are many instances of local populations resisting recreational developments for this reason. It must be admitted that the reconciliation of such conflicting interests is not always easy.

Another aspect of the land problem is price inflation. As Peters has said: "If ... a small country such as the Lebanon, with much urban development and considerable speculative appeal for outside capital, needed land for tourism development purposes, there could be inflation in land prices. The development of comprehensive projects will ... require land currently being used for other purposes ... [and] ... inflated prices could threaten the viability of many projects."[19] The French Government in planning its Languedoc–Roussillon Project secretly bought up land along the coast before it publicised the scheme to prevent speculators from moving in and causing inflation in land values. The Tunisian Government has taken similar action to control tourism development.

The seasonal nature of tourism means that land and many facilities are intensively used for only a restricted part of the year. Clearly, this is a wasteful use of resources and efforts are being made to introduce alternative or supplementary activities which can absorb the work force during the off-season. Reliance upon a single industry anywhere is an inherent economic weakness and a measure of diversification must be introduced into regional tourist economies to safeguard their prosperity; for instance, efforts have been made by the Fylde tourist resorts to attract suitable industries to provide a more balanced economy. It must be recognised that certain industries are incompatible with tourism, for instance, heavy industries or industries emitting dust or fumes or noise, but small-scale manufacturing, which is unobtrusive and can be discreetly hidden can be successfully introduced. This, yet again, is at once an economic and a planning problem.

Nowadays, it is often as cheap—sometimes even cheaper—to holiday abroad than at home. The introduction of package tours has so cut the cost of foreign holidays that not only has the domestic tourist industry suffered but the country's economy as a whole is weakened by the export of money to foreign countries. In Britain, for example, the domestic holiday industry was hit hard by the introduction of Value Added Tax in 1973 which resulted in hotel prices going up by between 3 and 10 per cent. Tourism is an activity which reacts sharply to costs and such things as price adjustments, currency exchange rates, cheaper transport, etc. have quite significant impacts upon tourist choices.

THE SOCIAL SIGNIFICANCE OF TOURISM

So far, little work has been done on the social impact of tourism and this is a fruitful field of enquiry; however, some of the more obvious effects are clear, *e.g.* on settlement, cultural exchange and enrichment, social changes.

One of the most important and obvious effects of tourism has been on settlement. Tourism has been responsible for the creation of many settlements which previously did not exist. In France, writes Pinchemel "tourism has given rise to more new urban developments than industry has done."[20] And in Spain numerous tiny coastal settlements have grown into flourishing resorts.

Tourism growth has also led to a spate of building. In England, for example, there are now relatively few stretches of coast that are not marred by the uncontrolled building of permanent and second homes. In Spain extensive tracts of the Mediterranean coast have been completely transformed within a few years: small, scattered coastal villages, such as Benidorm, Lloret del Mar and Torremolinos, have sprouted hotels in dozens and development is still proceeding fast. Many hitherto rather remote and unspoiled stretches of coast, such as the Algarve and Corsica, in addition have come under threat of colonisation by semi-permanent tourists. Properties for foreign residents, though by no means always ugly, seem to fit uncomfortably into the landscape; as Cosgrove and Jackson say: "Since such settlements have leisured rather than agricultural communities as their inhabitants, so their sites, situation, aspect, layout and overall form must inevitably differ from pre-existing forms."[21] Such settlements seldom seem to improve on the pre-existing forms.

The growth of second homes especially in rural areas has had important social repercussions. This development has already occurred on a wide scale in Denmark, Sweden, France and the United States but is now growing also in Britain. This development, at least in Britain, has had two somewhat paradoxical effects: on the one hand, the demand for rural properties has led to an escalation in the price of cottages and has resulted in numerous farm workers being forced off the land simply because they are unable to compete in the property market with the more affluent urban immigrants; on the other hand, numerous hamlets and small villages which, because of the drift from the land, seemed destined to decline and disappear as settlements have had a new lease of life, for many of their properties have been improved and renovated, and the appearance of the decaying villages has been transformed. However, such villages are often only "weekend villages," coming to life on Friday afternoon and becoming empty again on Monday morning.

Tourism development in a region, town or village may result in a conflict between the needs of tourists and the interests of the resident population. The larger the influx of visitors to a place, the greater becomes the risk of inconvenience and reduction in amenities and facilities to the permanent residents. Alfred Sherman has drawn attention to the disamenities created for Londoners by the massive influx of visitors in summer "Coaches exacerbate congestion in Inner London. . . . Public transport is crowded throughout the day, defeating all attempts to stagger journeys and miss rush-hours. The streets are ever more crowded and littered."[22] There are other clashes of interest which are often difficult to reconcile but the social problems involved can frequently be mitigated by careful planning. It should also be emphasised that any loss of amenity suffered by those living in the region or town is usually more than compensated for by the other and perhaps not equally obvious advantages which accrue from tourism.

Tourism may have an important cultural significance for it brings into contact peoples of differing races, nationalities and backgrounds and "cultural exchanges and the enrichment both of those who travel and of those who are at the receiving end"[23] may occur. Contacts of this kind may have beneficial effects, but they may also be socially disturbing. Native cultures and traditional ways of life may be weakened and even destroyed, by the impact of tourism; as Aalen and Bird in their survey of tourism in eastern Eire point out, local life, traditions and cultural individuality—valuable tourist attractions in themselves—must not be swamped by the growth of tourism.[24] But in many areas alien cultural features have been imported to the detriment of local cultures.

In other ways, too, contacts may bring undesirable social effects; the development of luxury tourism in countries or areas where living standards are low may create social unrest, as occurred in the Bahamas, and ultimately led to independence.

The impact of tourism manifests itself in numerous, and often unexpected ways. Niddrie has commented upon what has happened in Puerto Rico since tourism developed in that island. "Tourists on holiday in the Caribbean seldom eat the local foods. Every island seeking this trade must therefore allow considerable quantities of frozen, tinned or fresh food and Scotch whisky to be imported. Since these are also displayed in the local retail shop, they become part of an islander's regular purchases . . . Puerto Rico has almost abandoned its 'native' foods in favour of those imported from Miami in ever-increasing quantities."[25] The great increase in wine consumption in Britain in recent years may be attributed in part at least to the influence of Continental holidaying, while the occurrence of fish-and-chip shops on the Costa Brava is assuredly the outcome of the British invasion of that coast. As Medlik says: "When the tourist comes in contact with the place he visits and its population, a *social* exchange takes place. His social background affects the social structure and mode of life of his destination; he is in turn affected by it and sometimes carries back home with him new habits and ways of life."[26]

This has always been the case: Fairburn has shown how in an earlier age young Britons making the Grand Tour of Europe were strongly affected by foreign influences: "... the paintings of Reynolds and other contemporaries reflected the influence of France and particularly Italy, as did the colonnaded and porticoed mansions of the age. With the growth of a wealthy, proud and cultured aristocracy, decoration in art and architecture flourished under the ... stimuli of riches and the Latin influences acquired on the Tour.... The Tour was an education in elegance, an indispensable finishing-school for the aristocracy. Some of the young men ... only learnt foreign fashions, a fastidious accent and an affected manner."[27]

NOTES

1. G. Richards, "How Important is Tourism in Real Terms?" *Catering Times*, 3rd August, 1972.

2. M. Peters, *International Tourism*, Hutchinson, 1969, pp. 242–3.

3. I. Cosgrove and R. Jackson, *The Geography of Recreation and Leisure*, Hutchinson, 1972, p. 50.

4. *Op. cit.*, p. 241.

5. *Ibid.*

6. *Tourism: Principles, Practices, Philosophies*, p. 182.

7. *Op. cit.*

8. "Economic Importance of Tourism," University of Surrey, 1972.

9. F. Mitchell, *The Costs and Benefits of Tourism in Kenya*. Report prepared for Kenya Tourist Development Corporation, Institute of Development Studies, Nairobi, 1968.

10. G. H. Blake and R. I. Lawless, "Algeria's Tourist Industry," *Geography*, Vol. 57, April, 1972, pp. 148–52.

11. *Profile of the Hotel and Catering Industry*, Heinemann, 1972, p. 118.

12. *Idem*, p. 120.

13. *Op. cit.*, p. 244.

14. *Op. cit.*, p. 182.

15. *Op. cit.*, p. 187.

16. *Op. cit.*, Appendix M, p. 246.

17. W. Christaller, "Some Considerations of Tourist Location in Europe," *Papers Regional Science Association* XII, 1964, pp. 95–105.

18. I. B. Thompson, *Modern France: A Social and Economic Geography*, Butterworth, 1971, p. 319.

19. *Op. cit.*, p. 245.

20. P. Pinchemel, *France, A Geographical Survey*, G. Bell and Sons, 1969, p. 383.

21. *Op. cit.*, p. 55.

22. "Are Tourists Really Worth It?" *Daily Telegraph*, 2nd June, 1973.

23. S. Medlik, "Economic Importance of Tourism," University of Surrey, 1972.

24. F. H. A. Aalen and J. C. Bird, Tourism in Ireland—East: Guidelines for Development, Eastern Regional Tourism Organisation, 1969, p. 3.

25. The Caribbean in *Latin America: Geographical Perspectives*, ed. H. Blakemore and C. T. Smith, Methuen, 1971, p. 110.

26. *Op. cit.*

27. "The Grand Tour," *Geographical Magazine*, Vol. XXIV, 1951, pp. 118–27.

Chapter X

Planning for Tourism

"PROSPECTS for the future expansion of the world tourist industry, in the long-term, seem almost limitless."[1] If one takes into consideration the factors of increasing leisure, higher incomes and higher standards of living, improved education and better transport facilities, which have resulted in the growth in tourism at both the domestic and international levels during the past two decades, it would appear that the prospects are, indeed, almost limitless. Projections can only be based upon recent and current trends, and if we accept these trends, then a vast expansion in tourism in the future seems inevitable.

TOURISM IN THE DEVELOPING COUNTRIES

Until quite recently tourism was principally a feature of, and was largely confined to, the developed countries. Latterly, however, many of the developing countries have seen the possibilities in tourism development and introduced tourism development programmes. Unfortunately, some of these programmes have been embarked upon without sufficiently careful consideration or appreciation of the advantages and disadvantages involved. To quote the Report of the Estoril Seminar: "In the light of this ever-growing movement to seek out new and varied places for the enjoyment of leisure, there is perhaps a tendency for developing countries which are possessed of the two basic attractions of sunshine and ocean, to see in tourism an easy, natural resource for economic development and a ready-made solution to balance-of-payments difficulties. By the same token, it is sometimes suggested that international tourism represents an easy and painless way for the world's richer countries to help redress the situation of the poorer. This, of course, is far from being the case. Very often the developing countries who would have most to gain from being able to develop a vigorous tourist trade as a much-needed additional national resource are those which, in practice, are likely to be most handicapped for doing so.

Countries that are geographically remote from the high income areas, whose climates (despite the prevalence of sunshine) are unpleasantly extreme, and whose low level of overall development means that they lack the basic facilities and attractions that tourism requires, cannot expect to be able to build up a tourist industry of any appreciable size without considerable difficulty."[2] On the other hand, the United Nations Conference on Trade and Development (U.N.C.T.A.D.) in 1965 emphasised the particular promise which tourism held out for the developing countries, although this applies more especially to the more favourably located ones. For some countries, indeed, tourism offers a major opportunity since it provides employment for many, it stimulates investment and is a source of foreign exchange. Mexico and Tunisia, for example, have already benefited enormously through the development of the tourist sector, but it has become clear, both in these and other developing countries, that careful planning is a pre-requisite for complete success.

THE IMPERATIVE OF PLANNING

The Third I.U.O.T.O. Travel Research Seminar, held in Prague in 1964, examined in great detail the many problems involved in the development of a tourist industry and concluded that planning, whether at national, regional or local level, was indispensable. It concluded that all tourist planning should be based on "two classes of preliminary surveys: (*i*) detailed surveys of the characteristics of the area being considered for development and, in particular, of its tourist resources; (*ii*) studies of future customers based on surveys and forecasts."[3]

The planning process, fundamentally, involves five things (*see* Fig. 10): (*i*) it must make an inventory of all the facilities available and of the potential facilities; (*ii*) it must assess the tourism markets and attempt a projection of future tourist flows; (*iii*) it must look for areas where the demand is greater than the supply; (*iv*) it must investigate investment possibilities, both domestic and foreign, for the financial commitment in tourism development is likely to be substantial; and (*v*) it must attempt to conserve (as well as promote) the natural endowment, cultural legacy and social amenities. Planning, after all, is really about supply and demand, and the planning process requires an assessment of the supply of resources and the potential demand upon them.

It will have already become clear that the complexities of the tourist activity—the manifold resources and facilities required to meet the

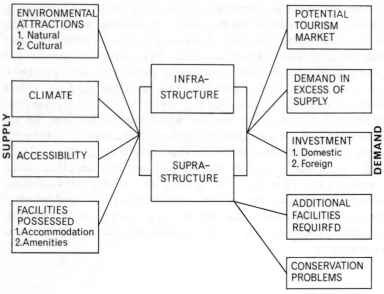

FIG. 10.—*Planning model.*

demands of the market—are such that joint planning becomes essential to ensure the co-ordinated development of the various inter-dependent sectors.

Most countries which are involved to any extent in tourism have a National Tourist Organisation (*see* pp. 82–5).

No matter which body is responsible for the planning of tourism development, it is important that any plans "should be conceived within a larger geographical context and be integrated into the national plan for economic development."[4] This is precisely what the French did in their Languedoc–Roussillon scheme. The development of major tourism projects often is beyond the powers and resources of private enterprise and requires State participation in respect of innovation, financing and co-ordination. In the case of the developing countries it would seem that State intervention is imperative for the successful launching of any tourism development.

THE FORMULATION OF A TOURISM PROGRAMME

Any country, whether it already has an active tourist industry or is thinking of developing a tourist sector, has many problems to face and resolve. The government has to decide upon the rate of growth of the tourism sector, whether indeed it wishes to encourage mass tourism or develop it more slowly and selectively. Such a decision may, of course, be taken for it by circumstances that already exist; for instance, a country with an incipient industry simply cannot cope with a vast influx of tourists since it does not possess the tourist plant capable of dealing with large numbers. Secondly, it must make a decision as to the importance which tourism is to have in the national economy and how its development and growth is to fit in with the plans for national and regional development; for instance, is it envisaged that it will be a major or only a supporting minor industry and is it the intention to focus it in the developed areas of the country (where there is already considerable infrastructure) or to develop it in economically retarded areas with a view to correcting regional economic imbalance? Thirdly, it must decide what are to be the respective roles of the public and the private sector in the development of the industry; the public sector as we have seen will almost certainly have to provide the necessary costly infrastructure before the private sector can begin to operate. Fourthly, it has to determine the roles to be played by domestic and foreign capital. It may be that foreign investment is essential if the country's financial resources are strictly limited, although dependence upon outside investment will greatly reduce the benefits which will accrue since the payment of interest rates will constitute a serious leakage (*see* p. 126). Fifthly, a decision must be made as to whether the tourist industry should be treated in the same way as other industries or whether the peculiar character of the industry warrants it being given special administrative and financial arrangements.

The O.E.C.D. Seminar at Estoril focused its attention on all these basic issues: "Much of the discussion ... [said the Report] turned on the fact that tourism is by its nature somewhat different from other sectors of the economy, since it is an industry based on movement of people rather than of goods. For this reason, it is particularly susceptible to subjective considerations quite apart from the play of economic forces. Politics and social pressures (seemingly very remote sometimes from the tourist industry itself), psychological attitudes, changes of fashion, may all influence the course of tourism development markedly and unpredictably. It is essential therefore that the tourism industry should be as flexible as possible to be able to adapt to changing conditions and requirements. As a corollary, the government's management of the tourism industry should also be as flexible as possible, with the relevant administrative structure and credit institutions geared to operate accordingly."[5]

The discussions at the Seminar also drew attention to the fact that tourism involves several considerations which are essentially non-economic: "Tourism often has significant cultural implications (for example, the restoration of ancient monuments); aesthetic (the preservation of beauties of landscape and the safeguarding of the nation's heritage); social (the provision of recreational facilities for the health and welfare of the people); and political (the improvement of international understanding)."[6]

In conclusion, it may be said that any government in formulating its tourism policy must (*i*) be perfectly clear as to the objectives of tourism development, (*ii*) be guided, primarily, by economic considerations, that is, the benefits which tourism development will bring to the national economy, and (*iii*) make a very careful study of the potential market.

THE ASSESSMENT OF NATIONAL TOURIST ATTRACTIONS

"Without a full study of the attractions a country possesses, and [their evaluation in terms of] ... potential future types of tourists," writes Peters, "countries cannot begin to plan for the future expansion of their tourist trade."[7] It is, then, of fundamental importance that a very careful assessment be made of all the attractions—physical, historical, cultural—that a country possesses. Following this inventory, says Peters, "legislation for the preservation, protection and development of outstanding natural attractions is essential to prevent piecemeal development, which may ruin the international competitiveness of the country."[8]

Peters lays down a number of principles on which assessment should be based.[9] First, it is highly desirable that the attractions should be developed progressively throughout the entire country so that tourism is spread as widely as possible; in this way the benefits which accrue from the industry are also widely spread and most parts of the country benefit. In many countries, Yugoslavia and Jordan, for example, tourism was highly concentrated in particular and fairly localised areas, to the economic and social detriment of the country as a whole. Secondly, areas and attractions which are singled out for special development should appeal to "the widest possible cross-section of tourists over the longest possible season."[10] By adhering to this principle, over-dependence upon a particular type of tourist, specific national group or particular season of the year will be avoided. Thirdly, priority should be given those attractions which can be most easily and most successfully developed. Such development should be equated with both the potential volume of visitor traffic and the probable expenditures by tourists. For example, it would be wise and more economic to develop those attractions which can be based upon the existing infrastructural services or those planned for other socio-economic developments; in this way distinct, and often large, economies in development costs can be made. Fourthly, since it is impossible to develop all the potential attractions at the same time, it is important that similar or competing attractions should not be embarked upon until the volume of visitors can justify them; too many alternative or competing attractions may well jeopardise the success of others if the numbers and spending power of the tourists are not large enough to sustain them. Clearly, great care must be taken over priorities. Fifthly, in planning tourism development it would be sensible to take into consideration "the future probable travel and recreational needs of the local population ... to ensure that tourism projects are backed by local custom and hence stand a better chance of being viable economic propositions."[11] Finally, it may be emphasised that the tourist is usually seeking something new; he desires new experiences, different environments, new thrills, different faces. Any country possessing attractions which are unique or out of the ordinary should attempt to capitalise on these for they are likely to have great drawing power. The great success of Tunisia as a European tourist attraction lies not a little in the fact that it offers an entirely different world, strange, fascinating and exotic.

ESSENTIAL BASIC SERVICES

These fall into two categories: infrastructure and suprastructure.

The term "infrastructure" refers literally to all those built-in services which are essential for modern social life and economic development; they include transport facilities such as roads, railways and airports, water supplies and sewerage systems, supplies of energy such as electricity and gas, and communications facilities such as telephone services. Since countries embarking upon tourism development programmes cannot afford to do everything at once they must, of necessity, select certain areas for development; if they are prudent they will choose areas where an infrastructure already exists. Tourism potential, however, is often related to peripheral, remote and economically underdeveloped areas and the transformation of such areas into viable tourist propositions in the future calls for heavy initial investment in infrastructure.

The Estoril Seminar Report commented that "The return is likely to be not only quicker but greater in relation to the new investment involved, if the tourism plan concentrates on expanding and improving facilities in existing tourist regions first." [12]

In addition to the infrastructure, tourism development also needs suprastructural services such as access facilities for transport, *e.g.* airport terminals, rail and coach stations, hotels, motels and other accommodation units, restaurants, cafés, bars and sport recreation facilities, and entertainments. These services, in contrast to the infrastructural services which are commonly supplied by the public authorities, are usually provided by private companies or individuals, although sometimes central and local government will lend or give financial or other aid. A case in point is the Hotel Development Incentives Scheme in the United Kingdom.

INVESTMENT PLANNING

In the case of countries which already possess an active tourist industry or have a proven potential for increased tourism development, investment capital will usually be readily available; however, in the case of the developing countries, which are desirous of developing tourism, the provision of adequate resources of capital may present something of a problem, as the demands upon their limited resources are many. "The development of the tourism sector will be only one of a number of options for development before a government. Since government resources will inevitably be inadequate for all the competing claims upon them, it is essential that the tourism option be presented in quantified terms as for the other sectors of the economy. The proposed investment in tourism must ... be demonstrably justified in terms of its anticipated contribution to the economic development of the country." [13]

Except in centrally planned economies, such as the Communist countries, public investment will be supported by private investment as happens in the mixed economies of, for instance, Britain and France. The Government may take the initiative in project developments but it will hope for private investment support. If the government is anxious to promote an active tourist industry it will be as helpful as possible to the private investor. There are two ways at least in which it can do this: first, it can create a favourable climate for investment by ensuring that conditions reassure the private investor and, second, it can help the private investor to consider tourism development as an attractive investment proposition by offering special financial inducements such as subsidies, credits, tax concessions, preferential rates of interest, special facilities for land purchase, etc.[14]

I.U.O.T.O. has suggested that greater attention should be focused upon three economic criteria which could be used to guide tourism expansion in developing countries: the gestation period of investments, the efficiency of capital utilisation and the labour intensity of investments.

By the gestation period of investments is meant the time lapse between the date of investment and the date when revenue begins to be returned; one of the chief attractions of investments for developing countries lies in the shortness of the gestation period before returns accrue. However, "this great advantage must not be allowed to obscure the fact that investments in tourism, unless they are effectively planned, can be an inefficient way of using scarce capital resources."[15] It is especially important that capital which is not easy to come by should not be squandered or inefficiently used. It is possible to measure the efficiency of capital investment in terms of the amount of capital required to produce each unit of output. When measured in these terms the "capital coefficient" or rate of return of investments in hotels may compare not unfavourably with most other forms of investment, although lavish investment in prestige hotels, where the capital coefficient is high, should be discouraged and emphasis put on the building of lower-cost tourist accommodation. Furthermore, it is very necessary to consider the total investment demanded by any new tourism project for "a project which requires a large investment in infrastructure—even though this infrastructure may eventually be of great value to the economy as a whole—must be regarded as a less efficient use of scarce capital than a project which is founded upon existing infrastructural facilities."[16] Finally, it is important to consider the amount of employment which is created by each unit of capital invested—a matter already discussed in the chapter on the economics of tourism. Although the direct employment in accommodation units is not especially high, the indirect employment which is created in other areas which service hotels may be very substantial. However, as the I.U.O.T.O. Report comments: "the full benefits of economic development from investments in tourist facilities will only be achieved if there is overall planning of these projects to ensure that (*a*) maximum encouragement is given to local auxiliary tourist activities like handicrafts and entertainments and (*b*) maximum use is made of local products and materials."[17]

THE MANAGEMENT OF TOURISM

Although the government may be responsible for the promotion of tourism in a country and for the formulation of a tourist programme of development, it also has responsibilities in connection with its implementation. Governments are inevitably involved, for such matters as passports and visas, customs regulations, foreign currency allowances, statutory holidays, the number of weekly working hours, etc. are all matters likely to affect the development of tourism. With the tremendous expansion in tourism, governments are becoming increasingly concerned with the industry. In Britain, for example, where a *laissez-faire* attitude prevailed formerly, the government has set up the British Tourist Authority and given important financial support to the industry. It will be readily appreciated that in countries where the tourism sector forms an important part of the national development plan, as in the case of France, Yugoslavia and Tunisia, the government will wish to involve itself directly in the actual management of tourism, over and above its general regulatory functions.

A fundamental issue which the government will have to resolve is the division of responsibilities between the public and private sectors. Much will depend upon the degree of development of the country concerned: in a well-developed country, where, traditionally, there is a thriving private sector, a lesser measure of direct government intervention will be needed than in an underdeveloped country where the private sector is both weak and relatively inactive. In the latter case the government is likely to have to take over many of the functions and responsibilities usually undertaken by private enterprise. At the Estoril Seminar it was generally accepted by the participants that "... direct intervention by the government was not only desirable but indispensable." [18] It was generally agreed that if operations were left solely in the hands of the private sector the government could not reasonably expect tourism development to either follow the lines or to proceed at the pace laid down by the national tourism programme. The main reason for this lies in the fact that investment is prone to lag behind the growth in demand since private investors are apt to be cautious when it comes to sinking capital in tourism enterprises. Accordingly, if this imbalance between demand and supply is to be corrected, state action must be invoked.

The Estoril Seminar came to the conclusion that there were five functions which could properly be considered to be the responsibility of the government in assisting tourism development: (*i*) Basic market research into future tourism demand. It was impossible for private investors to be cognisant of market prospects and it was precisely this uncertainty about the demand factor which strongly militated against them investing in tourism. (*ii*) The publicity promoting the country and its tourist assets and creating those conditions of good-will, interest, ease of entry, etc. which will not only attract the tourist but ensure that when he has been he will go away with a good impression and wish to return. (*iii*) The regulation and control of the manifold services which make up the industry, perhaps even co-ordination of the activities of the numerous private interests concerned; this co-ordination might be best achieved through the liaison machinery of the national tourist organisation; certainly its success would depend upon the mutual co-operation and confidence existing between the public and private sectors. (*iv*) The economic and social implications of tourism development in relation to the community; the interests of the resident population must not be jeopardised and appropriate action must be taken to ensure that their welfare is not adversely affected for, as the Seminar concluded "The introduction into a small and unsophisticated community of large numbers of people of very different standards and requirements may involve serious social strains."[19] (*v*) Making whatever arrangements are deemed necessary for tourism promotion with other governments, whether it be establishing cordial relationships, facilitating exchange movements or co-operating with neighbouring governments to attract a regional market; here, clearly, is a case "where government action must precede and support the initiatives of the private sector."[20]

OVERALL CONCLUSIONS

It would seem very desirable that some degree of planning should take place. It is perhaps easier to have planned development in countries where there is a potential which is only just beginning to be realised, if only for the reason that the government is likely to be substantially involved right from the start. But it has become increasingly apparent that even in those countries with a long-established and highly developed tourist industry, much of it in the hands of the private sector, some measure of planning is necessary. Planning is essential these days for three main reasons: first, most countries, to a lesser or greater degree, have planned economies and if tourism development is to be part and parcel of national economic development then this sector of the economy also should be subjected to planning; secondly, the success of tourism development depends very largely upon appropriate facilities being available in the right place at the right time and these can only be

provided by adequate research into national tourist assets and markets
—as Peters says, "Research has an extremely important role to play in
the future planning of tourism development";[21] and, thirdly, planning is
required to ensure that the natural and created assets are conserved and
protected to maintain tourist appeal, for lack of care and co-ordinated
development may impair and even ruin those assets upon which the
tourist industry is founded.

NOTES

1. *Tourism Development and Economic Growth*, Estoril Seminar, O.E.C.D.,
Paris, 1967, p. 11.

2. *Idem*, p. 12.

3. I.U.O.T.O. Travel Research Seminar, Prague, 1964.

4. *Tourism Development and Economic Growth*, Estoril Seminar, O.E.C.D.,
Paris, 1967, p. 21.

5. P. 13.

6. *Ibid.*

7. *International Tourism*, p. 150.

8. *Ibid.*

9. *Idem*, pp. 150–1.

10. *Ibid.*

11. *Ibid.*

12. *Tourism Development and Economic Growth*, p. 17.

13. I.U.O.T.O. *Economic Review of World Tourism*, 1972.

14. Travel Research Seminar, Prague, 1964.

15. *Idem.*

16. *Idem.*

17. *Idem.*

18. *Tourism Development and Economic Growth*, p. 23.

19. *Idem*, p. 25.

20. *Ibid.*

21. *Op. cit.*, p. 146.

Part Four

THE TOURIST AND THE ENVIRONMENT

Chapter XI

The Tourist and the Town

TOURIST RESORTS

"FOR generations," writes Peters, "spas, winter-sports centres and coastal resorts have existed, developed around a few outstanding natural features and aimed at specialised markets."[1] Both Bath and Buxton were Roman health and recreational centres and may lay some claim to be very early English resorts. However, resorts as a special town type are of relatively new development and many are of very recent growth. Providing an adequate definition of a tourist resort is not easy, for resorts vary widely in their character and size: they may be large urban centres, such as Blackpool or Nice with varied and sophisticated amenities, or they may be newly developed centres, such as La Grande Motte and Leucate–Barcares in Languedoc, which have been developed from scratch, as it were. Again, a tourist centre is not necessarily a resort town: Grasmere in the English Lake District is an important tourist centre but could never be called a resort town and Cambridge attracts large numbers of tourists but is decidedly not a resort. Clearly precise definition is elusive but as satisfactory a definition as any is that given by Professor Markovic, quoted by Peters. Tourist resorts are "places which attract large numbers of tourists and which tourism endows with special characteristics so that direct and indirect revenue produced by tourism plays a very important and even decisive role in their existence and development."[2]

Resorts also have morphological characteristics which help to distinguish them. Many grew from small and humble beginnings—a mineral spring, an unusual natural feature, a fishing hamlet, an hotel (as in the case of the Lancashire resort of Southport which had its origins in an hotel built by a man called Sutton in 1792); many have remained relatively small although a few may become quite large urban centres. When in 1841 Dr A. B. Granville prepared a map of English seaside resorts there were, according to his reckoning, thirty-six.[3] The factors necessary for the development of a resort, according to Granville, were a flat, sandy beach, cliffs to provide scenic interest and a position removed from a river mouth; however, as Cosgrove and Jackson have suggested, these "... were somewhat biased by his desire to promote the interests of Bournemouth."[4] Particular physical factors have without doubt stimulated resort development in some cases but, as Professor Gilbert has said, most resorts "do not have one physical feature in common other than being on the coast."[5] The establishment and successful growth of resorts has been as often due to historical accident, to individual enterprise, to whims of fashion, to governmental decision, as to physical attractions.

The origins of holiday resorts, as Smailes has said, antedate modern urban development but the great expansion of the seaside resorts waited upon the arrival of the railways.[6] At first, the resorts catered almost solely for the nobility and the wealthy, indeed many as we know grew to fame as a result of aristocratic patronage, but the railways were very largely responsible for facilitating the mass seasonal migration to the coast, which became such a pronounced feature of British social life, and were instrumental in concentrating this migration at particular points along the coast, *i.e.* at the termini of the railway lines. The importance of railways in influencing the growth of resorts is illustrated by the growth of the North Wales holiday resorts and by the late development of many of the Lincolnshire and East Anglian resorts, *e.g.* Cleethorpes, Mablethorpe and Skegness, which had no railway links with their hinterland until the turn of the century.

While many of the newer resorts were deliberately planned, the majority have grown up around some pre-existing settlement, a village or small port. "In accounting for the siting of many seaside towns, the existence of an earlier nucleus of settlement to which the modern town is attached must be recognised. As the trade or fishing, which had been the mainstay of these not necessarily urban settlements decayed during the course of the nineteenth century, they embarked upon a new career as resorts by developing adjacent stretches of the sea-front. Their nineteenth-century expansion was dominated by the positions of the marine promenade and the railway station. Among many examples are Scarborough and Aberystwyth and, on a much greater scale, Nice. Fortified headland, small harbour and adjacent foreshore are common site features...."[7]

After 1945 many of the older resorts began to lose their appeal, although some, in an attempt to regain their former popularity, have undertaken extensive redevelopment in order to meet new tastes. In many areas, however, especially in the newer tourist areas of the

Caribbean, North Africa, the Near East, East Africa and the Indian Ocean, completely new resorts are being established. Some of these "continue to be based on specific local features while [others,] . . . areas rather than centres, provide attractions, recreations and entertainment facilities, appealing to a wide range of tourists from many different markets."[8] Although the essential function of the resort—to provide recreational facilities—has not altered its particular activities and operations are very closely related to the market from which it derives its custom.

THE ATTRIBUTES OF RESORT TOWNS

All recreational towns, whether seaside resorts, mountain centres or watering places, have certain attributes in common. All mainly depend for their existence upon their ability to offer a different and usually contrasting environment from that to which most of their patrons are accustomed. Resort towns seldom possess well-developed manufacturing industries and these are often entirely absent; if manufactures do occur they are generally light, small-scale and unobtrusive. A very significant proportion of the gainfully employed population finds work in tertiary occupations and another distinguishing feature is the high proportion of elderly, retired people: this is especially true of some English resorts, such as Morecambe and Eastbourne. This feature is especially marked where resorts are located in the warmer and more equable areas—Devon and Cornwall in England, the Riviera in France and California and Florida in the United States. Yet another social feature of many resorts is the presence of a large commuter population, especially if the resort is not too far removed from a large urban centre of population. Southport, for instance, is a residential town for large numbers of professional people working in Liverpool, as the smaller resorts of the Wirral, *e.g.* West Kirby, are for those engaged in business in Birkenhead and Liverpool. In the West Riding, the spa towns of Harrogate, Knaresborough, Boston Spa and Ilkley are today very largely residential dormitories for Bradford and Leeds.

A further distinguishing feature of the typical resort town is a marked seasonal rhythm of activity and employment, with a high proportion of casual work. In countries located in higher latitudes, where the climates are cooler, as in Belgium, the Netherlands, Britain, Eire, Norway and Iceland, summer is the busy season and during the rest of the year resorts, with few exceptions, are moribund. The only exceptions are resorts in mountain areas which can capitalise upon winter sporting activities, *e.g.* Aviemore in Scotland, or resorts with suitable accommodation and facilities to attract conferences, *e.g.* Harrogate and Brighton. In contrast, in areas of warmer climates the cooler season is often preferred for holiday-making and in places such as Madeira and the Canaries, Jamaica and Florida the peak tourist season falls in winter and spring. Where summer heat is fierce or enervating people have always taken advantage of cooler, adjacent highlands: in India it has long been customary for the privileged classes of Delhi to move up to the hill stations of Simla and Darjeeling to escape the hot season. Many inhabitants of New York motor up into the Catskills while those of Sydney flock to the Blue Mountains. Some resorts are fortunate in having a double season, for example, Davos, St Moritz and Zermatt in Switzerland, and Banff and Jasper in the Canadian Rockies, which provide summer recreation in addition to winter-sports facilities and hence "are organised to handle one influx of visitors from December to March, and another from June to September."[9] Changes in tourism, growing out of increased leisure, affluence and mobility, have prolonged the tourist season in certain tourist areas: perhaps the best example is the Riviera, which first grew to importance as a wintering area for the titled and wealthy but which, since about 1960, has come to receive a clientele of middle- and working-class holiday-makers in the summer season.

Finally, resort towns tend, as a whole, to be small towns. Of the 200 or so English and Welsh resorts only a few attain any reasonable size in terms of their constant, as opposed to their temporary, residents. Easy access to large centres of population has frequently promoted the growth of some resorts and Brighton, Bournemouth, Southend and Blackpool, the largest English resorts, are in fairly close proximity to substantial populations and are well served by roads and railways. But even these can hardly be termed large towns, for their populations are around the 150,000 mark.

FACILITIES AND AMENITIES

Since the earliest seaside resorts developed as a result of the medical profession's recommendation of the therapeutic value of sea bathing, the beach became the focus of activity. Sea bathing, sometimes boating, and playing on the beach, together with a walk along the promenade (where there was one) to look at the sea and take deep breaths of ozone, formed the principal, sometimes the only, activities of the holiday-makers. Additional amenities quickly came to be offered, however—donkeys for the young to ride, beach stalls for those who wished to partake of an oyster or a saucer of whelks, and minstrels and pierrot shows. The donkey-ride, the highlight of many a child's holiday, seems first to have made its appearance at Margate around 1800.

Gradually various recreational facilities and amenities began to be introduced. These piers, amusement parks, swimming pools, theatres, etc. were man-made or created resources, in contrast to the natural resources of sea and sand. "As in many other aspects of economic geography," write Cosgrove and Jackson "so in leisure and recreation one may see a progression in the location of activity from resource- to market-based development."[10] Extensive investment, both private and public, came as we know to be put into the building of places of amusement, and so elaborate was this provision that in many cases the focus of the resort moved away from the beach to the built-up area behind it.

Nothing is more characteristic of the Victorian seaside resort than the pier. The first seaside piers were merely timber landing stages for boats, and perhaps the first true seaside pier was the Chain Pier at Brighton—built by a naval officer, Captain Samuel Browne, and opened in 1823. Other early piers were built at Southend (1830) and at Herne Bay (1831). Southend Pier was subsequently extended to one and one-third miles in length, the longest pleasure pier in the world. A number of piers were built during the 1850s but mostly for the use of vessels than for promenaders. The custom of building pleasure piers grew during the 1860s, as it was considered that no seaside resort worthy of the name should be without one and in the 1870s and 1880s there was a spate of pier building. The craze for piers subsequently subsided and among the last to be built was that at Weston-super-Mare in 1904.

A long list of attractions, including towers (at Blackpool and New Brighton), fairgrounds, swimming pools and zoos, were introduced and local authorities spent large sums on promenade construction and landscaping. There is no need to describe in detail the numerous facilities and amenities required by a resort but the more important may be listed as follows:

(*i*) accessibility and ease of transport to the resort;
(*ii*) accommodation to meet the demands of all social levels and pockets;
(*iii*) car parks and parking facilities for visitors and day excursionists;
(*iv*) internal transport facilities: tramways, bus services, taxi services, and cliff-lifts;
(*v*) open-spaces: parks, recreation areas, beaches;
(*vi*) promenades;

  (*vii*) gardens and floral displays;
 (*viii*) amusement facilities: theatres, cinemas, funfairs, piers, min-
          iature railways;
   (*ix*) games facilities: boating, water skiing, golf, tennis, bowls;
    (*x*) bathing facilities: sea bathing and swimming pools;
   (*xi*) shopping facilities;
  (*xii*) catering facilities: restaurants, cafés, bars;
 (*xiii*) seating arrangements: permanent seats and benches and deck
          chairs;
  (*xiv*) toilets;
   (*xv*) enquiry office and information centres.

MORPHOLOGY AND SHAPE

Smailes, discussing the origins and bases of modern towns, wrote:
"Not only is the service element a generally prominent feature of the
occupational structure of towns, specialised types of towns, notably
holiday resorts, have arisen to discharge particular service functions. ... A concomitant of the intense industrialisation and urbanisation of Great Britain, an island country with stretches of seaside now
within easy reach of all major concentrations of population, has been
the development of resorts on a scale unmatched in any other country.
As a class of towns, resorts are here both more numerous and more
highly specialised in function."[11]

Resorts in all other countries tend to display certain common
features of morphology and shape. Although certain site advantages,
such as fine beaches for bathing and ease of access to the shore, have
sometimes been responsible for the development of a seaside resort,
physical advantages of site have probably been less significant than in
the case of many other types of towns. As Smailes points out, there is
often little difference in site conditions along considerable stretches
of coast—think, for example, of the Yorkshire coast between
Flamborough Head and Spurn Point or the Sussex coast between
Beachy Head and Selsey Bill—hence local advantages of one place over
another are frequently of much less significance than other factors
which are responsible for urban growth.[12] Nevertheless, varying coastal
settings (Southport, Torquay) naturally lent themselves to differing
town layout and physical appearance, with the result that each resort
has tended to acquire its own particular individuality.[13]

Seaside resorts, by and large, possess a distinctive shape: they tend to
be long and narrow with their greatest inland dimension roughly in the

middle. This is, perhaps, what we should expect since the sea front with its bathing beach was the focus of the resort. Resorts which grew out of an old nucleus, as, for example Scarborough, quickly expanded away from this ancient core and spread along the line of the shore. As a result of such lateral extension, Brighton, as early as 1841, had over 4·8 km (3 miles) of built sea frontage. Today, Blackpool boasts of her 11-km (7-mile) long sea front. But as the lateral wings extend, they show a gradually decreasing inland extension. This narrow, attenuated form is distinctly recognisable in the cases of Morecambe, Blackpool, Brighton and Bournemouth and in many smaller resorts (*see* Fig. 11). Not all

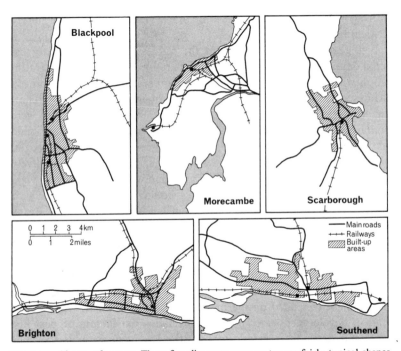

FIG. 11.—*Shapes of resorts.* These five diagrams represent some fairly typical shapes of seaside resorts. Four show the attenuated shape characteristic of many; Scarborough, built around a headland and two bays and based on an older fishing settlement, does not have the elongated shape of the others. Note how, in most cases, railways come close to the sea front.

resorts, of course, conform to this pattern for sometimes the local topography has hindered lateral extension along the shore or modified the regularity of the resort's growth, as in the case of Dawlish or Whitby. Another factor which has strongly influenced the shape and

structure of resorts is the railway. It was at the time of railway development that many resorts acquired a characteristic "T-shape," the stem
of the T being the main street leading from the railway station to the
promenade.[14] The railway was often brought as near to the sea front as
possible and in some cases the station is actually on the promenade, *e.g.*
Morecambe, or very near it, *e.g.* Blackpool. The railways, too, were
sometimes responsible for the breaking up of the continuity of the built-
up area of the resort and in some cases the beach and promenade are
separated from the town behind by a railway which runs closely parallel
with the shore, *e.g.* Colwyn Bay, Dawlish. ". . . its course often marks
the separation of a coastal belt of hotels and boarding houses, together
with shopping streets and places of amusement, from a more purely
residential area inland."[15]

It is also interesting to see how the resorts as they grew and prospered developed a concentric pattern of architectural and social stratification which is clearly discernible in many seaside towns. Williamson
has described this very well; he says: "Although geographical circumstances varied, and the coast towns differed in their setting, there were
similarities in their social growth. What we may call the aboriginal
inhabitants, the fishermen and small tradesmen who saw it all begin,
were usually located near the water's edge, but they had no lively
appreciation of salt winds and a sea view and were quite ready to yield
such amenities to the newcomers who would pay for them. The new
towns therefore developed as terraces of tall houses and hotels strung
out along the sea front, with other although less desirable penetrations
up valleys leading inland. Behind the sea front would lie an area of
shops selling good quality wares, and lodging-houses for the poorer
visitors. Behind that again, reaching sometimes far inland, would grow
rows of meaner streets housing the new working population whose
employment depended on the money of the sea front. It was a simple
kind of development uncomplicated by industrial factors or past history, and depending on one motive, the sea front with its view, its
spacious promenade and its bathing."[16]

Seaside resorts as a type, more than most other kinds of urban
centres, display a readily distinguishable and highly individual morphological pattern. This is principally the result of three conditions:
first, they had a coastal location which offered a unique combination of
landscape and seascape; secondly, they were frequently developed on
virgin sites and so did not have to adapt themselves to already existing
nuclei; and, thirdly, they were often planned by developers and
architects who could give rein to their imagination and create something

pleasing and distinctive.[17] Even where a seaside resort grew out of an original settlement, the newer resort part tends to exhibit a "resort layout," as can clearly be seen in the case of Scarborough or Whitby, displaying all the concepts of Victorian resort design: the grid-iron plan (Southport, Llandudno, Skegness, etc.), wide, often tree-lined, streets, crescents and terraces, substantial and often imposing hotels, *e.g.* the Grand Hotel, Scarborough, villas and houses, promenades and formal gardens.

ARCHITECTURE AND LANDSCAPE FEATURES

Resorts in Britain, whether inland or coastal, have developed their own rather unique architectural styles. Mixtures of architectural styles are common features, as Ewart Johns has illustrated in the small Devonshire resort of Dawlish. These are not always incompatible and may produce townscapes of singular attractiveness. "The story of design in town-building," writes Johns, "is one of overlapping phases, rather than of clearly separated periods. ... In Britain today, a town whose foundation precedes the year 1850 will contain, for certain, some inheritance of Classical form, and some of Romantic style. These two elements are the main threads in the pattern of architectural shapes in our towns, closely interwoven and sometimes almost indistinguishable from one another, but each, from time to time, emerging as the chief component."[18] In our seaside resorts there is also a strong mixture of architectural styles partly because in some—the older-established such as Scarborough and Whitby—a new part was grafted on to the older nucleus and partly because the wealthy residents could indulge their whims and build in unorthodox styles.

In the latter part of the eighteenth century "many smaller towns emerged from their village beginnings, and, in particular, many spas and resorts appeared [following] ... the lead of Bath. In tiny seaside places as remote as Aberayron on Cardigan Bay, and in the great resorts of Brighton and Cheltenham, in Sidmouth in Devon and in Scarborough in the North Riding of Yorkshire, there appeared a new type of townscape."[19] This townscape was Georgian. Prior to 1800, this Georgian building was "architecturally chaste and almost unadorned" but in "the first decades of the nineteenth [there appeared] an increasing tendency towards the abandonment of pure Renaissance formulae. The decoration of façades of buildings, the use of wrought-iron work, rich cornices, canopies, shutters, bow windows, rounded bays and even sculpture, produced an entirely new prospect in the urban scene."[20] Many of the spas and resorts, *e.g.* Bath, Cheltenham, Brighton, Scarborough, provide in their ordered and elegant terraces and crescents superb examples of Georgian architecture. Even some of the smaller resorts such as Boston Spa which is almost wholly in the Classical mould, are gems of the Georgian style of building. "Towns that were built at this time," says Johns, "retain an air of spacious ease, and foster the appreciation of good living."[21]

No comment upon resort architecture would be complete without some reference to Brighton's famed Royal Pavilion. Built, or rather remodelled and elaborated from an earlier structure, for the Prince of Wales, later George IV, during the first two decades of the nineteenth century, the Pavilion is an architectural extravaganza which seems perfectly fitting in Brighton and gives to the town a touch of glamour not to be found in many seaside resorts.

After the mid-nineteenth century the Gothic revival in architecture dominated most building, though there was still much mixing of borrowed styles. This was the time of rapid growth for many seaside resorts and industrial towns and they clearly reflect this changing style. "The kind of building that was typical of good-class residential development in the mid-century is well illustrated in Torquay.... Torquay experienced its first major building boom, as a resort for wealthy invalids and holiday-makers, in the middle decades of the nineteenth century. A good deal of terrace-building and the first stages of villa-construction had been completed by the time the railway reached the town in 1848.... Gothic villas of this early date are scattered on the hill-sides among the other splendid domestic architecture of this beautifully sited town, but the favourite style of the 1840s and 1850s was undoubtedly that borrowed from Italy. The country or suburban residence was chosen as a pattern, and the irregular masses produced by asymmetrically placed towers, gables and wings was an indication of the Victorian preference for Romantic arrangement even when Classical detail was being used. Although an excellent building-stone was quarried near at hand in the beds of Devonian limestone, it was only in the Gothic building that its colour and texture were preferred to the stucco which covered it in the Italianate houses. The surface features of the majority of villas in the Warberry Hill and Lincombe Hill Drives, and in the more closely built streets of Torre, where the slightly less wealthy buyer found smaller sites near the railway, add up to townscapes of superficial resemblance to those of Mediterranean Rivieras."[22]

In many northern resorts Victorian architecture is often dominant. A perfectly delightful example is provided by the small resort of Lytham, a few miles to the south of Blackpool. The place is essentially, almost totally, Victorian and provides an excellent example of how attractive Victorian building can be. Built almost exclusively in red brick, Lytham, with its tree-lined square and streets and spacious green, has a rare charm. Unfortunately there are few other Victorian resorts which can compare with it. Nearby Blackpool, for example, has been severely (and perhaps a little unfairly) criticised: it "is not an essay in taste or style. It was built in the last hundred years and must be one of the most extended essays in concrete in the world." [23]

The piers, pieces of "Victorian inconsequential extravagance," according to John Betjeman, were the work of civil engineers, not architects, and their elegant cast iron tracery provided the resort with a unique townscape feature.

Another characteristic feature of the seaside resort is the large hotel. These mostly have a sea frontage and occupy commanding positions, e.g. the Grand Hotel at Scarborough. The promenade of most resorts is usually lined to landward by the higher quality hotels; behind them lie the smaller private hotels and boarding-houses, though the latter are now rapidly being converted into flatlets as holiday-makers' demands and tastes change.

PARKS AND PLAYGROUNDS

"Within the town," writes Patmore "open space fulfils two main functions: firstly it provides opportunity for recreation of both active and passive, and formal and informal kinds: secondly, and less tangibly, it has a visual and psychological role in enhancing the whole quality of the urban environment. . . . Playing fields, sports and recreation grounds cater for active sport. More passive needs are served by parks . . . whether ornamental gardens, informal open spaces or areas of woodland and common. Children's playgrounds, allotments and golf courses fulfil more specific needs, while areas of water may enhance amenity and provide further opportunities for recreation." [24] It might be thought that towns having the most attractive environments, such as resorts, would have the most generous provision of open space but this is by no means always the case. As Patmore points out, Morecambe has only 1·8 acres while Manchester has 3·4 acres. [25] Again says Patmore "There is a close relationship between the total population of a local authority and its acreage of parks and gardens, for generosity of provision tends to be directly proportional to the size of population. . . ." [26]

Since resort towns are, as a class, typically small this relationship may help to explain the limited open space in many resorts. On the other hand, most coastal resorts possess extensive stretches of open beach which tends to obviate the necessity for providing large urban recreation areas.

Some resorts are very fortunate in possessing generous recreation areas. Harrogate, for instance, has its Stray, a park-like common of 215 acres which was secured to the inhabitants by the *Act of Enclosure* of 1770. This large open space with its avenues of trees is one of the most attractive features of the town. Few spas were as generously endowed with open spaces of this kind but most had their pleasure gardens and parades, for promenading was a characteristic of the social life of the spas. Other places were sometimes fortunate in possessing common lands which were preserved for recreational purposes. One of the chief attractions of the small Lancashire resort of Lytham is the expansive Green which stretches all the way along the front. Here is a valuable recreational area, for the estuarine muds make the foreshore practically unusable.

The park was essentially a Victorian innovation—the first urban park was laid out in Derby in 1839—which originally took the form of a landscaped area providing pleasing vistas and promenades for strolling. Primarily they were designed for aesthetic purposes and passive enjoyment. After the Second World War, parks increasingly began to cater for the more active needs of the population; Patmore draws an interesting comparison between Birkenhead Park, designed by Joseph Paxton in 1844, and Stanley Park, Blackpool, designed by Thomas Mawson in 1922; in the latter "The whole area was conceived as an organised playing space; passive enjoyment is obviously still possible, but the park is not primarily a landscape created for that enjoyment." [27] Most resorts possess at least one park with floral gardens and games areas. Much of the appeal of Scarborough lies in its parks and gardens and the resort is indebted to H. W. Smith, a talented landscape gardener who was largely responsible for the laying out of the municipal gardens. Terraced walks and flower gardens are to be found in both the North and South Bays while Peasholm Park and Northstead Manor Gardens—the latter containing a fine open-air theatre—are especially attractive. Some resorts such as Eastbourne have made a feature of their floral gardens. In Southport, the receding sea left a wide expanse of sandy beach which has been put to excellent use by the Corporation who created from it flower gardens, games areas, *e.g.* putting greens and parking spaces.

CULTURAL, SOCIAL AND HISTORICAL ATTRACTIONS

Resorts live primarily upon their tourist visitors and, accordingly, use many devices to lure the holiday-maker. Advertising is a common means and a nationally well-known holiday advertisement was the poster designed by Arthur Hassall—"Skegness Is So Bracing." Many resorts have come to hold annual festivals or sporting events to attract the visitor. The small resort of Aldeburgh has its famous music festival, while Harrogate has developed drama and music festivals. Stratford-on-Avon is not perhaps a resort in the usual meaning of the term but its association with Shakespeare and its Theatre ensure a continuing clientele. Southport Flower Show is an annual event of some importance in the North and attracts thousands of visitors in addition to the usual holiday-makers and day-trippers. The small Cornish resorts of St Ives, Polperro, etc. have become popular haunts for artists and those who like to watch the artist at work.

The small Welsh seaside resort of Portmeirion, designed, created and built by Clough Williams-Ellis and described by him as "a little essay in the architecture of pleasure," draws thousands of visitors annually simply because it is a charming Italianate fantasy—an architect's dream—in a Welsh setting.[28]

Sporting activities of various kinds are associated with many resorts. Redcar and Cheltenham have horse-racing, Scarborough an annual motor-cycle race and Monte Carlo has its Rally. Yachting has become a very popular activity and centres such as Scarborough and Salcombe become miniature Cowes during their regatta weeks. Conway, Poole, Broadstairs and Windermere are important sailing centres, while Burnham-on-Crouch, once a quiet back-water, has become a mecca for yachtsmen. Annual golf (St Andrews) and tennis (Bournemouth) tournaments help to swell the numbers of visitors to these resorts. Some resorts, notably Blackpool and Morecambe, introduced end-of-season "illuminations" with conspicuous success.

A few resorts have notable historical attractions and while these in themselves may not actually attract visitors provide added attractions within the resorts. Scarborough Castle, magnificently situated on the high plateau separating the North and South Bays, receives a greater number of visitors each year than any other ruined remains in the country.

Such resorts as Blackpool, Rhyl and Southend, make capital out of their "pagan pleasures" which attract large numbers of people bent on having a good time, others which attract their clientele by adopting and cultivating a pose of upper-middle-class gentility and sobriety as, for instance, Filey, Frinton, Eastbourne, St Annes-on-Sea (there are no public houses), and Grange-over-Sands.

CLASSIFICATION OF RESORTS

It is not an easy matter to classify resorts. Though as a town type they are clearly distinguishable as a separate group, they tend to be like ports, having rather specialised and, sometimes, varied functions. A broad twofold division can be made:

(*i*) centres which have developed purely and simply as tourist resorts and which claim to be little else, *e.g.* Blackpool, Monte Carlo, Atlantic City, St Moritz and Bowness on Windermere; and

(*ii*) towns which have developed a tourist industry as an incidental part of their normal functions, *e.g.* old ports, such as Whitby and Falmouth, places with cultural and historical attractions, such as York and Stratford-on-Avon, and many capital cities.

Ignoring capitals, resorts within these two broad divisions may be further classified into five main types: seaside, scenic, sports centres, watering places and historical–cultural centres. Though this is a useful grouping, there is nothing exclusive about it since many resorts share one or more of the basic attractions: Scarborough is a delectable seaside resort which, until fairly recently, was also a notable spa and which can also claim to have significant historical attractions and minor annual sporting attractions (tennis tournament, cricket, motor-cycle racing).

Seaside Resorts

These are the coastal resorts which rely basically upon the attractions of the sea and the shore. Stretches of fine, clean, firm sand form an especial attraction and are much to be preferred to shingle beaches. Traditionally the beach has been the main focus of attraction and even today when the weather is warm and sunny this is where the bulk of the holiday-makers congregate. Gently shelving beaches with shallow water provide good bathing facilities and fine seascapes. A cliffed coastline and rocky foreshore with sandy coves, as in the Gower Peninsula or around Tor Bay and Mounts Bay in Devon and Cornwall, provides a most attractive seaside location.

Seaside resorts of the past hundred years or so, grew largely out of their beach facilities, but most seaside resorts have undergone some sort of "development," *e.g.* the provision of promenades, piers, gardens, parks, bathing-pools, sporting facilities, theatres, fun-fairs, etc. This "development" has progressed to such an extent that nowadays many holiday-makers go to the seaside resorts to take advantage of these facilities and amusements rather than the basic attractions.

The seaside resort is more particularly a European development which has been diffused on a wider scale. Notable examples are Blackpool and Brighton, Ostend in Belgium, Biarritz and Cannes in France, Estoril in Portugal, Rimini in Italy, Atlantic City and Miami Beach in the United States, and Punta del Este, near Montevideo, in Uruguay.

Scenic Resorts

Many resorts grew up originally because of the attractions of the local scenery—mountains, lakes, waterfalls, etc. or some natural wonder—volcanic activity, subterranean caverns, unique geological formations, etc. Subsequently, many of these old scenic resorts developed other attractive features such as sporting facilities.

To large numbers of people a holiday means an escape to a rural retreat with long and leisurely walks over fields or fells or a caravanning or camping holiday in some unspoilt corner of the countryside; indeed, the number of people choosing a "country holiday," as distinct from the traditional seaside holiday, has increased substantially since the war. Nor must we forget that a growing proportion of people now possess a weekend cottage in a country village.

\Many scenic resorts developed as centres of tourism as a result of their location in areas of outstanding scenic beauty. Especially favourable resort sites are lakeside situations in or near to spectacular mountain country, *e.g.* Ambleside and Keswick in the English Lake District, Lugano and Interlaken in Switzerland, Bariloche in Argentina's Southern Lake District. Some of the lakeside resorts have undergone such "development" that they now resemble the seaside resort, *e.g.* Lugano. Other British scenic resorts include Pitlochry in Scotland, Ingleton in Yorkshire, Castleton in Derbyshire, Llangollen and Bettws-y-Coed in Wales. Bretton Woods in a fashionable resort in the mountain country (Presidential Range) of New Hampshire in the United States. Rotorua, in the centre of North Island, New Zealand, is a well-known resort in an area famous for its crater lakes, geysers and steam vents, together with the Maori villages of Ohinemuru and Whakarerewa.

Sports Centres

These fall into two sub-types: the winter-sports centres and other sporting areas. At the winter-sports centres a variety of activities, such as skiing, skating, curling, tobogganing and climbing, attract the tourist. Many of these centres, *e.g.* Davos in Switzerland, began as health resorts, since the clear, dry mountain air and bright winter sunshine were health-giving. Under such invigorating conditions, the jaded body becomes refreshed, the mind relaxed; small wonder many people, time and money permitting, seek a mid-winter holiday in the Alps or some other mountain area. A point worth mentioning is the changed character of the modern tourist: not only is he more venturesome but he tends also to be much more active and prepared to exert himself physically. The winter-sports centres continue to flourish but their clientele is gradually changing—the upper class no longer enjoys a monopoly. Outstanding examples among the winter-sports centres are St Moritz, Gstaad, Klosters and Zermatt in Switzerland, Chamonix in France and Banff and Jasper in Canada.

Apart from the winter-sports centres, there are some centres which have become renowned as places associated with a particular sporting or recreational activities. At Cowes in the Isle of Wight there is a tourist centre which may fairly claim to be devoted almost exclusively to yachting. Poole, in Dorset, with its spacious sheltered harbour, has become another important centre of sailing. There are, of course, numerous seaside and scenic resorts which also share this popular activity, such as the Norfolk Broads, which every year attract thousands who love "messing about in boats."

Golf has become an important sporting activity. Many people participate in golfing holidays and a number of centres have gained an international reputation, *e.g.* St Andrews—its Royal and Ancient Club is the most celebrated golf club in the world—Gleneagles, situated in a beautiful valley in south Perthshire, and Turnberry in Ayrshire. There are very few other games which can claim to be almost purely a tourist attraction.

Certain areas are noted for their fishing facilities as, for instance, Deeside in Scotland and the Norfolk Broads. The safari holiday is of growing popularity, providing the tourist with the opportunity of seeing, and taking ciné pictures of, wild life in its natural habitat. Grouse-shooting in Scotland is also a well-organised attraction.

Watering Places

The eighteenth century was the great age of spas in England, but on the Continent they continued to flourish into the nineteenth century since they frequently became noted as much for gambling as for healing. Visits by royalty continued to maintain their popularity; for example,

Kaiser Wilhelm II visited Homburg, Napoleon III Plombières and Vichy and Edward VII Marianske Lazny (Marienbad). In the nineteenth century the spas received a new lease of life through their adoption of hydropathic treatment. Modern spas are more scientific and usually offer a wide range of sophisticated treatments ranging from massage and manipulative exercises to electrical and light treatments as well as the older practices of water drinking and immersion.

Gardens, music salons, recreative facilities, etc. have now added to the attraction of their curative functions and latterly some spas, such as Vichy, have made determined attempts to attract younger visitors by providing greater opportunities for sport. But water continues still to hold out its ancient promise of healing and rejuvenation and thousands make their pilgrimages to the spas every year thereby ensuring their continuing popularity. English spas have greatly declined in their importance and are by no means as popular as they were half a century ago; this is very largely because they have become centres of retirement for the elderly, genteel and wealthy and have seldom attempted to cater for younger people. On the Continent, however, they continue to flourish: Germany has over 200 spas and France over 50 principal watering places.

Historical–Cultural Centres

Frequently visitors here are of a more transient character than those visiting the pleasure resorts, and the centres themselves are seldom purely centres of tourism; though they may have important attractions for the tourist, such towns usually have other functions. Places of pilgrimage, ecclesiastical centres, educational centres and ancient cities with notable historical associations commonly fall into this category.

Outstanding are many capital cities of which London is perhaps the most conspicuous example, although Rome, Paris, Brussels, Athens and Vienna can all claim to be major centres of attraction. Each became the capital of its respective country as a result of significant geographical as well as historical influences. Inevitably as centres of government major cultural activities became focused in them which, together with their unrivalled shopping facilities, have caused them to become excellent tourist centres.

Religious centres and holy cities attract numerous visitors. As Hudson has written: "Jerusalem, an ancient fortress town as well as the historic centre of Judaism and an important seat of the Moslem faith, is probably today more of an administrative, commercial and educational town than a strategic base or holy city. Rome, the headquarters of the Roman Catholic Church, Benares, sacred to the Hindus, Amritsar, the hub of the Sikh religion, and the more recently established Salt Lake City, the leading city of the Mormon faith, are all notable pilgrimage centres, but their permanent populations today are more concerned with administration, trade and industry than with the practice of religious rites and the propagation of sacred beliefs. Mecca, the birthplace of Mohammedanism, remains a more purely religious city, but an even better example was, until recently, provided by Lhasa in Tibet, the transcendental monastic city. The reputations of many religious centres, *e.g.* Canterbury and Cîteaux, derive from the planting of early churches or abbeys on their sites. Others, like Lourdes, have acquired sanctity because of the visions observed there and the supposed miraculous value of their holy waters, or like Kandy, because of their religious relics (in that case a tooth of Buddha), or like Bethlehem, because of a holy birth. Canterbury, besides being the seat of the first English church, gained added importance as a place of pilgrimage when Thomas à Becket, canonised in 1172, was buried there."[29] Such religious centres, then, especially if they are located in attractive surroundings, stimulate a considerable tourist trade but "even the least significant of cathedral cities derive some benefit from tourists."[30]

As with religious centres, so with educational centres: secular culture is no longer the dominant function but their prestige as centres of learning, their delightful college precincts (as in the case of Cambridge), together with their museums, libraries and book shops, frequently attract the discriminating tourist. Places such as Oxford, Cambridge and St Andrews in Britain, Heidelburg, Marburg and Tübingen in Germany, Bologna in Italy and Salamanca in Spain are visited each year by thousands of people.

Then there are places such as Stratford-on-Avon with its close associations with Shakespeare or Haworth in the West Riding of Yorkshire, the home of the Brontës, which attract an endless stream of tourists.

Finally, there are the historic centres, ancient towns with their walls and fortifications, their castles and old houses, their narrow streets and winding ways, market crosses and ancient monuments, which exert a great fascination for many. Such places as Petra, Carthage, Aigues-Mortes, Carcassonne, Toledo and York, Chester, Warwick and Durham in England, are a "must" for many tourists.

PROBLEMS OF A RESORT: BLACKPOOL

Blackpool has been described as the foremost seaside resort in Britain; certainly only Brighton could hope to rival it. Blackpool was almost non-existent before the coming of the railway and even as late as 1871 it was only a small place of some 6000 inhabitants. In origin it was essentially a middle-class creation patronised by the prosperous industrialists and businessmen of Lancashire and the West Riding but after about 1870 it began to attract the working classes in ever-increasing numbers. Frank Singleton aptly described it as "a study in vitality" where "pleasure is offered, organised and insisted on."[31] Today, it is, after Brighton, the largest resort town in Britain with a resident population of 151,000. Incredibly, it has 32 million visitors each year!

Until the outbreak of war in 1939 Blackpool was prosperous and go-ahead (it was the first resort in the country to introduce illuminations to extend its season) and the Tower was not only a famous landmark but a symbol of the resort's pre-eminence. As with many other things, the war changed the established pattern of social behaviour and the resort began to lose its traditional clientele. Longer holidays, motorisation and new trends in holiday-making affected Blackpool just as they affected numerous other resorts. A recent report has revealed that the resort now appeals mainly to "the middle-aged working class," an image which does not commend itself to the city corporation.[32] It is realised that the resort, which is so dependent upon the holiday trade, cannot continue to look back on the good old days but must kindle afresh that vitality and showmanship which originally made Blackpool great. Certain develop-ments have already been proposed and effected; for example, a big new zoo near Stanley Park has recently been opened as an additional attrac-tion while a new modern super-pier of unorthodox design has been envisaged; also the redevelopment of the Tower site. But the problem lies less in creating new physical attractions than in clientele. Young people are the big money-spenders these days and Blackpool Corporation is seriously considering what action can be taken to attract younger people, for there is a growing realisation that unless Blackpool can attract young people its future as Britain's premier resort will be in jeopardy. A corporation decision to lift its ban on pop festivals is the first move to boost the resort's image.

Blackpool has other problems. In the height of the season when the resort is choked with tens of thousands of trippers, the promenade and streets are clogged with thousands of cars and traffic in and out of Blackpool is reduced to an irritating crawl. Enlarged and improved traffic facilities are not only desirable but essential. Another threat to the resort is the proposed closure of one of its railway lines. Proposals to close Blackpool North, the biggest and best of the resort's stations would be fiercely opposed by the Council and the holiday industry but the closing of the Kirkham–Blackpool South line, used by the Lytham St Annes commuters who travel to Manchester, would also be vigorously opposed. It seems very likely, however, that one or the other will be axed by British Rail since it is costing the taxpayer nearly £900,000 a year to keep both lines open. On the other hand, when the M6 Fylde Motorway link is built communications will be greatly improved.

Two other problems, common to many resorts, may be mentioned. Over one-quarter of the resident population is retired (in the adjacent resorts of Thornton Clevelys and Lytham St Annes the figure approaches one-third) while large numbers live in Blackpool but commute to Preston and Manchester. Again, there is seasonal unemployment and a lack of industrial and commercial opportunities to keep or attract young wage-earners. Traditionally the attitude of the Blackpool Council has been "the holiday industry comes first" but now determined efforts are being made to attract new light industries to the resort.

CONSERVATION OF URBAN AMENITIES

From any point of view, but particularly from that of the tourist, the important elements of amenity are traffic, open space, urban character and urban aesthetics. Unfortunately, tourism itself may be the ruin of cities. Konrad Smigielski, Leicester's chief planning officer, speaking at a British Tourist Authority conference in London in September, 1972, expressed the opinion that the pressures of tourism have degraded some cities to the point where tourists are greater polluters of the environment than industry. He drew attention to Rome where, he said "numerous coaches discharge . . . tourists from all over the world onto St Peter's Square, the most beautiful pedestrian piazza of Europe. Cars are allowed to park on the Campidoglio in Rome—a great tourist attraction, an open air space of supreme quality which was designed for the sole use of pedestrians." And of Amsterdam he said, "Once a gracious city with pedestrian promenades along its canals, today it is packed with double rows of parked cars, and is not worth visiting any more." Strong words these, but there is more than an element of truth in them: many beautiful and attractive towns are blighted by traffic problems and utterly spoiled by the need for large parking areas for motor cars. Jean Cocteau has said of Paris: "It used to be the agora [market place] of the world. Now, it has become a parking garage. . . ." But the tourist without his motor car is also a problem. Venice, for example, receives such an influx of visitors that the French architect Le

Corbusier has proposed the closure of the city to tourists, who would be admitted only in limited numbers upon the payment of an entrance fee and according to a strict timetable. London in a year now draws as many visitors as it has population—7 million. One way of coping with the flood of visitors to London was put to the 1972 B.T.A. Conference by Sir Desmond Plummer who suggested that racecourses and "other suitable sites" might be used as tent cities for tourists!

It is customary to think of the pollution created by motor vehicles as that of exhaust fumes and noise, but there is also "a sense in which the presence of motor vehicles, by their numbers, penetration and voracious demand for space, itself constitutes a form of pollution."[33] As motorisation increases—the number of vehicles almost quadrupled between 1950 and 1970, from 4·4 million to 15·2 million—cities are being strangled by their traffic-clogged streets. Every town and city in the country needs traffic-free precincts and more unobtrusive parking spaces, in some cases traffic might be prevented from entering certain areas, and in many instances towns could be avoided altogether by the construction of well-planned by-passes. Britain has been slow to adopt such devices, much slower than many Continental countries, although it would be foolish to pretend that the latter have solved all their traffic problems. If our towns are to be preserved as attractive and pleasant places, not only for tourists but also for the local inhabitants, something has got to be done.

Such open spaces as exist in towns should be assiduously preserved and any encroachment upon them most vigorously resisted. It is sad that in the post-war phase of town rebuilding, new structures have gone up on the old sites and on the old building-lines. A golden opportunity to create open spaces and wider roads in our town centres, not to mention underground car parks, has, all too often, been lost. The usual excuse is economic: towns cannot afford to lose rents.

It is frequently averred that all towns are beginning to look alike, that the same glass and concrete boxes masquerading as "architecture" mushroom everywhere, and that the individual character of towns and cities is rapidly disappearing. It is indeed depressing to see the environmental damage done to urban centres in the name of progress by high-level roads, new office blocks and the demolition of old buildings of character and value. Much greater care should be taken over new building and planners should concern themselves with the urban environment as a whole; as the report *How Do You Want to Live?* says: "A huge slab block might look reasonable in Brasilia or set against the hills of Hongkong, but it can look totally incongruous towering over attractive Edwardian buildings." Aldous in his book *Battle for the Environment* has emphasised the importance of looking at the urban environment as a whole. While formerly, he says, emphasis was placed upon the preservation of individual old buildings, with usually only an implied reference to the townscape of which it was a part, people are now beginning to realise that it is not enough to safeguard and cherish an individual building if its setting is completely changed. For example, a group of Tudor cottages or a Georgian terrace, however attractive or graceful in themselves can be utterly spoiled if a glossy supermarket is built alongside, a concrete office block overtowers them or their gardens are shorn away by widened thoroughfares. The group, or townscape, is in need of protection and enhancement, says Aldous, not merely individual buildings, no matter how much they are valued for their architectural merits or their historical connections.[34] However, the difficulty is that we shall soon reach a point where nothing more can be done to some towns.

Again, much can be done to rehabilitate intrinsically attractive but run-down areas and streets. Civic Trusts have often pioneered the way in urban renovation. Streets can be dramatically improved by barring traffic, removing signs, advertisements and other urban clutter, repainting them in carefully chosen colours, emphasising especially attractive features or introducing trees, window boxes or flower cradles. A particularly interesting case is New Walk in Leicester, a fine Georgian thoroughfare, three-quarters of a mile in length which had become grossly neglected and degraded but which, in five years, was completely transformed. "New Walk today is a different place," writes Aldous. "The City's expenditure was, for what it had achieved, surprisingly modest: £25,000 spent judiciously on putting down a replacement for the grim sea of asphalt—new red tarmac broken by lateral strips of paving; repairing and replacing the Victorian street lamps and railings: getting rid of vandal-proof but ugly ... concrete seats, chicken wire and broken-down hedges and fences; and planting trees and grass."[35] The process of decline was halted and pushed into reverse and property owners have begun to take a pride in their properties, restoring, repairing and repainting them. To quote Aldous again: "The public now use and enjoy New Walk as it was meant to be. On any fine day at lunchtime, it is full of strolling groups and couples. They come and sit and eat their lunch, or just use it as a pleasant, traffic-free route through town. Vandalism continues, but much abated. There are more people around, and ... elegant, attractive surroundings command a certain respect—just as rundown surroundings invite abuse.... New Walk,

Leicester, so nearly one of conservation's defeats, stands out today as a victory and an object lesson."[36]

NOTES

1. *International Tourism*, Hutchinson, 1969, p. 157.
2. *Ibid.*
3. *The Spas of England and Principal Sea-Bathing Places*, 1841.
4. *The Geography of Recreation and Leisure*, Hutchinson, 1972, p. 36.
5. "The Holiday Industry and Seaside Towns in England and Wales," *Festschrift Leopold G. Scheidl zum 60 Geburstag*, Wien.
6. *The Geography of Towns*, Hutchinson, 1953, p. 29.
7. *Op. cit.*, p. 50.
8. Peters, *op. cit.*, p. 157.
9. F. S. Hudson, *A Geography of Settlements*, Macdonald & Evans, 1970, p. 215.
10. *Op. cit.*, p. 39.
11. *Op. cit.*, pp. 29–30.
12. *Idem*, p. 49.
13. A. Robinson, "Towns Beside the Seaside," *Geographical Magazine*, Vol. XLV September, 1973, pp. 877–85.
14. *The Planning of the Coastline*, Countryside Commission, H.S.M.O., 1970, p. 18.
15. Smailes, *op. cit.*, p. 130.
16. *The English Channel*, Collins, 1959, p. 327.
17. Robinson, *op. cit.*
18. *British Townscapes*, Arnold, 1965, p. 114.
19. Johns, *op. cit.*, p. 76.
20. *Ibid.*
21. *Ibid.*
22. Johns, *op. cit.*, p. 116.
23. F. Singleton, *Lancashire and the Pennines*, Batsford, 1952, p. 42.
24. *Land and Leisure*, David & Charles, 1970, p. 77.
25. *Op. cit.*, p. 81.
26. *Ibid.*
27. *Op. cit.*, p. 37.
28. *The Pleasures of Architecture*, revised edition 1954, Cape, p. 200.
29. *The Geography of Settlements*, pp. 205–7.
30. Hudson, *op. cit.*, p. 207.
31. *Op. cit.*, p. 42.
32. *North-West Tourist Board Report*, 1972.
33. T. Aldous, *Battle for the Environment*, Fontana, 1972, p. 43.
34. *Op. cit.*, p. 146.
35. *Idem*, p. 174.
36. *Idem*, p. 175.

Chapter XII

The Tourist and the Countryside

THE RESOURCES OF THE COUNTRYSIDE

A L L areas of the countryside are the result of two factors or influences: natural and human; there are few areas where the landscape remains in its natural condition untouched by the hand of man. The degree to which the natural landscape has been altered by man depends to a very large extent upon its location, accessibility and utility. The physical conditions of the landscape—its form, shape and colour, its water element, its flora and fauna—are the outcome basically of the geological and climatic conditions. Sir Dudley Stamp in his book *Britain's Structure and Scenery* drew attention to the fact that the British Isles epitomised in miniature the geological history of the earth and that this geological spectrum was in no small measure responsible for the extremely varied, if small-scale, physical conditions and scenery. It is these landscape miniatures which provide the British Isles with such varied scenery and which charm the foreign visitor. The landscape is never so vast as to become monotonous and satiate the viewer.

The geography of the British Isles is the unique product of a long human, as well as physical, history and man's activities and interferences have played a part in the shaping and character of the land. The pattern of fields, the patches of woodland, the hedgerows of the south, the walls of the north, the stately mansions, the hamlets and villages, the ruins of castles and monasteries, the standing stones and circles, the bridges and roads, the windmills and waterwheels, are all the outward visible sign of man's impact on the natural landscape. Professor W. G. Hoskins in his delightful study *The Making of the English Landscape* has shown how the land is a palimpsest, and that its cultural features are the handiwork of many men through long centuries.

John Drinkwater in his *Robinson of England* described felicitously the essential quality of: "a landscape that was moderate. . . . Not moderate in its beauty, which was infinitely tender and varied, but in scale and sensationalism. There were no longest rivers or highest mountains or broadest lakes, no uncharted deserts or impenetrable forests, no iron-bound frosts or torrid heats. It was an equable, friendly landscape from end to end of which one could walk without difficulty or danger. Green fields and a silver stream with willows, pines on the crest of a little hill, smooth downs cropped by sheep to their sea-margins, crooked lanes with tall hedges, rooks in the elm-tops, mill pools with the trout rising, copses yellow with primroses, valleys of fruit blossom and small acres of golden sheaves, quiet villages with a steeple and a bar, these were the features of a countryside whose loveliness still defied the great outcrop of urban development." [1] The British Isles have no Matterhorn, no Grand Canyon, no Iguassu Falls, no Kruger National Park but they do have gentle, green and homely landscapes.

Sir Francis Younghusband declared in the 1920s that it was one of the duties of the geographer to undertake the analytical study of beauty in scenery. Most geographers, by the very nature of their training, are alive to the beauty of scenery be it raw and natural or artificial and man-made but few have turned their hand to the analysis of landscape beauty. Vaughan Cornish was an exception and spent much of the later years of his life investigating the problem. [2] He attempted to establish the principles of the subject of aesthetic geography and illustrated their application to the essentially practical matter of the preservation of beauty in town and country.

Dr Bracey, discussing the tourist, says: "they seek out the beauties of nature as well as the masterpieces of man's art and craftsmanship." [3] That man is aesthetically starved and has a basic craving for the beauty of nature is suggested by his mass exodus into the countryside on fine days and his predeliction, if he can afford it, for a home in a rural or semi-rural environment. The motor car has, of course, made both possible but "the townsman on his excursions sometimes desecrates the country that he loves, but whose economy and necessities he does not understand" [4] while his desire to escape from urban imprisonment leads him to build in rural areas where very often "through bad design or clumsy siting he . . . spoils a part of the countryside for others." [5] This is the conflict which modern planners are attempting to resolve. Amenity and recreation are inescapably linked with the countryside and though they frequently conflict this does not mean that they need necessarily do so. The attributes of the countryside—space, beauty, quiet, wildlife—could be preserved for the enjoyment of all.

The treasures of the countryside fall into three principal categories:

(*i*) *natural* treasures, geological or physiographic features of particular interest, rare plants and animals and ecological features deemed worthy of preservation and areas of special scenic appeal;

(*ii*) *man-made*, pre-historic sites (camps, earthworks), ancient monuments (stone circles, monoliths, historic buildings and ruins, and monuments and memorials), and features of industrial archaeological interest;

(*iii*) *allusive*, those places possessing historic, biographical, artistic and literary associations.

All these are not only a part of the national heritage worthy of preservation and conservation but often also a great source of attraction to the foreigner and of special relevance to tourism.

MAN'S USE OF THE COUNTRYSIDE

What does the tourist consumer want from the country? what use does he make of it? His demands and his uses fall into five main categories. (*i*) The holiday-maker frequently desires space, quiet and the peace of nature for the refreshment of body and mind; this helps to explain why so many love wilderness country and tramp the lonely fells, why so many are attracted by farmhouse and village holidays. The pressures of modern life are such that many turn to the countryside for tranquillity, rest and recuperation: it is an escape, a return to sanity, an environment for rejuvenation. (*ii*) A fine day or weekend will entice urbanites in their hundreds of thousands to the country. The motor car and coach have made the sight-seeing tour a possibility and there are many who explore Wales, the Yorkshire Dales, the Border Country and the Highlands of Scotland in this way. There are many motorists indeed who will travel quite considerable distances to some vantage point giving wide-spreading views and, having arrived, will do no more than wind down the car window; but they are content, relaxing, taking in the view. (*iii*) Outdoor activities and holidays have been growing in popularity, these are very dependent upon the countryside: hunting, shooting, fishing, pony-trekking, canoeing, sailing, gliding, climbing, potholing, etc. It would seem that ever-increasing demands will be put on the rural environment for sporting activities and facilities as the amount of leisure time and disposable income increases. (*iv*) Considerable use is made of the countryside for educational reasons. There are many who are deeply interested in "the scenery of civilisation," as Vaughan Cornish termed it; the remains of the past—megalithic monuments, Roman remains, medieval castles, monastic sites, old churches and many features of industrial archaeology. There are others fascinated by great country houses, ancient market towns and rural architecture for "one of the pleasures of travelling in England is the crossing of geological boundaries into new scenery and to fresh styles in ancient architecture."[6] There are yet others who botanise or bird-watch, who put brush to canvas, drawing inspiration from nature's contours, colour and light, or who enjoy a flirtation with an archaeological site. (v) Finally, and increasingly, man is beginning to use the country for "second homes" whether these be permanently sited caravans or country cottages.

PRESSURES AND PROBLEMS

If there were vast spaces of country available for use, the pressure on the countryside would be greatly reduced but not necessarily entirely eliminated. Accessibility, volume of visitors and frequency of visits are the three main problems. Many of the most attractive areas are near to large urban concentrations and so feel the weight of the urban exodus at weekends. The second factor relates to the volume of visitors. An environment can absorb a small number of visitors and create no real problem but not a huge influx. Damage in terms of footpath wear and tear, walls knocked down, grass trampled, wild flowers picked, not to mention litter left behind, may be very substantial.

This environmental damage is aggravated by frequency of visits: if pressure is regular and heavy the flora and fauna have little or no chance of regeneration, walls cannot be patched up, paths repaired or litter collected and before long the ecological balance is completely disrupted, the natural drainage disturbed and erosion promoted. And if the land happens to be farmed, broken fences and walls may cause animals to stray, broken glass and other litter may cause injury to animals, growing crops may be badly damaged and water supplies polluted.

Table 27 shows the growth of membership of societies closely linked with environmental pressure.

TABLE 27
Growing membership of societies

	1950	1960	1968	1971
Royal Society for the Protection of Birds	6,500 (1951)	14,200 (1961)	41,260	87,448
County Naturalists Trusts	825	3,006	33,272	58,000 (end 1970)
National Trust	25,000	95,000	160,000	278,277
Caravan Club	11,000 (1951)	44,000 (1961)	95,276	100,000
Camping Club of Great Britain	13,800	52,000	120,000	111,000 (1970)
Royal Yachting Association	2,380	10,543	26,327	34,419

Source: Geographical Magazine, October, 1973, p. 42.

It would seem that if such environmental pressure is to be relieved, careful planning and management of the more popular areas is required. It may be possible to channel traffic, to divert it or disperse it; it may be desirable to restrict entry or movement of cars; it may be helpful to provide car parks at particular locations or camping sites or picnic spots. In the successful management of any area it is important that its resource capacity is very carefully assessed since user pressure bears a close relationship to capacity: the greater the variety of its resources, the greater, in general, is its capacity to absorb the pressure.

SECOND HOMES

The boom in second-home buying is the outcome of a number of factors: increased family incomes, increased car ownership, more leisure time and a wish to escape from the pressures of urban life.

No comprehensive survey, and therefore no precise figures, of second homes in Britain are available. Professor Wibberley has made a sample study for the Countryside Commission which was published in 1973.[7] Ian Martin, a county planner for Denbighshire, made an estimate that 7 per cent of the rural homes in Wales—a total of some 8700—belong to weekenders.[8] It would be unwise to take this percentage as being representative of Britain as a whole; all that may be said is that second-home ownership is increasing. Information about second homes in some other developed countries is more precise and Clout has written: "Sweden contains 500,000 second homes, with one urban family in every five having a country cottage. The proportion is similar in France where there are 1,600,000 second homes. Over 3,000,000 families in the U.S.A. (5 per cent of the total) own purpose-built second homes."[9]

Clout, discussing the problem of where people seek second homes, says: "Experience in Europe and North America as well as in Britain shows that three types of location are particularly popular for second homes: countryside within easy access of large cities (the Weald and other parts of South-Eastern England, the Peak District, north and central Wales); the coastline (East Anglia, the West Country and many other areas); and remote upland regions with attractive scenery, such as parts of the Pennines and the Scottish Highlands, which are too distant for weekend visits but attract summer occupants."[10] The Crofters' Commission is having to deal increasingly with applications from Englishmen for second homes in the Highlands. Such people are doomed to be disappointed, however, since crofts are reserved for *bona fide* farmers who are prepared to pay £50 a year for their small-holding and work it in accordance with ancient Scottish crofting law. Nevertheless, there are many cottages in Scotland which are not reserved in this way and are open for purchase by anyone.

Local authority grants can be obtained for renovating old property and the building societies have been prepared to grant second mortgages. The opening up of the country through motorway construction has also made long-distance travel easy and quick, so that distance nowadays is not the inhibiting factor it was even a short time ago.

The proliferation of second homes has produced important socio-economic problems. It is alleged that the buying up of rural properties by town-dwellers denies the local population, *e.g.* young married couples, the chance to acquire a home in their own locality, especially since the demand has led to an inflation in property values. There is much truth in this, although it should also be remembered that many dilapidated cottages, which would never have been considered as possible homes by the local residents, have been bought, renovated, almost rebuilt, by outsiders. Often, too, such properties lie remote and out of the way and would never be occupied by local people. Even so, the pressure from the town-dweller for a cottage in the country must accelerate the trend that is driving the countryman from the countryside.

Another problem lies in the threat to rural community life. Most town-based property owners visit their countryside second homes only at weekends or for a few weeks during the summer months; hence many villages are largely dead for most of the week and for the greater part of the year. The villages come into life on Friday evening and relapse into somnolence again on Sunday evening when the temporary residents trek back to the towns. "Comers in," as they are often called, may also tend to undermine and destroy local culture—dialect, customs, ways of life, etc. "Welsh culture, already weakened by decades of depopulation," says Clout, "was threatened by further dilution by the temporary invasion of the English. Fears for the cultural distinctiveness of rural Wales heighten the problems surrounding this important form of rural/urban interaction. Such emotions are probably not experienced quite so powerfully in any other part of Britain, but invasion by 'outsiders' and increases in property prices are matters of general concern." [11]

The new, second homes built in villages and hamlets may be out of keeping with the local style of building, either in style or material, and so destroy the natural harmony of the settlement. Many villages, it is true, are protected, but there are many cases where the damage has already been done. There is a stage beyond this which so far is only embryonic in Britain; if we may quote Clout again: "Britain, with a predominance of old properties that have been restored for occasional use, has reached only an early stage in second-home development. In the U.S.A. the emphasis has shifted to specially constructed, single-family homes sited either in isolation or on estates of second homes which have been developed in coastal and mountain areas, and around lakes and reservoirs.... In 1970–71 one-half of American second-home buyers chose to purchase lots or houses in planned recreational developments. A number of planners in Britain advocate a similar policy to cater for the growing demand for second homes. Estate development minimises costs involved in installing piped water and sewerage systems, avoids widespread visual degradation and permits sports facilities and other services to be provided. However, it recreates an 'urban' type of environment which, in the past at least, was what most second-home occupants were trying to escape from." [12]

So far we have been concerned with the unfortunate and undesirable effects of second-home developments, but we should also recognise some of the advantages. Large numbers of individual rural properties, even entire hamlets and villages, have been saved from decay and possible extinction and have been carefully, often expensively, renovated. Second-home occupants also bring distinct economic advantages to the countryside. The purchase of goods and services brings extra income to local stores and additional employment. A Denbighshire study estimates that the owners of the 8700 second properties in Wales spent £4·2m annually; the survey also showed that weekend families spent an average of £10 at each weekend visit, and an average of £27 during a week-long visit. Such figures clearly indicate a considerable injection of economic capital into the countryside; and many depressed rural areas benefit very considerably. The social repercussions should not be overlooked either. The temporary residents bring often more sophisticated ways of life with them into the country. While many rural folk, especially the more elderly and conservative, resent the "comers-in," the younger element often welcome the weekenders who bring a touch of gaiety and zestful living with them. Such contact, not only with the "outsiders" but also with their material possessions, may lead to the disenchantment of young country folk with rural life and tempt them to migrate to the towns which offer better wages and greater social attractions.

THE FRAMEWORK OF COUNTRYSIDE CONTROL

As more and more people are using the countryside for tourism, recreation and leisure pursuits, two somewhat contradictory issues emerge: first, the growing concern about access to open spaces, common land and forest areas and, second, the anxiety over landscape preservation and the conservation of amenities. At first sight, it would seem that these two issues are incompatible, but this is not necessarily so. Dr Bracey has described the *Countryside Act* of 1968 as the townsman's charter for the greater use of the countryside for recreation [13] and while this is very desirable there are two implicit constraints: that this increased use shall not be to the detriment of the countryside and the claims of country people, and that this increased use shall be carefully monitored and controlled and the countryside adequately managed to ensure that the amenities of the countryside are fully protected and conserved.

Prince Philip has said: "The quickest way to destroy the countryside is through ignorance, neglect, apathy and exploitation." [14] Two solutions would, therefore, seem to present themselves: people, especially townspeople, must be educated in the use, value and problems of the countryside, and there must be planning and management of its extended use for recreational purposes. As Bracey says "Britain enjoys, or is cursed by ... what is probably the most comprehensive and highly organised system of land-use planning in the world and one which is, rightly or wrongly, the envy of many foreign countries." [15] Concerning the aspect of education there is still much to be done, although many are now aware of the need to treat the countryside with care and respect.

Town and country planning in Britain falls into two categories: development planning and development control, the former involving the preparation of plans and schemes, relating to the use to which land may be put, by local planning authorities, *i.e.* the counties and county boroughs, the latter being concerned with the detail of planning and with the granting or refusal of planning permission by the responsible planning authority. Planning has been in operation in Britain for a quarter of a century, and planning policy has tended to be one of negative rather than positive control, not very imaginative and forward-looking, but without the restrictive planning controls of the post-war years there would have been great inroads into, and much highly undesirable development in, the countryside.

With reference to future land-use planning, Bracey has written: "All evidence suggests that pressures on the countryside arising from changes in social factors affecting land use between now and the end of the century will increase in staggering degree: one-third increase in total population, fourfold increase in car ownership, a substantial increase in average income per head and an undetermined increase in the desire to live and/or seek recreation in the countryside. Agriculture and forestry will, no doubt, remain the largest single users of land in rural areas, but we can expect to see more and more land demanded for motorways, gas and electricity fuel transmission [and] ... power stations, industrial plants and places for active recreation."[16] In view of this escalation and the increasing demands upon what is after all a relatively limited land resource, will the planning system we have in Britain, which has coped reasonably effectively with the relatively limited pressures of the past quarter of a century, be able to meet and master the immeasurably greater pressures of the next quarter century?

Let us now turn our attention to some aspects of rural land-use which have been the subject of parliamentary enactments and special development controls. Until the *Royal Commission on Common Land* was set up in 1955, no one knew precisely how much common land remained in England and Wales. The Commission reported that about $1\frac{1}{2}$ million acres existed, rather more than two-thirds of it in England (most of it with the exceptions of Devon, Hampshire and Surrey in northern counties) and was spread over 4,515 separate units, but Wales generally had a much higher percentage of land in each county as common land. Some 10 per cent of all commons in England was used for amenity and recreation purposes. Both Bracey and Patmore have useful discussions on the many difficulties and problems pertaining to common land. Common land is a most valuable recreational resource, but, as Wager found out, it is mostly used, from the recreational point of view, in a casual way, *e.g.* for car-parking, picnicking, walking and the occasional playing of games;[17] in other words, it is used informally by the public for simple, unorganised outdoor recreation. Basically the commons are simply open spaces, though some may possess special attributes, *e.g.* they may have scenic attractions, as do some village greens, or features of archaeological or historical interest.

In appearance much of the English landscape seems well-wooded but this is really an optical illusion produced by the tree-lined hedgerows. Britain, indeed, is one of the least wooded countries in Europe with only about $4\frac{1}{2}$ million acres or some 8 per cent of the area under forest and woodland. Despite its small extent, it is very important—think of the rich greens of spring and the autumnal colours—and the woodlands also provide a valuable recreational resource. Woodlands are coming under increasing pressure for recreational purposes and areas such as the Forest of Dean attract large numbers of trippers and tourists; it is estimated that on a fine summer's day as many as 100,000 people visit the New Forest. Formerly, it was not part of the Forestry

Commission's job to provide amenities for visitors although it did recognise that some people might wish to enjoy the peace and quiet of the forests and began to make some provision for them; as a result, today some 5 million people use Commission land annually. There are eight national forest parks, the first of which was established in 1936, and comprise 430,000 acres; they offer a wide range of facilities including bird-watching, fishing, pony-trekking, forest walks, nature trails, as well as car parks, picnic spots and camping sites (used by nearly half a million campers annually). "One of the great advantages of the use of forests for recreation," says Peter Garthwaite "is their capacity to absorb and hide a large number of people and their cars, tents, caravans and the facilities for them—huts, toilets, car parks. Visitors, in numbers that would wreck the visual amenities of wild, open country, can be accepted into forested areas without damage. But to be acceptable to visitors the forests must be managed in a way that creates or perpetuates landscape values. Those who come to the forest to camp, walk, ride, rest or climb, study nature or otherwise enjoy themselves, react unconsciously to the forest environment." [18]

Although Yellowstone Park was established in the United States in 1892, it was not until 1949, when the *National Parks and Access to the Countryside Act* was passed, that positive action was taken in Britain. Between 1951 and 1957 ten National Parks were designated in England and Wales; all were extensive areas of beautiful, relatively wild and, with the exception of Pembrokeshire, upland country. Together they make up nearly 10 per cent of the area of England and Wales, 13,365 km^2 (5258 sq. miles). A Cambrian Mountains Park in mid-Wales has been suggested and there are some who would like to see the Norfolk Broads area and the South Downs accepted as additional Parks. Provision of National Parks in Scotland has been delayed so far. The point should be made that the National Parks of England and Wales differ greatly from many of the National Parks established abroad which frequently were set up principally as nature or game reserves.

"1. They comprise [says Bracey] huge areas of virgin land, especially in the American and African continents.

2. In almost all foreign national parks the land has been appropriated by, or already belonged to, the respective national or state Governments.

3. Considerable emphasis is given to providing facilities for recreation and enjoyment in addition to a basic concern for wild-life conservation." [19]

National Parks
Areas of outstanding natural beauty
Heritage coast

0   km   150
0   miles   100

Northumberland

Lake District

Yorkshire Dales

North York Moors

Peak District

Snowdonia

Pembroke-shire Coast

Brecon Beacons

Exmoor

Dartmoor

Fig. 12.—*National Parks and Areas of Outstanding Natural Beauty in England and Wales.* The map shows the ten National Parks, the Areas of Outstanding Natural Beauty, and the Heritage Coasts of England and Wales.

Britain's ten national parks attract some 25 million visitors annually (*see* Fig. 12). The Parks, however, face various pressures and have a number of problems. Since they include "not only farms and towns but industrial establishments; and the land within them is privately owned,"[20] there are to begin with very varied interests at stake. One of the basic premises of John Dower's Report (1945) was that established farming use should be effectively maintained and over a quarter of a million people live and work in the Parks in farming, forestry and rural industries. Clearly there will be problems of access to, and use of, the countryside which often conflict with farming. Another problem relates to industrial and kindred developments which have affected the Parks. The Ramblers' Association have listed numerous developments, including power stations, cement works, a potash mine, reservoirs, defence installations, radio masts, road widening schemes and caravan sites, which have intruded into areas of great natural beauty and designed for peace and quiet and the Association claims that the Parks have fallen short of the objectives for which they were established. They have also claimed that the Parks are being invaded by the motor car and have urged that drastic control measures should be taken. The majority of motorists who visit the Parks merely drive around and enjoy the scenery and pose no great threat to the farming and rural communities except through their sheer numbers, although a minority may act destructively and be a nuisance.

Finally, there is the problem of the administration and financing of the National Parks. Sir Jack Longland has argued (*Longland Report* on the future of the National Parks) that if the National Parks are to be effective and not subject to interference from county councils and commercial developers, they must have a much greater degree of autonomy and he has recommended that each Park should be managed by its own autonomous planning authority. "The days are long past," says Christopher Hall, Secretary of the Ramblers' Association, "when the Parks could be left to preserve themselves. Only ... a career national parks service can enable them to meet increasing public demand on their space while still preserving their beauty and dwindling remoteness. But no such service is possible while national park planning remains a part-time job for county staff."[21] The Peak Park, by far the most successful in terms of planning, management and information services, offers an approximation to the ideal model which could well be adopted for all. Furthermore, the parsimony which has characterised National Park care and maintenance should be ended and a substantial increase in the total resources devoted to the Parks be made.

As the motorised population grows and as the motorway network spreads and makes areas more accessible, the pressure on the Parks will continue to grow and there are many who believe that something ought to be done now to safeguard our Parks before it is too late. One suggestion, which has much to commend it, is that certain areas—core areas—within the Parks should be "cordoned off"; in other words, these core areas, often mountainous or wild waste, should be forbidden to the motor car, rendered accessible only to the walker and placed out-of-bounds to any form of commercial enterprise. Only by such stringent measures, it is claimed, will the natural beauty and tranquillity be kept sacrosanct and the landscape preserved from degradation. Such areas—the High Peak, Snowdon, the central Lake District, central Dartmoor—would be cherished and rendered as inviolate as it is possible to make them.

AREAS OF OUTSTANDING NATURAL BEAUTY

In addition to the National Parks there are other areas of variable size which have been officially designated Areas of Outstanding Natural Beauty. In England and Wales there are thirty-two A.O.N.B.s covering more than 14,245 km^2 (5500 sq. miles); they include areas of mountain, fell and dale, cliffs, sand-dunes and tidal flats, with woods and wildlife, historic remains and delightful villages. A further ten areas have been proposed for designation but still awaited official ratification in 1973. While in theory the A.O.N.B.s are protected against desecration and creeping industrial development, in practice there is little real protection and insidious exploitation and spoliation continues. Swift and effective action is needed if these choice areas of countryside (*see* Appendix II) are to be saved; delay may mean they will be violated beyond redemption and our heritage countryside lost for ever.

ENCROACHMENT ON THE COUNTRYSIDE

Travelling in Britain, one is often surprised at the amount of open, rural country still remaining. In spite of industrialisation, urbanisation and communications there remain ample areas of country. However, we should heed the rate at which the rural areas are being encroached upon. Urban expansion and the creation of new towns since 1945 have taken a sizeable area, and it has been estimated that the motorway programme has been responsible for the loss of countryside equivalent in area to the county of Dorset.

Take Dartmoor, for instance. Dartmoor is a splendid area of wilderness and farming country and when it was designated a National Park in 1951 most lovers of the area believed that it would be protected from further encroachments—for there had already been many—on its natural beauty. But the "creeping appropriation" did not end and, as Sylvia Sayer has written, "wild Dartmoor is still anything but safe. No honest description of this national park can ignore this unhappy fact. Dartmoor's natural character has actually suffered more erosion and serious threat since its designation as a national park than ever before. Since designation, it has had imposed upon it the 230-m television mast on Hessary Tor; the ... construction of a vast network of [military] roads on northern Dartmoor bringing hordes of cars into its wildest area; the stepping-up of military activities generally, low-flying jet aircraft and helicopters; the Taw Marsh pumping station; commercial afforestation of the moor by private forestry syndicates combined with widespread felling of natural valley woodlands; the new fencing and ploughing of open moorland ['improvement' again]; the spreading growth of substandard speculative building in the villages; the china clay mining expansion; the particularly indefensible Meldon reservoir; the rising and ineffectively controlled tide of motor vehicles—cars, lorries, coaches, mobile canteens, caravans—jamming the ancient lanes and trespassing on to the open moorland.... More major waterworks [are planned], and an Okehampton bypass totally destructive of rare and splendid landscape. The metal mining speculators hover just around the corner."[21] Similar encroachments have been made on the natural beauty of the North York Moors, *e.g.* the Fylingdales early warning complex, potash mining on the coast and the threat of a reservoir in Rosedale.

In densely peopled countries, such as England, where there is a limited amount of land and many claims upon it, great vigilance is needed to ensure that right and proper use is made. Since, it is estimated, some 800,000 ha (2 million acres) will be needed for new towns by the end of the century together with over 200,000 ha (half a million acres) for motorways, not to to mention water supply undertakings and new or extended airfields, it becomes obvious that some very careful planning (and some stringent controls) is required. Already some 20,000 ha (50,000 acres) are being lost annually, land that is valuable agriculturally or scenically, for suburbia, industrial development, reservoirs, roads, etc. Although the Council for the Preservation of Rural England battles to keep the land green and unsullied it does not always win the fight: lost causes include I.C.I.'s reservoir at Cow Green in Yorkshire, the 1600 ha (4000 acres) earmarked for flooding at Empingham, Rutland, the 240 ha (600 acres) at Bovey Tracey, Dartmoor, taken over by a ball-clay works, and of the potash-mining developments on the north Yorkshire coast. The real difficulty, of course, lies in putting a hard economic value on losses of this kind, of balancing ". . . the profit of doing something with the erosion of peace and quiet, beauty and so on that it will cause. . . . I.C.I. wanted to build a reservoir in this Yorkshire moor [Cow Green] to provide water for a new factory. It meant jobs, products, profits, exports—all computable in an accountant's balance sheet. It also meant drowning some rare Alpine plants, the last survivors of the Ice Age. Opponents of the scheme could put no hard value on these; all they could say was that their loss would be like knocking down a cathedral or burning a Shakespeare first folio. They lost. Similarly, how do you compare the risks of shattering the stained glass of Chartres or waking up babies in the night with the profits and quick-travel advantages of Concorde? Or the wonder of a child seeing a butterfly for the first time against the cash value of using insecticides?"[22]

USE OF WATER AREAS

If we *must* use precious land for afforestation, water supplies or anything else, we should also try to see if they can be put to dual or multi-purpose use. For example, there are many lakes and reservoirs and even inundated gravel pits and disused canals which could be put to good recreational use. Although water authorites in the past were rather chary about allowing public access to their catchment areas for fear of contamination, this is an inadmissable fear nowadays and the reservoirs could be opened up for recreational purposes. The Goyt Valley experiment showed how a happy marriage could be arranged. The Goyt Valley in the Peak District National Park was flooded by the Stockport and District Water Board to provide water supplies but, at the same time, the Board undertook a "sensitive treatment of the landscape" for which it won a Civic Trust Award.[23] Previously the valley, though attractive, lay rather off the beaten track and was not much visited. However, after the scheme was finished, large numbers of visitors began to threaten its beauty and tranquillity. Accordingly, an experiment was tried: cars were denied free access but parking spaces were provided; special minibuses took visitors into the valley; and marked walks were tracked out. The whole experiment proved to be a success and showed what could be done with a little careful management. Some Water Boards, notably the Bristol Waterworks Company, have encouraged the recreational use of the water areas under their control but the majority of water undertakings have tended to drag their feet in this matter. Even as far back as 1948, the *Heneage Committee* recommended that sailing should be permitted on domestic water supply reservoirs subject to water board discretion and adequate control but relatively few authorities even today allow sailing on their reservoirs: in 1966 only 20 out of 75 authorities permitted it. In recent years the pressure for sailing facilities has increased and the growing number of sailing clubs are finding difficulty in procuring suitable stretches of water for their activities. Greater use should, and could, be made of reservoirs for recreational boating, especially since they often provide excellent conditions and are often near to the towns.

Disused clay and gravel pits which have become filled with water could, in many cases, be used for water-based recreational activities. The immediate environs of many of these ground holes are unattractive and frequently untidy but with a little ingenuity and landscaping they could be made visually attractive and pleasant places for sailing, fishing, bird-watching, etc.

Some 4800 km (3000 miles) of navigable canals and waterways, relics of Britain's industrial revolution, link the four great estuaries of England and stretch across the heart of the country (*see* Fig. 13). Intended to serve the growing industrial towns, they nevertheless traverse wide areas of pleasant rural country. Since, because of their restricted width and their locks, they would appear to have only a very minor role to play in the future transport system—many of the canals have indeed already fallen into disuse—the time has come to use them for other purposes. Colin Buchanan has said: "as a recreational asset the waterways have enormous potential for a variety of open air pursuits—boating, angling, walking and natural history. And they are full of interest to anyone concerned with our industrial history."[24] Already the movement to realise the recreational assets of the waterway network has begun. The Inland Waterways Association fosters public interest in the waterway network, while many local societies and clubs work to restore the canals or try to prevent others from falling into decay. For example, in Huddersfield, a private venture has turned Aspley Basin, the old canal wharf, into a small pleasant marina.

The British Waterways Board is responsible for some 3200 km (2000 miles) of canals in Britain but some 2575 km (1600 miles) is either disused or barely used commercially. Much of this disused mileage is unnavigable either in whole or in part. To keep the commercially unused canals clear, clean and navigable for pleasure craft

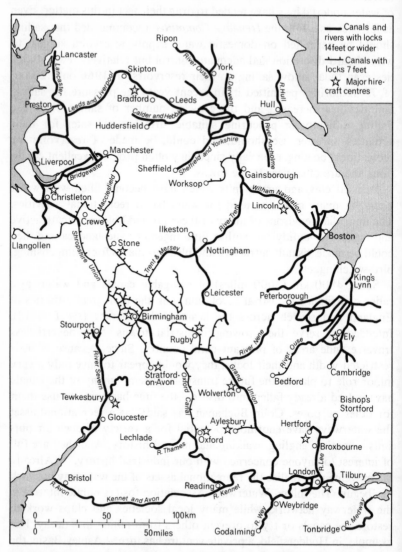

Fig. 13.—*Inland waterways.* There are many hundreds of miles of inland waterways—rivers and canals—which are negotiable by craft and offer excellent opportunities for recreation and leisure pursuits and for holiday cruising. In addition, there are, of course, the Norfolk Broads not shown on this map.

entails a heavy financial burden. Although certain charges are levied for the use of the canals by pleasure craft and although this income could be considerably increased as a result of greater use, the income would fall far short of maintenance costs and the Board inevitably would require Governmental financial assistance. It has been estimated that something of the order of £1m annually would be needed to keep the canals open for recreation and amenity. But in view of the manifold uses to which the canals could be put and the growing demand for recreational facilities, the sum required may be judged not unreasonable. Buchanan concludes: "There cannot be the slightest doubt that Britain will eventually need every mile of this ... pattern of waterways to assist in the provision of worthwhile recreational outlets.... Further decay of this invaluable national asset must be halted by any means possible."[25]

THE BROADS

The Broads comprise some 320 km (200 miles) of intercommunicating inland waterways based upon the rivers Waveney, Yare, Bure, Ant and Thurne, although many of the channels and wide stretches of shallow water are the handiwork of man, the outcome of the excavation of peat in earlier times. To this area each year come 100,000 holiday-makers but the numbers of tourists as well as the craft—some 2000 cabin-hire craft and 8000 privately owned boats—increases annually and an environmental problem is beginning to emerge for the space, beauty, peace and quiet and wildlife are being threatened. The increasing popularity of Broadland is resulting in overcrowding and many lovers of this unique corner of England fear that its natural attractiveness will be destroyed. The real threat to Broadland, however, probably comes less from accelerating numbers of holiday-makers and craft as from the insidious side-effects of the use of the waterways.

At one time the majority of craft were sailing boats but these have been almost totally displaced by power-driven vessels. The latter, together with their increased size and not infrequently inefficient hull design, not only churn up the bottom mud and keep it in a state of constant suspension but create excessive wash which damages the banks. The agitated muddy water kills off fish and steadily chokes the vegetation which provides the habitat for wildlife. In addition, spillage of oil and other pollutants poison the water to the detriment of fish and fowl alike. Increased litter, noise and vandalism though perhaps less serious, all assist in the degradation of the environment.

In an attempt to face the problem of overcrowding, it has been suggested that the Broads should be enlarged. It is claimed, probably correctly, that the waterways are being reduced each year as a result of natural processes and induced silting and some stretches have been almost entirely overgrown. A campaign has begun for the re-opening of 40 km (25 miles) of abandoned navigation which would add appreciably to the existing waterways and, besides alleviating the congestion elsewhere on the Broads, would bring the tourist trade to Aylsham, Bungay and North Walsham.

Commercial interests, such as the hire-craft owners, hoteliers and shopkeepers, oppose any limitation upon the numbers of craft plying on the Broads, for obvious reasons, but do suggest closer supervision of casual private boat-owners and the banning of certain types of undesirable water craft. It is important that the livelihood of the local people should be carefully considered for after all they largely depend upon the £7m spent annually by holiday-makers. Tourism has brought a substantial measure of prosperity to an area which half a century ago was one of great poverty.

FARMHOUSE HOLIDAYS

Farmhouse holidays have grown steadily in popularity during the past decade and the reasons are several and sometimes subtle. There is a paradox in British farming: though the industry as a whole is economically healthier than perhaps ever before and though the large lowland farms are prosperous, it is otherwise with the small, especially the hill, farmers. Between 1963–73 some 40,000 small farmers sold their properties, thereby reducing the number of farms from 185,000 in 1964 to 145,000 in 1974. Many smaller farmers have been compelled to seek additional sources of income to help maintain their farms and their standard of living: some have provided caravan sites for which they get a small rental; others have started farm shops, selling their own fresh produce; yet others have turned to offering farmhouse holidays. Realising the city dweller's desire to escape from the town and to find peace and quiet, the farmer has gradually come to see the possibility of reaping a "cash crop" from visitors. Precisely how many farmers offer holidays (especially in Devon, Cornwall, Wales and the Lake District) is not known but the British Tourist Authority has suggested a total running into several thousands and it has been estimated that the "industry" is growing at the rate of 8 per cent a year.

The Country Landowners' Association (whose 40,000 members own most of the upland farming land), maintain that farming alone does not give an adequate living for its farmers, needed to maintain the life and prosperity of the hill areas of Britain and they have urged that the Government should offer help and aid to the farmers willing to offer accommodation and leisure facilities to tourists. In a recent report prepared by the C.L.A. a number of recommendations for Government action were put forward: these included improved roads and public transport, special grants to stimulate and support rural industries and the development of such countryside activities as fishing, pony-trekking and nature walks. Aid of this kind, it is maintained, will greatly help to preserve the life and beauty of the country's upland regions, and without it the economic difficulties of upland farming will almost inevitably result in depopulation and decay. In 1970, the C.L.A. introduced a farm buildings award scheme to encourage farmers and landowners to pay more attention to the siting and design of new buildings, for farm buildings, even if they have to be functional, need not be eyesores.

LAND LOST FOR RECREATION

With mounting pressure on the land for recreational purposes, it is important that the best possible use is made of such land as we have. The Ministry of Defence holds more than 300,000 ha (750,000 acres) of land and, for the most part, the public is denied access to it. There are, of course, valid reasons for this but many question whether so much land should be withheld from public use, especially since so many of the areas under the control of the Ministry of Defence are beauty spots. An enquiry, led by Lord Nugent, put forward a number of recommendations in 1974; while his report re-affirmed the claims of the Defence Ministry for adequate practice and testing grounds, it urged that 12,400 ha (31,000 acres) could be surrendered.

The report recommended that forty sites should be vacated altogether and that some land could be released on another fifty-seven. Withdrawal from some sites would result in a number of beauty spots in Dorset, on Dartmoor, Salisbury Plain, the Isle of Wight, the North York Moors and in the Pentland Hills, being made available to the public. Some 2,800 ha (7000 acres) in Dorset adjacent to Lulworth Cove is used as a gunnery range and the release of this would mean that Lulworth Cove, one of the loveliest spots in Britain, would be made fully open to the public for the first time since the Second World War. The report, moreover, suggested that the Government should spend up to £14m to make it safe for walkers and campers. The report also emphasised that the Ministry of Defence should devote more attention to improving the appearance of its defence sites and to reducing noise and goes so far as to suggest that a conservation officer should be appointed to improve the amenities and initiate conservation in the training areas.

THE LEA VALLEY REGIONAL PARK

Even derelict and urban areas offer reasonable possibilities of rehabilitation and potential for conversion to recreational use. This is the philosophy behind the Civic Trust Plan for the Lea Valley, which is a bold and imaginative exercise in recreational planning to serve the needs of urban dwellers.

The scheme was really the brainchild of the late Sir Patrick Abercrombie who thirty years ago saw the potential which the Lea Valley offered as a linear park for London. The 40-km (25-mile) long river valley was, however, at that time under the control of eighteen different local authorities and this was the principal factor preventing the idea being taken up. In 1963, ten of the local authorities finally met and discussed the possibilities of unified development for recreation and in the following year a Civic Trust report, *A Lea Valley Regional Park*, was published, and in 1967 an "Authority" was constituted to translate the proposal into reality.

The area which was to be developed, defined by an Act of Parliament, was 40 km (25 miles) long and 4000 ha (10,000 acres) in area, and the scheme involved the creation of a continuous linear zone from Ware virtually to the point where the River Lea entered the Thames. The area had an initial natural advantage in that it comprised a relatively green area extending from the rural countryside of Hertfordshire into the very heart of London; on the other hand, much of it was in a rundown and semi-derelict condition, large areas were given over to water storage, the river itself was fouled by sewage effluent and the landscape was marred by electricity pylons. The condition of the zone can be appraised from the Civic Trust's report which described it as "London's kitchen garden, its well, its privy and its workshop." Nevertheless, there were numerous large and small areas of open land—some already used as playing fields—and many water areas—some already used for sailing. Thus the possibilities were there. The Civic Trust identified sixteen sites each of which were capable of being developed and it was proposed that these should be planned as a whole, forming a linear park, giving space and facilities for recreation and enjoyment to many of the capital's population. In advocating this development, the report, says Arvill, "has postulated some new concepts which bid fair to become the yardstick for any future planning of a high-quality environment."[26]

The plan for the Lea Valley Regional Park includes two main developments: first, the use of the northern section for water-based sporting activities, such as canoeing and sailing and water-skiing, and for the provision of golf courses, walking and picnic areas and since "horticulture has been a feature of land use in the Lea Valley it is hoped this could be linked with visitors and tourists as is done in Holland";[27] secondly, in the southern sector, there would be more varied recreational activities and amenities, such as sports stadia, swimming pools, skating rinks, motor-racing arenas, rifle ranges, amusement centres as well as playing-fields, golf courses and parks and gardens.

"The theme running through the planning for the Regional Park," writes Bracey "is the preparation of a series of multi-purpose sports and recreation areas concentrated near centres of communication separated by areas of quieter activity, the whole linked by the river, the park road and its associated footpaths."[28] The project is a long-term one, taking twenty years, though it is aimed to complete the intensive use areas within twelve to fifteen years. It is estimated that the overall cost of the project will amount to some £40m (probably considerably more in view of current inflation).

NOTES

1. P. 31.
2. See *The Beauties of Scenery*, Muller, 4th ed., 1946.
3. H. E. Bracey, *People and the Countryside*, Routledge & Kegan Paul, 1970, p. 256.
4. F. J. Osborne in the Introduction to V. Cornish's *The Beauties of Scenery*.
5. *Ibid.*
6. H. V. Morton, *I Saw Two Englands*, Methuen, 1942, p. 153.
7. Wibberley's Report was published in 1973, after this book was written.
8. *The Denbighshire Study.*
9. "Threat to rural communities," *Geographical Magazine*, Vol. XLV, November, 1972, pp. 98–102.
10. *Ibid.*
11. *Ibid.*
12. *Ibid.*
13. *Op. cit.*, p. 245.
14. Foreword to Bracey's *People and the Countryside.*
15. *Op. cit.*, p. 112.
16. *Op. cit.*, p. 124.

17. J. Wager, "The Use of Common Land for Recreation," Paper given to the Research Conference: Planning for the Countryside, Town Planning Institute, October, 1967.

18. Quoted by Bracey, *op. cit.*, p. 211.

19. *Op. cit.*, p. 233.

20. D. Lowenthal and H. C. Price, "The English Landscape," *The Geographical Review*, Vol. 54, No. 3, 1963, p. 334.

21. "Predators on the Dartmoor Wilderness," *Geographical Magazine*, Vol. XLV, June, 1973, pp. 743–8.

22. P. Laurie, "World in Danger," *Sunday Times Magazine*, 17th November, 1968.

23. T. Aldous, *Battle for the Environment*, Fontana, 1972, p. 196.

24. "Wide World of the Narrow Way," *Drive*, Autumn, 1967, pp. 69–71.

25. *Ibid.*

26. R. Arvill, *Man And Environment*, Penguin Books, 1967, p. 168.

27. Bracey, *op. cit.*, p. 183.

28. *Op. cit.*, p. 183.

Chapter XIII

The Tourist and the Coast

THE USE OF THE COAST

F ROM the point of view of recreation, the coast may be deemed Britain's most important resource: it is a tremendous asset providing various facilities for recreational activities. "The coastline is, and ... will continue to remain, our main national playground."[1] Since no part of England and Wales is more than 120 km (75 miles) from tide water and since the country has a fine network of communications, the coast is readily accessible and able to meet a very substantial proportion of the total out-of-doors recreational demand. As the *Pilot National Recreation Survey* (1967) indicated, 20 per cent of half-day trips and 32 per cent of day trips had the coast as their destination; and if to these percentages are added the fact that some 75 per cent of all holidays are spent at the seaside it will be clear that the sea coast has an extraordinary attraction. For long now in Britain "going away on holiday" meant, at least for some three-quarters of the population, "going to the seaside." Although according to B.T.A. statistics there was little change during the 1960s in the total number of main holidays taken away from home by the British people (in Britain as distinct from overseas holidays), it is forecast that by 1980 there will be a substantial increase in the numbers visiting the coast. According to the Countryside Commission on the *Planning of the Coastline* (1970), "there could well be an increase of 60–100 per cent in the demand for bed space by 1980."[2] Certainly with the growing use of the motor car, short visits to the coast must show a substantial increase.

Why do people visit the coast? What attractions has it? We can discern at least three principal ones: (*i*) the sea itself which has a magical quality for most British people; (*ii*) coastal scenery in infinite variety; and (*iii*) the facilities for recreational activities, especially water sports. The sea exerts a fascination for the landsman: he watches it in awe when it is in angry mood lashing the rocks and throwing up great fountains of spray or is mesmerised by the gently curling, foam-capped waves as they slowly roll ashore; in summer, under a blue sky, he marvels at the azure, turquoise and ultramarine colours.

On any stretch of coast one can always see onlookers, enthralled by the fascinating rhythm of the sea. Here, to be sure, is one reason why so many people visit the coast. The coastline also offers a wonderful variety of scenery. The coast forms the zone of contact between the land and the sea: of endless variety and tremendous attraction. Sometimes the coast is almost perfectly straight for miles, at other times it curves in and out in a quite bewildering fashion; sometimes the land meets the sea in awe-inspiring abruptness where cliffs, hundreds of feet in height, plunge almost vertically into the sea, at other times land and sea merge almost imperceptibly. Where it is cliffed and rocky, it may display a wealth of erosional features such as caves, arches, sea stacks and wave-cut platforms; where it is low and gently shelving the shoreline may consist of sand-flats and sand dunes or salt marshes and mudflats. And, in addition to the different shapes and sizes of the coastal landforms, there are the variegated colours of the rocks and pebbles which litter the beach.

PRESSURES ON THE COAST

In the heyday of the railways the influx of visitors was concentrated upon certain coastal spots—the seaside resorts—and the remainder of the coast was largely untouched; as Patmore has said: "the railway by its very nature concentrated rather than dispersed and though it brought greatly increased freedom of movement the channels of that movement were still relatively restricted."[3] With the coming of the motor car the situation was changed quite radically: for the majority of the population the nearest stretch of coast was rarely much more than two, or at the most, three, hours' drive away; and a much greater length of coastline could be reached because of the mobility which the car provided: now even the quietest and most remote coves became accessible. Patmore's comment which we quoted earlier has equal relevance here: ". . . the car brought incomparably greater freedom to recreational travel, freedom in the choice of destination, freedom in the timing of journeys, freedom to pause at a moment's whim."[4] These advantages of increased mobility and greater freedom, however, lie at the root of many of the problems of recreational land use.

Not only is there great pressure on coastal resources from the holiday-maker and the day-tripper, but also, it should be remembered, a considerable proportion of the population, including a high percentage of the retired, live permanently on or near to the coast. The car has made it possible for workers to commute between resort and city, for

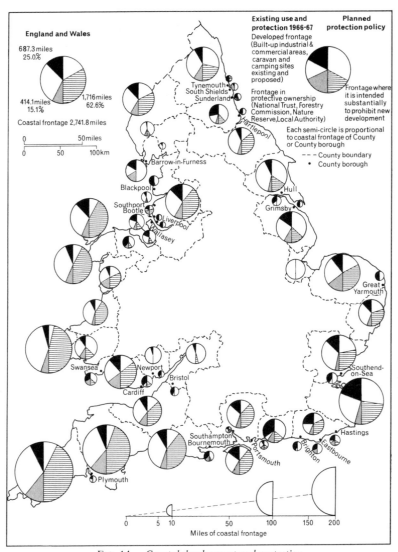

England and Wales

687.3 miles
25.0%

414.1 miles
15.1%

1,716 miles
62.6%

Coastal frontage 2,741.8 miles

0   50 miles
0   50   100 km

Existing use and protection 1966-67

Developed frontage (Built-up industrial & commercial areas, caravan and camping sites existing and proposed)

Frontage in protective ownership (National Trust, Forestry Commission, Nature Reserve, Local Authority)

Planned protection policy

Frontage where it is intended substantially to prohibit new development

Each semi-circle is proportional to coastal frontage of County or County borough

--- County boundary
• County borough

Tynemouth
South Shields
Sunderland
Hartlepool
Barrow-in-Furness
Blackpool
Southport
Bootle
Liverpool
Wallasey
Hull
Grimsby
Great Yarmouth
Swansea
Newport
Bristol
Cardiff
Southend-on-Sea
Southampton
Bournemouth
Portsmouth
Brighton
Eastbourne
Hastings
Plymouth

0   5   10   50   100   150   200

Miles of coastal frontage

FIG. 14.—*Coastal development and protection.*

instance, between Liverpool and Southport or the small resorts of the Wirral or between Preston and Lytham St Annes and Blackpool. In almost every coastal resort and village one can see tentacles of bricks and mortar stretching out along the shoreline (*see* Fig. 14). This pressure on the coast can only grow greater as the population (and expectation of life) increases.

Of a total, in England and Wales, of some 4400 km (2742 miles) of coast there is at the present time an available length of only 8·89 cm (3½ in.) per person! And for spots with high amenity value the length works out at about an inch each! "Happily, demand at peak periods is not yet absolute, and the shore itself has breadth as well as length, but it does at least highlight the very real pressures which exist."[5]

However, lest it should be thought that the growing leisure industry is responsible for all coastal ills, it should be emphasised that there are other important and growing demands for coastal land; from mining, industry, transport and shipping. The exploitation of offshore oil and natural gas resources means pipes and installations at points along the coast. The recent developments in bulk transport of commodities such as petroleum and ores have necessitated the construction of deep-water terminals, often on previously undeveloped coasts. Many power stations constructed in recent years have been located at coastal sites because of their greedy water needs. Much industrial development has occurred in great estuaries, especially Severnside and Humberside, since 1945, and the British Iron and Steel Corporation plans to seek new coastal sites for its projected massive integrated plants. And to all these "increasing demands for development generated by commerce and industry, must be added the demands, as yet unknown, that will be stimulated by future technological changes."[6]

Few of these developmental pressures are not in conflict with the need to preserve the natural beauty and amenity of the coast and the desire to maintain and secure public access to it.

THE STATE OF THE COAST

It is frequently asserted that Britain's coastline is rapidly being violated and spoiled by urban growth, industrial development and caravan parks. It is true that something of the order of 9 km (6 miles) of coast are becoming built-up areas each year, that industrial installations increasingly are moving towards coastal locations and that camping and caravan sites are mushrooming up all around the coast. It is nevertheless important that we should take a balanced view of the problem. The facts and figures collected by the Countryside Commission help to place the coastal problem in its proper perspective and nail the lie that our coast is rapidly being eroded by urbanisation, industrialisation and all the various manifestations of growing recreational activity and that a crisis point in relation to coastal usage is imminent.

The coastline of mainland Britain, some 9600 km (6000 miles) in length—roughly equivalent to the distance from London to Cape Town—still has some two-thirds of its extent undeveloped and unspoilt and a high proportion of this remains in its natural unaltered state. Thus, taking Britain as a whole, there is still a great deal of undeveloped coast. Much of this, however, occurs in Scotland, particularly the western coast, which is far removed from large concentrations of population and remains relatively remote and inaccessible. When we look at the picture for England and Wales the situation is much less reassuring although even here the *developed* frontage of the coast amounts to only about 25 per cent (26·5 per cent in the case of England, 21 per cent for Wales).[7]

The distribution of the developed and undeveloped sections of the coastline are, however, very unevenly spread; there are extensive stretches which have been developed and disfigured: on the other hand, there are extended areas which still show very little development. "Development" embraces all urban built-up areas, areas for industrial and commercial usages, *e.g.* mining and quarrying operations, power stations, port installations, holiday camps and caravan sites. The degree to which the coast of each country or county borough is developed (and protected) is shown in Fig. 17. The 1968 statistical report of the Countryside Commission showed that the most intensively developed coastal areas in England were West Sussex (68 per cent built on), Durham (53), and East Sussex (50), while the central and southern sections of the Lancashire coast were also very intensively developed. In Wales, Denbighshire (72 per cent) topped the national list. Conversely, there were some counties where the amount of developed frontage was relatively small: in fact, there was one county in England, the Holland part of Lincolnshire, that had no buildings along its coast. In the list of little-developed English counties were Gloucestershire (13·2 per cent), Devon (14·7), Northumberland (15·8) and the North Riding of Yorkshire (16·8). In Wales, Monmouthshire, whose coast was only 6 per cent developed, topped the list although more large-scale industrial development is planned in the future here. Next in order come Pembrokeshire (with 10 per cent), Caernarvonshire (15·3), Cardiganshire (15·6) and Merionethshire (16·5).

Patmore has drawn a map, Fig. 15, to illustrate the use which is made of the beaches of England and Wales; he distinguishes three categories of use: beaches that are intensively used, those that are moderately used and those that are of restricted use because the beach consists

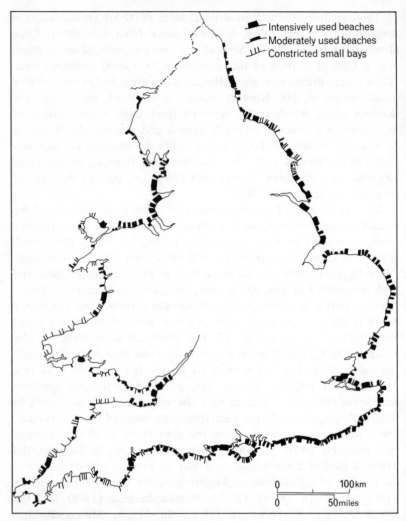

Intensively used beaches
Moderately used beaches
Constricted small bays

0   100km
0   50miles

FIG. 15.—*The use of beaches.* England and Wales have a coastal frontage of some 4422 km (2742 miles). Most of the beaches are used, some intensively, *e.g.* the Fylde and Torbay coasts. The Wash, Humber and Northumbrian coasts are the least used.

of restricted small bays.[8] If one compares Patmore's map with a topographical map, one can discern a measure of correlation between them; the least-used stretches are those distinguished by high, cliffed coasts such as the North Yorkshire coast, the North Devon coast and the coast of Pembrokeshire or by mudflats and salt marshes in estuarine areas such as the Humber, the Wash and part of the coast of Essex;

conversely, the most intensively used beaches tend to coincide with coasts which are gently shelving with expansive foreshores such as those of the Fylde district and the north-eastern coast of Kent.

"THE MESS ON THE COAST"

Planning policies have tended to show increasing concern with the preservation of such remaining stretches of unspoiled coast as we still possess but there has been little real corresponding concern to improve those sections of the coast which have been subjected to unsightly development or are marred by eyesores. A special study of poor-quality development, which has been referred to as "mess on the coast," has been made (1968–69) by local planning authorities but, unfortunately, each authority was left to decide what it thought was undesirable and unsightly and, as a result, this subjectivity brought widespread disparities in the individual reports. For example, Durham excluded collieries and industrial buildings from their list of derelict and unsightly structures while East Sussex included modern bungalow development! Table 28 summarises the information which was gathered by the survey but, clearly, it cannot be accepted as a completely objective or accurate picture.

Broadly, the problem may be said to fall into the following categories:

(*i*) derelict land, *e.g.* former quarries, gravel workings, colliery waste tips;

(*ii*) industrial plant and port installations;

(*iii*) military eyesores, *e.g.* pill-boxes, gun emplacements and other wartime relics;

(*iv*) old dilapidated shacks and similar holiday dwellings which disfigure the landscape;

(*v*) caravan and camping sites;

(*vi*) pollution, *e.g.* sewage, oil and rubbish generally which foul the beaches.

It must be recognised that we must sometimes use the coast for industrial and port development, for terminals and oil installations, but with careful planning the minimum of damage could be done to the coast and with a little care and effort such installations could be screened or partially hidden from view—a successful case in point is Fawley. Again, it is important that, so far as is possible, such developments should be concentrated and not allowed to develop at random around the coast.

TABLE 28
Coastal eyesores by geographical county[1]

| Geographical county | Derelict and unsightly buildings | | | Incompatible unauthorised development Holiday accommodation incl. caravans, chalets | | Total |
	Military origin	Derelict Other	In Use		Other	
Kent	46	33	5	—	—	84
Sussex	4	1	13	—	—	18
Hampshire and Isle of Wight	34	28	34	5	—	101
Devon	14	16	18	7	3	58
Dorset			2 unidentified sites			2
Cornwall	11	—	4	14	—	29
Monmouthshire	1	—	—	—	—	1
Glamorgan	2	—	8	—	1	11
Carmarthenshire			1 unidentified site			1
Pembrokeshire	42	7	13	3	—	65
Merioneth	3	2	—	—	—	5
Anglesey	3	2	4	—	—	9
Caernarvonshire	5	20	2	4	8	39
Flintshire			4 unidentified sites			4
Cheshire	1	1	1	—	—	3
Lancashire	2	—	4	—	—	6
Cumberland	1	16	3	2	—	22
Durham	12	7	6	—	2	27
Yorkshire	9	8	3	—	—	20
Lincolnshire	40	10	—	—	—	50
Norfolk	43	3	—	8	5	59
Suffolk	44	7	3	—	—	54
Essex	4	6	12	5	6	33
TOTAL	321	167	133	48	25	701

Includes 7 unidentified sites.

1. The local planning authorities recorded no eyesores or incompatible unauthorised development on the coasts of Somerset, Gloucestershire, Cardiganshire, Denbighshire or Northumberland.

There are many examples of slate and limestone quarries, sand and gravel workings and spoil heaps (e.g. the old alum workings near Whitby, although these, through the passing of time have acquired a cover of vegetation and their presence is well-masked). Some of these disfigurements are difficult, if not impossible, to eradicate but in some cases they could be made less obvious and less of an eyesore, e.g. by infilling, removing the old buildings and works, judicious tree-planting, etc. One of the most intractable problems of coastal "mess" is the colliery waste which blackens the foreshore for many miles in Northumberland and Durham.

More easy to deal with are the collections of old, rundown holiday huts and derelict or near-derelict properties. Planning authorities must strongly resist the proliferation of further caravan and camping sites in coastal locations where their presence would detract from the beauty of the coast; those which already exist and create eyesores should be moved to alternative sites.

The Ministry of Defence controls 235 km (146 miles) of coastline together with a further 68 km (42 miles) of estuary and creek land. Parts of the coast of Lincolnshire, Essex, Dorset, Pembroke and Carmarthenshire are wholly or partly sealed off. There are several other stretches of coast with valuable landscape features[9] and of considerable potential for recreation which are reserved to the Ministry of Defence, one is tempted to wonder with what real justification.

More attention and positive action must be directed against coastal pollution. Many coastal towns continue to dump sewage and other effluent directly into coastal waters, the tidal stretch of the Thames receives 200 million litres (440 million gallons) of sewage every day, much of it flowing back and forth with the tides for three months before getting through to the open sea, while Edinburgh daily discharges 50 million gallons of untreated sewage into the Forth estuary. Miles of beach are thereby contaminated by urban sludge and slime and the offshore waters rendered unfit for bathing. Domestic sewage and industrial effluent are the direct result of modern urbanised, industrial society and thus it is becoming imperative that adequate control and processing of waste material be undertaken, since such controls as do exist are totally inadequate for current conditions. Domestic sewage and industrial effluents are, in general, the most serious pollutants, but there are others which affect the coast and coastal waters. Some nuclear installations, *e.g.* Dounreay, Windscale, Winfrith, discharge radioactive waste into the sea, while power stations, whether nuclear or conventional, pour heated water into estuaries and the sea which has serious effects on local marine life. Oil is another, and very serious pollutant. It would be much worse had not measures been introduced to prevent tankers flushing their tanks at sea, but in spite of such precautions, there is little evidence to indicate that the fouling of beaches by oil is being reduced, and the coasts of Britain, and of north-western Europe generally, are increasingly threatened. The wreck of the *Torrey Canyon* in 1967 was an example of the disastrous effects oil can have on the whole marine environment. The far-reaching nature of the problem is shown by the fact that in the summer of 1972 many miles of the Riviera coast were closed to the holiday-maker because of pollution.

PLANNING POLICIES

Not surprisingly, therefore, considerable concern has arisen over what is to happen to the coasts, a concern by no means limited to ardent conservationists. It seems very clear that active planning is required if we are not only going to protect our coasts but to see that the best possible use is made of them. What has already been done to protect the coast? What policies are being adopted for protecting the remaining areas of undeveloped coast? What can be done to improve the situation where damage has already occurred.

Largely as a result of the *laissez-faire* attitude which dominated political thinking in Britain in the nineteenth century few controls were placed upon land use. The result was that developments took place at random and much of the desecration of the coast occurred during the inter-war period, when few were committed to the ideas of either control or planning. However, the *Town and Country Planning Act* of 1932 made it possible for local authorities to prepare schemes for their own areas if they so wished. A further Act, passed in 1943, placed under control all those areas which the local authorities had not resolved to plan. These Acts had precious little practical effect, especially on the coast, and their real significance was perhaps that they established the principle that positive and constructive planning was good. Until 1947, when a new *Town and Country Planning Act* was passed, the onus of protecting the public interest in the use and development of the land was left very largely in the hands of a few public-spirited voluntary organisations. However, the 1947 Act decreed that any material development of the land required the permission of the local planning authority.

The *Town and Country Planning Act* of 1968 laid down that "Structure Plans" embodying policies and proposals for each authority's area should be submitted to the appropriate Government Department for approval. Before this act became law, the Minister of Housing and Local Government had requested (Circular No. 56/63) all planning authorites having maritime boundaries to review their planning policies and to:

(*i*) ascertain which sections of their coasts needed safeguarding in order that full enjoyment of their natural attractions should be possible;

(*ii*) decide where it would be best to locate and concentrate facilities for recreational purposes and other coastal developments;

(*iii*) make efforts to restore as far as was possible such amenities as had been lost and to create new ones;

(*iv*) take due cognisance of the potential impact of new proposals upon any areas of scientific interest.

Following upon the local authorities' replies to Circular No. 56/63, the Minister, in another Circular (No. 7/6y) commented upon the unevenness of progress, the need for fuller information, the need for better co-ordination between the plans of different authorities and, furthermore, the need to locate additional stretches of coast which it might seem desirable to protect as well as those already protected by planning policies. Clearly at Departmental level there was considerable anxiety about the position.

Out of a total coastal frontage in England and Wales of 4413 km (2742 miles), 1106 km (687 miles) were substantially built-up areas or used industrially in 1968; in England this amounted to some 27 per cent of the coastline, in Wales 21 per cent. However, the degree of development varied very widely between counties. Of the 3307 km (2055 miles) of coastal frontage remaining, the greater part was protected by planning policies and in the case of eight counties, including Devon and Cornwall, the whole undeveloped part of the coast was to be protected; but there were some 544 km (339 miles) (12·5 per cent of the total frontage) which did not appear to be protected and, indeed, in the case of three counties none of the open frontage was apparently scheduled at all for protection.

While it is the general aim of all the thirty-four maritime county councils* to safeguard the coasts and to prohibit all but "essential development," the definition of what they regard as essential development is highly variable and one is forced to the conclusion that reliable protective policies cannot be ensured until, and unless, "essential development" is precisely spelled out and common denominators adopted by all the authorities. The Report of the Countryside Commission on *The Planning of the Coastline* (1970) came to the conclusion that the existing policies were essentially vague and negative, vague because they were imprecise and lacked definition, negative because they were too "preservationist" in character. The coast should be opened up as far as was possible and with the least constraints upon recreational use so far as was consonant with their protection.

These two aims are not necessarily incompatibleg as the 1970 Report commented: "We would prefer to see constructive policies which point to the kinds of uses and activities that could with advantage take place in protected areas and are consistent with the principles of conservation."

* This was the position before the Local Government reorganisation in 1973.

The conservation of protected land implies more than stringent development control: it implies, also, careful, efficient but flexible management. Future planning, to safeguard the quality of the coastal environment, must be active concerning three things: (*i*) to identify those sites where growth is anticipated for recreational purposes and prepare suitable management schemes; (*ii*) to plan appropriate action to regulate activities in such areas as seem likely to be threatened with degradation by excessive use; and (*iii*) to ensure that adequate provisions are made well in advance of demand to ease, or even drastically to reduce, the pressures on a particularly vulnerable area.

HERITAGE COASTS

Anxious about our coasts and recognising that many long stretches had already been despoiled, the Countryside Commission, considering that "some stretches of coastline where the scenery . . . is of the highest order, merit special attention" and fearful that such coasts "though substantially undeveloped at present, are likely to be increasingly threatened by development and recreation pressure" made proposals that these particular stretches of coast should be given special protection and designated "Heritage Coasts."[10] Altogether the Commission recognised thirty-four areas extending along some 1168 km (730 miles) of coast or 27 per cent of the total coastal frontage. These Heritage Coasts contained not only from a scenic point of view the most impressive coastal scenery in England and Wales but included a very wide variety of coastal environments ranging from majestic cliffs to flat sand-dunes.

Although the Government accepted in principle the idea of Heritage Coasts and also the Commission's selection of the individual sites, the Department of the Environment has since rather dragged its feet over the implementation of the scheme. The original proposals put forward by the Countryside Commission in *The Planning of the Coastline* and *The Coastal Heritage* envisaged that the Heritage Coasts should be planned and controlled by the county councils but this idea has been heavily criticised by some environmental conservation pressure groups. It is feared that powerful commercial interests may be able to bring such pressure to bear upon the county councils that they may not be able to resist successfully the exploitation of the present unspoiled coasts; accordingly, it has been advocated that there should be an independent or a few independent planning bodies who would have overall planning control. A subcommittee of the Committee for Environmental Conservation—a body established to provide a single voice to the principal conservation groups in the country—has recommended that Heritage Coast management committees should be given sufficient powers to ensure that their planning control and decisions are paramount, and it has been further suggested that the management committees should be given a measure of autonomy similar to that enjoyed by the Peak Park Board. It has also been urged that the Heritage Coasts should not be delimited simply to the narrow coastal margins but should embrace also fringes of hinterland where adequate car-parking and other facilites could be ensured, and that the thirty-four selected sites should be grouped for the purposes of effective and efficient planning control into eight larger regional groups.

THE COAST OF NORTH WALES AND TOURISM

To conclude this chapter on the Tourist and the Coast, it may be useful to take a stretch of coast where tourism is of some considerable importance and to look at the reasons for its development and the problems to which it has given rise.

Any account of the human geography of North Wales must take into consideration the impact and effects of external influences, for these have to a very appreciable extent fashioned the present-day cultural landscape. Here we are interested only in the tourist industry of North Wales, which is certainly strongly entrenched in many areas, having grown rapidly in importance during the present century. This development has helped to shape the geography of the North Wales coast and even of areas in the immediate hinterland.

The proximity of the North Wales coast to the densely populated industrial areas of south Lancashire and the west Midlands together with the coming of the Chester–Holyhead railway provided a great impetus for the development of tourism, particularly in Flintshire and Denbighshire but also, though to a much lesser extent, in Caernarvonshire and Anglesey. This accessibility, coupled with the advantages of an equable climate, relatively low rainfall and a high number of hours of sunshine and the scenically attractive nature of many stretches of the coast and the hinterland, especially Snowdonia and the Vale of Llangollen, led almost inevitably to the growth of tourism (*see* Fig. 16). The tourist industry has produced the larger resorts of Prestatyn, Rhyl, Colwyn Bay (which grew out of the old settlement of Old Colwyn), and Llandudno, the smaller centres (as much residential as holiday places), of Abergele, Llandulas and Rhos-on-sea, and, in more recent years, the caravans on the sandy shores linking

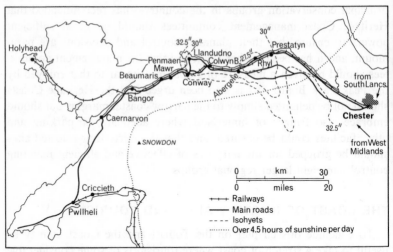

Fig. 16.—*The coast of North Wales.* Fine bays and beaches, magnificent hill country behind, a small rainfall, a mean daily average of 4–4½ hours' sunshine, together with a fairly easy accessibility to the large populations of South Lancashire and the West Midlands have made the North Wales coast a very popular holiday zone.

this string of resorts. Of the various resorts, Llandudno, elegantly Victorian in a fine setting, is much the largest, far exceeding the others in accommodation capacity. We have already seen that Denbighshire has 72 per cent of its coastline developed—the highest for Wales.

Beyond the River Conway the character of tourism changes quite sharply. To the west there are no major resorts, though the larger centres, Conway, Bangor and Caernarvon, are tourist centres. Penmaenmawr and Llanfairfechen have dual functions as small residential and resort towns. Caernarvonshire, rather distant from the main generating areas of tourists, suffered relatively little from the recreational pressures of the inter-war period and, apart from a few scattered caravan sites, there was scant tourism development. The result has been a tourist industry of a much quieter kind. The Isle of Anglesey and the Lleyn Peninsula cater for a different kind of clientele—those preferring self-catering types of holidays—and provide a more "rural" type of tourism. In the Lleyn Peninsula there are several small resorts, *e.g.* Portmadoc, Criccieth and Abersoch, but only Pwllheli, situated at a railhead, can in any way compare with the larger resorts of the Denbigh and Flint coasts. In the Isle of Anglesey, the small harbours, formerly sharing in the shipping of local cargoes, are now, except for a little fishing, mostly reliant upon summer tourists.

Tourism is of great importance to this northern coast of Wales: in financial terms tourist expenditure is now in excess of £50m (in 1966 it was £36m) while a significant proportion of the employed population is directly engaged in the tourist industry, although for many it is a seasonal occupation. Many others also benefit indirectly from the industry, *e.g.* farmers, transport firms, garage proprietors, builders. In recent years holiday and recreation traffic has increased substantially, giving rise to the obvious problems of traffic congestion and car parking. The building of an "expressway" from the English border to Bangor would ease the traffic flow as, indeed, the by-pass at St Asaph has eliminated an awful bottleneck (incidentally, it has brought back tranquillity to the small cathedral town), but the construction of such a coastal highway could well aggravate rather than alleviate some traffic problems by attracting yet more traffic. Changes in the character of the North Wales coastal region must follow as a result of any such improved communications: one development would certainly be the opening up of the coastal region west of Conway for the motorist would be encouraged to penetrate more deeply into the region. As a result, one could anticipate that the smaller resorts of Lleyn would see an upsurge in their popularity; on the other hand, the by-passing of Colwyn Bay might well lead to that resort losing some of its attraction.

Another serious problem arises out of the seasonal nature of tourism. Seasonal unemployment is widespread, and in addition facilities such as public services, water supply, sewage and lighting have to be provided for a large transient holiday population by a small resident population; Local Authorities are generally reluctant to make investments in infrastructure from which there is little direct return. Since tourism plant is in operation for only about half the year big profits can seldom be made to meet heavy annual rent and rate demands, and suggestions have been made that grants based on the peak holiday numbers, as distinct from the permanent resident population, should be provided to help Local Authorities fulfil their responsibilities.

In contrast to Denbighshire, Caernarvonshire has only a quarter of its coastline developed:

	per cent
Urban centres and resorts	16
Detached holiday development	3
Rural coastal settlements	5
Industrial development	1
TOTAL	25

These figures indicate that the coastal development is essentially recreational (if one includes the urban centres as being also tourist centres, which they mostly are) and that there is still considerable room for further development. In anticipation of increased development, it becomes highly desirable that the intensity of recreational use, the potential for recreational development, and total capacity which the area can provide should be carefully assessed and that conservation measures should be taken to preserve areas of high landscape value and scenic beauty. With respect to the latter, much of the Lleyn area has been designated an Area of Outstanding Natural Beauty (*see* Appendix II) and the Great Orme an Area of Great Landscape Value and, accordingly, they are protected and subject to development control, but there are other areas too which call for some sort of protection before despoliation gets out of hand. Some recreational developments have already been suggested such as a proposed marina at Pwllheli and Port Penrhyn.

The Isle of Anglesey has not yet felt the full impact of tourism but the pressure of traffic has been mounting gradually and between 1955 and 1970 the number of vehicles entering the island during the peak summer period quadrupled. Tourism has already significantly affected the form and character of many of the coastal settlements but fortunately the island has not suffered from unsightly caravan development. So far only 2·4 per cent of the coastline is used for holiday camping and caravanning and 90 per cent of the caravan sites are located within a one-mile stretch of coast. A high proportion of the coast of Anglesey is already protected as an Area of Outstanding Natural Beauty and on the northwestern side there are stretches of heritage coast, but with the intention of controlling development and preserving the amenities of the island a number of planning proposals have been outlined: (*i*) the minimum of interference in agriculture, (*ii*) the prevention of linear coastal development, (*iii*) the provision of adequate car-parking facilities, (*iv*) the development of potential sailing areas; (*v*) the avoidance, unless absolutely necessary, of road widening; and (*vi*) developmental control and conservation in the Menai Strait area.

It seems fairly clear that the Denbighshire coast has virtually reached saturation point and that any further development would be undesirable since it would be likely to have degrading effects upon the landscape and aggravate many of the problems which already beset this stretch of coast; on the other hand, Caernarvonshire and Anglesey could stand, and would be likely to benefit from, a further injection of tourism, although any such expansion would have to be carefully monitored, due regard paid to the provision of adequate and carefully selected and sited facilities and amenities, and a strong measure of control enforced to preserve zones of enhanced landscape value and to conserve the natural beauty and rural character of the areas.

NOTES

1. *The Planning of the Coastline*, Countryside Commission, H.M.S.O., 1970, p. 1.

2. P. 11.

3. *Land and Leisure*, David & Charles, 1970, p. 27.

4. *Idem*, p. 28.

5. Patmore, *op. cit.*, p. 211.

6. *The Planning of the Coastline*, p. 1.

7. *The Coasts of England and Wales*, Countryside Commission, H.M.S.O., 1968.

8. *Op. cit.*, p. 215.

9. As a result of the Nugent Report, this land may well be released by the Ministry.

10. *The Planning of the Coastline*, p. 73.

Part Five

REGIONAL TOURIST DEVELOPMENT

Chapter XIV

Tourism in the United Kingdom

DOMESTIC TOURISM

The Size of the British Holiday Market

FOR the majority of people, the annual holiday is something to be planned, saved up for and pleasurably anticipated. In 1973 some 48·75 million took a holiday of four nights or more; while the vast majority, 40·5 million, spent their holiday within the confines of the United Kingdom, a substantial minority, nearly 8·25 million, went abroad. Altogether, about 120 million trips were spent in the United Kingdom.

The habit of holiday-making which, as we have already seen, grew at first gradually, received an impetus after the Second World War; this was perhaps partly a reaction after the austerity of the war years but it was also due to new social attitudes, holidays with pay and increased transport facilities. The proportion taking a holiday away from home rose from approximately 50 per cent of the population in 1951 to 62 per cent in 1972. While the proportion of the population taking a holiday in Great Britain remained fairly stable for many years, growth commenced in 1970 and there was a marked increase in 1972. The

TABLE 29

Numbers of the population taking a holiday at home or abroad (m)

Year	In Britain	Abroad	Total
1951	25	1·5	26·5
1955	25	2	27
1960	31·5	3·5	35
1965	30	5	35
1966	31	5·5	36·5
1967	30	5	35
1968	30	5	35
1969	30·5	5·75	36·25
1970	34·5	5·75	40·25
1971	34	7·25	41·25
1972	37·5	8·5	46
1973	40·5	8·25	48·75

Source: British Tourist Authority.

proportion holidaying abroad, which at first also remained fairly stable, increased from 10 per cent in 1970 to 15 per cent in 1972.

Variations in the numbers holidaying at home (and abroad also) were linked with various socio-economic conditions such as economic recessions, the cutting of the foreign travel allowance (which probably diverted many would-be travellers abroad to the home market), and increased length of paid holiday (for example, in the 1950s some 4 million workers were granted a second week's holiday with pay).

One important point which needs emphasising is that the increase in the number of holidays being taken since 1970 is more especially an outcome of the increase in the number of second holidays being taken, rather than an increase in the proportion of the population taking a holiday. In 1968, for instance, the total number of holidays taken in Britain totalled 30 million: of these, 26 million were principal holidays and 4 million additional or second holidays (*see* Fig. 17). Thus, while the number of principal holidays seems to have attained a measure of stability, the growth of second, and even of third, holidays is increasing; for example, the proportion of the population taking more than one

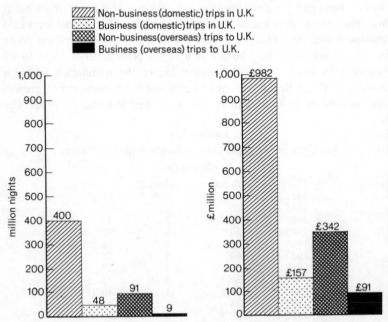

FIG. 17.—*Tourism flows in the U.K. in millions of nights and millions of pounds (1970).*

holiday in the late 1960s was around 7 per cent but by 1970 it had almost doubled to 13 per cent, and by 1972 to 19 per cent (*see* Table 30).

Even this, however, would appear to be an understatement, for the official figures relate to holidays of four consecutive nights or more away from home and do not include shorter-term breaks. In this connection it may be noted that the B.T.A.'s small-scale pilot survey carried out in 1968 indicated that around 10 million took short holidays of up to three nights away from home, although it would seem that about 60 per cent of such holidays were spent with relatives or friends who provided the accommodation.[1]

TABLE 30

Proportion of U.K. population taking holidays (%)

	1966	1967	1968	1969	1970	1971	1972
All taking							
One holiday	50	48	51	49	46	44	43
Two holidays	6	6	6	7	10	12	14
Three or more	1	1	1	1	3	3	5
All taking one or more	56	56	58	58	59	59	62

Source: British Tourist Authority.

The value of the British holiday market

The amount spent on holidays by British people increased threefold during the years from 1951 to 71: from £380m in 1951 to £1448m in 1971. The most astonishing development, however, has been the amount spent on holidays abroad which rocketed from £60m in 1951 to £528m in 1970, more than an eightfold increase. According to the B.T.A., the *per capita* cost, in 1951, of a holiday in Britain was approximately £11 and that of a holiday abroad just over £41, while the comparable figures for 1970 were £23 and £80. Table 31 gives the estimated holiday expenditure over the twenty-year period.

Attention should be drawn to the fact that these figures relate only to direct expenditure, *i.e.* money spent on accommodation and cost of travel to and from the holiday destination, on holidays of four nights or more away from home. They are exclusive of money (estimated at £175m in 1971) spent on shorter-term holidays or day excursions. The total holiday expenditure will, clearly, be considerably in excess of these figures. The rather sharp increase in holiday expenditure in Great Britain between 1969 and 1971 is attributable in part to an increase in the average *per capita* expenditure on holidays and in part to the rapidly accelerating increase in the taking of additional holidays. About 19 per cent more of the population had at least one extra holiday in 1972, as against 15 per cent in 1971.

TABLE 31

Estimated holiday expenditure 1951–71

	Britain (£m)	Abroad (£m)	Total (£m)
1951	320	60	380
1955	365	100	465
1960	400	150	550
1961	440	180	620
1962	450	200	650
1963	430	225	655
1964	430	245	675
1965	460	265	725
1966	550	320	870
1967	560	300	860
1968	570	320	890
1969	600	390	990
1970	790	470	1260
1971	920	528	1448

Source: British Tourist Authority.

Destinations of Holiday-makers

At one time the holiday-maker inevitably made for the nearest seaside resort: the Londoner went to Margate, Southend or Brighton, the Lancastrian went to Blackpool or Southport, and the Yorkshireman to either the East Coast or to Morecambe. Though this is not nearly so true now as formerly, since increasing numbers are extending their ambitions and seeking new horizons, it is still an ingrained habit with many; in the north of England the factory-workers make a bee-line for Blackpool, Bridlington and Whitley Bay: in London the non-professional worker goes to Brighton, Margate or Southend. Another characteristic of the northerner, though this, too, is much less strong than a generation or two ago, is his habit of visiting the same place year after year, with an obstinate loyalty and monotonous regularity. But times are changing and so are holiday habits.

Notwithstanding these changes, the sea coast remains the great magnet which attracts the holiday-maker. Approximately 70 per cent of all main holidays in Britain involve a stay by the seaside, usually in one of the large resorts;[2] the remaining 30 per cent of the population spend their holidays in rural areas, in the mountains or by lakes or rivers, or in inland locations such as Edinburgh, Stratford or the spas. A survey has stated that the proportions choosing coastal or inland locations vary between different social classes: whereas 78 per cent of the manual workers show a preference for the sea, only 69 per cent of the professional and upper-middle class choose the coast; by contrast 21 per cent of the latter but a mere 8 per cent of the former participate in country holidays where mountains and moorlands, lakes and streams are the attraction.[3]

The destination of holiday-makers vary considerably regionally. Patmore has said that the twin magnets of accessibility and climate may pull in opposing directions.[4] The increasing accessibility of the South-West, resulting from increased motor transport, new motorways and motor-rail facilities, has led to it becoming the most important single tourist region. The easy accessibility of the Lancashire and Yorkshire coasts from the industrial conurbations of the North exert a clear attraction to the peoples living in the industrial towns. On the other hand, the warmer and sunnier conditions of the South exert a strong pull and this seems to be reflected in the reluctance of Southerners to travel northwards for their holidays.

Figs. 18 and 20 illustrates the percentages of British holiday-makers

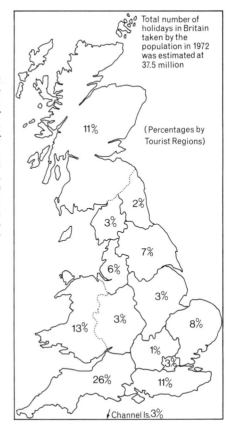

FIG. 18.—*Percentages of British holiday-makers visiting the various regions (1970)*. The map brings out the particular importance of the South-West Region as a tourist destination: more than a quarter of all British holiday-makers there. The popularity of the South-East is due, to a very considerable extent, to its nearness to London: some 40 per cent of its visitors come from neighbouring Regions. Apart from the essentially rural Thames–Chiltern Region, the least popular of all is Northumbria.

Total number of holidays in Britain taken by the population in 1972 was estimated at 37.5 million

(Percentages by Tourist Regions)

11%

2%

3%

7%

6%

3%

13%

3%

8%

1%

3%

26%

11%

Channel Is. 3%

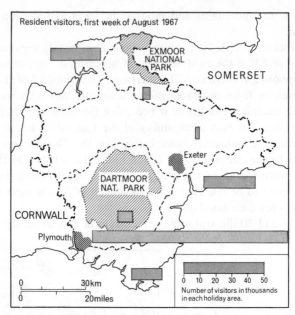

FIG. 19.—*Destination of holiday-makers in Devon.* Note the concentration of holiday-makers along the south coast, and especially in the Torbay district, which accounted for 40 per cent of all visitors. The four coastal zones accounted for 93 per cent of total visitors.

visiting the various regions. The data are supplied by the British Tourist Authority. It should be noted, however, that the B.T.A. does not differentiate between the varied destinations within the respective regions but it becomes clear when one studies the destinations of holiday-makers in individual counties, such as that in Devon (Fig. 19), that the attraction of the coast is usually paramount.

The South-West Region (Cornwall, Devon, Somerset, Wiltshire, Gloucestershire) is by a considerable margin the most important single region. It has led in popularity since the war. Even in 1951, with 13·5 per cent of the total of British holiday-makers, it ranked first, beating the South-East Region by 0·5 per cent. The early 1950s witnessed a sudden increase in the South-West Region's share of the market and by 1960 it had 17 per cent; growth since that time has continued, though at a much slower rate, and in 1970 the Region's share was 22 per cent. Devon and Cornwall, however, are the dominant destinations and these two counties alone (in 1973) accounted for 25 per cent of all British holidays. In spite of much fine country scenery in Dartmoor, Exmoor, the Mendips and the Cotswolds, the great lure in the South-West is the coast.

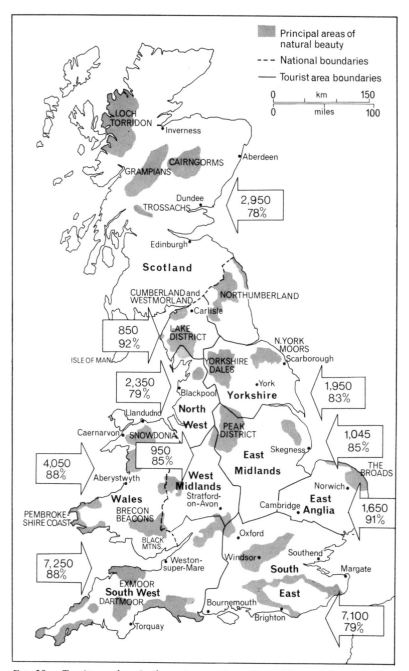

Fig. 20.—*Tourist numbers in the various tourist regions of Great Britain.* The map shows: (*a*) the main tourist areas and centres, (*b*) the number of people visiting each area for part of their holiday in 1968 and (*c*) the percentage travelling to their holiday destination by road.

The South Region (Dorset, Hampshire, Berkshire, Buckinghamshire and Oxfordshire) was the third most popular holiday region in 1951— only marginally behind the South-East which ranked second. The South made little progress during the 1950s, and even declined in some years, but after 1960 it began to increase its share and in 1970 this stood at 16 per cent of the total. Here again the coast, with the important resorts of Bournemouth, Poole, Weymouth and the Isle of Wight resorts, is the principal attraction, although the New Forest and such inland centres as Salisbury, Winchester, Windsor and Oxford are important. It seems rather strange that the attractions of Dorset, one of our loveliest and most interesting counties, should be so largely confined to the coast. The South Region has the great advantage of summer warmth and a mean daily average duration of sunshine, at least in its coastal parts, of $4\frac{1}{2}$ hours sunshine.

The South-East Region (Kent, Surrey and Sussex) had 13 per cent of the tourist market in 1951. Since then its share has declined, dropping to 11 per cent in 1960 and to 9 per cent in 1970. This decline is not easy to explain for this region has ease of accessibility from the metropolis, a string of well-established seaside resorts—Margate, Ramsgate, Dover, Folkestone, Hastings, Bexhill, Eastbourne, Brighton and Worthing—and just about the best summer weather in the country. No doubt the region has lost many of its visitors to the South and South-West Regions while many Londoners who formerly patronised the nearby coastal resorts are now going abroad.

The other tourist regions have shown little change over the period with the exception of the London Region which has declined rather sharply and somewhat surprisingly: its share of the home tourist market has dropped from 7 per cent in 1951 to 3 per cent in 1970. Both Wales and Scotland have registered a moderate increase, the former from 8·5 per cent in 1951 to 12 per cent in 1972, the latter from 10 to 11 per cent. The North-West Region (Cheshire, Lancashire, Cumberland and Westmorland) has remained more or less stable, although this is likely to show an increase in the future as a result of motorway construction which will make the Lake District much more accessible from the Midlands. The North and North-East Region (Yorkshire, Durham, Northumberland) has, likewise, remained stable with around 10 per cent. The East Region (Bedfordshire, Cambridgeshire, Huntingshire, Hertfordshire, Essex, Suffolk and Norfolk) has increased marginally from 8·5 per cent in 1951 to 9 per cent in 1970. The Midlands Region has remained almost static with around 7 per cent.

As Patmore has said: "temperature may matter but little in scenic inland areas such as the Lake District, but it certainly does when enjoyment of an open beach is concerned under somewhat marginal British conditions."[5] It is interesting to note that the South-East and South besides being the most popular regions for main holidays are also the most visited regions with regard to additional holidays; between them, in 1970, they accounted for 32 per cent.

An analysis of the actual movements of holiday-makers in Britain shows that such movements are, in fact, comparatively localised. This is so notwithstanding the increased mobility which the motor car has brought. Only a small proportion indulge in touring around and only 8 per cent sojourn in three or more places. Some interesting maps drawn by Patmore (*see* Fig. 21) from data supplied by the B.T.A. show a number of significant features: (*i*) there is a distinct tendency for an area to be most attractive to those living nearest to it; (*ii*) the local pull is greatest in the case of Yorkshire and the North-West; (*iii*) the South-West particularly exerts a disproportionate attraction viewing the country as a whole; and (*iv*) there is an obvious reluctance for southerners to travel northwards. In general terms, it would seem that easy accessibility is the preponderant factor affecting holiday travel. In the case of most regions, the majority of the holiday-makers come from near by; only a few regions, such as the South-West, by reason of better climate and amenities, induce people to travel further to reach them.

What will be the future patterns of holiday-making in Britain? One can only draw attention to a number of factors which may have effects upon people's choice of holiday destination: (*i*) the extension of the national motorway network and ever-increasing car ownership may tempt holiday-makers to visit more distant areas as they become, in terms of travelling time, more accessible; (*ii*) the introduction by British Rail of motor-rail services, which enable people to put their cars upon the railway and so obviate long, tiresome road journeys, are almost certain to increase in popularity and this, so long as rates remain reasonable, is again likely to cause people to travel further afield; (*iii*) the astonishing growth in popularity of caravanning holidays may lead tourists to explore the less popular areas; (*iv*) the greater emphasis these days on "activity" holidays involving touring, sight-seeing, interest and sports activities, may lead the holiday-maker to lesser known inland locations; (*v*) frequent holidays abroad may bring about its own satiation and result in the holiday-maker re-exploring his own homeland and visiting areas which he had hitherto neglected; and (*vi*) the effectiveness with which the new Tourist Boards can "sell" their regions by developing them and attracting the visitor.

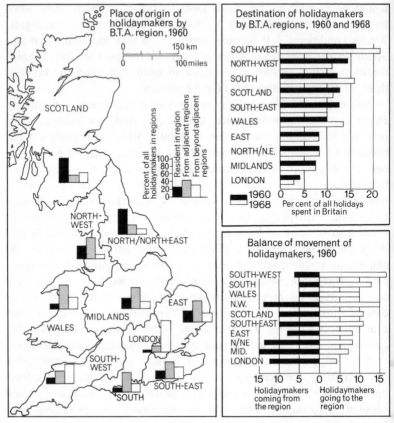

Fig. 21.—*Origins and destinations of holiday-makers in Britain (1968).* This map drawn by Professor Patmore from data issued by the British Travel Association is now rather dated, but the present-day picture has not altered all that much, apart from the South-West which has substantially increased its share. The map illustrates the pull which accessibility and climate exert.

The Timing of Holidays

The holiday season in Britain is encompassed within a very brief period. Ninety per cent of all main holidays are taken between June and September, while, in 1970, 65 per cent were crowded into the two most important holiday months of July and August. These proportions, incidentally, have altered little over the years: in 1951, for instance, the percentages were 92 and 64 respectively. "Even when all holidays are considered," says Patmore "and a mild area favoured for out-of-season holidays is taken as an example, the basic problem is but little alleviated.

In Devon 52·4 per cent of all visitors came during July and August in 1968, 86 per cent between June and September."[6]

This concentration of holiday-making within such a short period brings great disadvantages. (*i*) From the end of July right through August, in a normal year, there is insufficient room in Britain's resorts for all the people who want to go there, hence many, unable to secure accommodation, may have to forfeit their holiday and stay at home. (*ii*) It is impossible for all these people to cram the resorts and other holiday places and hope to get decent bedrooms, well-prepared food or travel in comfort; how can they expect to receive individual service in restaurants, one square yard of beach to call their own, or a seat of their choice in the theatre? (*iii*) Because of the shortness of the season the holiday industry is compelled to cash in quickly, and sometimes ruthlessly, on that proportion of the nation which does get away from home; prices are often higher than they might be. (*iv*) Economically it is unsound, for although facilities are intensively operated (and usually at great profit) for a short spell they are very much under-used for the greater part of the year; extreme fluctuations of this kind are undesirable to say the least from the point of view of employment, transport services, shops, etc.

Lest it be thought that this holiday rush is something peculiar to British holiday-making, it should be pointed out that a similar pattern occurs in other European countries. As Patmore says: "The seasonal peak is far from a uniquely British phenomenon. Less than 5 per cent of the French who go on holiday do so entirely outside the summer season, and the peak is reached in the first half of August when more than 10 million out of a total population of 50 million are on holiday. In Sweden, 90 per cent of those who went on holiday in 1963 did so in the June–August period."[7]

Why do the British mostly holiday in August? The basic constraints are fairly obvious: first, the shortness of the British summer and the (erroneous) belief that the best weather is to be had in August; second, because of the continuing influence of an out-of-date Victorian institution—the August Bank Holiday; third, because of factory and works closures during this period; and, fourth, the limitation of school term. The summer period, granted, is short in Britain but fair weather may be had between May and late September. But the general impression that August provides the best holiday weather is a myth, a myth, however, that is difficult to explode. The introduction of an August Bank Holiday—the first Monday in August—was a good idea in 1871. The working classes came to take a holiday in August week since they had to take one day without pay anyway, and if they opted to take the full week then they chose a "short week." Holidays with pay, however, have obviated the necessity for that, but industry, apart from that in many North Country towns, has clung rather rigidly to the convention of closing down during the early part of August. The moving in 1971 of the August Bank Holiday break to the last Monday in the month in an attempt to relieve the pressure in early August has not, so far, met with conspicuous success for ingrained habits are difficult to change. The most important factor of all, however, is the incidence of school holidays which are in part related to the closures decided by industry and in part to the school examinations. In 1968, of those who holidayed during the months of July and August 73 per cent had children.[8] It would seem that as long as the schools, colleges and universities stick to their present term-times the majority of British holiday-makers will be thrust into the late July–August bottleneck. Industrial holidays should be switched and school terms should be reorganised but, although there has been considerable discussion about these matters for nearly twenty years, the prospect of any radical change seems as far off as ever.

TABLE 32 (A)

Timing of holidays in Britain: Main holidays

Holidays beginning in:	1951	1955	1960	1965	1967 (%)	1968	1969	1970
May	4	4	3	5	6	4	6	5
June	17	14	15	17	15	18	16	16
July	32	29	37	37	34	32	31	33
August	32	36	28	27	30	30	32	32
September	11	13	11	10	12	11	11	10
Other months	4	4	4	5	3	4	2	4

TABLE 32 (B)

Timing of holidays in Britain: Additional holidays

Holidays beginning in:	1967	1968 (%)	1969	1970
May	15	12	15	16
June	12	15	12	11
July	10	10	9	8
August	19	16	19	19
September	23	19	20	19
Other months	20	26	24	27

Source: British Tourist Authority.

Table 32 brings out quite clearly the following points: (*i*) the monthly distribution of holidays has recently changed over the period 1951–70; (*ii*) 96 per cent of all main holidays are taken during the five-month May to September period; (*iii*) the high summer peak of July/August is as strongly marked as ever, with almost two-thirds of all main holidays occurring then; (*iv*) additional holidays are more evenly distributed than main holidays but nearly three-quarters of these are taken between May and September; and (*v*) approximately one-quarter of the additional holidays are taken in the winter half of the year (November to April), in contrast to a mere 4 per cent of main holidays.

Accommodation

Unless one is content to live "rough," some form of accommodation is required by the holiday-maker. Either he pays for his accommodation by staying in an hotel, boarding establishment, etc. or he provides his own by means of a caravan or a tent, or he contrives his board and lodging by staying with relatives and friends. The British Tourist Authority (*see* Table 33) recognises eight main categories of accommodation.

TABLE 33
Accommodation used on main holidays in Britain

	1951	1955	1960	1965	1968	1970
			(%)			
Licensed hotel/motel	10	14	13	13	14	15
Unlicensed hotel, boarding house, etc.	31	27	35	28	23	16
Friends'/relations' home	36	31	32	25	25	24
Caravan	na	8	na	13	16	18
Rented accommodation	8	7	na	8	9	11
Holiday camp	3	4	na	6	5	6
Camping	4	3	na	4	4	6
Paying guest in private house	na	na	na	3	4	7

Figure 22 shows the national pattern of demand and it brings out very clearly the great pressure upon holiday accommodation during the peak holiday period.

One of the most interesting features revealed by Table 33 is the changing pattern of accommodation used by the tourists. It will be observed that the larger hotels, with their superior accommodation, food and facilities, have maintained their ground, even marginally increased it. The smaller private hotels and boarding houses have witnessed a substantial decrease in their share of the market. Indeed, their trade has been so badly hit that large numbers of establishments have turned themselves into flatlet houses which are rented out. Another sharp decline is to be seen in the percentages of holidays spent with friends or relations over the past two decades, although the proportion —about 25 per cent—has tended to remain fairly stable during the past

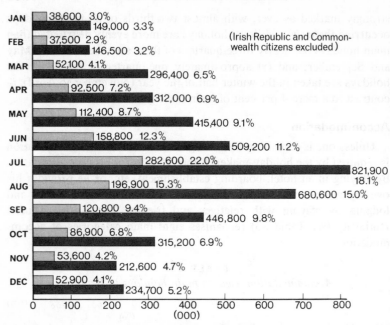

FIG. 22.—*Seasonality of foreign visitor arrivals in Britain.* Visitor arrivals are concentrated in the summer months and particularly in July and August. However, as the graphs show, there has been a greater spread of arrivals throughout the year thanks to the efforts of the B.T.A. to encourage foreign visitors outside the summer season. Notwithstanding continued midsummer peaking, there is now a much more equitable spread of arrivals.

five years. The overall decrease, however, is most probably related to the general rise in real incomes. Contrasting with these decreases, the popularity of informal and self-catering accommodation, *e.g.* caravans, rented accommodation and holiday camps, has increased appreciably. Statistics relating to the number and use of caravans in 1951 are not available; by 1955, however, some 2 million people were using caravans for holidays, which accounted for about 8 per cent of tourist accommodation; ten years later the figure had almost doubled and caravans accounted for 13 per cent of the accommodation; and in 1970 the total had risen to over 5 million accounting for 18 per cent of main holidays. This rapid growth in the more informal types of accommodation, whether it be in caravans, camps or in rented premises, reflects the changed attitudes to holiday-making; at the same time it gives the tourist an increased measure of freedom and substantially cuts holiday expenses.

The geographical distribution of holiday accommodation reflects two, often conflicting, conditions: demand and planning constraints. The great majority of hotels and boarding houses are to be found of course in the urban resorts and these provide almost one-third of the total accommodation. Motels, as one might expect, are closely tied to the great motor highways and are often located near to important road junctions. "The needs of various types of clientele are seen in the respective locations of youth hostels and holiday camps. The network of hostels ... [serves] the needs of walkers and cyclists, with particular concentrations in the most scenic areas. Holiday camps, in contrast, cater for a more gregarious and static form of holiday: their location is exclusively coastal, with ready access to suitable beaches of prime importance."[9] In 1970 there were seventy-two holiday camps in England and Wales which accounted for 6 per cent of the holiday accommodation. The rapid growth of caravanning has created a major problem: the physical difficulty of accommodating caravans in large numbers and, second, the preservation of visual amenity. The problem of disfigurement of coast and countryside had already begun in pre-war days when chalets, converted railway coaches and other holiday dwellings appeared. This uncontrolled development was halted by the 1960 *Caravan Sites and Control of Development Act*. "Any constraint of this kind will bring conflicting pressures of demand," says Patmore, "but it has effectively limited and channelled growth in many areas."[10]

FOREIGN TOURISM

United Kingdom Travellers Abroad

The number of Britons taking holidays abroad has increased very substantially since 1950; the rate of increase has moreover been an accelerating one, except between 1968 and 1970, a period of temporary stagnation. The numbers participating in foreign travel, according to B.T.A. estimates, have increased from 1·5 million in 1951 to 5 million in 1966, to over 8·0 million in 1971 and to 10·5 million in 1974. While the 1967 figure showed an increase of only 4 per cent over 1966, the 1969 figure showed an increase of 10 per cent over 1968, and those of 1971 an increase of 14 per cent over 1970. The increases between 1967 and 1969 were all the more remarkable since currency restrictions were in force in the non-sterling area. It is obvious that the United Kingdom is now one of the world's greatest generators of international tourism. In 1967, 71 per cent of visits abroad were for holidays, 13 per cent in connection with business and 16 per cent for miscellaneous other purposes.

The rapid growth in the numbers of United Kingdom residents going abroad is very largely a reflection of the growth of inclusive tours which are able to offer cut-price holidays. It is interesting to note that the percentage of British visitors who travel abroad on inclusive tours is considerably greater than the percentage of foreigners visiting Britain who take advantage of similar facilities. The average length of stay for holidays abroad is about a fortnight, although business visits are commonly of shorter duration while visits to friends and relatives tend to be longer. Where the holiday destination lies outside of Europe the stay is usually longer than two weeks; for example, visitors to North America average a four- to five-week duration. For several years the average length of stay abroad has remained fairly stable at about a fortnight but we can probably expect to see this *average* duration decrease as short winter season holidays grow in importance.

Where are the destinations of the British tourist? The great majority go to the Continent, especially to the countries of Western Europe and, in fact, only about 10 per cent of the destinations are outside Europe. Whereas in the 1950s the principal European destinations were France and Switzerland, today the most popular destination by a considerable margin is Spain (2 million visits in 1974); Spain, in 1974, accounted for 21 per cent of the total visitors holidaying in Europe. In 1974 France took 17 per cent, Italy 7 per cent and West Germany 6 per cent of the foreign trips. 1969 saw a striking increase in the number of visitors to the then Sterling Area destinations of Gibraltar, Malta and Cyprus: numbers increased by over one-third. In the case of Malta there was a quite spectacular increase, visitors going up from slightly more than 100,000 to 150,000. Substantial increases were also registered in the numbers of people visiting Greece and Yugoslavia and in both cases a total of 100,000 was reached for the first time. 235,000 visited North America, approximately two-thirds going to the United States, the remaining third to Canada. About 150,000 spent their holidays on cruise ships.

Table 34 gives a breakdown of the visits of United Kingdom residents to the countries of Europe for the period 1965 to 1969.

Since 1969 the most notable developments have been a continuing increase in the numbers visiting Spain and the growth of numbers visiting the newly developing tourist destinations such as Yugoslavia, Turkey, Tunisia and Morocco.

In 1969 British tourists spent £324m on holidays abroad, in 1970 £470m, in 1971 £528m and in 1972 over £650m. These figures represent approximately one-third of the total amount spent by British

TABLE 34

Main European destinations of British holiday-makers

Country visited	Number of visits (000)				
	1965	1966	1967	1968	1969
France	829	864	918	754	919
West Germany	373	405	434	452	525
Italy	703	756	637	538	604
Belgium and Luxembourg	318	294	329	306	324
Netherlands	260	292	301	314	375
Austria	245	295	284	271	246
Denmark, Norway and Sweden	174	203	210	215	205
Switzerland	348	331	309	272	302
Spain	803	958	1060	1282	1506
Other countries	223	276	258	253	330
TOTAL	4276	4674	4740	4657	5336

Source: British Travel Authority.

people on holiday. If we compare these figures with those of two decades ago—in 1951 £320m was spent on holidays at home and £60m on holidays abroad—we see a quite astonishing increase in the expenditure on holidays outside the United Kingdom. In fact, until 1970 the British spent more on holidays abroad than was earned by foreign visitors holidaying in Britain. In 1971 there was a credit of £52m on the internal travel account.

Tourists Visiting the United Kingdom

Let us turn now to the tourists who visited the United Kingdom. In summary, 7·6 million overseas visitors came in 1973, including slightly more than three-quarters of a million from Eire, and they spent a record £872m.

In 1951, by contrast, some 700,000 people visited Britain either for pleasure or business: the visitors were mainly Americans, French, Scandinavians and Dutch. These holiday-makers did not compete with the average British holiday-maker for accommodation, partly because they did not use the same kind of accommodation and partly because they did not frequent the same places. The foreign visitor was typically a person of substance who stayed at three- and four-star hotels and who came to Britain in search of the historic and the picturesque. The chief destination of these visitors was London; the principal other places to which they went were Windsor, York, Edinburgh, Oxford, Cambridge, Stratford-on-Avon, Bath, Bristol, the cathedral towns of Canterbury, Winchester, Salisbury, Exeter and Chester, and the large cities of Glasgow, Manchester and Birmingham. Only two resorts, Brighton and Bournemouth received appreciable numbers of foreign visitors.

The growth of the overseas tourist trade was steady but rather slow—in the early 1950s only about 20,000 came a year—but by 1960 the flow had begun significantly to improve and by 1965 $3\frac{1}{2}$ million visitors were coming to Britain. By 1968 the figure had reached 5 million, in 1970 $6\frac{3}{4}$ million and in 1973 in excess of 8 million. This growth rate has been quite remarkable but the annual rate of growth during the present decade is not expected to be as high as that during the 1960s. The B.T.A. comments: "As tourism grows so it becomes more competitive and more difficult to maintain the impetus of the growth. However, it seems reasonable to estimate that the growth in tourism to the U.K. during the 1970s will be something like ten per cent per annum up to 1975 and then five per cent per annum up to 1980."[11]

Table 35 gives details of the number of overseas visitors analysed by country of permanent residence for the period 1965 to 1969.

Scrutiny of these figures reveals some interesting facts and features. Over this five-year period, there was an accelerating growth in the number of visitors to Great Britain: the 1969 figure showed an increase of approximately 65 per cent over 1965. There was a substantial increase in the number coming from the United States and Canada—the number of visitors almost doubled. Visitors from Western Europe grew steadily, if rather slowly, at nearly 200,000 per year until 1967 after which date the growth increased to around 300,000 per year. Among the European countries, the Dutch, the Swiss and the Italians showed the greatest growth. Visitors from Eire remained fairly constant at around 700,000, while visitors from South Africa, Australia and New Zealand were fairly small in total, though between 1968 and 1969 there was a substantial increase in the number of South Africans who visited Britain. Finally, visitors from other non-sterling areas almost doubled over the five-year period.

Is it possible to discern any reasons behind this pattern of tourism? The large number of Americans and Canadians who visit Britain come mainly because of ethnic, cultural and historical ties; in 1967, for example, 1,800,000 North Americans came to Europe but 1,104,000 of them visited Britain. Western Europe in 1969 provided some 60 per cent of our overseas visitors and here, clearly, we can see the geographical factor at play. The largest number of visitors came from Eire and physical propinquity would obviously seem to be a major factor. Again, Britain has larger numbers of visitors from her near European neighbours than from such countries as Austria, Switzerland and Italy which are more distant. On the other hand, Spain, notwithstanding her

TABLE 35
Overseas visitors to the U.K.

Country of origin	Number of visits (000)				
	1965	1966	1967	1968	1969
United States	713	833	904	963	1295
Canada	184	215	200	276	361
NORTH AMERICA	897	1048	1104	1239	1656
France	354	384	418	458	543
West Germany	342	383	397	463	570
Italy	86	112	127	142	180
Belgium and Luxembourg	138	133	176	209	257
Netherlands	186	195	229	286	357
Austria	31	29	29	31	36
Denmark, Norway and Sweden	167	211	226	272	287
Switzerland	86	97	111	123	156
Spain	37	42	42	57	72
Other Western Europe	45	57	67	82	99
WESTERN EUROPE	1472	1643	1822	2123	2557
OTHER NON-STERLING AREA	178	215	245	280	360
Irish Republic	702	697	732	783	764
Australia and New Zealand	89	99	107	106	126
South Africa	52	57	66	63	81
Other Sterling Area	207	208	213	234	277
OVERSEAS STERLING AREA	1050	1061	1118	1186	1248
ALL COUNTRIES	3597	3967	4289	4828	5821

nearness to Britain, sends few visitors; standards of living are lower in Spain than in most Western European countries and consequently fewer holiday abroad, the climate of Britain is scarcely one to tempt Spaniards to come here. Sheer distance and high travel cost, clearly militates against large numbers of visitors from Australia, New Zealand and South Africa.

Nearly two-thirds of the overseas visitors to Britain come for the purposes of enjoyment and entertainment; approximately one-fifth come for business reasons. The average length of stay is about 15 days, and has tended to decline during recent years. On the other hand, the average expenditure per visit has increased and is now running at just over £60. Total receipts from tourism were in 1973 £872m or 12 per cent of invisible exports. The majority of visitors (55 per cent), came in the four months of June, July, August and September, but there is some indication of a slight change in the seasonal pattern, more visits now being made in spring. Nearly twice as many visitors travel by air as by sea, and over 80 per cent of the visitors from North America come by air.

Advantages and Disadvantages

Having reviewed the patterns of tourism in the United Kingdom, it will be useful to conclude this account with some of the advantages and disadvantages which can accrue. Some of the advantages are fairly obvious and frequently extolled, but not everyone is agreed that the country's rapidly growing tourist industry is a good thing and draw attention to some of the drawbacks it brings in its wake.

In 1973 8 million visitors from abroad visited Britain and, if fares to British carriers are included, total receipts from foreign tourism amounted to something around £872m. Thus tourism is responsible for about 12 per cent of the country's invisible earnings and about 4·5 per cent of all exports. Discounting the spending on travel fares which was around £180m, internal spending by visitors amounted to about £650m. The following figures, which are estimates for the year 1971, give a breakdown of this expenditure:

	£m
Hotels	120
Eating in restaurants	120
Shopping	140
Internal transport	40
Other	50
	470

It will be clear that many sections of the community benefit from this injection of additional wealth that tourism brings. Furthermore, if we take into consideration the multiplier effect of this expenditure, then the value of foreign tourism to the country is greater. It may be argued that against this credit income we should set the debit expenditure of British foreign holiday-making but in actual fact between 1968 and 1971 the country earned more from overseas visitors than Britons spent abroad (*see* p. 236).

The demands of the foreign and the domestic tourist provide employment for large numbers of people in a wide variety of occupations (hotel and catering, entertainment, transport, souvenirs, building trades, etc.). Moreover, there are many peripheral areas which rely substantially upon the tourist trade for their livelihood and but for tourism would be in a very depressed condition.

Tourism, too, exerts a favourable effect in that it stimulates the appropriate authorities to look after the national treasures, *e.g.* historic buildings, ancient monuments, places of special scenic value.

One complaint is that great numbers of visitors emphasise an already existing congestion and lead to increases in prices: many feel, in fact, that they are subsidising overseas visitors. But, as Morrison Halcrow has pointed out, life would be less attractive and more expensive without the tourists: "A big market can put up prices; but it can also bring the benefits of mass-marketing, and the size of the tourist market in London has reached the point where this is beginning to be true in many of the services available."[12] Tourism brings a wider range of goods in the shops, more taxis, more restaurants, more theatres, etc. And, as Halcrow says, "... if the West End theatres had to depend on suburbia for their support, the theatre would be in even more serious financial difficulties...."[13] There may be some loss of amenity for the Londoner, but there are compensating gains.

Against the advantages must be listed the disadvantages, above all the problems of congestion, housing shortages, employment and conservation. The great influx of tourists in summer, especially in London, exacerbate the congestion on the capital's thoroughfares and underground system, although tourists tend to use public transport mostly during off-peak periods. "A more serious objection to the growth of London as a tourist centre," says Halcrow, "is that houses and flats in the centre of the city increasingly tend to find themselves turned into hotels, to the detriment of the housing situation."[14] Another complaint is that the industry, especially its hotel and catering side, employs large numbers of foreigners who compete with the indigenous population for houses and other types of accommodation. Such foreign labour enjoys all the social benefits of the British social security system yet send a high proportion of earnings back to the native country as remittances. Many of these problems, however, result simply from the fact that the distribution of tourists is geographically unbalanced: there are too many concentrated in London.

An important issue, closely related to tourism, is the problem of conservation. Our towns and villages, our coasts and countryside, our historical monuments, our ways of life all to a greater or lesser degree experience the impact (in terms of wear and tear, vandalism, litter, filling stations, wayside cafés, signposts, etc.) of the tourist. Dr T. J. O'Driscoll, Executive Director of the European Travel Commission, discussing conservation and tourism, has said: "There is a cliché in our tourism activities that nobody travels to sit in an aeroplane seat or to sleep in an hotel bedroom. What they are interested in, what is the impelling attraction is the 'destination activity.' Ideally tourism should have little effect on the virtues of the destination and its inhabitants. Countries should simply 'be themselves' accepted and accepting, but facilities for visitors must be provided and those of us concerned with providing them know too well how delicate a task it is to change standards without altering the essential character one wishes to retain. As more people seek to share directly in tourism income this becomes even more difficult. National characteristics and natural and man-made amenities are the basic raw materials of tourism. They cannot be allowed to be eroded whether through ignorance or through commercialism. Increasing attention must be given to analysing and researching the situations which arise so that solutions compatible with accepted conservation principles can be found. Not only the physical environment but the cultural environment is ... involved."[15] Tourism by its very nature raises environmental issues of both a natural and cultural kind and it becomes imperative that these issues are faced and dealt with imaginatively and effectively with a minimum of change and dislocation.

NOTES

1. *Tourism in Wales*, Welsh Tourist Board, 1967, p. 8.
2. *The Planning of the Coastline*, Countryside Commission, H.M.S.O., p. 9.
3. J. A. Patmore, *Land and Leisure*, David & Charles, 1970, p. 156.
4. *Op. cit.*, p. 157.
5. *Idem*, p. 158.
6. *Idem*, p. 161.
7. *Idem*, p. 164.
8. *Idem*, p.161.
9. Patmore, *op. cit.*, p. 166.
10. *Op. cit.*, p. 169.
11. *British Travel News*, No. 37, Spring, 1972, p. 4.
12. "Tourism: the Hidden Assets," *Daily Telegraph*, 15th September, 1972.
13. *Ibid.*
14. *Ibid.*
15. Address at the opening of the Europa Nostra Conference, reproduced in *British Travel News*, No. 39, Autumn, 1972, p. 19.

Chapter XV

Introduction to Tourism in Europe

THE EUROPEAN TRAVEL MARKET

T H E European Travel Market Study (1972) provides a valuable source of information about tourism in Europe and much of what follows is based upon it.[1] It gives a description of the flows of European tourism and highlights some of the principal characteristics of the European travel market. Taking the three years 1960, 1965 and 1970, data is given to show:

(*i*) the internal flow of travel within Western Europe;

(*ii*) the outward flow from Western Europe to other regions of the world;

(*iii*) the inward flow into Western Europe from other parts of the world.

In 1969 some 155 million West Europeans took a holiday of at least four days away from home. Such holidays, expressed as percentages of national populations, ranged from 60 per cent in the cases of the United Kingdom, Switzerland and the Scandinavian countries, to as little as 15 per cent in the case of Spain, Yugoslavia and Greece. However, out of the 155 million taking holidays, 122 million (80 per cent) were domestic: only about 33 million went on foreign travel (by 1973 the figure had risen to about 55 million). West Germany, France and the United Kingdom, in that order, were the three greatest generators of foreign traffic, and between them they accounted for 60 per cent of total intra-European traffic. On the receiving end, the outstanding feature in the flow pattern has been the rapid growth in the traffic to Spain—from 6 to 21 million—and the dominating share which Spain now has in intra-European traffic. If short-period excursions are excluded, the market shares of both Italy and Scandinavia witnessed a marked reduction over the decade 1960–70.

Total intra-European arrivals grew at an average rate of 10 per cent a year—from 33 million in 1960 to 94 million in 1970.

There has been little significant change in the seasonal pattern of tourist arrivals, apart from a slight improvement in the "shoulder" months; the car provides the chief mode of transport and accounts for about half of the transport market, notwithstanding the boom in holiday charter flights; and the hotel remains the dominant form of accommodation with about half of the market.

Looking at the global picture, Europe is the principal tourist destination receiving over 150 million arrivals or over 75 per cent of international tourist movements. The major generating regions are North-West Europe and North America. Table 36 shows the West European foreign holiday traffic for three sample years during the decade 1960–70.

TABLE 36
European foreign holiday traffic

	Numbers of tourists holidaying abroad (m)		
Country	1962	1966	1970
West Germany	6·3	11·2	23·0
France	2·0	4·2	12·0
United Kingdom	2·5	4·0	5·7
Netherlands	1·5	2·5	3·0
Scandinavia	1·2	2·5	3·0
Italy	0·5	0·8	2·6
Switzerland	1·0	1·7	2·8

It will be noted that with the limited exception of Italy, none of the Mediterranean countries is of any real consequence as a generator of tourism. Portugal, Spain, Yugoslavia and Greece have scarcely participated at all in international tourism so far, although with the growth of tourism and growing prosperity they have now begun for the first time to contribute significantly to the international tourist flow. For example, in 1970 some 3 million Yugoslavs visited Italy and nearly 2 million Portuguese visited Spain, although in both cases the figures include short-period excursions. Figures 23–26 show the flow of tourists to and within the various regions of Europe.

If there has been a rapid growth in intra-European travel, there has been an equally rapid growth of travel from extra-European countries into Europe. The total number of arrivals rose from some 9 million in 1960 to around 23 million in 1970, although these figures undoubtedly include an element of duplication: the Travel Market Study suggests that the number of unduplicated journeys to Europe from outside probably rose from 3 million in 1960 to 8 million in 1970. Half of these extra-European arrivals in 1970 were North Americans. Italy, throughout the decade, led as the chief European destination for overseas visitors, although France, the United Kingdom and Spain all exhibited a high sustained growth.

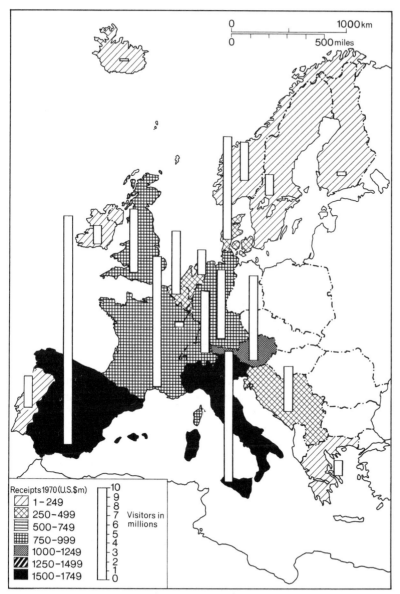

FIG. 23.—*Europe: map of tourist arrivals and receipts (1970).*

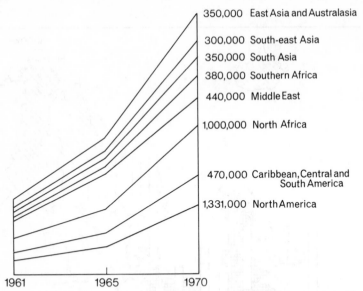

350,000   East Asia and Australasia

300,000   South-east Asia

350,000   South Asia

380,000   Southern Africa

440,000   Middle East

1,000,000 North Africa

470,000   Caribbean, Central and
          South America

1,331,000 North America

1961   1965   1970

FIG. 24.—*Arrivals of West Europeans outside Europe.* Within the decade 1960–70 the numbers of West Europeans travelling outside of Europe more than trebled. Over $4\frac{1}{2}$ million travelled to other regions but chiefly to North America and North Africa. The greatest increases over the decade were to North America where there was almost a fivefold increase, to North Africa where there was a fourfold increase, while to the other regions, the Middle East excepted, there was a roughly threefold increase. The increase to the Middle East scarcely doubled.

The rate of growth of travel from Europe to other regions of the world has proceeded even faster than either intra-European travel or travel to Europe. In 1960 2 million people travelled out of Europe to extra-European destinations; by 1970 the figure had risen to 9 million. North America (mainly to Canada, the United States and the Caribbean) and Africa (principally to the Atlas Countries, the offshore Atlantic islands and East Africa) were the chief destinations.

Since the early 1950s there has been a gradually accelerating growth in international tourism in Europe—except in 1967 and 1968 when there was an overall slackening. Such things as political upheavals, currency changes and limitations on foreign holiday spending have had important repercussions on the tourist trade of individual countries. For example, the military coup in Greece temporarily affected that country's growing tourist trade and Portugal was adversely affected during the late 1960s by the devalution of the Spanish peseta and U.K. sterling and, also, by the imposition of currency limits on U.K. citizens travelling outside the sterling area. This general slackening in tourism growth

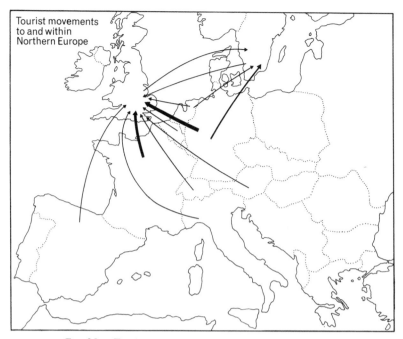

FIG. 25.—*Tourist movements to and within Northern Europe.*

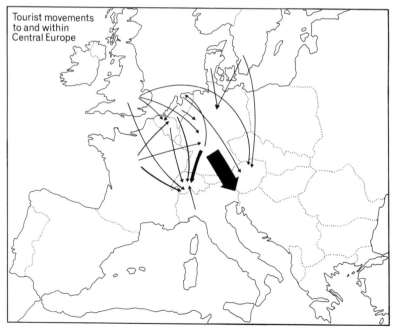

FIG. 26.—*Tourist movements to and within Central Europe.*

in Europe however proved to be merely a temporary decline and in 1969 the upward trend re-established itself and each year since has witnessed substantial gains.

Trends in Recent Years

Let us now enquire a little more closely into the trends in tourism in Western Europe during recent years (*see also* Figs. 27 and 28).

Study of Table 37 shows that in terms of percentage growth the United Kingdom very comfortably outstripped all other countries offering a comparable product (scenery/history/culture) and, in fact, was only rivalled by Spain whose visitor traffic is dominated by a very different product (sun/sea/sand) based on mass package holidays. During the period 1964–70 visitor traffic to Spain increased by 108 per cent, that to the United Kingdom by 107 per cent. No other country listed could show an increase of even 50 per cent; Austria came nearest with 44 per cent. Italy's and Switzerland's rate of growth was very sluggish, only 22 and 17 per cent respectively. Not only did Spain and the United Kingdom show the fastest growth rate but they had the

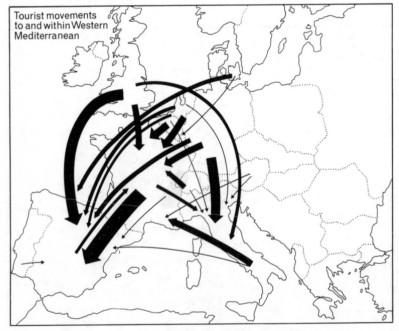

FIG. 27.—*Tourist movements to and within the Western Mediterranean.*

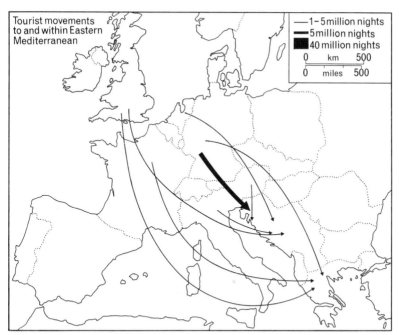

FIG. 28.—*Tourist movements to and within the Eastern Mediterranean.*

smoothest rate of growth—they were the only countries in which foreign visitor arrivals increased each year. The particular success of Spain and the United Kingdom may well partly reflect the devaluations of the peseta and the pound sterling in 1969 and 1967 respectively.

Table 38 shows that Spain and the United Kingdom also had most success in terms of the percentage growth of their tourist traffic from other O.E.C.D. European countries. In each case the overall growth in the period exceeded 100 per cent. The other countries lagged even further behind Spain and the United Kingdom than they did in terms of their total traffic. "The percentage growth of intra-European tourist traffic has in fact been smaller than that of total traffic in *all* the countries under review except the two leaders. Again, only the United Kingdom and Spain have recorded an increase from 1965 onwards. In Italy the number of European visitors attracted has fallen in each of the last four years [to 1970]. Switzerland, another traditional magnet for tourists, has also experienced a decline in European traffic in the latter half of the . . . [1960s], the level of 1964 only being regained in 1970."[2]

Table 39 indicates that tourist traffic to Europe from North America increased at a greater rate than intra-European tourism. Spain alone of

TABLE 37

Visitors to European countries (from all countries)

	1964 Nos. (000)	1964 Index[1]	1965 Nos. (000)	1965 Index[1]	1966 Nos. (000)	1966 Index[1]	1967 Nos. (000)	1967 Index[1]	1968 Nos. (000)	1968 Index[1]	1969 Nos. (000)	1969 Index[1]	1970 Nos. (000)	1970 Index[1]
Austria A	6,158	100	6,413	104	6,865	111	6,673	108	7,344	119	7,842	127	8,867	144
France F	10,250	100	11,100	108	11,800	115	12,000	117	10,800	105	12,100	118	13,700	134
W. Germany A	6,129	100	6,410	105	6,676	109	6,621	108	6,557	107	7,022	115	7,715	126
Italy F	11,613	100	11,100	96	12,700	109	12,600	108	12,600	108	13,500	116	14,189	122
Netherlands A	1,762	100	1,820	103	1,868	106	1,869	106	2,065	117	2,197	125	2,339	136
Spain F	11,601	100	13,072	113	17,252	149	17,859	154	19,184	165	21,682	187	24,105	208
Switzerland A	5,837	100	5,688	97	5,924	101	5,901	101	6,000	103	6,259	107	6,840	117
United Kingdom F	3,257	100	3,597	110	3,967	122	4,289	132	4,828	148	5,821	179	6,730	207

Source: All figures as quoted in O.E.C.D. "Tourism in Member Countries" 1965–1971.
A: Accommodation check. F: Frontier check.
1. Base = 100 in 1964.
2. Estimate.
3. Total Western Europe (O.E.C.D. Europe residents are not separately identified).

TABLE 38

Visitors to European countries (from other O.E.C.D. European countries)

	1964 Nos. (000)	1964 Index[1]	1965 Nos. (000)	1965 Index[1]	1966 Nos. (000)	1966 Index[1]	1967 Nos. (000)	1967 Index[1]	1968 Nos. (000)	1968 Index[1]	1969 Nos. (000)	1969 Index[1]	1970 Nos. (000)	1970 Index[1]
Austria A	5,488	100	5,667	103	6,024	110	5,778	105	6,387	116	6,725	123	7,658	140
France F	8,228	100	8,824	107	9,381	114	9,310	113	8,280	101	9,110	111	10,050	122

	Nos.	Index	Nos.	Index	Nos.	Index	Nos.	Index	Nos.	Index	Nos.	Index	Nos.	Index
W. Germany A	4,504	100	4,710	105	4,838	107	4,784	106	4,727	105	4,844	108	5,185	115
Italy F	8,326[2]	100	7,958	96	8,678	104	7,445	89	6,797	82	6,308	76	6,170	74
Netherlands A	1,270	100	1,282	101	1,291	102	1,264	100	1,382	109	1,398	110	1,499	118
Spain F	9,942	100	11,391	115	15,445	155	16,021	161	17,191	173	19,297	194	21,275	214
Switzerland A	4,768	100	4,618	97	4,749	100	4,649	98	4,658	98	4,632	97	4,948	104
United Kingdom F[3]	1,342	100	1,472	110	1,643	122	1,822	136	2,123	158	2,557	191	2,975	222

For sources and footnotes see Table 37.

TABLE 39

Visitors to European countries (from the U.S.A. and Canada)

	1964		1965		1966		1967		1968		1969		1970	
	Nos. (000)	Index 1	Nos. (000)	Index[1]	Nos. (000)	Index[1]	Nos. (000)	Index[1]	Nos. (000)	Index[1]	Nos. (000)	Index[1]	Nos. (000)	Index[1]
Austria A	362	100	412	114	475	131	487	135	505	140	603	167	737	204
France F	1017	100	1088	107	1156	114	1180	116	920	90	1240	122	1530	150
W. Germany A	1052	100	1113	106	1191	113	1231	117	1173	112	1395	133	1665	158
Italy F	1280	100	1330	104	1468	115	1509	118	1589	124	1987	155	2083	163
Netherlands A	343	100	366	107	394	115	419	122	462	135	547	159	616	180
Spain F	780	100	734	94	786	101	763	98	796	102	1006	129	1154	148
Switzerland A	706	100	714	101	768	109	824	117	839	119	1051	149	1273	180
United Kingdom F	767	100	897	117	1048	137	1104	144	1239	162	1656	216	1975	257

For sources and footnotes see Table 37.

the eight countries failed to see a higher rate of growth among North Americans than among Europeans—the increase in North American tourists over the period was less than 50 per cent. On the other hand, the United Kingdom enjoyed the highest rate of growth with a percentage increase over the period of 157 per cent. Austria came a good second with 104 per cent increase, while both Switzerland and the Netherlands showed appreciable increases of 80 per cent each.

Tourist Receipts

International tourist receipts (and expenditures) of European countries for 1969 and 1970 are given in Table 40. These figures are taken from the O.E.C.D. Tourism Report (1971). Following the stagnation in 1967 and 1968, tourism picked up in 1969 and 1970. In 1970 foreign currency receipts among the European members of O.E.C.D. increased by 16 per cent to $10·4 billion over the 1969 figures.

"International tourism in O.E.C.D. countries during 1970 benefited from a sustained rate of economic expansion generally, a relatively calm social scene, the lifting of travel allowance restrictions in the United Kingdom and their easing in France. Expenditure on tourist travel abroad continued to be sustained by the buoyancy of private consumption although part of the high rate of growth in total O.E.C.D. expen-

TABLE 40

International tourist receipts and expenditures of European countries
(rounded figures in U.S.$m)

	Receipts			Expenditure		
	1969	*1970*	%	*1969*	*1970*	%
Austria	785	999	27	296	323	9
Belgium and Luxembourg	314	348	11	454	492	8
Denmark	260	314	21	248	273	10
Finland	84	120	43	83	86	4
France	1072	1192	11	1039	1057	2
West Germany	915	1024	12	1900	2493	31
Greece	150	194	30	48	55	15
Iceland	4	na	na	3	5	96
Eire	188	193	3	91	na	na
Italy	1632	1639	—	493	727	48
Netherlands	334	421	26	540	598	11
Norway	128	156	22	115	140	22
Spain	1311	1681	28	86	113	31
Portugal	167	222	33	74	98	32
Sweden	127	143	13	365	481	32
Switzerland	643	733	14	275	309	12
Yugoslavia	242	275	14	74	113	53
United Kingdom	862	1040	21	778	931	20

Source: Annual Report of Tourism Committee, O.E.C.D., 1971.

diture on foreign tourism must be ascribed to the sharp general rise in prices experienced throughout 1970. Moreover, the revaluation of the Deutsche Mark in October, 1969, stimulated travel abroad by German tourists in 1970 while the devaluation of the French Franc in August, 1969, still made itself felt on foreign travel to France in 1970."[3]

Table 40 reveals that every country enjoyed increased receipts although in the case of Eire general inflation no doubt cancelled out the small percentage increase. A few countries, notably Belgium, Luxembourg, France and West Germany, showed only a moderate increase. On the other hand, Austria, Finland, Greece, Spain and Portugal had handsome increases. It is worth noting that West Germany, Spain, Sweden and Yugoslavia show an expenditure on international tourism that is greater than their receipts. Noteworthy, too, is the fact that the United Kingdom continued to increase its share of the European market.

Between the various countries of Europe there are very wide variations in the receipts from international tourism as a proportion of their total exports of goods and services. Table 41 clearly demonstrates that some countries depend much more than others upon tourism for their exports.

CURRENT TRENDS AND PROBLEMS

Until 1972 tourist trends and patterns in Europe seemed stable and expanding: for many years the flows in traffic had continued to increase and the industry had prospered. Minor fluctuations and temporary recessions had occurred as, for instance in 1967–68, but on the whole the keynote was one of expansion. In 1973 a series of events took place—currency problems, domestic troubles in the United States, the Middle East War, the energy crisis—which gave the tourist industry a severe

TABLE 41

Receipts from international tourism as a proportion of exports of goods and services (%—1969)

Spain	33·6	France	5·9
Portugal	22·3	Finland	3·7
Austria	22·1	U.K.	3·3
Greece	14·3	Norway	3·0
Ireland	13·5	Netherlands	2·7
Switzerland	11·3	West Germany	2·6
Yugoslavia	10·3	Belgium and Luxembourg	2·5
Italy	9·7	Sweden	1·8
Denmark	6·5		

Source: O.E.C.D. quoted in D. McEwen, *The European Tourist Markets*, Tourism Planning and Research Ltd., 1971.

jolt and which may presage a big change in the European tourist business. It is too early to see what precisely will be the effect, but certainly there have been some pointers since 1972 to the fact that the tourism boom might be slackening off.

As Arthur Sandles has pointed out, for a generation European tourism development, especially in the more expensive end of the market, was largely geared to the American tourist trade.[4] Until 1972 a steady flood of affluent Americans poured into Europe. But in that year the numbers of Americans travelling across the North Atlantic began to slow down, and in 1973 there was an actual decline. The United States dollar problems in the spring and summer of 1973 and the domestic upheaval of the Watergate affair must have contributed, and there would seem to be a strong possibility of an at least temporary contraction in the American overseas travel market; any such contraction would deal a severe blow to the European tourist business.

There are other discernible changes. The prosperity of the Federal Republic of Germany has made that country the greatest generator of tourism in Europe. Once content with Switzerland and Austria, Germans are now travelling much further afield—to Spain, Italy and Yugoslavia—with the result that "British tour operators have considerable difficulty in competing with the Germans in the purchase of . . . [accommodation] in Spain."[5] Increasing numbers of West Germans are also coming to Britain, attracted by the cheapness of British holidays since the devaluation of the pound. The weakness of the pound may well also lead to a decrease in the number of Britons travelling to the continent; costs in 1974 were up by some 15–20 per cent over summer 1973 figures.

The energy crisis made itself felt with dramatic suddenness. The shortage of aircraft fuel drastically curtailed air services and petrol costs may well cut back holiday motor travel. The cumulative effect may alter considerably all existing trends in European tourism.

NOTES

1. Published by the European Travel Commission, 1972.

2. "Tourism in Britain and Europe Compared," Research Newsletter, No. 4, 1972, in *British Travel News*, No. 37, Spring, 1972.

3. "Organisation for Economic Co-operation and Development Report 1971," Research Newsletter, No. 2, Autumn, 1971, in *British Travel News*, No. 35, Autumn, 1971.

4. "All Change in the Holiday Business," Financial Times Survey: Europe II, *The Financial Times*, 17th December, 1973.

5. Sandles, *op. cit.*

Chapter XVI

Tourism in Western and Central Europe

EIRE

EIRE, or the Republic of Ireland, cannot be counted among the major tourist countries since the total number of visitors is only 2 million a year, yet from the point of view of Eire's economy tourism is of exceptional importance for it is the country's biggest money-earner after agriculture and plays a vital role in the balance of payments: Austria and Spain apart, tourism plays a more important role in balancing the Republic's international payments than in any other European country. Until the troubles in Northern Ireland started, Irish tourism had expanded rapidly. Between 1960 and 1970 the income from tourism just about doubled—from around £50m in 1960 to around £100m in 1970: the receipts for 1971 totalled £103m. The vast majority of tourists to Eire—around 90 per cent—have come from her near neighbours, Great Britain and Northern Ireland. For example, in 1971, there were 1,115,000 visitors from Great Britain, who spent some £33m, and 325,000 from Northern Ireland, who spent £8m; the remaining half a million or so visitors were accounted for mainly by the United States, which is Eire's second best market.

The troubles in Northern Ireland have had crippling effects upon the Irish tourist industry. Large numbers of British holiday-makers have been either frightened off or angered by terrorist violence and cancelled their holiday bookings in Eire. 1972 was a bad year for Irish tourism. The Wallace Arnold Company, the biggest coach tour company handling holidays in Ireland, struck Eire off its schedule; the C.I.E., the Irish Transport Company, was compelled to close down two of its three offices in Britain; the British and Irish Line, the Dublin-based shipping company, had its traffic reduced by a third; Aer Lingus, the Irish airline, estimated a drop in revenue of £4m; while more than 100 hotels in Eire were faced with closure and appealed to the Irish Government for loans of almost £1m to ward off disaster. In 1972 estimated earnings dropped by one-fifth. There were 212,000 fewer British visitors, which meant a loss in revenue of £25m. Clearly, if the troubles in Ulster are not resolved, the Irish tourist industry is likely to suffer a very serious dislocation which may take many years to overcome.

Tourism has in the past been an important sector of growth in the Irish economy. Eire has long suffered from an ill-balanced and under-developed economy as well as continuing depopulation. Much has been done during the past fifty years, especially since the Second World War, to revitalise the economy, and in this revitalisation, tourism has a very important role to play—for perhaps more than anything else, and certainly more quickly than anything else, it can facilitate and develop the spatial redistribution of economic activity in the country. Many parts of Eire offer possibilities for enhanced tourist development but it is in western Eire that the major areas of tourism growth and potential lie; development in the west "has the outstanding merit of providing employment in areas traditionally dominated by a declining farm economy."[1] Tourism must not be looked upon as a panacea for the economic problems and difficulties of the west, but it could alleviate some of the troubles and help to stem the drift from the land. It is not easy to estimate with any precision how many people are employed in tourism but the Irish Tourist Board (*Board Failte Eireann*) quotes some 200,000 or 15 per cent of all those employed in the country.[2]

"The leisurely English tourists of the eighteenth and nineteenth centuries," write Cosgrove and Jackson "established the attractions of Ireland ... the lakes and mountains of Cork and Kerry, the wild cove-studded coasts of Galway and Mayo, the montane peasantry of Donegal, and the innumerable monasteries and castles spread throughout the island."[3] The present-day attractions of Eire are basically twofold: a green, unspoiled landscape, peaceful and tranquil, and the distinctiveness of Celtic life and culture. Eire's cultural individuality is a strongly attractive feature. As Aalen and Bird have written: "... there is an appeal ... in the distinctiveness of Irish life. British people come to see something 'different,' to experience a country with a unique 'atmosphere,' and atmosphere is an almost indefinable thing—a subtle amalgam of scenic and social characteristics."[4]

Although the tourist industry in Eire has considerable potential and its further development is being assiduously planned, care should be taken to ensure that it does not become over-developed, for two reasons: any gross expansion or institutionalisation of tourism would be likely to undermine, even destroy, local life with its inherited customs and traditions which are in themselves tourist attractions of great significance while, secondly, wholesale development resulting in large influxes of tourists "to particular locations can lead to visual and ecological deterioration which, in time, erodes their attractive qualities."[5] Since Eire's basic attractions are its fine landscape, its cultural individuality and its placid and relaxed way of life, it would be folly to develop tourism to the point where these are placed in jeopardy. Tourism is being especially developed in western Eire with the very desirable aim of trying to resuscitate the rundown economy, but this creates its own dilemma for, as Cosgrove and Jackson point out "First, it directs the bulk of the tourist revenue to the most backward areas. Since the tourist is unlikely to have the Gaelic, the Gael must use English more and more. Secondly, traditional housing, by definition, cannot house large numbers of comfort-seeking foreigners. Both these goals are self-defeating ... the greatest amount of economic good is being directed to those geographic areas susceptible to the greatest amount of social change. The West is poor and rigidly traditional. Bord Failte cannot sell traditionalism and cannot swell the West's purse *and* retain the honest sod roof and the Gaelic vernacular."[6]

The development of Irish tourism owes much of its success to the Bord Failte Eireann, established in 1955 as a state-supported body which has an overall responsibility for promotion, development and marketing. The great success which attended its efforts led, in 1964, to the setting up of eight regional tourist organisations. These latter not only encourage and co-ordinate local efforts in promoting tourism but provide information services and accommodation reservation facilities which are present in almost every town and frequently in many smaller settlements. Both the Board Failte and the Regional Organisations have developed a high degree of efficiency and have established an enviable reputation.

THE SCANDINAVIAN COUNTRIES, FINLAND AND ICELAND

Between Norway, Sweden and Denmark there are no frontier constraints and this has meant that there are no official tourist counts of visiting Scandinavians, and precise tourist statistics are not easy to come by. Table 42 summarises some significant features.

On the whole, Norway is a harsh land of limited opportunities and in the past its wealth lay mainly in its forests and fisheries. Today it has a much more balanced economy, but the Norwegians have had to struggle hard to maintain their high living standards. The industry which they have assiduously developed is tourism. "The tourist trade began with the handful of mid-nineteenth-century fishermen and hunters who

TABLE 42

Tourism in the countries of Northern Europe

Country	Tourist arrivals			Percentage change between 1971 and 1972	Receipts (1970) (U.S.$m)
	1964	1971	1972		
Norway ⎫					156
Sweden ⎭	9,809,054	10,183,876	10,602,636[1]	4·1	143
Denmark		9,346,938	9,466,265[2]	1·3	314
Finland		3,691,696	4,627,492	25·3	120
Iceland					4

1. Arrivals of non-Scandinavian visitors only, including a large number of excursionists from the Federal Republic of Germany (83·9 per cent in 1971)

2. Arrivals of non-Scandinavian visitors only.

established the legend of the English 'lords,' proceeded through late nineteenth-century climbers and less energetic travellers who sought the verandahs of villas and hotels 'Victoria', to a contemporary trade in 3 million visitors a year. The tourist trade is also partly a winter enterprise. The word *ski* is Norwegian, and Norway initiated skiing as a sport. Oslo's Holmenkollen, where ski-jumping competitions began, remains a European show place. Norway has come into its own as the continent's 'northern playground,' an epithet given to it by W. C. Slingsby, a legendary climber who has literally left his name upon the map of Vestlandet."[7]

Besides its snow slopes and winter sporting attractions, Norway possesses magnificent scenery, especially along her Atlantic coast. Few countries can compete with her when it comes to natural splendour, dazzling beauty and haunting tranquillity, and she has capitalised upon these natural assets. But Norway has other tourist assets, too, the old town of Bergen, the Viking museums in Oslo, the fine stave churches, excellent food and the rare hospitality of the Norwegian people. The tourist industry also supports varied craft industries such as hand-knitted woollen goods, seal-skin slippers, wood carving and pewter-ware.

About 60 per cent of Norwegians take at least one holiday of four nights or more away from home—all workers in Norway are entitled to four weeks' holiday a year—but the majority are taken in the homeland since many possess summer huts or chalets. During the main summer holiday period, only 12 per cent of the population go abroad. Total expenditure on foreign holidays in 1970 amounted to $140m. Thus Norway had a net balance of $15m on her travel account. The young, fairly wealthy, upper-class Norwegians are those most usually holidaying abroad. Substantial numbers visit Britain, rather less than one-third come on a package tour and nearly half travel independently.[8]

Sweden is an interesting case. The Swedes have a curious attitude to tourism: they do not believe their country has much to offer the tourist and are surprised that anyone should want to visit their homeland; moreover, when it has been suggested that heavier investment should be put into the tourist industry the idea has usually received little credence. Sweden, it is true, does not have the spectacular scenery of Norway but it does possess an unspoilt countryside—it is perhaps the least spoilt tourist country in Europe—and a spaciousness which will come to have ever-increasing value as the traditional tourist lands of southern Europe become ever more jammed with tourists.

Nearly 3 million foreigners visit Sweden annually. About $1\frac{1}{2}$ million are other Scandinavian neighbours, chiefly Danes and Finns. Of the remainder some 150,000–200,000 are British, although a substantial proportion are businessmen. In recent years, the official attitude has been to promote tourism, as it is a useful earner of foreign currency, and in 1968 the Swedish tourist industry launched a campaign to attract more tourists; four markets—Germany, Finland, Britain and Denmark—were specially selected for intensive attack. Perhaps the chief drawbacks in the past have been foreigners' mistaken ideas about Sweden's climate, a lack of proper holiday facilities (these now are rapidly being remedied), and the expensiveness of holidaying in Sweden (this is still true though the traveller usually gets good value for his money).

Chief interest in Sweden, however, probably centres on the large number of Swedes travelling abroad. Swedish tourist expenditure abroad as a percentage of disposable income amounts to more than 2 per cent—one of the largest expenditures among European countries. Total overseas tourist expenditure in 1970 was U.S.$481m (as against tourist receipts of U.S.$143m), a figure which gives Sweden a very substantial deficit (U.S.$338m) on her travel account.

Denmark receives 10 million visitors a year, although a high proporation are short-stay travellers from West Germany in transit to other destinations. Income from tourism, however, is substantial—US$314m in 1970. Copenhagen is the great centre for tourists visiting Denmark.

For some years now the Finns have been cultivating a tourist trade, with a considerable measure of success. Arrivals in 1971 totalled $3\frac{1}{2}$ million and in 1972 over $4\frac{1}{2}$ million, an increase of 25 per cent over the previous year; this rate of increase was one of the highest in Europe, even higher than that for Greece, one of the great tourism boom countries. According to the *Tilastotiedotus Statistik Rapport, 1973*, in 1972 11·5 per cent travelled by air, 54·6 per cent by sea and 33·9 per cent by land. Tourists came chiefly from Sweden, followed by West Germany, Norway, the United States and Britain. Tourism is now a major earner of foreign currency.

Until a few years ago, the tourist visiting Finland went to Helsinki, the capital, and perhaps made a trip to the old town of Turku. But gradually the quiet beauty and magical colouring of the lake country began to be appreciated. More recently still, Finish Lappland has been discovered. The Finnish Government, partly to help settlement and economic development in this northern territory, which was badly ravaged during the Second World War, has done much to develop tourism. The result is, surprisingly, a fairly well-developed tourist industry in this Arctic land. Finnish Lappland now receives more than 500,000 visitors a year, about a quarter of them foreigners. Near Rovaniemi, the administrative capital of the north, a tourist complex based on the present ski slopes of Ounasvaara Hill and a modern motel, is to be developed: "a new project of extraordinarily ambitious proportions is afoot to carve a new world of over 2000 acres inside the hill. It is called Joulupukinmaa, or Father Christmas Land, and will take 10 to 20 years to build and cost upwards of £600,000 in its first phase."[9] It is planned that here eventually will be a great sports and recreation centre.

Iceland, a lone island in the North Atlantic which is heavily dependent upon its cod fisheries, desperately needs an additional source of income. Tourism might well provide it. Some 10,000 tourists visit Iceland annually. Many stop over on their Atlantic flights. Some visit Iceland seeking escape from the twentieth century in Iceland's empty solitudes. Others avail themselves of tourist day-trips from Iceland to the *ultima Thule* of the Greenland ice-cap beyond.[10]

THE BENELUX COUNTRIES

The Netherlands, Belgium and Luxembourg all have a substantial tourist trade, though the nature of the industry varies considerably between them. In the Netherlands the industry is concentrated in the polderlands and its historic towns, especially Amsterdam; in Belgium it is largely concentrated on the sea coast, in the historic towns of Flanders and in the capital, Brussels; while in the Grand Duchy, Luxembourg is the great attraction. Because of their location at one of the most important cross-roads of Europe, each of the three countries has a big transit trade, travellers often staying overnight or for a day or two *en route* elsewhere.

The Belgian coast provides one of the finest beaches in Europe—

some 40 miles of broad, firm sand which stretch almost unbroken from France to the Netherlands. The coast and its fringing sand dunes, which in places are up to a mile wide, is an important recreational asset to Belgium: the beaches form an almost continuous holiday resort from Coxyde near the French border to Knokke near the Dutch—it can hardly pretend to be beautiful but is ideal for family holidays. Many resorts have grown up along this coast, chief of which are Ostend and Blankenberghe, both catering primarily for summer visitors when their populations may increase tenfold; during the winter period many of the apartment blocks, hotels and shops close down.[11] In summer large numbers of British day-trippers cross from Dover to Ostend and the English impact manifests itself in the presence of tea shops, fish and chips and bingo.

In the Plain of Flanders are many small towns of medieval origin most famous of which is Bruges, once a flourishing port and prosperous Hanseatic city but now a quiet backwater. It must be counted one of the loveliest towns in Europe for this "city of bridges" has kept much of its medieval character. The Belgian capital, Brussels, is a large, handsome city with many fine buildings including medieval guild houses, a cathedral founded in A.D. 1010 and the magnificent Hotel de Ville built in the fifteenth century. As with all capital cities, it attracts a large quota of visitors and now it is the focus of the Common Market is likely to see its tourist potential grow even more.

In southern Belgium are the rolling, richly wooded Ardennes. In summer the region has a notable tourist trade for there are several designated parks and nature reserves and some of the small well-sited settlements are tourist centres, e.g. Spar, Rochefort, Dinant, St Hubert, Houffalize, Bastogne and Bouillon. Spar is the most famous; it has mineral springs which have been known since the third century A.D. and may lay claim to being the oldest European watering-place of any importance—so renowned did it become that its name came to be applied to health resorts in general. For the tourist there is much of interest besides the wooded country and the rushing streams: historic associations, several finely placed citadels, numerous attractive châteaux, and the famous Grottoes of Han, a system of interconnected underground caverns, eaten out of the limestone, through which the River Lesse follows a subterranean course. Stalactites and stalagmites form an underground architecture of grandeur and great interest.

In 1964 Belgium attracted 4,696,000 visitors; in 1970 the number was in excess of 5 million. Many of her visitors are day excursionists or short-stay visitors from northern France and England. The combined tourist receipts of Belgium and Luxembourg totalled U.S.$348m in 1970. Expenditure on tourism is greater, however, and in the same year amounted to U.S.$492m.

Luxembourg with its delightful countryside, charming villages, châteaux and churches, not to speak of the capital itself, offers much to the tourist and the industry has grown greatly since 1960. The tourist trade brings in a useful additional source of income to this small country. The Oesling or hill country in the northern third of the Duchy—really an extension of the Ardennes massif—and the small area known as the *Petite Suisse*, in the north-eastern part of the Gutland or Bon Pays in the south of the country, possesses an astonishing variety of scenery within a very restricted area. Here is not only superb scenery and tranquil beauty but good fishing and boating. Wiltz, Clervaux and Vianden are small centres of tourism. Luxembourg itself has grown to be a great tourist centre partly because of the intrinsic attraction of its fairytale atmosphere, partly because of its historic role as a fortress point and its impressive complex of fortifications, and partly because it is well-placed for exploring the country as a whole.

In 1964 the Netherlands had 1,762,000 visitors: in 1970 the total had risen to 2,399,000. The rate of tourist growth between these years was 36 per cent, marginally better than France's, appreciably better than West Germany's and Italy's and much better than that of Switzerland. About 1½ million of the Netherland's visitors come from other European countries, of which nearly 400,000 are British tourists. Over the period 1964–70 the number of American visitors to the Netherlands almost doubled. Dutch receipts from tourism in 1970 totalled U.S.$421m. However, expenditure on tourism reached U.S.$598m.

The attractions of the Netherlands lie mainly in the quiet charm of the country, its picturesque villages such as Volendam, in the friendly hospitality of the Dutch and in Amsterdam. This historic city is a graceful town, though terribly cluttered nowadays with cars. Its canals, water-taxis, bridges, gardens, richly decorated merchants' houses and fine warehouses, which testify to the prosperity of former times, give it a charm which makes it one of the most attractive and interesting cities in Western Europe. In the area around Haarlem are the famous bulb fields which in spring attract numerous tourists. The Netherlands has few large seaside resorts, but on the seaward side of the dune belt in Nord Holland are some small resorts and fishing centres, *e.g.* Scheveningen, Noordwijk and Zandvoort.

FRANCE

France ranks with Italy and Spain as one of the three leading tourist countries of Europe, receiving annually in excess of 13 million foreign visitors. With its fortunate location, its strongly marked regional variety and its rich cultural legacy, France was made for tourism. The country has great natural beauty: spectacular mountain scenery in the Alps and Pyrenees, attractive rocky broken coasts and extensive beaches and gentle wooded valleys; it has climatic conditions which are on the whole moderate, invariably give a delightful spring and which, in the Midi at any rate, provide ideal holiday weather; it possesses a rich cultural heritage of prehistoric monuments and cave paintings, well-preserved architectural remains of Roman times, splendid medieval cathedrals and castles, and fine châteaux and palaces; and it has a cuisine of worldwide renown. France, indeed, could hardly help becoming an important tourist destination. The French tourist industry employs some 400,000 persons and has an annual turnover of over 10,000 m francs: accordingly, it is an important sector of the country's economy and one of its chief sources of foreign currency.

Historical Development and Organisation

France has a long and well-established tradition of tourism. In the days of the Grand Tour, young aristocrats, in order to improve their education, visited France, at that time the most advanced and most civilised country in Europe. Modern tourism goes back to the latter part of the nineteenth century, when deliberate attempts began to be made to foster centres of tourism. France recognised the importance of tourism earlier than most other countries and by 1910 a National Tourist Office had already come into being. The scope and functions of this body, as indeed, its name, have suffered change on several occasions but its present form was established in 1963 when the *Commissariat Général au Tourisme* was officially set up. This is the direct responsibility of the Premier, although in effect it is delegated to a Secretary of State, the Minister being the Director of the Commissariat. The Office aims to promote France as a tourist destination to foreign travellers, it has the task of creating and improving the tourist infrastructure in the country, it co-ordinates the activities and work of various organisations participating in tourism, *e.g.* tour operators, travel agencies and hotels, it is engaged in the planning and development of national, regional and local developments, and it administers the Government's financial investment in tourism. From this it will be clear that there is a high degree of centralisation within the tourist activity and industry. "In terms of tourist organisation, in contrast to a largely non-governmental approach such as exists in Britain, the French concept represents strong central direction, planning and co-ordination of tourism. There is in France a very full realisation of the value of tourism and of the role of the State in its promotion and development."[12]

Supporting the French N.T.O. are other bodies or associations concerned with tourism. The Higher Council for Tourism is an advisory body at national level, set up in 1952. Then there are the *syndicats d'initiative*, numbering some 1500, which are non-profit-making associations and which aim to support and develop tourism in communes or resorts chiefly by publicising the place and by providing local information bureaux. The first of these *syndicats d'initiative* was founded in Grenoble in 1889. Finally, there are the resort tourist offices (*Offices du Tourisme*) which, by an Act of 1964, were allowed to be established by scheduled resorts; they are "public commercial establishments and, as such, can borrow, make capital investments, run tourist or sports services or installations and receive part of the yield from the 'taxe de sejour'* or, in winter sports resorts, from the tax on the use of ropeway installations. They are usually set up to take over from private initiative in tourist matters, when the latter is inadequate, and can be run as business concerns."[13]

If one ignores the spa developments, the Riviera was the first and most important tourist area and in pre-war days was especially important as a winter resort area, although there were fashionable centres elsewhere in the country, *e.g.* Le Touquet and Deauville on the Channel coast, Biarritz on the Biscayan coast and, of course, incomparable Paris. Until the Second World War the foreign tourist, as also indeed the domestic tourist, belonged essentially to the more affluent classes of society. France's clientele was of a cosmopolitan kind, although there was always a strong English contingent. In those days the domestic tourist industry was not very highly developed and certainly much less so than in Britain. Since the Second World War there has been a quite spectacular growth in the domestic tourism although, paradoxically, the foreign tourist trade has tended to flag. France, however, has a tremendous tourist potential and the Government is taking vigorous steps to realise it.

Domestic Tourism

"An essential distinction must be made," says Thompson, "between traditional commercial tourism, based on hotels and for the most part in

---

* A daily tax applicable to non-residents staying in a commune on a paying basis.

established coastal resorts, spas and historic towns, and the more recent growth of popular tourism."[14] Until 1936 France's domestic tourist industry was very substantially dependent upon the wealthier strata of the community. The year 1936 may be said to mark a turning point and, had it not been for the outbreak of the Second World War in 1939, it would have been a more emphatic turning point than it was. 1936 saw the legal provision in France of fifteen days of holiday a year for all workers and this had the effect of widening the social groups participating in holiday-making. After the immediate post-war years, France witnessed a period of economic expansion which brought increased prosperity. At the same time, the institution of four-week holidays with pay gave greatly increased leisure. These two factors were responsible for a sudden increase in popular tourism which, in turn, called new forms of holiday-making into being. The increasing prosperity of the French worker resulted, as in Britain, in a pronounced increase in car ownership which led to a greater mobility of the population and new forms of holiday-making based upon car usage. By the mid-1960s, for instance, some two-thirds of French holiday-makers were travelling by their own cars. There is now widespread travel by motor-coach, private car, motor cycle and scooter and this has been facilitated by the existence of a good road network which is being maintained and improved to meet the continuing increase in tourist activity.

An official enquiry in 1966 revealed that out of a total population of 49 million less than 45 per cent (21·5 million) took a holiday away from home. By 1970, just over half the population (25 million) enjoyed holidays away from home. Continuing prosperity will, in all likelihood, see this percentage increase. However, there are certain distinctive features applicable to the French holiday-maker. Although increased leisure time has helped to promote increased tourism, long holidays, especially for the family man with several children, are expensive and this has created a demand for cheaper forms of holiday which in France has largely manifested itself in camping. By using their own cars, sleeping in caravans or tents and catering for themselves they can economise on costs. This has had important and beneficial economic effects: it has dispersed the tourist much more widely, often bringing a measure of prosperity to the more remote areas, for he must make purchases of provisions and petrol and pay parking rents. The popularity of this form of holiday, however, is a threat to certain resorts which have been highly dependent on hotel clientele. So long as tourist travel was dominated by railway routes, tourist activity was largely channelled to the resorts served by them, but with the rapid growth of motor transport the tourist now goes wherever the mood takes him.

A second distinctive feature associated with French holiday-making is also related to costs: as Thompson says: ". . . expense also plays the dominant role in the growth of collective holidays available at cheap rates to members of various industrial, professional or social organisations. The most rudimentary form is the '*colonie de vacances*'—a hostel for young children, possessing limited amenities, but invariably located in countryside suitable for outdoor recreation. Such institutions are commonly sponsored by industrial firms and religious bodies and make holidays for children possible for the most modest income groups. At the other end of the scale, many professional organisations own fully equipped holiday apartments and villas, available to members at rates far below those of their commercial equivalents." [15]

Thirdly, again probably partly because of expense, a high proportion of French holiday-makers—41 per cent in the later 1960s—stay with relatives, although the point may be made that many urban dwellers have only lately left the countryside and so still have close family connections with those living in rural areas.

The percentages of the French people taking holidays varies widely from one category to another: from about 20 per cent in the rural communes to more than 80 per cent in Paris and (according to estimates made in 1964 and now perhaps a little changed) from 11 per cent among farmers, to 44 per cent among manual workers, 63 per cent among clerical workers and 86 per cent among managerial and professional people. [16] The map (Fig. 29) shows the destinations of French holiday-makers both within France and abroad in 1966.

There are other holiday features, not uniquely French however, which characterise the French holiday industry. First, France, like Britain, suffers from seasonal congestion. July and August are the peak months for domestic tourism and this creates undue congestion and strain upon resources. Tourists naturally are more attracted to Aquitaine and the Midi where the climatic conditions are more favourable than to Brittany and the Channel coast where the weather is more uncertain. The resorts of northern France are doubly penalised for, in addition to the weather hazard, which may dissuade holiday-makers from risking a vacation there, the holiday season is of shorter duration than that enjoyed by Mediterranean resorts. Congestion in the more popular tourist areas also leads to seasonal increases in prices though such it is claimed with some justification is an unavoidable outcome of the necessity to achieve maximum profits in a short-term period of intense activity. More fortunate are the Riviera resorts which enjoy a winter as well as a summer season and many of the Alpine and Pyrenean resorts which have all-year-round custom. Clearly, there is need to stagger the holiday period so that tourism can be more equitably spread throughout the year or a greater part of the year, an extension which would help to relieve the undue congestion and bring down prices by providing income and employment over a longer period. The present

FIG. 29.—*France: stays in various regions and abroad.*

Courtesy the French Embassy

situation is uneconomic in that "France must provide a tourist equipment, in terms of hotels, camp sites and other amenities, capable of serving the August peak but representing a considerable surplus capacity outside this month."[17]

Finally we may refer to the growing numbers of Frenchmen who are holidaying abroad. This growth, which has been increasing rapidly in recent years, has been a response to the rising standard of living in France. France now ranks, in fact, as the world's third most important tourist generating country (after the United States and West Germany) with more than 12 million Frenchmen travelling abroad annually. The principal destinations of those who go abroad are Spain (8·2 million) and Italy (4·3 million) and these two countries account for the bulk of French holidays abroad. In 1974 some 880,000 Frenchmen visited the United Kingdom. Total expenditure on foreign travel amounted to $1056·8m in 1970.

Foreign Tourism

Reference has already been made to the fact that France has a long tradition of tourism. In the seventeenth and eighteenth centuries the sons of the English aristocracy visited France when making their Grand Tours and Arthur Young in his *Travels in France* 1787–89 stated that by the 1780s the affluent and titled English were already sojourning on the Riviera for long periods. During the nineteenth century France became the premier tourist destination in Europe. This was due in part to the natural attractions of the country but more especially to the tremendous expertise which the French possessed for managing tourism and to the dictates of fashion which at that time made France a "must." Paris, which has always been a major focus of tourism, apart, the most important centre of attraction has always been the Riviera. At first it developed chiefly as a winter resort area but, subsequently, as it became more readily accessible through improved communications and as it became fashionable to acquire a sun-tan, large numbers began to flock to the Côte d'Azure.

Although as a tourist destination France, relatively, has lost ground, she continues to attract in excess of 13 million foreign visitors a year. Americans form the largest group of foreign visitors, over $1\frac{1}{2}$ million annually. Williams and Zelinsky explain the peculiar attraction of France to the Americans as follows: "American's image of France as a long-term ally of the United States, coupled with that country's well-known attractions and the special place Paris holds in many Americans' hearts and minds may have prevented a decline in the flow of U.S. tourists to France over the past decade of tense relations and frequent recriminations."[18] Americans make up a smaller proportion of France's tourists now than in the past, though there has been an absolute increase in U.S. tourists (1,530,000 in 1970). There is a strong flow of tourists to France from neighbouring countries and "about one half of the total

TABLE 43
Frontier arrivals in France (1970)

West Germany	1,900,000
U.K. and Ireland	1,750,000
Italy	1,650,000
Belgium and Luxembourg	1,600,000
U.S.A.	1,350,000
Netherlands	1,100,000
Spain and Portugal	850,000
Switzerland	750,000
Scandinavia	300,000
Latin America	270,000
Canada	180,000
Austria	150,000
Other countries	1,850,000
TOTAL	13,700,000

Source: Commissariat Général au Tourisme, Paris.

foreign arrivals in France come in almost equal proportions from Germany, United Kingdom and the Benelux countries."[19] In 1969, 919,000 British tourists visited France. In 1973 the figure was around 2 million, most of them going to Normandy and Brittany which are the most popular areas for British holiday-makers; only about 600,000 go to the Côte d'Azur. Total receipts from foreign tourism in 1970 amounted to $1191·5m.

TOURIST REGIONS

The Channel Coast

The Channel Coast (here taken as extending from the Belgian border to the Golfe de St Malo, for Brittany will be dealt with separately as a tourist region), has a long tradition of tourism although its importance varies between one stretch of the coast and another; moreover, the popularity of many of the resorts along this coast has been strongly affected by the passing whims of fashion. The Channel coast can be divided into four sections: from the Belgian frontier to the mouth of the Seine, the coast of the Baie de la Seine, the coast of the northern portion of Cotentin and the Cotentin coast south of Carteret fronting the Golfe de St Malo. The coastline to the east of the Seine has limited natural amenities for tourism. Along the coast of Artois are a number of small seaside resorts, such as Rosendael, St Pol-sur-Mer, Le Touquet, Paris Plage and Berck which largely serve the industrial populations of the Nord industrial region. In the 1920s, Le Touquet was a very fashionable resort for English tourists but the watering place has little popularity now.

The flat, dune-backed coast of French Flanders gives way further south to cliffs and west of the Somme the littoral of Haute-Normandie shows an impressive cliffed chalk coast. The chief tourist centres along this stretch of coast are Le Treport, Saint Valery en Caux and Etretat, although all are small. "The coastal tourist industry has experienced a relative decline, and in terms of total hotel capacity, number of visitors and the number of secondary holiday homes is far outranked by the coast of Basse-Normandie."[20]

The coast to the west of the Seine, on the edge of the Baie de la Seine, has seen popularity, subsequent decline and popularity again. The existence of underdeveloped coastal sites, nearness to Paris and growing demand for second homes by more affluent dwellers from the capital and also from Caen are distinct advantages which are likely to promote increased tourism. "The tourist industry of Basse-Normandie is of long standing," writes Thompson. ". . . Conceived initially as watering places for a wealthy and cosmopolitan clientele, the resorts of Deauville and Trouville, situated closest to Paris, were the first to develop. Since the Second World War, tourism has developed intensively along the littoral between Honfleur and Courseulles, but the character of the industry has changed. Villas, rented apartments, camp sites and secondary homes have replaced the . . . industry based on fashionable high-quality hotels. A distinction may be made between the 'Cote Fleurie,' containing the original centres and backed by a pleasant hinterland in the Pays d'Augue and the 'Cote de Nacre,' west of the mouth of the Orne, of more recent expansion. Here camping and nautical sports are the principal attractions together with the historical and architectural interests of Bayeux."[21]

The coast of the Cotentin peninsula falls, from both a physical and a tourist point of view, into two contrasting parts. The northern section, roughly from St Vaast-le-Hague on the eastern side of the peninsula to Carteret on the western has cliffed coast, and extensive beaches are of very restricted extent. There are few resorts, although the small port of Barfleur combines fishing with tourism. South of Carteret to the Point du Roc, a distance of some 64 km (40 miles), a dune belt fringes the coast and many camping and holiday centres have arisen since 1945. Granville and Avranches are small towns which have witnessed tourist growth since 1960. Mont St Michel, a rocky islet in the bay of the same name crowned by a fortified monastery, is one of the most popular centres of tourist interest in the whole of France.

In the *département* of Manche in particular, which largely relies on pastoral farming, the expansion of tourism would bring some benefits although Cotentin as a whole has a relatively short holiday season and there are problems of relating a fairly heavy investment in tourist infrastructure to a low utilisation outside the peak period—mid-June to the end of August.

Brittany

Brittany is the French counterpart of the south-western peninsula of England with which it shares many geological, topographical, climatic, economic and cultural characteristics. "At once both a peripheral and a terminal region, Brittany has remained apart from the mainstream of economic trends, preserving a specific cultural and social identity. Eccentric location, internal isolation, the absence of indigenous energy resources and remoteness from the hearths of both the industrial and agricultural revolutions, combined to retard the economic evolution of Brittany, promoting a large-scale exodus of population."[22] In this economic backwater, in which agriculture and fishing have been the traditional bases of Breton livelihood, tourism has an important role to play. Not that tourism is not already considerable, for over 2 million tourists visit Brittany each year while the industry is responsible for more than 5 per cent of the region's revenue. Nevertheless, there is considerable potential for further expansion and the C.O.D.E.R. (*Commission de Développement Economique Régional*) plan aims at a substantial development of the industry.

The region has both advantages and disadvantages. Brittany has an extensive broken and rugged coast, the result of its Hercynian origins and later slight submergence, giving spacious rias and innumerable sheltered coves and sandy bays often separated by high castellated cliffs. The possibilities for yachting and water sports are great, and indeed these form the basis of tourist expansion. As in Cornwall, the small fishing villages can be easily adapted to the demands of tourism. The Breton culture and certain pre-historic remains such as those around Carnac (stone monuments including long rows of menhirs, circles and dolmens) are a source of attraction to many.

The chief disadvantages relate to geographical position. Exposed to air masses moving in from the Atlantic, the region is characterised by a high degree of humidity, cloudiness and drizzling rains, although the littoral is mild in winter and free from frost. Such winter mildness, however, has not so far fostered a winter tourist trade, largely because much more favourable winter climates can be found elsewhere in

France. Brittany's relative physical isolation and its remoteness from the more densely populated regions have also tended to militate against tourism, although the growth in motor transport has helped to make it more accessible. Another serious disadvantage is the shortness of the tourist season, which compares very unfavourably with that in the Mediterranean region.

Some 80 per cent of the present tourist activity is concentrated on the littoral in centres such as St Malo, Dinard, Brignogan Plage and a number of other *plages*, since the interior has little in the way of picturesque scenery to attract the holiday-maker; however, a regional park has recently been designated in interior Finistere and this may well serve to attract tourists as well as to provide a recreational area for the people of Brest and Quimper. Mention should also be made of La Baule, not far from St Nazaire, which is an important family holiday resort. Notwithstanding the efforts of C.O.D.E.R. to develop the tourist industry in Brittany, "the expansion of tourism is unlikely," concludes Thompson, "to make a far-reaching impact on the fundamental disequilibrium of the Breton economy. The employment created is highly seasonal and the chief benefits are felt indirectly, through the stimulus to the construction industry and the revenue derived from general tourist spending."[23]

Aquitaine

The Biscayan coast of Aquitaine, gently shelving and backed by a six-mile wide belt of sand-dunes, remained for years almost undeveloped but recently there has been a rapid growth of the tourist industry. Holiday-makers now throng the beaches in summer and a number of small coast settlements have grown into seaside resorts. In the extreme south is Biarritz, a fashionable summer and winter resort with mineral baths, and Basque town of St Jean-de-Luz, a former fishing port which is now mainly a resort. Not far inland, on the Andour, is Dax, a small spa.

A plan to develop the Aquitaine coast for tourism was approved in 1970. The Aquitaine coast scheme (less ambitious than the Languedoc–Roussillon scheme) consisted originally of a number of separate developments such as the open-air centre at Bombannes, the resort at Seignosse, the harbour works at Peyrehorade and the regional park at La Leyre but these have now been included in a comprehensive tourism development scheme which includes the creation (already begun) of a 150-km Trans-Aquitaine Canal, running parallel with the coast, which will become one of the finest holiday canals, providing sailing and water-sports, in Europe.[24]

The Massif Central

In south central France lies the Central Plateau or Massif Central, a region of varied geology, structure and relief which can be geographically subdivided into four main areas: (*i*) the eastern margins, from Morvan in the north to the southern end of the Cevennes; (*ii*) the limestone Grandes Causses and the crystalline uplands of the Segalas plateau, Monts de Lacaune and Montagne Noire; (*iii*) the plateau and slightly elevated rolling plains country of Limousin in the west and north-west; and (*iv*) the centre of the Massif, Auvergne, together with the upper valleys of the Allier and Loire. It is the latter area more particularly with its complex landscape, physical fragmentation and volcanic forms which is important from the tourist point of view although there are other areas of fine scenery and high recreational value that are beginning to attract visitors.

The volcanic region of Auvergne has long been a significant tourist district. As Thompson writes: "the suitability of the region ... is adventitious rather than material, but nevertheless is of growing significance in the ... economy. ... The reputation of the mineral waters for the treatment of specific illnesses and of mountain resorts for the alleviation of respiratory complaints led to the creation of fashionable resorts at Vichy, La Bourboule, Chatel-Guyon, Mont-Dore, Royat and St Nectaire. ... The popularity of the thermal resorts has waned ... [but it] stimulated a much wider form of tourism which is by no means fully exploited as yet. The attractions of the mountains of the Chaines-des-Puys, Cantal and Mont-Dore for summer holidays has now been extended to the creation of winter sports and a proliferation of secondary holiday residences. From a specific origin in thermalism, the natural attractions of Auvergne are now the basis of a major tourist industry in full expansion."[25]

Much of the centre and north of the Massif Central was subjected to vulcanism during the Tertiary period and into Quaternary times when volcanoes were piled up and basalt was poured out on to the surface. The Puy de Sancy 1913 m (6186 ft) forms the highest point of the Massif Central. The older volcanoes have been subjected to prolonged erosion and often only the plugs remain, some of which are surmounted by small chapels and churches, but the volcanoes of Quaternary times, *e.g.* those of the Chaine des Puys, are very well preserved. This volcanic landscape, often of a bizarre character, has greatly attracted the tourist.

The resources of the Massif Central are limited and conditions often difficult leading to emigration to the richer and more attractive parts of

France. In an attempt to stem the drift and to turn what natural advantages it has to good account, a company "*La Société pour la Mise en Valeur de la Région Auvergne–Limousin*," known in short as SOMIVAL, was established in 1964, to undertake rural development and improvement. SOMIVAL is organised into three sections which are concerned with agriculture, forestry and tourism. The company concerned itself not with the already established centres of tourism but rather with the extension of tourism into the lesser known rural areas which were undeveloped and unspoiled; it is hoped that, once enticed by the physical attractions of the country, tourism will become more widely dispersed and that this, in turn, will augment the income of those dependent upon a not very rewarding agriculture. In its attempts to diffuse tourism more widely throughout Auvergne, SOMIVAL has undertaken some forty development projects. "The type of development favoured is that of holiday villages, consisting of individual chalets and secondary homes, in some instances aligned round artificial lakes, possessing communal services. The objective is to afford inexpensive holidays in quiet surroundings as compared with the more animated and expensive established resorts. In this way, tourism is seen as the final stage in integrated rural development, absorbing some of the produce of an improved agriculture and employing a proportion of the labour displaced through agricultural improvement schemes."[26]

The Côte d'Azur

The Côte d'Azur, commonly called the Riviera, is the rocky broken coast of Provence extending from Toulon to the Italian frontier. Along most of the coast the hills come right down to the sea to give steep cliffs—between Nice and Menton 306 m (1000 ft) high—but here and there tiny patches of plain occur. This attractive coast has become world famous. Backed by hills and mountains, which protect the coast from chill north winds, and facing southwards, it is a warm, sunny, sheltered littoral zone where sub-tropical vegetation can flourish. These highly favourable conditions, along with the enticements of a warm and deep blue sea, have led to the growth of a string of fashionable resorts, such as St Tropez, St Raphael, Cannes, Antibes, Nice, Menton and Monte Carlo in the enclave of the Principality of Monaco.

Because of its equable winter climate and winter sunshine, the Riviera first developed as a winter resort area which was patronised by the titled and the wealthy and was very cosmopolitan. Its heyday was the Edwardian era but it continued to be popular as a winter holiday area until the Second World War. After the war it largely changed its function, becoming a summer resort area and the volume of its summer visitors is now probably three times greater than that of its winter visitors. Moreover, its clientele has substantially changed. While some of the smaller more exclusive resorts continue to attract the affluent, package holidays have led to an influx of middle- and lower-class tourists. Over 2 million tourists visited the Riviera in summer 1970.

A railway, from Marseilles, skirts the Riviera coast from Fréjus to the Italian frontier and continues beyond along the Riviera di Ponente and Riviera di Levante as far as La Spezia. A road, the Corniche, runs along the hill slopes; dating from Roman times but developed by Napoleon, it originally connected Nice with Genoa. A motorway now runs from just west of Fréjus to Nice. Nice itself is served by an airport.

Monte Carlo is one of the three communes of the Principality of Monaco. A century ago Monte Carlo did not exist but by the beginning of the present century it had become established as an exclusive resort for royalty and the rich. Its famous Casino for long financed almost everything in the Principality. Monaco is a strange, exotic and almost artificial corner of the world. It is a practically man-made principality; even the soil of its sub-tropical gardens—among the botanical marvels of the world—was imported. Here, too, is the famous Oceanographical Museum, opened in 1910, which houses a wonderful aquarium. Over three-quarters of a million visitors went to Monte Carlo in 1970.

Famed as the Riviera is as a tourist region, it faces many problems. Its popularity has led to urban growth along the narrow littoral zone, to such an extent that there is now almost a continuous linear agglomeration. This urban expansion has brought communication problems and considerable congestion during the peak season which the new motorway has helped to alleviate but by no means cured. A second problem is that of soaring and grossly inflated land values; this arises, in part, from an absolute shortage of land along the coast. One effect has been for development to encroach inland and many former agricultural villages in the hilly hinterland have now also become holiday centres. Another effect of the high prices in real estate has been to deter industrial development (of an appropriate kind, for industry and tourism are not compatible), which would mitigate seasonal unemployment. A third problem is that of growing pollution: stretches of beach have been closed to the public because they have become polluted and unfit to use.

Urbanisation is not the only problem with which the coast has to contend. In more recent years, newer and cheaper forms of holiday-making, such as camping and caravanning, have become fashionable and hotel accommodation is in less demand. Again, whereas at one time visitors would spend many weeks, even months, on the Riviera, nowadays the average length of stay is under a week. Thus, while there are more visitors than ever before, the tourist revenue is less. Many of the older resorts are not equipped to cope with, neither have they adjusted to, the newer demands in tourism—cheap, more informal, activity-based types of holiday. And, in addition to these handicaps, the Riviera has had to face keen competition from the comparable Italian and Spanish coastal holiday zones.

Languedoc–Roussillon

The most ambitious single tourism development operation in Europe is currently being undertaken along the Languedoc–Roussillon coast of Mediterranean France (*see* Fig. 30). A narrow coastal strip 193 km (120 miles) long, extending from Aigues-Mortes to the Spanish frontier, straight and flat, frequently fringed with sand-dunes and backed by mosquito-infested lagoons, marshes and water channels, sparsely

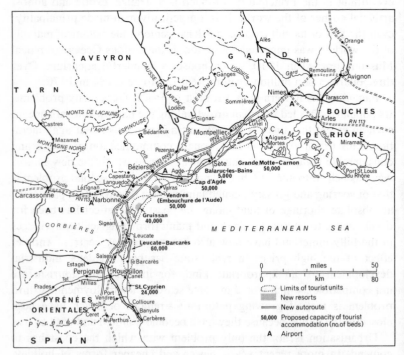

FIG. 30.—*Tourism development in Languedoc–Roussillon.* It is estimated that a million tourists visited this new holiday coast in 1973. It may well come to rival the Côte d'Azur eventually.

populated and little known, is being transformed into a vast new tourist complex. This hitherto unattractive littoral zone seems destined to become one of the largest holiday resort areas in Europe. Although the coastal zone possessed many disadvantages from the point of view of tourism development, it also had some advantages: it was thinly peopled, the chief towns—Montpellier, Béziers, Narbonne and Perpignan—lay inland, there are extensive beaches of fine sand, while the numerous lagoons offer expansive areas for the development of water-sports. Until the French Government turned their attention to this area, tourism had made little impact on it although, as Hazel Thurston commented "This Mediterranean vacuum must have tantalised the appetites of speculators since the tourist boom first gained impetus in the post-war years. Yet the problems of land reclamation and communications were so enormous in terms of finance and civil engineering that little was done."[27] The Languedoc–Roussillon Project is of singular importance not only to the French economy and French regional development but "the methods adopted by the French authorities to deal with it have an obvious relevance to less advanced countries faced with the problems of developing a new tourist area."[28]

The project, initiated in 1961, envisaged the creation of six new holiday resorts, strung out at intervals along the Languedoc–Roussillon coast; these were to be La Grande Motte, Cap d'Agde, Embouchure de l'Aude, Gruissan, Leucate-Barcarès and Saint Cyprien. In every case the resorts are adjacent to *étangs* and it is proposed that the recreative activities will be focused as much on sailing and water sports as on beach life. The proposed capacity of tourist accommodation, in numbers of beds, was around 50,000 in the case of each resort, except for Saint Cyprien which will have half this capacity. This will mean that the resorts will be able to accommodate 450,000 visitors. It has been estimated that by around 1980 the region will probably be receiving a million tourists annually. This vast and far-sighted tourism enterprise must attract large numbers of holiday-makers and become an extremely popular tourist area during the later 1970s, altering very appreciably tourist flows in Europe.

The Languedoc–Roussillon Project was officially approved in March, 1964, but before that date action had secretly been taken to purchase all the available land in the proposed development zones. Some 4000 ha (9880 acres) of land were secured at low agricultural land-use prices prior to the public announcement of the development plan: this was to prevent undesirable speculation in land. Furthermore, a law was passed which gave land purchase priority and compulsory purchase powers to the *Mission Interministrielle pour l'Amenagement Touristique du Littoral Languedoc–Roussillon*, a body set up by the French Government. Immediately after the initial purchase of land, a further 30,000 ha (74,000 acres) were acquired by the Mission "either for deferred development or to act as a protection against uncoordinated speculation."[29] The government authorised an expenditure of £60m over two five-year periods (1965–75) for the acquisition of land and the provision of basic infrastructure. Once the infrastructure had been completed, and this included swamp clearance and the eradication of the mosquito, harbour construction, highway development, the construction of airports and the laying of electricity and water mains, the Mission was empowered to sell land to private investors at a price which included the infrastructural development cost. Since the Mission is not concerned with profit-making, the private developer gets land at a very reasonable price with the added advantages of infrastructure, although he has an obligation to develop once he has acquired land and is forbidden to resell unused land. "Under these arrangements, the Government keeps control without having a monopoly of execution. It has a coherent policy of land acquisition, it controls physical planning and development and it maintains a financial co-ordination over investment in the area."[30]

Accessibility is clearly an important factor in the scheme and a new road system, already largely completed by 1970, was carefully planned. A new motorway running parallel with the coast but lying about ten miles inland has been constructed to give easy access to the new resorts. From the autoroute, access roads serve each of the tourist centres, although in each case the roads terminate well behind the beach; the intention has been to keep motor traffic away from the shore and to discourage ribbon development. In addition to the new motor roads, four new airports had by 1972 been built to serve the resort areas.

The first of the new tourist units to take shape was La Grande Motte in the east, some 16 km (10 miles) south-east of Montpellier. The scheme here was completed in 1970 and indicates the general pattern of development. Located in a sheltered position on the Gulf of Grau du Roi where there is a 5-km (3-mile) unbroken stretch of gently shelving sandy beach, La Grande Motte has been developed around two water areas, the port and the Étang du Ponant. The new Port de Plaisance, which is the principal focal point of the resort, possesses a yachting harbour capable of accommodating 1000 craft together with a small outer harbour with sufficient draught of water for larger vessels. The Étang du Ponant is the other main centre of interest. The Étang in its natural state was a marshy salt-water lagoon but this has been dredged and deepened to give a fine 150-ha (470-acre) area of water with a navigable depth of 3 m. Thus the emphasis has been on the provision of sailing and water sports facilities. Mention should also be made of the extensive lagoon, the Étang de Maugio, which lies immediately to the north of La Grande Motte and is suitable for aquatic sports. The shores around the Étang have been designated a nature conservation area. La Grande Motte has a tourist accommodation of around 50,000 beds. Careful thought has gone into the planning not only of the siting and provision of infrastructure of the new resort but also into its layout, for a zoning system has been adopted with specific areas allocated to hotels, private villas and blocks of flats, camping and caravan sites, sporting activities, shopping facilities and municipal services. Leucate-Barcarès, near Perpignan, based on the two small settlements of Leucate and Le Barcarès and the Étang de Leucate, is in a well-advanced state of development and has in fact been accommodating visitors for four years. When finally completed it will have a capacity of 60,000 beds. A third resort, Cap d'Agde, near Béziers, has also been started. Already, by 1970, the total number of tourists received on the Languedoc coast was estimated at more than 800,000.

The Languedoc–Roussillon scheme should, if planned targets are met, be fully completed and operative by 1975. £350m of public and private capital will have been invested in the project, whose success would seem to be assured. From the geographical point of view the project has already made "a major impact on the fauna, flora, topography and economy of the little-known and hitherto uneconomic Languedoc–Roussillon coast."[31]

The Alps and the Pyrenees

The Alps and the Pyrenees are notable centres for tourism, more particularly for winter sports (*see* Fig. 31). In the Pyrenees there are many formerly fashionable but now decayed small spas, such as Aix les Thermes, Eaux Bonnes and Eaux Chaudes. Bagnères de Luchon, which began as a Roman spa, has been more fortunate for it is linked by funicular to Superbagnères, a winter sports resort, and so has an all-year-round season. Mention should be made of Lourdes, in the foothills, which attracts large numbers of visitors every year.

Tourism is one of the mainstays of the Alpine economy. The earliest tourist centres were at such places as Aix-les-Bains, Annecy and Evian in the Pre-Alps. The coming of the railway, which threaded the Alpine valleys, made places more accessible and was responsible for the greater

SWITZERLAND

Lake Geneva

Geneva

Annecy

Avoriaz
Morzine
Flaine
Chamonix
La Clusaz
Megève
Saint-Gervais

Bourg-Saint-Maurice
La Plagne
Les Arcs
Courchevel
Moutiers
Tignes
Val d'Isère
Méribel-les-Allues
Saint-Martin-de-Belleville
Pralognan

Grenoble
Chamrousse
L'Alpe D'Huez
Les Deux-Alpes

ITALY

Serre-Chevalier
Briançon

Vars

Gap

Pra-Loup
Le Sauze
Le Super-Sauze
Allos

Nice

Rhône
Dranse
Arve
Isère
Arc
Romanche
Drac
Guisane
Ubaye
Durance
Verdon

km 50
0
0 miles 30

⊙ Main resorts developed around existing village
⊖ Main resorts created since 1946
○ New resorts under construction
■ Altitude of more than 1500m.
░ Land over 2000m

[*Courtesy the French Embassy*

FIG. 31.—*French winter sports resorts in the Alps.* There are some 200 winter sports resorts in France, offering altogether 2000 hotels.

development of tourism, especially winter sports centres such as Chamonix.

The 12-km (7·25-mile) road tunnel beneath Mont Blanc between Chamonix and Courmayeur has placed Chamonix on a major trans-Alpine route although some fears were expressed by its citizens that the new road tunnel might adversely affect its tourist trade: instead of visitors halting in Chamonix, they might decide to carry on into Italy.

The growth in winter sporting activities has had one very important geographical result: the creation of new settlements in areas which were suffering depopulation. "Until a few years ago," writes Pinchemel, "no one thought of creating a winter-sports station *ex nihilo*, away from all existing habitation, however today one can list as new resorts Flaine, Avoriaz, Corbier, St Martin Belleville and Super Bevoluy, in the Alps, all resulting from private initiative or through the intervention of public bodies."[32]

France has some 200 winter sports centres, including some forty "super-resorts."[33]

Corsica

Economically, Corsica has for long been something of a backwater. In the early 1950s the French Government began to prepare plans for the economic rehabilitation and development of the island. An ambitious new development project, begun in 1957 and spread over five years, covered land reclamation, afforestation, agricultural improvement, extended communications and the stimulation of the tourist trade. Corsica's tourist potential is considerable and in an effort to foster the industry a development corporation was set up to build 100 new hotels and develop the thermal springs of the island. Tourism growth was slower to materialise than was first thought and in 1966 Corsica could only claim 1 per cent of the holiday stays in the various regions of France: this amounted to less than 200,000 visitors. However, at the beginning of 1970, Corsica became a separate planning region and is now the object of an overall development programme which includes further tourism growth: indeed, by 1972 a start had already been made on a plan to build more hotels and holiday villages, to develop yachting harbours and water sports facilities and to provide infrastructure for future tourist development.[34]

WEST GERMANY

West Germany is remarkable because it vies with the United States as the world's greatest generator of tourism: in excess of 20 million

Germans, out of a total of nearly 60 million nationals, travel abroad. This, in terms of proportion, makes the Germans the world's greatest travellers. The very large number engaging in foreign travel is a reflection, primarily, of the economic prosperity of West Germany but, also, to some extent, of the country's geographical location—an almost land-locked position in central Europe having frontiers with nine other countries. West Germany accounts for about one-sixth of world tourist arrivals but, unlike the United States, nearly half of whose citizens travel to another region—mainly Europe—West Germans holiday preponderantly within the European region. German tourism is principally intra-regional and as a proportion of the total travel only some 2 or 3 per cent is of an inter-regional nature. It should be noted, however, that because of West Germany's industrial and commercial importance, a substantial number of German tourists are business travellers. The chief European recipients of West German tourists are given in Table 44. In 1974, 969,000 Germans visited Britain.

TABLE 44

West German tourist destinations and expenditures (1970)

Chief country visited	Number of visitors	Expenditure in country ($m)
Austria	5,379,065	544·8
Denmark[1]	9,245,650	66·3
France	1,900,000	153·5
Italy	2,052,202	450·8
Netherlands	551,505	123·8
Spain	2,075,094	197·8
Switzerland	1,557,879	347·8
Britain	663,000	76·2
U.S.A	177,272	174·9

1. Mainly border excursionists.

In 1970, the United States received 184,000 West Germans, Canada 41,300. From the destination countries' point of view, German tourists are important because they are great spenders, commonly spending more *per capita* than any other national group, the Americans excepted. The West Germans spent some $2500m in 1970, approximately one-quarter of the total expenditure incurred by all European countries outside the Iron Curtain and rather more than half the amount spent by U.S. citizens on foreign tourism.

As a tourist destination itself West Germany is not of major ranking, although in 1970 she received 7,715,000 visitors, placing her fourth among the European countries, though a long way behind Spain, Italy and France. In that year she had a million fewer visitors than Austria but a million more than Britain. West Germany's visitor traffic grew only moderately during 1960–70 in contrast to that of Britain which just about doubled.

However, despite the nearly 7·75 million visitors in 1970, the total nights in accommodation only reached 16,376,000; this gives an average length of stay of just over two nights and clearly indicates that much of the tourist traffic is in transit to other destinations. West Germany's income from foreign tourism amounted in 1970 to $1024m, as against an expenditure of $2500m: thus there is a very substantial deficit on the travel account.

TABLE 45

Principal visitors to the West German Federal Republic (1970)

U.S.A.	1,550,215
Netherlands	1,026,175
United Kingdom	860,055
France	582,714
Denmark	472,337
Belgium and Luxembourg	421,185
Sweden	382,764
Switzerland	369,945
Italy	342,938
Austria	279,526

West Germany's chief attractions are scenic and cultural. Germany's pre-war coastline, on both the North and Baltic Seas, was greatly reduced after the Second World War. This short stretch of sea coast is not highly developed with respect to resorts, although there are a few centres, such as Norderney, Cuxhaven and the island of Heligoland, which are patronised by the Germans. The chief tourist areas are the Rhine Gorge region, the hill country of the Rift Valley and Bavaria. The ancient rocks which flank the Rhine Gorge between Bingen and Bonn have given rise to memorable scenery. The crags have been crowned with castles, associated with legend and romance. Vulcanism in the region created mineral springs, around which spas developed, such as Bad Godesberg, Kripp, Neider, Ober Breisig and Bad Honningen. Many of the villages, *e.g.* St Goar, Oberwesel, Bacharach and Rüdesheim, are centres of viticulture. The last named is an old wine town with a well-known wine festival which has now become one of the foremost tourist centres of the Rhineland. Other centres of note are Konigswinter (magnificent scenery) and Boppard. At Coblenz, the Mosel joins the Rhine, and yacht cruising is a holiday feature of both rivers.

Further upstream are the forested Hercynian massifs along the edge of the Rhine Rift Valley. These wooded hills are attractive to the tourist (especially the area around Lake Titisee) and in some parts, such as the Black Forest, there are many Youth Hostels. There are several towns of note, *e.g.* Wiesbaden, a residential, spa and tourist town, Heidelberg, a delightful old university town much frequented by tourists, Freiburg, a tourist centre for the Black Forest, and Freudenstadt.

Mention should be made of the famous *Romantische Strasse*—the "Romantic Highway"—which runs for 360 km (225 miles) from Würzburg to Fussen in the foothills of the Alps, north–south across the Swabian and Franconian Scarplands and Bavaria and which follows the Via Claudia of the Romans and the great medieval trade route. Along, or near it, are some very interesting places such as Rothenburg, an almost perfect medieval town with its walls, towers and gates intact, moated Dinkelsbuhl, Nördlingen, another old walled town with its medieval gates still remaining, which lies in the centre of the fertile Ries basin and commands the gap through the scarplands, and the fantastic, fairytale castle of Neuschwanstein built by Ludwig II, King of Bavaria.

The Alps extend for a distance of nearly 320 km (200 miles) along West Germany's Southern frontier. Ice erosion has fretted the limestone mountains into jagged ridges and pinnacled summits with âretes, cirques and precipices. Here is found the Zugspitze 2200 m (9720 ft), the highest mountain in Germany. This is a popular tourist area and Garmisch-Partenkirchen is a famous winter sports centre. Not far away is Oberammergau, another resort, where the Passion Play is enacted every ten years.

More than 8 million domestic and foreign holiday-makers visit Bavaria annually. The Munich Olympics of 1972 may well have helped to boost Bavaria's tourist trade. To Bavaria the tourist industry is worth DM2100m (about £250m). The tourist industry is twice as important to the Bavarian economy as it is to any other state in West Germany.[35]

The Organisation of German Tourism

In contrast to the strong central direction, planning and co-ordination of the tourist industry found in France and Spain, the tourist organisation in West Germany is looser and much more decentralised. "Germany is a Federal State and the degree of devolution on the individual States in the field of tourism is considerable," says Medlik. "Local initiative is strong and tourist organisation is based on the one hand on the States, regions and cities, and on the other hand on national sectional bodies. Two central organisations provide for co-ordination at Federal level. Promotion abroad is the main function of the German National Tourist Office (*Deutsche Zentrale für Fremdenverkehr—Z.F.V.*). Internal travel promotion by the population of the country and questions of internal development, organisation and representation are the functions of the German Tourist Federation (*Deutscher Fremdenverkehrsband—D.F.V.*)."[36] It is the task of the National Tourist Office to bring together and co-ordinate the various sectional activities and interests of tourism. The N.T.O. is largely financed by the Federal Government. On the other hand, the Tourist Federation is supported financially by contributions from the various regional and civic tourist organisations whose interests it serves.

Because of the large numbers of Germans holidaying abroad, tour promotion is big business in West Germany. An interesting development was the entry into the travel business in the early 1960s of two large mail-order companies, Quelle and Neckermann. At first selling mainly travel goods and recreational equipment, they quickly moved into selling holidays. "They specialise almost entirely in air-inclusive tours. Catalogues are sent to their formidable list of mail-order customers who can ask for advice and make their booking at any of the company's department stores (most important towns in Germany have one). They are also using travel agents to boost their coverage, but this considerably affects the profit margin. By concentrating on a relatively limited number of well-tried holiday resorts, the German mail-order firms can produce high-quality trips at prices cut by nearly a quarter. . . . These firms have been very ambitious and have opened up new areas, unfettered by 'Provision 1' restrictions. Thus Neckermann opened up Rumania, Quelle found Portugal."[37] As a result of the severe competition from the mail-order concerns, the leading German tour operators—Touropa, Scharnow, Hummel and Dr Tigges—merged to form a massive combined travel organisation; this integration has enabled them "to set up a central computer system and the air-charter arrangements and hotel accommodation of the four operators are pooled."[38] This integration has also made it possible for the four operators to rationalise their business and to specialise to an even greater degree in the particular fields of tourist activity they had developed, *i.e.* Touropa on sea travel, Scharnow on air and rail travel, Hummel on youth travel and Dr Tigges on country holidays. A point of interest is that in West Germany integration has tended to be "horizontal" in its nature in contrast to the "vertical" integration which since 1968 has begun to manifest itself in the United Kingdom.

SWITZERLAND

Switzerland has often been described as "the playground of Europe" and for a century or so tourism has been a significant factor in the national economy. The origins of the foreign tourist industry go back to medieval times when some of the mineral springs began to attract visitors. However, the modern tourist industry is over 100 years old for it was in 1865 that the very first winter visitors arrived in Davos and St Moritz (*see* Fig. 32).[39] About this time, also, the Matterhorn was first

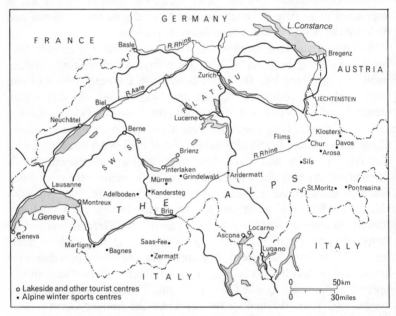

FIG. 32.—*Switzerland: tourist centres and communications.* In a broad way, the Swiss holiday resorts fall into two groups: (*a*) the summer resorts of the Swiss Plateau and the Italian lakes (*b*) the alpine winter sports centres.

climbed by the English mountaineer Edward Whymper and his six fellow climbers, an event which drew attention to the Alps. Indeed, to a very considerable extent, the Swiss tourist industry may be said to have been initiated by the British who provided the first trickle of mountaineering enthusiasts: the Swiss Alpine Club pioneered the "golden age of mountain-eering." The Swiss themselves commemorated these anniversaries in 1965 and the Swiss National Tourist Office christened 1965 as "The Year of the Alps," an excellent publicity idea which enabled the Swiss to focus attention once more on the tourism advantages offered by their mountains.

It is of some interest to recall that the early climbers were resented by the mountain Swiss, but they quickly began to see in mountaineering the possibilities of a new or additional source of income, and in this poorly endowed land the opportunity was not lost: the Swiss offered their services as guides—the two Zermatt guides Taugwalder father and son had accompanied Whymper on his ascent of the Matterhorn—and began to convert mountain inns into hotels. Soon villages such as Zermatt, which was originally nothing more than a collection of wooden chalets, became thriving winter sports centres. Davos grew very rapidly and in the late 1960s between $1\frac{1}{2}$ and 2 million tourist bed-nights were being passed there annually.[40] The mountain resort of Villars was also discovered for the tourist traffic and began to flourish. However, the first visitors, who were more especially mountaineering enthusiasts, soon began to be outnumbered by visitors who were either enthralled by Alpine scenery or attracted by winter sports, which grew in popularity, especially after the First World War.

As we saw in Chapter I (p. 44), mountains were once viewed with awe and dread and until this attitude was changed it was unlikely that travellers would visit the Swiss Alps. Dr Albrecht von Haller, a Bernese physician, sought in his book, *The Alps*, to awaken in his contemporaries a new appreciation of mountains and nature. In this he had some success for he managed to dispel some of the fear and horror of mountains which had prevailed until this time. But, as Dr P. Risch commented: "numerous great foreign writers—Goethe, Schiller, Lord Byron ... also did much to bring the sublime Alpine world closer to their many readers everywhere and to implant the desire to see and experience it at first hand."[41]

The Swiss tourist industry in its early days was not exclusively Alpine; such lakeside centres as Locarno and Lugano were also catering for summer holiday-makers—as early as 1801 the latter had eighteen hotels.[42] Cosgrove and Jackson have written: "The British popularised mountaineering holidays. Ski-ing was introduced from Norway in the 1870s and skating from Holland in the 1880s. The original summer resorts, like Villard de Lans, attempted first to ... [provide for] the new winter sports and later to introduce, with more success, forms of tourism such as 'climatism' and health cures which were especially popular among German tourists. Wealthy individuals, selecting a secluded village for their resort, bequeathed ... a legacy of tourist amenity to their favoured valleys. Thus, the development of Megeve owed much to the personal favour of the Rothschild family ... [after] 1916...."[43]

Winter and Summer Tourism

Switzerland is fortunate in that it has both winter tourists who come principally for the winter sports in the Alpine areas and summer holiday-makers who visit more especially the lakeside resorts of the Swiss Plateau and the southern margins of the Alps. This seasonal tourism thus brings benefits to two different parts of the country. Summers are generally warm and sunny, though not infrequently showery; winters are cold but usually dry and in the mountains, at least at higher elevations, there can be much sunshine. Autumn is typically misty and can be chilly and damp and this is the off-season for tourists. The winter sports season extends from about Christmas to April, the summer season from May to October.

The chief Alpine resorts and sports centres lie in the Bernese Oberland, the Pennine Alps and the Grisons in the east, all renowned tourist areas. On the northern margins of the Oberland, where the valleys open out on to the Swiss Plateau or *mittelland*, are many resorts, some popular in both winter and summer. Here are fashionable Gstaad, Adelboden, Kandersteg (the curling-centre), Mürren, Grindelwald and Wengen. In the Pennine Alps, in the Valais, are some of Switzerland's best winter sports centres (and summer climbing centres) such as Zermatt at the foot of the Matterhorn, Saas-Fee in the Saas valley, Zinal in the Val D'Anniviers and Arolla in the Val d'Hérens, each possessing their own ski schools and mountain guides. Away to the east, in the large canton of Grisons, is another important tourist area. Here the winters are snowy and harder, though sunny and invigorating, and the Grisons has therefore become the leading health centre in addition to being renowned for winter sports. St Moritz, long a resort of international renown, Davos-Platz, Klosters, Arosa and Pontresina are all famous. "During this century the Upper Engadine has become a very popular district for tourists, with highly developed winter sports and mountaineering, notably among the peaks and snowfields of the Bernina group, such as Piz Bernina, Piz Palu and Piz Morteratsch."[44]

The majority of tourists, and certainly the summer tourists, tend not to penetrate very deeply into the Alps: they congregate in the towns of the *mittelland* such as Berne and Zurich or the lakeside centres of Geneva, Montreux, Lucerne, Lausanne and Interlaken or the resorts on the lakes at the foot of the mountains, *e.g.* Locarno on Lake Maggiore, Lugano on Lake Lugano. Because of their more southerly situation and sheltered position, these resorts are more affected by Mediterranean influences and enjoy more sunshine both in summer and winter; partly for this reason and partly because they are more easily accessible, they tend to attract many visitors from Italy and Yugoslavia.

Switzerland also possesses a number of more purely health resorts, often located where medicinal springs occur, *e.g.* at Scuols-Tarasp in the Engadine and Bad Ragaz, near Sargans in Graubünden.

Reasons For the Growth of Swiss Tourism

Switzerland, located almost at the geographical centre of Western Europe, is well situated to capture much of the European holiday traffic through its control of trans-Alpine communications. The country is also richly endowed with natural attractions: mountains, glaciers, rivers and lakes. The Swiss Alps offer magnificent mountain scenery, the finest in Europe; the climate, too, is healthful and invigorating in winter, cold but dry and often sunny. The lakes are yet another natural attraction. In the *mittelland* are a number of historic cities, *e.g.* Bern, Lucerne, Solothurn.

One element that cannot be under-emphasised is the scrupulous attention the Swiss have always paid to food, accommodation and service. Once tourists began to visit Switzerland, the Swiss quickly became experts in hotel management, an expertise which they have cherished and maintained. Cleanliness and comfort, good food and service became the hallmark of the Swiss hotelier. As a result, clientele, appreciative of such qualities, have remained faithful. At the same time the Swiss have adopted a sensible price policy and, by and large, for the services and facilities rendered, hotel charges are moderate.

The tourist industry has also been greatly assisted by the widespread development of hydro-electric power and of a transport system which makes even the more remote areas readily accessible. The electrification of the railway system was completed by 1961. The building of roads, especially mountain roads, the driving of trans-Alpine tunnels, the construction of rack-and-pinion railways and the development of electrically driven chairlifts, ski-lifts and aerial cableways, which enabled tourists to reach without effort many of the mountain peaks and enjoy the magnificent scenery, greatly enhanced the development of tourism.

Finally, though not perhaps a factor related directly to tourism, there is the fact that Switzerland has long been a cultural oasis and a refuge in the centre of an often intolerant Europe. Switzerland's neutrality and prosperity have been responsible for drawing large numbers of foreigners to the country who live there more or less permanently. Dr A. Martin, Director of the Swiss Federal Transport Office, wrote: "It is all too easily forgotten—and this is a problem facing the promotion of a tourist industry in the developing countries—what a great contribution was made to foreign tourism in Switzerland by the fact that it was a country of law and order, with security and safety forming a background of confidence. The life and property of the visitor were protected; freedom of speech and movement were guaranteed from the outset.... It may well be said that tourism ... was just the very thing for the Swiss, a people whose hospitality had earned the praise of Montaigne centuries before. For Switzerland is the melting-pot of so many different currents of thought—the *liberty* of Rousseau, who hoped to cure the ills of society with his 'back to nature' movement, the *educational ideas* of Pestalozzi, Fellenberg and Père Girard, which led to the introduction of elementary public education, the *feeling of unity* of the German, French and Italian-speaking sections of the population of the Federal State in 1848. It would be a grave error to imagine that tourism in Switzerland owed its origin to purely commercial motives. The urge to visit this land ... this remarkable little republic ... in the heart of Europe, existed long before the advent of modern tourist propaganda."[45]

Tourism and its Present-day Importance

It has been estimated that around 1850 the number of foreign visitors to Switzerland was between 30,000–40,000 a year. In 1970, the figure was about 6 million visitors annually, half of whom went to the Swiss Alps. The Alps, also, it is worth noting, received an annual average of more than $1\frac{1}{2}$ million "home" tourists.

Swiss tourism had an early start and up to the Second World War largely dominated Alpine tourism. The war years brought a temporary halt but by the early 1950s the holiday industry was once again in full swing. The interlude, however, brought very significant changes and the Swiss found themselves having to adapt their industry to tourism's changing image. Not only had the Swiss to meet an increased volume of tourist traffic but, also, changes in tourist demand, *e.g.* hotel bedrooms with baths, non-hotel accommodation and increased amenities and facilities for amusement and sporting activities. Thus the Swiss had to make a reappraisal and readjustment of their industry and since 1950 there has been much streamlining of hotels, a big expansion in the provision of non-hotel accommodation (even by 1965 the person-per-night figure for non-hotel accommodation totalled 15 million or about half of the relevant figure for hotels and pensions),[46] greatly increased recreational facilities and vastly improved transport. All this has meant a very heavy investment in tourism. Even so, Switzerland as a tourist destination has lost ground relatively and in respect of Alpine tourism it has barely managed to maintain its lead; as Cosgrove and Jackson have

TABLE 46
Switzerland: foreign arrivals (1970)

West Germany	1,557,879
U.S.A.	1,176,927
France	894,953
Italy	667,480
United Kingdom and Ireland	628,410
Belgium and Luxembourg	330,940
Netherlands	326,402
Scandinavia	186,473
Austria	147,250
Spain and Portugal	123,744
Japan	100,455
Canada	95,734
Israel	63,310
Yugoslavia	55,618
Other countries	484,284
	6,839,859

said: "Switzerland, as a whole, has suffered in recent years from a general stagnation in the industry and a decline in the number of summer visitors. It is usually said that Alpine summer tourism suffers greatly from the absence of sunny sea beaches and certainly the down-valley, old-established summer resorts are the weak links in the regional tourist network."[47]

Tourism is a major Swiss industry which makes a very significant contribution to the country's balance of payments. In 1970 the revenue from the tourist industry was 1500m Swiss francs ($733m). Notwithstanding the substantial volume of Swiss travel abroad—over 2 million tourists a year—Switzerland has a large surplus on its balance of payments account: in 1970 there was a net surplus on the travel account of $478m. Income from the industry amounts to about 8 per cent of the total national income and is equal to one-fifth of the total export commodities, normally ranking second to the exports of the products of the machine industry.

The Swiss tourist industry is also very important in the internal economy of the country, for it provides employment for 140,000–150,000 people, approximately half of whom are employed directly in the hotel industry. Tourism is therefore responsible for the employment of 5–6 per cent of the actively engaged population. And many more—food producers, transport workers, those engaged in hotel maintenance and furnishings, etc.—benefit indirectly.

The Organisation of Tourism

The highly developed character of Swiss tourism owes much to its organisation. There are two complementary top-level organisations:

the *Schweizerische Verkehrszentrale* or Swiss National Tourist Office, which is primarily concerned with the promotion of Switzerland abroad and is largely financed by the Federal Government, and the *Schweizerischer Fremdenverkehrsband* or Swiss Tourist Federation which deals principally with internal tourist development and its co-ordination and which is supported by various national, regional and local associations together with certain other large organisations who together finance its activities.

"The Federal character of Switzerland is reflected in its highly developed tourist organisation," says Medlik. "At local and regional level there is a long tradition of tourist associations and offices, which are concerned with promotion and development of their respective areas. They cover towns as well as villages and represent a solid basis for the co-ordination of local tourist interests and for the provision of information services to visitors. . . . The highly developed character of Swiss tourism is also evident from the existence of several organisations such as the Swiss Travel Savings Bank, two hotel credit organisations and others with specific functions in tourism."[48]

AUSTRIA

Austria is essentially an Alpine country, for mountains occupy some 70 per cent of the total area. To the north lies the Danube valley and, beyond, a portion of the Bohemian Forest: to the east the low-lying Vienna Basin and the Burgenland; to the south-east the sub-Alpine basins of Klagenfurt and Graz (*see* Fig. 33). Apart from the attractions

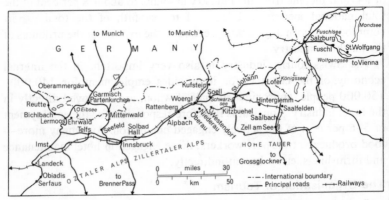

Fig. 33.—*Austria: tourist centres.* The map shows some of the more important winter sports centres.

of Vienna, the capital, the Alpine region, which in every respect is the most picturesque part of the country, forms the tourist centre. The mountain ranges—the Otztaler Alpen, the Hohe Tauern and the Niedere Tauern—trend in a general east–west direction, separated by the deep, trench-like valley of the River Inn which provides a geological boundary also, since to the north the mountains are formed of intensely folded limestone whereas to the south the higher massifs are composed of crystalline rocks. The mountains of Austria, like those of Switzerland, have been heavily glaciated and show, especially in the west, spiked peaks, serrated ridges, great cirques, snowfields and glaciers; on the northern and southern margins lie many finger lakes. Alpine Austria is a land of scenic splendour: towering, rocky, snow-capped mountains, with coniferous forests on the lower slopes, and green valleys with picturesque villages, landscapes as dramatic and as pleasing as can be found anywhere in Europe.

Three areas in particular are important for tourism: the Western Tyrol, the Central Tyrol and the Austrian Lake District; other areas of note are Vorarlberg, Carinthia and Styria, although in the last area the majority of the visitors are Austrians. The province of Vorarlberg in the extreme west is cut off by mountains from the neighbouring province of Tyrol but the Arlberg Pass, crossed by both road and rail, provides a link between them. The Vorarlberg slopes and looks westwards towards Switzerland and there is a strong Swiss influence in the province. Vorarlberg is mountainous but well wooded and has very attractive scenery; among its tourist resorts are Bregenz, on the shores of Lake Constance, Bludenz and Schruns. The province of Tyrol is one of the most popular tourist areas, with magnificent scenery and on the lower mountain slopes wonderful facilities for winter sports. In the Western Tyrol are many small towns and villages which have become winter sports centres, *e.g.* Bichlbach, Lermoos and Ehrwald (which lies at the foot of the Zugspitze), Serfaus and Seefeld, while Innsbruck has become a great tourist centre for both winter and summer visitors. In the Central Tyrol are Alpbach, Auffach, Oberau, Niederau, Soell and Kitzbühel. The area to the east of Salzburg is Austria's Lakeland and here are numerous delightful resorts, many of them clustered round the lake shores, *e.g.* Fuschl, St Wolfgang. The town of Salzburg itself is a very old settlement, occupying a historically strategic position. During the sixteenth and seventeenth centuries it flourished and its prosperity at that time is reflected in the baroque architecture of its cathedral, bishop's palace and merchants' houses. Salzburg is famed as the birth-place of Mozart and for its International Musical Festival.

The beautiful city of Vienna, which grew up as the capital of a great Empire, has long been a great centre of art and music and developed numerous luxury trades. Although Vienna has now lost much of its former glamour and importance, it has numerous fine buildings, shops, museums, parks and other attractions for tourists.

In the pre-Second World War years Austria had begun to build up a significant tourist industry but the war and its aftermath were disastrous for Austrian tourism. During the first decade after the war the number of tourists lagged behind pre-war figures, then in the mid-1950s a marked revival commenced. The Austrians were not slow to take advantage of the post-war growth in travel and the government, as soon as it was able, put the construction and repair of hotels, inns and other kinds of holiday accommodation high on the list of priorities. Since the mid-1950s Austria has experienced a truly astonishing development, overtaking her neighbour, Switzerland, by a considerable margin. By 1964 Austria was receiving slightly more than 6 million visitors: by 1970 rather more than $8\frac{3}{4}$ million, while in 1973 the figure approached 10 million. Austria's visitor traffic grew by 44 per cent over the seven-year period 1964–70, as compared with only 17 per cent in the case of Switzerland. In terms of percentage growth only Spain and the United Kingdom, among European countries, were able to show a faster growth rate than Austria.

In terms of income, Austria's receipts in 1970 amounted to $999m, as against $785m in the previous year—an increase of 27 per cent.[49] The value of Austria's tourism is approximately one-third of the value of its commodity exports. The industry is the largest single earner of foreign currency, so is a very valuable invisible export and the earnings from tourism help very substantially to meet the deficit on Austria's balance of trade. The volume of Austrian nationals who travel abroad is

TABLE 47
Principal arrivals in Austria (1970)

West Germany	5,379,065
U.S.A.	678,248
United Kingdom	610,671
Netherlands	468,770
France	238,474
Switzerland	216,456
Italy	211,514
Belgium and Luxembourg	164,603
Yugoslavia	142,103
Sweden	136,231
Denmark	118,223
Other countries	502,619
TOTAL	8,866,977

relatively small, hence the favourable effect of tourism on the country's balance of payments is greatly enhanced. The great majority of foreign tourists—almost two-thirds in fact in 1970—came from West Germany. The next two most important sources of tourist traffic were the United States and the United Kingdom; in both cases the traffic was around 600,000 annually.

Tourist organisation in Austria reflects the federal character of the state. Each of the nine provinces has its own tourist board which concerns itself generally with all matters relating to tourism within its area. Each tourist board is financed by the provincial governments. However, in the case of individual resorts the promotion and provision of tourist facilities normally lies in the hands of local councils. The Central Federal Government only comes into the picture in framing national tourist policy, in controlling transport facilities and in the financing of tourism.[50] These activities are shared by the Federal Ministry of Trade and Reconstruction and the Federal Ministry of Transport and Electricity Industry, the former concerning itself more particularly with tourist policy and finance and the promotion of tourism abroad, the latter with transport and communications facilities.

NOTES

1. F. H. A. Aalen and J. C. Bird, *Tourism in Ireland—East, Guidelines for Development*, Eastern Region Tourism Organisation, 1969, p. 3.

2. Annual Report for 1967–8.

3. *The Geography of Recreation and Leisure*, p. 62.

4. Aalen and Bird, *op. cit.*, p. 3.

5. *Idem*, p. 5.

6. *The Geography of Recreation and Leisure*, p. 63.

7. W. R. Mead, *An Advanced Geography of Northern and Western Europe*, Hulton Press, 1967, p. 111.

8. *British Travel News*, No. 40, Winter, 1972.

9. S. Nickels, "Far from the space-age race," *The Times*, 13th May, 1971.

10. W. R. Mead, *op. cit.*, p. 130.

11. G. R. P. Lawrence, *An Advanced Geography of Northern and Western Europe*, Hulton Press, 1967, p. 316.

12. S. Medlik, "Organisation of Tourism In Six European Countries," University of Surrey, 1966.

13. *The French Tourist Industry*, Ambassade de France, Service de Presse et d'Information, p. 6.

14. I. B. Thompson, *Modern France I: a Social and Economic Geography*, Butterworth, 1970, p. 118.

15. *Op. cit.*, pp. 182–3.

16. *The French Tourist Industry*, Ambassade de France, Service de Presse et d'Information, p. 18.

17. Thompson, *op. cit.*, p. 184.

18. J. E. Williams and W. Zelinsky, "On Some Patterns of International Tourist Flows," *Economic Geography*, October, 1970, pp. 549–67.

19. Medlik, *op. cit.*

20. Thompson, *op. cit.*, p. 269.

21. *Op. cit.*, p. 339.

22. Thompson, *op. cit.*, p. 341.

23. *Op. cit.*, p. 351.

24. *French Regional Development*, Ambassade de France, Service de Presse et d'Information, p. 11.

25. *Op. cit.*, p. 378.

26. *Op. cit.*, p. 382.

27. H. Thurston, "France finds a new holiday coast," *Geographical Magazine*, Vol. XLI, February, 1969, pp. 339–45.

28. *Tourism Development and Economic Growth*, O.E.C.D. Estoril Seminar, 1966, p. 33.

29. Thurston, *op. cit.*

30. *Idem.*

31. *Idem.*

32. P. Pinchemel, *France, A Geographical Survey*, G. Bell & Sons, 1969, p. 383.

33. *The French Tourist Industry*, Ambassade de France, Service de Presse et d'Information, p. 22.

34. *French Regional Development*, Ambassade de France, Service de Presse et d'Information, p. 14.

35. I. Macdonald, "Bavaria: a Special Report," *The Guardian*, 6th March, 1972.

36. Medlik, *op. cit.*

37. M. Peters, *International Tourism*, Hutchinson, 1969, pp. 232–3.

38. *Ibid.*

·39. W. Kaempfen, "Switzerland for Holidays in the Alpine Year 1965," *Swiss Industry and Trade*, No. 1, 1965, p. 3.

40. J. Marion and J. Loup, "Cent ans de tourisme alpine," *Rev. Geog. Alp.*, 1965, p. 423.

41. P. Risch, "Rejuvenation of Switzerland's Tourist Industry," *Swiss Industry and Trade*, No. 1, 1965, p. 5.

42. J. Billet, "La montagne, chance du tourisme tessinois de demain," *Rev. Geog. Alp.*, 1966, p. 373.

43. *Op. cit.*, p. 56.

44. F. J. Monkhouse, *The Countries of Northwestern Europe*, Longman, 1965, p. 398.

45. A. Martin, "Swiss Transport Facilities in the Service of the Tourist Industry," *Swiss Industry and Trade*, No. 1, 1965, p. 17.

46. Risch, *op. cit.*, p. 11.

47. *Op. cit.*, p. 57.

48. Medlik, *op. cit.*

49. O.E.C.D. Tourism Report, 1971.

50. Medlik, *op. cit.*

Chapter XVII

Tourism in Southern Europe

SPAIN

The Growth of Tourism

PRIOR to the Second World War, Spain was unimportant as a tourist country and during the 1930s the average annual number of foreign visitors was not much more than a quarter of a million. The Spanish Civil War and the Second World War obviously precluded any tourism development, and in 1947 the number of tourists was still around the quarter of a million mark. Two years later, however, the number had doubled and in 1950 the million mark was reached. The 1950s showed a rapid expansion in the number of visitors and between 1951–8 there was an annual increase of about 16 per cent. After 1959, largely as a result of the stabilisation of the peseta, the real holiday boom began (*see* Fig. 34). Naylon wrote: "A striking jump can be seen after the successful Stabilisation Plan of July 1959; between 1958 and 1963 there was a 145 per cent rise in the number of tourists arriving in Spain, compared with France (60 per cent), Italy (32 per cent) and West Germany (17 per cent)."[1] After 1964 there was a levelling-off in the rate of increase and the number of tourists settled down to around 14 million; Spain had anticipated 16 million tourists in 1965 but the actual figure was almost 2 million short. Naylon commented that this levelling-off seemed to indicate that "the period of easy spontaneous gains is over" and that the Spanish success had "stimulated new competitors and roused old campaigners such as France and Italy."[2] However, this lull proved to be only temporary and in 1967 Spain received 17·9 million visitors and in 1969 21·6 million. Since 1969 there seems to have been a further truly astonishing growth and in 1973 the number of arrivals was around 28 million (one estimate in fact gave 34 million).

The French have always formed the predominant national group visiting Spain and in the early 1960s France supplied about half of foreign visitor traffic, although in more recent years this proportion has declined to around one-third. The British form the second largest national group of visitors, rising from 803,000 in 1965 to 4 million in 1973. Spain, including Majorca and the other Balearic Islands, is now

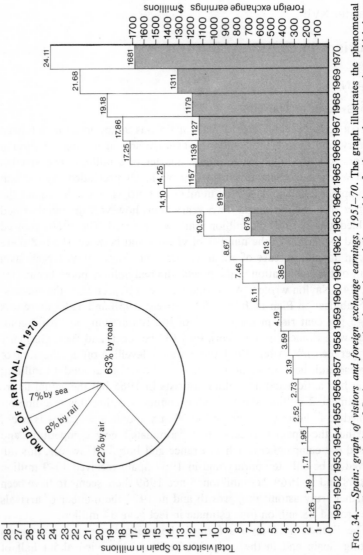

Fig. 34.—*Spain: graph of visitors and foreign exchange earnings, 1951–70.* The graph illustrates the phenomenal growth in popularity of Spain as a tourist destination and the resulting foreign exchange earnings which have transformed the Spanish economy. The inset pie-graph shows the mode of travel by visitors to Spain in 1970.

TABLE 48

Spain: tourism by nationalities

National group	1968	1969	1970
French	7,782,981	8,216,122	8,826,172
British	2,285,471	2,564,505	2,618,068
Portuguese	1,490,770	1,992,227	na
Germans	1,389,148	1,800,681	2,075,094
Americans	719,843	901,656	1,030,437
Dutch	545,672	805,341	874,511
Belgians	502,109	656,428	614,316
Italians	160,878	492,457	505,606

by far the most popular foreign holiday destination, accounting for 30 per cent of all holidays taken abroad in 1970 by the British. Table 48 shows the main national groups visiting Spain in 1968, 1969 and 1970.

The large number of French and Portuguese visitors is explained in part by close geographical proximity, although it is interesting that so many Portuguese visit Spain where conditions are very like those obtaining in their own homeland. Especially noteworthy is the very considerable increase in the number of Italians visiting Spain.

Reasons for the Growth of Tourism

The quite phenomenal growth and popularity of Spain as a tourist destination is difficult to explain. The climatic conditions of the Mediterranean coastlands with their assured sunshine obviously exert a tremendous attraction to sun-starved Britons but the British form only a comparatively small proportion of the total number of tourists. It would be difficult to convince anyone that the French and Portuguese go to Spain because of the sunshine. Any attempt to explain Spain's success in tourism in terms of weather alone cannot be accepted. Of much greater importance is the relative cheapness of holidays in Spain. Low prices must always be a powerful factor in generating tourist flow. Spain was late in developing tourism, hence prices were much lower than in France and Italy which had a long-established and well-developed tourist trade. When tourism began to grow in Spain during the early 1950s, the French tourist was "the pioneer who first exploited such low prices on the Costa Brava on any scale."[3] With the coming of charter flights, North Europeans found they could holiday on the Costa Brava at scarcely any greater expense than that involved in holidaying at home. Although costs in Spain have gone up quite appreciably since the late 1960s, it is still true to say that they compare very favourably with those in other West European countries.

A third factor would seem to be fashion. In Britain at least it became very fashionable in the 1960s to holiday on the Costa Brava. Once the trend was set, the tour operators began to exploit the situation and their coloured brochures beckoned the holiday-maker to the sunny bays and beaches of this mountain coast. It should not, however, be forgotten that when a place becomes too fashionable there is the probability of a reaction setting in and of the place becoming *de trop*.

Finally, one should take into consideration the Government's role although, as Naylon said "it is debatable how much of Spanish success in attracting visitors . . . [was] due to the Government's organisation and expansion of facilities under its National Tourism Plans of 1953 and 1959."[4] The effects of State encouragement, intervention and promotion must have been of some benefit to the tourist industry but such measures in themselves cannot explain the phenomenal success of Spanish tourism.

The Organisation of Spanish Tourism

This is dominated by the Government. Prior to 1951 the promotion of tourism was in the hands of the *Patronato Nacional de Turismo* but in that year direct government intervention was established when tourism became the responsibility of a cabinet minister. In 1962 an Under-Secretariat of Tourism was established under the Ministry of Information and Tourism and it is this body, the *Subsecretaria de Turismo*, which has powers "to develop, regulate and supervise all activities concerned with the organisation of tourism, the hotel industry, services related to tourism and information, entertainment and publicity abroad."[5]

As early as the 1930s the significance of tourism began to be appreciated, and the *Patronato* began to build some state inns (*albergues*) and hotels (*paradores*) along the newly built highways. This initial progress, however, was greatly handicapped first by the Civil War in Spain and then by the Second World War and it was not until the early 1950s that any further significant progress could be made. Under the National Tourism Plans of 1953 and 1959 improved organisation and facilities greatly assisted the already booming tourist industry but, as Naylon comments "although the Tourism Plans provided a sort of institutional framework, state support generally lagged behind actual growth and catering for the increasing flow of visitors was left, on the whole, to private initiative, which built more or less adequate facilities, all of which proved profitable despite official price-fixing."[6]

The National Development Plan 1964–67 provided for substantial increases and developments in tourist facilities, amenities and services generally. There was an urgent need for greatly increased accommodation—Spanish hotel capacity was only about one-third that of Italy—for the greater dispersion of the industry especially into areas suitable for tourism but which were undeveloped, for improved communications of every sort and for more adequate professional training. Since 1968, much has been done and many improvements effected: for example, hotel construction has grown rapidly, new areas such as Mar Menor in Murcia have been opened up, new motorways such as the *Autopista de Levante* have been built, an Institute of Tourist Studies has been set up and several professional training schools (such as that established in Palma (Majorca) in 1965), opened. The industry, however, has developed so rapidly that it has often been impossible to keep pace with the demand.

The Importance of Tourism

The single most important effect of the growth of tourism in Spain has been its influence upon the Spanish economy, since tourism earns about half Spain's foreign currency and is invaluable in compensating for the unfavourable visible balance of trade. Tourist receipts from January to November, 1973 were $2951m, 26·6 per cent higher than the corresponding period in 1972. The income from tourism in fact exceeds that gained from all the country's exports. Tourism has thus brought a measure of prosperity to Spain undreamt of a quarter of a century ago. The Spanish economy is now buoyant and the outlook for Spain's continuing economic expansion seems to be exceptionally good. Doubts have, of course, been expressed about tourism forming a sound basis for serious economic development planning but, as Naylon says, tourism is probably no more fickle or risky than any other aspect of international commerce.[7] Tourism in Spain is still far off reaching saturation point and it seems fairly clear that the country can look forward to a continuing tourist-based prosperity for a long time to come. The Economist Intelligence Unit Report has said: "As far as the future is concerned, the prospects for growth in the medium term are good. Political development will not be allowed to affect tourism. Over the longer term to 1980, a total of 50 million visitors may be reached, with $5 billion in foreign exchange receipts. By that time, however, Spain should have moved up-market to some extent, and may have attained a position similar to that of Italy or France today."[8]

"Without tourism, imports would have to be held back to around two-thirds of their present level, and as three-quarters of imports are industrial inputs and capital goods the growth of the economy would be seriously impaired. In round terms, the average rate of growth of the economy in the decade [1960–70 was] ... 6 per cent per annum. Without tourism this might have been reduced to 4 per cent. The importance of tourism is therefore not in its direct effect upon the economy, but in the way in which it allows natural resources such as labour, food and beaches to be converted into machine tools and chemical feedstock via the international market. It is in this sense that tourism is one of the keys to Spain's rapid economic growth since the war."[9]

Although tourism is undoubtedly of great significance, constituting the first export industry, it is easy to exaggerate its direct importance to the Spanish economy. The report mentioned above points out: "The value added in the entire tourist sector cannot be more than 100 billion pesetas, which is only 5 per cent of the total Spanish G.D.P. at factor cost (approximately 2000 billion pesetas in 1970) and 10 per cent of the service sector. Employment in hotels and restaurants is officially estimated at some 0·3 million, and with other related employment (shops, bars, etc.) the total may be as much as 0·5 million, but this is only 12 per cent of employment in the service industries and 4 per cent of total employment. Output per head is therefore somewhat lower than the service sector as a whole. On the other hand, the industry is highly labour-intensive and employs a great deal of essentially unskilled labour."[10]

One must, however, recognise that tourism affects many other industries, notably transportation, construction and food, each of which have benefited substantially and grown rapidly as a result of the strong demands made upon them. Tourism has provided work for low-income groups and many shopkeepers, entertainers and the like have benefited from tourist spending. When one considers these benefits in relation to regional distribution, however, it is unfortunate that the greatest have occurred in areas which already possess higher than average income levels while the poorer areas of the country which are in need of a monetary injection are the ones which have gained least.

The social effects which the growth of tourism has had are nonetheless significant. Considerable areas have been completely transformed: "Benidorm was moribund in 1945; today it has over 4 million annual visitors in its region. The erstwhile coastal village of Lloret del Mar has today more hotels than Barcelona and almost as many as Madrid."[11] Thus settlement patterns have been drastically altered. Spain has been brought into closer touch with the rest of Europe and the Spaniards have been confronted with and possibly influenced by, some of the more liberal, progressive and permissive attitudes of their fellow Europeans; the comment has been made that "only the worst aspects of modernisation have in fact been imported."[12]

The Regional Importance of Tourism

Tourist activity is largely concentrated in a few areas of Spain, more particularly the Mediterranean coast and islands (*see* Fig. 35). With the

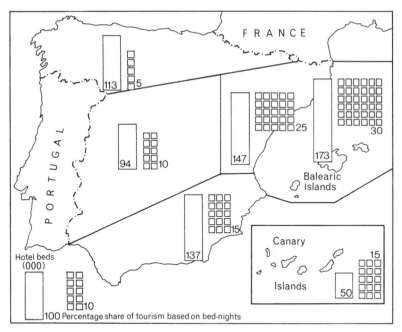

FIG. 35.—*Spain: regional distribution of tourism.*

exception of Madrid, the capital and itself a centre of attraction as well as a good base for visiting some of Spain's historic cities—Segovia, Avila, Salamanca and Toledo—the Meseta makes only a small contribution to the tourist trade. One or two other plateau towns receive tourists although largely because they lie on main routes between coast and capital, *e.g.* Burgos which is on the main road from the French frontier town of Irun to Madrid, and Zaragoza which is situated on the main highway from Barcelona to the capital. Scenically the Meseta is not very attractive but many of the towns have a rich cultural legacy; the Spanish Government has been trying to tempt the tourist into the interior and many new hotels have been built during recent years.

The Biscayan and Atlantic coasts of Spain have much to offer the tourist but the industry has rather languished here, at least in comparison with that in the south. The three Basque provinces are the least typically Spanish and on the Basque coast are several delightful resorts, notably Laredo, Castro Urdiales and San Sebastian. The latter, located on an almost perfectly semi-circular bay, La Concha, has the reputation of being the most elegant resort in the country and is frequented by the "smart set" to avoid the summer heat. In the *ria* country of the north-west, with its mild and pleasant, if sometimes damp, climate, there are several fine resorts, often beautifully situated, with splendid beaches and sheltered bays ideal for sailing, *e.g.* La Toja. Pontevedra is the most important province in the north-west for tourism. Inland is the interesting ancient town of Santiago de Compostela, one of the great centres of medieval pilgrimage. Further along the coast towards the east, in the old province of Asturias, are the resorts of Gijón and Santander, both possessing fine beaches. Not far from Santander are the famous caves of Altamira with their prehistoric wall paintings. This northern maritime fringe of Spain, as Naylon has pointed out, is exclusively a summer holiday area and so suffers on this account; it is, moreover, "traditionally frequented by Spaniards themselves and only recently has begun to be favoured by French and other foreign visitors."[13]

As in France, the Pyrenean country has both summer and winter attractions and several tourist centres and resorts. There are several old medieval towns in the foothills, often quiet backwaters of great charm set in very attractive surroundings. Candanchu, near the frontier town of Canfranc, is a winter resort with ski-runs and ski-lifts. The National Park of Ordesa, a game reserve, also lies near the French frontier.

The Mediterranean coastlands and the Balearic Islands form *the* great tourist zone of Spain: the Costa Brava, the Costa Blanca, the Costa del Sol and the Costa de la Luz. The world-famous Costa Brava (Rocky Coast) stretches all the way from Port Bou at the French border to Blanes some 64 km (40 miles) east of Barcelona. Until the early 1950s this coast of Gerona Province attracted few foreigners and was frequented almost solely by the Catalans. Then it was discovered by the French and with astonishing rapidity it became a rival to the French Riviera. This stretch of coast has great intrinsic natural beauty still not entirely marred by the *urbanización* which has taken place since 1960, although the rapid development has brought acute congestion. The Costa Blanca, with its ideal climate, lies some 80 km (50 miles) either side of Alicante. Until very recently it was essentially a Spanish playground but it has now become an international centre with such places as Calpe, Benidorm, Villajoyosa and Playa San Juan developing fast. The area around the Mar Menor is being transformed as rapid urbanisation occurs. Malaga is the focal point of the Costa del Sol, a stretch of coast enjoying abundant and almost continuous sunshine, very little rain and very mild winters. Originally the Costa del Sol comprised the coastal strip between Torremolinos and Estepona in Malaga Province but development has taken place on both sides of Malaga and the Costa now extends for a distance of about 160 km (100 miles) from Motril in the east to Estepona in the west. The expansion of tourism on this stretch of Andalusian coast has been quite phenomenal but the greatest concentration of resorts occurs to the west of Malaga on the original Costa where development is practically continuous from Torremolinos through Marbella to Estepona. In the ten-year period 1955–65 £70m worth of Spanish Government and private foreign investment was put into properties along the Costa del Sol. It is not improbable that before very long the entire embayment between Almeria and Algeçiras will comprise a continuous string of resorts. Whereas formerly the eccentric position of the Costa del Sol and the travelling time involved militated against development, the coming of cheap jet transport—there is an airport at Malaga—altered the picture completely.

Behind the sun-scorched, golden beaches of the Costa lie the mountains of Granada and the plains of Andalusia. "The Andalucian triangle of Cordoba–Sevilla–Granada," says Naylon "has a sound basis for tourism . . . medieval Arab architecture and a folklore unique in Europe. At present holiday-makers appear to spend not more than a week in these centres before heading for the Costa del Sol: but the full integration of the two zones by improved road and rail communications could make Andalucia the most important touring region in Europe."[14]

The Balearic Islands (Mallorca, Menorca, Ibiza and Formentera) are the principal destination for many tourists and account for one-third of all nights spent by tourists in Spain. Some 70,000 Britons go to these islands, which have about a quarter of all the hotel places in the country. Tourism development has been spectacular, especially in Mallorca (or Majorca as it is perhaps more commonly called in Britain), which is now suffering acutely from congestion. This in part has been responsible for the development of the neighbouring islands. There are good and frequent air services to Mallorca and Palma airport is one of the busiest in the world but the other islands are not well-served; in fact the inadequacy of inter-island shipping and water shortage problems have tended to handicap tourism development there.

PROBLEMS AND FUTURE PLANNING

The National Report on Spain by the Economic Intelligence Unit summarised the official tourist policy thus:

"(*i*) to ensure recognition of the central position of tourism in the Spanish economy;
(*ii*) to develop domestic tourism;

(*iii*) to intensify promotion abroad in order to increase both numbers and unit expenditure;

(*iv*) to attempt to reduce the problem of seasonality and improve capacity utilisation by promoting all-year zones, creating new off-peak demand (winter sports, hunting, etc.) and by attracting other activities (*e.g.* conferences) to hotel capacity;

(*v*) to diversify supply in a selective manner, filling in gaps and creating new zones;

(*vi*) to control real estate speculation and environmental pollution, using participation as a stimulating force." [15]

Although the tourist industry in Spain is thriving and potential remains great, the country has many problems. First there is heavy regional concentration, with the Balearic Islands and the Costa Brava receiving about half the foreign tourists (*see* Fig. 36). The Costa Blanca and the Costa del Sol together account for a further 20 per cent. There is, as Naylon has said "a pressing need to alleviate the present concentration and congestion ... by promoting other areas which are still underdeveloped in relation to their possibilities." [16] Since the basic tourist demand in Spain is for sunshine, it would seem that the less-developed sectors of the Mediterranean coastline should be considered. "Filling in" the gaps along the eastern coast, *i.e.* along the Costa Dorada and the Costa Azahar, is already proceeding with the result that the only stretch of undeveloped coast is that from the Strait of Gibraltar to the Portuguese frontier. The Spanish Government has already begun to promote this last section as the Costa de la Luz. This 80-km (50-mile) stretch of coast with its extensive sandy pine-fringed beaches and almost continuous sunshine holds out great promise as another holiday playground. Developments are well in hand to provide accommodation and holiday amenities for some 350,000 visitors. But an even wider dispersion of the industry is desirable and it would be advantageous to Spain if more of the tourist traffic could be encouraged to visit the Biscayan and Atlantic coasts and the interior areas. These regions are not without notable natural and cultural attractions. In 1970 the Spanish Government designated certain areas as "Zones and Centres of National Tourist Interest" and the intention was to develop these to help relieve congestion elsewhere. "Development of the designated areas is being strictly controlled with a view to the preservation of their charm, but at the same time they are being opened up and provided with transport and accommodation both by supporting local initiative (*Crédito Hotelero*) and by direct state action through its own enter-

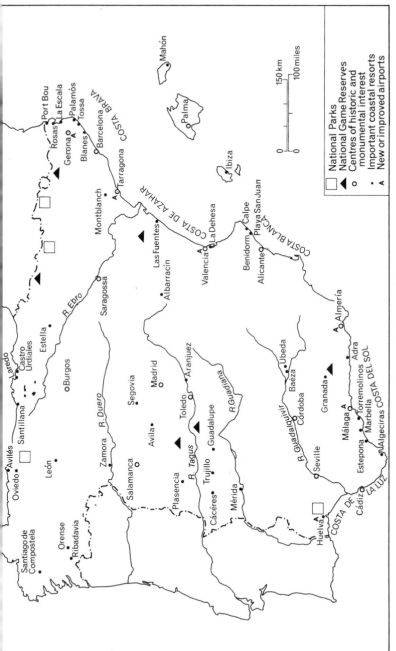

FIG. 36.—*Spain: tourism features.*

prises."[17] Two examples may be cited of areas or centres which offer considerable scope for tourist development. First, there is the possibility of developing further the winter sports centres in the mountain areas, *e.g.* the Pyrenees and Sierra Nevada; here are great natural attractions but until very recently they offered few facilities. With their eye on the fast-growing international winter sports market, however, the Spanish tourist authorities have begun vigorously to promote the country's skiing potential. By the end of 1972 Spain had twenty-seven skiing centres and another sixteen are planned. Secondly, the demand for water for irrigation and for hydro-electric power have resulted in the creation of numerous reservoirs: these are often located in areas of great natural beauty and in addition to offering scenic attractions could be used for boating and water sports. Here, then, are two possibilities which so far have scarcely begun to be exploited.

Another serious problem relates to the seasonality of the tourist industry. If one excludes the overseas territories, the industry suffers from a severe seasonal peaking of demand. Over 60 per cent of tourist arrivals come within the four-month June–September period, with some 23 per cent in August alone. This coincides of course with domestic tourism and so the problem is exacerbated. Hotel capacity is not used to the full because of this seasonal demand and many hotels are compelled to close down in the winter period. Attempts are being made to try to overcome this problem, for example, the Government has encouraged its nationals to stagger their holidays, tried to attract international conferences in the slack season and introduced short reduced-price winter holidays which many Britons have begun to take advantage of.

A third problem relates to the provision of adequate communications and transport facilities. These are a crucial feature in the further expansion of the tourist trade. In 1970, 63 per cent of tourists came to Spain by road, 22 per cent by air, 8 per cent by rail and 7 per cent by sea; hence it will be clear that transport infrastructures, especially those relating to motor roads and airports, are of fundamental importance. Spain has a reasonably good road system but improvements are needed to meet the demands of the travelling tourist: for instance, there is need to speed up holiday traffic in some areas and to provide roads in areas which are deficient. The Autopista de Levante runs all the way down the Mediterranean coast to Cadiz but there is need of a similar highway along the northern coast. There are some areas of considerable tourist potential which remain, if not inaccessible, difficult of access and improved roads with service stations would be of great benefit. Air traffic, however, is growing faster than road traffic and in view of the increasing importance of air transport and especially of jet aircraft, many Spanish airports are inadequate for both the volume of traffic they have to deal with and the type of craft they have to receive. Under the Development Plans new airports were scheduled for construction, *e.g.* at Reus, Valencia, Alicante, Almeria, Malaga and Huelva, but until recently "the lack of any airfields at all, added to difficult land communications, impeded the growth of tourism."[18] The airport at Palma in Mallorca has been heavily criticised because of the inadequate provision of terminal facilities.

It is very clear that Spanish tourism has had a major impact upon the cultural landscape of the Costas. Some of the development has been unsightly and completely out of character. The Spanish Government, however, is alive to the process of *urbanización* and the problems it brings and has taken measures to ensure that uncontrolled development does not continue and tourism, therefore, is exerting some influence upon regional planning.

THE CANARY ISLANDS

The Canary Islands comprise a group of mountainous islands with rocky coasts and wild scenery some 160 km (100 miles) off the north-west African coast. The chief islands are Teneriffe, Grand Canary, Palma, Hierro and Gomera. The archipelago, known to the Romans as the Fortunate Islands, was occupied by Spain in 1496; today, for administrative purposes, the islands are considered part of Spain. The total area of the Canaries is 7270 km^2 (2807 sq. miles) and the population close on a million.

Teneriffe, with an area of 2380 km^2 (919 sq. miles), is the largest of the islands forming the archipelago. It lies around latitude 28° N. Its native inhabitants number about 440,000. Teneriffe has spectacular scenery and particularly interesting geological formations. Volcanic in origin, the island rises in a series of terraces to Las Canadas, an immense sunken crater forming a circular plain 12 km (8 miles) in diameter at an elevation of 2900 m (6500 ft) and in the centre of this rises the great cone of Mt Teide which attains 3700 m (12,152 ft) and whose summit is snow-covered for the greater part of the year. At lower levels, the climate of Teneriffe is delightful with little rainfall, although this means that water is often scarce. Green in spring, the landscape takes on an arid, burnt dun colour as the seasons wear on and neither Teneriffe nor the other islands enjoy the lush all-year-round greenness of Madeira.

Tourism has grown spectacularly since 1960 and has had a big impact upon the economy of the islands: "the Canary Islands are rapidly being overtaken by modern cosmopolitan development. An all-the-year-round invasion of tourists, whose numbers are growing at the rate of about 40 per cent annually, has replaced the small luxury tourist trade confined to the winter months. This revolution has been created by rising standards of living, increased leisure and cheaper and swifter transport, bringing the archipelago within easy reach of most of Europe. The growth of tourism has given rise to a boom in property construction, particularly on the islands of Teneriffe, Grand Canary and La Palma, financed mainly by British, Belgian, German, Spanish and Swedish interests. Hotels are springing up, not only in the principal towns, but also in new resorts by the sea, which are being connected to the main centres by modern motor roads. Several projects aimed at private buyers are under way, with prices starting at around £3000." [19] The large number of visitors has meant that the volume of air traffic has increased phenomenally and has necessitated the extension of the two international airports at Las Palmas and Teneriffe. The busy ports of Las Palmas and Santa Cruz de Teneriffe, where one can always see holiday liners moored, are being enlarged to cater for the increased traffic on the shipping routes to Africa and South America. Outside the thriving tourist centres the traditional way of life persists but, as in Madeira, local industries, such as fruit growing, cigar making, the manufacture of filigree jewellery, inlay work and drawn-thread work, have benefited through increasing sales to tourists.

PORTUGAL

Portugal, and more particularly the Atlantic island of Madeira, has a long tradition of tourism but it is only since the 1960s that the industry has come to assume considerable significance. Accurate figures of visitors to Portugal are not easy to come by, as it is only since 1967 that the method of collecting data recommended by O.E.C.D. has been adopted by Portugal. Table 49 shows the number of foreigners spending

TABLE 49
Visitors: Portugal with Madeira (000)

Mode of entry	1968	1969	1970	1971
Land	967·0	1141·9	1320·7	1513·2
Air	33·6	31·5	38·2	38·7
Sea (excluding cruise vessels)	9·2	9·9	4·3	4·4
Sea (cruise ships)	398·4	416·1	393·2	348·1
TOTAL	1408·2	1599·4	1756·4	1904·4

Source: Direcção Geral de Segurança: National Institute of Statistics.

some time in Portugal, either as holiday-makers, short-stay stop-over or cruise visitors.

A large number of the visits, however, are of short duration. Day trippers are foreign motorists crossing over from Spain, shore visits by ship passengers and short stop-overs by air passengers in transit. The vast majority of these short-stay visitors are Spanish; in 1971 they accounted for 90 per cent of the total. Many of the visits are to see relatives and friends and usually involve little expenditure, so they do not bring much money into the country. Cruise business, on the other hand, provides a fairly large market and there is appreciable expenditure by visitors; however, cruise traffic is concentrated in Lisbon and Funchal and 1971 figures show a falling-off. In 1971 Funchal handled three times as many cruise passengers as long-stay tourists arriving in Madeira.[20] The market is largely dominated by British cruise passengers. Portuguese statistics also include a significant but unquantified element of business, conference and diplomatic traffic. Furthermore, the recent rapid growth in permanent and semi-permanent holiday and retirement flats and villas is a factor of increasing importance. Frontier arrivals and hotel arrivals in consequence show very different totals.

TABLE 50
Frontier and hotel arrivals (000)

	1967	1968	1969	1970	1971
Frontier arrivals	1025·4	1102·4	1186·0	1586·4	1962·6
Hotel arrivals	1002·5	912·6	1024·3	1190·7	1287·4

Source Direcção Geral de Segurança: National Institute of Statistics.

Although the most accurate measure of tourism growth is perhaps in terms of earnings—$305m in 1971, as against $206m in 1966—tourist revenue has fluctuated. The general slackening in tourism growth which affected Europe in 1967 and 1968 influenced Portugal more than most countries; the devaluations of the Spanish peseta and U.K. sterling and the imposition of currency restrictions on British citizens travelling outside the sterling area hit Portugal severely, especially since her tourist industry depended to a very considerable extent upon Spanish and British markets. Since 1970, however, the position has improved: 1972 saw a 17 per cent increase in tourist arrivals over the previous year and foreign currency receipts from long-stay tourists totalled more than £140m. It remains to be seen what effect the recent political changes will have but it seems inevitable that they will adversely affect Portugal's tourist industry.

The Portuguese have developed their own particular approach to tourism development: they have cultivated the more sophisticated upper end of the market, played down the low-cost charter traffic and avoided the proliferation of concrete which has marred other stretches of the Mediterranean coast. The Portuguese have also encouraged the permanent foreign resident and "second home" tourist. As Arthur Sandles has written: "The way to a tourist's pocket is through his heart. It is for this reason that the Portuguese property business and Portuguese tourism are inextricably intermingled. The authorities have encouraged development, knowing that once a visitor has sufficiently fallen for the country to buy a 'second home' there he will return again and again, sending his friends and relatives and probably spending far more on local services than any package tourist. The other advantage for the host country in second home development is that it can draw investment which requires relatively little Government support—just a little guidance here and there. But whatever the reasons the expansion of the past few years has given Portugal a vast pool of villa accommodation, particularly along the Algarve strip, which should stand it in good stead in an age which seems to be moving in favour of that style of holiday capacity."[21]

The Spanish rank first among Portugal's tourist clientele. Traditionally they have been Portugal's most numerous visitors and as we have already seen, account for the bulk of the short-stay traffic. The volume of this border day-trip traffic, however, should not be allowed to obscure the significance of the Spanish market as a source of long-stay tourism since in fact they also form the largest national group staying in Portugal for five days or more, "the 214,000 Spanish tourists in this category in 1971 topping their nearest rivals, the British, by 29,000."[22] The Spanish share of total bed-nights in Portugal is small, only 6·5 in 1971, and they tend to occupy the more modest types of accommodation. The yield from the Spanish market is relatively low but it would be unwise to underestimate the role of the Spanish market since, with increasing prosperity and higher standards of living in Spain, its importance must increase. Ranking second in volume, yielding the highest earnings, and since 1970 the most active, is the United States market. U.S. visitors account for about one-quarter of the total foreign hotel traffic and stay mostly in the higher-grade hotels. The American market is essentially a luxury market (to be assiduously cultivated) but the Americans seldom stay long in one place, preferring to move around from centre to centre. The British market ranks third: ". . . [its] main characteristic . . . is that to the traditional flow of business travel and high-yield old-style tourism, both of which are kept alive, has been added the new long-stay, one-resort concept of tourism."[23] The West

German and Scandinavian markets are increasing, although the latter remains small. The West Germans are big spenders and form an important long-stay market. The French market remains relatively stagnant; the French tend to visit in the high season and a large proportion of them are campers. Table 51 summarises foreign tourist movement by nationalities.

TABLE 51

Foreign tourist movements by nationality (1971) (000)

	Spain	U.S./Canada	U.K.	W. Germany	France	Benelux	Scan-dinavia [2]	Total [3]
Short-stay visitors [1]	1407·3	67·3	185·4	35·4	37·6	14·9	12·4	1904·4
Tourist arrivals at frontier [4]	648·5	350·8	271·9	134·6	177·8	73·3	69·2	1962·6
of which: staying over 5 days	214·0	109·0	185·0	90·4	108·4	—	42·2	—
Tourist arrivals at hotels [5]	154·0	414·3	182·6	97·7	132·2	62·4	54·2	1287·4
Hotel bed-nights	305·4	1137·1	1138·7	608·8	346·9	211·6	412·1	4724·0
Ratio of hotel bed-nights to frontier tourist arrivals	0·47	3·2	4·2	4·5	1·9	2·9	6·0	2·4
Ratio of hotel bed-nights to tourist arrivals at hotels	2·0	2·7	6·2	6·2	2·6	3·4	7·6	3·7

1. Staying under 24 hours, including cruise passengers.
2. Denmark, Sweden, Norway, Finland.
3. Including other nationalities.
4. Staying over 24 hours, arrivals at frontiers.
5. All names of accommodation except holiday camps, youth hostels and camping sites.

Source: Secretaria de Estado da Informação e Turismo.

Because of the geographical position of mainland Portugal and the insular location of Madeira, Portugal's tourism development depends to a considerable and increasing degree upon air transport. The new airports at Faro and in Madeira have had a very important impact upon tourism development in both the Algarve and Madeira. In 1971 tourist arrivals by land (rail, coach and car) and air were 1,270,000 and 656,500 respectively, as compared with 692,400 and 293,400 in 1967.

Tourism activity is heavily concentrated in three main areas: in Lisbon and its environs, in the Algarve and in the island of Madeira. Although there are other parts of the country receiving visitors and other areas have great potential for tourism development, the trend has been towards increasing concentration in these three; indeed, the share of tourism traffic outside them has witnessed a gradual decline and in 1972 accounted for under 3 per cent of tourist bed-nights.[24]

Lisbon, the capital, and the nearby Tagus estuary coast (known as the Costa del Sol) is the principal reception area. Lisbon, as the country's chief centre of administration, business and diplomatic activity, is a natural tourist attraction in itself. Estoril nearby, with its casino, sporting facilities, etc. is a fashionable resort. Adjacent to Estoril are the beaches of Cascais, a fishing village rapidly being transformed into a beach resort, while inland is the old, picturesque town of Cintra. "The Costa del Sol has traditionally attracted the Portuguese well-to-do, the British and assorted royalty and nobility."[25] The tourist attraction of this area continued to grow and in terms of tourist bed-nights has expanded in recent years at the rate of 7·4 per cent annually.

The development of the Algarve, which stretches from Sagres in the extreme west as far as the Spanish frontier in the east, a distance of 160 km (100 miles), is essentially a recent phenomenon. Here on this sheltered, south-facing coastal strip, a holiday zone has emerged, virtually from scratch, within the space of the fifteen years 1955–70. A string of small towns and fishing villages—Lagos, Portimao, Albufeira, Faro, Olhao, Tavira, Vila Real de St Antonio—have developed as resorts. The growth of the Algarve has meant that Lisbon's share of the total tourist market has contracted: in fact in 1972 the Algarve's share of the tourist bed-nights amounted to around 45 per cent of the total. The Algarve has flourished more particularly on long-stay holidays such as two-week package tours and even longer-term rented villas. The opening of the airport at Faro in 1965, marked the real coming of age of the Algarve as a holiday coast; indeed, since then foreign tourist bed-nights have risen from 273,500 to 1,370,958 (1971). The Algarve offers a relatively restricted choice of accommodation (mostly of top- and higher-grade hotels) and thus the renting of private houses has been especially important in this area. Leisure facilities—other than beach, sea and some outdoor sporting activities—are rather restricted, hence the appeal of the area has been largely to families holidaying with young children.[26] Although some two-thirds of the visitors come between April and September, there has also been successful promotion of the Algarve as a winter resort area.

Madeira, a volcanic island lying approximately 640 km (400 miles) from the coast of Morocco, forms Portugal's third tourist area. Its mild, equable climate, moderate rainfall confined largely to the early part of the year, mountainous countryside with deep ravines, vineyards and banana groves, pines and eucalyptus woods and the profusion of flowers in spring all make Madeira an almost perfect island. Madeira attracts a very different clientele from Lisbon and the Algarve. "Links with the U.K. have always been strong: British residents in Madeira inspired the lace industry and imported Madeira cake in exchange. Reid's Hotel has a Somerset Maugham air and the breezes have continued to waft an older generation of British tourists to the island."[27] These days, however,

Madeira's clientele is much more cosmopolitan and the island is much favoured by the Germans and Swedes. Until the 1960s, the only way for the tourist to get to Madeira was by boat but a new airstrip, literally built out into the sea because of the lack of level land on the island, has been constructed at Funchal, so that now Madeira can be reached by air and there are regular services from Lisbon airport. Although Madeira has tourists all the year round, the important season is April–June when the island is at its best, ablaze with flowers. This is the season of the opulent tourist. Madeira has much of interest to offer the tourist apart from its wonderful climate and scenery. Excursions can be taken to all the notable places of interest, including Terreiro da Lucta, nearly 914 m (3000 ft) high, from which there are magnificent views and from where one can take a thrilling toboggan ride down the mountainside to Pombal. Noteworthy, too, are the strange, long-lived Dragon Trees. Madeira is famous for its embroidery and wickerwork and Madeira wine (the chief export) and tourism helps to support these native crafts and products. Cruise traffic is important: short-stay cruise passengers outnumber considerably the long-stay holiday-makers. Nevertheless, the hotel trade is booming as ever-increasing numbers come by air; for example, tourist bed-nights have increased from 355,435 in 1968 to 637,300 in 1971 and in 1972 traffic grew faster in Madeira than in either of the other two principal reception areas of Portugal. "Madeira's geography confines tourism to the capital, Funchal, where Reid's Hotel and the Savoy—now upgraded to a 5-star hotel—reflect the taste of the traditional market. However, as a result of considerable hotel investment which boosted capacity by almost a third in two years, total bed capacity was up to 5000 in mid-1972. Of the international hotel chains, Hilton, Sheraton and Holiday Inns are all represented." [28]

Sustained growth in the Algarve and Madeira would seem to be assured if the present political problem can be resolved although the Lisbon area may remain stagnant. Since trans-Atlantic fares are tumbling it may well be that Portugal will be able to tap the American market. Care must be taken to cherish the Algarve and to prevent it deteriorating into just another Mediterranean Costa. The Atlantic coast of Portugal, with extensive, fine, clean beaches, though slightly cooler, offers an unrealised potential for tourism as does much of the attractive country in the north although before such areas can be developed there is need of heavy investment in infrastructure.

Portugal's other Atlantic islands, the Azores, a group of nine small volcanic islands covering less than a thousand square miles, are some 1440 km (900 miles) west of Portugal. The islands are mountainous and, though the climate is mild, the weather is not especially favourable for tourism. A tourist industry is just beginning to manifest itself and as yet "the U.S. air force base at Lajes is the only real source of revenue from foreign leisure spending."[29] The prospects of any major tourist development taking place in the Azores seem questionable.

ITALY

Until overtaken by Spain in 1964, Italy had more foreign visitors than any other country in the world, so the tourist industry is clearly of great importance. Like its neighbours France and Switzerland, Italy has been at the centre of international tourist traffic for more than a century —in the days of the Grand Tour Italy was the ultimate destination of all Continental travellers.

Large numbers of tourists (chiefly the affluent and the cultured) visited Italy during the years prior to the Second World War, but the war severely interrupted and disorganised the Italian tourist industry. After the war the industry was rapidly resuscitated, however, and by the early 1960s some 20 million people a year were visiting the country, although approximately half of these were day excursionists from adjoining countries, particularly France and Switzerland. Nevertheless, even some 10 million long-period visitors annually was a very substantial figure in those days. In 1972 13·5 million tourists visited Italy, and probably a similar number crossed Italy's frontiers. In 1969, registrations at hotels and at other overnight lodgings totalled 65 million: this was an increase of 3·7 million on the previous year. Table 52 shows the numbers of visitors to Italy from the most important originating countries for 1962, 1970 and 1973.

TABLE 52
Visitors to Italy

Country	1962	1970	1973
West Germany	4·6	6·5	5·6
France	2·0	4·5	3·8
Switzerland	2·3	4·1	3·4
Austria	2·1	3·3	2·8
Yugoslavia		3·5	2·2
United Kingdom	1·5	1·8	1·3
United States		1·7	1·3

Between 1964 and 1970 visitor traffic increased by 22 per cent (an average annual rate of 3·75 per cent); this was a slow rate of growth compared with Spain's which increased by 108 per cent (for the same period) and with the United Kingdom's 107 per cent. The recession in foreign tourism which hit Italy in 1966–67 appears to have been temporary, for in the late 1960s visitor arrivals picked up and the annual average rate of increase in 1970 was 4·75 per cent. If not spectacular, overall, Italian tourism may be said to be in a reasonably healthy state.

Three-quarters of all the tourist arrivals come from other O.E.C.D. countries. A high proportion—21·3 per cent—come from West Germany; moreover, German visitors spend the greatest amount of time in Italy. However, the growth in the number of tourists from the Federal Republic has tended to slow down since 1968, especially among those in the lower income bracket; again, many German tourists have taken to camping. As Table 52 shows numbers for 1973 are smaller by just under a million compared with those for 1970. From each of her immediate neighbours, France, Switzerland and Yugoslavia, Italy receives between 2 and 4 million visitors annually (see Fig. 37), although a considerable proportion of these are excursionists. Special mention should be made of the rapid growth in the number of Yugoslav visitors in recent years: this is largely "a result of efforts to smooth out the red tape involved in crossing the frontier." [30] The number of Britons visiting Italy has remained fairly stable since 1960 at around 1½ mil-

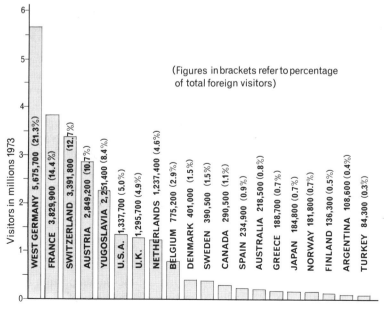

FIG. 37.—Italy: bar graph of foreign visitors.

lion; half or more of the British visitors are attracted to the coastal resorts of the north. Visitors from the United States and Canada increased from 1,280,000 in 1964 to 2,083,000 in 1970, a growth of 63 per cent over the period—although, Spain apart, this was the lowest rate of growth among the countries of Western Europe. 1973 figures show that the numbers of North American visitors have dropped by nearly 25 per cent since 1970, a clear reflection of the economic recession in the United States. Although numbers of visitors from the traditional originating countries have fallen, Italy has more than made up for this drop by increased numbers from other sources, such as Japan: nearly 185,000 Japanese visited Italy in 1973.

Tourist Attractions

More than any other country, Italy's success in tourism is based upon its ability to attract visitors all the year round. Italy appeals as a tourist destination because of its climate, coasts and scenery and its historical and cultural heritage[31] but also, to a very considerable extent, because these attractions can be enjoyed comparatively inexpensively, although costs are not as low as those in Spain or Greece. Nevertheless, Italian tourism has been substantially helped by the competitive pricing of its tourist services. The cost of an Italian holiday for a week was in 1970 typically between £40–£60, a figure still below average rates in most of the other traditional tourist areas.

Although Italy is known to its inhabitants as *il bel paese*—the beautiful country—and although many parts, *e.g.* the Alpine areas and Tuscany, are undeniably beautiful, the natural scenery cannot be counted as a major attraction in the way that the climate can.

Italy is rich in archaeological, historical, artistic and cultural attractions: the glories of Venice, Florence, Siena, Rome and Naples are popular all the year round. There is Rome and the Vatican City, Assisi with its association with St Francis and other holy places. Also, Italy has 150 or so hot-spring areas and world-famous spas and health cure centres exploit the thermal and mineralised waters. Italy, in fact, offers a choice of holidays to suit practically all tastes.

Tourist Environments

The mountain areas attracting tourists are the Italian portion of the Alps, although the scenically attractive hill country of the central Apennines also forms a minor area drawing tourists. The snowy winters and cooler conditions in summer serve to entice many visitors (and Italians, too) to Italy's mountain areas. The Italian Alps share with the alpine parts of France, Switzerland and Austria excellent conditions and facilities for winter sports and the alpine resorts of Sestriere, Bardonecchia, Courmayeur and Breil in the Western Alps and Merano, Bressanone, Ortisei and Cortina d'Ampezzo in the Eastern Alps (the Dolomites) draw large numbers of visitors (*see* Fig. 38). Apart from these alpine and winter sports centres there are a number of mountain resorts which are popular in summer: Como, Stresa, Bolzano and Cortina d'Ampezzo (both as a winter and summer resort).

The coastal areas of some 8000 km (5000 miles) are attractive because of their generally mild winters—especially along the Italian Riviera and the western coasts, for the eastern side of Italy may on occasions suffer chill north-easterly and easterly winds—and their hot and sunny summers. For most of the year the weather in peninsular Italy is usually superior to that occurring in lands to the north of the Mediterranean. The Ligurian coasts—the Riviera di Ponente and the Riviera di Levante—and the coasts around the Gulfs of Naples and Salerno are rocky and backed by steeply sloping hills and are extremely alluring; the Adriatic coasts are much flatter and have extensive sandy beaches and are less scenically attractive. The most popular coastal zones are those of Liguria (where there is a string of resorts: San Remo, Alassio, Rapallo, Sestri Levante, etc.), Naples and Salerno (where are Capri, Positano and Sorrento) and that immediately south of the Po delta (where are the beach resorts of Rimini and Cattolica). Of lesser importance are the coasts of the Straits of Messina (although the resort of Taormina is becoming increasingly attractive to the foreigner) and that of the Agro Romano. Rome has its own seaside resorts, such as the Lido di Roma, though these tend to serve the domestic, rather than the foreign, holiday-maker.

"With regard to historic sites," wrote Cole "Italy is undoubtedly one of the richest areas in the world. . . . Greek [ruins] at Agrigento . . . Roman [around] . . . Rome itself; and Etruscan. . . . Towns . . . such as Lecce, with its baroque buildings, are exceptionally fine. Most of the larger surviving medieval towns are in the northern part of the Peninsula and in the North Italian Lowland, Venice and Florence being of outstanding interest."[32] There are numerous small, old towns fascinating to the discerning visitor: Verona, a beautiful town built of rose-red brick with a fine Roman arena, Vicenza, renowned for its Palladian architecture, Ravenna, famous for its fine mosaics and early Christian

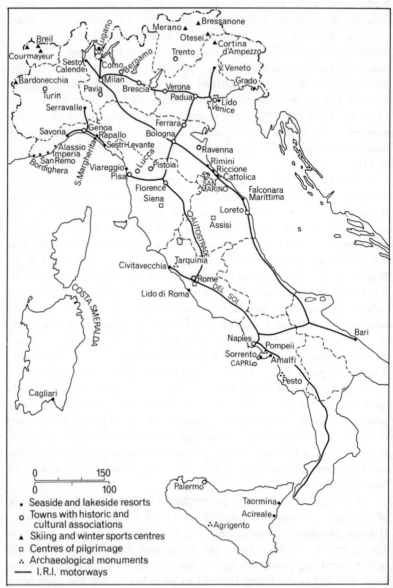

FIG. 38.—*Italy: tourism features*. Tourism is largely concentrated in the north. The government is trying to develop tourism in the poverty-stricken south to aid development. The new motorways should assist the growth of the tourist industry here.

art, Pisa, with its leaning tower, Siena, a walled town with a magnificent cathedral and many medieval mansions and palaces.

Tourism Problems

The Italian tourist industry is not without its problems, however. First, the industry faces a problem of great overcrowding in the high season (May–September) for there are too many visitors for them all to be accommodated in the comfort they seek. In spite of the fact that between 1950 and 1970 the number of hotels doubled, the number of bedrooms tripled and the number of beds quadrupled, there is still an acute shortage of accommodation. There appears to be a need of more medium-priced accommodation with better quality standards. The Government is helping by offering low-interest loans to investors prepared to build new hotels and to hoteliers wishing to expand and modernise their properties, while the State is also encouraging the development of new facilities. While there is overcrowding in summer, tourist plant is under-utilised in the off season. The Government, therefore, "would like to extend the tourist season, and, in particular, to encourage more Italians to take off-peak season holidays, to allow more space for visitors when the latter are best able to come; and also to effect a more economic use of plant, which on a year-round basis is only about 40 per cent employed."[33] The Italians show a preference for holidaying in mid-summer, at precisely the time of the greatest influx of foreign visitors, hence they contribute to the over-crowding.

A third problem is the need to spread the tourist industry more equitably throughout the country. At present it is predominantly concentrated in some half-dozen sites all of which, with the exception of the Rome and Naples areas, are in the northern half of the country. Southern Italy—the Mezzogiorno—has traditionally been an economic and social backwater, an underdeveloped and poverty-stricken part of the country. Since the Second World War the State has made determined efforts to redress the economic imbalance and tourism is seen as one particularly useful way. Accordingly, there have been efforts to create new centres of tourism in southern Italy and in the islands of Sicily and Sardinia as an integral part of the Government's programme of socio-economic development. Plans to build new tourist centres and applications to build new hotels in the South have received special favour and the results of these new investments are now beginning to manifest themselves: new resorts on the coast of Abruzzi, in Sicily and Sardinia have emerged and the Mezzogiorno "disposes of some 170,000 beds, an increase of 50,000 since 1965, and four times the total of twenty years earlier."[34] The building and extension southwards of the Autostrada del Sole has also made it much easier for the tourist to visit the South. But, though the percentage of tourists visiting the South is slowly increasing, it is still only about 12 per cent of all visitors to Italy. Special mention should perhaps be made of developments in Sardinia, for since 1970 the island has embarked upon a policy of tourism development which is already showing signs of success. Not far from Santa Margherita di Pula, Forte Village, a completely self-contained tourism complex has been established. This successful venture may well be a harbinger of things to come. Sardinia's chief drawback is that its links with the Italian mainland and the Continent at large are not very good, although there are air services to Cagliari, the island's capital.

Italy's receipts from tourism continue to grow: 950,000m lire (£630m) in 1969 and 1,135,000m lire in 1972. Since the Italians themselves spend something of the order of £160m in travel to other countries, the tourism account shows a net balance, a very useful contribution to the country's balance of payments. The value of tourism compared with that of commodity exports is around 15 per cent. One point, however, must be noted. Increasing numbers of Italians are now holidaying abroad and the country is faced with an outflow of foreign exchange. In 1972 receipts were reduced by nearly a half by these expenditures. While there still remains an impressive net balance, this is likely to be gradually reduced since, although incoming tourists are increasing at an annual rate of 4·75 per cent, the number of Italians going abroad has been increasing at 12·26 per cent since 1970.

Organisation and Promotion

Because tourism is a major Italian industry and the rate of tourism growth began to level off after 1965, the Government became alarmed. The recession in the flow of visitors in the late 1960s was part of the general recession which afflicted Western Europe as a whole, but before that, in 1963 and 1964, there had been a small decrease in the number of arrivals, while after 1968 numbers did not pick up so quickly as elsewhere. There are many reasons helping to explain this retarded growth: the increasing popularity of Spain and Yugoslavia as tourist destinations offering cheaper holidays, is certainly important; but there are many others, such as dirty beaches, polluted sea, hotel strikes, poor rail and air services and congestion, which have contributed. To ensure that the industry suffers no further setback the Government has taken several measures: for instance, new long-distance roads have been constructed and others improved, electricity has been installed in many areas, infrastructure for new development has been provided, great efforts have been made to attract investment to the tourist areas and special incentives, *e.g.* tax concessions or exemptions, loans and grants, etc. have been given to aid development. Furthermore, there has been research into tourists' desires and potential markets and an increase in propaganda and promotion by the Italian State Tourist Office, E.N.I.T., which was spending £1·25m annually in 1970.

The Government is anxious to sustain, and if possible to expand, the tourist industry. It believes there will be a strong growth in the domestic demand for tourism and that the tide will eventually turn once again in Italy's favour. The Five Year National Economic Programme (1971–75) included, therefore, plans for further tourism development. Among the more important objectives were: to encourage a more even distribution of the tourist flow, to reconstruct much of the existing accommodation to meet new types of demand, *e.g.* medium- to higher-class hotels, camping facilities, to improve tourist amenities and expand tourism development in the south and to begin building a network of marinas.

Because of the importance of tourism to the country, Italy has a Ministry of Tourism and Entertainment. Such matters as tourism policy, the administration of loans, the grading of hotels and the general co-ordination of tourist services all come under the control of the Directorate-General of Tourism, which is the tourist part of the Ministry. An important ancillary organisation is the Italian State Tourist Office (*Ente Nazionale Italicinio per il Turismo*) which is a semi-autonomous organisation. While the Ministry provides the bulk of its revenue, is responsible for certain appointments and exercises some general supervision of its activities, E.N.I.T. is in most respects a self-governing body; its chief functions are propaganda and promotion, although it has involved itself in some research activities. "Individual tourist interests are organised in some thirty national boards and associations, ranging from the hoteliers' association to the automobile club and from the student travel centre to various other bodies engaged in social tourism. Several major regions have their own regional tourist boards and there are also numerous provincial and local tourist boards and offices, as well as regional and local associations of individual interests engaged in tourism. Although the Ministry exercises a strong directing and controlling role, there appears to be a greater degree of decentralisation in the organisation of Italian tourism than, for example, in Spain, which also has a Ministry of Tourism. Not only local promotion but also the whole of tourist administration in individual regions, districts and towns is in the hands of local bodies with a substantial degree of autonomy, which are in turn represented at higher levels."[35]

YUGOSLAVIA

Until fairly recently Yugoslavia was not to be counted among the important tourist countries although, of course, there were some coastal resorts and watering places of long standing in the country. During the 1960s Yugoslavia was "discovered." Although tourism began to grow steadily after the Second World War, the influx of foreign visitors remained modest (in 1960 the number of foreign tourists was only 873,000); however, by 1963 the number had increased to 1·5 million and by 1972 was 5·5 million. Tourism brought in $360m in 1970, about 90 per cent of it in hard currency, and the industry has become Yugoslavia's biggest earner of foreign exchange. In 1973 Yugoslavia earned $630m but the rate of growth since 1970 has been somewhat slower than that which occurred in the late 1960s and hopes that the income from foreign tourism will reach $900m by 1975 have been found to be rather optimistic. Nevertheless, tourism is the fastest-growing sector of the country's economy and the prospects for continued growth are excellent, especially as the package tours from the countries of Western Europe become more common. Another important development which has had great repercussions on the growth of Yugoslavian tourism is the completion of the Adriatic Highway, or *Magistrale*, a fast, scenic coastal road, running from Rijeka to Titograd. The phenomenal increase in the number of motor cars entering Yugoslavia since 1965 clearly indicates the impact of the new Highway on the tourist trade. The next stage in these improved transport developments is the linking up of the Highway with new motor roads to the interior of the country. The independent line which Yugoslavia, a Communist state, has taken in relation to its political and economic associations has also profoundly affected its tourist industry: more than 80 per cent of the tourists who now visit Yugoslavia come from the West and, approximately in decreasing order of importance, the largest numbers come from West Germany, Italy, Austria, France, Britain, the United States, Czechoslovakia and Hungary. Yugoslavia is one of Europe's cheapest tourist countries and so has been able to draw visitors from her more expensive Mediterranean rivals. The Government also abolished visas and other bureaucratic procedures and formalities for all visitors in 1967.

The resource base for tourism development in Yugoslavia is excellent

TABLE 53
Yugoslavia: chief foreign arrivals (1970)

West Germany	1,216,270
Italy	786,605
Austria	557,853
France	314,712
Britain	262,825
Netherlands	207,445
U.S.A.	205,926
Czechoslovakia	165,620
Hungary	124,535
Switzerland	119,653
Turkey	82,217
Belgium	93,706
U.S.S.R.	75,592
Poland	70,582
Greece	70,403
Sweden	63,390
Denmark	50,541
Other countries	280,219
TOTAL	4,748,094

Source: Federal Bureau of Statistics and Federal Administration of Customs.

for the country possesses a great variety of natural scenery and history. There are many potential areas to be opened up, and at present foreign tourism is largely concentrated in the north, in Slovenia and along the Adriatic littoral.

In Slovenia in the north-western corner of the country where the mountains are majestic and the landscape enthrallingly beautiful is the Slovenian Lakeland where Lakes Bled and Bohinj are found. These lie in spectacular scenic surroundings and provide excellent centres for relaxation and rest. The resort of Bled, on the shore of Lake Bled, has been an alpine spa for over a century and was formerly a favourite holiday centre for the aristocracy of the Austro-Hungarian Empire. Not far away is the more sophisticated resort of Straza. In the extreme north-west is the mountain resort of Kranjska Gora. There are winter sports in the northern ranges, opportunities for hunting in the remote forested mountains and good fishing for perch, pike and bream almost everywhere. Also in the north are the Postojna Grottoes, a series of underground caves, galleries, lakes and waterfalls which stretch for a distance of 27 km (17 miles) and which are partly served by an underground railway. The regional capital, Ljubljana, an old city with Roman walls, a magnificent medieval castle and a fine church, is also a centre of tourist attraction.

The Adriatic coastland (*see* Fig. 39) is Yugoslavia's most important tourist area and the country's greatest asset. The sheltered position of the Dalmatian lowlands and offshore island festoons, lying in the lee of the Dinaric mountain karstlands, together with the Mediterranean

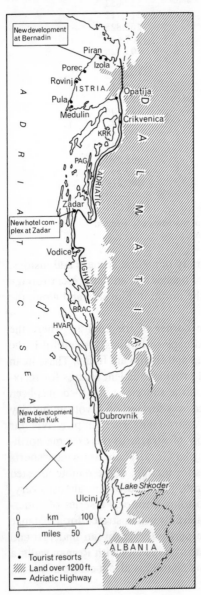

Fig. 39.—*The Dalmatian coast of Yugoslavia.* This is the golden holiday coast of Yugoslavia which has witnessed a rapid and continuing growth of tourism. New holiday complexes are being set up and the Adriatic Highway has given many small isolated centres a new accessibility.

climate of long, sunny, warm summers and warm winters, has made the region a most desirable location. In earlier times the harbours along this Dalmatian littoral throve on maritime commerce and cities such as Dubrovnik or Ragusa (the term "argosy" is a corruption of Ragusa) waxed fat on the carrying trade. The principal towns of this coast still retain their Mediterranean city sea-state characteristics and their architecture shows strong Italian influences. The physical landscape, the attractive climate and the historical legacy of this coast all form compelling tourist attractions. However, the small picturesque fishing villages and little Italianate towns on the coasts and islands of Dalmatia remained inaccessible except by sea until the construction of the Adriatic Highway; then, as Singleton has said, the *Magistrale* transformed Dalmatia and made many of these spots relatively easy to reach by motor car.[36]

The Adriatic coast forms an "almost continuous zone of tourist activity. Three sub-regions, however, are notable. The Istrian–Kvarner area is the foremost tourist region of Yugoslavia (28 per cent of all tourist nights) by reason of its good road and railway access from the main Yugoslav tourist markets of the north and from abroad (*see also* Fig. 40). Leading centres here are Opatija, Crikvenica, Pula, Rovinj, Porec, Rab and Portoroz. A second area in central Dalmatia (16 per cent) is developed around Biograd, Split, Hvar and Makarska and is accessible through Split, Sibenik and Zadar. A third area, southern Dalmatia and Montenegro (18 per cent) offers outstanding resorts in Dubrovnik, Hercegnovi, Budva and Ulcinj, which are accessible through the port (Gruz) and airport (Cilipi) at Dubrovnik and through Titograd airport."[37]

The Istrian Peninsula, at the head of the Adriatic, is a dry, limestone platform with an indented and rocky coast but little sand. Inland the region is little developed but along its 224-km (140-mile) coast running from the Italian boundary to Opatija, a few miles west of the port of Rijeka-Susak, are several attractive resorts. Starting from Portoroz on the Gulf of Trieste and going round the Istrian coast in an anti-clockwise direction are Pirano (a small medieval port), Porec (an old settlement of great charm situated on a small peninsula which has developed an extremely well-equipped holiday area called the Playa Laguna), Vrsar (a quiet little place with an attractive harbour), Rovinj (a quaint fishing village with steep, narrow, cobbled streets), Pula (a busy little port with many Roman remains), Medulin (which has the best beach in the whole of Istria) and Opatija. Opatija is the best known of all Yugoslavia's holiday resorts: it has many elegant hotels, avenues fringed with palm trees and pleasant waterside walks.

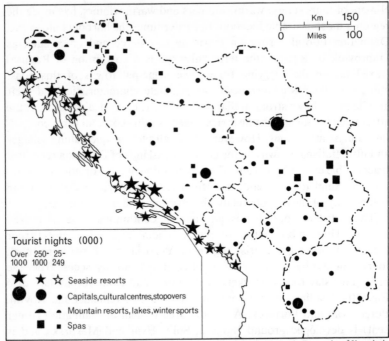

[*Reproduced by kind permission from I. Hamilton's* Economic Geography of Yugoslavia

FIG. 40.—*Numbers of nights spent by visitors at leading Yugoslavian tourist centres*
(*1965*). This map, though now a little dated, brings out the importance of the
Dalmatian coast. But the spas, lake and mountain resorts of Slovenia are also
important, as are the spa centres of Serbia. But the resorts of interior Yugoslavia
are mostly patronised by the Yugoslavs themselves.

The second concentration of resorts is around Split and on the
offshore islands of Brac, Hvar and Korcula. Split has a new airport and
the offshore islands are linked to the mainland by a hydrofoil service.
The third section of the Dalmatian coast, from Dubrovnik to the
Albanian frontier, has undergone great development since 1960. Here
the greatest tourist attraction is Dubrovnik, a superb example of a
medieval city and, after Venice, surely the most beautiful town on the
Adriatic. An important summer event is the Dubrovnik Festival. But
there are many other very attractive centres such as the lovely small
walled coastal ports of Budva and Kotor.

The tourist potential of this coastline is very great and increasing
numbers of tourists are being attracted to it. Much has been done to
develop it but much also still remains to be done. "The Yugoslavs claim
to have undertaken on the Adriatic an urbanisation project whose scale
is unique. In the past few years they and the United Nations have

carried out a comprehensive development survey of the southern part of the coast between Split and the Albanian border. Their report forecasts a sixfold rise in tourist accommodation to about 600,000 beds during the next 20–25 years. At the same time it recommends that other economic activities should be fostered to avoid a mono-cultural development, and that new building should blend harmoniously with the outstanding ... beauty of the area."[38] Now that a very considerable measure of success has been achieved in this southern sector of the coast, the next stage is the development of the northern sector from Split to Rijeka and a similar survey to that undertaken in the south has already begun.

"The opening up, in 1969, of a through road from Zagreb to the coast via the Lakes of Plitvice ... will bring many visitors to ... the spectacular beauty of ... [a] unique piece of natural 'civil engineering'. A staircase of seventeen lakes occupies a wooded gorge cut by the Korana river through the limestone of the Velika Kapela mountains. The water is held back by walls of travertine. . . ."[39] Further south, in Bosnia and Hercegovina, the rivers Vrbas, Neretva and Drina have carved other magnificent gorges which in due course will become showpieces for tourists, while in the south-western corner of Macedonia are two large and beautiful lakes, Ohrid and Prespa, in a magnificent mountain setting. Bosnia, Serbia and Macedonia are also rich in Byzantine and Moslem art and architecture, for there are numerous churches, monasteries and castles. Numerous spas in northern, central and eastern Yugoslavia have developed around mineral springs associated with crustal fracture lines and areas of former vulcanism; these attract few foreign tourists but they are popular resorts for Yugoslav nationals. Clearly, therefore, Yugoslavia has further rich tourist potential but as Hamilton has said: ". . . in many areas of highland Yugoslavia ... [it has] not yet been exploited because of poor accessibility or insufficient accommodation. This is as true of isolated regions in western and eastern Bosnia, west Serbia, northern Montenegro and south-eastern Macedonia as it is of the winter sports areas and the main national parks . . ."[40] where tourism is still in its infancy.

West Germany, Austria and Italy have traditionally been the chief tourist sources. As a tourist destination for Britons, Yugoslavia has only recently found favour, but each year sees increasing numbers of Britons going there. In 1970 2 per cent of British overseas tourists spent four days or more in Yugoslavia. In 1971 Yugoslavia received more than 300,000 British visitors—a 20 per cent increase over the 1970 figure. Britain's share of the total numbers visiting Yugoslavia has been increasing more rapidly than that of the other three traditional source areas and as British tour operators begin to develop more inclusive tours to Yugoslavia her share of the market should rapidly increase.

Visitors to Yugoslavia have in the past voiced two main complaints: the inadequacy of entertainments on the Adriatic coast and the high cost of extras over and above the basic package tour charge. Considerable investment has been put into the provision of swimming-pools, water-skiing facilities, tennis courts, miniature golf courses and similar sporting amenities and into discothèques and other evening entertainments for those who require more than sun and sea to satisfy them. The 20 per cent devaluation of the dinar in January, 1971 helped to offset the rapidly rising local prices. However, prices in Yugoslavia are not inordinately high; in terms of British prices, they are very reasonable. A fortnight's package tour in 1973 cost about £60 inclusive of air fares from Britain. The independent traveller could stay in a comfortable medium-grade hotel for around £4 a day full board or rent a family-size villa for about £6·50 a day or a flat for £5.

Tourism is now a significant factor in the Yugoslav economy. Its expansion has had important side effects in the development and improvement of motor road communications which hitherto were poor. "In the longer term, Yugoslavia hopes to extend the tourist season on the Adriatic. Winter sunshine holidays have started already and winter package tours from Britain . . . [began] in 1971–72. Construction of ski resorts will take second place until the coast is fully exploited. At present, expansion of mountain [areas] . . . is proceeding slowly . . . [because of] lack of funds."[41]

The Adriatic coast and its attendant islands, poor in natural resources and largely isolated from the interior of the country, seemed destined to suffer depopulation, progressive economic impoverishment and a gradually deteriorating cultural life. For example, in the Hvar group of islands, situated roughly mid-way along the Dalmatian coast, a natural decline in the population reinforced by outward migration had resulted in a steady fall of population up to 1950; however, the development of tourism has had the effect of halting and reversing this decline and, in fact, the planned 7400 new jobs in tourism is expected to lead to an increase in the population of over 75 per cent to 32,000 by 1980.[42]

GREECE

Greece has many attractions for the tourist but it is only since the early 1960s that the tourist industry has attained significant proportions. In 1960 a mere 500,000 tourists visited Greece but between 1960 and 1970 the numbers increased threefold, and the number of visitors in 1972 was $2\frac{1}{4}$ million. Greek authorities believe that this trend will accelerate and hope that Greece may look forward to receiving as many as 10 million visitors in 1980. Whether such a figure will be achieved is, however, more uncertain: a spectacular development in the tourist infrastructure will be required if such numbers are to be realised. "It is extremely doubtful whether Greece could cope with [such] an influx of tourists . . . even supposing that the demand potential is there. But there might be 7 million tourists before saturation point is reached—and that figure must be set against a native population of 8,700,000."[43]

Greece possesses beautiful, if somewhat austere, scenery, attractive islands, picturesque ports, unspoiled villages, a wealth of classical architectural remains, a most attractive climate, sun-drenched and temperate for most of the year (except in interior locations where it can be cold in winter) and a friendly and hospitable people. It seems therefore rather surprising that its tourist trade has traditionally been so limited. Distance from the main tourist-generating countries of Western Europe, a series of political problems in the post-war era and the inadequacy of the tourist infrastructure are the main explanation.

The immediate post-war years were followed by a civil war in Greece, and any prospects of developing tourism were impossible until a measure of internal political stability had been achieved. Gradually in the early 1950s tourists once again began to visit Greece but the numbers were small; for instance, in 1953 the total of foreign visitors, inclusive of cruise visitors, was only about 100,000. However, by 1960 the figure was approaching half a million and since that year the numbers have steadily risen and tourism as a whole has shown an average annual increase of 14 per cent a year. Not only has there been a substantial increase in foreign tourism but domestic tourism has also greatly increased. A severe setback to the industry occurred in 1967–68 as a result of another political upheaval and although the trade picked up again after 1968, it illustrates well the sensitivity of the tourist industry to domestic political disturbance. When the new military régime was set up in Greece decreases were registered in the numbers of visitors from Norway, Sweden, France, West Germany and Italy, where there was opposition to the Greek military government.

During the period 1968–70 revenue from tourism increased by about 60 per cent, and in 1972 it was estimated that tourism accounted for 4 per cent of the gross national product and employed more than 50,000 persons.

The United States is by far the most important source country: 300,000 Americans visited Greece in 1970. The United Kingdom ranked second with 166,900 visitors in 1970. West Germany was third with 142,000, France fourth with 116,000, Italy fifth with 76,000 and Switzerland sixth with 28,000 visitors. In 1966 some 52,000 Swedes visited Greece but numbers declined sharply in 1968 and in 1970 the total had only crept back to 18,000. These ". . . Swedish figures, and the fact that the U.K. has outstripped West Germany in recent years, reinforce the conclusion that conditions in Greece itself are more decisive in the development of Greek tourism than economic conditions in the source countries."[44]

A matter which may well affect the Greek tourist industry (and most other tourist countries) is that length of stay and average spending per head of tourists is gradually declining. These factors are tending to offset generally rising incomes and increasing numbers of people travelling abroad. The growth of package tours to Greece is a reflection of this general trend. For example, it is estimated that some two-thirds of U.K. visitors to Greece are currently doing so on a package basis, a quite startling development when one considers that in 1960 inclusive tours to Greece were almost unheard of. Further suggestive evidence of the changing pattern of tourists in relation to income groups and spending is provided by the distribution of hotel capacity by class of hotel: there seems to be a percentage decrease in the number of beds provided by luxury and first-class hotels and a marked increase in the number of beds provided by lower-class hotels and other types of holiday accommodation such as motels and bungalows.

These trends, and the fact that forecasts indicate a fivefold increase during the decade 1970–80 pose certain problems for the Greek tourist industry. Greece would almost certainly be unable to cope with mass tourism of the kind which Spain is experiencing and it might be more prudent for the industry to concentrate its energies on providing for high *per capita* spenders than on a larger number of low *per capita* spenders. Such a policy has a double advantage: in the first place the capital investment in tourism infrastructure tends to be reduced and, secondly, much less strain is imposed upon the available resources for an approximately equal return in tourist receipts. It remains to be seen which policy will be adopted, although there are indications that the Greek Government tends to favour the attraction of tourists from the higher income brackets. Such a policy is largely at variance with general trends but it must be recognised that the physical capacity of the country to handle a vast influx of visitors is uncertain and it is believed that even the 3 million visitors expected in 1975 will stretch the available facilities to the limit.

MALTA

After 150 years of British control and influence, Malta (and neighbouring Gozo and Comino) gained its independence in 1964. For a long time it had been an island fortress, strategically placed in the narrow waist of the Mediterranean Sea and an important military–naval base. Developments in modern warfare rendered Malta obsolete and the base which Britain had had there was run down. The decline in importance of Malta's military role brought economic problems and the island had to seek diversification of its economy. During the period of British rule Malta's economy was based upon defence expenditure; agriculture and industry were developed to provide visible exports and then, with the development of the European tourist boom, Malta began to realise its tourism potential which was heavily promoted in order to earn invisible exports.

It is important to realise that the tourist industry in Malta is of very recent growth: prior to independence the islands had few visitors, in 1962 there were only 23,000. By 1969 there were 170,000 tourists who spent some £10m. It was forecast that tourist arrivals would reach the quarter of a million mark by 1972–73. However, this has not proved to be the case and the 150,000 visitors in 1971 dropped to around 120,000 in 1972. In 1973 the net revenue from tourism was £8·5m.

Tourism, until 1970, had become the fastest-growing industry. In assessing the impact and importance of tourism on the islands it should be realised that the annual ordinary revenue collected by the Maltese Exchequer is only of the order of some £25m. Clearly tourism is of more than ordinary significance in the Maltese economy. It earns much-needed foreign currency, it provides employment and it stimulates other industries, notably construction and agriculture. Britain still provides substantial financial support, and is the chief trading partner. Some 75 per cent of the tourists are British, and the number of British residents retired in Malta is substantial (in 1969 there were 2900 who spent £2·5m a year).

In the travel agents' image Malta is presented as a holiday paradise with a beguiling climate and warm, blue seas. This is not really exaggerated for Malta and its associated islands, though topographically lean and bare, have plentiful sunshine, a rich cultural legacy, splendid hotels and many holiday amenities. The climate is warm in summer, sometimes very hot and cool, but never cold, in winter. Because it is insular, it tends to be breezy and in September the sirocco, blowing from North Africa, is unpleasant but on the whole the climatic conditions are attractive. There is plenty of interest for the sightseer: the lover of art and architecture, the historian and archaeologist all find much of interest in this small island, for the Phoenicians, Romans, Arabs, Normans, the Knights of St John, the French and the British have, in turn, held sway over her destiny and left something behind to make Malta's heritage. The growth of tourism has led to an impressive hotel building programme: in 1972 there were 100 compared with 25 in 1958 and although accommodation at all levels and prices is provided Malta can boast a number of first-class hotels, e.g. the Mellieha Bay, Hilton, Preluna, Phoenicia and Sheraton.

The rapid growth of Malta as a tourist destination has brought many problems and difficulties and these will have to be resolved if the island is to keep and increase its popularity. More beds are required—the target for 1972 was 13,500—to meet the demand, standards of service and cuisine, in some cases, are not as good as they might be, the beaches are for the most part neglected and sea and air communications are by no means entirely satisfactory. Above all, there is the problem of retaining the islands' individual character in the face of massive commercialisation.

None of Malta's problems is insurmountable but time and investment are needed. The Manoel Island marina development scheme, which aimed to turn Malta into the yachting centre of the Mediterranean, suffered prolonged delays but the Government has set up an Hotels and Catering Establishments Board to vet, license and classify all hotels and restaurants, and has made a determined attempt to sell Malta to a wider market, notably to the West Germans and Scandinavians. Realising the rewards which are to be had from tourism, the Government is actively participating in the development process.

NOTES

1. "Tourism—Spain's Most Important Industry," *Geography*, Vol. 52, January, 1967, pp. 23–40.

2. *Idem*, p. 26.

3. I. Cosgrove and R. Jackson, *The Geography of Recreation and Leisure*, Hutchinson, 1972, p. 60.

4. *Op. cit.*, p. 27.

5. S. Medlik, "Organisation of Tourism in Six European Countries," University of Surrey, 1966.

6. *Op. cit.*, p. 27.

7. *Op. cit.*, p. 33.

8. National Report No. 2: Spain, *International Tourism Quarterly*, No. 2, 1971, p. 8.

9. *Idem*, p. 25.

10. *Idem*, p. 24.

11. Cosgrove and Jackson, *op. cit.*, p. 59.

12. *I.T.Q.*, No. 2, 1971, p. 25.

13. *Op. cit.*, p. 32.

14. *Op. cit.*, p. 32.

15. *I.T.Q.*, No. 2, 1971, p. 26.

16. *Op. cit.*, p. 34.

17. Naylon, *op. cit.*, p. 36.

18. Naylon, *op. cit.*, p. 39.

19. *Barclay's Bank Review*, August, 1969, p. 55.

20. National Report No. 8: Portugal, *International Tourism Quarterly*, No. 1, 1973, p. 10.

21. "Tourism: looking for hearts as well as cheque books," Portugal: a *Financial Times Survey*, 4th June, 1973.

22. National Report No. 8: Portugal, *International Tourism Quarterly*, No. 1, 1973, p. 17.

23. *Idem*, p. 17.

24. *Idem*, p. 11.

25. *Idem*, p. 12.

26. *Idem*, p. 12.

27. *Idem*, p. 13.

28. *Idem*, p. 14.

29. *Idem*, p. 14.

30. "Tourism in Italy," Special Report, No. 8, *Marketing in Europe*, Vol. 63, January, 1968, pp. 39–47.

31. J. P. Cole, *Italy*, Christophers.

32. *Op. cit.*

33. N. Willat, "State Plan To Fight Tourist Overcrowding," *Financial Times*, 20th April, 1970.

34. Willat, *op. cit.*

35. Medlik, *op. cit.*

36. *Yugoslavia: the Country and its People*, Queen Anne Press Ltd., 1970, p. 101.

37. F. E. I. Hamilton, *Yugoslavia: Patterns of Economic Activity*, G. B. Bell & Sons, Ltd., 1968, p. 303.

38. *Times*, 23rd June, 1971.

39. Singleton, *op. cit.*, p. 103.

40. *Op. cit.*, p. 304.

41. *Times*, 23rd June, 1971.

42. Cosgrove and Jackson, *op. cit.*, p. 54.

43. National Report No. 1: Greece, *International Tourism Quarterly*, The Economic Intelligence Unit, No. 1, 1971, p. 8.

44. *Idem*, p. 13.

Chapter XVIII

Tourism in Eastern Europe and the Soviet Union

EASTERN EUROPE

THE first point which should be emphasised, and which is applicable to all the Eastern European countries, is that travel objectives and the purpose of tourist activity differ quite fundamentally from those in the West. "In Eastern Europe the tourist industry is considered more an important tool for publicising political and economic achievements—even if it is not officially admitted—than as a 'breadwinner' for earning of convertible (hard) currency. Such currency increases the country's potential to buy badly needed raw materials both for military and peaceful purposes. For these reasons, promotional expenditures to attract travellers to this area, as well as for travel market research abroad, is concentrated mainly in Western markets including those with ethnic groups less devoted to Eastern European countries and still less to states with a Communist government."[1] The Communist countries are eager to impress the Western World with their achievements and their progress under a socialist system: thus an attempt is made to seduce the Western traveller by offering him the best tourist facilities and adroitly conducting him to the "showpieces" of the country.

An important feature of the tourist industry in the Communist countries is that all foreign tourism, whether inward or outward, is under the firm control of the central government. The Government normally exercises a monopoly on all matters relating to tourism, from policy-making down to service institutions. State-sponsored organisations, such as *Intourist* in the Soviet Union, are multi-functional operating travel agencies, running hotels and restaurants, providing transport and numerous other tourism services and facilities. In the field of domestic tourism a similar control is exercised though often at lower levels, the service institutions being run by collective bodies such as co-operatives, youth organisations, etc.

The Communist governments exert a strict control over the movement of people, whether foreigners or their own nationals. Some are rather more liberal than others but the Soviet Union is particularly rigid in this respect. A national has no democratic right to leave his homeland to pursue a holiday abroad, certainly to a Western country. The people of East European Communist countries are allowed to visit other countries within the Communist bloc either on an organised travel group basis or individually to visit relatives or friends providing the visitor is funded by them. But if a person wishes to travel outside the Communist bloc a special exit visa of a limited time duration is required. Exit visas are not easy to acquire, hence very few manage to travel to Western countries for pleasure. Those who are fortunate are usually government officials, business representatives or artists, musicians, etc. Another factor militating against foreign travel by East Europeans, even if permitted and organised by official government agencies, is the great expense involved: "The cost of a 14-day escorted tour of Western Europe with accommodation in hotels of third category (three or four in a room) may amount to the aggregate of three to four months' salary . . . intercontinental trips are even more expensive and are usually organised [for] . . . events like Expo '67, Olympic games, etc. . . ."[2] Entrance by foreigners to the Eastern European Communist countries is also strictly regulated and visas are required which may or may not be granted, although in most cases these are readily forthcoming at fairly short notice, although the bureaucratic formalities to which Western travellers are sometimes subjected at frontier posts both on arrival and departure can be exasperating and humiliating, not to say unwelcoming. A point of interest is that Bulgaria, in 1967, to celebrate the United Nations International Year of Tourism, waived the necessity for all visas for visitors from all countries and this arrangement was continued with all those countries who were prepared to make it reciprocal.

Tourism development in the Eastern European countries is variable: in Czechoslovakia and Hungary, there is a long tradition of tourism; in Romania and Bulgaria, the industry is being rapidly developed and great efforts are being made to improve standards; but in East Germany and Poland[3] tourism, if not actually stagnant, is far behind. "Present resources of the tourist industry in these countries," says Jaczina "consist of the assets and experiences obtained by seizure from former owners and experts respectively. [When] . . . a Communist government took over, it . . . nationalised the most important tourist facilities . . . a relatively large network of well-equipped private hotels and restaurants was seized, the professional standard of which varied according to the tradition of the particular country. In addition to this, many former experts and in some cases owners who for family or other personal reasons could not leave the country, were temporarily [used] . . . to run the industry and to administer government offices and institutions responsible for tourist services. These persons were later gradually replaced by ... trained new personnel. ... Although many mistakes have been made during the first years after the Second World War ... [Eastern European] countries, mainly those with a good ... tourist industry background, have made considerable progress by further development of laws and facilities inherited and seized from the past regime."[4]

Czechoslovakia was traditionally famous for its spas, *e.g.* Karlovy Vary (Carlsbad) and Marianske Lazne (Marienbad) in Bohemia and Piest'any in Slovakia. High-quality services were a hallmark of the Czech spas and the Grand Hotel Pupp in Carlsbad had a world-famous reputation. But Czechoslovakia has much else to offer. In the Krkonose and Tatra Mountains winter sports facilities are highly developed and among the best in Europe, while the country is rich in wildlife and there is good shooting. Prague, the capital, is a beautiful city with some splendid architecture and a gay night life. *Cedok*, the Czechoslovak Travel Bureau, has a reputation for reliability, the Czechs are more Westernised and more prosperous than the peoples of the other East European countries and the traveller from Western Europe not only feels more at home here but also knows that he is genuinely welcomed. In 1972 Czechoslovakia had over 9 million visitors, two-thirds coming from the West, one-third from the Communist countries of Eastern Europe.

Bulgaria and Romania both have very little tradition of tourism, but have made notable progress in recent years and appear to be developing very successfully. With a minimum of tourism expertise and a deficient infrastructure Bulgaria had nevertheless attracted some $3\frac{1}{2}$ million tourists by 1973. The country, as yet little known to Westerners, has much to offer the tourist: beautiful natural scenery, an attractive coast of alternating rocky headlands and sheltered sandy beaches, a warm and sunny climate from April to October, numerous historical remains and monuments from a wide range of varied cultures, modern hotels giving excellent value for money and well-developed sports and entertainments for visitors. When the Bulgarians overcome their present problems of management and services, the prospects for a strong tourist industry would seem to be very promising. *Balkantourist*, the national state-sponsored tourist agency, supervises all tourism activities in the country on behalf of a government Tourist Board which has ministerial status and which directs tourism policy and planning.

Romania likewise has made great strides in recent years. *Carpati*,

TABLE 54

International tourist traffic to and from Czechoslovakia

International tourist traffic / active + passive −	±	1967 a	1967 b	1968 a	1968 b	1969 a	1969 b	1970 a	1970 b	1971 a	1971 b	1967% A	B	C	1968% A	B	C	1969% A	B	C	1970% A	B	C	1971% A	B	C
Austria	+	312,696	4.0	288,383	4.0	216,406	4.7	161,310	5.0	153,303	4.1	85.7	2.7	11.6	83.9	4.0	12.1	75.9	8.6	15.5	64.5	14.5	21.0	63.2	14.0	22.8
	−	132,626	9.0	204,685	8.3	287,914	6.6	46,429	12.0	32,840	12.6	81.8	18.2	—	86.7	13.3	—	85.7	14.3	—	36.6	63.4	—	39.5	60.5	—
France	+	40,255	9.0	35,840	9.5	33,158	9.8	35,452	7.5	35,372	6.6	68.0	11.2	22.8	70.7	11.8	17.5	74.6	10.9	14.5	66.7	11.7	21.6	62.0	12.4	25.6
	−	18,269	24.0	26,259	25.0	40,471	22.0	12,043	24.0	10,246	25.0	68.7	31.3	—	85.6	14.4	—	76.9	23.1	—	50.3	49.7	—	42.7	57.3	—
Ger. F.R.	+	248,415	7.0	232,809	7.0	225,106	7.6	264,827	6.7	292,818	6.0	89.3	4.0	6.7	88.8	7.7	3.5	87.2	9.1	3.7	83.7	11.5	4.8	81.9	12.1	6.0
	−	81,476	18.0	107,187	18.2	177,417	16.2	51,298	21.4	46,605	20.0	68.5	31.5	—	76.6	23.4	—	75.1	24.9	—	38.8	61.2	—	34.2	65.8	—
Great Britain	+	24,921	8.5	24,526	8.7	20,858	8.7	21,319	8.8	20,595	7.2	65.6	20.9	13.5	66.9	21.6	11.5	69.2	20.6	10.2	60.1	27.1	12.8	63.1	23.2	13.7
	−	9,331	29.0	14,557	32.0	20,927	33.6	8,285	36.0	6,588	24.0	63.1	36.9	—	65.4	34.6	—	69.0	31.0	—	43.2	56.8	—	23.7	76.3	—
Italy	+	30,765	5.3	34,121	6.0	35,762	6.3	38,200	6.0	45,555	5.2	59.1	8.9	32.0	64.7	9.9	25.4	64.1	10.0	25.9	60.4	12.1	27.5	60.7	10.3	29.0
	−	19,104	19.0	34,587	18.0	79,443	14.0	20,627	17.5	14,180	19.0	71.4	28.6	—	80.0	20.0	—	85.5	14.5	—	63.1	36.9	—	51.9	48.1	—
Sweden	+	21,774	5.5	22,219	5.7	18,278	6.1	21,200	5.2	21,009	45.0	60.0	9.4	30.6	67.9	11.1	24.0	58.1	14.8	27.1	60.6	14.7	24.7	51.1	13.9	35.0
	−	3,529	22.0	9,318	23.0	9,088	18.0	2,415	25	1,656	21.7	48.2	51.8	—	82.8	17.2	—	66.4	33.6	—	36.9	63.1	—	17.3	82.7	—
Switzerland	+	6,906	20.0	11,419	20.0	31,055	19.6	8,671	24.0	7,252	21.0	50.7	49.3	—	61.8	38.2	—	75.6	24.4	—	41.6	58.4	—	37.1	62.9	—
U.S.A.	+	35,276	8.5	36,469	9.1	38,350	8.0	43,800	7.8	46,112	7.5	84.0	4.9	11.1	82.5	7.7	9.8	83.0	7.1	9.9	80.2	10.5	9.3	80.7	7.9	11.4
Visitors: totals	+	714,102	7.0	674,367	6.5	587,918	7.0	586,108	6.8	614,764	6.3															
	−	271,241	19.0	408,012	17.5	646,315	15.0	149,768	26.0	149,367	27.0															
Visitors from other capitalist countries	+	124,145		149,958		136,636		144,486		177,677																
Visitors to other capitalist countries	−	32,138		41,742		69,041		38,046		29,522																

a + active: refers to number of visitors to Czechoslovakia from eight main countries.

− passive: refers to number of Czechs visiting foreign countries.

b refers to the average number of days spent by visitors in Czechoslovakia; and to average number of days spent abroad by Czechs.

A—tourist visit, holiday and spa visitors in percentage.

B—business trip or official delegation in percentage.

C—visitors in transit to other destinations.

TABLE 55

Visitors from Communist countries to Czechoslovakia and Czech visitors to Communist countries

Country		1967	Days	1968	Days	1969	Days	1970	Days	1971	Days	%1967 A	B	C	%1968 A	B	C	%1969 A	B	C	%1970 A	B	C	%1971 A	B	C
Bulgaria	+	49,469	7.8	69,086	4.0	92,135	5.0	105,708	6.3	140,921	5.7	73.6	4.4	22.0	71.0	9.7	19.3	82.2	5.9	11.9	76.0	6.7	17.3	80.5	5.9	13.6
	−	192,719	15.2	123,053	14.0	93,836	16.0	190,277	15.8	234,847	15.5	95.0	5.0	—	94.5	5.5	—	98.4	1.6	—	97.7	2.3	—	97.4	2.6	—
G.D.R.	+	1,307,459	3.1	1,282,839	3.3	289,152	3.0	375,303	3.6	1,093,719	4.1	88.9	2.9	8.2	90.3	3.2	6.5	76.0	4.4	19.6	79.6	5.8	14.6	83.5	5.3	11.2
	−	641,671	5.1	464,889	5.5	427,247	4.2	233,677	5.5	319,599	7.0	64.3	35.7	—	95.6	4.4	—	97.3	2.7	—	95.7	4.3	—	87.7	12.3	—
Hungary	+	1,351,951	3.2	1,111,506	3.5	719,489	3.0	1,281,102	3.6	1,408,371	4.0	56.5	34.5	9.0	89.8	4.2	6.0	81.9	4.0	14.1	78.7	7.2	14.1	83.0	4.7	12.3
	−	649,344	4.8	772,752	6.0	926,695	4.0	880,542	4.5	1,092,690	4.3	95.2	4.8	—	95.1	4.9	—	88.9	11.1	—	98.5	1.5	—	97.8	2.2	—
Poland	+	889,734	2.2	590,529	3.0	862,768	2.8	751,708	3.2	850,523	3.3	82.1	4.7	13.2	82.0	8.2	9.8	82.4	4.6	13.0	83.0	5.1	11.9	84.1	3.8	12.1
	−	327,879	3.8	232,866	5.0	226,374	7.5	237,705	5.0	254,058	6.0	97.4	2.6	—	95.6	4.4	—	98.3	1.7	—	96.0	4.0	—	92.8	7.2	—
Roumania	+	30,280	8.6	65,717	6.0	59,096	4.0	71,231	5.5	86,943	7.0	83.5	10.0	6.5	70.2	12.6	17.2	81.1	6.5	12.4	77.0	12.6	10.4	79.8	10.7	9.5
	−	34,982	12.3	54,574	14.0	161,175	15.0	142,191	14.7	125,596	17.2	94.9	3.3	1.8	95.9	4.1	—	98.4	1.6	—	97.8	2.2	—	96.9	3.1	—
U.S.S.R.	+	69,288	11.0	59,646	15.0	52,144	10.3	120,548	9.6	238,794	10.2	93.5	6.5	—	71.4	17.0	11.6	73.2	15.7	11.1	74.5	14.3	11.2	73.8	13.5	12.7
	−	87,479	14.3	72,877	15.0	59,230	15.0	87,682	16.0	104,297	16.0	68.5	14.8	16.7	96.9	3.1	—	90.3	9.7	—	86.6	13.4	—	80.2	19.8	—
Yugoslavia	+	51,166	6.5	96,914	5.0	78,108	4.6	83,285	5.0	53,602	6.6	95.0	5.0	—	73.3	10.1	16.6	81.0	6.2	12.7	77.0	13.2	9.8	80.6	8.9	10.5
	−	146,810	14.7	151,211	15.5	284,139	16.2	98,091	15.0	68,185	15.3	92.0	4.0	4.0	95.4	7.6	—	98.0	2.0	—	93.4	6.6	—	91.4	8.6	—
Others	+	16,094	4.0	65,495	4.2	21,767	6.5	25,940	7.2	34,077	8.0	90.8	9.2	—	66.9	10.1	23.0	73.6	10.4	16.0	69.6	12.9	17.5	72.6	14.3	13.1
	−	9,826	10.3	13,372	38.6	2,400	57.0	2,471	48.0	406	91.0				99.0	1.0	—	70.1	29.9	—	91.1	8.9	—	94.1	5.9	—
Number of visitors from other Communist countries	+	3,765,441	3.3	3,341,632	3.6	2,174,659	3.0	2,814,825	4.0	3,906,950	4.2															
Number of Czechs visiting other Communist countries	−	2,090,710	7.0	1,885,594	7.5	2,181,096	7.5	1,872,636	8.0	2,199,678	9.0															

+ active: refers to number of visitors from Communist countries to Czechoslovakia.
− passive: refers to number of Czechs visiting other Communist countries.
A—purpose of travel: tourist trip, holiday, spa visit.
B—purpose of travel: business trip, official delegation.
C—purpose of travel: visitors in transit to other destinations.

Romania's central agency for international tourism, has achieved great success in attracting visitors to the country's Black Sea coastal resorts of Mamaia, Eforie, Mangalia, Aurora, Olymp, Neptun, Saturn and Venus. But the Black Sea Riviera and Bucharest apart, the remainder of the country is little developed, although Romania's mountain region is especially attractive and there are some delightful quieter holiday centres there. There is excellent skiing in the Carpathians in winter at Brasov, Predeal and Sinaia. But the coastal strip of the Dobruja, only about 240 km (150 miles) in length, is the real focal point of Romania's tourist industry and here numerous resorts have sprung up. Tourism growth has been rapid and has been a development almost entirely of the decade 1960–70; the total number of foreign tourists in 1960 was merely 138,000 but by 1968 it had grown to $1\frac{1}{2}$ million and in 1972 reached $2\frac{1}{2}$ million. Most of the visitors, it is true, come from the other Communist countries of Eastern Europe but Romania is attracting Western tourists in increasing numbers, chiefly from Austria, West Germany, France, Britain and Italy, in that order of importance. The major proportion of the visitors, and certainly those from Western Europe, arrive by air, mostly on package tours. Costs are modest and the tourist gets good value for money. The rapid growth of the tourist industry presented Romania with an accommodation problem for in the late 1960s there were only 360 hotels in the country with a capacity for 50,000 visitors (although inns and private accommodation could accommodate a further 70,000), but the tourist authorities aimed to double the hotel accommodation by 1971.[5]

TABLE 56

Arrivals in East European countries

	1971	1972
Poland	663,462	3,652,190
Czechoslovakia	3,780,782	9,244,781
Hungary	5,215,900	5,532,300
Romania	2,394,082	2,542,363
Bulgaria	2,380,548	2,523,138

The wide difference in the annual totals in the case of Czechoslovakia reflects the political troubles in 1970.

RUSSIA

For several decades after the Revolution the Soviet Union was virtually closed to the international tourist. For the decade 1945–55 foreign travel in the Soviet Union was prohibited altogether (partly because of the "cold war" and partly because of the severe problems of post-war reconstruction) but foreign travel was permitted again in 1956. In that year only about 500,000 people visited the Soviet Union but in 1966 the figure was $1\frac{1}{2}$ million and in 1972 2·3 million. The tourist traffic between Britain and Russia, for example, showed a very rapid increase: during the period 1956–66 the number of British tourists increased twenty-fivefold (some 50,000 Britons visited the country in 1973). In 1970 the total number of foreign visitors was 2 million.

Though Russia is not scenically exciting, a land of vast spaces and monotonous horizons, there are many historical, human and cultural features to attract the foreigner. The tourist is interested in the Soviet peoples—there are over one hundered different nationalities—in the way of life under a Communist system and in the art and architectural treasures. There are many old and beautiful cities such as Moscow, Leningrad, Novgorod, Kiev, Tashkent and Samarkand, with unique architectural and historical buildings and fine theatres and museums.

Intourist, the Soviet state-sponsored tourist organisation, founded in 1929, covers practically every aspect of the tourist market and controls all foreign travel in the U.S.S.R. Not only does it provide the usual facilities offered by travel agencies and tour operators but runs hotels and restaurants, sells tickets for theatres, concerts and sporting events and provides transport services and interpreter-guides. Not only has the scope of the activities and services of Intourist expanded enormously since 1960 but it has itself done much to foster and promote the tourist industry. In 1964 the Soviet Board for Foreign Tourism was created, and Intourist sought the help of the Government to develop foreign tourism and succeeded in getting aid under the 1966–70 Five Year Plan: a fund of 300m roubles was provided to secure an additional 50,000 beds in hotels and motels, to train staff and to construct and improve roads. Whereas in 1957 the foreign tourist was largely limited to conducted group tours, for independent tourism was hedged by restrictions and very expensive, now there is much greater freedom of movement (although impulsive travel is still discouraged) and choice of facilities. All-inclusive coach, rail and air tours, cruises, etc. are available, while Intourist offers the independent motorist 8000 km (5000 miles) of routes equipped with hotels, motels, camping sites and petrol stations and repair facilities. Intourist has a large staff of linguists, who act as interpreters and guides for the non-Russian-speaking visitor. Another valuable service rendered by Intourist is to look after business travellers and those visiting the Soviet Union in order to attend conferences and international congresses. In the past, the shortage of accommodation, the limited services and the lack of experience militated strongly against the tourist industry but these drawbacks are gradually being overcome.

The more relaxed political situation has also made it possible for more Soviet citizens to travel abroad and in 1966 some 1,300,000 visited foreign countries—more than twice as many as went abroad in 1956. In 1972 almost 2 million Soviet citizens visited foreign countries. There is still, of course, a fairly tight grip on holidaying abroad and there are restrictions on tourist destinations outside Russia. While travel for pleasure is possible in Communist Eastern European countries, visits to the West are rigidly controlled. The privileged and the well-off, such as politicians, scientists, actors, dancers, composers and writers, manage to get abroad, many of them going to Karlovy Vary (Carlsbad), the Czechoslovakian spa, which since the Second World War has become a favourite resort.

Domestic tourism, as it exists in the West, scarcely exists in the Soviet Union partly because the pattern of an annual holiday at the seaside never developed, partly because standards of living have remained lower and partly because the private motor car is still very rare. Nevertheless, large numbers of workers are sent to resorts and sanatoria (really workers' holiday homes) for rest and recuperation. But it seems certain that as standards of living improve larger numbers of Soviet citizens will wish to participate in foreign tourism. The Soviet worker has on average a five-day, 41-hour week with an average annual paid holiday of three to four weeks, although his remuneration falls far below that in the West.

The Soviet Union is not lacking in holiday centres for there are more than 400 spa and other resorts and over 2000 sanatoria providing accommodation for some 300,000 people. There are also around 6000 summer camps for young people which cater for over 3 million boys and girls annually. Cruise vessels travel on the Volga and it is possible to take a holiday cruise between Kazan and Rostov-on-Don.

The principal tourist areas in the Soviet Union are Moscow, Leningrad and the Baltic Lands, the Crimea and the Caucasus region. Like most capital cities, Moscow is an important centre of attraction. The ancient Kremlin, built more than 800 years ago on a hill overlooking the Moskva River, is the heart of Moscow. The massive red-brick walls of this medieval fortress enclose palaces and churches and other buildings of interest. Immediately outside the Kremlin wall is the famous Red Square with the Cathedral of St Basil. Modern Moscow, however, is a very fine city with many imposing buildings, wide thoroughfares, numerous theatres and metro. Leningrad is a beautiful city situated on the banks of the Neva with some very fine architecture, spacious squares and many gardens and parks. The Hermitage Museum in the Winter Palace, formerly the residence of the Russian Tsars, has a world-famous art collection. Along the Baltic shores are other interesting cities, notably Tallinn and Riga. The old part of Tallinn has many buildings of interest and is a museum of medieval architecture while the ancient city of Riga, on the banks of the Daugava, is a much-frequented tourist centre. "The tourist industry, whether based on the historical and cultural attractions of Leningrad, Novgorod or Tallinn, or the more hedonistic attractions of the sandy beaches of Latvia, has a great deal of scope for development as living-standards rise."[6]

The southern coast of the Crimea is one of the most important resort areas in Russia. The wonderful sunny climate, Mediterranean-type vegetation, fine beaches and mountain background (which protects the coast from cold northerly winds) make the coastal strip of the Crimea a very attractive holiday region and people from all over the country throng the area all year round. Yalta is the most famous of the resorts but there are many others—Alupka, Miskhor, Livadia, Simeiz—all linked by excellent motor roads with Yalta. The Caucasus is another region important for tourism. Here are to be found two distinct types of resorts, both of which originated in Tsarist times but which have since been greatly expanded. First there are the coastal resorts of the Black Sea littoral such as Sochi, Gagry, Sukhumi and Butumi; here, as on the Crimean Riviera, the attractions are a combination of winter warmth, abundant sunshine, mountains, luxuriant sub-tropical vegetation and the sea. Sochi-and-Matsesta is the jewel of this holiday coast. The second type consists of the spas, founded originally on the warm sulphur springs, which occur in a volcanic region in the foothills of the northern flanks of the Caucasus; here are Pyatigorsk, Yessentuki, Mineralniye Vody and Kislovodsk, with hydrotherapy centres and sanatoria. These spa resorts, however, have not grown to anything like the extent of the Black Sea coastal resorts. "A third type, hitherto less developed but also offering considerable potential, is the skiing and climbing-resort of the high central Caucasus. Since health resorts are now firmly part of Soviet governmental policy and since the Caucasus has quite unusually rich assets in the Soviet context, located quite close to the main population centres, great expansion of this industry here is almost certain to take place."[7]

Another region where the tourist industry already has some significance and where the future potential is great is Middle Asia where are those famous cities of the past, the great trading centres of Samarkand,

Tashkent, Bukhara and Kokand. Tashkent has grown into a vast modern city but the others are rich in relics of their past, and still retain some of the atmosphere of a former age. The scope for tourism development in this region, given improved tourist provision, would seem to be great.

The tourist industry in the Soviet Union is a recent development but intensive efforts are being made to expand it and to catch up with those countries which have a well-established industry. Because of its lack of experience and shortage of trained personnel Soviet tourism has many shortcomings; these, with the best will in the world, cannot be surmounted overnight and it will be many years before the Soviet industry will be able to compare with those of most Western countries. There are, however, many built-in hindrances, resulting from political and social attitudes, which are likely to militate against the rapid and successful development of the tourist industry, *e.g.* the suspicion of the foreign traveller, the emphasis upon communal living and activity, the generally lower standards of travel, accommodation and food. A number of practical difficulties also face the foreign traveller. First, there is the problem of communication: unless the traveller is fluent in Russian he has difficulty in making himself understood for few of the personnel in the industry have much knowledge of foreign languages; accordingly, the tourist is usually obliged to go on a conducted tour which has the services of an interpreter-guide. Secondly, because of the general shortage of adequately trained personnel, the level of services provided in transport and in hotels often falls short, at least when measured by Western standards. Thirdly, the facilities for relaxed late-night entertainment hardly exist and the tourist has no option but to retire to bed, although usually after a day's exhausting sight-seeing with an Intourist guide he is ready for bed! Nevertheless, the opportunities for late-night drinking and frivolous entertainment are generally lacking. Fourthly, individual exploration is difficult (in some areas forbidden) and attempting to secure accommodation in an hotel which has not been arranged by Intourist is virtually impossible. The tourist industry in the Soviet Union, already massively organised, suffers from the lack of a tradition and properly trained personnel, but is an expanding one and if the present intensive development is sustained the future could well see large numbers of foreigners seeking to explore this little-known, exciting country.

NOTES

1. S. T. Jaczina, "Tourism in Eastern Europe," in R. W. McIntosh, *Tourism: Principles, Practices, Philosophies*, Grid. Inc., 1972, p. 166.
2. *Idem*, p. 170.

3. Strangely enough Poland, in 1972, had over $3\frac{1}{2}$ million visitors whereas in the previous year the total was only 663,462; the 1972 figure showed a percentage change of 450·5!

4. *Op. cit.*, p. 168.

5. R. McEwan, "The Friendly Frontier," Romania: Special Report, *The Times*, 24th March, 1970.

6. D. J. M. Hooson, *The Soviet Union*, University of London Press, 1966, p. 243.

7. Hooson, *op. cit.*, p. 264.

Chapter XIX

Tourism in North America

NORTH AMERICAN LEISURE

COSGROVE and Jackson have explored the philosophy behind American leisure. They point out that the original settlers in the mid-Atlantic States were largely of a Puritannical persuasion "who had no positive attitude towards leisure as an end in itself and believed in a religion of work."[1] The ascetism and work ethic of the Protestants directed and channelled the attitudes and efforts of the immigrant populations who were responsible for realising and accumulating the fabulous wealth of this New World. The Rockefellers and Vanderbilts built up vast fortunes but, though they lived in great style, they do not appear to have had any great desire to travel: "the first generation of the American leisured class consumed their wealth competitively and conspicuously at home."[2] The only people for whom foreign travel had any attraction were individuals such as Henry James and Walt Whitman, members of the small literary élite of the time.

During the early decades of the present century many Americans, for the first time, began to seek new horizons and to holiday outside their homeland. "A number of factors ... [produced] the vacation in Europe," write Cosgrove and Jackson. "The Atlantic had shrunk to a ... pool crossed by luxury liners, the second generation of American millionaires had grown up with inherited wealth, itself a powerful disincentive to ideas of the sacredness of work ... the mere possession of goods was no longer enough. Culture and experience were now the indices of status and they were to be found in Europe rather than North America."[3] Thus was initiated the "grand tour" of Europe which has now reached the ample proportions of some 4 million visitors a year and an American accent is a familiar sound in London and Paris, Oxford and Heidelberg, Venice and Rome.

The size of the United States, the affluence of the Americans and their mobility have produced leisure patterns which differ greatly from those which have emerged in Europe. As Cosgrove and Jackson point out "What to the British is a holiday abroad in terms of distance and cost is to the North American a weekend excursion to a cottage or camp site."[4] Because of these fundamental differences in scale, affluence and mobility there are appreciable differences between American attitudes to recreation and tourism and those prevailing in Europe.

DOMESTIC TOURISM

For these reasons the United States has a highly developed domestic tourist industry. Over 100 million Americans visit the National Parks annually, over 5 million skiers visit the country's snow-covered slopes, hundreds of thousands pour into the northern Appalachians in summer, large numbers flock to Florida and California in winter and, although these may be classed as foreign tourists since they cross the frontier, 50 million make brief trips to Mexico and 10 million go to Canada. It would need a book in itself to do full justice to the domestic tourist industry and here we must be content with highlighting the most important aspects.

There are within the United States three main areas where tourism is of special importance: the New England region with the Adirondack and Catskill Mts, Florida and California. The New York Metropolitan region with its 15 million inhabitants together with the 10 million who live in New England create a large tourist market and it is not surprising that both coast and mountain hinterland have developed an important tourism industry. The New England region has undoubted attractions. "New England is the only region of the North American continent where colonial history is more than a thin veneer. It has developed a distinctive architectural style of undeniable handsomeness ... quite apart from the settings on the rocky, ocean-swept coast, or against backdrops of forested mountains, the small settlements of New England are visually attractive in themselves. Scenery and buildings contribute alike to the tourist and recreational trades. Coastal resorts in summer double their populations by their intake of holiday-makers, while inland districts capitalise on forested mountains, on rivers and on lakes ... and on the 100 in. of winter snowfall which supports the operation of alpine playgrounds. Travel and tourism are easy enough to understand, given the scenic and recreational attractions of New England, its historical associations and the general affluence which makes travel and touring widely possible. But the deliberate promotion of the resort trades in New England also represents a response to an environment which is little less forbidding than that of the Maritime Provinces."[5]

Florida, because of its genial climate, has become a famous winter resort area. Large numbers of Americans escape to the sun and warmth of this sub-tropical peninsula. The Atlantic coast has a series of resorts—St Augustine, Daytona Beach, New Smyrna Beach, Vero Beach, West Palm Beach, Delray Beach, Fort Lauderdale and Miami Beach—which serve as holiday centres for sailing and fishing in summer and as winter or permanent retreats for the wealthy. Nowadays, the entire 160-km (100-mile) stretch from West Palm Beach to the Florida Keys is lined with smart hotels or high-grade private residences. Most famous of all the resorts is Miami which "aided by the vigorous promotion of tourism and by equally vigorous real-estate salesmanship, has raised itself in fifty years from the status of a Seminole Indian trading-post to that of a pre-eminent riviera resort."[6] The Gulf Coast of Florida, except for a few places such as Pensacola and the fishing centre of Biloxi in the north, has few resorts of importance but, inland from the west coast, Silver Springs, Sarasota Springs, Rainbow Springs, Waukulla Springs are centres of tourist activity.[7]

California has numerous tourist attractions and draws large numbers of tourists, although the state itself, with a population of around 20 million, also has an important domestic tourist industry. The Sierra Nevada offers many scenic attractions and sporting facilities. "The migrant population of tourists may, especially in summer, exceed the resident population, notably in the Lassen Volcano, Sequoia, General Grant, King's Canyon and Yosemite National Parks. . . . All the Parks are accessible by motor road and all are well-provided with accommodation, including motels."[8] The Yosemite National Park alone attracts some 2 million visitors annually.

But, spectacular as the mountains are, it is the sunshine and the sea, especially of the southern coast of California, which is the great magnet; the coast of central California with its cool waters (due to the cold southward flowing Californian Current) and its susceptibility to fog is handicapped. However, facing the Santa Barbara Channel and the San Pedro Channel of southern California are a whole series of beach resorts and residential towns such as Santa Barbara, Santa Monica, Redondo Beach, Long Beach, Newport Beach, Oceanside and San Diego. The warm winters and clear, dry, sunny weather also attract large numbers of tourists.

Special reference should be made to the impact which tourism has had in the opening up and economic life of the mountain and desert region of the American west. This rather remote and often inhospitable region, with thinly scattered natural resources but with a variety of splendid scenery, owes much to travel and tourism. "While commercial tourism in the west may be said to have begun in 1872, with the opening of Yellowstone National Park, its modern development has been based on the motor car and the extension of the region's road network. Yellowstone and Grand Canyon have become familiar to millions . . .; the distinctive cultures of the Spanish South-West and the Indian Reservations attract others. . . . Tourism has been responsible for the opening of large sections of the region which previously were both valueless and inaccessible. Lacking the profitable resource base of the lowlands, the mountain states have made capital out of their scenery. Settlements have sprung up to serve and house the tourists, and many of those who came as visitors have returned later, especially to the southern part of the region, as residents."[9] Apart from splendid scenery there are numerous attractions such as hunting and fishing, winter sports, etc. Some of the more important centres are Colorado Springs which originated as a health resort but which has grown into an important recreation centre, Las Vegas a notoriously brash, gambling, holiday centre, and Aspen and Vail, in Colorado, which are important skiing centres.

The American national parks differ from the British parks in two principal respects: first, in their vast size, and secondly in the fact that they are entirely natural, unlike the British parks which contain farmland, villages and even towns (see Fig. 41). Right from the outset, the aim in establishing the parks was "to combine the preservation of scenic areas with the provision of public access . . . and it is the rule for the parks to be staffed by rangers or wardens, and for the operating agencies to provide camp-grounds, picnic areas, roads and trails. Motels, hotels and lodges operate privately under lease."[10] The national parks are very popular and the number of visitors annually since 1920 has increased from 5 million to over 100 million; the Grand Canyon National Park attracts more than $1\frac{1}{2}$ million visitors a year.

A more recent development has been the setting up of National Nature Trails. Traditionally Americans have looked upon long hikes as journeys only to be taken on sufferance but this attitude is rapidly changing and in recent times increasing numbers of lovers of nature and the open air have strapped packs to their backs and put on their walking boots and begun tramping the countryside. Many, of course, stick to the neighbouring localities but increasing numbers are venturing into the wilderness. Some stalwarts are tackling the four-month trek from Canada to Mexico along the 3760-km (2350-mile) Pacific Crest Trail or the 3200-km (2000-mile) Appalachian Trail which runs from Maine to Georgia. Although the majority of hikers are young people, generally

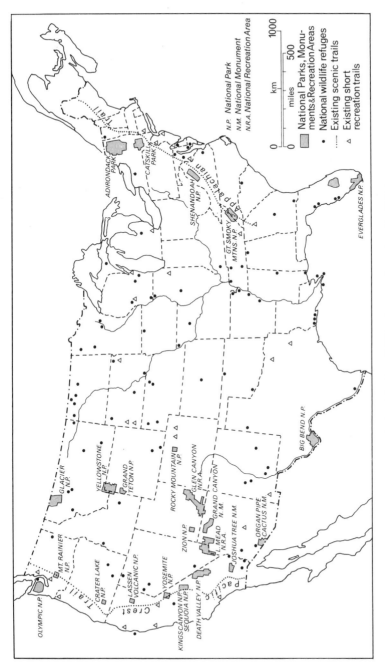

FIG. 41.—*National Parks, wildlife refuges and scenic trails, U.S.A.*

under thirty years of age, it is not uncommon to see entire families, young children to grandparents, following the trails.

The Pacific and Appalachian nature trails were designated by Congress in 1968 and the growing popularity of this kind of outdoor recreation has led to proposals for sixteen other possible National Scenic Trails. The Pacific Crest and Appalachian trails are the only ones officially marked on maps and maintained for public use, "but when the system is complete it will be possible to follow the route of Lewis and Clark across the Rockies or hike for 1320 km (825 miles) past Civil War and Revolutionary battle sites near the Potomac. Hardy footsloggers may also be able to trudge the length of the Chisholm Trail—one of the three main cattle routes of the old South-West—or retrace the exodus of the Mormons from Illinois to Salt Lake City."[11] In addition to these proposed long trails, the 1968 Act also provided for the setting up of short trails, often under 16 km (10 miles) in length, within easy reach of the cities. By the summer of 1972, thirty-three of these short-distance National Recreational Trails had been made available to hikers and horseriders.

Tramping and camping equipment sales—manufacturers have reported sales increases of as much as 400 per cent since 1970—testify to the new popularity of this sphere of outdoor recreation. Modern lightweight, streamlined equipment, specially designed to take much of the drudgery and backache out of hiking, has helped to entice people to go trailing. "Many Americans find overnight hiking trips an escape not only from the urban din but from the strident crowds that glut any campsite within reach by automobile."[12] Ironically, however, the trail walkers have themselves now begun to congest certain areas, thereby endangering the very wilderness they cherish. In popular areas, 95 per cent of the hikers appear to use the same 5 per cent of the trails and such over-use is leading to serious damage of the vegetation and even of the paths themselves: as one hiker commented "People are wearing out our rocks." The Appalachian Trail has been seriously affected in parts, so seriously that some constraints have had to be introduced, *e.g.* some areas have been closed to overnight campers while along some stretches of the trail permits have to be obtained.

According to a travel study carried out in 1970, 68 per cent of the adult population, *i.e.* over 18 years of age, took a holiday lasting a week or more and three-quarters of these travelled 160 km (100 miles) or more to their destination. Apart from holidays, trips of short duration were undertaken by 92 per cent of the population. Twelve per cent of the population or over 20 million travelled to other countries, either

Canada or Mexico or overseas; of these a quarter travelled overseas, mostly to Europe although a substantial number visited the Caribbean region.

THE AMERICAN OVERSEAS TOURIST

"With more discretionary income, leisure time and a higher degree of mobility than any other population," say Cosgrove and Jackson "North Americans play the largest role in the business of international tourism."[13] The United States is in fact the most important tourist-generating country and accounts for some 20 per cent of world tourist arrivals—over 20 million in 1970. And yet, in spite of this lead, we should heed what Peters has to say: "It is usual to consider Americans as having a high propensity to travel abroad. In fact, relative to the income level in the United States, foreign travel abroad is undeveloped. In terms of foreign travel generated per 1000 inhabitants, the U.S. comes very low in the table for developed countries."[14] The explanation for this, however, is not difficult to see for, visits to the neighbouring countries of Canada and Mexico excepted, U.S. citizens must, almost always, if they wish to engage in foreign travel go overseas which involves travelling great distances at considerable expense. Europeans, in contrast, are able to engage in international travel much more readily and only short trips may be involved as in the case of the Englishman who wants to go to France or the German who wishes to holiday in Switzerland. As Peters comments: "If a U.S. citizen travelled the [4160 km] 2600 miles from New York to San Francisco it would obviously be considered as a domestic trip. If the same traveller left London by land and covered [4160 km] 2600 miles, it would be possible to cross ten frontiers. From another point of view, if the fifty American states were considered as different countries, the comparative influence of North America in international tourism would be substantially greater."[15]

Large numbers—over 15 million—visited the U.S.'s immediate neighbours in 1970 but here we are more particularly concerned with the numbers travelling abroad who go overseas. During the past twenty years the numbers of those so doing has increased over eightfold and Table 57 shows this growth between 1951 and 1970.

Europe is the most important overseas destination area for tourists from the United States. The other main centres of attraction are the West Indies, Central America and, more recently, the Pacific and the Far East.

The American tourist has the reputation of being a big spender and in 1967 the $3\frac{1}{2}$ million U.S. overseas tourists spent the substantial

TABLE 57

U.S. travellers to overseas areas

Year	Number of travellers
1951	684,000
1955	1,075,000
1959	1,516,000
1963	1,990,000
1967	3,425,000
1970	5,260,000

amount of $1·5 billion, two-thirds of which was spent in the European/Mediterranean area. However, as more middle-class travellers engage in overseas tourism the amount spent *per capita* is decreasing.

TABLE 58

Destination of U.S. travellers overseas

	1960	1970
Base: all overseas travellers	1,634,000	5,260,000
Destination (%)		
Europe and Mediterranean	51	55
West Indies and Central America	39	32
South America	4	5
Other	6	9

Source: U.S. Department of Commerce: Office of Business Economics.

Peters draws some important conclusions with respect to the American tourist. He says that only slightly in excess of 1 per cent of the total population travel to overseas countries and that a large proportion of these make repeat visits; that the average age of visitors is decreasing, partly it would appear because of the increasing number of student travellers; that the average length of stay in Europe is decreasing and that travellers to Europe by air spend appreciably less than do those who travel by sea.[16]

Until 1965 France was the chief destination, but after that date the U.K. took precedence. Table 59 shows the five most popular countries and their ranking in 1970.

TABLE 59

U.S. travellers visiting selected European countries (1970)

Base: U.S. visitors to Europe and the Mediterranean	2,898,000
Destination (%)	
United Kingdom	47
France	34
West Germany	32
Italy	30
Switzerland	27

Source: U.S. Department of Commerce: Office of Business Economics.

In 1971 1,637,000 U.S. residents visited the U.K. This represented an increase of only 4 per cent over 1970 as against an increase of 21 per cent in 1970 over the 1969 arrivals; this drop, however, can be accounted for by the economic recession in the U.S. and the devaluation of the U.S. dollar. In 1971, however, U.S. visitors still represented nearly a quarter of all overseas visitors to the U.K. and their expenditure, which totalled £133m, accounted for 27 per cent of the total expenditure in the U.K. by overseas visitors. The average length of stay was about ten days and some two-thirds of the visits occurred between May and September.

The United States as a Tourist Receiving Country

From the viewpoint of international tourism, the United States is not a tourist-attracting country in the way that either the West Indies or Mediterranean Europe is; as a tourist destination it attracts a mere 8 per cent of world travellers. Moreover, out of a total of 13·2 million visitors (1970), some 9·8 million, or 75 per cent, of all visitors were Canadians.[17] Clearly then the United States' basic market for tourists is its immediate northern neighbour. Ignoring Canadians, the remaining 25 per cent or 3·4 million tourists comprise two distinct groups: 1·7 million who visit United States offshore states or possessions, *e.g.* Hawaii, Virgin Islands, and a further 1·7 million who visit continental United States.[18]

TABLE 60
Total visitor arrivals to U.S. (m)

	North American	Of which Canadian	Overseas	Total
1960	4·95	4·43	0·60	5·55
1963	5·25	4·98	0·85	6·10
1966	7·69	7·26	1·36	9·06
1969	10·43	9·40	2·01	12·44
1970	10·89	9·80	2·29	13·18

Source: United States Department of Commerce.

Traditionally, visitors to the United States have been in three principal categories: (*i*) relatives of recent immigrants who very often have had their holiday expenses supported by, or even entirely paid by, their family living in the United States, (*ii*) European artists, scholars, writers, together with students, who have visited the United States in order to see and experience the American way of life, and (*iii*) businessmen who have combined business with pleasure. Very few indeed seem to have been attracted to the United States in order to see its natural scenery, its art treasures or its historical monuments. As the *Economic Intelligence Unit Report* says: "In fact, after Siberia, the United States must have the lowest general image appeal to the average European tourist. The fact that the rest of the world is so full of American tourists somehow persuades Europeans that there can be little attraction in taking a holiday in the United States if the Americans all go abroad."[19]

It must be admitted that since the Second World War there has been little official interest in attracting foreign tourists to the United States; indeed it is possible to say that there has been actual discouragement of potential visitors. "There was no need to boost the tourist industry in the United States. Florida is already so overloaded with hotels, motels and vacation and retirement homes that much new building is on reclaimed land. California's tourist areas are suffering from overcrowding, as are Vermont's ski resorts and Cape Cod's summer places. Judging by the traffic jams in the summer on the Long Island Expressway, it is unlikely that more tourists would be welcome. . . . The National Parks are booming; historic Virginia rarely has enough spare beds for the casual tourist; the throughput in Washington, D.C., is continuous throughout the year despite appalling summer weather. So the hotel and tourist business is doing fine with the local customer and could not cope with any significant increase without substantial new investments."[20] Thus there were good reasons for not promoting foreign tourism. However, in 1961 the United States Travel Service was inaugurated as an agency of the State Department of Commerce to stimulate foreign tourist travel, although full recognition of U.S.T.S. and adequate funding was withheld until the late 1960s. In the meantime, however, the United States began to feel the burden of foreign exchange deficits which in 1971 resulted in the devaluation of the dollar. In order to check the drain on dollars, restriction on foreign travel by Americans was recommended, though this was never implemented; nevertheless, Americans were urged to holiday within their own country and to spend their dollars at home. At this time the net deficit on the travel account was running at some $2 billion annually and, with a view to offsetting this deficit, it was decided that foreign visitors should be attracted to the country, so that foreign exchange could be earned which would help reduce the deficit on travel.

It should be realised that whereas the United States attracted only 8 per cent of world travellers in 1970, it took 16 per cent of the world total tourist expenditure (the expenditures of visitors to the United States amounted in 1970 to $2·3 billion, of which around $0·9 billion came from overseas visitors, an average of $388 per head). Thus, in terms of the foreign payments situation, the receipts from foreign visitors already equalled the net deficit on the United States' international account and any additional tourist trade would bring positive gains.

Foreign Visitors

Table 61 shows the origins of overseas visitors to the United States over the past decade. Note that the Table covers all visitors—businessmen, students and those in transit as well as tourists proper.

TABLE 61
U.S.: origins of foreign overseas visitors (000)

Area	1959	1965	1970	Share of total 1970 (%)
Europe	221	563	982	42·8
South America	92	188	319	13·9
Central America	25	62	111	4·9
West Indies	125	199	373	16·3
Asia	47	110	357	15·6
Oceania	24	66	121	5·3
Africa	6	14	28	1·2
Total overseas	546	1202	2291	100·0

Source: U.S. Department of Justice, Immigration and Naturalisation Service.

Europe clearly provides the lion's share, almost 43 per cent, in 1970, of visitors to the United States. The largest single national group of arrivals was British with 12·8 per cent; the West Germans came second with 7·8 per cent; and the French third with 5·1 per cent. In view of the ethnic and cultural links between the United Kingdom and the United States, the dominance of British visitors is hardly surprising. Rather more surprising is the West Indies' position (West Indian visitors from Puerto Rico and the U.S. Virgin Islands are excluded). One reason may be that visiting arrivals are based on the visitor's last permanent address rather than by passport. Asia comes a close third with 9 per cent out of their total of 15·6 per cent being Japanese visitors. After the British visitors, the Japanese form the second largest national group visiting the United States: "the ... number of Japanese visitors, which grew tenfold between 1959 and 1970, indicates an exceptional interest in the U.S. not solely based on commercial ventures."[21]

Tourists from overseas (*i.e.* those arriving for the purposes of pleasure, as distinct from business or other reasons), totalling 1·7 million, formed almost 75 per cent of *total* arrivals to the U.S. in 1970. As might be expected, the leading sources of all arrivals (Table 61 above), are also the main origins of visiting tourists.

"The exchange rates and relative costs of living are the main constraints affecting the development of tourism from foreign countries into the United States. Only Canada, Britain, West Germany and Japan can provide the necessary income and population which make possible a large number of holiday trips ... and the European nations have a similar variety of climate, culture and landscape far closer to home. For many other nations, movement into the United States is for political, professional or business reasons only."[22]

Arrivals and Destinations

Of the $1\frac{3}{4}$ or so million overseas tourists who visit continental United States, 90 per cent arrive by air, and New York accounts for 40 per cent of the total arrivals. The other important arrival centre is Miami with 16·6 per cent. The Pacific coast cities (Seattle, San Francisco and Los Angeles) between them account for 12·9 per cent. Most of the visitors coming to the United States do so in the period May to September with July as the peak month. December stands out as a better-than-average month, because of family visits at Christmastime.

It is not easy to analyse the destinations of visiting tourists. A large proportion disperse to see their relatives who may live anywhere in the country and as the E.I.U. Report says, there does not appear to be any established pattern for foreign visitors. European visitors tend to concentrate their activities to the north-east, visiting New York, Washington and perhaps Boston. Relatively few get as far as the Pacific coast, despite the attractions of California. Time and cost are enemies unless the visitor is on an extended visit and is fairly affluent. "The poor student tends to get the best of the deal since he has the time to take a Greyhound bus, or hitch a ride 'from sea to shining sea,' but for the middle-class tourist who wants a modicum of comfort and ease, there is not the time and sometimes not the money to go another [4800 km] 3000 miles east of San Francisco, or west of the eastern seaboard."[23]

Canadian Tourism

Similar socio-economic factors influence Canadian and U.S. citizens: Canadians enjoy high standards of living, have long holidays, are mobile and prepared to spend a high proportion of their income on leisure pursuits. Not only is domestic tourism well developed but Canada ranks as one of the most important countries in generating tourist arrivals: she is fifth in rank and only a little behind the United Kingdom. Canadians spend about $3000m each year abroad, about half of this being spent on overseas tourism. Expenditure has increased greatly in recent years, almost doubling during the six-year period 1965–70 (in 1965 $796m, in 1970 $1437m), and these figures exclude international fare payments. Considerable numbers of Canadians visit Europe and especially Britain (in 1971 437,000 Canadians visited Britain and spent some £33m).

Two points relating to Canadian tourism are of particular interest. Rather more than half of all Canadian adults take a holiday and, although the great majority spend that holiday within their own country, about a fifth cross the border into the United States and about 8 per cent (1 million) travel overseas. Some 56 per cent of overseas travellers go to Europe, chiefly the United Kingdom, France, West Germany, Switzerland, the Netherlands and Italy; while, however, the total of Canadians visiting Europe continues to increase annually, since 1968 Europe's percentage share of Canadian overseas travellers has markedly declined. Certain other destinations, such as Bermuda, the Caribbean, Mexico and Hawaii, are also attracting a smaller share of the travel market. On the other hand, during recent years many Canadians have begun to broaden their horizons and are travelling to places other than the traditional destinations.

Partly because Canada is the immediate neighbour of the United States, partly because around 90 per cent of the Canadian population lives within a few hundred miles of the Canadian–United States frontier, partly because that frontier is no great barrier to movement and partly because communications links between the two countries are well developed, there is a great volume of tourist movement between them. Canadians account for about 75 per cent of the tourists who visit the United States (9·8 million in 1970). There are no records of how Canadians travel to the United States, but the great majority must use road and air transport. Although Canadians spend more than any other national group of visitors—$885m in 1970—the expenditure *per capita* is surprisingly low—a mere $90 in 1970.[24] This is largely accounted for by the fact that most travel to the United States is for relatively short excursions and Canadians on holiday tend to use their own cars as a travel base.

Apart from domestic tourism, Canada is increasingly becoming a tourist destination, especially for North Americans but also for other nationalities. In 1972 Canada received 738,204 visitors from overseas. "Tourism appears to be the most vigorous new industry, and is becoming a valuable supplementary source of income. The principal attractions are the forests, the sea, the ... shores dotted with picturesque villages, the sandy beaches, the 27-m (60-ft) tides of the Bay of Fundy, the famous Reversing Falls on the St John River and the tidal bore on the Petitcodiac River. Another attraction of Atlantic Canada is the Gaspe Peninsula, part of Quebec Province, famed for its wild, rocky, cliff-lined shores."[25]

The majority of Canada's population is concentrated in the St Lawrence Lowlands and in the Lake Peninsula and hence parts of southern Quebec and southern Ontario have become important as holiday areas. It is possible for the holiday-maker easily to get away from it all into the wilderness. In winter, the Laurentides, over 900 m (3000 ft) high and thickly covered with snow, form an important sports area in Quebec Province. In summer large numbers of tourists travel along the highways of southern Quebec and Ontario in search of river and lakeside sites where they can camp, picnic and swim, and also study animals and wildfowl in their natural habitat as, for example, in the Algonquin Provincial Park south of the River Ottawa, and in the Muskoka Lake country east of Georgian Bay.[26]

In the far west, the Canadian Rocky Mountains have spectacular secnery with peaks over 3000 m (10,000 ft) in height. The ranges have been shaped and fretted by glaciation which has left behind great U-shaped trenches and magnificent lakes and all the other landforms associated with ice action. Several national parks, like those of Banff, Jasper and Glacier, have been established in this region and many thousands of tourists visit the area every year.

Banff and Jasper, the main resorts, are readily accessible for they both lie on trans-mountain railway routes while the Banff–Jasper Highway, a feat of engineering skill, provides the tourist with views of some of the finest mountain scenery in the continent. In addition to these *headquarters resorts*, as they have been called, which serve as residential centres with a wide range of recreational resources, there are many other smaller centres (*objective resorts*), which are located usually in more out-of-the-way places and which usually have a single natural feature of attraction, *e.g.* Twin Falls, Radium Springs, Lake Louise.[27] New roads and service centres are constantly being opened up to provide improved facilities for the tourist. The following Tables show tourist arrivals and receipts for 1970.

TABLE 62
Tourist arrivals: Canada (1970) (000)

United States	13,648·0 (including short-term visitors)
United Kingdom	157·7
West Germany	41·3
France	36·9
Netherlands	28·0
Japan	22·0
Italy	18·6
Australia	17·0
Jamaica	11·4
Mexico	10·7
TOTAL	14,183·5

TABLE 63
Foreign tourist receipts by main visitor groups (1970) ($m)

United States	1082
United Kingdom	n.a.
Other O.E.C.D.	152
TOTAL	1234

NOTES

1. I. Cosgrove and R. Jackson, *The Geography of Recreation and Leisure*, Hutchinson, 1972, pp. 70–1.
2. *Ibid.*
3. *Ibid.*
4. *Idem*, p. 70.
5. G. H. Dury and R. Mathieson, *The United States and Canada*, Heinemann, 1970, pp. 187–8.
6. Dury and Mathieson, *op. cit.*, pp. 217–18.
7. *Idem*, p. 218.
8. F. S. Hudson, *North America*, Macdonald & Evans, 1974, p. 343.
9. J. H. Paterson, *North America*, Oxford University Press, 1960, p. 390.
10. Dury and Mathieson, *op. cit.*, p. 118.
11. *Time Magazine*, 24th July, 1972, pp. 53–4.
12. *Time Magazine*, 24th July, 1972, pp. 53–4.
13. *Op. cit.*, p. 73.
14. M. Peters, *International Tourism*, Hutchinson, 1969, p. 40.
15. *Ibid.*
16. *Op. cit.*, p. 46.

17. National Report No. 4: Visit the U.S.A., *International Tourism Quarterly*, Economic Intelligence Unit, No. 1, 1972, p. 11.

18. *Ibid.*

19. *Op. cit.*, p. 12.

20. *Ibid.*

21. *Idem*, p. 19.

22. Cosgrove and Jackson, *op. cit.*, p. 73.

23. National Report No. 4: Visit the U.S.A., *International Tourism Quarterly*, Economic Intelligence Unit, No. 1, 1972, p. 27.

24. *Idem*, p. 24.

25. *Larousse Encyclopedia of World Geography*, Paul Hamlyn, 1964, p. 581.

26. F. S. Hudson, *North America*, Macdonald & Evans, 1974, p. 89.

27. G. Taylor, *Urban Geography*, Methuen, 1949, pp. 342–4.

Chapter XX

Latin America

"LATIN America" refers to the Western Hemisphere lands south of the United States–Mexican frontier; it really embraces three areas: Mexico and the Central American Republics, the West Indian Islands of the Caribbean region and South America. Figures relating to tourism are frequently given separately for Central America (the Central American Republics and the West Indies but, often, not including Mexico) and for South America. Peters' work on tourism[1] has been drawn upon throughout the following discussion.

Broadly, a distinction may be made between the Central American area (Mexico, the Central American Republics and the West Indian Islands) where tourism is, in general, well-established and flourishing (it is least developed in the Central American Republics) and the South American area where, although there is sometimes a fairly well-developed domestic tourist industry, foreign and especially overseas tourism is not well-developed. The countries of South America are only really just beginning to participate in international tourism.

The following figures give the numbers of arrivals and the region's world share in percentages for selected years.

TABLE 64
Patterns of Latin American tourism

	1950	1960	1967	1970
Arrivals in Latin America (m)	1·3	2·7	4·7	5·5
World share (%)	5·2	3·8	3·4	3·0

In 1965, inter-regional arrivals, *i.e.* from outside the Latin American region, totalled 1,134,000, arrivals from within the region 526,000. In 1972, South America had 2 million foreign tourists, Central America and the West Indies (including the Bahamas) $2\frac{1}{2}$ million, while Mexico had 2·8 million. In Latin America more than half of the tourist arrivals are from regions outside the destination region, clearly, therefore, it is dependent to a large extent on long-haul traffic.

In spite of an absolute increase in the number of tourist arrivals over the past decade or so, the share of Latin America in international tourist arrivals has declined. Total receipts increased from £140m in 1950 to £650m in 1967, but Latin America's share of total receipts from international tourism dropped from 18·7 per cent in 1950 to 12·8 per cent in 1967.

MEXICO

During the decade 1960–70 Mexico embarked upon an ambitious tourism promotion policy. This seems to have been inspired principally by the need to solve the country's balance of payments problem. Although economic progress since 1950 has been very substantial, Mexico has a trading deficit on its visible account: for example, in 1969, exports totalled $1432m, imports $2078. However, largely because of the income from tourism (which in 1970 amounted to $575m) there was in that year a favourable balance of payments. The growth of tourism has been rapid and by the end of the 1960s foreign tourism had become the country's second largest source of foreign exchange revenue and was almost equal to the value of the commodity exports.

In 1973 it was written: "tourism generates more foreign exchange than the whole of the conventional export industry," and tourism "has proved to be a check on inflation as well as a prime mover of economic growth."[2]

Currently more than 2 million tourists visit the interior of Mexico but over 50 million United States citizens make day trips across the border! This border trade is by no means one-sided, however, for 80 million Mexicans a year cross the border into the United States.

Tables 65 and 66 summarise some of the main features of Mexican tourism.

Before proceeding to discuss Mexico's tourist industry, it will be useful to quote a Mexican's view of the impact which tourism has had on the country. "Though generally measured in terms of its contribution to the balance of payments, the economic and social influence of foreign tourism in Mexico, particularly in the second half of the 1960s, has enlarged its scope appreciably. Tourism, directly or indirectly, has affected the direction given to important amounts of public investment and determined the channelling of a significant part of private investment into the construction of hotels and other installations, and the provision of other tourist services. It has created demands—for goods, services and labour—that have changed the development course of certain economic activities and have influenced the programmes for the

TABLE 65
Selected tourist arrivals: Latin-American countries
(preliminary statistics)

	1971	1972	Change (%)
Central America			
Mexico	2,509,933	2,883,599	14·9
El Salvador	121,858	123,721	1·5
Panama	138,198	149,546	8·2
West Indies			
Bahamas	732,051	802,009	9·6
Jamaica	284,111	318,380	12·1
Netherlands Antilles	143,111	140,267	−2·0
Puerto Rico	604,401	646,773	7·0
Trinidad and Tobago	66,130	66,640	0·8
South America			
Brazil	211,305	234,549	11·0
Colombia	144,223	171,772	19·1
Peru	73,716	86,404	17·2

Note: Some of the 1972 figures are not for the full year.
Source: I.U.O.T.O. Technical Bulletin, February, 1973.

TABLE 66
Tourism account (U.S.$m)

	Gross revenue from tourism	of which		Tourists' gross expenditure	of which		Net revenue	Mean annual growth rate (%)
		Border trade	Tourism		Border trade	Tourism		
1960	521·3	366·0	155·3	261·5	221·0	40·5	259·8	—
1965	773·3	499·5	274·8	414·3	295·2	119·1	359·0	6·7
1969	1209·0	744·0	465·0	714·0	480·0	234·0	495·0	8·3

Source: Bank of Mexico.

formation of human resources. At other levels, foreign tourism has made itself felt in the consumption habits and the scale of values adopted by important segments of Mexican society; it has altered the landscape, modified the urban environment and, in some instances, has come into conflict with traditional Mexican government policies, such as the agrarian reform. These secondary effects of the tourism boom are generally little known and, up to now, have not been submitted to an overall assessment in terms of policy implications. . . . It appears, however, that the country's tourism development strategy has failed to take into account the complexity of factors involved. Some loose ends detectable in the policy may either make impossible the achievement of the basic balance of payments objective or alternatively may increase considerably its economic and social cost."[3]

Foreign Tourism

Ignoring for the moment weekend vacationists and day-trippers, more than 3·2 million tourists visited Mexico in 1973. Some 1·7 million were American tourists, chiefly from the United States. Visitors stay an average of eight days, and spend about $225 *per capita*.[4] Tourist expenditure in 1973 was $1·838m. Foreign tourist spending has been more or less stable since 1965 and this would seem to indicate that increasing numbers of visitors fall into the middle-income category. Although substantial numbers of American visitors arrive by air, there are four great road routes across the United States–Mexican frontier: the Gulf Route (by Pan-American Highway) via Nuevo Laredo, the first route to be opened and still the most important; the Eagle Pass–Piedras Negras Route; the El Paso–Ciudad Juarez or Central Route; and the Western Route via Nogales. All these main highways lead to Mexico City.

Tourism in Mexico is mainly concentrated in a small number of traditional tourist centres, especially Mexico City and Acapulco. Mexico City is one of the largest urban areas in the world ($8\frac{1}{2}$ million inhabitants); it is a city of startling contrasts with much of interest for the tourist—fine buildings, beautiful parks, a bull ring (the largest in the world), excellent museums and impressive remains of the old Aztec civilisation. The capital has numerous good hotels and many excellent restaurants and there is plenty of night-life. The tourist season is between November and March. Acapulco in recent years has become the most popular resort in Mexico. The town stretches along the coast in a series of bays for a distance of some 16 km (10 miles). "The hotels, of which there are 237, are mostly perched high to catch the breeze, for between 11.30 and 4.30 the heat is sizzling. They are filled to overflowing in January and February. It has all the paraphernalia of a booming resort: smart shops, night clubs, quaint red light district, golf club, touts and street vendors. There are some twenty beaches, all with fine, golden sand. The two most popular are the sickle-curved and shielded Caleta, with its smooth water, and the surf-pounded . . . beach of Los Hornos. One can swim and fish, the year round."[5] Acapulco is by no means the only coastal resort, however, there are many others including Ensenada, La Paz, Guaymas, Mazatlan, Puerto Vallarta and Manzanillo together with the islands Isla de Cozumel and Isla Mujeres, which lie off the coast of Yucatan.

Border Visitors

Special mention must be made of Mexico's border visitors: day-trippers and weekenders. In 1970, some 53 million visitors from the United States stayed for less than twenty-four hours in the northern frontier areas;[6] Tijuana, in the extreme west, received 15 million visitors (up to 130,000 on Sundays) from California.[7] Most of these short-stay visitors make repeated return trips. Since each border visitor spends, on average, $14 per head, the sum total—$744m—is very substantial. This border tourism supports a large industry which provides goods and services for the visitors—bars, restaurants, motels, service stations, racing, gambling and nightclubs. The provision of tourist services has become in fact an essential activity in border towns such as Tijuana and Ciudad Juarez. Navarrette, discussing border tourism, has said: "Though the Mexican income derived from border tourism has grown at a fast pace, 10·4 per cent yearly from 1965 to 1969, due largely to the increase in the number of U.S. visitors, the increment in Mexican border-crossers' spending has expanded even more quickly in the same period (12·9 per cent annually)."[8]

Domestic Tourism

Mexico had a population of 48·5 million in 1970—large by Latin American standards—and a fast-growing population—at 3·4 per cent per annum (1970) among the highest in the world. As already indicated there has been a steady expansion of the Mexican economy; nevertheless, by European standards, the distribution of wealth remains very uneven and only about 10 per cent of the people enjoy a high enough standard of discretionary income to enable them to purchase consumer durables such as motor cars or refrigerators, or to travel abroad. Even so, the market for travel abroad is gradually expanding. "Foreign travel is a status symbol in Mexico and is encouraged by a highly developed system of credit finance unparalleled in most other Latin American countries. The numbers of Mexican travellers leaving for foreign countries and staying outside Mexico for more than seventy-two hours (these figures eliminate the considerable number of very short-term U.SA./Mexico border crossings) has risen considerably ... from 69,479 in 1961 to 142,319 in 1966 and 295,242 in 1971."[9] The United States is by far the most important destination, and the Americas as a whole accounted for 82 per cent of all Mexicans travelling abroad in 1971. However, more are beginning to travel to Europe and the number of Mexicans visiting Britain, for instance, increased from

18,000 in 1968 to 26,000 in 1971. Mexican travel to Britain is overwhelmingly pleasure-orientated, less than 5 per cent coming for business reasons.[10] June to August are the most popular months for travel abroad, related, as in Europe, to the closure of the schools for the summer holidays. Mexico's international travel expenditure (excluding fares) increased from U.S.$119m in 1965 to U.S.$266m in 1970.

Problems of Mexican Tourism

Although the growth in gross revenue derived from tourism more than doubled between 1960 and 1970 and between 1965 and 1970 grew at a rate of slightly more than 14 per cent annually, unfortunately for Mexico it was overshadowed by an even faster expansion of Mexican tourist spending abroad—18·4 per cent a year over the latter period.[11] This has been due partly to the approximate doubling of the numbers of Mexicans travelling abroad and partly to the more than twofold rise in *per capita* spending between 1965 and 1970. The net contribution made by foreign tourism and the border trade to financing the country's balance of trade deficit is thus declining. Navarrette has said that in order to keep the current account deficit to manageable proportions, the gross revenue from foreign tourism and the border trade will have to grow at the rate of 15 per cent annually—a rather high rate to achieve.[12] What chance has Mexico of attaining such a fast growth? "The achievement of the objective ... does not, in principle, appear to be unattainable at a time when the rise in advanced countries' personal income levels and the generalised use of mass air transportation forecast a world tourism boom. The picture, however, seems less simple when the prerequisites for increased Mexican participation in the world tourism market—imperative in order to attain the indicated growth-rate—are examined."[13] Mexican tourist services are generally satisfactory in the major centres of attraction but are often far from adequate elsewhere. If other tourist areas are to be opened up and developed—as has been suggested in Baja California, along the Pacific littoral, and on the Caribbean coast of Yucatan (plans for the development of the island of Cancun as a tourist centre are already under way)—heavy investment in basic infrastructure and superstructure (hotels and other direct tourist services) will be required. The question, however, still remains "if, in terms of the country's global development needs, the priority given to public and private investment in tourism promotion does not represent a less than optimal application of Mexico's limited investment resources."[14] Foreign investment might come to the rescue but this would involve interest payments and such leakages would curtail the net tourist revenue while at the same time it would take some control of tourist activity out of Mexican hands. Another problem relates to customers: so far the United States has been Mexico's traditional market and she has had relatively little success in attracting tourism from other markets; but this she must do if she wishes to achieve the 15 per cent annual growth rate.

THE WEST INDIES

The Caribbean has become an important tourist region and for many of the islands tourism has become an item of considerable economic significance. The tourist industry, at least in some areas, goes back to the 1920s and developed steadily in the period 1918–39. The most spectacular growth, however, has occurred since 1945. At one time the West Indies were regarded as a place only for the rich, out of reach for the majority of European tourists. The situation has changed quite radically in recent years as air travel to the Caribbean has expanded. The North American tourist market still dominates the industry and more than 75 per cent of visitors come from the United States and Canada. Increasingly, however, Europeans are being attracted. If the Bahamas is included, an estimated 5–6 million tourists visited the Caribbean region in 1972. In one or two places, notably the Bahamas and the U.S. Virgin Islands, tourism ranks as the major industry and virtually dominates the economy; in other islands, as for example Puerto Rico and Jamaica, tourism is the second or third principal source of income, and in the remaining islands it has a potential in which the authorities place great hope.

The islands have much to offer the tourist: almost perfect weather, never too hot, never cold and abundant sunshine; beautiful and varied scenery with many superb beaches; superlative conditions for swimming, water-sports and sailing; a rich cultural background and much local colour. The natural attractions of the West Indies can scarcely be matched anywhere else in the world. But undoubtedly the most important factor in the growth of the West Indies' tourist trade has been the region's nearness to the prosperous United States: within a matter of hours wealthy Americans can exchange the oppressive heat of summer or the rigours of winter for the delightful conditions of the Caribbean islands. The continuing post-war prosperity of the United States, together with the greatly improved and speedy transportation facilities, have been instrumental in the rapid development of the Caribbean tourist trade.

Tourist Centres

Four million tourists visited the Caribbean region in 1970 by far the greatest share of this going to Puerto Rico, the U.S. Virgin Islands, Jamaica and Barbados. Puerto Rico and the Virgin Islands, both United States' possessions, have for some time been popular holiday centres for Americans. In the case of Puerto Rico, where the tourist industry began in the early 1940s, the number of visitors jumped from around 40,000 a year in 1940 to 400,000 in 1960. Whereas tourist receipts totalled a mere $13·7m in 1952, the figure had jumped to over $100m in 1965 when over 500,000 tourists visited the island.[15] Tourism has been one of Puerto Rico's biggest growth industries and ranks third after agriculture and manufacturing. The industry employs some 10,000 people.

Although Puerto Rico has great natural beauty—the Puerto Ricans call their island La Isla del Encanto (the Isle of Enchantment)—the great boom in the tourist trade really resulted from the efforts of the Government and the coincidence of a series of fortunate circumstances. In 1948 the Government built the Caribe-Hilton hotel (later leased to the Hilton organisation), which proved to be a highly successful venture, and followed this up with other hotels constructed at public expense.[16] These successful developments soon attracted private investment and hotel building began to increase; some of these hotels, such as the $9m Dorado Beach hotel built by Laurence Rockefeller, were the height of luxury.[17] The Cuban Revolution in 1959 diverted much of its tourist trade to Puerto Rico; the cheap air services between the island and the United States mainland (originally instituted to assist migrant Puerto Ricans) now offer cheap transportation for tourists; until 1970, continued prosperity enabled large numbers of Americans to afford Caribbean holidays. However, after twenty years of rapid expansion, the Puerto Rican tourist industry underwent a very severe recession and in San Juan, the capital and chief tourist centre, numerous hotels had to close down. However in 1973 the situation began to improve and in that year 638,000 tourists visited the island and spent $126m.

In much the same way as Puerto Rico, the American Virgin Islands (St Croix, St Thomas, St John) reaped great economic benefits from tourism: this is reflected in the fact that "*per capita* income rose from $412 in 1950, to $1,751 in 1964; and total annual income increased more than 500 per cent in the same 15-year period."[18] In the 10-year period 1952–62 tourist receipts increased from $5 million to $35 million.[19] In 1972 the islands had $1\frac{1}{4}$m visitors and earned $106m from tourism. The fact that the islands have free-port status means that visitors can purchase luxury articles at a very substantial discount on the prices paid on the United States mainland. Like Puerto Rico, the Virgins are at the moment suffering a setback, largely because of the activities of ruthless speculators. Professor G. K. Lewis wrote of these wheeler dealers "who move in ruthlessly to make their money [from] ... the unsuspecting tourist before the industry reaches its apex and then evacuate at the strategic moment, leaving behind a gaudy, unreal atmosphere and a permanently disgruntled local populace. The service motive rapidly gives way to the profit motive. As this happens there are signs that the American tourist, who generally is a shrewd analyst of the costs and benefits of what he spends, is rapidly disillusioned and will very likely shift his patronage to the new European travel schemes, which already are no more expensive than the increasing [in terms of costs] anachronistic Caribbean vacation tour."[20]

The first significant flow of tourists came to Jamaica in the mid-1920s. Before the Second World War, the greatest proportion of visitors came by sea, usually by cruising liners but sometimes by banana boats. In those days, the port of Port Antonio could lay claim to being a tourist centre since vessels in the banana trade called there.[21] After the Second World War, Jamaica increasingly became a favourite tourist destination for North American holiday-makers who in recent years accounted for about 85 per cent of all tourists. Only a very small proportion of Britons—slightly over 4 per cent of all visitors to Jamaica in 1972—visited the island, although their numbers are likely to grow with the expansion of U.K. inclusive tour holidays. Most tourists now come by air. The revolution in Cuba also gave the Jamaican tourist industry a great fillip and the Jamaican Government has since 1960 done much to encourage the development of the island as a popular tourist centre, especially since tourist receipts provide very significant and valuable foreign exchange. By 1960 Jamaica was receiving nearly 250,000 visitors annually; by 1967 the number had increased to 350,000 and tourism brought in $66m; by 1972 comparative figures were 374,625 and $108m, while in 1973 over half a million visitors brought in earnings of $115m. After bauxite mining and sugar production, tourism now ranks as the third most important industry, and tourism is the second largest foreign-exchange earner.[22] Kingston, Montego Bay and Ocho Rios are the principal tourist centres. An international airport has been built near Montego Bay and it is a busy terminal bringing visitors to the island. The town of Montego Bay has developed as a major high-class tourist resort, for the coast offers wonderful bathing and water-sports facilities. While vacation facilities are being expanded in the older resorts, new areas are being opened up to tourism as, for example, on the northern coast between Falmouth and Port Maria and in the extreme west in the Negril district.[23] In this connection due credit must be given to the Jamaica Tourist Board which is perhaps the best in the Caribbean.

Jamaica has much to offer the tourist: the historical attractions of Port Royal, magnificent beaches of pink and white sand, the interesting limestone features of the Cockpit Country, the forested Blue Mountains, Fern Valley and, for those who want something more exciting, rafting on the Rio Colorado.

Like Jamaica, Barbados has depended substantially in the past upon the American market (in fact for over 60 per cent of its tourist traffic), although the island, like many of the other small islands in the Lesser Antilles, has had a certain amount of British traffic, *e.g.* cruise ships frequently call. In 1970 some 8 per cent of all Barbados' visitors came from Britain. The Barbadians, like the Jamaicans, have since 1970 been trying, partly by advertising campaigns, to tempt more Britons and Europeans to the island. Barbados has traditionally been a holiday centre for West Indians from neighbouring islands. Barbados has more than fifty hotels, excellent shops and sophisticated entertainments. The modern airport at Seawell, ten miles from Bridgetown, is on direct air routes between London and the United States and these air services have been largely responsible for the recent rapid increase in the importance of tourism which brought in $30m a year in 1970.[24]

Most of the smaller West Indian islands, *e.g.* Antigua, Grenada, Dominica, St Lucia, St Vincent, Tobago, have some tradition of tourism and, endowed with great natural beauty, have great potential as holiday places. Important developments are already taking place. The British Virgin Islands, for example, more than sixty islands, islets and cays offering first-class sailing in light breezes and safe, protected anchorages together with warm, clear, unpolluted waters for every kind of water-sports, have already gone a long way towards becoming a full integrated and serviced water-sports environment. Frigate Bay on St Kitts is being developed into a great holiday complex with hotels, apartments, residential units, shops, a yachting marina and an 18-hole international-standard golf course. On St Lucia, British Court Line built two hotels, the Halcyon Days, with 256 rooms, and the Halcyon Beach Club, with eighty-eight rooms. Such developments are clearly harbingers of things to come.

Until the revolution in 1959 Cuba had a thriving tourist industry: tourism, in fact, was the second major industry. Largely because of

Cuba's close strategic, political and economic relations with the U.S., large numbers of Americans visited the island. "Increasing affluence brought thousands of North American tourists to Havana, only 145 km (90 miles) from Miami. Chicago gangsters opened casinos in Havana. After 1945 the boom increased. Hotels multiplied everywhere, in 1958 the Havana Riviera was built for gamblers who saw nothing of Cuba but the airport and the hotel gaming-tables and fruit machines. Cuba earned millions of dollars."[25] After the revolution, the disenchantment between Cuba and the United States led to the collapse of the tourist industry. Castro wished to see his country freed from dependence upon American tourism while the United States for her part proscribed American visits to Cuba.

Hispaniola and Trinidad have not so far interested themselves in tourism to any great extent although the potential is great. In the Dominican Republic the tourist trade also has a great potential, for the country has some splendid, varied scenery, including fine rugged mountains in the interior, beautiful beaches and an attractive capital city—Santo Domingo. A number of hotels were built in the 1960s in an attempt to stimulate a tourist trade but it never really developed.[26] Until quite recently Trinidad, too, had little in the way of a tourist industry but since 1960 the government has made determined efforts to encourage tourism. A number of hotels—the largest being the Trinidad-Hilton built in 1962—and guest houses have been built.[27] Trinidad's attractions include beautiful and colourful scenery and highly developed sporting and recreational facilities. Trinidad's small sister island Tobago, one of the jewels of the Caribbean, is an added attraction which is already being increasingly visited. Trinidad has excellent air services since it is a focus of air routes; this should aid tourism development, as hitherto much of the tourist trade was from "stop-over-visitors."[28] The government has established a Tourist Board to help promote the industry.

Strictly speaking, the Bahamas are not part of the West Indies but they have similar attractions. The Bahamas consist of an archipelago of some 3000 islands, islets and rocks scattered over some 1207 km² (750 sq. miles); they are coralline, generally long, narrow and low-lying. Subtropical climatic conditions prevail. Warmed by the Gulf Stream in winter and cooled by the sea breezes in summer, with clear blue skies, abundant sunshine and little rain, the climate is ideal; the winter climate is particularly delightful. This healthful climate is one of the Bahamas' chief assets, which it has capitalised to the full. There is first-class bathing, boating and fishing facilities and spectacular marine scenery.

Lacking any significant exports of agricultural or mineral commodities, the islands set out to exploit its natural beauty and salubrious climate and it has built up a prosperous tourist industry whose value was in 1970 estimated at over $100m annually. Tourism is the islands' principal foreign-exchange earner, receipts far exceeding the total of all visible exports.[29]

The first real expansion began in the 1950s and by 1958 the number of visitors was around 250,000. By 1963, it had risen to 500,000, by 1969 to nearly $1\frac{1}{2}$ million. The period 1960–69 saw a fivefold increase in the number of tourists with a 20 per cent increase in 1969 over 1968. The main reasons for this rapid development, given the attractive natural conditions, are the same as for Puerto Rico and Jamaica. Although proximity to the American market is a big advantage, "being so dependent on American tourists and investment (in industry and property), the Bahamas catch a cold about six months after the U.S. sneezes."[30] Not surprisingly, therefore, when economic recession afflicted the United States in 1970 the Bahamas suffered accordingly. 1970 saw a 15 per cent drop in the number of tourist arrivals and, as a result, "there was excess hotel capacity, the construction industry went into a decline (reflecting the climate in the property market also), unemployment grew and the Bahama Airways went into liquidation."[31] However, as the U.S. economy partly recovered in 1971 so the Bahamas tourist industry improved and in that year the number of visitors increased by 13 per cent; this trend continued in 1972 and the first half of the year showed an 18 per cent increase compared with the same period in 1971. In 1973 tourist arrivals totalled 1·4m.

Ninety per cent of the tourists come from the U.S. This overdependence on the U.S. market, together with the effects of the American recession, has caused the Bahamas to explore new markets and there has been increased advertising in Europe. This appears to have had some success, for arrivals from Europe increased by more than one-third in 1971. Although European tourists make up only 5 per cent of the total number of visitors, their average length of stay, 10 days, is approximately twice that of the North American visitor. Although there has been a slight drop in the overall length of stay of the American visitor from 6·3 to 5·7 days, expenditure per visit has risen (1972 figures).[32] The Bahamian Government is alive to the fact that in order to compete with the established European tourist areas it must be prepared and able to offer low- to medium-cost facilities.

The island of New Providence is the main attraction and Nassau, the capital, the principal resort and focus of tourism. All the ingredients necessary for a successful tourist industry—abundant sunshine, beautiful scenery, sparkling seas, fine beaches, sumptuous hotels—are here. Nassau itself is a strikingly beautiful town with numerous trees and gardens. However, with improving transportation links, more and more visitors are discovering the attractions of other islands and indeed some of the smaller outlying islands are beginning to be developed to cater for the more affluent clientele who have expensive tastes and desire exclusiveness.

An important role is played by the Bahamas as a residential and retirement haven, since the climate, abundant cheap land and lack of taxation have attracted many ". . . well-heeled permanent guests from the United States and elsewhere."[33] However, as so often happens, this development together with the expansion in the tourist industry has led to a property boom and much speculation in land while for British residents and companies at least the Bahamas are no longer the tax-free haven they once were.

Fearful that the Bahamas might become too dependent upon the tourist industry and that any major recession in tourism could have disastrous effects, the Government has attempted to diversify the economy—with some limited success. But tourism remains the mainstay of the economy accounting for 50 per cent of Government revenue and provides work for some 70 per cent of the actively engaged population.

Caribbean Cruising

"One of the most remarkable growth businesses of modern tourism has been Caribbean cruising. Year after year new ships have rushed to an area which seems at times to be specifically designed for the business. Passengers are increasingly attracted by the Caribbean which, for the moment, has only one real international competitor, the Greek islands. To some extent success has bred success. The popularity of island cruising has led to heavy investment in new and converted tonnage which, in turn, has increased the popularity of this type of holiday. Resorts have reacted to the commercial opportunities, and there have been extensive investments in port-side facilities, such as craft markets, shopping and restaurant areas, and provision for inland tours. Resorts around the islands are geared to the arrival of the next ship. Out roll the taxis and up go the shop blinds."[34]

The "island-hopping" cruise has largely replaced the traditional kind of cruise holiday—spending most of the time at sea with only one or two calls *en route*. Nowadays a cruise ship may take in as many places as there are days on board. Clearly cruise passengers are not likely to spend as much money as those who stay in a place for a week or more but their custom is not to be spurned. It has been estimated that in 1971 500,000 cruise passengers visited the Bahamas and the total spent by these visitors must have been considerable. Likewise any island visited by a cruise ship benefits, if only by selling water to the ship! But cruise calls may have another important side-effect: many cruise visitors find the places of call so attractive that they decide they will make a return visit for a much longer stay.

Caribbean Problems

"In North America the Caribbean has been regarded for years almost in the same light as the Mediterranean has been looked upon by British holiday-makers. An analysis of the air traffic pattern for the Caribbean region shows that by far the heaviest traffic is between New York and San Juan, Puerto Rico, with substantial traffic also between San Juan and Miami. But many of the Caribbean holiday islands also have substantial air traffic links with North America, notably New York and Miami, while there are also direct services to a number of them from Toronto and Montreal, reflecting the growing Canadian interest in this holiday market."[35] The majority of all tourists in the Caribbean region have come from the United States: for example, in Jamaica in 1970 more than 85 per cent of all tourists, and in Barbados over 60 per cent, came from North America. The Caribbean tourism industry has clearly therefore been too dependent upon the North American market, which was acceptable while the steady flow continued. Two developments have however occurred which have slowed down this flow: first, the recession in the United States reduced the number of holiday-makers travelling abroad and, secondly, the American tourist is increasingly being tempted to visit Europe by cheap air fares and tour prices. Thus, although American tourists brought a good deal of economic development and progress to the Caribbean region, at the same time it has made the industry extremely vulnerable.

These developments are creating substantial changes in the organisation of the industry: "The Caribbean tourist industry is in a period of such rapid and widespread change that those who are not quick to adapt to ... [new] circumstances and attitudes may well find themselves in the bankruptcy courts before they realise what has happened. Those who do respond to the new forces in the area will doubtless continue to make a rewarding living.

In the 1950s and 1960s the Caribbean, and particularly the Commonwealth Caribbean, was wide open to any sort of commercial tourist deal. The small territories, most of which were only just emerging from colonial rule, almost fell on their knees to get outside investment. Hotels were put up under regulations which permitted long tax holidays, beaches were often alienated out of the public domain into the hands of private interests. The result produced some quick fortunes, but it also produced a legacy of bitterness and resentment. . . .

Parallel with and related to the exhaustion of the first wave of tourist speculation has come a move towards nationalism in the islands as they have graduated to independence or semi-independence. Appalled by the legacy they are inheriting, those governments who can stand out against the pressures of the tourist industry are attempting to introduce a measure of control on the hoteliers and tour operators. The times when private proprietors could buy up stretches of beach or impose a colour bar are disappearing. The local people are realising that they are masters in their own house."[36]

The Europe–Caribbean Tourism Conference

In May 1972 a tourism conference held under the auspices of the West India Committee met in London to discuss tourist development in the West Indies (including Bermuda and the Bahamas) especially in relation to the European market. The Conference provided an opportunity for Caribbean tourist officials and hoteliers to discuss the potential of the European market, which could be as rich as that of North America, and to make contacts with European tour promoters and airline representatives. It was hoped that a Caribbean–Europe Travel Association would emerge as the result of the Conference.

Hitherto, the West Indies were rather remote and too expensive for the majority of European tourists but now "the increasingly affluent European tourist is tempted farther westwards as transatlantic air fares are forced lower and lower, and the possibility of visiting a romantic and exotic part of the world is . . . possible."[37]

However, reaping the full benefit from growing European tourist numbers is not without its problems. As Irene Hawkins has said: "As long as the cost of the other half of the package, the accommodation, cannot be brought down to a more reasonable level, Caribbean hoteliers will not succeed in signing the big package deals with Europe which they need to fill their empty beds in the slack summer months and to put their industry on a broader and thus a stabler basis. Caribbean hotel prices are high because of high cost of land, construction, finance, food, labour and overheads. Some problems, like land costs, can only be tackled by the governments. Others can be solved only by the hoteliers themselves by thoroughly reorganising their hotels and managing them more efficiently. But there is little doubt that the scope for real economies is fairly limited in most of the existing hotels, because they are almost entirely geared to North American expectations and purses. . . . The real hope for providing cheaper accommodation at Mediterranean prices will almost certainly have to lie with newly built hotels, tailor-made to European requirements, with smaller, but nevertheless well-equipped rooms, public rooms of a less generous, but adequate size, fixed menus and a smaller but much better trained and supervised staff."[38]

"The years ahead will . . . call for a great deal more thought and planning by the governments of the area. The islands will have to decide just what they want to get out of the tourist industry and where they want tourism to stop. Too energetic promotional efforts by some of the smaller islands, the population of many of which hardly reaches five figures, will necessarily bring about a complete swamping of their characters by a massive influx of strangers. Do islands like Montserrat or Grand Cayman or Grand Turk really want that? And do the islands want to replace an unhealthy dependence on one agricultural crop such as sugar or sea-island cotton with an equally unhealthy dependence on the tourist dollar, pound or mark? The various governments will also have to grasp more firmly the opportunity that the influx of tourists gives for a revitalisation of agriculture. . . .

The other main subject which the various governments must attend to with greater enthusiasm is the planning and conservation problem. As more tourists tramp round the islands so the natural resources and the historic monuments, from Port Royal to Brimstone Hill, must be better cared for within the possibilities of each island's budget. Once these opportunities are grasped and these safeguards adopted there is no reason why the Caribbean cannot settle down to a trouble-free and harmonious development of the tourist industry. After all some of the islands have precious little else to live off."[39]

SOUTH AMERICA

A claim could be made that South America possesses more potential attraction for tourism than any other area in the world. It has some of the most magnificent and varied scenery, fine beaches, more skiing areas than Europe, generally attractive climatic conditions, exotic wild life, some very impressive archaeological sites, a wide range of interesting towns and cities and a rich culture which finds a unique expression in the arts and crafts. In spite of this, both domestic and foreign tourism in South America is under-developed and the area received a mere 1 per cent of the total global tourist arrivals (200 million) in 1972.[40]

Brazil

Brazil is not only the largest country in South America but it possesses, in terms of tourist attractions, "the lion's share of the continent's natural resources."[41] Brazil had, however, only 291,000 visitors in 1971 and an estimated 323,000 in 1972—less than 0·2 per cent of world tourist arrivals. Nevertheless, the industry is beginning to grow and "Brazil is beginning to recognise the useful role carefully controlled tourism could play in its declared export-oriented economic policy. Consequently it has embarked upon a programme to create the conditions necessary to obtain these benefits. Learning from the mistakes of other countries who opened the floodgates before having developed the necessary infrastructure, Brazil's development will be gradual and closely controlled."[42] Forecasts of foreign tourist arrivals were put at 442,000 in 1975 and at 900,000 in 1980, but whether these numbers and a progressive healthy growth will materialise will depend very largely upon successful promotion and massive investment.

Brazil did not have a domestic tourist industry which might have provided a base on which a foreign tourist trade could have been founded. "Domestic tourism did not really begin in Brazil until the 1930s, when the spa water resorts were created, and frequented by the wealthy."[43] The State of Minas Gerais possesses the largest number of spas, among them are São Lourenco, Caxambu, Cambuquira, Araxa, Lambari and Pocos de Caldes (*see* Fig. 42). Araxa is one of the largest health and tourist resorts in the continent and the Grande Hotel de Araxa is among the finest and most luxurious in the whole of South America. And there are other notable spas, such as those of São Pedro, Prata, Lindoia and Serra Negra in the State of São Paulo, and others in the States of Bahia and Santa Catarina. Though late and slow to develop, "the . . . decade [1960–70] has seen a rapid spread in domestic tourism following the growth of education and a middle class, improvements to the road system and the complementary expansion of the indigenous automobile industry, and stimulated by Embratur's [the government tourist development agency] promotional programme."[44] Embratur (*Empresa Brasileira de Turismo*) is making a determined effort not only to stimulate the domestic tourist industry but to provide amenities and facilities for the domestic market, reasonably priced hotels are being built and camping sites developed. The growth of a vigorous domestic industry is seen as a necessary preliminary to the development of a foreign tourist industry and it is believed that a number of advantages will accrue from it; as the Economic Intelligence

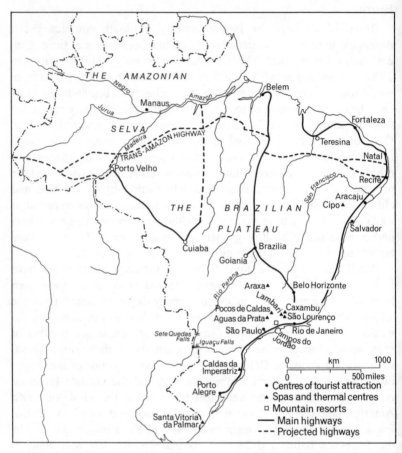

FIG. 42.—*Brazil: tourism features.*

Unit report on Brazil said: "(*i*) It provides finance towards the construction of tourist infrastructure for the world market. (*ii*) It creates jobs in tourism services in areas of high unemployment. (*iii*) It provides experience for staff before they deal with foreign tourists. (*iv*) It promotes labour movement from the rich to the poorer areas. (*v*) It protects the economy from the fluctuations of the international tourist market."[45]

Although the population of Brazil is over 95 million the average *per capita* income is low (about U.S.$400), but there is an increasingly large and influential middle-class in the urban centres and a small, rich élite. So far, it is these two groups who support the domestic tourist industry. It is also these two groups who provide the market for travel abroad. Precise statistics on the numbers of Brazilians travelling abroad are not easy to obtain, but international travel expenditure (excluding fare payments) was estimated to have risen substantially over the period 1965–70, from U.S.$30·8m to U.S.$160·3m. "The U.S. Department of Commerce sources suggest that the total number of Brazilian international air travellers in 1970 was 300,000 and that the total potential for international travel—to the United States, at least—is between one and two millions."[46] Relatively few Brazilians travel outside the Western Hemisphere, but 36,422 visited the United Kingdom in 1971. "More nationals of Brazil come to the U.K. than of any other South American country. Numbers ... [rose] dramatically over the 1960s. In fact, the increase in traffic from Brazil during this period rivals that of traffic from Japan. The 1961 visitor total of 4179 had risen to 13,237 by 1966 and in 1971 reached 36,422."[47] The majority of Brazilians visiting the United Kingdom come for pleasure rather than business.

Let us now turn to the foreign visitor tourist trade, and first try to account for its feeble development. One can point to three basic reasons (which apply equally to other South American countries).

(*i*) Both the United States and Europe lie some 4800 km (3000 miles) from Brazil and, therefore, travel costs are high; the air fares from these two major tourist-generating areas are still high on a mileage basis when compared with competing destination areas. The reason for this is that few charter flights for inclusive tours are sanctioned by the Brazilian authorities who place rather stringent conditions upon aviation.

(*ii*) Shortage of hotel or other kinds of accommodation has severely handicapped the industry. Rio de Janeiro has traditionally been the main point of entry for European and North American visitors and although Rio was formerly the capital there was until very recently a chronic shortage of hotel rooms. This situation was also typical of the other large cities and there was little or no tourist accommodation available in the states outside the "coffee region."

(*iii*) Seasonality has been a contributing factor. Because Brazil lies largely south of the equator, it has been regarded as a place to be visited in the northern winter; the fact that Brazil's climates are generally pleasant during the months of April to September seems not to be generally appreciated.

There are three main areas in Brazil offering possibilities for tourism development: Amazonia, the North-East and the Centre–South or heartland region of the country. Amazonia, with vast forests, exotic wildlife, Manaus, once the centre of the rubber industry, offers the excitement of probing what is still an inaccessible and little-known area. Trips up the Amazon have been provided by a British shipping line for very many years but the number of tourists taking advantage of this facility has always been small. At present, the two great drawbacks to tourist development are transportation and hotel capacity. "Most tourist accommodation is limited, at present, to the three main towns: Belem, Manaus and Porto Velho, and there are less than 30 hotels of more than adequate standard offering less than 1500 rooms in the whole region."[48] However, Embratur has supported the building of three additional hotels, two in Belem and the other at Manaus.

The North-East is a problem area in Brazil, where the development of tourism would bring, if not economic salvation at least very valuable economic help. The region possesses many natural resources which lend themselves to careful development: beautiful spacious beaches, perennial sunshine with high average mean temperatures (above 24° C (75° F)), splendid church architecture, local folklore and art and towns which have retained much of their colonial charm. Natal is strategically positioned to attract international tourists. Recife already receives some scheduled service flights from Europe, while the airport at São Salvador is capable of taking them with certain restrictions. However, the only states in the North-East where so far there is anything in the way of a tourist trade are Bahia (which had 20,000 foreign visitors in 1972) and Pernambuco. With the exception of these two states, tourist accommodation is very limited but Embratur is supporting new hotel developments throughout the region—six in Bahia, three in Pernambuco and nine in the three states of Alagoas, Piaui and Sergipe—while *Varig* (the Brazilian National Airline) has built an hotel in each of the states of Paraiba and Rio Grande do Norte.[49]

The Centre–South region is the most economically developed, most densely populated and most urbanised part of Brazil. Rio de Janeiro is the tourist capital of the country: not only is it the chief point of entry into the country but its magnificent situation, famed Copacabana Beach, architecture and monuments from colonial and imperial times, as well as some fine modern buildings, inevitably draw the tourist. Unfortunately, Rio's international airport leaves a great deal to be desired. There is a shortage of hotel accommodation; there were in 1973 52 hotels providing 5610 rooms and although six new hotels were projected to add a further 1675 rooms, the total provision was quite inadequate to meet the expected demand of half a million foreign tourist arrivals in 1974. "As the commercial centre of Brazil, São Paulo attracts the bulk of foreign business arrivals and, consequently, much of the hotel development there has catered for the business trade. Tourist hotels total 181 with 10,600 rooms and Embratur has supported the construction of twelve more offering an additional 2000 rooms."[50] Rio de Janeiro and São Paulo apart "the remainder of the Centre–South region contains a wide variety of tourist attractions ranging from Brazil's administrative centre and new capital, Brasilia, to the mountain resorts of the State of Rio de Janeiro—Nova Friburgo, Teresopolis and Petropolis—which are the weekend refuge of thousands of office workers from Rio and São Paulo."[51] The spectacular Iguassu Falls, on the border with Argentina and Paraguay, is a very popular tourist attraction, visited by 270,800 people in 1971.

Tourist numbers have increased at a modest rate from some 100,000 in 1962 to 291,000 in 1971, and business travellers have tended to predominate, for instance in 1971 only about one-third of the total visitors were primarily holiday-makers. Brazil has traditionally been dependent upon her southern neighbours, Argentina and Uruguay, for her foreign visitors and, as recently as 1971 over 40 per cent of the foreign tourist arrivals came from other South American countries.[52] European visitors counted for 28 per cent of the total and visitors from the United States 22 per cent. Table 67 gives a breakdown of the principal national groups visiting Brazil.

TABLE 67

Foreign tourist arrivals (1971) (000)

U.S.A.	55·6
Argentina	54·2
Uruguay	37·5
West Germany	16·0
Italy	12·7
France	10·8
U.K.	9·3
Portugal	8·8
Spain	7·6
Paraguay	6·6
Chile	6·4
Japan	6·2

Source: Anuario Estatistico, Embratur.

The chief mode of travel is by air: "over 72 per cent of Brazil's foreign tourists in 1971 travelled by air but from North America and Europe this proportion was significantly higher at 92 per cent and 87 per cent respectively."[53] Slightly more than half the South American tourists travelled to Brazil by road or rail in 1971.

Brazil's tourism account shows a very substantial deficit; although she received nearly $50m from foreign tourism in 1971, she spent over four times this sum on foreign travel. Brazil is anxious to cultivate the high-spending tourist markets of North America and Europe since the income from South American visitors is low.

Serious interest in international tourism dates from 1966 when Embratur was set up and the National Tourism Council (CNTur), a planning body, was established. As instruments of the Government, these two organisations have been concerned with carrying out the general policy of tourism development. Within the space of a few years much has been achieved but shortage of finance is a serious problem which seriously handicaps the industry's development. "The period from 1975 to 1980 is the time in which Brazil will shape itself as an international tourism centre. Before competing for the mass-market foreign tourist, Brazil needs more hotels, more resorts, more national parks and above all more trained staff."[54]

URUGUAY

Few people associate Uruguay with tourism, yet tourism ranks third as an "export." Some 17 per cent of Uruguay's foreign exchange earnings come from tourism. The tourist trade is not only an important source of foreign currency but a valuable service industry in a country which is primarily dependent upon pastoral and agricultural industries. Uruguay attracts about a quarter of a million tourists annually, although the visitors come overwhelmingly from Argentina. These are mostly the wealthier citizens of Buenos Aires who come to Uruguay to escape the summer heat. Convenient position is an important factor explaining this tourist trade and "Uruguay has little to offer the tourist from other nations."[55] However, between Montevideo and La Paloma, a stretch of rather more than 320 km (200 miles), Uruguay has some very fine beaches of clean white sand where the bathing is excellent. Montevideo itself has a whole series of beaches which extend along almost the entire metropolitan waterfront from Playa Ramirez to the Playa Carrasco at the eastern extremity. The fine highway, the Rambla Naciones Unidas, runs along the whole waterfront, joining up these beaches. Eastwards the coast provides a succession of small bays, beaches and promontories backed by hills and woods and here are the resorts of Atlantida, La Floresta, Solis, Piriapolis, Portezuelo, Punta Ballena, Punta del Este, Playa San Rafael and La Paloma. Punta del Este is "the largest, most fashionable and internationally best known of the resorts."[56] It has excellent bathing beaches and water-skiing, yachting and fishing facilities, golf courses and two casinos. In the woodland around the resort are thousands of villas and chalets, many owned by Argentinians. There are daily air services to and from Buenos Aires. Punta Ballena is a quiet, attractive residential resort.

CHILE

Tourism is already fairly important but there is great potential for tourism development in Chile. Some of South America's most beautiful scenery is to be found in the unspoiled, though increasingly frequented, Chilean–Argentinian Lake District. Blakemore writes that "already the Lake District is a major attraction for foreign visitors ... and ... as elsewhere in the republic, recent years have seen a great improvement of tourist facilities with government support. The region of the lakes, with ... superb volcanoes, and tree-clad slopes as ... a setting, is an outstanding area of scenic beauty, and tourism will undoubtedly contribute in the future a much larger proportion to the gross domestic product than the 2 per cent it provides at present."[57]

Portillo, in the Andes in central Chile, is already the greatest centre for skiing and winter-sports in the whole of South America. "The weather is ideal, the snow conditions excellent, the runs many and varied ... [and] the season is from June to October."[58] Portillo is easily reached from Santiago by rail, car or coach. Along Chile's extensive coastline are several resorts—Vina del Mar, close by Valparaiso, and its associated bathing resorts of El Recreo and Caleta Abarca, which attract large numbers of tourists from the capital and from Argentina; San Antonio, south of Valparaiso, which is a popular seaside resort; in northern Chile the attractive old town of La Serena has developed into a tourist resort and Los Vilos is a small, beautiful bathing resort.

PERU

Peru is a country of violent contrasts, both scenic and social. It has great potential for tourism, and 1971 saw a 17 per cent increase in the number of visitors over 1970. Table 68 gives a breakdown of the main visitors.

Air links to Peru from North America are fairly good and several shipping lines serve Peru. Internal communications, however, except by air, are difficult. The State Tourist Hotels and the high-class hotels are usually good. The main centres of tourism are Lima, the capital,

TABLE 68

Foreign visitor arrivals (1970 and 1971)

	S. America	N. America	Europe	Rest of the World	Total
1970	55,845	40,024	26,775	10,908	133,552
1971	66,204	43,986	33,133	13,054	156,377

which in spite of its tremendous growth still has many colonial buildings and plazas and fine churches; Cuzco, once the capital of the Inca Empire, rich in colonial churches and monasteries as well as extensive Inca ruins; and Macchu Picchu the lost city of the Incas which Hiram Bingham stumbled across in 1911. A number of coastal resorts are developing—not far from the port of Mollendo is the rapidly growing fashionable resort of Mejia, while on the coast near Lima there are a number of others with bathing and boating facilities.

ARGENTINA

Argentina ranks second in size and in population among the South American countries. Like the other A.B.C. countries, it is rather remote from the main tourist-generating areas and this is an important factor militating against tourism development. Indeed the numbers of Argentinians travelling abroad are greater than the number of visitors to the country. Recent figures of foreign visitors are not easy to procure but in 1966, 323,159 tourists visited the country and spent U.S.$52m. The number of Argentinians travelling abroad has shown a gradual increase in recent years, from 511,000 in 1968 to 550,000 in 1970.

Argentina has a number of important tourist attractions. The Iguassu Falls, which lie on the Iguassu River forming the boundary between Argentina and Brazil, have already been referred to. These surpass both Niagara and Victoria Falls in their grandeur and form the greatest scenic feature in the continent. The Falls can be reached by river, rail, road or air—there is a landing strip nearby—and already attract tens of thousands of visitors each year. The Lake District of western Argentina (comparable with that of Chile) lies in the Los Glaciares National Park. Here is a series of great lakes lying at the foot of the Andes in a majestic setting. Tourists go chiefly to the northern lakes and especially to Lake Nahuel Huapi, the largest. San Carlos de Bariloche is the best centre, with hotels of varied grading. There are many activities available, *e.g.* sailing, water-skiing, mountaineering, walking, horse-riding, golf, fishing and even hunting (though a special licence is needed), while in winter there is good skiing. The Lake District provides a popular holiday area for many Argentinians. Rather unexpectedly, Patagonia is showing signs of an embryonic tourist trade: "Tourism is opening up. There is now a steady, but still small, flow of visitors who travel by car to the tip of the Continent."[59] Another developing area is the North-West where there are some interesting and attractive colonial towns, *e.g.* Cordoba, Tucuman, Rosario de la Frontera, a popular resort, Salta and Jujuy. Tourism is "a new and important factor. . . . All travel agencies in Buenos Aires now sell ten- to fourteen-day package tours (mostly by bus) during the winter months to the provinces of Tucuman, Salta, Jujoy and Santiago del Estero, and all the year round to the Cordoba area. They have excellent plane services."[60]

Paramount among Argentina's seaside resorts is Mar del Plata, some 400 km (250 miles) from Buenos Aires. There are extensive beaches, fine plazas and numerous amentities, including a famous casino. "The normal population is 140,000, but during the summer months 1·5 million visitors stay there for an average of 14 to 20 days, for it is a popular resort with all classes."[61] Villa Gesell is a new resort of increasing popularity especially with young people and holiday-makers with children. Miramar is a summer bathing resort; Quequen possesses a first-class beach and good bathing; and, finally, there is Necochea, which ranks next to Mar del Plata in repute, with "about 100,000 tourists during the season, for the 24-km (15-mile) long beach is one of the best in the country."[62]

Most Argentinians who holiday abroad go to neighbouring countries, especially to Uruguay (200,000), Brazil (55,000) and Chile (1971 figures). The majority of Argentinians travelling overseas go to North America and Europe. In 1971, 27,494 Argentinians visited the United Kingdom and Argentina is the U.K.'s second most important market in South America, and "travel for non-business reasons is much more important than business travel and has been growing at a faster rate in recent years."[63] Rather more than half of Argentinian travellers abroad go by air.

NOTES

1. M. Peters, *International Tourism*, Hutchinson, 1969, pp. 34–8.

2. Special Article No. 8, "The Role of Tourism in Economic Development," *International Tourism Quarterly*, No. 2, 1973, reprinted from *Travel Research Journal*, I.U.O.T.O.

3. J. E. Navarrette, "Fast growth strategy for tourism," Special Supplement: Mexico, *Financial Times*, 4th June, 1970.

4. Navarrette, *op. cit.*

5. *South American Handbook*, ed. A. Marshall, 46th edition, 1970, p. 662.

6. Navarrette, *op. cit.*

7. *South American Handbook*, p. 672.

8. Navarrette, *op. cit.*

9. "The São Paulo Workshop—the Latin American Travel Market," Research Newsletter No. 7, Winter, 1972, p. vii in *British Travel News*, No. 40, Winter, 1972.

10. *Ibid.*

11. Navarrette, *op. cit.*

12. *Op. cit.*

13. *Op. cit.*

14. Navarrette, *op. cit.*

15. J. Rettie, "Puerto Rico," in *Latin America and the Caribbean: a Handbook*, ed. Claudio Véliz, Anthony Blond, 1968, p. 307.

16. R. C. West and J. P. Augelli, *Middle America: its Lands and Peoples*, Prentice-Hall Inc., 1966, p. 132.

17. West and Augelli, *op. cit.*, p. 132.

18. *Idem*, p. 221.

19. *Idem*, p. 222.

20. Quoted by Hugh O'Shaughnessy, "Islands adapt to new attitudes," in *Financial Times* survey "Tourism and the Caribbean," 1st May, 1972.

21. West and Augelli, *op. cit.*, p. 173.

22. C. Rickards, "The English Speaking West Indies," in *Latin America and the Caribbean: a Handbook*, p. 333.

23. West and Augelli, *op. cit.*, p. 173.

24. *Latin American Handbook*, 1970, p. 894.

25. J. H. Ferguson, "Cuba," in *Latin America and the Caribbean: a Handbook*, p. 251.

26. West and Augelli, *op. cit.*, p. 147.

27. *Idem*, p. 183.

28. *Ibid.*

29. *Bahamas*, Economic Report, National Westminster Bank, August, 1972.

30. *Ibid.*

31. *Ibid.*

32. *Ibid.*

33. West and Augelli, *op. cit.*, p. 226.

34. "Remarkable growth in the cruising business," Tourism and the Caribbean, Special Report, *Financial Times*, 1st May, 1972.

35. "Cheaper fares boost air travel," Tourism and the Caribbean, Special Report, *Financial Times*, 1st May, 1972.

36. "Islands adapt to new attitudes," Tourism and the Caribbean, Special Report, *Financial Times*, 1st May, 1972.

37. *Ibid.*

38. "Tempting the European," Tourism and the Caribbean, Special Report, *Financial Times*, 1st May, 1972.

39. "Islands adapt to new attitudes," Tourism and the Caribbean, Special Report, *Financial Times*, 1st May, 1972.

40. Regional Report No. 8: Brazil, *International Tourism Quarterly*, No. 1, 1973, The Economic Intelligence Unit, p. 29.

41. *Ibid.*

42. *Idem*, p. 30.

43. *Idem*, p. 37.

44. *Idem*, p. 37.

45. *Idem*, pp. 37–8.

46. "The São Paulo Workshop—the Latin American Travel Market," *British Travel News*, No. 40, Winter, 1972. British Tourist Authority, Research News Letter, No. 7, 1972, p. vi.

47. *Ibid.*

48. Regional Report No. 8: Brazil, *International Tourism Quarterly*, No. 1, 1973, The Economic Intelligence Unit, p. 30.

49. *Idem*, p. 31.

50. *Idem*, p. 32.

51. *Idem*, p. 32

52. *Idem*, p. 33.

53. *Idem*, p. 35.

54. *Idem*, p. 48.

55. J. C. Crossley, "The River Plate Countries," *Latin America: Geographical Perspectives*, ed. H. Blakemore and C. T. Smith, Methuen, 1971, p. 464.

56. *The South American Handbook*, ed. A. Marshall, 1970, p. 540.

57. H. Blakemore, "Chile," *Latin America: Geographical Perspectives*, ed. H. Blakemore and C. T. Smith, Methuen, 1971, p. 548.

58. *The South American Handbook*, ed. A. Marshall, 1970, p. 289.

59. *The South American Handbook*, p. 84.

60. *The South American Handbook*, p. 51.

61. *The South American Handbook*, p. 45.

62. *The South American Handbook*, p. 46.

63. "The São Paulo Workshop—The Latin American Travel Market," Research Newsletter, No. 7, Winter, 1972, p. vii, in *British Travel News*, No. 40, Winter, 1972.

Chapter XXI

Africa and the Near East

ONE of the most significant developments since 1960 has been the growth of tourism in Africa and the Near East. The total number of visitors, both arrivals from within the region and inter-regional arrivals, is still relatively small (7 million in 1972, compared with $2\frac{1}{2}$ million in 1965), but substantial growth is taking place. The countries dealt with here are all largely dependent upon long-haul traffic and more than half of the tourist arrivals come from regions outside the destination region. One can divide the region up into five main tourist areas: North Africa, the Levantine countries, West Africa, East Africa and Southern Africa, and Table 69 shows the numbers visiting each area and each country within these areas. Some of the other countries in the region, *e.g.* Ethiopia, receive tourists but numbers are small and do not materially affect the grand total for the region.

The countries of North Africa and the Near East have shared with other Mediterranean countries the great upsurge of tourism since 1960. Two developments above all—quick air transport and the introduction of inclusive tours—have speeded up their participation in the industry. But most are also developing countries and so have problems of infrastructure and provision of amenities. However, they see in tourism a partial and relatively speedy solution to their problems of earning foreign exchange, unemployment and regional economic imbalance. But the problems facing them should not be under-estimated: they are heavily dependent in most cases upon foreign investment, foreign imports and foreign expertise to help them develop and run their tourist industries and these leakages may result in a lower net return than anticipated.

The attractions in East Africa are of a rather different kind: a wildlife which is unique in the world and extensive areas of unspoiled nature (*see* Fig. 43). Distant from the great centres of tourist generation, the East African countries are dependent upon air transport and although services are for the most part adequate there is much room for improvement. While visitors from the European travel market are grow-

TABLE 69

Tourist arrivals in Africa and the Near East (1972)

North Africa		
Morocco	904,975	
Algeria	350,000 (est.)	
Tunisia	620,722	
Libya	123,634	
Egypt	416,433	
	2,415,764	2,415,764
Levant		
Turkey	814,015	
Lebanon	958,000	
Israel	549,172	
Jordan	209,186	
Syria	819,715	
	3,350,088	3,350,088
West Africa		
Senegal	51,031	
Ivory Coast	37,531	
Ghana	48,538	
Zaire	53,749	
	190,849	190,849
East Africa		
Uganda	80,363 (1970)	
Kenya	343,500 (1970)	
Tanzania	66,036 (1969)	
	489,899	489,899
Southern Africa		
Rhodesia	300,000 (est.)	
Republic of S. Africa	368,592	
	668,592	668,592
TOTAL		7,115,192

ing, the cost of travel to East Africa is still high and hence the East African countries have "to look for potential tourists only at individuals and families in higher income brackets."[1] North America is the other great generating region but "the vast and fast-growing American travel market has hardly been tapped seriously yet by the African countries";[2] indeed, out of the 5 million United States' residents who travel overseas only about 20,000 travel to Africa. Here, then, is a market to be assiduously cultivated.

The countries of West Africa have only a very poorly developed tourist trade but there are possibilities for considerable expansion. Rhodesia and particularly South Africa offer greater promise, although

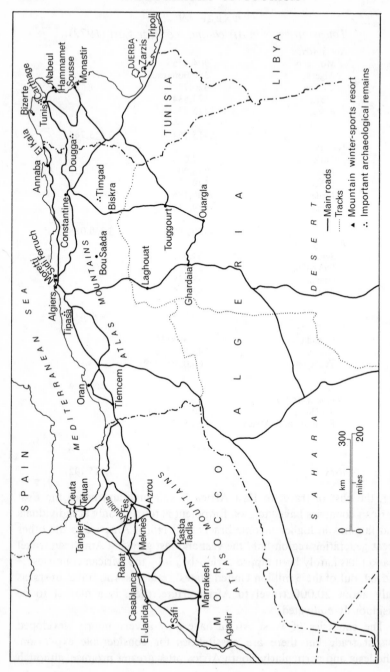

Fig. 43.— *Tourist centres in Morocco, Algeria and Tunisia.*

their tourist industry is likely to suffer considerably constraint until the problem of racial policy is solved.

THE ATLAS REGION

The Atlas lands of north-west Africa, the countries of Morocco, Algeria and Tunisia, comprise the region known to the Arabs as the Djezira-el-Maghreb or Island of the West. Surrounded and isolated by sea and desert, this mountainous area with its high plateaus and inter-montane depressions is very like an island. The peoples of the Maghreb are mainly either Arabs or Berbers although during French rule many immigrants from southern Europe settled in the region. French political control brought widespread and fundamental changes to the region and its impact produced great changes in the cultural landscape and in economic, social and political life. Morocco and Tunisia were recognised by France as sovereign independent states in 1956, Algeria in 1962. Since then all three states have been faced by many problems, and achieved different levels of political development and economic growth.

Each of the three countries has increasingly turned to tourism development to help solve some of its economic problems. "International tourism on a large scale in North Africa is of recent origin and essentially represents an extension of the southwards push from northern Europe towards the sun, which the southern littoral of the Mediterranean guarantees. The region's attractions, however, are by no means limited to sunny beaches, and include hot springs, ski resorts in the High Atlas and desert oases in the Sahara, while the architectural and archaeological legacy of the various cultures which have moved across it offers a completely different type of tourist activity."[3] The tourist trade was an asset of growing importance in Morocco in the 1950s and Tunisia developed an accelerating tourist business during the 1960s. Algeria came last, largely because of the disturbed conditions within the country, and it is only since 1970 that she has appeared on the scene as a tourist destination of any consequence. Table 70 shows the growth in tourist numbers for each of the three countries during the period 1966–72. It will be seen that the total number of visitors to the Maghreb more than doubled during this time and that in 1972 it was 1,876,000. Compared with Spain's total of 25 million in the same year the numbers are small, but the chances of rapid growth seem good.

With a view to consolidating and expanding tourism in the Maghreb, the three countries formed, in September, 1972, the *Confederation*

TABLE 70

Numbers of tourists entering the Maghreb 1966–72 (000) (*excluding visitors from cruise-ships*)

	Algeria	Morocco	Tunisia	Total
1966	127	424	219	770
1967	112	400	231	743
1968	137	481	330	948
1969	213	621	373	1207
1970	240 (est.)	747	411	1398
1971	315	823	608	1746
1972	350	905	621	1876

Source: *International Tourism Quarterly*, No. 4, 1972.

Maghrebine des Operateurs de Tourisme (C.M.O.T.); the objectives of this association were to sell North Africa to the tourist, to co-operate in market promotion and to pool their resources. This association "Would seem to be a natural and expected development between countries which share so close a geographical, historical and cultural heritage."[4]

Morocco

Morocco was, as we have seen, the first of the Atlas countries in the field of tourism. The industry began to grow in the 1950s and in the late 1960s the number of visitors had reached around half a million annually; in 1970 the total was nearly three-quarters of a million and this excluded cruise visitors, and the 1 million mark was almost topped in 1972.[5] Between 1961 and 1971 the growth rate averaged 17 per cent a year. The popularity of Morocco as a tourist destination for British tourists owed not a little to Sir Winston Churchill who on several occasions holidayed in Marrakesh and popularised the place. In 1967 Morocco obtained almost one-fifth of the value of its commodity exports from tourism; in other words, tourist receipts amounted to around £35m. In 1972 receipts were in excess of £60m. Thus tourism is already of some considerable importance in Morocco and with proper handling could become a very important factor in the economy. Until fairly recently Morocco was a destination for the wealthier tourist but with the expansion in mass tourism the country is likely to attract increasing numbers of middle- and lower-class groups.

Like all the Atlas countries, Morocco is a land where two worlds meet, and there are fascinating contrasts between old and new. It is, moreover, a country of quite startling physical and cultural contrasts. Running obliquely across the country is a series of high fold mountains, the Atlas ranges, within and around which are intermontane depressions and lowlands; the High Atlas, which culminate in sharply crested peaks over 3970 m (13,000 ft) in height, are snow-covered in winter and the Middle Atlas contain the "alpine" resorts of Ifrane and Azrou. Morocco has an Atlantic coast of over 800 km (500 miles): north of Essaourra (formerly Mogador) there are interminable stretches of sandy beach but to the south the coast is rugged and rocky and in places spectacularly cliffed. From the beaches, swimming is possible all the year round, for temperatures do not drop below $14 \cdot 5°$ C ($58°$ F) in winter. The chief Moroccan seaside resorts are Mohammedia in the north and Agadir in the south. New developments are taking place however as, for example, the Sun Dance holiday village on the outskirts of the old Barbary pirate port of Sale; this holiday village has been specially designed and built for the 18–35 age group. Morocco has many interesting towns offering attractions to the tourist: some, like Casablanca and Essaourra, planned and built by the French, are modern and others, such as Fez, Meknes and Marrakesh, old walled towns with narrow, labyrinthine streets and fascinating *souks* or markets in which are sold the products of various indigenous craft industries such as metal working, pottery, leather work and rug making. Morocco, too, has its Roman remains and not far from Fez are the ruins of Volubilis, once a great Roman city, while the country is rich in Moorish architecture. For the tourist who wants wild scenery, adventure and something different this colourful country has much to offer.

The chief sources of visitors to Morocco are the countries of Western Europe, especially France, the United Kingdom, West Germany and Spain, which together accounted for nearly half of the total visitors in 1971, the United States, and Algeria and Tunisia. Within the past year or two, there has been a rapid increase in the number of visitors from the United States. Table 71 gives a breakdown of the tourist arrivals in 1969 and 1971.

The methods by which tourists reach Morocco are fairly evenly spread, although slightly more arrive by air than by land or sea: in 1971 air $37 \cdot 1$ per cent, sea $32 \cdot 3$ per cent and land $30 \cdot 6$ per cent.[6] Many of the "land" arrivals are "trippers" coming by ferry from Spain who are making a brief visit to Tangier. In addition, Morocco receives 100,000 cruise passengers a year from liners calling at Moroccan ports. Seasonal variations in Moroccan tourism are still very apparent, with around two-thirds of the total visitors holidaying between April and September, although there is a perceptible, and desirable, growth in the number of winter visitors.

The Moroccan Government, through the Moroccan National Tourism Office (M.N.T.O.) has done much to develop the industry. In

TABLE 71

Tourist arrivals by country of origin

Country	1969	1971	Percentage of 1971 total
France	148,986	188,173	22·9
United States	94,125	136,744	16·6
United Kingdom	79,721	80,886	9·9
Algeria, Tunisia and Libya	48,665	70,062	8·2
West Germany	38,551	70,706	8·6
Spain	36,229	42,768	5·2
Scandinavian countries	31,599	20,741	2·5
Netherlands	23,227	24,481	3·1
Belgium	21,190	21,775	2·7
Switzerland	15,431	12,690	1·5
Italy	17,597	17,916	2·2
Canada	15,198	20,712	2·5
Others	50,487	115,600	14·1
	621,006	823,254	100·0

the country's five-year development plan £50m was allocated to tourism development. Possibly over-ambitious efforts were made to provide a total of 50,000 beds by 1972. But the M.N.T.O. has created tourist complexes along the formerly little-developed Mediterranean coast and established a chain of hotels in the Saharan oases of the far south. It has also done much to promote Morocco's ancient inland cities (Fez, Meknes and Marrakesh) as tourist centres. A network of camping sites to serve the motor tourist has been established along the Atlantic coast, a feature unique to Morocco and one, so far, not developed by either Algeria or Tunisia. Another point worthy of note and a matter in which Morocco differs from the other Maghreb countries, is the welcome given to United States' investment. Foreign investment by both the United States, and more recently by West Germany, has provided a valuable supplement to state investment.

What of the future? Morocco's Five-Year Plan (1973–77) clearly commits the country to an expanded tourism policy. The Plan lays down the guidelines and policy for further development—expansion of tourist areas, improvement of arrival terminals, provision of a further 50,000 beds, career training in the tourist industry, tax exemptions on goods imported for "tourist reasons" and government investment, provision of loans at preferential interest rates and encouragement of foreign investment.

The industry is turning increasingly to the mass tourist market and it is planned to receive 2·7 million visitors by 1977 (an annual increase of 21·6 per cent). It is estimated that the revenue from tourism will increase at the rate of 23·5 per cent a year; this means that in 1977 income from tourism will be around £150m.

Tunisia

Tunisia was a rather late and shy entrant into the tourist business but, perhaps prompted by the growing success of the Moroccan industry, the government decided in the early 1960s to embark upon the experiment. Following systematic studies of the potential demand and of the kind of visitors who would be likely to visit the country, an inventory of Tunisian tourism resources was made; this was then followed up by a planning programme. A projected ten-year development was formulated although firm plans for the first three years only were laid down. An important feature of the Tunisian plan was that it should be geared to regional development, that "tourism should benefit the maximum number of regions in the country in a balanced way."[7] Accordingly, the country was divided up into tourist zones and appropriate accommodation units programmed. However, it must be admitted that Tunisia has not the wide variety of natural assets possessed by either Algeria or Morocco and its tourism is based essentially on its beaches. It was agreed that the capital investment necessary for the establishment of the industry should come from both the public and private sectors, although it was realised that in the early stages the government would have to provide the bulk of the financial investment. Thus in the beginning the state provided approximately two-thirds of the finance, the private sector roughly one-third. "It is intended that this ratio should be reversed during the final stages of the ten-year plan. An important aspect of the Tunisian plan is that, of necessity, it began as a predominantly state plan and will end as a private one."[8] After ten years of conscious development, the Tunisians could feel gratified at the successful progress which had attended their efforts. The tourist industry is now beginning to boom and in 1971 Tunisia showed the fastest growth rate of any Mediterranean country. Between 1966 and 1972 the number of visitors trebled. In 1971, 600,000 people visited the country, an increase of 45 per cent over 1970. Estimates for 1972 were 820,000 visitors.[9] In 1972 British tourist agents reported a strong movement to Tunisia; for example, one firm, Hickie Borman, reported a 100 per cent jump in travel to that country. All the indications pointed to the fact that Tunisia is going to become increasingly popular as a tourist destination. Indeed there are plans to expand the industry in order to cater for $1\frac{1}{2}$ million tourists by 1976.

What are the factors behind this growth? Discounting the

promotional activities of the Tunisians, one can perceive a number of factors which have assisted expansion. First, tourists are becoming more adventurous and there seems to be a switch to medium- and long-distance holidays, especially where package tours are available. Secondly, many people are becoming a little tired of going to the same place, *e.g.* Spain, and of the growing crowds and congestion of some of the more popular centres. Thirdly, Tunisia has all the physical attractions of the Mediterranean tourist playgrounds—hot and abundant sunshine, spacious uncrowded beaches, warm blue seas. Fourthly, the country has a touch of the magic and mystery of another world, for notwithstanding Tunisia's progressive outlook and modern developments, old customs, traditions and ways of life remain.

Although Tunisia receives a considerable number of visitors from her immediate neighbours, Algeria and Libya—more than 50,000 in 1971—the overwhelming proportion of arrivals are true visitors from overseas. Table 72 shows the breakdown of tourist arrivals for 1961, 1965 and 1971. It will be noted that West Germany became the principal source of tourists, that France ranked second and the United Kingdom third. Of particular significance is the rapid expansion in the number of British holiday-makers visiting Tunisia, a result mainly of the growth of package tours. But, in general, it would seem that the phenomenal growth of Tunisian tourism is a reflection of the rapid increase in group tours and an I.T.A.L.–C.O.N.S.U.L.T survey in 1970 indicated that as many as 80 per cent of the arrivals were on group tours.[10]

TABLE 72

Tunisia: tourist arrivals 1961–71

Country	1961	1965	1971	Percentage of total (1971)
Algeria, Morocco and Libya	2,366	44,942	71,160	11·8
West Germany	5,414	22,388	153,828	25·3
France	15,923	34,494	132,360	21·8
United Kingdom	2,640	11,950	60,610	9·9
Italy	3,249	8,789	38,493	6·3
Belgium	762	4,477	26,501	4·3
Switzerland	1,925	12,603	25,841	4·2
Sweden	200	2,985	21,967	3·6
Netherlands	1,042	2,985	14,528	2·3
Denmark	160	497	10,061	1·9
Austria	842	2,653	8,565	1·4
United States			12,845	2·1
Others	5,587	17,077	31,447	5·1
	40,110	165,840	608,206	100·0

Source: Office national du tourisme et du thermalisme (O.N.T.T.).

The seasonal pattern of arrivals for 1971 was as follows: 11·6 per cent arrived January to March, 27·4 per cent April to June, 40·9 per cent July to September and 20·1 per cent October to December. Table 72 indicates that the great majority of visitors came from the countries of Western Europe and the seasonal pattern of arrivals closely reflected the incidence of public holiday periods in Europe. Winter tourism, however, is gradually gaining ground but more especially towards the end, rather than the beginning, of the year. The greater proportion of the arrivals, more than two-thirds, come by air, reflecting the predominance of the package tour holiday.

Gross receipts from tourism in 1971 were TD53·8m (£22m) and if deductions are made for the cost of imports used by the industry and for interest on capital loans then a net income of TD43m (approximately £17m) is left. Tourism brings in considerably more than any other major Tunisian commodity export and is the major foreign-exchange earner. It is estimated that the growth of tourism in Tunisia has resulted in generating, directly and indirectly, over 30,000 jobs (direct employment around 12,000).[11]

This sudden popularity of Tunisia has obviously brought its crop of problems, especially in respect of accommodation and catering. There was an acute shortage of hotels, so an hotel building programme was a priority. To help, the government offered tax rebates and technical assistance. Planning laws, however, are strict and there is a semi-official rule which says that no building must be higher than the tallest palm tree. The hotels, as Robert Troop pointed out, are usually discreet and handsome for "the Tunisians have a fine sense of architecture and colour, and the quality of building is high, using mainly local stone."[12] Hotels are usually one or two storeys high, with domed ceilings and Moorish arches. All hotels, restaurants and travel agencies are under the control of the *Société Hotelière et Touristique* which was established in 1959 with joint state and private capital. The company itself administers some hotels but has ultimate responsibility for all, although a private investor is not compelled to direct his investment through the Société. Another difficulty was the acute shortage of trained hotel staff but Tunisia has tackled this by establishing an hotel and catering school in Bizerta.

The northern coast of Tunisia is cliffed, rugged and rocky with virtually no natural harbours and there is little development here. South of Cape Bon, the shelving Sahel coast with its golden beaches was destined for tourism and here are several booming resorts, notably Hammamet, Sousse, Gammarth and Monastir. In the extreme south, in the Gulf of Gabès, lies the island of Djerba whose innumerable wells have turned it into an immense garden. Djerba has remained virtually unchanged since Ulysses named it the island of lotus-eaters but it is fast becoming popular as a tourist centre, and, for example, at Sidi Mahrès there are some fine modern hotels with varied amenities.

Villa and bungalow development for foreign tourists and residents has already been undertaken, and several major property schemes are already in hand. The government, however, is making determined efforts to discourage land speculation and to control development and so far there has been no undesirable seafront development; on the other hand, several areas have been zoned for tourist development and these include Nabeul and Hammamet on the northern shores of the Gulf of Hammamet and Sousse and Monastir (which possesses an airport) on the southern shore of the same embayment, together with the island of Djerba.

Algeria

Algeria was slow to exploit its natural beauty and rich cultural legacy for tourism and until the mid-1960s the tourist trade was negligible, in any event, the struggle for independence and the internal political difficulties immediately following made tourism impossible. Thus, compared with her immediate neighbours, Algeria was a late starter. "The turning point came," write Blake and Lawless, "in 1966, when President Boumedienne's government decided to stimulate tourism as part of an integrated plan for the maximisation of Algeria's economic potential. Algeria's 'Charter of Tourism' in 1966 proposed the expenditure of some £65m over a period of seven years, for the construction of facilities to cater for half a million visitors annually, and to train personnel to provide the appropriate services for large-scale tourism." Like other developing countries, Algeria needs foreign exchange, in spite of considerable earnings from oil exports. Tourism can also create employment opportunities; in Algeria one job will be directly created for every six new hotel beds, and many more indirectly. This is a particularly important fact for some of the less-favoured parts of the country, notably the south, where employment opportunities are severely limited. Thus tourism was to be an essential feature of regional economic development at least in respect of creating work. It was also hoped that tourism would help revive something of the rich Islamic culture of the Maghreb which the French did so much to erase in Algeria. The revitalisation of craft industries to furnish the new hotels, and the adoption of Moorish architectural styles in the construction of new buildings are part of the process of re-establishing Algerian cultural identity."[13] And to these factors one may possibly add the success of the growing tourist industry in Morocco and Tunisia; if it could thrive there, there was no reason why it should not succeed in Algeria. In the 1970–72 Plan a further substantial investment—2·5 per cent of the total planned investment—was put into tourism development.

S.O.N.A.T.O.U.R. is the state tourist organisation, which receives government financial aid. Private investment is not actively discouraged but, so far, the contribution of private capital to tourist development has been small, although once the tourist trade really begins to flourish there will almost certainly be no shortage of private investment. As can be readily understood, much of the increased hotel capacity is located in and around the city of Algiers. Some 32 km (20 miles) west of the capital are the resorts of Moretti and Sidi Ferruch, the former a well-established resort with all the usual amenities, the latter a small fishing village which is being transformed into a yachting centre. Each of these resorts has a new hotel, the El Minzah at Moretti and the Hotel Riadh at Sidi Ferruch, each built in Moorish style along the beach and first class in every respect. But fine, modern hotels are being built at many points along the Algerian coast, e.g. west of Oran and in the Annaba region near the Tunisian border.

Another specific governmental decision has been "to make substantial provision for beach holidays in the form of large 'complexes' including hotels and bungalows, together with sports and other recreational facilities. These represent a unique form of settlement designed for the twentieth-century nomad in search of sunshine and sand. This kind of tourism, focused on the beach, is most important in Algeria between May and October when average monthly temperatures on the coast remain generally above 18° C [64° F]."[14]

Although most of the developments so far have been in the coastal region, Algeria has not neglected the potential of its northern interior and the Saharan oases. "Winter sports can be enjoyed in the Kabylie mountains 100 km (62 miles) east of Algiers, which is also a favourite region for summer touring. There are many sites of historic and artistic interest such as the cave drawings of the Tassili, the extensive ruins of classical cities at Timgad and Tipasa and other ancient Islamic centres such as Tlemcen. Algeria's numerous hot springs, renowned for their curative properties since ancient times [exist] ... in five major centres where thermal baths and trained staff provide therapy for certain ailments."[15] But perhaps the most bold and enterprising development is the plan to promote Saharan tourism. Very few tourists have visited the oases of the interior but the Algerians intend to capitalise on the strange and fascinating Saharan landscapes, the quiet and solitude of the desert, the attraction of the oases and winter warmth and sunshine. "While continuing to cater for the short-stay visitor with a series of 'caravan-serai' or small hotels in Touggourt, Ain Sefra, Ouargla, El Golea, Timimoun and Beni Abbès, several luxury hotels are being built to attract longer-stay visitors. Those near completion or already open are at Biskra, Bou Saada, El-Oued, Tindouf and Laghouat [and] in addition to the hotel units mentioned, the Algerians plan to build three winter holiday villages for stays of 10–15 days in the Hoggar, Tassili and M'zab regions—the last near Ghardaia. These villages, capable of accommodating large groups of tourists, may well be the ideal form of arid-zone tourist development." [16]

All these developments anticipate a rapid growth in the number of tourists visiting Algeria: the Algerians expected around 400,000 in 1972. The number of beds available to international tourists in 1973 was of the order of 35,000—a quite spectacular increase compared with less than 5500 in 1966. The French and Moroccans have been the most important visitors so far, accounting for about half the total, but the West Germans, Americans and Tunisians formed other sizeable groups. The Economist Intelligence Unit's study of the industry has concluded: "In a country which is rapidly approaching economic independence and which is experiencing increasing industrialisation, tourism may always be expected to be a low-priority sector in terms of the overall economy. However, despite its late start, which at least enabled Algeria to benefit from the experience of its neighbours, it does appear that within the sector itself, growth is accelerating." [17]

Some of the problems associated with tourist development are, however, likely to be hard to overcome. First, Algeria's vast size creates difficulties although physical distances are to some extent mitigated by the good communications network that exists, a legacy of French rule; even so, as Blake and Lawless point out, it is not easy to combine a coastal holiday with a visit to the interior oases. [18] Secondly, the climatic conditions of the desert summer can be overpowering to those not acclimatised to them, although modern methods of air conditioning can do much to make the heat more tolerable. Thirdly, there is some evidence to suggest that the Algerians, relatively new to the industry, have not fully appreciated the needs of European tourists, *e.g.* sporting activities, social facilities, and that unless they cater for these needs the tourist is unlikely to pay a second visit. And lastly, "during the next few years the Algerians themselves will have to come to terms with two fundamental problems ... the apparent anomaly of luxury tourism in parts of the country where standards of living are low, and ... the problem of preserving Algeria's tourist assets from over-exploitation. Vigilance is particularly needed in the oases where a delicate balance has to be struck between providing facilities for tourists and preserving the 'other-worldliness' they go to enjoy." [19]

EGYPT

Egypt has for many decades attracted foreign visitors, as a country rich in antiquities—tombs and temples, obelisks and wall-carvings, not to mention the priceless art treasures discovered by the archaeologist (*see* Fig. 44). These antiquities—the three great pyramids of Gizeh, the Sphinx, the Temple of Karnak, the ruins of Luxor, the necropolis of Thebes, the Colossi of Memnon, and the gigantic carvings of Abu Simbel—are the principal attractions of Egypt, although the country has many other things of great interest to offer to the tourist, *e.g.* the mosques of Cairo, among the finest in the world, the citadel of Cairo, the museum at Alexandria, the catacombs of Alexandria and the Aswan Dam. Egypt has a Mediterranean and Red Sea coast, but these are not well-developed from the tourist viewpoint, although at Alexandria there is a 19-km (12-mile) long promenade looking over beaches which are thronged by Egyptians during the summer months.

The tourist industry, which in the early 1960s was gradually gaining momentum, was severely disrupted by the June 1967 war which cut tourist receipts by 50 per cent. After 1970 the number of tourists began to increase again—331,153 in 1971, 416,433 in 1972, a percentage increase of 25·8 per cent—and it was anticipated that the income in 1972 would roughly equal that in 1966. However, there has been a noticeable change in the visitor clientele: "the majority of visitors are now Arabs (44 per cent ... in 1966 ... 60 per cent ... in 1971)." [20] This reflects the growing prosperity, at least among some social classes of the Arab world, of the oil-rich countries. The comment has also been made that "the 'legalising' of the black market in foreign currency by providing a special premium tourist rate will add to Egypt's existing attractions of low prices and a long history, but the high hopes held for the industry could obviously be dashed by a resumption of hostilities." [21] This indeed occurred in 1973 with the Yom Kippur war, which caused another setback for Egypt's tourist industry.

Of the total arrivals in 1972, only about 50,000 visitors came from European countries and only slightly more than 20,000 from the United

Fig. 44.—*Tourist centres in the Near East.* The Near East is rich in Holy Places, Ancient and Classical remains, archaeological sites, Crusader castles, and these have been the traditional tourist attractions. Increasingly, however, "sun, sand and sea" are attracting visitors and many new coastal resorts are being developed, *e.g.* the holiday camp, club and hotel complexes at Antalya, Marmaris, Beirut, Aqaba, Eilat, Sharm el Sheikh.

States. The greater proportion of visitors came from the Arab countries, chiefly Libya 75,449, Sudan 31,011, Jordan 26,417 and Lebanon 23,549. The bulk of the visitors came by air (269,061), a fair proportion by road (71,989) and a few by sea (16,611). The average length of stay of visitors was thirteen nights, and total tourist receipts amounted to $65m.

Tourism is likely to become one of the main foreign-exchange earners in Egypt and the Government seems to be well aware of the benefits which an increased tourist industry could bring. A new tourist development plan was announced for the period 1973–82, indicating that Egypt intended to involve itself seriously in tourism promotion and activity. The objectives of the plan were "to raise tourist receipts to £E250m based on 5 million visitors a year and 50 million overnight stays at a cost of £E5 per overnight stay. To achieve this an additional 100,000 beds were needed, 30 per cent of the new accommodation being planned for the north-west coast and 10 per cent for the Red Sea area. The plan also envisaged the creation of 250,000 new jobs in the tourism sector, concentration of development into a few selected areas such as Luxor, Aswan and Abu Simbel, the Mediterranean coast west of Alexandria and the Red Sea coast, and the encouragement of foreign investment."[22]

TURKEY

Turkey has a wide range of attractions and opportunities for tourists—more, in fact, than most Mediterranean countries. Among these are a wonderful climate, at least on the Aegean and Levantine coasts, and a long season which in some areas extends up to ten months, splendid unspoilt beaches, mountains high enough for skiing resorts, numerous lakes on the interior plateau, the great city of Istanbul and archaeological sites and historic remains from a dozen different civilisations.

Turkey possesses a cultural blend of East and West which provides great attraction for many Europeans. In spite of these very considerable assets, tourism is not, as yet, highly developed in Turkey—the 1970 figure was around half a million visitors. Even so, there has been a very substantial increase in the number of visitors: from 94,000 in 1960 to 446,000 in 1970 (an increase of 374 per cent), and in the first four months of 1973 alone 238,000 arrived, representing an 36·3 per cent increase over the comparative figure for 1972; on the basis of that figure, the total for 1973 looked likely to reach a million. Turkey's hard currency gain from tourism in the first quarter of 1973 was almost $34m (slightly over 40 per cent more than the earnings in the corresponding period of 1972). Accordingly, receipts for 1973 as a whole looked likely to exceed $100m. Turkey has a great potential for tourism development and the indications are that it will become an increasingly popular holiday destination in the later 1970s. If the present rate of growth (around 18 per cent a year) were to be maintained the country could expect $3\frac{1}{2}$ million visitors by 1980.

A number of difficulties and problems face Turkey in its efforts to promote its tourist industry. First, Turkey is little known in the West. This unfamiliarity is due "not simply [to] an ignorance of the attractions of the country, but [to] a lack of knowledge about the allegiance of Turkey to the West and its rather odd position as a predominantly Asian and Moslem nation within Western economic and political alliances."[23] Secondly, Turkey's peripheral geographical position with respect to the most important tourist-generating countries of Western Europe has handicapped the growth of tourism. Until fairly recently most of the tourist arrivals came by road but it is a long haul from the countries of Western Europe by motor car and clearly the distance sets a limit to the numbers of visitors travelling in this fashion. The number of tourist arrivals coming by air has now overtaken those by road but until air fares are reduced travel costs impose an additional constraint upon the numbers of tourists who might like to visit Turkey. Thirdly, until the 1970s the major tour operators paid little attention to Turkey, concentrating their activities upon the Mediterranean countries of southern Europe and the Atlas Lands of North Africa. "Figures show that Turkey appeals at the moment to the rich, who need top-class accommodation, and the intellectual, student or teacher, who needs cheap accommodation and has long holidays. Medium-range accommodation, which could be most easily met by the private sector, is not much in demand."[24] It would seem that until the tour operators interest themselves more actively in Turkey and are prepared to organise package tours to that country the biggest potential market will remain untapped. Fourthly, on the domestic front Turkey is inadequately prepared to meet a large influx of tourists. Investment in infrastructure ... falls far short of what is required while there is a shortage of trained personnel to service the tourist industry. To a very considerable extent these deficiencies reflect the problem of scarce capital but they are also the outcome of imperfect planning: "Planning has been too optimistic and based more on hope than on fact."[25]

Table 73 shows the principal tourist-originating countries. These six dominated tourist arrivals over the five-year period 1966–70 and accounted for slightly more than half of the total number of visitors annually. It will be seen that West Germany and the United States are the most important sources, although France made an increasingly substantial contribution. The predominance of West Germany may be explained partly by the fact that the West Germans are great holidayers abroad and partly by the fact that there are substantial numbers of

TABLE 73
Country of origin of tourists

	1966	1967	1968	1969	1970
West Germany	51,863	47,373	45,403	56,674	64,425
United States	62,540	44,370	44,318	50,383	53,214
France	29,951	28,850	32,809	43,579	48,037
United Kingdom	28,377	20,526	23,927	28,202	32,236
Italy	19,003	13,462	17,959	24,390	24,121
Yugoslavia	36,881	54,083	17,295	32,068	26,501

Source: Ministry of Tourism, Ankara.

Turkish nationals working in West Germany, which has without doubt stimulated interest and curiosity in Turkey.

The tourists from neighbouring countries are numerically small but the figure is growing. However, only Lebanon, Syria and Iraq contribute in excess of 10,000 a year.[26]

The Turkish tourist industry suffers on three counts: first, the typical traveller is the professional man or the student and it appears that there are few family holiday-makers; secondly, the length of holiday stays is short—the average in 1970 from all countries was $5\frac{1}{2}$ days—but this is, without doubt largely explained by the distance of Turkey from the main tourist-generating countries; and, thirdly, the tourist season is short (half of the total being concentrated into the three months of July, August and September). The latest figures (July 1973) issued by the Ministry of Tourism strongly suggest that the season is being extended: for example, in the first quarter of 1973 238,000 tourists arrived, 110,000 of them in April.

The Government was slow to realise the potential of tourism and until the mid-1960s showed scant interest in the industry. However, in 1966 Turkey participated in the Estoril Seminar organised by O.E.C.D. and in the second five-year plan (1968–72) money was allocated for tourist development—promotion of the industry, hotel building and the development of tourist attractions.

One aim of the second five-year plan was to develop those areas of the country where tourism was already of some significance and could, therefore, be most easily exploited, *i.e.* the coastal regions of Marmara, the Aegean and Levantine Seas. Investment in these three regions was to be $67m, $84m and $112m respectively over the five years of the plan.[27] Ninety per cent of the total investment in tourism ($290m) was to be put into these coastal areas. This may be a sound policy decision, but it does mean that the interior plateau and the far eastern region, which has some exceedingly fine scenery, are being neglected; it also means that the benefits from tourism are going to those areas which from the economic point of view need them least. However, it must be appreciated that Turkey is a large country, that the industry is still small and that the availability of capital is restricted, hence emphasis must be placed on those areas which are likely to bring the greatest rewards. If the industry should undergo spectacular developments in the later 1970s then attention and development can be switched to other areas of tourism potential.

The Economic Intelligence Unit Report came to the conclusion that in spite of some far-sighted policies on the part of the Turkish Government, *e.g.* a concentration on the development of holiday villages, its concern to develop its rich heritage of archaeological sites and historical monuments, and its plans to rebuild Istanbul airport and improve the road network, insufficient investment was being ploughed into promotional activities and the hotel industry. It also came to the conclusion that any rapid growth of the tourist industry, at least in the immediate future, seemed unlikely and that it may be some considerable time before Turkey could attract substantially more visitors than at present. There is, however, one optimistic note: "Many observers see a close correlation between the development of tourism in Turkey and in Spain. The key in both countries is the package tour holiday, which puts the country within reach of the wider public in Western countries. It can be assumed that the Turkish economy will benefit from this as much as Spain does, but that it will not happen for some four or five years at least. The trend has to be seen over the longer term: perhaps fifteen to twenty years. This, far from being discouraging, should be seen as a period during which the country can prepare itself in terms of structures and, particularly, of personnel."[28]

LEBANON

In view of Lebanon's geographical position, climate, antiquities and Beirut's established reputation as a centre for pleasure, tourism was obviously ripe for development in the post-war era. Lebanon has many assets for a centre of tourism: a superb climate, fine scenery, a 240-km (150-mile) stretch of indented coast with good beaches and sea-bathing, mountains inland providing relief from the extreme heat of mid-summer, and high enough to provide skiing in winter, rich pre-historic and historic sites, a tradition of hospitality, a cuisine of a high order and plenty of night life, especially in Beirut, which alone has 120 nightclubs and 14,000 restaurants and cafés. Just outside the city is the Casino du Liban at Maameltain where there is gambling and a glittering floor show each night. Special mention should be made of Lebanon's archaeological and historic sites, since these are attracting large and increasing numbers of visitors. Byblos, one of the oldest towns in the world, has a wealth of remains—Egyptian, Phoenician and Roman. Baalbeck has a complex of splendid remains, including the temples of Jupiter and Bacchus (Baalbeck also mounts an outstanding musical festival each year). There are crusader castles at Sidon and Tripoli, the Palace of the Emir Shihab at Beiteddin, and Phoenician and Roman excavations at Tyre.

There are, however, two factors militating against Lebanese tourism. The first is its inevitable entanglement in the political and military Arab–Israeli dispute. Lebanon suffered a setback from the 1967 and 1973 wars. The Israeli occupation of the west bank of the Jordan meant that it was no longer possible to offer inclusive tours of Lebanon, Syria and the Holy Land. The fall in the number of American and European visitors was, however, partly offset by the increase in the numbers of visitors from the Arab countries (*see* Table 74). The National Tourism Council estimated that in 1974 visitors from Arab countries contributed two-thirds of its tourist revenue.

TABLE 74
Tourist arrivals (1968–72)

	1969	1970	1971	1972
Non-Arab visitors	317,379	288,097	396,601	470,977
Arab countries	459,756	534,250	619,171	577,176
Syrian visitors	810,050	863,832	1,241,625	1,232,903
TOTAL	1,587,185	1,686,179	2,257,397	2,281,056

Source: Conseil National de Tourisme, Département Recherches et Documentation, Lebanon.

Citizens of other Arab countries have for long been coming to the Lebanon. In pre-war days many were accustomed to spending part of the summer in the Lebanese mountains to escape the fierce heat, but since 1945 ever-increasing numbers have begun to visit the country. This is a reflection not only of the wealth derived from oil by the sheikdoms of the Middle East but also of the rapid emergence of a prosperous middle class in the region. After the war Lebanon made an attempt, with considerable success, to attract visitors from the West. "At one time there was a tendency for the Lebanese to under-estimate the economic importance of Arab tourism and to believe that the only important objective was to attract more visitors from the West. This is certainly no longer true today."[29] Even so, the Lebanese are vigorously promoting their country in the European market, and Middle East Airlines must carry much of the credit for the expansion of Lebanon's tourist industry. Middle East Airlines fly big jets every day from London and other major European cities to Beirut, and most international carriers, including British Air Lines, have Beirut on their schedules. The Arab visitors come chiefly from Jordan, Egypt, Saudi Arabia, Kuwait, Iraq, Sudan, Libya and Qatar (numerically in that order). The very large number of Syrian visitors include substantial numbers of tourists but also large numbers of workers and it is impossible to differentiate between the two. The chief West European visitors are French, British, West Germans, Italians, Swedes and Belgians (again in that order). Rather more than 92,000 U.S. tourists visited Lebanon in 1972. Whereas the non-Arab visitors go mainly to the resorts along the coast, the Arabs go mainly to the mountain resorts. While the Arab visitors in general spend less per day than Westerners, they tend to stay for longer periods and hence bring in a greater volume of tourist receipts. Another difference between the two groups is that the Western visitors tend to arrive throughout the year whereas the Arabs come mostly in the summer months.

The second factor which acts, or may act, unfavourably on Lebanese tourism is discussed in the Economic Intelligence Report: "The traditional Lebanese system of 'laissez-faire' economics and commercial freedom and tolerance of racial and religious minorities, which is doubtless the only one suited to its special circumstances, makes for a weak and unauthoritarian state. This has many obvious advantages, but it also means that the Government, which has less income than a handful of Lebanese millionaires, has great difficulty in planning and protecting the environment and in imposing the kinds of discipline on the ... Lebanese people which would protect the tourist from certain abuses. A little progress has been made towards controlling Lebanese taxi drivers, who have what is probably the most politically powerful trade union in the country, but their predatoriness is still internationally renowned. Some effort has been made to preserve a few outstanding examples of the Lebanese architecture which enchanted nineteenth-century travellers, but already the immense profits to be earned from real estate have led to the breakneck and often unsightly over-development of parts of the coastline and the western slopes of Mount Lebanon."[30] There are other problems too, especially the improvement and extensions in communications and the beach pollution which seriously affects the coast north of Beirut.

Short of some politico-military catastrophe, it seems fairly clear that Lebanon's future as a tourist centre is assured and that it has by no means reached the limit of its potential. New coastal developments, as at Jounieh Bay to the north of Beirut where a major tourist complex is emerging, and the expansion of the country's winter sports centres, as at the Cedars and Faraya, are indicative of the growing popularity of Lebanon and the faith in its future from the tourism viewpoint. Tourist receipts in 1972 were £L610m compared with £L566m in the previous year (9 per cent increase). When one compares the 1972 figure with that for 1966, when tourist receipts were around £L300m (nearly 10 per cent of the national income), it becomes obvious that tourism is now a thriving and major industry, in spite of the severe setback which this sector of the economy suffered from the 1967 and 1973 wars and the skirmishes with Israel since.

ISRAEL

Israel, like its immediate neighbours Lebanon and Jordon, has shared in the recent upsurge in tourism which has affected all the eastern Mediterranean countries. In addition to the common advantages—abundant sunshine, attractive beaches, varied scenery, historical monuments and art treasures—possessed by all the Levantine countries, Israel has the compelling "spiritual appeal of a country that contains . . . Holy Places of three monotheistic religions."[31] Jerusalem in particular is a city sacred to Arab, Christian and Jew alike. Pilgrimages to the Holy Land, as was noted in Chapter I, have occurred for nearly two thousand years but these travellers were rather differently motivated to the modern tourist, although many of the latter, it is true, still come to pay homage in the Holy Places. There are, however, other more secular motivations: some come to visit their families who have settled in Israel, others to visit their Jewish ancestral homeland, yet others to see the social and economic experiments carried out by the Jews, and yet others who out of sheer curiosity come to see what miracles the Jews have worked since the state of Israel was established.

Until 1960 Jews from other parts of the world formed the majority of the tourists visiting Israel. In 1960 the number of visitors first reached 100,000. Five years later the number had trebled. The Six Day War in June 1967 brought a setback but the outcome of this brief but decisive struggle gave an added impetus to the tourist industry, especially since the reunification of Jerusalem (formerly divided between Israel and Jordan) put all the Holy Places in Jewish hands. By 1971 the number of visitors had increased to 477,136; in 1972 the number totalled 549,172, a 15 per cent increase over the previous year.

The figure of 549,172 in 1972 is that given by the I.U.O.T.O. Technical Bulletin, February, 1973, but according to the London Israel Government Tourist Office the number of visitors in 1972 was 727,000 overseas visitors plus 160,000 visitors from across the border.[32] Tourists from the United States and Canada took first place, totalling 310,000 (43 per cent of all overseas traffic). Heading the list of visitors from Europe were the British (66,500), while the French were second (65,000), closely followed by the West Germans (43,000).

The outbreak of the Yom Kippur war in 1973 severely disrupted this promising upward trend. Income from tourism which in 1966 was in the region of $60m (exclusive of travel fares) is now in excess of $200m ($213m in 1972), a valuable source of much-needed foreign currency and a vital factor in improving the country's balance of payments.

Israel's relatively late arrival on the tourist scene can be explained partly by its relative remoteness, compared with places such as Tunisia, Greece and Cyprus, from the principal tourist-generating countries, partly by high travel costs and high cost of living in Israel, and partly by the late start made in developing tourist amenities. But once Israel became alive to the potential and rewards of tourism, she employed United States consultants to prepare her first tourism plan.

The decade 1960–70 saw a change in the tourist clientele: whereas up to 1960 approximately half of the visitors (frequently Jews) came from North America, more especially the United States, by 1965 the tourists from this region had dropped to 35 per cent of the total; on the other hand, the European share increased from 36 per cent in 1960 to 52 per cent in 1965.[33]

Another significant change relates to changing motivation: although Israel still continues to attract Christians and Jews in large numbers who are essentially spiritually motivated and come to visit the Holy Places, a large proportion of the tourists come for no other reason but a holiday: the increasing number of British, French, German and Scandinavian visitors suggests that Israel is now coming to be thought of as a new and unique tourist attraction. The majority of these visitors, who number some 40 per cent of the total, come on inclusive tours. Yet another aspect of Israel's changing image as a tourist country is its growing popularity as a conventions centre: "Not unexpectedly, in view of the country's achievements in the fields of science and technology, medicine and agriculture, Israel has become increasingly popular as a venue. . . . In 1972 the country was host to 59 conventions attended by some 38,000 overseas participants; more than 70 conventions have been announced for this year [1973], which are expected to bring an estimated 50,000 foreign delegates into the country."[34]

The average duration of tourist stay—seventeen days in 1972—is rather longer than is usual in the Levantine countries and is to be explained largely by the fact that many of the Jewish visitors, who form a fairly high proportion of the total, combine their holiday with visits to friends and relatives. Table 75 shows the average duration of tourist stays in 1967.

TABLE 75

Average duration of a tourist's stay (1967)
(one-day Mediterranean cruises not included)

Duration	Percentage
2–5 days	26·4
6–9 days	15·8
10–19 days	25·8
20–29 days	13·7
1–2 months	10·1
Over 2 months	8·2

Source: Yehuda Karmon, *Israel*, p. 137.

The foremost attraction, of course, is the city of Jerusalem: almost all visitors go to the Holy City. Before unification the town was divided into the Arab or Jordanian sector and the Israeli sector. The Arab sector, though much smaller, had twice as many hotel beds as the Israeli sector—"in 1967 West Jerusalem could offer 31 recognised tourist hotels with 1092 rooms, while East Jerusalem contained 35 hotels with 1894 rooms."[35] The reunification of Jerusalem is bound to have a beneficial effect on Israeli tourism: indeed, this has already proved to be the case. But there are many Biblical sites—Bethlehem, Jericho, Nazareth—which also attract the tourist. In addition, there are Crusader castles and churches and Arab palaces and mosques. "Two towns holy to the Jews ... have been repopulated and both have developed as a tourist attraction. Tiberias, [182 m] (600 ft) below sea-level, on the shore of the Sea of Galilee is a winter resort and contains hot springs which were famous already in the Roman time. Safed, [766 m] (2500 ft) above sea-level among wooded hills, is a summer station."[36] Elat, Israel's port on the Gulf of Aqaba, is also being developed as a popular tourist centre. Along the 187-km (117-mile) Mediterranean coast there are holiday resorts such as Ashkelon, Nahariya, Caesarea and Netanya, while holiday villages are springing up, *e.g.* the villages of the French Club Méditerranée, which are providing a new kind of free, popularly priced tourism, and the Caravan Village at Ophira (Sharm-esh-Sheikh). Barring further military conflict, it would seem that tourism will continue to expand and bring very real and valuable economic advantages to the country. According to Karmon "about 20,000 people are directly employed in the industry. It is not only a source of income but also an important factor of development, leading to the construction of new roads, water supply and recreational facilities. In some development towns like Zefat (Safed), Tiberias and Elat it has become already the strongest economic factor."[37]

The rapid growth in tourism has presented Israel with an accommodation problem. According to Karmon the number of recognised tourist hotels was 229 in 1967; these provided some 10,000 rooms.[38] The number of tourists at that time was around 300,000, but since that time the volume of tourists has at least doubled. Accordingly, there has been a boom in hotel building and in 1973 alone it was intended to increase hotel rooms by 4000, bringing the total up to 20,000. However, it should be noted that in addition to the hotel accommodation (which, incidentally, is mostly concentrated in Tel Aviv and Jerusalem) there are many youth hostels providing some 5300 beds, camping sites providing a further 2300 beds, while sixteen of the 240 kibbutzim have guest houses which can offer accommodation. Israel anticipated that 850,000 visitors would arrive in 1973, the twenty-fifth anniversary of its national foundation, and if they had come then every bed would have been occupied; however, the outbreak of the Yom Kippur War badly upset these calculations.

The money invested in tourism development has been very substantial. In hotel construction alone some $100m has been invested during the five years 1965–70. About half of this was provided by the Tourist Industry Development Corporation of the Ministry of Tourism in the form of grants and favourable long-term loans; the remainder came from foreign investment, largely American, French and German, which was encouraged by the Government by inducements such as tax exemptions and exemptions on import duties. The success of these measures may be gained from the fact that "in 1972 the hotel industry attracted 27 per cent of all foreign investments in Israel."[39]

JORDAN

Jordan is a country of strictly limited resources and since it achieved national sovereignty it has depended upon substantial foreign aid. Notwithstanding its poverty, the country has made great efforts in agricultural development, mineral exploitation and light industry and its seven-year development plan (1964–70) seemed to promise that eventually Jordan might come to have a self-sustaining economy. In this economic development, tourism played a valuable role and its significance was growing yearly. In 1967, as a result of the Arab–Israeli War, Jordan's progress was severely interrupted and set back: the West Bank Territories were lost to Israel, the economy had to bear heavy military costs and there was the legacy of a formidable refugee problem.

Tourism was practically destroyed overnight as a result of the loss of Jordan's sacred and historic sites in the Holy Land, and collapse of the industry was a severe blow to the national economy, for with a large balance-of-payments deficit the country naturally placed great importance on the valuable foreign exchange brought into the country by tourists. During the 1960s the number of tourists had been growing steadily and in the year prior to the war (1966) had reached 650,000, double the figure for 1963. Income from tourism in 1966 was JD11·3m (£14·12m). With improved communications and the building of new hotels, the Jordanian Government had hoped to reach a target of 827,000 visitors by 1970. The war and then the period of internal strife which followed led to a disastrous slump in the number of tourists and in tourist receipts: in 1971, the number of visitors dropped to 257,000 and the income from tourism to JD3·1m (£3·9m).

Jerusalem, Bethlehem and Jericho were the particular attractions lost, and it was realised too late that too much reliance had been placed on these Holy Sites (82 per cent of all hotel accommodation was concentrated on the West Bank), while there were insufficient technical and financial facilities available at the planning, promotional and administrative level. East Bank facilities were very limited and accommodation was largely restricted to seventeen classified hotels in Amman, the capital, and two in the Red Sea port of Aqaba, and to a number of "rest houses" only three of which included accommodation.

Jordan still has a number of important tourist attractions, however, and is now turning her attention to developing these more actively. The Ministry of Tourism and Antiquities has begun a vigorous promotion of the East Bank sites which formerly had been neglected and under a three-year development plan begun in 1972 some £6m was to be spent on developing the East Bank sites. It had been estimated that private investment would also contribute a further £4m. *Alia*, the Royal

Jordanian Airline, is also assisting in this promotion: it has services with many larger European cities, *e.g.* London, Paris, Frankfurt, and arrangements were made (in conjunction with Belgian *Sabena*) to start charter flights to bring United States' visitors to Jordan. In 1971 the airport at Aqaba was enlarged to receive jetliners. The war, in 1973, however, brought further setbacks to Jordanian tourism planning.

Jordan has been called "an open-air museum" since it possesses magnificent remains of interest to students of archaeology and history and to tourists generally. Foremost is Petra, the ancient Nabataean city, "lost" for several hundreds of years until it was rediscovered in 1812. It is approached through a spectacular 2-km (1½-mile) long defile. Petra's tombs and temples are carved out of solid multi-coloured rock tinted like watered silk. Jerash, a Graeco-Roman city, recovered from the desert sands, has a huge forum approached by a mile-long colonnaded avenue. Madaba has extensive and well-preserved mosaics, the floors of its early Christian Churches, while in the desert, especially around Amman, are several Ommayad castles. The austere but impressive desert scenery of the Wadi Rumm with its "mountains of the moon" is awe-inspiring and fascinating; prior to 1967 the tourist could engage a camel-back tour of the valley and stay overnight in a Bedouin tent. This camel safari lapsed after the war. In the vicinity of Aqaba in the far south of the country more orthodox tourist developments have taken place along the coast: here are good hotels and a complete tourist complex, designed by the Greek town-planner Doxiadis, and plenty of facilities for water sports, *e.g.* water skiing and scuba-diving. Another new planned development is a national park and wildlife reserve based on the desert oasis of Azraq east of Amman, while on the Dead Sea coast two new tourist sites are already well under way. As a result of all these efforts and developments to resuscitate and promote tourism receipts had reached some JD9m by 1973; it is hoped that the target receipts for 1975 will reach JD10m (£12·5m); even so, this total will still be less than that for 1966.

WEST AFRICA

Tourism is not well developed in West Africa and few countries, apart from the Ivory Coast, appear to have given much thought to the possibilities of tourism development. It will be seen from Table 76 that the number of visitors is low, and perhaps most of these are business visitors.

TABLE 76
Visitors to selected West African
countries (1972)

Senegal	51,031
Ivory Coast	37,531
Ghana	48,538
Zaire	53,749

All the countries of West Africa are "developing" countries and are therefore confronted with a shortage of foreign exchange and have consequent difficulties in financing their economic development. Since tourism is an important foreign-exchange earner, it might in every sense pay to explore their tourist potential and develop a tourism industry. A few years ago, distance from the tourism-generating markets was an important handicap but nowadays distance counts less and less; places such as Fiji and the Seychelles lie thousands of miles from their main sources of tourist supply, yet they have experienced a rapid growth rate. Furthermore, for some countries "inaccessibility can be an asset in securing low-volume/high expenditure tourism development."[40]

If the West African countries could develop some sort of joint promotional organisation such as that established by the Indian Ocean Islands or the Organisation of Central American States which set up a permanent secretariat for tourism (S.I.T.C.A.) to conduct a regional programme for promotion and publicity, it could well speed up their development of tourism. As Popovic has emphasised, effective travel promotion is an expensive business, especially for poor countries, and a joint organisation not only reduces costs to individual countries but is able to mount more effective campaigns; also, in bringing as large a number of tourists into the region as possible all of the countries in the region are likely to benefit.[41]

One major tourism development—the Riviera Project—is taking place in the Ivory Coast down the coast from Abidjan, the capital. "Total expenditure on the project could eventually rise to CFA Francs 5500 billion, but at present the finance does not seem to be available. However, there seems to be no urgency to have the scheme completed since shorter-term projects are already returning good dividends."[42] Although in 1973 foreign-exchange receipts in the Ivory Coast came to only around CFA Francs 333m, it is anticipated that by 1980 these should have risen to CFA Francs 1500m.[43] So far the tourist industry has concentrated upon the upper end of the tourist market but this has not proved to be particularly successful.

While tourism growth both in the Ivory Coast and elsewhere in West

Africa might bring some economic advantages, *e.g.* foreign exchange, additional employment opportunities, etc. the benefits must be measured against the high costs of infrastructure and capital goods needed to establish and expand the industry and the increasing costs of imported food and drink. Such leakages, as the industry in the Caribbean has shown, substantially reduce the net benefits which accrue from tourism. Clearly, it would be sensible for those countries in West Africa contemplating tourism development to call in specialist consultants, as Israel did, to explore the soundness of tourism development and to prepare development plans.

EAST AFRICA

Until the late 1950s only the more adventurous, and more affluent, members of society, along with the European settlers in Uganda, Kenya and Tanzania, were able to enjoy the attractions offered to the tourist by East Africa. The main factors inhibiting realisation of the considerable tourist potential of the area were its distance from the main areas of demand, the high cost of transport and the inadequacy of hotel accommodation and other essential tourist amenities. During the 1960s, however, largely because of government support and participation, appreciable development took place and East Africa has become a major growth point in international tourism since the beginning of the 1970s.

The governments of Uganda, Kenya and Tanzania, recognising the potential of their natural resources and appreciating the benefits which might accrue, set about planning, developing and promoting a tourist industry. Each of the three countries has established its tourist promotional organisation to guide and promote tourist development. The governments have encouraged private investment and provided public money for the building of adequate accommodation facilities, *e.g.* new hotels and safari lodges; they have sought to provide better transport facilities by, for example, building airports and improving existing airfields to enable international jet air traffic to bring tourists to East Africa, and beginning the construction and improvement of roads; and they have established tourist offices in overseas countries to carry out promotional and marketing activities.[44]

East African tourism, prior to 1965, was promoted by the East African Tourist Travel Association, a voluntary body which received financial and other support from state and private organisations. After 1965 each of the three East African territories set up their own tourist offices, *viz.* the Uganda Department of Tourism, the Kenya Tourist

Development Corporation (K.T.D.C.), and the Tanzania National Tourist Board which subsequently was absorbed by the Ministry of Information and Tourism. The Department of Tourism in Uganda, though under ministerial jurisdiction, is responsible for tourism and development in that country. The K.T.D.C. in Kenya has very wide responsibilities and functions which include even the protection and preservation of wildlife. In Tanzania, the Ministry of Information and Tourism, which formerly concerned itself primarily with policy formulation, has widened its scope and it is now responsible for all aspects of the tourist industry—strategy, organisation, marketing, etc. although the Tanzanian Tourist Corporation (T.T.C.), set up under the control of the Ministry, provides ". . . the requisite organisation of the planning, financing, operation and expansion of the hotels and tourist transport sector."[45]

It will be clear from this that the three East African countries are anxious to develop tourism. However, one point should be made: "their individual promotional activities must, whether intentionally or not, place them in direct competition with each other since they all offer . . . in varying degrees of sophistication and exploitation, the same types of attractions."[46] It seems equally clear that careful and imaginative administration and management can do much to advance the industry: "Prior to the reorganisation of the bodies with responsibilities for tourism in 1969, Tanzania was the poor relation to Kenya in terms of the numbers of tourists received and in the amenities provided. Since . . . , efforts . . . have been particularly noticeable and successful."[47]

In Kenya, the capital Nairobi, the Mount Kenya area, the Southern Game area and the coastal resorts of Mombasa and Malindi are the chief tourist areas. Nairobi, a fine city of over half a million inhabitants (1970), served by an international airport, is the main centre of tourist attraction (see Fig. 45); slightly more than 90 per cent of all tourists visit Nairobi which has some fifty hotels with, in 1970, 4456 hotel beds (some two-fifths of all the hotel beds available in Kenya). Nairobi has good shopping facilities, restaurants, cultural and sporting facilities but is far removed from the country's other main attractions, e.g. game parks, wildlife reserves and the coast. On the other hand, these are fairly easily accessible from Nairobi since it is the hub of the communications network in Kenya. Some 96 km (60 miles) north of Nairobi is Mount Kenya within the Mount Kenya National Park while not far away to the west and east respectively are the Aberdare National Park (famous for the Treetops Hotel) and the Meru Game Reserve. In south-east Kenya is the Southern Game area which comprises the Tsavo National Park

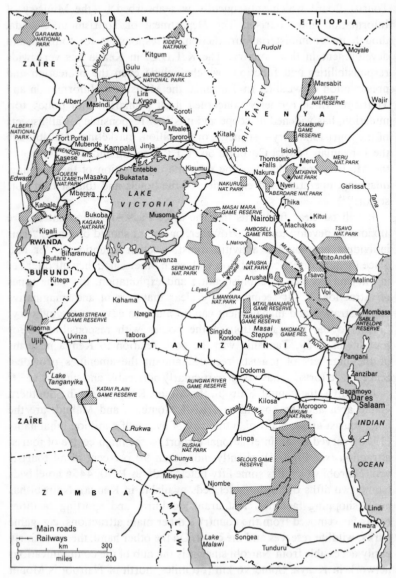

Fig. 45.—*National Parks and Game Reserves in East Africa.*

(with 20,000 elephants) and the smaller Amboseli National Park. The Tsavo National Park is conveniently situated, for it lies roughly midway between the coast and Nairobi, the main road and railway between Mombasa and the capital runs through it, and there are a number of hotels and safari lodges. Mombasa and Malindi are the two chief coastal resorts, and there are considerable stretches of coast near by which are capable of development. There are some fifty hotels in the coastal region with the majority concentrated on Mombasa Island. Such amenities as shopping facilities, aquatic sporting facilities and local tour facilities are well catered for, but there is a paucity of night-time entertainment. Already about one-quarter of all the tourists visiting Kenya include a stay at the coast and since the numbers of visitors should increase substantially with the development of package holidays, a more sophisticated tourist infrastructure could with value be introduced. Accommodation capacity in the game areas, along with poor roads, seem to have hampered the expansion of the tourist traffic. During the past decade tourism has developed rapidly and become a major source of foreign exchange generating around £30m annually since 1972. The longer term prospects for tourism remain favourable and the government is investing £10m in the industry to improve publicity and facilities.

Uganda has several areas offering attraction to tourists. Lake Victoria is obviously a major source of attraction for sailing and fishing although other facilities and amenities are somewhat restricted. The extinct volcano of Mount Elgon in eastern Uganda is an attraction; there are hotels at Mbale and an airstrip at Soroti. Climbing, fishing and an interesting mountain flora are the main attractions in the Mount Elgon area. Of the three national parks in Uganda, the Kidepo Valley in the extreme north is least developed from the tourist point of view: it is somewhat remote and of limited accessibility. While there are a number of self-service lodges and safari excursions are organised, other facilities and amenities are practically non-existent. The premier tourist attraction in Uganda is the Murchison Falls in the national park. The Park offers varied attractions, *e.g.* the Falls, fine scenery and a rich wildlife, and attracts about one-third of all the tourists who visit the country, and it is reasonably well served by communications and safari lodges. In the south-west of Uganda is the Queen Elizabeth National Park, with the Ruwenzori Mountains and the Bujumbura volcanoes. It is an area of splendid scenery and wildlife and there are mountaineering, hunting and fishing attractions. The Park receives about a quarter of Uganda's visitors. As in the Murchison Falls National Park, there is reasonably adequate accommodation and transport facilities but, again, little in the way of a developed tourist infrastructure. The current political régime is likely to antagonise would-be tourists and certainly British tourists.

Tanzania is the largest of the three East African countries but in the past was the least developed. Though slow to realise its tourist potential, rapid and successful strides have been made since 1970. The coastal area, including Dar-es-Salaam, the northern parks near to and adjoining the frontier with Kenya, and the parks and game reserves in the southern part of the country are of tourist value. Since 1969, the beginning of Tanzania's second Five Year Development Plan, tourism has gradually expanded and in 1973 over 100,000 tourists visited the country bringing revenue earnings of around £8m.

Table 77 shows the growth in the volume of tourists to the three East African countries. Even greater growth might accrue if more effective

TABLE 77

Foreign visitors in East African countries (000)

	1967	1968	1969	1970
Kenya	143·0	262·0	293·4	343·5
Tanzania	28·3[1]	34·6[1]	66·0	
Uganda	38·2	53·9	73·9	80·3

1. Excludes visitors from Kenya and Uganda.

promotion were carried out. Popovic strongly advocates the advantages: "joint promotion is the best way for small countries and countries at the incipient stage of tourism to be noticed on overseas travel markets and to attract tourists from there." If the East African countries are not to be handicapped they "should establish an efficient co-operation in travel promotion on overseas markets and create a permanent [joint] organisation."[48] Although inherently there is an element of competition between the three countries, visitors to East Africa, especially if they have travelled long distances, are likely to visit adjacent countries if only for short visits or on a stop-over basis; therefore, the promotion of the whole geographical area would seem sensible and perhaps be the most efficient way to attract overseas tourism.

THE REPUBLIC OF SOUTH AFRICA

In spite of its size and attractions, South Africa does not have nearly as many foreign tourists as the European countries, although those who do visit the Republic usually stay for a considerable period, being not merely in transit as is so often the case in European countries. One obvious reason for this is that South Africa lies far removed from the main centres of tourist supply. Similarly, because the Republic is situated a considerable distance from the tourist countries, the people domiciled there mainly prefer to take their holidays in their own country.

As a result of the introduction of jet airliners which are capable of transporting several hundred people on one flight and which reduce travelling time considerably, South African tourist traffic has great potential for expansion. South Africa has much to offer: abundant sunshine, blue skies, magnificent scenery, extensive beaches, unique wild life, good food and hospitality. One big advantage is that South Africa can offer sunshine during the European or North American winter.

Among South Africa's greatest attractions are the game reserves, such as the Kruger National Park and the Umfolozi Game Reserve in Natal (*see* Fig. 46). In these parks the wild animals and birds (850 species) can be seen in their natural habitat viewed from a motor car. There are, also, wild flower reserves protecting the wonderful variety of brilliant coloured native plants (18,000 species). Thanks to the efforts of the State Governments these parks act as sanctuaries for wild life.

There is much of human interest also: the older towns in the south-western part of Cape Province are rich in historic "Cape Dutch" architecture; Stellenbosch, the second oldest town in South Africa, has a famous annual festival commemorating pioneer days; Groote Schuur, bequeathed to the nation by Cecil Rhodes, is a beautiful and graceful residence (now the home of South Africa's premiers) and a repository of the country's cultural heritage; "the big hole," formerly the diamond mine of Kimberley and the deepest open pit in the world, has special observation posts for visitors; while Bantu villages and tribal dances can be seen. The would-be tourist, then, has much to interest him. However, tourists apart, South Africa's rapidly developing economy is attracting ever-increasing numbers of foreign businessmen who also, of course, contribute to the tourist industry.

Particular attention is now being paid to the hotel industry by the South African Government. "Not so long ago, when South Africa was a very cheap country to live in and a New York businessman could come to South Africa for a golfing holiday for what his flat rental cost him, it did not matter much just how the hotels went about their job. In those days South Africans still had the good old habit of spending their holidays with relatives. But those days have passed. Today the majority live in cities and towns, and the farming community is becoming sparser. In addition, the average city household cannot afford to entertain guests ad lib., although the tendency to visit is still strong. So, holidays at the sea, in a game reserve or at one of the numerous interior

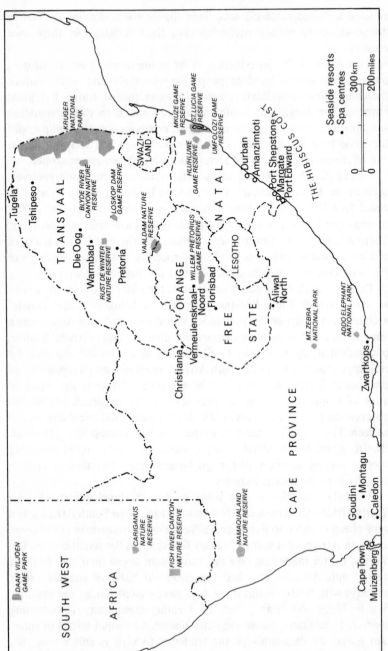

FIG. 46.—*South Africa: tourism features.*

holiday resorts which have come into existence in the meantime, have become the rule. Hotels, which were a luxury in the past, have now become an essential service."[49] The growing need for higher standards in the hotel business led to the passing of legislation in 1965 which brought the South African Hotel Board into existence. This Board has the legal right to inspect and grade hotels (recognising five categories; a five star hotel, of which there are six in the country, compares with the best in the world). The Board is also empowered to provide financial support for extensions, improvements and repairs to hotels. Furthermore, it has now been given the responsibility of planning and providing training facilities for hotel personnel at all levels. The object and purpose of the Board is in fact to ensure the highest possible standards of accommodation, meals and service in all hotels.

Since 1965 the hotel business has grown very rapidly and in 1971 represented a capital investment of R250m. During this period sixty new hotels were built. In 1971 there were 1195 graded hotels (924 one-star, 203 two-star, 55 three-star, seven four-star and six five-star). Altogether, there were more than 62,000 beds available in registered hotels. In addition to the hotels, there were 160 motels, botels and inns which also offer accommodation; these, too, must be registered with the Hotel Board. Thus from the point of view of accommodation it will be seen that the South African tourist industry is being efficiently served. Another measure of this success is seen in the degree to which large financial houses are now investing in the hotel business, an area which formerly they did not regard as being profitable. Something approaching R100m was put into projects 1971–75. The giant Southern Sun Hotel Corporation invested some R30m in higher grade hotels while other groups such as Cape Hotels and Amalgamated Hotels were also very active.

The inland holiday places may be divided into two categories: spas and country centres. Mineral water and hot springs occur throughout the Republic and in recent years these spa centres have become increasingly popular as holiday resorts. In total, there are over eighty centres (over half in the Transvaal, twenty-nine in Cape Province, five in Natal and four in the Orange Free State).[50] In addition, there are twenty-eight in South-West Africa. Except in the Transvaal, where the spas are State-owned, -developed and -run, most of the spas in the Republic of South Africa have been developed by private enterprise. The Republic's most elaborate spa is at Aliwal North where there are large open-air and covered swimming pools as well as elaborate treatment centres. Caledon, near Cape Town, is the oldest spa in South Africa and its popularity goes back to the nineteenth century. Many of those living on the coast go inland for their holidays—into the mountains or on to the veld to find a change of climate, to camp or to fish. Rondavels (huts) and bungalows, which are usually well-equipped and sited in pleasant localities, can be rented and these are a favourite type of accommodation for holiday-makers who wish to stay put for a while or who are on tour.

Just as those living by the sea like to go inland, so those living in the interior crowd into the coastal resorts in summer, especially during December and January. South Africa has 3200 km (2000 miles) of coastal beaches but the chief resort areas are the Cape region with its lovely beaches and the coast of Natal. Muizenberg some 24 km (15 miles) from Cape Town is one of the Republic's premier holiday resorts but there is a whole series of resorts around False Bay, e.g. St James, Kalk Bay, Fish Hoek, Buffels Bay. South of Durban, the South Coast has a whole string of resorts; this equable, warm sea coast attracted over 300,000 visitors annually (1970) but it has enormous potential.[51] The so-called Hibiscus Coast is the chief holiday zone: the focal point here is Margate, the largest of the resorts along the Natal South Coast; to the north lie Manaba Beach and Uvongo, to the south Ramsgate and Southbroom. Amanzimtoti is another rapidly growing resort which is also developing as a residential area; it lies some 25 km (17 miles) south of Durban. Kingsburgh, south of Amanzimtoti, is the centre of a number of small beach resorts. Scottburgh, over a century old, is one of Natal's oldest resorts.

The flow of holiday-makers from all parts of the Republic is increasing year by year and there is now a very substantial domestic tourist trade. But the foreign tourist trade is also beginning to grow: in 1968 there were 299,000 tourists, in 1972 368,592 and the annual growth rate is around 12 per cent. The South African Tourist Corporation has a target of one million foreign tourists a year by 1980.

A commentator, writing in the summer of 1970, said: "The [tourist] industry is dependent upon the Government for direction because of the State's stranglehold on transport, its power to introduce improvements in the Republic's entry and exit formalities, and to initiate regional planning schemes to accommodate a bigger influx of visitors to the major tourist centres."[52] Although the Government now appears committed to an expansionary tourism programme, not all the problems have been dissipated. The accommodation infrastructure which a few years ago was totally inadequate is being rapidly improved. The industry, however, especially the hotel industry, suffers from acute staffing shortages and although hotel training schools have been instituted these will not be able to produce all the staff needed. A Government decision in 1970 to ban Negroes from certain key hotel jobs can only hinder the problem. Furthermore, the Government has barred non-white tourists from the country except under what are impossibly restricting circumstances but, as has been pointed out, how does one ensure that only whites book to visit South Africa? Again, the Republic's apartheid policy may discourage large numbers who might otherwise like to visit the country.

Until the 1970s there was a lack of direction and co-ordination in the tourist industry but now the attitude of the Government is more positive and banking and industrial corporations are investing capital on a large scale. Travel agents, tour operators and charter organisations are gearing themselves for anticipated expansion and the South African Tourist Corporation (Satour) is launching promotional campaigns to sell the Republic abroad. The growth potential for tourism in South Africa is great and with proper handling could double or even treble its (1972) R 60m annual foreign exchange earnings; tourism could well replace wool as the second earner after gold.

NOTES

1. V. Popovic, *Tourism in Eastern Africa*, Weltforum Verlag, München, 1972, p. 19.

2. *Idem*, p. 21.

3. "North Africa," Regional Report No. 7, *International Tourism Quarterly*, No. 4, 1972, p. 22.

4. *Idem*, p. 19.

5. The million mark was not reached; the figure was 904,975, but this figure showed a 22·6 per cent increase over 1971. In 1973, however, the total was over 1·3 million, 25 per cent up on 1972.

6. "North Africa," Regional Report No. 7, *I.T.Q.*, No. 4, 1972, p. 29.

7. M. Peters, *International Tourism*, Hutchinson, 1969, p. 185.

8. *Ibid.*

9. 620,722 arrivals were in fact recorded, some 200,000 less than anticipated.

10. *I.T.Q.*, No. 4, 1972, p. 31.

11. "The Role of Tourism in Economic Development," Special Article No. 8, *I.T.Q.*, No. 2, 1973.

12. R. Troop, "Restraint in Tunisia," *Sunday Times*, 1972.

13. G. H. Blake and R. I. Lawless, "Algeria's Tourist Industry," *Geography*, Vol. 57, April, 1972, pp. 148–52.

14. Blake and Lawless, *op. cit.*

15. Blake and Lawless, *op. cit.*

16. Blake and Lawless, *op. cit.*

17. "North Africa," Regional Report No. 7, *I.T.Q.*, No. 4, 1972, p. 25.

18. *Op. cit.*

19. *Op. cit.*

20. *Egypt*, Economic Report, National Westminster Bank, August, 1972.

21. *Ibid.*

22. *I.T.Q.* No. 2, 1973, p. 3.

23. "Turkey," National Report No. 3, *I.T.Q.* No. 3, 1971, p. 9.

24. *Ibid.*

25. *Idem*, p. 8.

26. *Idem*, p. 11.

27. "Turkey," National Report No. 3, *I.T.Q.*, No. 3, 1971, p. 19.

28. *Idem*, p. 9.

29. "Lebanon," National Report No. 9, *I.T.Q.*, No. 2, 1973, p. 7.

30. *Idem*, p. 6.

31. Y. Karmon, *Israel: A Regional Geography*, Wiley–Interscience, 1971, p. 137.

32. *Sunday Times*, 11th March, 1973.

33. Karmon, *op. cit.*, p. 138.

34. E. Gidron, "Big Increase in Tourist Revenue," Special Report: Israel, *The Financial Times*, 7th May, 1973.

35. Karmon, *op. cit.*, p. 137.

36. "Israel Now," *British Survey*, No. 225, 1967, p. 4.

37. *Op. cit.*, p. 139.

38. *Op. cit.*, p. 138.

39. Gidron, *op. cit.*

40. "The Role of Tourism in Economic Development," *I.T.Q.* No. 2, 1973, p. 58.

41. V. Popovic, *op. cit.*, p. 194.

42. "Ivory Coast," Economic Report, National Westminster Bank, October, 1972.

43. *Ibid.*

44. East Africa, Regional Report No. 1, *I.T.Q.*, No. 1, 1972, p. 26.

45. *Idem*, p. 28.

46. *Idem*, p. 26.

47. *Idem*, p. 28.

48. Popovic, *op. cit.*, pp. 55–6.

49. *Panorama*, Vol. 16, April, 1971, pp. 27–33.

50. "Waters of Healing," *Panorama*, Vol. 14, July, 1969, pp. 16–19.

51. "South of Durban," *Panorama*, Vol. 14, October, 1969, pp. 26–31.

52. M. Taylor, Special Supplement: South Africa, *The Financial Times*, 22nd June, 1970, pp. 26–7.

Chapter XXII

Tourism in the Rest of the World

IN this chapter we are concerned with tourism in the islands of the Indian Ocean, the monsoon lands of Asia, and Australasia. The intention has been to select particular countries showing interesting developments and tourism problems. This vast area has a number of features shared in common: (*i*) although some of the countries have for long received tourists, in the main they are all in the stage of initiating or developing a tourist industry; (*ii*) all lie far removed from the principal centres of tourism generation, hence a large proportion of their business is of the long-haul type; (*iii*) with the exception of a few countries, such as Australia, most lack adequate financial resources and are dependent to a very considerable extent upon foreign investment; and (*iv*) most countries, apart from Australia, New Zealand and Japan, have no well-developed domestic tourist industry, partly because tourism is not a developed social characteristic as it is in the West and partly because of low incomes and standards of living.

While the islands of the Indian and Pacific Oceans have "island paradise" appeal, the marginal mainland countries have, in most cases, truly splendid natural scenery with unique cultures. The Oriental world in particular has attractions of the strongest appeal to Western tourists. Although this Asian/Australasian area received only some 3 to 4 million visitors or about 2·5 per cent of international tourist movements (1970), future expansion is assured, although the regional proportion may not show much increase because of the continuing growth of tourism elsewhere. A feature of the years since 1970 has been the rapid growth in long-distance tourism to this area, though so far the tourists have been mainly in the higher income bracket. However, with the growth of package tours to far-away places, more people in lower income groups will be tempted further afield.

In an attempt to stimulate and develop their tourism industries many of the countries have joined co-operative organisations for promoting travel. Joint marketing and publicity arrangements have been established by the Indian Ocean Islands of Madagascar, Mauritius, Réunion, the Comores and the Seychelles through the Indian Ocean Tourist Alliance (1967), and by the Far Eastern countries of Japan, South Korea, Hong Kong, Macao, The Philippines and Thailand, who set up the East Asian Travel Association (1966).

TABLE 78

Tourist arrivals and receipts in Asia and Australia (1970)

Country	Number of arrivals	Receipts ($m)
Afghanistan	100,233	7·8
Iran	298,633	42·2
India	280,821	50·8
Sri Lanka (Ceylon)	46,247	3·6
Thailand	628,671	104·3
Khmer Rep. (Cambodia)	20,895	1·35
Malaysia	76,374	9·23
Singapore	521,654	—
Indonesia	129,319	16·2
Philippines	144,071	32·0
S. Vietnam	72,474	10·8
Taiwan	400,000 (est.)	70·0 (est.)
Hong Kong	927,256	293·0
China	472,452	89·7
S. Korea	150,000 (est.)	50·0 (est.)
Japan	770,573	232·0
Australia	338,395	105·0

Table 78 shows the numbers of visitors and the receipts accruing from tourism in most of the countries in the eastern hemisphere. Apart from Hong Kong, Japan, Thailand and Singapore, no country exceeded half a million visitors a year, and eight had less than quarter of a million visitors in 1970. Sri Lanka, the Khmer Republic and Nepal, not mentioned above, received less than 50,000 tourists annually. The hostilities which afflicted South Vietnam and the Khmer Republic have seriously affected tourism in these two countries. The rapid growth of tourism in Hong Kong and Singapore is closely related to their locations on important air routes; their trade, however, also suffers on this account and tourists' visits are of short duration, about two–three days duration. Of the mainland countries of South-East Asia, Thailand has the best developed tourist industry and it has great growth potential. In 1973 visitors totalled 1m, generating expenditure of just over $2000m. The Republic of Indonesia has many assets, natural and cultural, for an important tourist industry but tourism is only feebly developed. Most of these countries will enjoy increased tourism developments in the future but as developing countries they almost all are seriously lacking in tourism infrastructure and short of capital for investment in the industry, so that to a very considerable extent, future developments will be dependent upon outside investment.

THE INDIAN OCEAN ISLANDS

With the exception perhaps of the Malagasy Republic, there has hardly been any history of tourism in this region. The Regional Report on the Indian Ocean Islands by the Economist Intelligence Unit (March, 1972) traced the past trends in tourism in the component members of I.O.T.A. and explored the potential and probable future developments among them, and the following account draws heavily upon the Report.

Before examining the developments which have taken place, it will be useful to look at the attractions which the Indian Ocean Islands have for the tourist. Leaving Madagascar aside for the moment, the other island groups have an "island paradise" image. If a tropical island is everybody's dream, then these Indian Ocean Islands come pretty near to fulfilling it. All the islands, excepting Madagascar, are of volcanic origin but are fringed by coral reefs and have beaches of white sand with graceful palm trees swaying gently in the breeze. Because they are all located within the Tropics, they have high day-time and night-time temperatures which hardly vary throughout the year, clear blue skies, abundant sunshine and warm blue seas. Most of them, too, have a mixed population of African, Asian and European origin with a distinct French flavour which adds an element of fascination to the natural scene. Madagascar differs markedly from the other islands in the association if only because of its size—it is a very large island; over 650,000 km^2 (250,000 sq. miles) in area—and exhibits very varied landscapes, although tourism is concentrated in Tananarive, the capital, and around the offshore island of Nossi Bé and the town of Diego Suarez in the extreme north. Until the establishment of air links, all these islands were far removed from tourist markets and the only means of access was by boat, which was slow and irregular. The coming of air transport has revolutionised the situation and the trends in tourist arrivals since 1970 suggest the possibility of an explosive development in tourism over the next decade.

Because of the general lack of tourism in the past and the very recent development of tourism in the Indian Ocean Islands there are few and incomplete statistics and even where they exist "the small scale of the islands' tourism prevents statistical analysis from being especially meaningful."[1] Table 79 summarises such information as is available.

TABLE 79

Tourist arrivals in the Indian Ocean Alliance

	1967	1968	1969	1970	1971
Mauritius [1]	14,814	15,553	20,587	27,650	35,000 [2]
Madagascar [3]	—	6,000	9,000	17,000	24,000
Seychelles	—	—	—	—	2,500 [4]
Reunion	—	—	—	6,000 [4]	
Comores				4,000 [4]	

1. Includes business visitors, estimated by M.G.T.O. to constitute about one-eighth of the total.
2. Provisional figures.
3. Estimates by C.T.A.T. of holiday visitors.
4. Estimates, based on partial data and air and sea traffic.

Sources: Mauritius Government Tourist Office (M.G.T.O.); Commissariat au Tourisme et aux Arts Traditionnels, Madagascar (C.T.A.T.): Statistical Commission, Seychelles. *From: International Tourism Quarterly*, No. 1, March, 1972.

Madagascar has potentially much more to offer the tourist than the smaller islands. The country's sheer size, however, has been a significant factor militating against tourist development, for its internal communications, with the exception of one railway line leading from the coast to Tananarive, the capital, and continued beyond to the small mountain resort of Antsirabe, consist of poor roads. Air Madagascar now provides internal flights and this is really the only reliable mode of transport for the visitor. Tananarive, a town of some 250,000 inhabitants, situated on a hill high on the central plateau at an altitude of 1371 m (4500 ft) is an interesting city with several hotels, including a 200-room Hilton, many restaurants and night clubs, and is visited by most tourists. About 160 km (100 miles) to the south of the capital is the spa centre of Antsirabe, high up in the mountains, which possesses a good hotel and golf and tennis facilities. Apart from the capital, tourism is concentrated at Nossi Bé, a volcanic "paradise" island, and at Diego Suarez, on a bay fringed with coral reefs. Palm Beach at Nossi Bé is a popular centre with a variety of entertainments, a casino and a swimming pool but is apt to be overcrowded. In an attempt to stimulate tourist development the Malagasy Government encouraged foreign developers and, for example, the South African hotel group, Southern Sun, built a 150-room hotel at Nossi Bé. An extensive tourism complex, served by a new airport, was also being planned at Nossi Bé with the help of substantial financial support from the Republic of South Africa.[2]

Madagascar is aware of its potential as a tourist area and, although the tourist industry is still young C.T.A.T. is already working out development policies for the next thirty years. The country's immediate needs focus upon improved hotel resources, particularly in the already established resorts. Madagascar enjoys fairly wide and rapidly expanding air links with the rest of the world which should enable it to tap valuable tourist markets in Europe and South Africa, which Madagascar sees as the most important. Within a short space of time, and working from a very limited base, Madagascar's tourist industry has made rapid strides but it faces many problems, especially in relation to adequate accommodation and communications; moreover, the cost of living is very high in the island and this means that its market is more strictly confined to the more affluent tourists.

Mauritius seems to have been the first of the islands in the south-west Indian Ocean to recognise the possibilities of tourism and to begin exploiting its potential. This small but densely populated island is built of volcanic rocks which have formed a central dome some 610 m (2000 ft) high. The relief is not dramatic, as in neighbouring Réunion, but it has considerable scenic variety—volcanic stumps, lakes, waterfalls and caverns. Mauritius is encircled by coral reefs and its embayed coast has good beaches and first-class swimming and underwater fishing facilities. "The island contains some excellent buildings, and there is a fine museum, a race course and a theatre in Port Louis, the capital, while the botanical gardens at Pamplemousses are world-renowned. Unfortunately, the tourism infrastructure does not yet measure up to the natural attractions of the island."[3] There is a network of reasonably good roads served by buses and cars can be hired at a moderate cost but accommodation facilities leave much to be desired. Mauritius has fifteen hotels which in 1970–71 provided 860 beds, but none of these are of international tourist standard. Herein lies a fundamental weakness, but one fully appreciated by the Government Tourist Office, which is encouraging outside investment. As a result of this encouragement "The Blyth Group, Kennwood and the International Finance Corporation, which has put up $600,000, are ... involved in projects which will add a further 724 beds to the island's existing 860 hotel beds, and forty-seven holiday bungalow beds. Two of the new hotels will be at Curepipe, a third at Tamarin and the fourth, described as 'very luxurious,' at Belle Mare. In addition, two smaller holiday bungalow projects are under way. Furthermore, New Mauritius Hotels is itself planning a 600-room hotel at Grand-Sable."[4] Other amenities, such as water sports facilities, restaurants and evening entertainments, seem to be superior in Mauritius to those available in the other islands. Furthermore, these considerable developments in hotel construction will without doubt lead to greatly enhanced facilities for sporting activities and entertainment. Of the tourists who holiday in Mauritius, the Réunionais from the neighbouring island dominate the arrivals, accounting for about 40 per cent of the total (in 1970, 11,405 out of 27,650). Visitors from South Africa form the next largest group (3637 in 1970) and the Mauritians look to the Republic to provide the bulk of the growth in tourist arrivals. The total number of European visitors is small (4319 in 1970) but growing; the United Kingdom and France provide the most tourists, 1740 and 1437 respectively in 1970.[5]

Réunion, which is French, has a small tourist industry but the total number of visitors was only around 6000 a year in 1970. But it is only since 1971 that any real attention has been paid to tourism. Such facilities as exist are of a reasonable standard but limited in quantity, although a drawback from the visitor's point of view are the high prices. The island, dominated by an active volcano, the Piton des Neiges 3069 m (10,068 ft) high, has quite spectacular scenery and Burning Crater, the impressive gorges carved in the slopes, the mountain torrents and tropical vegetation provide natural attractions of interest. The roughly circular island has a pebbly coast and the only area of beach is to be found around St Gilles-les-Bains. There were plans (1972) to build a 150-bed Club Mediterranée village near St Giles.[6]

The Comores lie between the African mainland and Madagascar; they comprise four small islands, Mayotte, Moheli, Anjouan and Grand Comoro. The archipelago has a mixed population of Africans, Arabs, Indians, Malays and Chinese as well as Europeans. The total population (around a quarter of a million), is dependent upon agriculture and the development of tourism could be a great blessing. The Comoro Archipelago is volcanic and on Grand Comoro there is an active volcano which rises up to 243 m (8000 ft). Tourism is in its infancy (an estimated 4000 visitors in 1970), and there were only four hotels with 200 beds. Near Dzaoudzi, on Mayotte, a holiday camp was opened in 1968. The islands, especially Anjouan, are naturally very attractive and many of the small towns have much local colour. Transport between the islands is provided by Air Comores but air communications with the outside world are not good; even so, the tourist future of the Comores would seem to be largely linked with "island-hopping tours."

The Seychelles, which belong to Great Britain, comprise a group of 100 volcanic islands and atolls, some 800 km (500 miles) north-east of Madagascar. So far, tourism is mainly concentrated on Mahé, the largest of the islands, but facilities are being developed on the islands of Raslin, La Digue and Bird. Until 1971 very few travellers indeed visited the Seychelles, and then only after a three-day, 1600-km (1000-mile) journey by boat from Mombasa. Thus, there was no tourist industry.

However, in the summer of 1971 an international airport was opened on Mahé and this, in effect, ended centuries of inaccessibility and isolation overnight. Almost immediately aircraft began to bring full loads of visitors. The package-tour operators were quick to see the potential and firms such as Cooks and Houlder Bros began to offer inclusive tours for under £200 for a fortnight's holiday. The journey from London takes fourteen hours, and the case of the Seychelles well illustrates the vital role which air transport can play in the development of island tourism. The Seychelles possess great beauty and have a wonderful climate and for the tourist who yearns to "get away from it all" and also wants a South Sea Island paradise this British Colony will take some beating. Development promises to be rapid and the authorities are giving careful thought to tourism policy. A target of 150,000 visitors by 1985 has been set but it is realised that detailed planning is required. There is, as one might expect, a lack of infrastructure needed to support the industry and a first priority is hotel accommodation. The new 300-bed Reef Hotel on Mahé is of full international standard, and another 200-bed hotel was opened in January, 1973; but several more will be required. The future for tourism in the Seychelles looks very bright although the colony's economy could become too heavily dependent upon tourism; indeed there has already been some strong reaction from certain groups who are fearful of what tourism may mean and may bring to the Seychelles. Approximately 15,000 tourists visited the Seychelles in 1972 and the provisional figure for 1973 was 20,000.

I.O.T.A. is the co-ordinating body which represents the interests of members in all the islands and through which general policy and promotional activity is channelled, although its achievements have been hampered by its lack of resources. Helpful as this co-operation and co-ordination undoubtedly is, it must be acknowledged that most of the tourism development that has taken place has been achieved through the efforts of the organisations set up by the individual members of I.O.T.A. It is perhaps too early for coherent tourism policies to emerge, although Madagascar, Mauritius and the Seychelles have gone a long way towards developing such policies; in Réunion and the Comores considerable thought but little decision has emerged. Because of costs, especially in relation to long travelling distance, it would seem that the islands will have to depend on the higher-class tourist as their main customer. The aim is to attract West Europeans and also Australians and North Americans if they can, but in particular the islands are hoping to attract the wealthier whites of southern Africa, *i.e.* the Republic of South Africa and Rhodesia; they see in those two countries possibly their most important future markets. The I.O.T.A. members realise that their future is likely to be closely tied up with tourism but they realise also that their natural beauty is their greatest asset and are investigating tourist capacity with considerable care: they do not wish to spoil, or completely destroy, the very attractions which are the principal magnet drawing tourists to them.

The E.I.U. Report sums up the future prospects as follows: "Although tourism is still in its infancy in the Indian Ocean islands, future prospects are good if the right development and promotional policies can be pursued. Comparison with tourism in the Caribbean islands is inevitable, the main point of difference being that the Indian Ocean islands do not have the advantage of the neighbouring North American market. Nevertheless, given probable growth in disposable incomes and lower air fares, tourists from Europe, Asia, Southern Africa and Australia should provide a sufficient guarantee of the future profitability of both public and private tourism investment.

"But, so far, inadequate financial resources have led to neglect of the all-important promotional aspects of tourism development. The Seychelles probably offer the greatest prospect for growth, followed by the already more developed Mauritius and Madagascar markets. Comores and Réunion are likely to continue to benefit mainly from the visits of an increasing number of 'island-hopping,' short-stay visitors, although Réunion places some hope—as does Seychelles—in a declared 'open sky' policy for charter airlines." [7]

INDIA

Centre of an age-old, highly developed and unique civilisation in which are woven Hindu, Moslem and European strands, India has an overwhelming personality and the moment the foreign traveller places his foot in the country he is made abundantly aware that this is a land at once beautiful and ugly, vibrant and inert, exotic and earthy. For the tourist, however, apart from a surfeit of local colour, India has perhaps two special attractions which few other countries can offer: rich and varied wildlife and a wealth of ancient monuments.[8] Paradoxically, in spite of long human occupance of the country and a teeming population, India retains a substantial wildlife. Though many species of animal are declining (for example, the Indian lion is all but extinct and the last *keddah* or round-up of wild elephants took place in 1962), it is still possible to see elephants, rhinoceros, leopards, tigers and birdlife in their natural habitat. The authorities have already taken steps to safeguard this natural resource and have set up a series of wildlife parks and bird sanctuaries, partly with a view to preserving her animal population and partly as a tourist attraction. Above all, however, the country is a treasure house of monuments ranging from the pre-historic period to the time of the British Raj. There are the remains and relics of the pre-historic Indus Valley civilisation at Lothal and Kalibangan; the temples, sculptures and holy sites associated with Buddha, especially at Benares and Patna; the Hindu temples and caves at Ellora, Elephanta, Khajuraho and Tanjore; the monuments, palaces and forts of Muslim rule—not forgetting the exquisite Taj Mahal—notably at Agra and Delhi; and the remains of European occupation and rule, *e.g.* the Portuguese forts and churches at Goa and Diu, and the British factories, forts and residencies at such places as Madras, Surat and Lucknow. Most of India's ancient monuments are now protected by the Government: they have been scheduled for preservation and placed in the hands of the Archaeological Survey which is responsible for the care and maintenance of national monuments.

Tourism in India comes under the aegis of the Department of Tourism and its associate the India Tourism Development Corporation (I.T.D.C.). Both are concerned with the promotion of Indian tourism abroad, with the development of facilities for tourism, such as transport and accommodation, and with the opening up of new areas to tourism. Among its many activities I.T.D.C. looks after the approach roads at much-frequented sites, provides tourist bungalow accommodation at important out-station sites, such as at Bodh Gaya, Khajuraho and Sanchi, restaurants and guide services at many sites visited by tourists, car-hire services at important centres and guide-books and brochures of the places of interest.[9]

There is a growing appreciation of the need to meet the demands of the foreign tourist and to make it possible for him to see as much as possible of India during a brief stay; also of the value of tourism to the national economy in terms of earning much-needed foreign currency, attracting capital investment and providing employment. The Department of Tourism has been responsible for injecting dynamism and enthusiasm into the industry. Certainly the tourist is enthusiastically welcomed—airport placards declare "Tourists are our honoured guests"—and cared for with the greatest courtesy and hospitality. The Department is, however, well aware of the many shortcomings, more especially in relation to the shortage of hotels, cuisine, the difficulty of procuring alcoholic drinks and the paucity of nightlife and lighter entertainments for the visitor.

India is a long way from its main sources of tourism. The high air fares (around £300 return economy flight between the United Kingdom and India in 1971), militate against large numbers of Britons visiting India. India is otherwise a relatively inexpensive country to tour. In 1971 foreign tourist arrivals totalled 301,000 (chief visitors—55,000 from the United States, 40,000 from the United Kingdom and 18,000 from West Germany). In 1970, the receipts from foreign tourism were $50·8m (nearly $7m up on the previous year), but this is a very low figure only comparable with those received by Kenya and Romania.

The great size of India and the sheer number of its attractions presents a difficulty, and the short-term visitor is limited in the distances he can travel and in the amount he can see. For these reasons, the tourist is encouraged to follow the usual packaged circuit—visits to Bombay, Udaipur, Jaipur, Agra, Benares and Delhi which are easily linked by air and rail services. "As rich in colour as a maharajah's jewels, this tour well displays the elephants-and-mogul-palaces image of India, but lacks scenery in which to relax." [10] However, serious attempts are now being made by the Indian Government to develop a greater spatial spread of tourism and attention at present is being directed to the expansion of the industry in Kashmir, in Goa and along the Malabar Coast which has attractive beaches. It is intended that these places shall cater more particularly for the cheaper, stay-put type of holiday; by taking advantage of new lower group fares, the cost of a two weeks' holiday could be about £175 per head for people from the United Kingdom (1972).

SRI LANKA

The brochures describe Sri Lanka, more commonly known as Ceylon, as a delightful unspoilt treasure island, with tropical palm-fringed beaches, mighty monuments, mysterious festivals, spectacular tropical scenery and charming friendly people, and for all its "promotional" tone, this description is substantially true. Sri Lanka *is* a beautiful island, with coasts and beaches that compare with those in the Caribbean. It has wonderful ancient monuments, shrines and remains—the old sacred city of Anuradhapura, the rock fortress of Sigiriya, the temple at Kandy containing Buddha's tooth, the shrines and statues of Polonnaruwa. Its biogeography is rich and beautiful and the climate for much of the year delightful. Holidaying in the country is also relatively cheap since tourists, as an inducement to come, get privileged exchange rates.

In 1970 over 100,000 foreign tourists visited Sri Lanka. In 1971, because of internal political troubles, the total dropped by 77,000. By 1972 the inward flow of tourists began to recover and there were 37,588 visitors (37·4 per cent increase upon the previous year). Until 1970, Britons topped the list of foreign tourists; the West Germans now take first place. Most visitors tend to visit Sri Lanka in the winter half of the year, between December and April especially; June and July (the time of the south-west monsoon) are the least popular months.

The Government is planning to develop the tourism industry and provision was made in the Five-Year Plan (1972–76) for investment in tourism. Tourism, incidentally, is one of the areas in which foreign private investment is allowed without restriction. It is generally believed that tourism has reached the "take-off" stage in Sri Lanka and great faith is being placed in its future development; by 1976 the industry should be in a really thriving condition. One reason for the promotion of tourism relates to Sri Lanka's high dependence upon three staples —tea, rubber and coconut products—which are highly susceptible to fluctuations in world demand and therefore in prices. It is hoped that tourism will not only reduce the country's reliance upon these commodities (which normally provide 90 per cent of export revenue) but bring in foreign exchange, encourage foreign investment and provide additional employment. "In some quarters it is expected that tourism will become the country's third largest foreign exchange earner, replacing coconuts, by 1976, when revenue from tourism will total Rs160m (at 1971 prices) according to the Five-Year Plan."[11]

Although considerable investment will be required in infrastructure, Sri Lanka is not starting from scratch: she has been a participator in tourism activity for a long time. A well-established superstructure already exists which in recent years has been improved. For example, the Intercontinental Hotel was opened in Colombo in 1972 and the Bentota Beach Hotel, built by one of the country's best designers matches up to the highest international standards. Along the south-west coast there is in fact a string of luxurious hotels but Bentota Beach, some 60 km (38 miles) from Colombo, is a well-established resort with hotels, restaurants, shops, souvenirs, etc. everything, in fact, that the tourist needs. In addition, for the visitor who wishes to explore the interior of the island, the Tourist Board has established rest houses (although the majority of these offer only basic facilities, they are cheap) and set up camping sites in jungle clearings. On the whole, the prospects for Sri Lanka's success in the field of tourism appear very promising.

SINGAPORE

By 1972 the number of tourists in Singapore was fast approaching the million mark. The main reason is that Singapore is a stop-over point for tourists bound for eastern Asia, Indonesia and Australia, and many tourists pause for few days before proceeding to their final destination. The average length of stay is about three days, and this short-period sojourn is characteristic of the nature of tourism there. Just as formerly Singapore was a great, strategic shipping focus, now it has become an important international airways centre and lies on the air routes to the Far East and Australasia. It has the finest airport in South-East Asia.

The Federation of Malaysia came into being in September, 1963, and, at first, Singapore was a part of the Federation; however, subsequently it withdrew and gained complete independence in 1964. The State of Singapore consists of Singapore Island together with some nearby islets; it has a total area of only about 579 km² (225 sq. miles) with a population of $2\frac{1}{2}$ million. Singapore, lying at a major crossroads, was ideally situated to become a great centre of commerce and, accordingly, developed as a great entrepôt centre. Latterly, however, its entrepôt function has declined and as a means of solving a serious unemployment problem Singapore turned to industrialisation and, like Hong Kong, it has seen spectacular developments in manufacturing industry. More recently, it has developed a flourishing tourist trade.

This growth in tourism has really come as something of a surprise to the Government who did not believe that the small republic could possibly compete with neighbouring countries such as Malaya, Cambodia, Thailand or Indonesia as an attractive tourist destination, for touristically it has relatively little to offer. However, it has the advantages of an important location at the hub of international routes, splendid modern hotels and duty-free shopping facilities.

In 1970 the number of visitors topped the 500,000 mark, while in the following year tourists increased by 21 per cent to 632,000; in 1972 the total was 783,015, 23·9 per cent more than in 1971. 1973 looked likely to see the arrivals coming close to the million mark. In 1972, arrivals by country of residence came chiefly from Australia (17·8 per cent), Indonesia (13·7 per cent), Malaysia (11·2 per cent), United States (11·1 per cent), Japan (9·1 per cent) and Britain (8·4 per cent).[12] The income from tourism is substantial—S$397m in 1972 (an increase of 21·4 per cent over 1971), contributing 5 per cent of the G.D.P.—with visitors spending on average S$494 per head.[13] About half the total expenditure of tourists went on shop purchases especially of clothes and textiles, stereophonic and sound equipment, ciné cameras and other photographic equipment, and watches. Tourist arrivals are fairly evenly spread throughout the year, although June, July and December are the peak months. Nearly 95 per cent of Singapore's tourists arrive by air.

The Tourist Board has been concerned about the "stop-over" nature of tourism and is trying to create attractions which hold the tourist's interest and keep him in Singapore for a longer period. Some of the developments which have taken place, apart from the scheduling of certain national monuments, are "the Jurong Bird Park on the Jurong industrial estate, the Jurong Japanese and Chinese gardens with an eighteen-hole golf course, the Mandai Zoological Gardens, the Changi Beach complex, the Kallang Park National Stadium and sports complex, the seaside Collyer Quay overhead shopping bridge, Singapore's self-created mascot the Merlion, a half-fish, half-lion, sculptured monument ... and the Soochow Gardens. ... The single project most likely to boost length of stay is the Sentosa Island development. This small island was scheduled to become a pleasure complex by 1975, equipped with hotels, a golf course, coralarium, gun museum, maritime museum, swimming lagoon and cable-car link with the main island." [14]

The Tourist Board is also concentrating some of its energies into making Singapore the "convention capital" for South-East Asia. Already it has had a measure of success in this respect and is exceptionally well-placed, in view of its communications links, for development along these lines. Its principal handicap is the lack of facilities for conventions where the numbers of delegates are in excess of 2000. Conventions have two great advantages: delegates form a captive group so to speak for the duration of the conference and, secondly, conventions can often be planned during the off-peak season, thus improving the occupancy rates for the hotels (around 60 per cent in 1972). But there has been an hotel building boom—Singapore by 1972 had seventy hotels providing some 8350 rooms—and accommodation is increasing at an annual rate of just over 10 per cent. The result has been that a large proportion of the hotels are operating at a low, uneconomic occupancy rate and have been undercutting one another. [15] There have been justifiable fears that the expansion will exceed the growth of tourism, and lead to an excess of hotel rooms. At this rate Singapore should have 12,350 rooms by 1977. One other problem is that the ratio of luxury hotels to medium-range tourist hotels is too high.

A drive has been made to capture a larger part of the Australian and Japanese markets and this has proved successful; in 1973 similar moves were made to tempt New Zealanders and West Germans—"In a link-up with the major German travel wholesalers, Touropa and Scharnow, the Board ... [channelled] inclusive tour programmes direct to Singapore from Frankfurt."[16] Notwithstanding their problems, the Tourist Board has adopted a realistic approach and hopes to receive more than 2 million tourists a year by 1992.

HONG KONG

The Crown Colony of Hong Kong consists of a number of islands, of which only the largest, Hong Kong Island, is important, together with a part of the mainland facing them. The entire Colony, including the islands, Kowloon Peninsula and the New Territories, leased to Great Britain by China, has an area slightly less than 1036 km² (400 sq. miles). Most of the Colony is mountainous and with over 4 million inhabitants, is bursting at the seams. Originally Hong Kong functioned as a great entrepôt centre, as a major distributing point for a variety of miscellaneous goods exported from, and imported into, China. Since the setting up of the Communist régime in China the whole basis and character of Hong Kong's economy has been changed; to offset the loss of its trade, the Colony turned, successfully, to industrial expansion. Recently, another source of income has emerged—tourism; it is now claimed that tourist receipts form the Colony's second largest "export," and it is an important foreign-exchange earner.

Hong Kong conjures up all the colour and magic of the Far East: its very name is evocative of oriental romance and excitement. There is in fact much to interest and titillate the tourist. Victoria seethes with activity and is a shopping paradise but not far away are wooded heights giving breathing space and magnificent views. On the nearby islands there are good beaches for sunbathing and swimming. Restaurants are everywhere and one can dine on a wide variety of Chinese and cosmopolitan food. Night life is prolific. There are numerous new, often elegant hotels giving excellent service to the increasing number of tourists pouring into Hong Kong, since its location makes the Colony a very important stop-over point.

Tourism began to grow during the 1960s and during the later years of the decade the number of visitors began to creep up towards the million mark. 1970 was an exceptional year because of stop-overs by travellers bound to or from Japan's Expo '70: visitors totalled well over 900,000. In 1971 there was a slight decrease (2·2 per cent) in the number of arrivals, which totalled 907,295, although this figure showed an increase of 18·6 per cent on the 1969 figure. In 1972 the figure of 1 million arrivals was reached. 1972 saw a percentage growth of 13·3 per cent over the previous year, and 1973 a 17 per cent increase over 1972.

In 1972 half of the arrivals were accounted for by Japanese and United States' visitors; the former numbered 349,212 (32·3 per cent of the total arrivals), the latter 216,690 (19·6 per cent). "While the number of Japanese tourists increased by 51·3 per cent [over 1971], that of U.S. tourists decreased by 6·1 per cent, in large part a result of the termination in October, 1971 of the Rest and Recreation programme for U.S. military personnel in Vietnam [who had counted as 'tourists' when in Hong Kong]."[17] Apart from these two major groups, Australasians counted for 6·6 per cent and visitors from Western Europe for 14·7 per cent of the total.

The current trend seems to indicate that the American market is contracting but that the European market is expanding quite rapidly as, also, is the South-East Asian market. The Japanese are continuing to arrive in increasing numbers, nearly half a million in 1973, while they are also the largest spenders. Table 80 gives a breakdown of the reasons for visits from the four chief originating areas.

TABLE 80

Visitors to Hong Kong (1972) (%)

From country or area	Vacation	Visiting friends/relatives	In transit to main holiday	Business
S.E. Asia	20	28	19	30
Western Europe	49	16	15	19
U.S.A.	71	6	9	14
Japan	74	4	9	12

Source: *International Tourism Quarterly*, No. 4, 1972.

It is estimated that this high percentage growth rate will flatten out somewhat to between 10·5 to 8·5 per cent during the later 1970s; nevertheless, projected arrivals for 1980 are forecast at more than 2 million.[18]

Hotel development has proceeded rapidly since 1965 and there are many skyscraper hotels: in 1966 there were 6089 beds, in 1971 9047. In 1972 two new major hotels were opened in Causeway Bay adding a further 2000 beds, and the shortage of accommodation experienced after 1970 has now been considerably alleviated (in 1973 the percentage occupancy rate was running at around 85 per cent).

Hong Kong shares with Singapore the disadvantage of short-stay tourism. The average length of stay here is also not much more than three days. Various attempts are being made to persuade visitors to lengthen their stay, *e.g.* resort projects for Lantau and other outlying areas. "Carefully planned resort areas, taking advantage of Hong Kong's beaches, natural resources and potential sporting facilities, would go a long way towards maintaining Hong Kong's position as the leading tourist destination in Asia, as well as providing recreational facilities for local residents."[19] In addition, there are moves to develop Hong Kong as a convention city and a local consortium announced plans for the construction of a major trade and conference centre in Causeway Bay, where the new cross-harbour tunnel gives a direct link with Kaitak Airport on the northern part of Kowloon Bay. Such improvements in communications—Kaitak Airport was extended in 1970—are important, for the single most important factor affecting the Colony's tourist industry has been the steady increase in recent years in the number of relatively inexpensive charter flights to Hong Kong.

TAIWAN

Since Chiang Kai-shek with his Nationalist forces retreated to Taiwan in 1947, the economy of this East Asian offshore island has been transformed. At first bolstered up by American aid, Taiwan is now a thriving country with an economic growth rate of around 10 per cent. In this economic development tourism has played a notable role, becoming a leading export through the foreign exchange it earns. The tourist industry during the period of the fourth four-year Economic Development Plan (1965–68) averaged an annual growth slightly in excess of 33 per cent. It was projected that this very rapid growth would decline slightly during the fifth four-year plan (1969–72) and the Tourism Council of the Ministry of Communications forecasted a 20 per cent growth annually.[20] This has proved to be too optimistic. In 1972 arrivals totalled 582,000, as against a projected 631,000, although the 1972 total still represented a 7·5 per cent increase over the 1971 figures.

$57·65m out of the $4500m budgeted for the 1969–72 Plan was allocated for tourism: development and improvement of scenic areas, highway construction and improvement, investment in hotels and international promotion of Taiwan as a desirable tourist destination.[21]

When Portuguese navigators in the sixteenth century first visited Taiwan they were enthralled by its natural beauty and called it "Ilha Formosa"—Beautiful Island! The Tourism Council in their campaign to place Taiwan on the tourist map have emphasised the island's great natural beauty but have also claimed that it "combines the best of old and modern China and is the only part of China open to travellers."

Scenically, Taiwan has much to offer: in addition to great beauty there are magnificent physical features such as the Taroko Gorge, claimed to be one of the wonders of the world, and the mighty vertical cliffs along the east coast which are said to be the highest in the world. The National Palace Museum in Taipei has a superb collection of Chinese art treasures. The island also has many first-class hotels with an excellent Chinese cuisine. Taiwan also has the advantage of lying on one of the major air routes of the Far East and is in easy reach of Hong Kong and Japan.

The growth in the number of visitors and in the income derived from tourism is given in Table 81:

TABLE 81
Visitors to Taiwan

Year	No. of visitors	Estimated revenue
1959	19,328	$1·2m
1968	301,770	$53·3m
1969	365,000	$64·4m
1972	582,000	$100·0m

Note: The numbers for 1968 and 1969 do not include United States' military personnel who came to Taiwan on rest and recreation visits. About 30,000 visits a year were made, which brought in an estimated $11·4m annually.

The very rapid expansion in tourism in Taiwan has brought some problems chief of which relate to accommodation. There are some misgivings as to whether Taiwan has sufficient hotel accommodation to meet the demands of the increasing influx of visitors requiring international tourist standard accommodation, in spite of a boom in hotel construction—1969–70 saw the building of twenty new hotels which increased the accommodation by over 3400 rooms.

So far, Taiwan has depended very largely upon United States' and Japanese visitors: in 1968, 30·4 per cent were American, 41·19 per cent Japanese. In 1972 the chief foreign visitors were: Japanese 277,704 (55·6 per cent of arrivals), 121,805 United States tourists and 80,000 overseas Chinese. Among the other nationalities visiting Taiwan are Filipinos, Malaysians and Australians. The Tourism Council would like to see more people from other parts of the world visiting Taiwan and special efforts are being made to attract visitors from places outside the traditional sources of supply.

KOREA

Tourism is Korea's newest industry. Until the Korean War ended in 1953, tourism was out of the question, although it had not ever really existed before the hostilities began. The war, of course, had devastated much of the country and until a measure of reorganisation and reconstruction had taken·place, the tourist industry could not begin to develop: for instance, there were no hotels. Even in 1968 there were only 2213 hotel rooms in the country (in 1962 there were no more than 700), but by 1972 there were more than 6000. At least five new hotels had been built by 1970 in Seoul, the capital, the largest of which was the eighteen-storey Chosun Hotel. This hotel expansion is, in itself, an indication of the growth of the tourist industry in South Korea. In 1965, 33,464 foreign tourists visited the country; by 1968 the number had reached 102,748; by 1971 171,000; and by 1972 252,628. Such numbers may seem small but the annual increase in recent years has been impressive (around 20 per cent annually and between 1971 and 1972 47·7 per cent) and it is this rate of growth which is really significant.

When, in 1966, normal diplomatic relations were re-established between Korea and Japan, Japanese tourists began to arrive in substantial numbers. Of the tourists visiting South Korea in 1968, the Japanese came first (42·5 per cent of the total); Americans second (40·7 per cent); other visitors were Formosan Chinese (3·7 per cent), Britons (1·8 per cent) and West Germans (1·3 per cent). Earnings from tourism increased from $20·7m in 1965 to $35·4m in 1968, although it should be noted that these figures include money spent by American diplomats, military personnel, economic advisers, etc. who are not tourists in the strict sense; if purely tourist earnings were to be extracted they would be appreciably less.[22]

JAPAN

International tourism in Japan, both incoming and outgoing, expanded very rapidly during the years 1960–74, especially since Japan became a member of the International Monetary Fund. Until 1964 there had been government restrictions on foreign travel but in that year they began to be relaxed and in 1971 were removed altogether. Partly because of this, Japan has emerged as a major tourist-generating market. But this extraordinarily rapid increase also reflects the increasing affluence of the Japanese people (family incomes increased 2·3 times during 1965–73).[23] With this increased income has come increased leisure time and therefore longer holidays. Another factor which has stimulated travel is that there are now more low-priced all-inclusive tours available. Basically, however, this growth in tourism is the outcome of national prosperity; as Devas has written: "The causes of this rapid market development are fundamentally linked with the economic development of post-war Japan. The economy has been expanding continuously at a rate of around 10 per cent *per annum* in real terms— that is after allowing for inflationary effects—compared with a rate of growth of roughly half that amount in the United States and the advanced European countries. This has resulted in a consumer market emerging in Japan with incomes broadly similar to those in Europe. Japanese overseas trading led to the early appearance of substantial business travel to and from Japan, and this traffic continues to form the foundation on which the excellent air services linking Japan and the rest of the world are built." [24]

Outward tourism has grown much more rapidly than incoming tourism (*see* Fig. 47). Since 1964, when some 220,000 Japanese went abroad—most of them for business purposes—there has been an increase of over 20 per cent a year. In 1968 some 541,716 holidayed overseas (this included some 198,000 who visited Okinawa). In 1970 the total travelling overseas reached 663,500; rather more than half travelled for pleasure rather than business. In 1971, when all restrictions on travel abroad were lifted, the total reached about 960,000 and

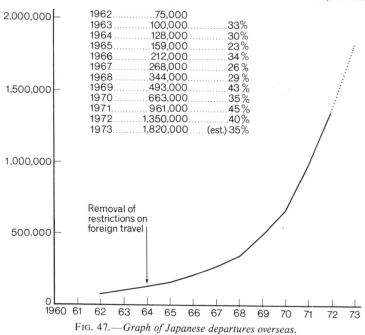

1962	75,000	
1963	100,000	33%
1964	128,000	30%
1965	159,000	23%
1966	212,000	34%
1967	268,000	26%
1968	344,000	29%
1969	493,000	43%
1970	663,000	35%
1971	961,000	45%
1972	1,350,000	40%
1973	1,820,000	(est.) 35%

Removal of restrictions on foreign travel

FIG. 47.—*Graph of Japanese departures overseas.*

in 1972 it had climbed to 1,392,000—an increase of 40 per cent on the previous year. It was forecast that 1973 would see the total reach 1,820,000: in fact, the total was 2,288,966. Table 82 shows the principal destinations of Japanese travellers in 1972.

TABLE 82

Major destinations of Japanese travellers (1972)
(rounded figures)

Hong Kong	500,000
United States	343,000
Taiwan	277,000
United Kingdom	133,000
Korea	94,000 (1971)
Spain	52,000
Canada	20,000
Singapore	17,000
Australia	15,000
Brazil	6,000

An analysis of the quite spectacular increase in the Japanese overseas travel market since 1970 has been prepared by the sales planning and research division of Japan Air Lines. The report shows that the great majority of the travellers come from the major commercial and industrial centres in Honshu, the main island. Honshu provides about three-quarters of the total travellers: 54 per cent from Tokyo and its vicinity (the Kanto area), and 21 per cent from Osaka and its surrounding area (the Kinsai).[25] The Kyushu area, which covers the southernmost island in the Japanese archipelago, provides rather less than 15 per cent, and the number of tourists from the rest of the country is insignificant. From this it would appear that it is the more sophisticated, better-paid urbanites who are engaging in foreign tourism. At present, the most favoured destinations are South-East Asia, the United States and Europe, but destination preferences may well change; for instance, Europe, which currently receives 15 per cent of the market, is gaining ground rapidly and the numbers visiting Britain, for example, are nearly doubling annually. Rather surprising, too, is the fact that 52,000 Japanese visited Spain in 1972.

At present rather more than two-thirds of Japanese tourists going abroad are of middle age, but this proportion is likely to decline, though slowly, since the fastest growing travel age-group is that between 20 and 30 years. Moreover, most overseas travellers are males, a clear reflection of the significance of business traffic; only slightly more than one-fifth of the overseas travel market consists of females, but the proportion of women travellers is likely to show a marked increase as pleasure travel gets into its stride. Devas comments that there is no marked seasonal pattern in respect of Japanese travel abroad: merely that Asia tends to be preferred in winter and North America and Europe in summer. Holiday travel, too, tends to be of rather short duration; for example, group tours to Europe are often of no more than ten days.[26]

As mentioned above, the development of inclusive tours has been an important factor in the growth of Japanese holidays abroad. "A major impact has been made by group tours as a result of two principal factors. Firstly, they offer good value, and have in fact, declined in price at a time of rapid inflation and increasing personal income. Secondly, the success of group tours is a reflection of their convenience for people who often have never travelled abroad and who are unfamiliar with foreign languages, customs and foods. Japanese Airlines have estimated that 52 per cent of all air travellers in 1971 were doing so for the first time."[27]

Whereas the increase in outgoing tourism has been nothing short of dramatic, incoming tourism, though expanding, has been much more gradual. In 1968 Japan received 519,000 foreign visitors; this represented an increase of 9 per cent over the previous year. Expo '70, held in Osaka, no doubt encouraged the foreign tourist to visit Japan, although the impact does not appear to have been as great as one might have expected, for the tourist arrivals in 1972 (from January to September) totalled 538,000. Arrivals during 1970–73 suggest that the growth rate is of the order of 10 per cent a year. One of the chief factors militating against a more rapid growth is the great distance which separates Japan from the major generating countries, which means high transport costs. Moreover, the neighbouring countries of eastern Asia, with very few exceptions, are not in a position to provide overseas tourists: for political or economic reasons the majority of Asians are restricted in their movement. In 1968, for the first time, the total of Japanese tourists going abroad exceeded the number of tourists visiting Japan; today overseas tourists outnumber visitors by more than three to one.

Increased prosperity and increased leisure together with, one suspects, increased familiarity with Western culture and habits, have greatly affected the lives of the Japanese people and encouraged them in the habit of holiday-making. Even so, it must be recognised that the Japanese have long visited certain historic centres and places of natural beauty; for example, Nara City, the ancient eighth-century capital of Japan and the cradle of Japanese arts and crafts, possesses numerous shrines and temples and several million visitors come to look at Nara's treasures every year.[28] Already very large numbers are participating in leisure activities: golf, angling, mountain climbing and skiing.[29] "In 1971 the Japanese made an estimated 442 million trips within the country for non-business purposes, and 83 million of these lasted one or more nights away from home."[30] Hence, as Devas comments: "The present boom in overseas travel is founded on a well-established domestic touring trade. Adopting and adapting many aspects of Western culture, as the Japanese have, they possess an intense interest and curiosity about the way of life and cultures of other countries, not just of the relatively accessible nearby Asian countries such as Hong Kong, but also of Western lands."[31]

Finally, reference may be made to the recreational aspects of the National Development Plan adopted in 1969. This Plan aimed at comprehensive development to be gradually effected over a fifteen-year period and to be implemented by 1985. An important feature of the Plan is to ensure a desirable environment throughout the country and a high quality of life. The protection of nature and the creation of amenities will be stressed. It is realised that working hours will become progressively shorter, that leisure time will increase and that living standards will be raised; hence it is intended that sporting and recreational facilities will be provided. It is intended that the natural and cultural heritage shall be protected and every effort is to be made to reduce pollution and spoliation of the environment. Coastal and inland recreation areas are planned for swimming, yachting, walking, camping, etc.[32]

AUSTRALIA

Tourism in Australia is an industry bringing in around $A1500m annually. About 10 per cent of this total is accounted for by the expenditure of foreign visitors. It was reported that "In 1968, the composition of the tourist cake was split as follows: expenditure on holiday motoring 38 per cent; expenditure for accommodation, meals, sight-seeing 39 per cent; domestic airline passenger services 10 per cent; expenditure by overseas visitors 8 per cent; inter-state passenger trains 4 per cent; road coach services 1 per cent."[33] Although there is a substantial domestic tourist industry, the number of overseas visitors is small, mainly because of the remoteness of Australia from the major tourist-generating countries. Nevertheless the number of foreign visitors is gradually increasing and during the past decade they have doubled over each five-year period.

In 1964 the forerunner of the Australian Tourist Commission sought the advice of some travel consultants who were commissioned to study and advise upon travel and tourist developments in Australia. The consultants' report predicted that international travel to Australia would increase from 132,000 in 1964 to 320,000 in 1970, and that by 1975 the total would have reached 607,000.[34] The figure for 1970 was in fact reached by 1968, although this was mainly due to short-term recreational leave granted to United States' soldiers stationed in South Vietnam during the Vietnam War. The Australian Tourist Commission had set a target of 316,000 visitors for 1968 but this proved to be exceeded by 10,000; it did, however, include some 26,000 short-term pleasure cruise visitors and some 63,000 United States' servicemen. In 1972 the number of arrivals was 426,403. Tables 83 and 84 show the numbers of visitors, the purpose of the visit and the lengths of stay.

From Tables 83 and 84 a number of significant facts emerge: (*i*) some two-thirds of the total arrivals are holiday tourists, although no doubt a

TABLE 83

Tourist statistics: Australia

	1963		1968	
	000	%	000	%
MODE OF TRANSPORT				
Sea	18	14	19	6
Air	107	86	281	94
	125	100	300	100
PURPOSE OF JOURNEY				
In transit	27	22	38	13
Business	22	18	45	15
Holiday	61	48	191	64
Education	7	5	9	3
Other and not stated	8	7	17	5
	125	100	300	100
LENGTH OF STAY				
Under 1 week	26	21	114	38
1–2 weeks	15	12	39	13
2 weeks–1 month	24	19	58	19
1–2 months	17	14	29	10
2–4 months	18	14	29	10
4 months–1 year	13	10	18	6
Indefinite, not stated	12	10	13	4
	125	100	300	100
Average length of stay	55 days		36 days[1]	

1. Excluding Service personnel, the average length of stay is 43 days.

Source: The Financial Times, 2nd September, 1969.

TABLE 84

Principal overseas visitors (1971/72)

Country	1971 No. of arrivals	% of total	1972 No. of arrivals	% of total
New Zealand	98,457	25·3	111,168	26·1
United States	83,283	21·5	77,827	18·3
U.K. and Eire	44,224	11·4	57,448	13·5
Papua/New Guinea	33,812	8·8	36,004	8·4
Japan	16,042	4·1	15,335	3·6
Canada	12,515	3·2	14,737	3·5
Malaysia/Singapore	12,687	3·3	13,716	3·2
West Germany	6,767	1·7	8,217	1·9
Hong Kong	6,795	1·7	7,823	1·8
Netherlands	5,489	1·4	7,640	1·8
Fiji	5,109	1·3	5,673	1·3
South Africa	4,842	1·2	5,383	1·3
All countries	388,660	100·0	426,403	100·0

Source: Australian Tourist Commission.

substantial proportion of these are visiting relatives; (*ii*) the overwhelming majority (94 per cent) travel by air, with the proportion travelling by sea rapidly declining; (*iii*) New Zealanders account for slightly more than one-quarter of all visitors; (*iv*) a further quarter come from North America (U.S. and Canadian visitors); (*v*) perhaps rather surprisingly, substantial numbers come from Papua, New Guinea and Malaysia; (*vi*) notwithstanding the remoteness of Australia from the British Isles, over 50,000 tourists from the latter visit Australia each year; and (*vii*) although the average length of stay has declined in recent years, it is still over one month in duration.

Although Australia has a variety of natural attractions, *e.g.* the Great Barrier Reef, Ayer's Rock, these are not normally the reasons for foreigners visiting the country. Analysis shows that visitors come mainly for three reasons: first, many, especially from the British Isles and New Zealand, visit in order to see relatives and friends; secondly, large numbers from neighbouring lands visit Australia for a change of physical and social environment and recreation; and, thirdly, about one-sixth come for business reasons but combine their business with pleasure.

It would seem that the projected increase of visitors to 600,000 by 1975 has been more than fulfilled. A number of factors are likely to promote increased tourist arrivals, most important of which are the introduction of jumbo jet services, the inception of flights between the United States and Australia by American Airlines, the increase in services to and from Japan, with whom Australia is developing increasing contacts, and the likelihood of more charter flights to Australia.

TABLE 85
Source of arrivals

Source	1963 (%)	1969 (%)	1972 (%)
North America	16	19	22·5
South Pacific neighbours	50	29	39·5
(New Zealand, New Guinea, Fiji)			
Europe	20	18[1]	22·5[1]
Asia	12	35	13·5
Africa	2	31	2·1

1. Approximately two-thirds come from the United Kingdom, one-third from Continental Europe.
Source: Australian Tourist Commission.

During the period 1963–69 the source of arrivals showed relatively little change except in two instances: the arrivals from Australia's neighbours, which showed a big drop, and those coming from Asia, which increased very substantially, though this is a temporary increase resulting from American servicemen spending leave in Australia; now that American participation in the Vietnam War is over, this source of visitors will dry up. It would seem that the greatest potential for Australian tourism is from North American visitors, but the increasing commercial contacts between Australia and Japan may well lead to considerable increases in Japanese visitors for holiday as well as business purposes.

Australia's share of international tourist receipts—less than 1 per cent of the total—is extremely small, and international tourism, though expected to grow, is unlikely to play any significant role in the Australian economy for a long time to come.

NEW ZEALAND

The prime attraction for tourism in New Zealand is natural: the country possesses much fine and spectacular scenery, both mountain and coastal, together with inland lakes and volcanic phenomena in North Island. There are excellent opportunities for sport, especially hunting and fishing, skiing and sailing. Maori settlement, arts and crafts are of great interest also. The climate favours out-of-doors activities throughout most of the year and large numbers of New Zealanders spend their holidays and weekends camping and caravanning. There is already a fairly well-developed domestic tourist industry but the Government which came into power in 1972 made a pledge that it would support and expand tourism development for New Zealanders as well as for foreign visitors. The Government's objective is "to make every New Zealander a potential tourist, seeing his own country first, and to put the utmost vigour into promoting New Zealand as a tourist attraction." Already moves have been made to attain these objectives. On the home front there has been a campaign, costing $100,000, to promote internal domestic travel and a programme to build low-cost holiday accommodation while a number of measures have been taken to given an impetus to foreign tourism to New Zealand.[35] Relatively little seems to be known about the domestic tourist industry but estimates indicate that holiday and business travel are valued at about $NZ200m a year.

Foreign tourism to New Zealand is gradually growing. During the 1972–73 season 254,644 foreign tourists visited New Zealand of whom some 125,000 came from Australia and around 54,000 from the United States. The total arrivals showed an increase of $11 \cdot 9$ per cent on the previous season—an increase on a par with the world average. The growing U.S. traffic declined slightly, probably mainly due to the devaluation of the U.S. dollar which made international travel more expensive. Foreign earnings for the 1972–73 season amounted to $NZ57 \cdot 4m$. Almost half of New Zealand's visitors are Australians and Australia will probably continue to be the principal source of tourists. The New Zealanders, however, have their eye on the rapidly expanding Japanese market and interest has already been shown by the Japanese. The Government, committed to a policy of tourism expansion, believes that by the early 1980s New Zealand will be receiving around half a million visitors annually.

If this target is to be achieved, New Zealand must remedy the deficiencies in its facilities: a shortage of hotels and other types of tourist accommodation and a shortage of personnel adequately trained for the service industry. It has been estimated that an additional 12,000 rooms will be required to meet the demands of half a million tourists and this will entail an investment of around $NZ115m.[36] The Tourist Hotel Commission, a government corporation, is to purchase hotels and build new ones and, although the intention is to compete with the private sector, it is not the Government's aim to exercise a monopoly in the field of tourist accommodation. The shortage of trained personnel is especially serious, for in the prosperous and egalitarian society of New Zealand it is difficult to find workers who are prepared to work in the hotel service industry; in the hotels run by the Tourist Hotel Commission "there is a preponderance of foreign workers on short-term jobs" while "in the private sector there is a high turnover."[37] Clearly not only is it essential to establish training colleges and centres to turn out properly trained staff but it is necessary to improve the image and status of the hotel and service industry so that young people will be attracted and prepared to make a career in it.

There are a number of other problems, too, which will have to be resolved. One is the attitude to charter flights which it is feared may undermine the successful operation of the domestically owned airline Air New Zealand. Another is the problem of the seasonal character of the tourist trade which puts strain upon the tourism plant and places it in low gear for much of the year; to redress the balance of this diseconomy efforts are being made to promote an all-year-round flow of visitors. Yet another issue that worries many is that the Government's decision to promote foreign tourism may lead to a wholesale influx of foreign visitors which may give rise to undesirable social effects even though their presence is economically desirable.

NOTES

1. "Indian Ocean Islands," Regional Report No. 4, *International Tourism Quarterly*, No. 1, 1972, p. 36.

2. *Idem*, p. 34.

3. *Idem*, p. 32.

4. *Idem*, p. 33.

5. *Idem*, p. 38.

6. *Idem*, p. 35.

7. *Idem*, p. 45.

8. R. Allchin, "History in Monuments," Special Report: India, *Times*, 13th October, 1969, p. xviii.

9. *Ibid.*

10. C. Wright, "Mulligatawny in Mogul Palaces," Special Report: India, *Times*, 13th October, 1969, p. xx.

11. Sri Lanka, Economic Report, National Westminster Bank, January, 1973.

12. I. Sharpe, "Realistic Approach to Tourism," Singapore: Special Report, *The Financial Times*, 1st October, 1973.

13. *Ibid.*

14. *Ibid.*

15. *Ibid.*

16. *Ibid.*

17. Hong Kong, Economic Report, National Westminister Bank, September, 1972.

18. Hong Kong, National Report, *International Tourism Quarterly*, No. 4, 1972.

19. *Hong Kong Year Book*, p. 122.

20. "Tourism Leaps Ahead," Taiwan, Special Report: *Times*, 9th December, 1969.

21. *Ibid.*

22. *International Tourism Quarterly*, No. 2, 1973, p. 75.

23. Sharpe, *op. cit.*

24. E. Devas, "Japan: The Fastest Growing Travel Market," *British Travel News*, No. 43, Autumn, 1973, pp. 17–18.

25. Research Newsletter, p. iv, in *British Travel News*, No. 39, Winter, 1973.

26. Devas, *op. cit.*

27. *Idem.*

28. H. Robinson, *Monsoon Asia*, Macdonald & Evans, 2nd. edn. 1972, p. 545.

29. Devas, *op. cit.*

30. *Idem.*

31. *Op. cit.*

32. Robinson, *op. cit.*, p. 531.

33. Australia and New Zealand, Regional Report No. 3, *International Tourism Quarterly*, No. 3, 1971.

34. *Idem.*

35. M. Southern, "Fresh Impetus for Tourism," New Zealand Survey, *The Financial Times*, 23rd October, 1973.

36. *Idem.*

37. *Idem.*

Appendix I

Bibliography

BOOKS

Addison, W., *English Spas*, Batsford, 1951.

Aldous, T., *Battle for the Environment*, Fontana, 1972.

Beckinsale, R. P. and Houston, J. M., eds. *Urbanization and its Problems*, Blackwell, 1968.

Blakemore, H. and Smith, C. T., eds. *Latin America: Geographical Perspectives*, Methuen, 1971.

Bracey, H. E., *People and the Countryside*, Routledge and Kegan Paul, 1970.

Burton, T. L., ed., *Recreation Research and Planning*, Allen and Unwin, 1970.

Clawson, M. and Knetsch, J. L., *Economics of Outdoor Recreation*, John Hopkins Press, 1966.

Cornish, V., *The Beauties of Scenery*, 4th edition, Muller, 1946.

Cosgrove, I. and Jackson, R., *The Geography of Recreation and Leisure*, Hutchinson, 1972.

Devas, E., *Japan—a major tourist market*, Tourism Planning and Research Ltd., 1973.

Dury, G. H. and Mathieson, R., *The United States and Canada*, Heinemann, 1970.

Dumazedier, J., *Towards a Society of Leisure*, Free Press, New York, 1967.

George, P., *France: a Geographical Study*, Martin Robertson, 1973.

Hamilton, F. E. I., *Yugoslavia: Patterns of Economic Activity*, G. B. Bell and Sons, 1968.

Hudson, F. S., *A Geography of Settlement*, Macdonald & Evans, 1970.

Hudson, F. S., *North America*, Macdonald & Evans, 1974.

Johns, E., *British Townscapes*, Arnold, 1965.

Karmon, Y., *Israel: A Regional Geography*, Wiley–Interscience, 1971.

Lansing, J. B. and Blood, D. M., *The Changing Travel Market*, University of Michigan, 1964.

McIntosh, R. W., *Tourism: Principles, Practices, Philosophies*, Grid Inc., 1972.

Medlik, S., *Profile of the Hotel and Catering Industry*, Heinemann, 1972.

Morgan, W. T. W., ed., *East Africa: its Peoples and Resources*, Oxford University Press, 1969.

Paterson, J. H., *North America*, Oxford University Press, 1960, p. 390.

Patmore, J. A., *Land and Leisure*, David and Charles, 1970.

Peters, M., *International Tourism*, Hutchinson, 1969.

Pimlott, J. A. R., *The Englishman's Holiday*, Faber and Faber, 1947.

Popovic, V., *Tourism in Eastern Africa*, Ifo-Institut für Wirtschafts-forschung München Afrika-Studienstelle, Weltforum Verlag, München, 1972.

Sigaux, G., *History of Tourism*, Leisure Art, London, 1966.

Singleton, F., *Yugoslavia: the Country and its People*, Queen Anne Press, 1970.

Smailes, A. E., *The Geography of Towns*, Hutchinson, 1953.

Smith, G. H., ed., *Conservation of Natural Resources*, 4th edition, Wiley, 1971.

Thompson, I. B., *Modern France: a Social and Economic Geography*, Butterworth, 1971.

Véliz, C., ed., *Latin America and the Caribbean: a Handbook*, Anthony Blond, 1968.

West, R. C. and Augelli, J. P., *Middle America: its Lands and Peoples*, Prentice-Hall, 1966.

Young, Sir G., *Accommodation Services in Britain 1970–1980*. N.U.E., London, 1970.

White, J., *History of Tourism*, Leisure Art, London, 1967.

ARTICLES AND PAPERS

Bell, M., "Land Conservation for a Nation of Town Dwellers," *Geographical Magazine*, Vol. VXLVI, October, 1973, pp. 41–7.

Billet, J., "La montagne, chance du tourisme tessinois de demain," *Rev. Geog. Alp.*, 1966.

Blake, G. H. and Lawless, R. I., "Algeria's Tourist Industry," *Geography*, Vol. 57, April, 1972, pp. 148–52.

Board, C. and Morgan, B., "Parks for People," *Geographical Magazine*, Vol. XLIII, June, 1971, pp. 640–8.

Buchanan, C., "Wide World of the Narrow Way," *Drive*, Autumn, 1967, pp. 69–71.

Burkart, A. J., "Package Holidays by Air," University of Surrey, 1971.

Christaller, W., "Some Considerations of Tourist Location in Europe," *Papers Regional Science Association*, Vol. XII, 1964, pp. 95–105.

Clout, H., "Threat to Rural Communities," *Geographical Magazine*, Vol. XLV, November, 1972, pp. 98–102.

Dower, M., "Leisure—its Impact on Man and the Land," *Geography*, Vol. 55, 1970, pp. 253–60.

Escritt, E. A. and Gittins, J., "Limits of a Nature Reserve," *Geographical Magazine*, Vol. XLVI, October, 1973, pp. 48–50.

Fairburn, A. N., "The Grand Tour," *Geographical Magazine*, Vol, XXIV, 1951, pp. 118–27.

Furmidge, J., "Planning for Recreation in the Countryside," *Journal of the Town Planning Institute*, Vol. 55, 1968, p. 65.

Gilbert, E. W., "The Growth of Inland and Seaside Health Resorts," *Scottish Geographical Magazine*, January, 1939.

Jackson, R. T., "Problems of Tourist Industry Development on the Kenyan Coast," *Geography*, Vol. 58, January, 1973, pp. 62–4.

Janata, G., "Tourism in H.N.D. Hotel and Catering Administration Courses," given at Ealing Technical College, 1971.

Kaempfen, W., "Switzerland for Holidays in the Alpine Year 1965," *Swiss Trade and Industry*, No. 1, 1965, p. 3.

Lowenthal, D. and Price, H. C., "The English Landscape," *Geographical Review*, Vol. 54, No. 3, 1963, p. 334.

McIntosh, R. W., "Some Tourism Economics," *The Cornell Quarterly*, Vol. 14, No. 2, August, 1973, pp. 2–4.

Marion, J. and Loup, J., "Cent ans de tourisme alpine," *Rev. Geog. Alp.*, 1965.

Martin, A., "Swiss Transport Facilities in the Service of the Tourist Industry," *Swiss Industry and Trade*, No. 1, 1965, pp. 17–24.

Medlik, S., "Organisation of Tourism in Six European Countries," University of Surrey, 1966.

"The Economic Importance of Tourism," University of Surrey, 1972.

Mercer, D. C., "The Geography of Leisure—A Contemporary Growth-Point," *Geography*, Vol. 55, 1970, pp. 261–72.

Naylon, J., "Tourism—Spain's Most Important Industry," *Geography*, Vol. 52, January, 1967, pp. 23–40.

Richards, G., "How Important is Tourism in Real Terms?", *Catering Times*, 3rd August, 1972.

Risch, P., "Rejuvenation of Switzerland's Tourist Industry," *Swiss Trade and Industry*, No. 1, 1965, pp. 5–15.

Robinson, A., "Towns Beside the Seaside," *Geographical Magazine*, Vol. XLV, September, 1973, pp. 877–85.

Sayer, S., "Wild Uplands of the South-West," *Geographical Magazine*, Vol. XLV, July, 1973, pp. 743–8.

Schaleman, H. J., "Man's Stamp on Florida Keys," *Geographical Magazine*, Vol. XLV, March, 1973, pp. 433–7.

Sinclair, D. J., "Affluent Adventurers," *Geographical Magazine*, Vol. XLI, March, 1969, pp. 438–9.

Sinclair, D. J. and Sinclair, M., "Land in Trust," *Geographical Magazine*, Vol. XLII, January, 1970, pp. 304–5.

Tanner, J. C., "Trends in car ownership and traffic flow," Road Research Laboratory, 1970.

Temple, A., "Tunisian Mosaic," *Geographical Magazine*, Vol. XLV, September, 1973, pp. 857–61.

Thurston, H., "France Finds a new Holiday Coast," *Geographical Magazine*, Vol. XLI, February, 1969, pp. 339–45.

Tolley, R. S., "New Technology and Transport Geography," *Geography*, Vol. 58, July, 1973, pp. 227–36.

Ullman, E. L., "The Role of Transportation and the Bases for Interaction," in *Man's Role in Changing the Face of the Earth*, ed. Thomas, W. L. University of Chicago Press, 1956.

Wager, J., "The Use of Common Land for Recreation," *Journal of the Town Planning Institute*, Vol. 53, October, 1967, p. 398.

Williams, J. E. D., "Holiday Traffic by Air," Brancker Memorial Lecture, 1968.

Williams, J. E. and Zelinsky, W., "On Some Patterns of International Tourist Flows," *Economic Geography*, October, 1970, pp. 549–67.

Wolfe, R. I., "Recreational Travel: the New Migration," *Canadian Geographer*, Vol. x, No. 1, 1966, pp. 1–14.

REPORTS, ETC.

Aalen, F. H. A. and Bird, J. C., *Tourism in Ireland—East: Guidelines for Development*, Eastern Regional Tourism Organisation, 1969.

British Air Transport in the 'Seventies, H.M.S.O., 1969.

British Waterways: recreation and amenity, Ministry of Transport, H.M.S.O., 1967.

Economic Review of World Tourism, I.U.O.T.O., 1970 and 1972.

North-West Tourist Board Report, 1972.

Tourism and Economic Growth, Estoril Seminar, 1967.

Tourism in Wales, Welsh Tourist Board, 1967.

The Coasts of England and Wales, Countryside Commission, H.M.S.O., 1968.

The Planning of the Coastline, Countryside Commission, H.M.S.O., 1970.

Roads and Tourism, A British Road Federation Report published in association with the British Tourist Authority, 1970.

The French Tourist Industry, Ambassade de France, Service de Presse et d'Information.

French Regional Development, Ambassade de France, Service de Presse et d'Information.

Coastal Recreation and Holidays, Countryside Commission, H.M.S.O., 1969.

Town and Country Planning in Britain, Central Office of Information, H.M.S.O., 1968.

Development of Tourism Act 1969, H.M.S.O., 1969.

The South American Handbook, ed. A. Marshall, Trade and Travel Publications, 1970.

International Travel Statistics, I.U.O.T.O., Geneva, 1970.

Digest of Tourist Statistics, British Tourist Authority.

B.T.A. and Keele University, *Pilot National Recreation Survey*, Vols. I and II, British Tourist Authority, 1967 and 1969.

Patterns of British Holidaymaking 1951–68, British Tourist Authority, 1970.

International Tourism Quarterly, 1971–73.

British Travel News.

The European Tourist Markets, Tourism Planning and Research Limited, London, 1971.

Areas of Outstanding Natural Beauty

Anglesey:	Most of the coast of the island with its rocky coves, unspoiled beaches and bird colonies.
Arnside and Silverdale:	The limestone hills and tidal flats, with wildfowl around the Kent estuary, Morecambe Bay.
Cannock Chase:	A small oasis of wilderness country in Staffordshire; heathland, beech and oakwoods with wild deer.
Chichester Harbour:	An area of sea creeks and tidal flats; a yachtsman's playground with the old, attractive town of Bosham.
Chiltern Hills:	Chalk downs and magnificent beechwoods with many good vantage points.
Cornwall:	Many tracts of fine coastal scenery and attractive coastal settlements together with Bodmin Moor.
Cotswolds:	Britain's second largest A.O.N.B.; an area of limestone hill country bejewelled with attractive Cotswold-stone towns and villages.
Dedham Vale:	Constable country around Dedham, Flatford Mill and Stoke-by-Nayland; tranquil country of water meadows, ponds, trees and picturesque buildings.
East Devon:	The coast of Lyme Bay from Exmouth to Dorset and the high-quality hill country immediately behind the coast.
South Devon:	South Hams and the scenic estuaries of the Dart, Avon, Erme and Yealm together with interesting coastal features such as cliffs and leys.
North Devon:	Craggy cliffs and dune stretches with fine seascapes from Hartland Point around Bideford Bay to Combe Martin.
Dorset:	Magnificent coastal scenery all the way from the Isle of Purbeck to the Devon boundary plus the rich, rolling country of the Dorset Downs and their attractive villages.
Forest of Bowland:	A stretch of fine, wild, open country between the Lune and the Ribble.
Gower Peninsula:	An attractive area of scenic variety with steep limestone cliffs, wooded ravines and sandy bays.
East Hampshire:	The pleasant rolling hill country between Winchester and the Sussex border with its mixture of woodlands and farmlands.
South Hampshire Coast:	The attractive Solent coast from Hurst Castle to Calshot Castle and the Beaulieu River including Bucler's Hard and Beaulieu Abbey.

Kent Downs:
A 96-km (60-mile) stretch of the Downs, including several outstanding National Trust properties.

Lincolnshire Wolds:
The pleasant, gently undulating chalk wold country from Caistor in the north to Spilsby in the south.

Lleyn Peninsula:
The northern and western coastal areas are of great scenic value while the coasts of the western end of Lleyn are classed as heritage coasts.

Malvern Hills:
The 13-km (9-mile) ridge of the Malverns, richly wooded in parts provides excellent walking country and some splendid views.

Mendip Hills:
The limestone hills, already scarred in places by quarrying, contains Cheddar Gorge and Wookey Hole.

Norfolk Coast:
A unique coastal area of sand-dunes, shingle ridges, mud flats and saltings with rich bird life.

Northumbrian Coast:
A superb stretch of coast with wonderful beaches and projecting rocks crowned with splendid castles; offshore are the Farne Islands with their seals and seabirds.

Quantock Hills:
A 20-km (12-mile) ridge of woods, heath and moorland in Somerset providing good walking country.

Shropshire Hills:
They include Long Mynd, Wenlock Edge and the Wrekin, Clee Hills and Clun Forest, fine windy heights rising above delectable rural valleys, providing good views and tramping country.

Solway Coast:
A beautiful and tranquil stretch of coast haunted by wildfowl, as yet hardly discovered and visited by very few.

Isle of Wight:
Not all the island but some of its finest parts such as the downs and the south-west coast including the Needles.

Surrey Hills:
Attractive and, in places, still unspoilt landscape of farmlands, woodlands and downland but under increasing pressure from the great conurbation.

North Wessex Downs:
The country's largest A.O.N.B.; an area of swelling downs, pastoral vales and patches of forest, *e.g.* Savernake with many features of pre-historic interest.

Sussex Downs:
The rolling chalk hills extending from East Hampshire, across West Sussex into the southern part of East Sussex terminating at the Seven Sisters and Beachy Head.

Wye Valley:
A superbly beautiful stretch of country with winding stream, river-cut gorges and wooded slopes culminating in Symonds Yat and Tintern Abbey.

Suffolk Coast:
The little frequented coast, estuaries and backing heathlands between Felixstowe and Lowestoft, including Orford Ness and the little ancient towns of Southwold, Dunwich and Aldeburgh.

Index

A

Accessibility, 15, 23, 41, 47, 81, 97–9, 159, 181, 225, 229, 278, 327, 349, 382, 417, 450

Accommodation, 40, 47–8, 56, 58, 64, 74, 81, 89, 131, 159, 233–5, 237, 244, 277, 279, 283, 285, 289–90, 300, 312, 321, 329, 337, 349, 399, 406, 414–15, 425, 433, 441, 445, 454

'Activity' holidays, 16, 34, 229

Adriatic Highway, 85, 107, 324, 326–7

Affluence, 21–5

Age and tourism, 25–6

Airports, 147, 275, 305, 307–9, 313–14, 328, 372, 382, 408, 418–19, 440

Air Transport Licensing Board (A.T.L.B.), 111, 115–16

Air travel, 24, 47, 76, 98–9, *110–17*, 239, 285, 305, 313, 315, 323, 334, 341, 359, 366, 369, 371, 376, 381, 384–6, 390, 399, 410, 433–4, 441, 451–2

Albergues, 300

Aldeburgh, 167

Algarve, 47, 75, 138, 313–15

Algeria, 98, 130, 291, 396, 398, *400–3*

Alps, *270–81*, 286–7, 318–19

Amenities, tourist, 15, 45–6, 81, 159–60, 229, 267, 330, 378, 412, 421

Amsterdam, 29, 174, 262

Andorra, 47

Angkor, 46

Architecture of resorts, 163–5, 167

Areas of Outstanding Natural Beauty, 188, 190, 216, 461–2

Argentina, 383, *386–7*

Antiquities, 42, 320, 324, 405, 408–9, 415–16, 437–8

Athens, 171

Atlantic City, 168

Atlas Lands, 67, 392–4

August Bank Holiday, 231

Australia, 239, 361, 429–30, 448, *450–3*
Austria, 32, 43, 48, 64, 67–8, 72, 123, 228–9, 248, 252, 255, 291, *292–5*, 324–5, 398
Autobahnen, 105

B

Bahamas, 43, 139, 363, 365, 369, *373–5*
Balance of Payments, 57, *121–3*, 255, 291, 322, 364, 366
Bali, 92
Balkantourist, 338
Banff, 158, 170, 387
Bank Holidays, 5, 19, 47, 61, 231–2
Barbados, *372*
Bariloche, 168, 387
Bath, 7–10, 163–4, 237
Beeching Report, 100
Behavioural aspects of tourism, *30–2*
Belgium, 45, 64, 67, 157, 252–3, *260–2*, 283, 291, 294, 325, 396, 398
Benidorm, 302, 304
Bermuda, 47, 359
Blackpool, 11, 14–16, 31, 35, 46–7, 98, 103, 155, 158, 161–2, 165, *172–4*, 224
Boston Spa, 8, 157, 164
Bournemouth, 161, 228, 237
Brazil, 62, 76, 92, 365, *379–84*, 387, 448
Bridlington, 14, 224
Brighton, 9–11, 14, 35, 47, 98, 158, 161, 164, 237
British National Travel Survey, 57
British Tourist Authority (B.T.A.), 57, 83, 85–6, 102, 150, 223, 226–9, 235, 238
British Tourist Regions, 225, 230
British Travel Association, 83, 85–6
British Waterways Board, 193
Brittany, 74, 286, 271–2
Broads, 45, 170, *195–6*
Bruges, 29, 46, 261
Bulgaria, 49, *337–8*
Business travel, *59–60*
Buxton, 8

C

California, 43, 97, 157, 348–9, 358, 367

Cambodia, 46

Camping, 16, 37, 48, 169, 204, 209, 233, 235, 265, 270, 313, 323, 342, 352, 360, 396, 426, 439, 450, 453

Canada, 63, 67–8, 236, 238–9, 246, 282, 291, 318, 348, 353, *358–61*, 369, 396, 448, 452

Canals, 193–5, 272

Canary Islands, 25, 158, 303, *309–10*

Caravanning, 16, 37, 48, 169, 204, 209, 229, 235, 265, 279, 453

Caribbean, 99, 109, 139, 157, 246, 359, 370, 376–7, 418

Carpati, 338

Cedok, 338

Channel Tunnel, 101, 109

Charter flights, 74, 113, 244, 285, 299, 381, 416, 444, 455

Cheltenham, 8, 163–4, 167

Chile, 383, *385*, 387

Civil Aviation Licensing Act, 1960, 111

Cleethorpes, 14, 156

Climate, 29–30, 33, 41, 43–4, 73–4, 95, 157–8, 168, 170, 225, 228, 231, 271, 274, 288–9, 304, 314, 316, 319, 327, 334, 344, 402

Club Méditerranée, 92, 434

Coastal eyesores, 208

C.O.D.E.R., 271–2

Colombia, 365

Colonie de vacances, 266

Colwyn Bay, 15, 162, 213–15

Comores, *432–6*

Conservation, 174–7, 241, 400, 419

Conventions, 36, 60–1, 306, 212–13, 441, 444

Copacabana Beach, 48

Cornish Riviera, 33, 43

Corsica, 48, 138, 281

Costa Azahar, 306–7

Costa Blanca, 306–7

Costa Brava, 110, 129, 299, 304, 306–7

Costa Dorada, 306–7

Costa de la Luz, 306–7

Costa del Sol, 304–6

Cote d'Azur, 268, 274–6

Countryside Act, 1968, 185

Cowes, 11, 167, 170
Crete, 47
Cruises, 43, 46, 99, 109, 236, 283, 311, 315, 343, 375–6
Cuba, 370–3
Cunard, Sir Samuel, 108
Currency restrictions, 59
Czechoslovakia, 325, 337–8

D

Dartmoor, 188, 191–2, 197, 226
Davos, 33, 158, 170, 286–7
Dawlish, 161–2
Day excursions, 19, 312, 367
Deauville, 31, 270
Denmark, 138, 252–3, 257, *259*, 283, 294, 398
Development of Tourism Act, 1969, 85–6, 134
Dimensions of world tourism, *64–6*
Dinsdale-on-Tees, 8
Dover, 14
Dragon trees, 315
Duke of Edinburgh, 18, 185

E

East Africa, 76, 246
East Anglia Tourist Board, 88
Eastbourne, 11, 157, 168, 228
East Midlands Tourist Region, 88, 228
Edinburgh, 224, 237
Education and tourism, 26–7
Egypt, 46, 92, 98, 391, *403–5*
Eire, 58, 68, 122–3, 127, 139, 157, 237–8, 252–3, *255–7*
El Salvador, 365
Embratur, 379, 382, 384
Employment, 128–30, 240, 258, 291, 302, 399–400
Energy crisis, 253–4
English Tourist Board, 134, 136
E.N.I.T., 323
Environmental damage, 181–2, 352
Epsom, 8–9

Estoril Seminar, 34, 145, 148, 150
Ethnocentrism, 31
Excursionists, 54, 312, 367, 395
Excursion trains, 13

F

Farmhouse holidays, 100, 196–7
Filey, 168
Finland, 75, 98, 252–3, *258–60*
Fiji, 417, 452
Fleetwood, 15
Florence, 11, 13, 318, 320
Florida, 43, 97, 157, 348
Floyer, Sir John, 10
Forest of Dean, 186
France, 13, 64, 67–8, 72, 92, 138, 150, 171, 182, 237, 243, 252–3, 261, *263–81*, 283, 291, 297, 317, 324–5, 331–2, 341, 354, 359, 361, 383, 395–6, 398, 406–7, 434
Frinton, 16
Functions of the N.T.O., 82

G

Gailhard, John, 13
Game reserves, 304, 420–2, 423–4
Gardens, 16, 46
Geneva, 11
Generators of tourism, 14, 66, 235, 243, 254, 268
Genoa, 13, 288
Geographical components of tourism, 41–2
Germany, Federal Republic of, 64, 66, 68, 72–3, 91, 123, 171, 239, 243, 252–3, 268–9, *281–5*, 291, 297, 324–5, 331–2, 341, 354, 359, 361, 383, 395–6, 398, 406–7, 438, 452
Gower Peninsula, 15, 168
Grand Canyon, 45, 179
Grand Metropolitan Hotels, 133
Grand Tour, 4, 11–13, 140, 236, 316, 347
Granville, Dr A. B., 155
Greece, 43, 46, 58, 75, 92, 117, 123, 127, 236, 244, 252–3, 318, *330–3*, 412

H

Handicaps to travel, 36–8
Haller, Dr A. von, 287
Harrogate, 8, 157–8, 166–7
Hastings, 14
Hawaii, 92, 127, 359
Heidelburg, 29, 284
Heritage Coasts, 188, 212–13
Hibiscus Coast, 426
Highlands and Islands Development Board, 134
Hill station resorts, 44, 158, 381, 410, 413
Historical–cultural centres, 171–2, 284, 294, 303, 319–21
Holiday camps, 30, 92, 235
Holidays with Pay Act, 21
Holiday villages, 274, 281, 322, 395, 402, 408, 413
Holy wells, 7
Hong Kong, 62, 175, 430, 440, *442–4*, 445, 448, 452
Hotels, 15, 271, 281, 290, 294, 301, 308, 310, 321, 334, 338, 341, 345, 366, 370, 372–3, 377, 379, 382–3, 386, 396, 399, 401, 414–15, 419–21, 423–5, 432–3, 439, 441, 443, 446, 454
Hungary, 337, 341
Hydrotherapy, 9

I

Iceland, 47, 157, 252–3, 258, *260*
Iguassu Falls, 179, 383, 386
Ilkley, 8, 157
Inclusive tours, 16, 59, 110, 112, 115, 236, 285, 330, 332, 342, 390, 435, 442, 446, 449
Income and tourism, *26*
India, 430, 436–8
Indian Ocean Islands, 76, *431–6*
Indonesia, 113, 440
Industrial Revolution, 5
Infrastructure, 85, 125, 147–8, 263, 278–9, 281, 331, 368, 379, 390, 406, 418, 422, 433, 435
Inland waterways, *193–6*
International Air Transport Association, 111, 116
International Civil Aviation Organisation, 112

International tourist growth, 66
International tourist movements, *66–9*
Intervening opportunities, 75, 97
Intourist, 336, 342
Investment, 15, *130–6*, 145, 148–9, 159, 279, 364, 368, 396, 401, 405, 407, 414–15, 418, 429, 454
Irish Tourist Board, 256–7
Israel, 92, 291, 391, *411–14*, 418
Italy, 12–13, 20, 43, 46, 64, 67–8, 75, 107, 238–9, 244, 248, 263, 291, 297, *316–25*, 331–2, 354, 359, 361, 383, 396, 407
I.U.O.T.O., 54, 57, 63, 70, 149
Ivory Coast, 391, 417

J

Jamaica, 62, 158, 361, 365, 369, *371–2*, 376
Japan, 62–3, 67, 75–6, 291, 361, 383, 429–30, 440, 443, *445–50*, 452
Jasper, 158, 170, 360
Jerusalem, 36, 171, 411, 413
John Dower Report, 1945, 189
Jordan, 146, 391, *414–16*

K

Kenya, 391, *418–22*, 438
Khmer Republic, 430
Kislovodsk, 33, 344
Korea, South, *445–6*, 448
Kruger National Park, 179

L

Lake Counties Tourist Board, 87
Lake District
    England, 47, 155, 169, 196, 225, 229
    Argentina, 169, 387
    Chile, 385
Languedoc-Roussillon, 107, 128, 132, 137, 144, *276–9*
Lea Valley Regional Park, 198–9
Leakages, 121, 126, 418

Lebanon, 127, 136, 391, *408–10*
Legal constraints, 49
Libya, 391
Llandrindod Wells, 8
Llandudno, 14–15, 163, 214
London, 9, 14, 29, 46, 113, 117, 174–5, 198, 237, 347
London Tourist Region, 85, 228
Long-haul traffic, 67–8, 429
Longland Report, 189
Lourdes, 36, 172
Lubbock, Sir John, 19
Luxembourg, 64, 260, *262*, 283, 294
Lytham, 165–6, 174, 203

M

Mablethorpe, 14, 156
Macchu Picchu, 386
Madagascar, 429, 431, *432–6*
Madeira, 33, 99, 158, 313–15
Magistrale, 107, 324, 327
Majorca, 35, 47, 92, 117
Malta, 25, *233–4*, 236
Mar del Plata, 387
Margate, 11, 14, 23, 31, 224
Marinas, 193, 323, 334
Market analysis, *59–60*
Malaysia, 430, 440, 452
Mauritius, 92, 429, *432–6*
Measurement of tourism, *53–9*
Mexico, 67, 76, 122, 348, 353, 359, 363, *364–9*
Mezzogiornio, 128, 321
Middle East, 67–9, 70–1, 246
Midlands Tourist Region, 85
Milan, 13, 320
Mineral waters, 6–7, 261, 273, 329
Mobility, 13, 18–19, 23–5, 37, 158, 229, 265
Monte Carlo, 167–8, 274–5
Morecambe, 157, 161–2, 165, 167, 224
Morroco, 95, 236, 391, *394–7*, 401
Motels, 235
Motorail, 25, 229

Motor-car, 15–16, 23–5, 76, 98, 101, 103, 118, 175, 179, 191, 201–2, 244, 265, 324, 327, 343, 406
Motorways, 47, 102, 105–6, 118, 174, 191, 225, 235, 275, 301, 320, 322
Multiple holidays, 20
Multiplier effect, *126–7*, 240

N

Napoleonic Wars, 11
Nash, Richard 'Beau', 8
National Parks, 41, *187–90*, 261, 304, 348, 350–51, 360, 387, 416, 419–22
National Tourist Office functions, *83–5*
National Tourism Organisation, 82–5, 144, 263, 285, 323
Nature Reserves, 261
Nature Trails, 350–1
Nepal, 430
Netherlands, 32, 48, 64, 157, 252–3, *262*, 283, 291, 359, 361, 396, 398, 452
New Forest, 186, 228
New Zealand, 169, 239, 429, 452, *453–5*
Norway, 64, 98, 157, 252–3, *257–8*, 260, 331
North-east Tourist Region, 85, 87
North Midlands Tourist Region, 85
North-west Tourist Region, 85, 228

O

Oberammagau, 26, 284

P

Package tours, 16, 27, 74, 90, 110, 137, 248, 275, 324, 330, 332, 341, 387, 398–9, 406, 408, 429
Palm Beach, 45
Panama, 365
Paradores, 300
Paris, 11, 13, 46, 171, 268, 347
Parks, 15, *165–6*, 261, 272, 294, 350, 366, 419
Patterns of tourist flows, *72–5*
Peak District, 182
Peru, 365, *385–6*

Petite Suisse, 262

Petra, 46, 172

Piers, 15, 46, *159*

Pilgrimages, 4, 7, 35–6, 411

Pilot National Recreation Survey, 22, 26, 201

Plages, 272

Poland, 341

Political influences, 11, 13, 16, 49, 58, 76, 246, 331, 337, 403, 409, 411–12, 415, 422, 453

Pollution, 207, 209, 275, 322, 410

Poole, 167, 170, 228

Portmeirion, 167

Portugal, 56, 58–9, 62, 73, 123, 244, 252–3, 291, *310–16*, 383

Prince Regent, 10–11

Promenades, 16, 46, 156, 159, 162–3, 165

Puerto Rico, 139, 365, *369–70*

Pullman, G. M., 100

Punta del Este, 169, 385

Pyramids, 45–6

R

Railways, 13–15, 23–4, 99–101, 118, 147, 156, 162, 173, 279, 289, 308, 385, 387, 432

Redcar, 14–15, 167

Receipts from world tourism, *69–71*

Regional parks, 272

Religion and holidays, 4–6, 171–2

Religious centres, 171–2

Resorts, *155–75*
  attributes of, 157–8
  morphology of, 160–3
  origins of, 156, 161

Réunion, *432–6*

Rhodesia, 391, 435

Rhyl, 14–15, 167, 213

Riviera
  French, 74, 157–8, 209, 264, 268, *274–6*, 304
  English, 43

Roads, 3–4, 13, 47, *105–8*, 118, 147, 191, 308, 324, 344, 387, 404, 408, 414, 432–3

Romania, 285, 337, *341*, 438

Romantische Strasse, 284
Rome, 11, 13, 29, 46, 171, 174, 318–19, 347
Russell, Dr Richard, 10
Russia, *341–5*

S

Safari holidays, 170, 416, 418, 421
Sailing, 30–4, 45, 167, 193, 195, 198, 272, 277, 279, 349, 369, 372, 386, 421, 453
Saltburn, 14
Sanatoria, 33, 343
Saturnalia, 5
Scandinavia, 35, 74
Scarborough, 7, 9, 11, 14, 161, 163, 165, 167–8
Scenery, 44–5, 73, 169, 263, 283, 289, 293, 318, 325, 329, 331, 349, 360, 369, 373, 421, 423, 434, 445
Scenic trails, 351–2
Scottish Tourist Board, 89, 134
Sea-bathing, 9–11, 45, 158, 160
Seaside resorts, 9–11, 13, 43, 46, 103, 155, 162, *168–9*, 261, 270, 272, 274, 319, 341, 344, 385, 387, 399, 413, 421, 426
Seasonality, *60–3*, 90, 231, 234, 381, 399, 407, 455
Seasonal unemployment, 61, 91, 103, 215, 275
Senegal, 391, 417
Seychelles, 95, 99, 407, 430, *432–6*
Second holidays, 222
Second homes, 20, 138, *181–4*, 270, 312
Short-haul traffic, 67
Singapore, 113, 430, *440–2*, 448, 452
Skegness, 14, 156, 163, 167
Social class and tourism, 26, 224
SOMIVAL, 274
S.O.N.A.T.O.U.R., 401
South Africa, 76, 239, 391, *422–7*, 435, 452
South-east Tourist Region, 85, 225, 228
Southend, 11, 98, 159, 161, 167, 224
Southern Tourist Region, 85, 225, 228
South-west Tourist Region, 85, 225–8, 230
Soviet Union, 33, 35, 73, 81, *341–5*
Spain, 43, 64, 67, 73, 75, 81, 98, 112–13, 122–3, 125, 138, 236–9, 242, 244, 248–9, 252–3, 255, 261, 291, *297–310*, 318, 383, 395–6, 398, 448

Spas, 7–11, 33, 41, 157, 166, 170–1, 224, 272, 283–4, 318, 325, 328–9, 338, 343, 379, 401, 425, 432

Sports centres, 169–70

Sri Lanka, 430, *438–9*

St Moritz, 158, 170, 286, 288

Stratford-on-Avon, 46, 103, 167–8, 172, 224

Structure of British hotel industry, 133

Sweden, 67, 117, 128, 182, 257, *259*, 283, 294, 331

Swimming pools, 16, 159–60, 199

Swiss Alpine Club, 286

Switzerland, 32–3, 43, 48, 64, 67–8, 82, 98, 125, 158, 237, 238–9, 242, 248, 262, 283, *286–72*, 317, 325, 354, 398

Syndicats d'initiative, 264

Syria, 391, 407

Taiwan, 430, *444–5*, 448

Tanzania, 391, *418–22*

Thailand, 430, 440

Thames and Chilterns Tourist Board, 88, 225

Therapeutic value of bathing, 9–10

Timing of holidays in U.K., 230–3

Thomas Cook, 24, 89, 99

Tourism, international value of *69–72*
    management, *150–1*
    motivation, *29–38*
    organisation, *81–92*, 284–5, 291–2, 295, 300, 322–3, 338
    planning, 58, *142–52*, 278–9, 323, 397, 399, 401, 418–19
    social impact of, 137–40, 146, 256–7

Tourist
    agents, 397, 399
    attractions, 41, 81
    Boards, 299
    counting, 55–6
    definition of, 53–5
    flows, *64–80*, 243, 247–9, 268
    generating countries, 64, 66, 331
    promotion, 84–5, 89, 300, 323, 349, 407, 435, 439, 444, 454
    receipts, 124, 239, 252–3, 255, 258–9, 262, 269, 283, 291, 294, 311, 322, 333, 364–5, 367, 386, 397, 399, 403, 405, 411–12, 415, 417, 421, 438–9, 440, 445, 454

Tour operators, 89–91, 116, 285, 377, 406

Torquay, 160

Trade Unions, 19–20

Traffic congestion, 24, 103, 139, 174–5, 215, 262, 275, 322, 356

Transport, 13–14, 40, 58, 76, 89, *94–118*, 240
Travel, 3–4, 12–13, 23
Travel agents, *89–91*
Trinidad, 365, 373
Trust House Forte, 133
Tunbridge Wells, 7–9
Tunisia, 25, 35, 147, 150, 236, 391, *397–400*, 401, 412
Turkey, 92, 236, 391, *405–8*

U

Uganda, 391, *418–22*
United Kingdom, 66, 68, 242, 248–9, 268–9, 285, 295, 316, 332, 354, 359,
    381, 383, 387, 395, 398, 407, 434, 438, 448, 452
  destinations of holidaymakers, 224–30
  domestic tourism, 221–35
  expenditure on holidays abroad, 236–7
  timing of holidays, 230–3
  value of holiday market, 223–4
United States, 20, 37, 43, 47, 68, 99, 123, 138, 182, 238–9, 246, 255, 282–3,
    291, 295, 312, 316, 318, 324–5, 332, *347–58*, 366, 369, 373–5, 383,
    395–6, 406–7, 412, 428, 443, 448, 452
U.S. Virgin Islands, 369, *370–1*
Uruguay, 383, *384–5*, 387

V

Value of international tourism, *69–72*
Venice, 12, 29, 174, 328, 347
Vienna, 101, 294
Volkerwanderung, 4

W

Wakes weeks, 5
Water sports, 199, 272, 277, 279, 281, 308, 369, 371–2, 387, 416, 433
Water transport, *108–10*, 118, 193
Weather and tourism, 42–4
Welsh Tourist Board, 89, 134
West Africa, *416–18*

West Indies, 43, 123, 353, *369–78*

West Midlands Tourist Board, 88

Weymouth, 11, 228

Whitby, 161, 163, 168, 208

Whittie, Dr Robert, 10

Wildlife, 4, 42, 351, 380, 419, 423, 436–7

Windermere, 45, 167–8

Winter sports, 199, 272, 277, 279, 281, 308, 369, 371–2, 387, 416, 433
    centres, 29, 33, 43, 155, 169–70, 264, 273, 280–1, 284, 286, 288, 304,
        319, 325, 360, 401, 411, 413

Woodhall Spa, 9

Worthing, 11

Y

Yellowstone Park, 187, 350–1

Yom Kippur War, 403, 412

York, 29, 103, 168, 237

Yorkshire Tourist Board, 87

Yugoslavia, 49, 64, 68, 75, 85, 92, 107, 125, 147, 150, 236, 242, 252–3, 294,
    324–30, 317, 407

Z

Zaire, 391, 417

Zoos, 159